W9-BEB-187

THE NEW AMERICAN COMMENTARY

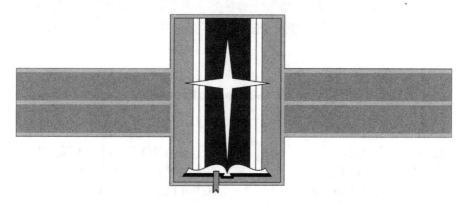

An Exegetical and Theological
Exposition of Holy Scripture

General Editor
E. RAY CLENDENEN

Assistant General Editors, OT
KENNETH A. MATHEWS

Assistant General Editor, NT
DAVID S. DOCKERY

Consulting Editors

Old Testament
L. RUSS BUSH
DUANE A. GARRETT
LARRY L. WALKER

New Testament
RICHARD R. MELICK, JR.
PAIGE PATTERSON
CURTIS VAUGHAN

Manuscript Editors
LINDA L. SCOTT
MARC A. JOLLEY

THE NEW AMERICAN COMMENTARY

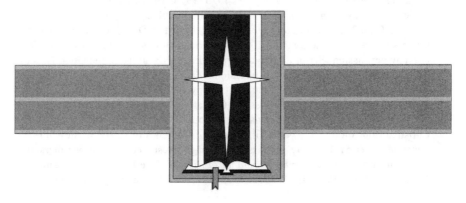

Volume
8

1, 2 KINGS

Paul R. House

B&H
PUBLISHING GROUP
Nashville, Tennessee

© Copyright 1995 • Broadman & Holman Publishers
All rights reserved
4201-8
ISBN 10: 0-8054-0108-3
ISBN 13: 978-08054-0108-0
Dewey Decimal Classification: 222.5
Subject Heading: BIBLE. O.T. KINGS
Library of Congress Catalog Card Number: 94-47508
Printed in the United States of America
14 13 12 11 10 13 12 11 10 9

Unless otherwise indicated, Scripture quotations are from the Holy Bible, *New International Version* (NIV), copyright © 1973, 1978, 1984 by International Bible Society. Used by permission of Zondervan Bible Publishers. Quotations marked NEB are from *The New English Bible*. Copyright © The Delegates of the Oxford University Press and the Syndics of the Cambridge University Press, 1961, 1970. Used by permission. Scripture quotations marked GNB are from the Good News Bible, the Bible in Today's English Version. Old Testament: Copyright © American Bible Society 1976; New Testament: Copyright © American Bible Society 1966, 1971, 1976. Used by permission. Quotations marked NRSV are from the *New Revised Standard Version of the Bible,* copyright © 1989 by the Division of Christian Education of the National Council of Churches of Christ in the United States of America. Used by permission. All rights reserved. Quotations marked NASB are from the *New American Standard Bible*. © The Lockman Foundation, 1960, 1962, 1963, 1968, 1971, 1972, 1973, 1975, 1977. Used by permission.

Library of Congress Cataloging-in-Publication Data

House, Paul R., 1958–
1, 2 Kings / Paul R. House.
p. cm. — (The New American commentary ; vol. 8)
Includes bibliographical references and indexes.
ISBN 0-8054-0108-3 (hardcover)
1. Bible. O.T. Kings—Commentaries. I. Title. II. Title: First, second Kings. III. Series: The New American commentary ; v. 8.
BS1335.3.H68 1995
222'.5077—dc20

To Jim Dixon, Drew Hayes, Tim McCoy, and Mike Tucker
Old Friends, Reading Pastors, Men of God

Editors' Preface

God's Word does not change. God's world, however, changes in every generation. These changes, in addition to new findings by scholars and a new variety of challenges to the gospel message, call for the church in each generation to interpret and apply God's Word for God's people. Thus, THE NEW AMERICAN COMMENTARY is introduced to bridge the twentieth and twenty-first centuries. This new series has been designed primarily to enable pastors, teachers, and students to read the Bible with clarity and proclaim it with power.

In one sense THE NEW AMERICAN COMMENTARY is not new, for it represents the continuation of a heritage rich in biblical and theological exposition. The title of this forty-volume set points to the continuity of this series with an important commentary project published at the end of the nineteenth century called AN AMERICAN COMMENTARY, edited by Alvah Hovey. The older series included, among other significant contributions, the outstanding volume on Matthew by John A. Broadus, from whom the publisher of the new series, Broadman Press, partly derives its name. The former series was authored and edited by scholars committed to the infallibility of Scripture, making it a solid foundation for the present project. In line with this heritage, all NAC authors affirm the divine inspiration, inerrancy, complete truthfulness, and full authority of the Bible. The perspective of the NAC is unapologetically confessional and rooted in the evangelical tradition.

Since a commentary is a fundamental tool for the expositor or teacher who seeks to interpret and apply Scripture in the church or classroom, the NAC focuses on communicating the theological structure and content of each biblical book. The writers seek to illuminate both the historical meaning and contemporary significance of Holy Scripture.

In its attempt to make a unique contribution to the Christian community, the NAC focuses on two concerns. First, the commentary emphasizes how each section of a book fits together so that the reader becomes aware of the theological unity of each book and of Scripture as a whole. The writers, however, remain aware of the Bible's inherently rich variety. Second, the NAC is produced with the conviction that the Bible primarily belongs to the church. We believe that scholarship and the academy provide an indispensable foundation for biblical understanding and the service of Christ, but the editors and authors of this series have attempted to communicate the findings of their research in a manner that will build up the whole body of Christ. Thus, the commentary concentrates on theological exegesis while providing practical, applicable exposition.

THE NEW AMERICAN COMMENTARY's theological focus enables the reader to see the parts as well as the whole of Scripture. The biblical books vary in content, context, literary type, and style. In addition to this rich variety, the editors and authors recognize that the doctrinal emphasis and use of the biblical books differs in various places, contexts, and cultures among God's people. These factors, as well as other concerns, have led the editors to give freedom to the writers to wrestle with the issues raised by the scholarly community surrounding each book and to determine the appropriate shape and length of the introductory materials. Moreover, each writer has developed the structure of the commentary in a way best suited for expounding the basic structure and the meaning of the biblical books for our day. Generally, discussions relating to contemporary scholarship and technical points of grammar and syntax appear in the footnotes and not in the text of the commentary. This format allows pastors and interested laypersons, scholars and teachers, and serious college and seminary students to profit from the commentary at various levels. This approach has been employed because we believe that all Christians have the privilege and responsibility to read and seek to understand the Bible for themselves.

Consistent with the desire to produce a readable, up-to-date commentary, the editors selected the *New International Version* as the standard translation for the commentary series. The selection was made primarily because of the NIV's faithfulness to the original languages and its beautiful and readable style. The authors, however, have been given the liberty to differ at places from the NIV as they develop their own translations from the Greek and Hebrew texts.

The NAC reflects the vision and leadership of those who provide oversight for Broadman Press, who in 1987 called for a new commentary series that would evidence a commitment to the inerrancy of Scripture and a faithfulness to the classic Christian tradition. While the commentary adopts an "American" name, it should be noted some writers represent countries outside the United States, giving the commentary an international perspective. The diverse group of writers includes scholars, teachers, and administrators from almost twenty different colleges and seminaries, as well as pastors, missionaries, and a layperson.

The editors and writers hope that THE NEW AMERICAN COMMENTARY will be helpful and instructive for pastors and teachers, scholars and students, for men and women in the churches who study and teach God's Word in various settings. We trust that for editors, authors, and readers alike, the commentary will be used to build up the church, encourage obedience, and bring renewal to God's people. Above all, we pray that the NAC will bring glory and honor to our Lord who has graciously redeemed us and faithfully revealed himself to us in his Holy Word.

SOLI DEO GLORIA
The Editors

Acknowledgments

Several people deserve thanks for their help in this project. My family has always supported my writing projects, and this time was no exception. Becky, my wife, and Molly, my daughter, exhorted me to work hard and finish on time. Both were a source of joy and inspiration. They are infinitely worth whatever commitments I have made to them. Roy House, my father, offered some solid suggestions and read a large portion of the manuscript. His support has been lifelong, at least so far.

My colleagues at Taylor University were also quite helpful. Each member of the departments of Biblical Studies, Christian Education, and Philosophy extended real and needed encouragement. Joanne Giger typed the manuscript with great efficiency and offered sage commentary on the commentary. Taylor University's administration, led by Daryl Yost, Bob Pitts, and Dwight Jessup, allowed me a course reduction during the semester the manuscript was due. I work with good people, a fact I appreciate and hope never to take for granted.

The editors at Broadman & Holman were kind as well. Ray Clendenen, Marc Jolley, and Trent Butler were all very strategic counselors, and Ray and Marc, as well as Linda Scott, saw the manuscript through to completion with patience and grace. Indeed they made the volume a better book than it would have been. These and other persons at Broadman & Holman made this project a good experience for me.

Certain friends must also be thanked. Scott Hafemann, Jim Dixon, Carol Mott, Gordon Kingsley, and Suzanne House Kingsley kept me going when I wanted to stop writing, among other things. Their goodness to me mediated God's presence, which is the highest compliment I know how to give.

The volume is dedicated to four special friends, each of whom is supposed to be a member of the "reading pastor" target group this series tries to address. I met these men at Southern Seminary in the 1980s, where we stuck together during difficult days. I have enjoyed ministering with them from time to time over the past decade. They were then and are now good people and good ministers, good conversationalists and good listeners, good Christians and good companions.

For these and other kindnesses I am extremely grateful.

Paul R. House
Taylor University
Upland, Indiana

Author's Preface

Few biblical books are as neglected by the church as 1, 2 Kings. There are several reasons for this situation. First, some preachers find it difficult to construct sermons from Old Testament texts. Second, misconceptions about Old Testament history, such as its supposedly boring, nontheological nature, cause laypersons to question the books' value for devotional reading. Third, Christians from all walks of life doubt the practicality of studying events that occurred three thousand years ago. Fourth, even diligent Bible students may get discouraged trying to fit the kings, foreign enemies, and relevant dates into a coherent whole. Fifth, commentaries on 1, 2 Kings often explain chronological and compositional matters without exploring the books' theological and literary richness.

These barriers can be overcome. Pastors *can* learn to prepare doctrinally sound, relevant messages from 1, 2 Kings. How? By developing the ability to read the books' stories[1] as mirrors of today's world. Historical situations such as war, poverty, political corruption, and oppression are permanent symptoms of the human condition. Likewise faithfulness, loyalty, and obedience remain marks of God's people. Also, crucial Bible doctrines like God's sovereignty, redemption, wrath, and love permeate 1, 2 Kings. Creative, insightful communicators will quickly grasp the many ways these books can enrich their hearers' lives.

Once pastors proclaim the books' value, laypersons will begin to read 1, 2 Kings with renewed interest and enthusiasm. Characters from Israel's history will become instructors, even companions, rather than obscure, forbidding figures from the past. Guidance for life will emerge as these books are understood to contain real life stories written for people involved in real life.

Scholars also can help by approaching 1, 2 Kings in a more holistic fashion. Background issues such as chronology, composition, ancient history, and textual criticism are, and will always be, important for interpreting 1, 2 Kings. Yet they need to become parts of an integrated approach to the books, an approach that uses background material to inform, not replace, literary and theological analysis. Similarly, expositors must make their interpretations of texts consistent with historical facts. Sloppy, unfounded applications are as inexcusable as dry, grindingly boring presentations of historical data.[2]

Obviously, these lofty goals for scholars, pastors, and laypersons will not

---

[1] Calling the accounts in 1, 2 Kings "stories" is in no way a negative comment on their historical trustworthiness. "Story" is simply a descriptive term in this commentary.

[2] This commentary rejects the notion that history is not exciting or that literary concerns must be divorced from historical reality.

be met by accident. Thus, this commentary will follow a format designed to integrate the major elements of thorough "theological exegesis."[3] These elements include historical, literary, canonical, theological, and applicational concerns.[4] Each of these categories is important for a scholarly and useful study of 1, 2 Kings, and each will be stressed in the introduction and analysis of the books, so it is appropriate to outline them now.

HISTORICAL DETAILS

It is impossible to interpret 1, 2 Kings properly without some knowledge of its historical context. The very nature of the literature dictates this conviction. Kings made decisions based on historical, social, and political realities. Nations reacted to one another for the same reasons. Prophets and prophecy arose within specific cultural contexts. What happened before and after the event in question often determined that event's significance.

Obviously, a work like 1, 2 Kings that covers roughly four hundred years of history cannot possibly include *every* occurrence within its time frame. The author had to select what events would receive attention. Thus, it is vital to theorize about the author's era, situation, and theology. These details may explain why the history has been shaped into its current form. Like all authors, historians seek objectivity yet remain, at least partially, products of their own times. They write in part, then, to fit the perspectives and needs of those times.

Skilled interpreters soon learn the value of historical research. Indeed, they find that discovering what a passage meant to its original audience is the first step to its application to present-day congregations. Accurate historical knowledge guards against fanciful or heretical readings of texts, for, as Stuart and Fee cogently conclude, "a text cannot mean what it never meant."[5] Knowing how a passage affected ancient readers leads to uncovering ways the text can impact readers now.

LITERARY DETAILS

Literary analysis of the Old Testament has become quite prominent during the past quarter century.[6] This development should aid the interpretation of

---

[3] "Theological exegesis" is the stated goal for each volume of the NAC.

[4] For information on OT exegesis see D. Stuart, *Old Testament Exegesis: A Primer for Students and Pastors*, 2d ed. (Philadelphia: Westminster, 1984); W. C. Kaiser, Jr., *Toward an Exegetical Theology: Biblical Exegesis for Preaching and Teaching* (Grand Rapids: Baker, 1981); C. Westermann, ed., *Essays on Old Testament Hermeneutics* (Atlanta: John Knox, 1979); and B. S. Childs, *Biblical Theology in Crisis* (Philadelphia: Westminster, 1970).

[5] D. Stuart and G. Fee, *How to Read the Bible for All Its Worth* (Grand Rapids: Zondervan, 1982) 27.

[6] Cf. P. House, ed., *Beyond Form Criticism: Essays in Old Testament Literary Criticism* (Winona Lake, Ind.: Eisenbrauns, 1992).

1, 2 Kings in a number of ways. First, literary criticism focuses on how causes and effects in stories create plots. Certainly 1, 2 Kings present Israel's history as a series of events that describe how and why the nation fell from the heights of national prosperity to the depths of conquest and exile. Second, literary criticism stresses characterization, or how authors present characters. Solomon, Jeroboam, Elijah, Elisha, Jezebel, and others are well-developed, compelling individuals. They require, indeed they deserve, careful analysis.

Third, literary studies uncover important themes. These themes unite characters and plot and also provide structural links between major narrative sections. In biblical texts themes often divulge theological emphases. First and Second Kings emphasize certain ideas repeatedly, all of which indicate the author's theological perspective on Israel's history. Fourth, literary criticism explores a story's narrative viewpoint or what commentary a book offers on the events it describes. At several key points in the story, the author of 1, 2 Kings explains the significance of important events. Such editorial comments do offer hints about the books' composition, but they also give information regarding plot and theme.

There is no need to pit historical studies and literary analysis against each other when analyzing 1, 2 Kings. Rather, each can inform the other. Characters, themes, and commentary tell Israel's story. Historical data gives this story content and context. How the author combines these components determines the books' literary, historical, theological, and pedagogical effectiveness.

CANONICAL DETAILS

First and Second Kings are considered sacred within both Judaism and Christianity. In the Hebrew Bible they are part of what is called the former prophets, which includes Joshua, Judges, 1, 2 Samuel, and 1, 2 Kings. Clearly, in this scheme they conclude the history of Israel that begins with the conquest of the promised land. Thus, they comment on previous books and provide information that subsequent books may discuss. Of course, Christians add the New Testament to their list of inspired books, which means that twenty-seven more books may reflect on the events and teachings found in 1, 2 Kings.

Given these facts, it is improper to interpret 1, 2 Kings only in isolation. Rather, they must be examined with their canonical role in mind. Interpreters must note how they help explain other books and how the rest of the Bible explains them. This type of analysis, called canonical criticism, is, like literary criticism, fairly new.[7] Its proponents seek to interpret texts within their

---

[7] Canonical criticism of the OT emerged in the 1970s with the publication of Childs' *Biblical Theology in Crisis* and J. A. Sanders' *Torah and Canon* (Philadelphia: Fortress, 1973), and it was established in the 1980s, particularly through Childs' *Introduction to the Old Testament as Scripture* (Philadelphia: Fortress, 1980).

own historical context, but then to note how an individual passage's theology relates to the rest of the Bible.[8] In this way the Bible is allowed to interpret itself whenever possible.

Canonical analysis aids 1, 2 Kings studies in at least five ways. First, it helps demonstrate the similarities and differences in the accounts in 1, 2 Kings and 1, 2 Chronicles. Second, it shows how 1, 2 Kings fits into the former prophets. Third, it suggests ways that the New Testament's use of 1, 2 Kings illuminates the books' meaning. Fourth, it helps exegetes develop a biblical theology. Fifth, besides these benefits, it forwards the exegetical process begun by examining historical and literary details. Historical data explains information vital for understanding the original author and audience's situation. It also discusses details readers need to know to read a text intelligently. In other words, it deals with pretextual matters. Literary data examines the text itself, for it deals with the text as it stands. Canonical interpretation, then, explains how later biblical audiences interpreted this historical, literary document. It thus deals with posttextual issues in a way that leads interpreters closer to an appropriate application of the text for current audiences.

THEOLOGICAL DETAILS

Theology can be defined in a number of ways. For example, it is an academic discipline, a personal belief system, or a school of thought all at the same time. At its most basic level, however, the word means "a study of God." Therefore, as an academic or exegetical exercise the term "seems to signify a special science, a very special science, whose task is 'to apprehend, understand, and speak of God.'"[9] Because of God's obvious importance for theology, this concern impacts every other aspect of interpretation.[10]

For example, understanding God's nature helps explain the human race's sinfulness and need for salvation and God's desire to redeem these sinners. Further, knowing that a merciful God attempted to make and keep a covenant with Israel explains the Lord's anger with that nation's idolatry in 1, 2 Kings. Finally, grasping the notion that God created the entire world and thus has dominion over it explains why the Lord rules all nations and can direct their actions in 1, 2 Kings. Clearly, individuals, nations, and thus history are all impacted by a proper understanding of God.

Theology also acts as a link between the ancient world and today because

---

[8] Good examples of canonical exegesis include B. Childs, *The Book of Exodus*, OTL (Philadelphia: Westminster, 1974), and J. Sailhamer, "Genesis," EBC (Grand Rapids: Zondervan, 1990).

[9] K. Barth, *Evangelical Theology*, trans. G. Foley (Grand Rapids: Eerdmans, 1980) 3.

[10] Ibid., 3-4.

its emphasis on the eternal God gives it a timeless quality vital for applying texts to current situations. God remains holy, just, and merciful. Human beings continue to need salvation and discipline. Nations still need to obey their Creator. Interpreters maintain their relevance and effectiveness only by examining their own situations in a manner similar to the author of 1, 2 Kings.

In this way theological reflection continues the process from pretextual studies to application of texts. It uses the material collected from historical analysis to understand the situation that spawned the theological conclusions found in the Bible. It analyzes literary data to learn how themes, characters, plots, and settings portray sin, salvation, and God's sovereignty. It utilizes the whole Bible's interpretation of individual passages to build a coherent pattern of thought. In short, theology gathers up the various exegetical strands and makes them available for application.

This emphasis on theology is particularly important for reclaiming 1, 2 Kings as Scripture the church should heed. For too long these books have been viewed as arid historical documents. When their theological value is recognized, though, this misunderstanding will be at least partially erased. Preaching will be enriched by theologically based application that will replace self-help based on individual opinions. Every segment of the church will thereby benefit.

Applicational Details

Only when historical, literary, canonical, and theological data have been gathered can an expositor make logical and valid application of a text. Also the applicational task then becomes much simpler. The expositor knows how the text emerged in history and what cultural factors impacted its initial creation. The passage's distinct means of presentation has been acknowledged, and intellectually and spiritually stimulating characters and situations have been identified. What the Bible itself says about the text has been determined and the major doctrinal ideas gathered.

With all this information at hand, the interpreter can compare the biblical situation to that of a current audience in order to determine a text's significance. "Significance" means the way biblical material attempts to impact readers. Many types of significances appear in Scripture, but perhaps four basic ones will help at this point. First, a text's significance may lie in its portrayal of a positive or negative example. Solomon's choice of wisdom over wealth or fame in 1 Kgs 3:4–15 is an example of wise decision making. His fascination with idols in 1 Kgs 11:1–13, though, warns readers against taking similar actions themselves. Second, a passage's significance may lie in the fact that it contains a command. For instance, in 1 Kgs 18:40 Elijah commands the people to expel Baal worship (idolatry) from their midst.

Third, a text's significance may come from its description of an event. Elijah's ascension to heaven in a chariot of fire indicates the prophet's preeminence without stating that truth explicitly. Fourth, a text's significance may be stated directly by the book's narrator. For example, the author of 1, 2 Kings constantly evaluates kings and nations. Summary passages like 2 Kings 17 tell the reader why important events occur so that no misconception can arise.

When a text's significance has been determined, expositors can then compare their findings to the needs of their audience. They can then note how the original audience's composition, age, situation, and character traits compare to their audience's. For instance, if 1, 2 Kings addresses an audience that was prone to take God for granted, does the current audience have similar failings? If the ancient audience needed to seek the Lord's forgiveness after a long period of sinfulness, then that text could speak to a like situation in a current audience. More positively, if God approves of actions taken in 1, 2 Kings, perhaps an expositor can encourage a contemporary group in the same way.

Other suggestions will be made during the actual analysis of 1, 2 Kings. It must be noted, however, that commentaries can only mention *possible* applications of texts. They cannot do the expositors' work for them, since the commentator does not know the speakers' audiences. It is the individual interpreter's responsibility, then, to gather and apply the data found in the commentary.

CONCLUSION

This commentary will seek to model the exegetical principles outlined above. *Every* text will not receive exhaustive treatment, lest the volume become too long and unusable. Still, where new sections and situations occur, the historical situation will be noted. Major and minor characters will be analyzed, main plot elements highlighted, and vital themes exposed. At the end of appropriate sections will be found remarks on how the texts are understood by other passages and their theological significance. Possible applications then will be suggested briefly. Readers should be aware of this method in order to gain maximum use of the studies whether reading the commentary from cover to cover or using it to study an individual passage.

The New American Commentary seeks to meet the needs of many types of readers. But chief among these is the "reading pastor." This designated audience assumes that pastors must be serious students and skilled communicators. If this commentary fulfills its purpose, it will provide the kind of research scholarly pastors demand from a reference tool and also will address the exciting and demanding tasks of preaching and teaching. No book can meet the needs of every reader, but the methodology outlined in this section is intended to help as many individuals as possible as they study this portion of God's Word.

Abbreviations

Bible Books

Gen
Exod
Lev
Num
Deut
Josh
Judg
Ruth
1, 2 Sam
1, 2 Kgs
1, 2 Chr
Ezra
Neh
Esth
Job
Ps (pl. Pss)
Prov
Eccl
Song
Isa
Jer
Lam
Ezek
Dan
Hos
Joel
Amos
Obad
Jonah
Mic
Nah
Hab
Zeph
Hag
Zech
Mal
Matt
Mark
Luke
John
Acts
Rom
1, 2 Cor
Gal
Eph
Phil
Col
1, 2 Thess
1, 2 Tim
Titus
Phlm
Heb
Jas
1, 2 Pet
1, 2, 3 John
Jude
Rev

Apocrypha

Add Esth	*The Additions to the Book of Esther*
Bar	*Baruch*
Bel	*Bel and the Dragon*
1,2 Esdr	*1,2 Esdras*
4 Ezra	*4 Ezra*
Jdt	*Judith*
Ep Jer	*Epistle of Jeremiah*
1,2,3,4 Mac	*1,2,3,4 Maccabees*
Pr Azar	*Prayer of Azariah and the Song of the Three Jews*
Pr Man	*Prayer of Manasseh*
Sir	*Sirach, Ecclesiasticus*
Sus	*Susanna*
Tob	*Tobit*
Wis	*The Wisdom of Solomon*

Commonly Used Sources

AASOR	Annual of the American Schools of Oriental Research
AB	Anchor Bible
ABD	*Anchor Bible Dictionary*
ABW	*Archaeology and the Biblical World*
AC	An American Commentary, ed. A. Hovey
AcOr	*Acta orientalia*
AEL	M. Lichtheim, *Ancient Egyptian Literature*
AJSL	*American Journal of Semitic Languages and Literature*
Akk.	Akkadian
AnBib	Analecta Biblica
ANET	J. B. Pritchard, ed., *Ancient Near Eastern Texts*
AOAT	Alter Orient und Altes Testament
AOTS	*Archaeology and Old Testament Study,* ed. D. W. Thomas
ArOr	Archiv orientální
ATD	Das Alte Testament Deutsch
ATR	*Anglican Theological Review*
AusBR	*Australian Biblical Review*
BA	*Biblical Archaeologist*
BAGD	W. Bauer, W. F. Arndt, F. W. Gingrich, and F. W. Danker, *Greek-English Lexicon of the New Testament*
BALS	Bible and Literature Series
BARev	*Biblical Archaeology Review*
BASOR	*Bulletin of the American Schools of Oriental Research*
BDB	F. Brown, S. R. Driver, and C. A. Briggs, *Hebrew and English Lexicon of the Old Testament*
BETL	Bibliotheca ephemeridum theologicarum lovaniensium
BFT	Biblical Foundations in Theology
BHS	*Biblia hebraica stuttgartensia*
Bib	*Biblica*
BKAT	Biblischer Kommentar: Altes Testament
BO	*Bibliotheca orientalis*
BSac	*Bibliotheca Sacra*
BSC	Bible Study Commentary
BT	*Bible Translator*
BurH	*Buried History*
BZ	*Biblische Zeitschrift*
BZAW	Beihefte zur ZAW
CAD	*The Assyrian Dictionary of the Oriental Institute of the University of Chicago*

CAH	*Cambridge Ancient History*
CB	Century Bible
CBSC	Cambridge Bible for Schools and Colleges
CBC	Cambridge Bible Commentary
CBQ	*Catholic Biblical Quarterly*
CC	The Communicator's Commentary
CCK	*Chronicles of Chaldean Kings,* D. J. Wiseman
CHAL	*Concise Hebrew and Aramic Lexicon,* ed. W. L. Holladay
COT	Commentary on the Old Testament, C. F. Keil and F. Delitzsch
CTR	*Criswell Theological Review*
DOTT	*Documents from Old Testament Times,* ed. D. W. Thomas
EAEHL	*Encyclopedia of Archaeological Excavations in the Holy Land,* ed. M. Avi-Yonah
DSS	Dead Sea Scrolls
EBC	Expositor's Bible Commentary
Ebib	Etudes bibliques
ETL	*Ephermerides theologicae lovanienses*
EvBC	Everyman's Bible Commentary
FB	Forschung zur Bibel
FOTL	Forms of Old Testament Literature
GKC	Gesenius' Hebrew Grammar, ed. E. Kautzsch, tr. A. E. Cowley
GTJ	*Grace Theological Journal*
HAR	*Hebrew Annual Review*
HAT	Handbuch zum Alten Testament
HBT	*Horizons in Biblical Theology*
HDR	Harvard Dissertations in Religion
Her	Hermeneia
HKAT	Handkommentar zum Alten Testament
HSM	Harvard Semitic Monographs
HT	Helps for Translators
HTR	*Harvard Theological Review*
HUCA	*Hebrew Union College Annual*
IB	*Interpreter's Bible*
IBC	Interpretation: A Bible Commentary for Teaching and Preaching
ICC	International Critical Commentary
IDB	*Interpreter's Dictionary of the Bible,* ed. G. A. Buttrick, et al.

IDBSup	Supplementary volume to *IDB*
IBHS	B. K. Waltke and M. O'Connor, *Introduction to Biblical Hebrew Syntax*
IEJ	*Israel Exploration Journal*
IES	Israel Exploration Society
Int	*Interpretation*
ITC	International Theological Commentary
IOS	*Israel Oriental Society*
ISBE	*International Standard Bible Encyclopedia,* rev. ed. G. W. Bromiley
IJT	*Indian Journal of Theology*
ITC	International Theological Commentary
JANES	*Journal of Ancient Near Eastern Society*
JAOS	*Journal of the American Oriental Society*
JBL	*Journal of Biblical Literature*
JBR	*Journal of Bible and Religion*
JCS	*Journal of Cuneiform Studies*
JEA	*Journal of Egyptian Archaeology*
JETS	*Journal of the Evangelical Theological Society*
JJS	*Journal of Jewish Studies*
JNES	*Journal of Near Eastern Studies*
JNSL	*Journal of Northwest Semitic Languages*
JPOS	*Journal of Palestine Oriental Society*
JSJ	*Journal for the Study of Judaism in the Persian, Hellenistic, and Roman Period*
JSOR	*Journal of the Society for Oriental Research*
JSOT	*Journal for the Study of the Old Testament*
JSOTSup	JSOT—Supplement Series
JSS	*Journal of Semitic Studies*
JTS	*Journal of Theological Studies*
JTSNS	*Journal of Theological Studies, New Series*
KAT	Kommentar zum Alten Testament
KB	Koehler and W. Baumgartner, *Lexicon in Veteris Testamenti libros*
LBI	Library of Biblical Interpretation
LCC	Library of Christian Classics
LLAVT	E. Vogt, *Lexicon Linguae Aramaicae Veteris Testamenti*
LTQ	*Lexington Theological Quarterly*
MT	Masoretic Text
NAC	New American Commentary
NB	*Nebuchadrezzar and Babylon,* D. J. Wiseman

NBD	*New Bible Dictionary*
NCBC	New Century Bible Commentary
NICOT	New International Commentary on the Old Testament
NJPS	New Jewish Publication Society Version
NKZ	*Neue kirchliche Zeitschrift*
NovT	*Novum Testamentum*
NTS	*New Testament Studies*
Or	*Orientalia*
OTL	Old Testament Library
OTP	*The Old Testament Pseudepigrapha,* ed. J. H. Charlesworth
OTS	*Oudtestamentische Studiën*
OTWSA	*Ou-Testamentiese Werkgemeenskap in Suid-Afrika*
PCB	*Peake's Commentary on the Bible,* ed. M. Black and H. H. Rowley
PEQ	*Palestine Exploration Quarterly*
POTT	*Peoples of Old Testament Times,* ed. D. J. Wiseman
PTR	*Princeton Theological Review*
Pss. Sol.	*Psalms of Solomon*
RA	Revue d'assyriologie et d'archéologie orientale
RB	*Revue biblique*
ResQ	*Restoration Quarterly*
RevExp	*Review and Expositor*
RSR	Recherches de science religieuse
SANE	Sources from the Ancient Near East
SBLDS	Society of Biblical Literature Dissertation Series
SOTI	*A Survey of Old Testament Introduction,* G. L. Archer
SBT	Studies in Biblical Theology
SJT	*Scottish Journal of Theology*
SP	Samaritan Pentateuch
SR	Studies in Religion/Sciences religieuses
ST	*Studia theologica*
STJD	Studies on the Texts of the Desert of Judah
Syr	Syriac
TDOT	*Theological Dictionary of the Old Testament,* ed. G. J. Botterweck and H. Ringgren
Tg	Targum
TJNS	Trinity Journal—New Series
TrinJ	*Trinity Journal*
TLZ	*Theologische Literaturzeitung*
TOTC	Tyndale Old Testament Commentaries
TS	*Theological Studies*

TWAT	*Theologisches Wörterbuch zum Alten Testament,* ed. G. J. Botterweck and H. Ringgren
TWOT	*Theological Wordbook of the Old Testament*
TynBul	*Tyndale Bulletin*
UF	*Ugarit-Forschungen*
Vg	Vulgate
VT	*Vetus Testamentum*
VTSup	Vetus Testamentum, Supplements
WBC	Word Biblical Commentaries
WEC	Wycliffe Exegetical Commentary
WTJ	*Westminster Theological Journal*
WMANT	Wissenschaftliche Monographien zum Alten und Neuen Testament
ZAW	*Zeitschrift für die alttestamentliche Wissenschaft*
ZDMG	*Zeitschrift der deutschen morgenländischen Gesellschaft*
ZDPV	*Zeitschrift des deutschen Palätina-Vereing*
ZKT	*Zeitschrift für katholische Theologie*

Contents

The Divided Monarchy
Sidon
Damascus
Zarephath
MT. HERMON
MT. LEBANON
Tyre
ARAM
Dan
BASHAN
Hazor
Acco
Sea of Galilee
Wadi Yarmuk
MT. CARMEL
MT. TABOR
Megiddo
Jezreel
Beth-shan
Mediterranean Sea
Jordan River
Samaria
ISRAEL
GILEAD
AMMON
Shechem
EPHRAIM
Aphek
Shiloh
Joppa
Bethel
Ai
Gilgal
Rabbath-Ammon
Mizpah
Heshbon
Ramah
Jericho
BENJAMIN
MT. NEBO
Gibeon
Anathoth (Anata)
Ekron
Jerusalem
Ashdod
Beth-hakkerem
Medeba
Beth-shemesh
Bethlehem
Baal-meon
Ashkelon
Azekah
Tekoa
Lachish
Dibon
Hebron
Gaza
JUDAH
Dead Sea
Wadi Arnon
Aroer
Gath
MOAB
Beersheba
Kir-Hareseth
Honoraim
The Negev
Zoar
Ije-abarim
Wadi Zered
The Arabah
EDOM
Bozrah
Scale of Miles
0 5 10 20

1, 2 Kings

INTRODUCTION OUTLINE

INTRODUCTION

First and Second Kings conclude a history of Israel that, generally speaking, begins in Genesis. This history has an amazing scope, for it includes the human race's origins, Israel's emergence through Abraham and Sarah's family, the exodus, the conquest, the monarchy, and the nation's destruction.[1] More specifically, 1, 2 Kings explain how and why Israel lost the land it fought so hard to win in Joshua and worked so hard to organize in Judges and 1, 2 Samuel. These books focus on *Israel's* successes and failures, of course, yet also comment on world politics. Scholars of virtually every theological stripe are impressed with the accuracy of the historical details in 1, 2 Kings. Thus, it is appropriate to begin any analysis of these books with a section on historical issues.

Introduction to Historical Issues

First and Second Kings are not disinterested, flat historical works. Rather, they emphasize most of Scripture's great theological truths. They stress God's sovereignty over Israel and all other nations. They claim that God created the earth and therefore has every right to rule the earth. This rule unfolds in accordance with the Lord's character, which means that mercy, justice, righteousness, and salvation work together when God fashions world events.

This section addresses five traditional background issues. First, the difficult matter of authorship and date will be discussed. Though this subject gets complicated at times, interpreters need to weigh authorial options in order to gain a better understanding of the books' original purpose. Second, the chronologies in 1, 2 Kings will be treated. Even a casual reader will notice some apparent difficulties in the Kings' dates, so some sense of the author's methodology must be gained. Third, the political situations depicted in 1, 2 Kings will be

[1] This statement certainly reflects the obvious nature of the OT canon, but note E. G. Newing, "The Rhetoric of Hope: The Theological Structure of Genesis–2 Kings," *Colloquium* (Australia: NZ) 17, no. 2, 1–15, for an argument for the literary, structural, and theological unity of Genesis-Kings.

noted to help explain why Israel experienced success during some eras and dismal defeat in others. Fourth, textual problems related to 1, 2 Kings will be examined. Fifth, the role of miracles in the books will be analyzed to determine whether 1, 2 Kings always divulges historical material or sometimes relates legendary tales.

1. The Authorship and Date of 1, 2 Kings

The identity and viewpoint of the author of 1, 2 Kings have sparked lively debate over the past fifty years. This debate has basically been divided into scholars who think the books were written by a single author who carefully crafted the history using accurate sources and those who believe the texts were composed by two or more careful editors writing at different stages of Israel's history. These commentators include a variety of data in their discussions but usually begin with the evidence the books themselves provide.

(1) Internal Evidence

No author is ever mentioned in the text itself. There is not even a major character in the story that stands out as a possible composer of the books. Given this situation, it is necessary to examine other types of information provided in the accounts in order to determine when 1, 2 Kings were written. Three elements in the books may provide some idea of when the author may have lived. The first element is the scope of events covered in the books. Roughly four hundred years unfold. Solomon's rise to the throne of his father David, which occurs ca. 970 B.C., is the initial event in 1 Kings. Second Kings concludes with a description of how Jehoiachin, a Judahite king exiled in 597 B.C., is given kind treatment in the thirty-seventh year of his imprisonment in Babylon (2 Kgs 25:27–30). This notation sets the author of that section beyond 560 B.C. Therefore, it is safe to conclude that the books were completed sometime after that date. Since no other events are mentioned, the author of the books could have written the material by 550 B.C.

The second element is the many instances of "until this day" or some variation of that phrase.[2] Taken at face value, this editorial comment may mean that the situation the author describes still existed when the books were composed. The phrase appears at least twelve times in the two books (1 Kgs 8:8;

[2]Cf. B. Childs, "A Study of the Formula, 'Until This Day,'" *JBL* 82 (1963) 279–92. Childs notes that the formula has both historical and theological implications, yet "seldom has an etiological function of justifying an existing phenomenon, but in the great majority of cases is a formula of personal testimony added to, and confirming, a received tradition" (p. 292). Thus, the phrase confirms what was true whenever the source the author used was written, or when the author composed his own material.

9:13,21; 12:19; 2 Kgs 2:22; 8:22; 10:27; 14:7; 16:6; 17:23,34,41). One reference describes a portion of the temple (1 Kgs 8:8). Four of them comment on place names (1 Kgs 9:13; 2 Kgs 2:22; 10:27; 14:7). Three refer to a foreign nation's attitude toward Israel (1 Kgs 9:21; 2 Kgs 8:21; 16:6), and four occur in denunciation of activities and attitudes in Samaria.

All of these references except 1 Kgs 8:8 and 9:21 depict situations and opinions that still could have been true after 560 B.C. Place names do not necessarily change over time. Likewise, Edom's hatred of Israel (2 Kgs 8:22) and habitation of Elath (2 Kgs 16:6) were both still intact by the mid-sixth century B.C.[3] Also the Samaritan idolatry and hatred of their southern brothers and sisters (2 Kgs 12:19; 17:23,34,41) was quite possibly continuing after 560 B.C. Given their nature, then, these texts do not clearly determine when 1, 2 Kings were written.

Since the temple itself was destroyed in 587 B.C., it seems unlikely that the statement in 1 Kgs 8:8 that the poles that held the ark of the covenant "could be seen from the Holy Place in front of the inner sanctuary . . . and they are still there today" could not have been written after that time. Two solutions are possible. First, some Greek translations of the Old Testament omit this phrase, so textual criticism may remove the problem.[4] Second, authors who write a history covering several centuries normally use written sources. The books mention three such sources (see below). Thus, 1 Kgs 8:8 simply states what was true when the author's source was written. In other words, the author accurately quotes a source here. Either solution is possible, though the latter one encounters the least difficulties.

Likewise, 1 Kgs 9:21 says Solomon conscripted certain nations for forced labor and that they remain so "to this day." Again, after Israel ceased to exist in 587 B.C., this statement would be out of place. It is likely, therefore, that the author confirms the source's accuracy in this verse as well. In modern terminology the writer "footnotes" the source.

Because of the ambiguous nature of these references, then, it is impossible to use them as clear indicators of the books' authorship and date. The formula does, however, encourage readers to trust the historical information included in the text. It also invites a careful inspection of the books' stated sources and how they are used in the story.

The third element relating to authorship and date is that three written sources are mentioned in 1, 2 Kings. The Book of the Acts of Solomon is listed in 1 Kgs 11:41 and seems to be cited as the main source for most if not all of the Solomonic material in chaps. 1–11. The Book of the Chronicles of the

---

[3] J. A. Montgomery and H. S. Gehman, *A Critical and Exegetical Commentary on the Book of Kings*, ICC (1951; reprint, Edinburgh: T & T Clark, 1986) 458.

[4] The BHS editors suggest that the formula may belong after 8:9 instead of 8:8.

Kings of Israel is claimed as a source for every northern king's reign except for Jehoram and Hoshea, while the Book of the Chronicles of the Kings of Judah is cited as a source of information on the Southern rulers except for Ahaziah, Athaliah, Jehoahaz, Jehoiachin, and Zedekiah.[5] In each instance where these three sources appear, the author leaves the impression that further details on each king's era was available in those works. This impression leaves the true nature of the source material very much in doubt, which has allowed various scholarly opinions to arise.

In the decades after J. Wellhausen popularized source criticism of the Pentateuch, several scholars, following Wellhausen himself,[6] sought to divide 1, 2 Kings into a number of possible documents. Some critics argued that the same J and E sources supposedly found in the Pentateuch also run throughout 1, 2 Kings.[7] Other commentators largely rejected the J and E hypothesis and chose to focus on identifying all the possible unstated sources that might have been used to write the books.[8] Most writers correctly concluded that so-called Pentateuchal sources were not present in 1, 2 Kings, based on the difficulty of determining what the three sources, and any other unstated sources, may have actually contained. As G. H. Jones declares, "The variety of the sources that can be traced is the precise reason why the Pentateuchal documentary hypothesis is inadequate to deal with Kings."[9]

If the hypothetical Pentateuchal documents are not used in 1, 2 Kings, then what is the nature and number of the books' actual sources? Interpreters must exercise caution and humility when answering these questions. Though only three sources are explicitly revealed, other data may have been used. After all, the stated sources all refer to the activity of kings. The books also include several narratives about prophets, which makes it possible that the author also gathered written or oral materials from prophetic circles. If so, more than three

[5] Cf. J. Skinner, *1, 2 Kings,* CB, rev. ed. (Edinburgh: T & T Clark, 1904) 23.

[6] J. Wellhausen, *Prolegomena to the History of Ancient Israel,* rev. ed., trans. Menzies and Black (1883; reprint, Gloucester, Mass.: Peter Smith, 1973) 228–94. Wellhausen's theories exploded on the theological scene in 1878 with the first edition of this volume.

[7] E.g., O. Eissfeldt concluded that J, E, and an older lay (L) source are evident in Genesis-Kings (*The Old Testament: An Introduction,* 3d ed., trans. P. Ackroyd [New York: Harper & Row, 1966] 241–48, 297–99). Cf. I. Benzinger, "Jahwist und Elohist in den Königsbüchern," BZAW II, 2 (Berlin: Töpelmann, 1921); G. Hölscher, "Das Buch der Könige, seine Quellen und seine Redaktion," *Eucharisterion Hermann Gunkel zum 60 Geburstag,* FRLANT 36 (Göttingen: Vandenhoeck & Ruprecht, 1927), and R. Smend, "JE in den geschichtlichen Büchern des Alten Testament, herausgegeben von H. Holzinger," *ZAW* 39 (1921) 204–15, for variations of the J and E theory.

[8] Prominent proponents of this type of analysis include S. R. Driver, *An Introduction to the Literature of the Old Testament* (1891; reprint, Gloucester, Mass.: Peter Smith, 1972) 188–89, who adds prophetic and temple sources to the three stated sources, and Skinner, *1, 2 Kings,* 23–33, who also adds prophetic, priestly, political, and succession sources.

[9] G. H. Jones, *1 and 2 Kings,* NCB (Grand Rapids: Eerdmans, 1984) 1:47. Jones offers the most complete introduction to source and dating issues of any current commentary.

sources were used.[10] As for the nature of the stated sources, 1 Kgs 11:41 indicates that the Book of the Acts of Solomon "comprised contemporary annals, biographical material, and extracts from records in the Temple archives."[11] The Books of the Chronicles of the Kings of Israel and Judah probably contained similar details, since they are said to chronicle dates, royal achievements, and important events (e.g., 2 Kgs 13:8). Whether or not these "events" include the prophets' lives and teachings is impossible to determine. Thus, it is appropriate to conclude that the exact nature of the author's sources is also unknown.

Do such conclusions lessen the historical value of 1, 2 Kings? No, for archaeological evidence found in the past one hundred years demonstrates that the historical data remains accurate and reliable. The author simply chose appropriate material from available sources to tell Israel's story and even cited the documents in case readers wanted to peruse them. Certainly the author produced a theological history, but this fact does not automatically mean the history is inaccurate.[12] Indeed theological concern may lead to an even greater concern for truth and accuracy. There is no reason, then, to doubt that the author of 1, 2 Kings used accurate sources to write the books, even though their exact nature and age cannot be recovered.

Several conclusions emerge from this discussion of the internal evidence about the authorship and date of 1, 2 Kings. First, the books were written anonymously (see next section) after Jerusalem's destruction. Second, this author freely admits using sources for this history spanning over four hundred years, claims the sources are accurate, and invites inspection of these sources. Third, the books' theological interests do not negate their historicity, or vice versa. Fourth, more explicit knowledge of the author's intentions in writing must be gleaned by examining the books' literary and theological characteristics.

(2) Single-Author Theories

Several commentators think that a single individual working about 550 B.C.

---

[10] Though they differ over specifics, scholars from a wide variety of critical and theological positions agree that the author of Kings used more than three sources. Materials from David's court and from prophetic circles are commonly listed as possibilities. Cf. R. K. Harrison, *Introduction to the Old Testament* (Grand Rapids: Eerdmans, 1969) 726–29; A. E. Hill and J. H. Walton, *A Survey of the Old Testament* (Grand Rapids: Zondervan, 1991) 203–4; G. R. Jones, *1, 2 Kings,* 47–77; and J. Gray, *1 and 2 Kings,* OTL (Philadelphia: Westminster, 1963) 20–43.

[11] Harrison, *Introduction to the Old Testament,* 726.

[12] See the "Introduction to Literary Issues" in this Introduction and discussions such as those found in S. J. DeVries, *1 Kings,* WBC (Waco: Word, 1985) xxxiii–xxxiv, and G. Rice, *Nations under God: A Commentary on the Book of 1 Kings,* ITC (Grand Rapids: Eerdmans, 1990) 2–3. Even scholars who think 1, 2 Kings include "legendary" material still consider them to be mostly solid, trustworthy accounts. E.g., S. Szikszai, "Kings, 1 and 2," *IDB* (Nashville: Abingdon, 1962) 3:31. Many writers who call material "legendary" or "mythic" seem to write with antisupernaturalist presuppositions.

collected relevant source data, arranged the material into a coherent whole, and then wrote 1, 2 Kings as a conclusion to the history of Israel begun in Joshua, Judges, and 1, 2 Samuel. Some of these scholars believe that this person wrote only 1, 2 Kings, while others contend that the individual wrote all these books. Obviously, in either case this author must have possessed tremendous historical, literary, and theological abilities.

Nineteenth-century advocates of the single-author position tended to assert that the author of 1, 2 Kings did not compose all the former prophets. For instance, C. F. Keil argues that 1, 2 Kings display a united theological perspective "of the kingdom of God under the kings," as well as a unity of language.[13] This theological and linguistic unity led Keil to conclude that a single individual wrote 1, 2 Kings and that this person "was a prophet living in the Babylonian exile" during "the second half of the Babylonian captivity."[14] Yet Keil states that the "peculiarities of the language of the different prophetic books of history do furnish decisive evidence" against the notion that this same author wrote all of Joshua-Kings.[15] Keil also argues for multiple authorship because Spinoza and other antisupernaturalists held the opposite position.[16]

S. R. Driver also thought that 1, 2 Kings exhibit a distinct, unified theology and unique linguistic features. Driver claimed that the books' author/compiler was greatly influenced by Deuteronomy and its power to reform in both the past and the future.[17] He also noted the distinctive phraseology the author uses to convey this theological viewpoint.[18] Driver did not think this compiler also wrote the other former prophets, however, because he accepted the source-critical opinion that the hypothetical sources JEDP run throughout Genesis to Joshua, thus forming a Hexateuch.[19]

Clearly, Keil and Driver present certain common conclusions. First, they agree that theology and phraseology unite 1, 2 Kings. Second, they do not believe that these elements are sufficiently visible in Joshua, Judges, and Samuel to conclude that all the books have the same author. Third, they state that the author's viewpoint is in part determined by the exile. Though parts of their studies are flawed, it is sufficient at this point to observe their agreements.

---

[13] C. F. Keil, "I and II Kings," COT, trans. J. Martin (1876; reprint, Grand Rapids: Eerdmans, 1980) 3:5, 9.

[14] Ibid., 11.

[15] C. F. Keil and F. Delitzsch, "The Book of Samuel," COT, trans. J. Martin (1857; reprint, Grand Rapids: Eerdmans, 1975) 2:11.

[16] Ibid., 12.

[17] Driver states: "Deuteronomy is the standard by which the compiler judges both men and actions; and the history, from the beginning of Solomon's reign, is presented, not in a purely 'objective' form (as, e.g., in 2 Sa. 9–20), but from the point of view of the Deuteronomic code" (*An Introduction,* 199).

[18] Ibid., 200–203.

[19] Ibid., 103–59.

In 1943 M. Noth set a new agenda for the authorship discussion by claiming that one author wrote all of Joshua, Judges, Samuel, and Kings.[20] His theory was clear, concise, and in step with then-current critical opinions on the Pentateuch and the Prophets. Noth claimed that the author was heavily influenced by the language and thinking "found in the Deuteronomic Law and the admonitory speeches which precede and follow the Law,"[21] an opinion already stated by Driver and others. Because of this influence, Noth called the author "the Deuteronomist." Further, Noth said the "Deuteronomist" selected source materials that were then carefully crafted into a unified whole.[22] This process included writing Deuteronomy 1–4, providing links between "books" and composing strategic speeches that summarize and advance the story's plot.[23] Finally, Noth stated that the "Deuteronomist" had witnessed the fall of Jerusalem (and thus must have written the history by 550 B.C.)[24] and therefore wrote in order to explain to future generations how Israel lost its land.[25] The "Deuteronomist" was a careful, theologically astute individual who chronicled the negative side of Israel's history.

Various critiques of Noth's ideas soon surfaced. Some of these argued for multiple authors of the books (see next section). Others accepted Noth's basic theses but modified certain theological or compositional details. For example, G. von Rad and H. W. Wolff observed that the history's theology may be more hopeful than Noth thinks. Von Rad claimed that the "Deuteronomist" was fascinated by how God fulfilled prophetic words (predictions) in history and that the great historian believed that God would continue to work with and through David's descendants because of the promises made to David in 2 Sam 7:13.[26] According to von Rad, the partially hopeful ending of 2 Kings (25:27–30) implies "that the line of David has not yet come to an irrevocable end."[27]

---

[20] M. Noth, *The Deuteronomistic History,* trans. D. Orton, JSOTSup 15 (Sheffield: Sheffield Academic Press, 1981).

[21] Ibid., 4. Indeed Noth believed the "Deuteronomist" wrote Deut 1–4 as an introduction to the then-existing book of Deuteronomy, which then served as an introduction to the history as a whole (*The Deuteronomistic History,* 14–17).

[22] Noth says, "Dtr. was not merely an editor but the author of a history which brought together material from highly varied traditions and arranged it according to a carefully conceived plan. In general Dtr. simply reproduced the literary sources available to him and merely provided a connecting narrative for isolated passages. We can prove, however, that in places he made a deliberate selection from the material at his disposal" (*The Deuteronomistic History,* 10).

[23] Cf. Noth, *The Deuteronomistic History,* 9, for a discussion of how the author created transitions between books and p. 5 for opinions about the role of the key speeches in the history.

[24] Ibid., 99.

[25] Ibid., 90–92.

[26] G. von Rad, *Studies in Deuteronomy,* SBT 9, trans. D. Stalker (1948; reprint, London: SCM Press, 1963) 74–91. Von Rad thinks that 2 Sam 7:13 is the first and greatest of eleven prophetic promises in the "deuteronomistic" history. See the sections on theology and structure in this Introduction for more implications of von Rad's insights.

[27] Ibid., 90–91.

Wolff locates his positive theology in the many texts that encourage Israel to repent and turn to the Lord.[28] These passages indicate that God still cares for Israel and calls this special nation back to a relationship with its Lord. These and other[29] studies helped balance Noth's presentation of the books' theology.

R. K. Harrison provided an evangelical's perspective on Noth's work in his comprehensive *Introduction to the Old Testament* (1969). While agreeing that one person heavily influenced by covenant thinking and the Book of Deuteronomy wrote Joshua-Kings, Harrison correctly noted that this conclusion need not be based on an acceptance of source-critical theories of the Pentateuch.[30] In fact, "the term 'Deuteronomist' can only be applied unexceptionally to Kings in the sense that the author recognized with Moses (Deut 28:1ff.), that obedience to God brought blessing, while disobedience resulted in calamity."[31] Still, Harrison and Noth both stressed the unity of Joshua-Kings, the overriding theology of these books, and their probable composition by 550 B.C.

Recently, B. Long has argued for a single author because of Noth's conclusions and because of the literary form of ancient historical documents. Long finds arguments for multiple editions of the history wanting, particularly because these theories are based on minor linguistic variations, on the assumption that ancient authors wrote toward a climactic conclusion, and on the presumption that the longer a document is the more hands have written it.[32] Long critiques these criteria and cites Herodotus's ancient history of Greece[33] as an example of an ancient historical account that, like 1, 2 Kings, "carefully connected traditions with one another, preserved the multiplicity of factors in each account while stressing one point or another, and suggested connections to other portions" of the whole work.[34] In other words, Herodotus carefully com-

---

[28] H. W. Wolff, "The Kerygma of the Deuteronomic Historical Work," trans. F. C. Prussner, in *The Vitality of Old Testament Traditions,* ed. W. Brueggemann and H. W. Wolff (Atlanta: John Knox, 1975) 83–100. Note Wolff's summary of the historian's main theological points on p. 98.

[29] Cf. D. J. McCarthy, "II Samuel 7 and the Structure of the Deuteronomic History," *JBL* 84 (1965) 131–38, for an analysis of both the positive and negative aspects of God's promise to David within 1, 2 Samuel and 1, 2 Kings. See H. A. Kenick, *Design for Kingship: The Deuteronomistic Narrative Technique in 1 Kings 3:4–15,* SBLDS (Chico, Cal.: Scholars Press, 1983) for a representative work on how the "deuteronomist" shaped important speeches.

[30] Harrison, *Introduction to the Old Testament,* 732.

[31] Ibid. For significant arguments in favor of Mosaic authorship of Deuteronomy, see M. G. Kline, *Treaty of the Great King: The Covenant Structure of Deuteronomy* (Grand Rapids: Eerdmans, 1963); P. C. Craigie, *The Book of Deuteronomy,* NICOT (Grand Rapids: Eerdmans, 1976) 24–69; and R. K. Harrison, *Introduction to the Old Testament,* 495–541, 637–62.

[32] B. O. Long, *1 Kings, with an Introduction to Historical Literature,* FOTL (Grand Rapids: Eerdmans, 1984) 16–18.

[33] Herodotus was born between 490 and 480 B.C. Like the author of 1, 2 Kings, his history was based on oral tradition and written sources. He also attributes many events to divine powers. Cf. Herodotus, *The Histories,* trans. and introduced by A. de Selincourt (Baltimore: Penguin, 1954). Selincourt notes, "Herodotus' greatness lies in the mastery by which he has reduced his enormous mass of heterogeneous material to a single artistic whole of unsurpassed beauty and grace" (p. 9).

[34] Long, *1 Kings,* 19.

bined diverse sources into a coherent whole. Long also notes that Sumerian and Assyrian records show that sources can be updated "many centuries with extreme fidelity to a received tradition."[35] Thus, Long finds no compelling reason to interpret 1, 2 Kings as books collected by a series of editors rather than as a unified work compiled and arranged by one author.

A fairly distinct authorial portrait emerges from these discussions. The author is an anonymous individual[36] who carefully collected source data and shaped this material into a great history that, despite the objections of Keil, Driver, and others, spans Joshua-Kings. This author wrote about 550 B.C. and was influenced by covenant theology such as that found in Deuteronomy and the prophets. The historian's main idea was the loss of the promised land, a theme that includes God's ongoing concern for Israel. It is not necessary to accept source-critical viewpoints about the authorship of Deuteronomy to accept the single-author theory. As was stated earlier, this individual must have possessed outstanding literary, historical, and spiritual depth.

(3) Multiple-Author Theories

Several scholars have concluded that the "deuteronomic history" and, thus, 1, 2 Kings, passed through more than one editor's hands. These editors are said to have completed separate histories that had distinct theological viewpoints and distinct conclusions. A later editor then added his own historical details, smoothed over some rough transitions, and thereby produced 1, 2 Kings as it now stands.

Long before Noth's hypothesis appeared, some commentators believed that there had once existed an early version of 1, 2 Kings that only included preexilic materials. Both A. Kuenen and J. Wellhausen thought that the formula "unto this day," the apparent lack of awareness in 1 Kings 8 that the temple would be destroyed, and the possible presupposing of the exile in other texts indicate at least two editions of the "deuteronomic history."[37] For similar reasons J. Skinner identified two editors of the material, the first writing just

---

[35] Ibid., 18.

[36] One Jewish tradition says Jeremiah wrote 1, 2 Kings. G. Archer, *A Survey of Old Testament Introduction,* rev. ed. (Chicago: Moody, 1974), and R. D. Patterson and H. J. Austel, "1 & 2 Kings," EBC (Grand Rapids: Zondervan, 1988), argue for the plausibility of Jeremianic authorship based on the covenant and prophetic emphases in 1, 2 Kings. The lack of any mention of Jeremiah in 1, 2 Kings is a serious blow to this theory, especially since Jeremiah's prophecy is never shy about mentioning the prophet by name in either first- (autobiographical) or third-person accounts.

[37] Cf. A. Kuenen, *Historisch-Kritische Einleitung in die Bücher des Alten Testaments,* trans. T. Weber (Leipzig: Otto Schulze, 1886–1894); J. Wellhausen, *Die Composition des Hexateuchs und der historischen Bücher des Alten Testaments* (Berlin: Georg Reimer, 1889); and Wellhausen, *Prolegomena.* For an outstanding summary of these and other multiredactional theories, see R. D. Nelson, *The Double Redaction of the Deuteronomistic History,* JSOTSup 18 (Sheffield: Sheffield Academic Press, 1981). Nelson's own ideas are discussed later.

before the fall of Jerusalem and the second between 561 B.C. and 536 B.C.[38] Despite his conclusions Skinner warns that the two editors "are so much alike in their principles and their cast of thought that it is not always possible to assign an editorial insertion with confidence to the one rather than to the other."[39]

Eissfeldt proposed that the hypothetical sources JE, plus a third source (L), continued into Joshua-Kings from the Pentateuch. This initial edition was then expanded over several decades until the material reached its final form.[40] His hypothesis never enjoyed widespread acceptance, but the two-editor theory was embraced by many thinkers and even led some writers to postulate three editions of 1, 2 Kings. A. Jepsen located two editors in the books, one with a priestly perspective and one with prophetic convictions.[41] Like Skinner, though, Jepsen could not be sure where one spoke and the other did not. R. Smend agreed with Jepsen's concept of prophetic and priestly editors and added another compiler who displays keen interest in the law. Thus, Smend claimed that a prophetic editor wrote an initial history after Jerusalem's fall (587 B.C.), a priestly compiler reworked the history about 580–560 B.C., and a law-oriented editor completed the work after 560 B.C.[42] These individuals were all heavily influenced by "deuteronomic" thought, which explains the books' coherence. G. H. Jones basically agrees with Smend's conclusions because he thinks this theory explains both the unity that Noth emphasizes and the diversity inherent in the text.[43] Jones therefore believes that a "deuteronomic school," or movement, may have produced this history after several decades of theological reflection.[44]

Following F. M. Cross's suggestion that there is no explanatory text for Jerusalem's fall to match the one for Samaria's demise (2 Kgs 17), R. D. Nel-

---

[38] Skinner, *1 Kings,* 18–23, 30–33.

[39] Ibid., 22.

[40] Eissfeldt, *The Old Testament: An Introduction,* 297–99.

[41] A. Jepsen, *Die Quellen der Königsbuches* (Halle: Niemeyer, 1953).

[42] Cf. R. Smend, "Das Gesetz und die Völker: Ein Beitrag zur deuteronomistischen Redaktionsgeschichte," in *Probleme Biblischer Theologie: Gerhard von Rad zum 70. Geburstag,* ed. H. W. Wolff (Munich: Chr. Kaiser, 1971) 494–509; and *Die Enstehung des Alten Testaments* (Stuttgart: Kohlhammer, 1978) 110–25. Smend's ideas were adopted and adapted by W. Dietrich, *Prophetie und Geschichte. Eine redaktionsgeschichtliche Untersuchung zum deuteronomistischen Geschichtswerk,* FRLANT 108 (Göttingen: Vandenhoeck & Ruprecht, 1972), and T. Veijola, *Das Königtum in der Beurteilung der deuteronomistischen Historiographie* (Helsinki: Suomalainen Tieddeakatemia, 1977). H. Weippert suggests another three-editor theory in "Die 'deuteronomistischen' Beurteilungen der Könige von Israel und Juda und das Problem der Redaktion der Königsbücher," *Bib* 53 (1972) 301–39. Weippert thinks that a first edition appeared at the time of Samaria's destruction (722 B.C.), a second near Josiah's era (640–609 B.C.), and a third after Jerusalem's fall.

[43] Jones, *1 and 2 Kings,* 1:43–44.

[44] Ibid., 44.

son said that one pro-David editor wrote during Josiah's time and was followed by an exilic writer who explains how and why the monarchy ended. Nelson based his arguments on detailed structural, theological, and linguistic grounds.[45] This 1981 volume stated the two-author theory more carefully than it had been in the past yet also generally agreed with other commentators who advocated the multiple-authorship position.[46]

Two scenarios emerge from the multiple-author theories. The first is based on historical developments, the most important of which are the fall of Samaria and the fall of Jerusalem. A first edition of 1, 2 Kings was composed to explain Samaria's destruction, and a second edition included Jerusalem's destruction and intended to warn the survivors of future judgment and to offer hope beyond that devastation. The second scenario also focuses on critical historical events yet stresses theological viewpoints a bit more. This scheme has prophetic, priestly, and legal minds producing an ever-growing document along similar theological lines.

(4) Conclusion

Though it is prudent to be cautious about the authorship of an anonymous document, the single-author approach to the issue probably is the best solution to the problem. At least four reasons point to this conclusion. First, this position best explains the unity of Joshua-Kings in general and 1, 2 Kings in particular. As is evident from the texts themselves, each new "book" in this great history is linked to its predecessor. Thus, Moses' death links Joshua to Deuteronomy, Joshua's death ties Judges to Joshua, Samuel's acting as the last judge unites Judges and 1, 2 Samuel, and David's final days helps 2 Samuel flow into 1, 2 Kings. Other linkages also hold the books together, such as conquering the land, God's promises to David, and Israel's loss of land through their worship of idols. Multiple authors/editors could possibly achieve this type of unity, but critical scholars themselves struggle to suggest ways that several writers could produce such a coherent story.

Second, the single-author theory adequately explains the history's diversity. Because the author used source material that spans from the conquest of Canaan (either ca. 1400 or 1250 B.C.) to the Babylonian conquest of Jerusalem

---

[45] Cf. F. M. Cross, "The Themes of the Book of Kings and the Structure of the Deuteronomistic History," in *Canaanite Myth and Hebrew Epic* (Cambridge: Harvard University Press, 1973) 274–89, and R. D. Nelson, *The Double Redaction of the Deuteronomistic History.* Gray also claims there were two redactions, one c. 597 B.C. and one after 587 B.C., in *I and II Kings,* 38. In *1 Kings* (WBC [Waco: Word, 1985]) DeVries says that a first edition was written by "a contemporary of King Josiah" (xlii) and was "revised by a member of the same school living during the Babylonian exile, ca. 550 B.C." (xliii).

[46] Though I do not share Nelson's preference for the double redaction theory, his book is careful, balanced, and quick to point out the weaknesses of other multiple author positions.

(587 B.C.), some diversity is to be expected. It is also true that the author had to include various ideological viewpoints to portray accurately Israel's theological heritage. Third, as Long has stated, the single-author hypothesis fits the nature of ancient historiography. Indeed, ancient historians often used diverse types of material to present a series of scenes that create the author's main arguments.[47] Seen this way, what some scholars consider evidence for two or more editors can actually be viewed as part of a carefully structured whole (see section two below).

Fourth, the single-author theory retains its scholarly attractiveness without encountering the difficulties of the multiple-author position. Scholars advocating multiple authors do not agree on the number, date, or criteria of the proposed redactions. They are forced to posit "schools" that last for decades to account for the unity in the books, or they must utilize highly selective and sensitive criteria to separate one edition from the other.[48] These tendencies appear to be based more on a preference for a modified source criticism than on the final form of the text itself. Certainly the single-author viewpoint has difficulties of its own, such as accounting for the books' various theological emphases, but it does deal resourcefully with theological, historical, and literary issues.

Therefore, this commentary will analyze the text with a single author in mind. Using many ancient sources this author composed Joshua-Kings as a sweeping account of Israel's tragic loss of the land it was promised in the Pentateuch.[49] Though this loss was a quite negative event, the author did not view the situation as permanent. Living after the nation's defeat, this great writer looked to God's earlier promises as proof that Israel was not finished. As several commentators have observed, the author was influenced by Deuteronomy and the covenant concept. It is unnecessary, however, to conclude that the historian wrote any part of the Book of Deuteronomy. That book's influence is sufficient to explain the emphases in Joshua-Kings. Seen this way, then, the author wrote 1, 2 Kings as the capstone to a compelling story. These books depict Israel's glory, failures, and enduring hope.

2. The Chronology of 1, 2 Kings

Even a casual reading of 1, 2 Kings produces some apparent chronological questions. For example, the author lists how long the kings of Israel and Judah

---

[47] Cf. Long, *1 Kings,* 16–21.

[48] Cf. Jones, *1 and 2 Kings,* 1:44, and Nelson, *The Double Redaction of the Deuteronomistic History,* 43–98.

[49] For two thorough analyses of the role of the land motif in the Pentateuch, see D. J. A. Clines, *The Theme of the Pentateuch,* JSOTSup 10 (Sheffield: Sheffield Academic Press, 1978) and, especially, J. H. Sailhamer, *The Pentateuch as Narrative: A Biblical-Theological Commentary,* LBI 4 (Grand Rapids: Zondervan, 1992).

reigned and synchronizes the monarchs with one another. Oddly, however, when these numbers are added, one kingdom seems to have more years than the other. Just as strangely, 2 Kgs 9:29 says Ahaziah became king of Judah during Joram's eleventh year as king of Israel, while 2 Kgs 8:25 places Ahaziah's reign in Joram's twelfth year. Similar statements are made about Ahab's son Joram in 2 Kgs 1:17; 3:1; and 8:16. The length of Omri's reign does not seem to coincide with the author's synchronization of Omri with Asa (cf. 1 Kgs 16:28–29), nor does the biblical account of Hezekiah's deeds match Assyrian records at first glance. These and other difficulties have led some scholars to take a dim view of the books' accuracy. J. Gray represents this attitude when he writes that "these precise figures often confuse rather than elucidate chronology, which in consequence is one of the notorious problems of Old Testament scholarship."[50]

Fortunately, these difficulties can be explained by consulting other ancient chronologies and by examining how Judah and Israel counted the length of a monarch's reign. R. K. Harrison notes that Assyrian records set the date for the battle of Qarqar at 853 B.C., which is the same year Ahab died.[51] This fixed date helps scholars figure the years before and after 853 B.C. M. Cogan and H. Tadmor add that other Assyrian texts "preserve the names of three kings of Israel: Menahem, Pekah, Hoshea, and one king of Judah: Ahaz."[52] They also add that Assyrian inscriptions and Babylonian documents clarify events surrounding the last years of both Israel and Judah and help set dates for the destruction of Samaria and Jerusalem.[53] Studies like these have the dual effect of establishing the basic veracity of the biblical texts and of identifying fixed dates that help synchronize the biblical data.

Perhaps the most significant analysis of the chronological methodology employed in 1, 2 Kings is E. R. Thiele's *Mysterious Numbers of the Hebrew Kings*.[54] Certainly other studies have made significant contributions to this issue,[55] but Thiele's work examines the most problems, deals with the issues fairly, and presents answers with great clarity. Thiele claims that most synchronic problems can be solved when readers realize that Judah and Israel counted the beginning of reigns differently. Normally, Judah used the accession-year

---

[50] Gray, *I and II Kings*, 56.

[51] Harrison, *Introduction to the Old Testament*, 733.

[52] M. Cogan and H. Tadmor, *II Kings*, AB 11 (New York: Doubleday, 1988) 5.

[53] Ibid., 5–6.

[54] E. R. Thiele, *The Mysterious Numbers of the Hebrew Kings*, 3d ed. (Grand Rapids: Zondervan, 1983).

[55] Cf. W. F. Albright, "The Chronology of the Divided Monarchy of Israel," *BASOR* 100 (1945) 16–22; K. A. Kitchen and T. C. Mitchell, "Chronology of the Old Testament," *NBD* (Grand Rapids: Eerdmans, 1962); and J. Begrich, *Die Chronologie der Könige von Israel und Judah und die Quellen des Rahmens des Königsbucher* (Tübingen: Mohr, 1929). For a recent summary of the issues, see T. R. Hobbs, *2 Kings*, WBC 13 (Waco: Word: 1985) xxxviii–xliv.

system, which began counting a king's first year at the first of the calendar year. Israel, on the other hand, began counting the regnal years from when the reign *began*. Thus, a year's difference could exist even when two kings began to rule on the same day. During one period both nations used the same system.[56] Further, the nations began their calendar year six months apart, which also would affect the counting of years.[57] Finally, some kings acted as coregents with their fathers before the older man's death.[58] Again, this factor, if unknown to the reader, would seemingly make some synchronisms impossible to accept.

Because of the information offered by the Assyrian and Babylonian records and by studies like Thiele's, it is possible for most commentators to affirm the historical reliability of the chronologies in 1, 2 Kings.[59] It has also become possible for scholars to present an accurate table of when the kings ruled. Disagreements remain but usually do not entail a significant shift of years for any important date. The chart in "The Divided Kingdom" section presents the kings' dates, including any coregency that may have occurred. Thiele's conclusions have been followed most of the time, and major divergencies are explained in the footnotes. Specific dating issues are discussed in the commentary.

3. The Political Situation in 1, 2 Kings

Domestic and foreign politics play a significant role in the events recounted in 1, 2 Kings. Regional conflicts, superpower expansionism, and petty internal squabbles all affect how Israel's history unfolds. To read 1, 2 Kings intelligently, then, it is necessary to note some key nations and events that impact the books' telling of the story. Though these nations and events take place in a "secular" context, the author constantly reminds readers that the Lord determines who rules at what point in history.

(1) The United Kingdom

Except for a description of David's last days (1 Kgs 1–2), Israel only exists

---

[56] Thiele, *Mysterious Numbers of the Hebrew Kings,* 21, 44.

[57] Ibid., 45.

[58] Ibid., 61–65. Thiele summarizes his system when he says: "The essential points of the chronological scheme we will present are in brief as follows: Judah began with the accession-year system, both for its own kings and its synchronisms with Israel. At a time of alliance and intermarriage with Israel, the system of Israel was adopted by Judah and was used through four reigns, after which Judah returned to its original system of reckoning. Regnal years in Judah began with the month of Tishri. In Israel the nonaccession-year system was used for the length of reign in Israel and the synchronisms with Judah. When Judah shifted back to the accession-year system, Israel also adopted that method. Regnal years in Israel began with the month of Nisan. In both Judah and Israel a number of co-regencies occurred, and in Israel there were two instances of rival reigns" (p. 21).

[59] E.g., Eissfeldt says that "the synchronistic dates of the books of Kings have also proved themselves to be old and basically reliable" (*The Old Testament: An Introduction,* 283).

as a unified, twelve-tribe nation during Solomon's reign (970–930 B.C.) in 1, 2 Kings. Unity had been difficult for David to achieve after Saul's death (cf. 2 Sam 2–4), and tribal tensions never died completely. Therefore, Solomon's ability to govern all twelve tribes for forty years was in itself a major achievement. Of course, the absence of wars and the emergence of economic prosperity probably helped the people accept his leadership more readily.

Solomon's foreign policy also was effective. He made peace with Egypt, the main threat from the south, through a marriage alliance (1 Kgs 3:1). Though this practice came to haunt him, marriage alliances were keys to peace with other neighboring countries as well (1 Kgs 11:1). Solomon also continued David's vital relationship with Tyre (1 Kgs 5:1–7). Tyre helped Solomon with his building projects, and he in turn paid them in wages and with a few small cities (1 Kgs 5:6; 9:10–14). The text indicates few external problems in the first decades of Solomon's reign.

In his old age, however, Solomon encountered several difficulties, which the author attributes to Solomon's idolatry (1 Kgs 11:1–8). God decided to punish Solomon but left David's descendants a portion of Israel to govern (1 Kgs 11:9–13). As a domestic punishment God allowed Jeroboam to emerge as a rebel leader (1 Kgs 11:26–40). More will be heard from him later. As a further punishment the Lord "raises up" (1 Kgs 11:14) Edomite foes to the southeast (1 Kgs 11:14–22) and Aramean enemies in the north (1 Kgs 11:23–25). Worse still, Solomon's allies in Egypt were overthrown by Shishak, who supported Solomon's domestic and foreign enemies (1 Kgs 11:14–40).[60] Clearly, Solomon's death found Israel in a weakened condition both at home and abroad.

(2) The Divided Kingdom

Immediately after Solomon's death the nation split into two parts. Jeroboam managed to take ten northern tribes, while Rehoboam, Solomon's son, retained Judah and Benjamin—two southern tribes (1 Kgs 12:1–17). Tensions had always existed in Israel, yet the author states that the division occurred as a direct result of Solomon's sin (1 Kgs 11:9–13) and according to God's word through Ahijah the prophet (1 Kgs 11:29–39). Once again the Lord directs human events. After the split "Israel" became two nations, with two names, with two capitals, in two separate regions (see following chart).

KINGS OF JUDAH	KINGS OF ISRAEL
Rehoboam (930–913)	Jeroboam I (930–909)

[60] J. Bright, *A History of Israel,* 2d ed. (Philadelphia: Westminster, 1972) 229. Bright's account of Israel's history from Solomon to Jehoiachin (cf. pp. 206–339) is clear, concise, and accurate.

Abijah (913–910)	
Asa (910–869)	Nadab (909–908)
	Baasha (908–885)
	Elah (885–884)
	Zimri (884)
	Tibni (884–880)
	Civil Unrest (884–880)[61]
	Omri (880–874)
Coregency (872–869)	Ahab (874–853)
Jehoshaphat (869–848)	Ahaziah (853–852)
Coregency (853–848)	Joram (852–841)
Jehoram (848–841)	
Ahaziah (841)	Jehu (841–814)
Athaliah (841–835)	
Joash (835–796)	Jehoahaz (814–798)
	Jehoash (798–782)
Amaziah (796–767)	
Coregency (792–767)[62]	Coregency (793–782)
	Jeroboam II (782–753)
Azariah/Uzziah (767–740)	Zechariah (753–752)
	Shallum (752)
Coregency (750–740)	Menahem (752–742)
	Pekahiah (742–740)
Jotham (740–731)	Pekah (740–732)[63]
Coregency (735–731)	Hoshea (732–722)
Ahaz (731–715)	
Hezekiah (715–687)	
Coregency (697–687)	

[61] Omri and Tibni apparently rule rival factions in Israel from 884 to 880 B.C. (cf. 1 Kgs 16:21–22). Thus, in effect, two "kings" existed at the same time.

[62] Amaziah's and Uzziah's dates are particularly difficult to determine. The text gives Amaziah twenty-nine years (2 Kgs 14:2); it says Uzziah succeeds his father at age sixteen (2 Kgs 14:21) and then rules for fifty-two years (2 Kgs 15:2). Some coregency must have occurred for other fixed dates, such as Samaria's fall, to be correct. How many years the coregency lasted and Uzziah's age during the coregency, though, continue to puzzle interpreters. Cf. Thiele, *Mysterious Numbers of the Hebrew Kings,* 199–200.

[63] First Kings 15:27–31 says Pekah ruled for twenty years and equates these years with Jotham's first twenty years. Some coregency occurred, but its length is hard to uncover since the kings that precede him rule for short periods of time.

Manasseh (687–642)
Amon (642–640)
Josiah (640–609)
Jehoahaz (609)
Jehoiakim (609–598)
Jehoiachin (598–597)
Zedekiah (597–587)[64]

Israel and Judah warred periodically until Israel was destroyed by Assyria in 722 B.C. Jeroboam and Rehoboam fought one another (1 Kgs 15:6), as did Asa and Baasha (1 Kgs 15:16–17) and Jehoash and Amaziah (2 Kgs 14:8–14). Yet at times the two nations fought together against common foes (e.g., 1 Kgs 22:1–40; 2 Kgs 3:1–27; 2 Kgs 8:28–29) and were allied through marriage (2 Kgs 8:25–27). Obviously, then, Israel and Judah were both friends and enemies through the centuries. The greatest threat to the two countries, however, came from other powers.

(3) Egypt

Egypt impacted Israel's history most during the years after Solomon's reign and during the decades just before the great destruction of Jerusalem. In Rehoboam's fifth year (925 B.C.) Shishak invaded Jerusalem and stripped the temple of its gold (1 Kgs 14:25–27). Though the biblical text does not mention any other cities being affected by this attack, J. Bright notes that Egyptian records claim that up to 150 places were taken.[65] Shishak's invasion kept Judah too weak to attack Israel, which helped keep the two nations apart.

In 609 B.C. Pharaoh Neco marched north to aid Assyria's efforts against Babylon (2 Kgs 23:29). For reasons not stated in the text, Josiah, Judah's last righteous king, confronted Neco and was killed (2 Kgs 23:29–30). Egypt could not overcome Babylon at this time but was able to dominate Judah's political scene until 605 B.C. Thus, just as Shishak's invasion partially sealed the nation's division, so Neco's killing of Josiah effectively removed Judah's last godly king and paved the way for the people's final destruction.

(4) Aram (Syria)

Syria posed a great threat to the Northern Kingdom's security during the ninth century B.C. Two powerful kings, Ben-Hadad I (ca. 880–840 B.C.) and Hazael (ca. 840–805),[66] led Syria to become perhaps the chief power in north-

[64] The 587 B.C. date for Jerusalem's destruction differs from Thiele's 586 B.C. designation for that event.

[65] Bright, *A History of Israel,* 230.

[66] These dates are deliberately "rounded off" to avoid long discussions of Syrian chronology.

east Palestine. Ben-Hadad first enters the biblical story when he breaks an alliance with Israel's King Baasha to ally himself with Judah's King Asa (1 Kgs 15:9–22). Ben-Hadad's friendship was costly, since Asa was forced to strip the palace and temple of its gold and silver to purchase the Syrian's "loyalty" (15:18–19). With Judah's money in hand, Ben-Hadad gladly annexed several of Israel's cities (15:20).[67] Omri took steps to ward off the Syrian threat, including marrying his son Ahab to Tyre's princess Jezebel, thus linking Israel with another anti-Syrian country (16:31).[68] Indeed, the Syrian problem remained so serious that Israel and Judah joined together to fight Syria during the days of Ahab and Jehoshaphat (22:1–4), and Ahab died fighting this long-term foe (22:29–40).

Syria continued its dominance under Hazael. Though annoyed for a time by Assyria,[69] Syria ravaged Israel during Jehu's reign (2 Kgs 10:32–33), captured Gath of Philistia (12:17), and only spared Jerusalem because Joash paid him a large sum of money (12:18).[70] Syria's power was finally broken after Hazael's death, when Assyria laid siege to Damascus and forced the king to pay tribute money.[71] Assyria did not threaten Israel and Judah at this time, however, so those nations enjoyed a half-century of peace and prosperity.

(5) Assyria

Assyria probably was the fiercest, most cruel, and most oppressive foreign power ever to threaten Israel and Judah. This ambitious, seemingly relentless nation terrorized Palestine from the mid-eighth century B.C. to the late seventh century B.C. Assyria's power was especially devastating to Israel, since Assyria conquered and destroyed the entire nation in 722 B.C. Judah also felt the sting of Assyrian oppression in 701 B.C. when the Assyrians nearly captured Jerusalem. Only a miracle of God saved the city (2 Kgs 18:17–19:37).

Three Assyrian kings figured prominently in Israel and Judah's history during the period from 750 to 700 B.C. First, Tiglath-Pileser III (745–727 B.C.) began a new foreign policy. J. Bright observes, "The campaigns of Tiglath-Pileser differed from those of his predecessors in that they were not tribute-gathering expeditions, but permanent conquests."[72] This new policy made the

---

[67] Cf. H. Donner, "The Separate States of Israel and Judah," in *Israelite and Judean History*, ed. J. H. Hayes and J. M. Miller (Philadelphia: Westminster, 1977) 390, for a good description of Ben-Hadad's many military ventures.

[68] Cf. M. Noth, *The History of Israel*, 2d ed., trans. P. R. Ackroyd (New York: Harper & Row, 1960) 241–42.

[69] Cf. Bright, *History of Israel*, 237. Assyria checked Syria's progress for a time, but Syria's apparent success at Qarqar in 853 B.C. forced Assyria to withdraw from the region.

[70] Ibid., 250–52; Donner, "The Separate States of Israel and Judah," 394.

[71] Cf. Noth, *History of Israel*, 249.

[72] Bright, *History of Israel*, 269.

Assyrians more dangerous than other invading armies. Syria, Israel, Philistia, and a few other small nations opposed Tiglath, but Judah's king Ahaz adopted a pro-Assyrian foreign policy (2 Kgs 16:7–9).[73] Tiglath invaded the area from 734 to 732 B.C. and punished the coalition by defeating Gaza and Damascus (2 Kgs 16:9) and by annexing parts of northern Israel (cf. 2 Kgs 15:29).[74] Judah's pact with Assyria saved them, but Israel was now in serious trouble.

Shalmaneser V (727–722 B.C.) finished what Tiglath began in Israel. After Tiglath's death Hoshea sought to free Israel from Assyrian domination. In a colossal miscalculation Hoshea withheld tribute money from Shalmaneser (2 Kgs 17:3–4), then depended on Egypt for help (cf. Isa 30–31). Egypt, always a poor ally to Israel, failed to respond, and Assyria laid siege to Samaria. After three years the city surrendered (2 Kgs 17:5–6). Then, M. Grant notes: "The city was burnt to the ground; and the state of Israel was abolished and absorbed into the Assyrian empire. No less that 27,290 of its inhabitants . . . were reportedly taken off to Assyria and Media."[75] Tiny Judah was all that remained of the covenant nation.

Sennacherib (704–681) nearly obliterated Judah in 701 B.C. Judah's King Hezekiah decided to break with Assyria when the old oppressor had difficulties with Babylon.[76] Though exact details are difficult to gather,[77] Sennacherib invaded Judah, took several cities, and laid siege to Jerusalem (2 Kgs 18:1–17). Isaiah the prophet counseled Hezekiah to resist, trusting only in the Lord's power (2 Kgs 19:20–34; Isa 37:31–35). Because Hezekiah obeyed, God killed 185,000 Assyrian soldiers, then removed Sennacherib from power (2 Kgs 19:35–37). After Hezekiah's death, however, Manasseh reverted to appeasing Assyria and not trusting the Lord (2 Kgs 21:1–18).

Assyria's prominence in Israel's history is reflected in the many biblical references to its pride, power, and viciousness. When Assyria fell, Judah celebrated (cf. Nahum), as did the rest of the ancient world. Though God loved Assyria (cf. Jonah and Isa 19:19–25), Babylon was allowed to destroy this great destroyer of others.

(6) Babylon

Like Assyria, Babylon exerted its power and influence intermittently over several centuries. It was from 605 to 539 B.C., however, that this nation impacted Judah the most. In 612 B.C., Babylon conquered Nineveh, Assyria's

[73] For an excellent overview of the events of 750–700 B.C., see J. H. Hayes and S. A. Irvine, *Isaiah the Eighth-Century Prophet: His Times and His Preaching* (Nashville: Abingdon, 1987) 19–24.

[74] Ibid., 23–24.

[75] M. Grant, *The History of Ancient Israel* (New York: Scribners, 1984) 121.

[76] Bright, *History of Israel,* 283.

[77] Cf. Hayes and Irvine, *Isaiah the Eighth-Century Prophet,* 373–76.

capital, thus becoming the dominant force in the ancient world. It took the Babylonians until 610 B.C. to eliminate Assyrian opposition[78] and until 605 B.C. to place Judah under servitude, but once in control they did not relinquish power for nearly seven decades.

When Nebuchadnezzar subdued Egypt at Carchemish in 605 B.C. (Jer 46:2), thus establishing Babylon's power in the region (2 Kgs 24:7), he found Jehoiakim, hand picked by Egypt (2 Kgs 23:31–35), on Judah's throne. At this time Babylon took some exiles, including Daniel and his friends (Dan 1:1–2). Jehoiakim served Babylon for three years, then rebelled (2 Kgs 24:1). Though according to 2 Kgs 24:2–4 God sent various raiders from neighboring lands to harass Jehoiakim, Babylon itself did not move to punish this rebellion until 598 B.C., the year Jehoiachin succeeded his father (2 Kgs 24:8).[79] Nebuchadnezzar removed Jehoiachin from power in 597 B.C., deported more Israelites (e.g., Ezekiel), stripped the temple of its wealth, and placed Zedekiah on the throne (2 Kgs 24:10–17; Jer 24–29). Thus, Babylon gave Judah one more chance to be a loyal vassal.

Zedekiah governed Judah during its last decade of existence. The only notice 2 Kings offers about why Babylon finally decided to destroy Jerusalem is the brief comment, "Now Zedekiah rebelled against the king of Babylon" (2 Kgs 24:20). Perhaps nationalistic fervor had risen, but no clear reason for this rebellion can be discerned.[80] Regardless of the reasons for Zedekiah's actions, his decisions caused Nebuchadnezzar to eliminate his troublesome vassal. He captured the city, burned its walls and important buildings, including the temple, and appointed his own governor (25:1–24). Zedekiah was blinded but only after seeing his sons killed (25:6–7). No part of Israel or Judah was left free. All twelve tribes were now in exile or enslaved in their own land. Hope for the future remained (cf. 25:27–30; Jer 31–34), but that hope was blunted by the present reality that God had "thrust them from his presence" (2 Kgs 24:20).

4. The Text of 1, 2 Kings

This commentary, like all the Old Testament volumes in *The New American Commentary,* interprets the NIV text, which is based on the Masoretic Text (MT) of the Hebrew Bible.[81] The Masoretes were scribes who copied the

---

[78] Cf. Bright, *History of Israel,* 323, for an account of how Assyria kept trying to defeat Babylon and regain its former authority.

[79] For possible reasons for Babylon's delay in chastising Israel, see Noth, *History of Israel,* 282, and Bright, *History of Israel,* 326.

[80] Cf. Bright, *History of Israel,* 328–29.

[81] This commentary uses the 1967 *Biblia Hebraica Stuttgartensia* edition of the Hebrew Scriptures as the basis for all textual, exegetical, and translation comments.

Hebrew Scriptures in A.D. 500–1200, long after Hebrew had ceased to be a spoken language.[82] At least two schools of Masoretes existed, one led by a scholar named Ben Asher and the other by one called Ben Naphtali. The Ben Asher school's A.D. 1009 version of 1, 2 Kings is the standard Hebrew text of the books. A few scattered verses from 1, 2 Kings were discovered among the Dead Sea Scrolls, but these few references neither add substantially to nor subtract significantly from the MT.[83]

Most scholars believe the MT of 1, 2 Kings is a basically sound, well-preserved manuscript. They draw this conclusion because the vast majority of the text requires no alteration[84] and because parallel texts in 1, 2 Chronicles, Isaiah 36–39, and Jeremiah 52 essentially support the accounts in 1, 2 Kings.[85] Some writers note, however, that while the MT is mostly reliable, significant differences exist between the Hebrew text and the Greek translation of the books. These variations must be considered before an assessment of the full reliability of the MT can be accepted.

Commonly known as the Septuagint (LXX),[86] the Greek Old Testament was first translated from Hebrew perhaps as early as 250 B.C.[87] The version was used widely, and its influence is evident in the New Testament. Its translation of 1, 2 Kings differs from the MT in several ways. For instance, certain details about Solomon's administrative prowess are rearranged, and the LXX has Solomon finishing the temple *before* completing his palace.[88] Also, 1 Kings 20 and 21 are transposed to show that Ahab was swiftly punished for killing Naboth.[89] Further, the LXX makes Jeroboam I, the first northern king, look much worse than the MT, for the LXX claims his mother was a prostitute and that no prophet predicted his rise to power.[90] Finally, the LXX tries to har-

---

[82] For a survey of the Masoretes and their work consult J. A. Thompson, "Textual Criticism in the Old Testament," *IDBSup* (Nashville: Abingdon, 1976) 886–91, and J. Weingreen, *Introduction to the Critical Study of the Text of the Hebrew Bible* (New York: Oxford University Press, 1982).

[83] Jones, *1 and 2 Kings,* 1:3–4. Jones does think that the DSS do provide evidence that helps determine the age and accuracy of other versions of 1 and 2 Kings.

[84] Montgomery and Gehman, *The Book of Kings,* 23.

[85] Gray, *I and II Kings,* 43–44.

[86] This name comes from the tradition that claims that seventy (LXX) scholars translated the OT into Greek. For a fuller explanation of the Septuagint's origins see H. B. Swete, *An Introduction to the Old Testament in Greek,* 2d ed. (Cambridge: Cambridge University Press, 1902) 8–28. For differing analyses of how the LXX was formed and impacted the church, consult A. C. Sundberg, *The Old Testament of the Early Church,* HTS 20 (Cambridge: Harvard University Press, 1964), and R. Beckwith, *The Old Testament Canon of the New Testament Church* (Grand Rapids: Eerdmans, 1985).

[87] R. W. Klein, *Textual Criticism of the Old Testament: The Septuagint after Qumran* (Philadelphia: Fortress, 1974) 2–3.

[88] Gray, *I and II Kings,* 45.

[89] Ibid., 45.

[90] Montgomery and Gehman, *The Book of Kings,* 253.

monize historical difficulties in one case by transposing when Jehoshaphat lived.[91]

One of the major differences between the Hebrew and Greek versions of 1, 2 Kings occurs in the order and details of the Jeroboam stories. The Greek text places virtually all of the Jeroboam information, such as his work for Solomon, his rise to power, and his son's death, after the notation of Solomon's death and Rehoboam's succession. Thus, the order of the stories in 1 Kgs (LXX) is as follows: (1) Solomon dies, and Rehoboam succeeds him; (2) Jeroboam, the son of a harlot, works for Solomon yet desires to be king, so Solomon seeks to kill him; (3) Jeroboam flees to Egypt, where he is given the king's oldest daughter as his wife; (4) Jeroboam's son becomes ill, so Jeroboam sends his wife to Ahijah; (5) Ahijah says the boy will die and denounces Jeroboam's lineage; (6) Shemaiah the prophet gives Jeroboam ten pieces of the kingdom; (7) Jeroboam becomes king, partly due to Rehoboam's folly; (8) Shemaiah warns Rehoboam not to fight Jeroboam. Besides the different order, the LXX adds details such as Jeroboam's mother being a harlot, Jeroboam's desire to be king (which tries to explain 1 Kgs 11:40), and the name of Jeroboam's wife. It also gives much of Ahijah's work to Shemaiah.

Summarizing the work of J. W. Wevers and others, G. H. Jones notes "six hermeneutical principles" that emerge from an analysis of the LXX text of Kings:

> A clear tendency towards harmonisation and rationalisations; exaltation of the heroes of antiquity; condemnation of Joab, Jeroboam, the northern kingdom and Ahab; cultic correctness; condemnation of paganism; the emphasising of God's transcendence.[92]

Those who support the primacy of the MT point out that political ideology may have motivated the anti-Israel materials,[93] that a misunderstanding of ancient chronological methodology could explain the harmonization attempts,[94] and that embarrassment over Solomon's portrayal might have led to changes in his characterization. Though such concerns may be valid, they do not merit changing the text.

On the other hand, J. D. Shenkel argues vigorously and carefully that some LXX readings are older than the MT. In particular he thinks the Old Greek chronology was already present in the Hebrew *Vorlage* (the text used by translators)[95] and must therefore be taken very seriously. He therefore disagrees

---

[91] DeVries, *I Kings,* lix.

[92] Jones, *1 and 2 Kings,* 1:7. Cf. J. W. Wevers, "Exegetical Principles Underlying the Septuagint Text of I Kings ii.12–xxi. 43," *OSt* 8 (1950) 300–322.

[93] Montgomery and Gehman, *The Book of Kings,* 253–54.

[94] Cf. Thiele, *Mysterious Numbers of the Hebrew Kings.*

[95] J. D. Shenkel, *Chronology and Recensional Development in the Greek Text of Kings* (Cambridge, Mass.: Harvard University Press, 1964) 110.

with Thiele's reconstructions of the chronologies[96] yet at the same time offers his own evidence for the general agreement between the LXX and the MT.

The MT deserves to be used as the basis for commentaries on 1, 2 Kings. It is based on an ancient and accurate manuscript tradition and is an honest, open portrayal of Israel's history. The LXX helps interpreters assess variant readings, though, and must be used as a corrective when necessary.[97] But it should not replace the MT, since it sounds at times like a reinterpretation of an already established story. Still, humility must be exercised by honest interpreters whenever especially difficult variations occur.

C. F. Burney rightly questions the Greek text's use of Jeroboam's son's illness and wonders why the text omits any mention of Jeroboam's death, yet he does claim that certain details of Jeroboam's time in Egypt may be more thorough than the Hebrew text.[98] S. L. McKenzie believes the Greek text has been rewritten from the MT, primarily because of the cursing of Jeroboam's dynasty before Jeroboam comes to power, because of the confusion of prophetic stories, and because of the vilification of Jeroboam and his mother.[99] D. W. Gooding concludes that the Greek version adapts the story to make Solomon look better at Jeroboam's expense.[100]

5. Miracles in 1, 2 Kings

Various accounts in 1, 2 Kings raise the issue of the presence of the miraculous in historical writing. For example, prophets such as Ahijah predicted the future (1 Kgs 11:29–33), and in 1 Kgs 13:2–3 an anonymous prophet even predicted the very name and specific activities of King Josiah (640–609 B.C.) during the reign of Jeroboam I (930–909 B.C.). Elijah received sustenance from ravens (1 Kgs 17:2–6), called fire down from heaven on more than one occasion (1 Kgs 18:38; 2 Kgs 1:10,12), and raised the dead (1 Kgs 17:19–24). Elisha performed similar miracles through God's power, and the list could be extended to include the Lord's absolute domination of world events. The supernatural is never far from the action in these accounts. Since the prophets' miracle stories are the most prominent type of supernatural event in 1, 2 Kings,

[96] Ibid., 4.

[97] This commentary basically adopts the attitude of T. R. Hobbs, who says: "The practice in the textual Notes in this commentary has been to offer the important variants from the MT and to comment upon them where necessary, but we have avoided emendation unless it is deemed absolutely necessary. . . . The most important work for our purposes has been the study of Shenkel, and consideration is taken of his contribution" (*2 Kings,* [xlv]).

[98] C. F. Burney, *Notes on the Hebrew Text of the Book of Kings* (Oxford: Clarendon Press, 1903) 166–69.

[99] S. L. McKenzie, *The Trouble with Kings: The Composition of the Book of Kings in the Deuteronomistic History,* VTSup 42 (Leiden: Brill, 199)] 21–40.

[100] D. W. Gooding, "The Septuagint's Rival Versions of Jeroboam's Rise to Power," *VT* 17 (1967) 173–89.

it is appropriate to focus on their interpretation when discussing the plausibility of miracles in history.

Several authors quite frankly describe the accounts in 1, 2 Kings that include miraculous elements as "legends." B. Long takes this position and offers the following fairly comprehensive definition of "legend":

> A narrative concerned primarily with the wondrous, miraculous and exemplary. Legend is aimed at edification rather than merely entertainment, instruction, or even imaginative exploration of the storyteller's art. . . . Legend differs from history and historical story in its refusal to be bound by a drive to recount real events as they happened; it differs from the more artistic story in giving less attention to developed points of narrative interest, such as description, artistic structure, and plot. Legend belongs to the world of oral folklore and storytellers. Legends took varied forms and were told in royal court, at religious shrines, in family and tribal settings, and on pilgrimages to holy sites."[101]

More specifically, Long calls the prophetic miracles examples of a "prophetic legend," which he believes "focuses both the teller's and the reader's interest on wonderful attributes and miraculous action of God and his prophet."[102] For Long the chief differences between "legends" and "historical stories" or even "history" itself are that history recounts what actually happened while at best legend is *based* on something that may have happened, that the legend includes miraculous events, while historically based forms of writing do not, and that legends have less artistic development than other texts.

In general, A. Rofé, O. H. Steck, and J. Gray[103] agree with Long's rather clear formal distinctions, although each scholar contributes certain details of his own. For instance, Rofé thinks "legenda" usually include a crisis that requires supernatural intervention, a plea to the prophet for help, a doubt that the miracle will occur, and a miraculous deliverance effected by God's messenger.[104] Such stories are also short, unconnected to the surrounding context, thin on character development, and concerned with a single miracle.[105] Steck stresses how the "legends" are fitted into the book by its editors.[106] Gray believes that the miraculous events attributed to Elijah and Elisha are

---

[101] Long, *1 Kings,* 252.

[102] Ibid., 181.

[103] A. Rofé, *The Prophetical Stories: The Narratives about the Prophets in the Hebrew Bible, Their Literary Types and History,* trans. D. Levy (Jerusalem: Magnes, 1988); O. H. Steck, *Uberlieferung und Zeitsgeschichte in den Elia-Erzählungen,* WMANT 26 (Neukirchen-Vluyn: Neukirchener, 1968) 142–44; Gray, *1 and 2 Kings,* 32–33.

[104] Rofé, *The Prophetical Stories,* 13.

[105] Ibid.

[106] Steck, *Uberlieferung und Zeitsgeschichte in den Elia-Erzählungen,* 131–47.

part of rivalries between various localities, each claiming priority over the other through their association with the prophets.[107] At the heart of each of these viewpoints is the conviction that the presence of the miraculous alerts readers that the legend form is being used.

Though these ideas are carefully argued, they have certain literary, theological, and philosophical difficulties. Many arguments for the legend form are made, of course, on literary grounds. Rofé, in particular, finds differences between longer historical narratives and shorter, legendary material. Such distinctions are hard to maintain. Short, pithy, barely developed, character-poor accounts of kings appear regularly too (e.g., 1 Kgs 15:1–6,25–31; 16:1–7,8–14; 2 Kgs 8:16–24,25–29; 14:23–29; 15:1–7). These annalistic texts also have set formulae of how the king reigned, died, and so forth; yet their historical validity is seldom questioned. Both the brief prophetic accounts and the short royal accounts have the same function, which is to move the plot between major events. Further, many of the miraculous accounts fit the ongoing story carefully, as is the case in 1 Kings 17–19 and 2 Kings 3. Removing them from the plot changes the face of the story from a war between God, who can do in real life what his opponent Baal could only do in mythology, to a battle between competing sociological and religious figures. These accounts are also sometimes as lengthy as any "historical" narrative. Finally, except for the miracles, there is no difference between how the author depicts cause and effect and time in the miraculous accounts and the nonmiracle stories. The author includes these texts in the overall fabric of the story with no indication that they are less believable than the rest of the history. One might argue that these events never occurred, but the evidence cannot be deduced from the text's *literary form*.

One historical detail that relates to the literary issue also should be noted. Many Old Testament literary forms have ancient Near Eastern parallels. For instance, Hebrew poetry reads like that of other nations. Wisdom literature existed in many lands outside Israel. Such parallels help scholars determine the basic forms that Israel used. Quite significantly, there were prophets in the surrounding countries, and many prophetic texts have survived.[108] But no prophetic legends have been uncovered. Rofé admits:

> To the best of my knowledge the general *gattung* of stories about prophets and other holy men has not yet been identified in ancient Near Eastern literatures. And since the writings of Mesopotamia, Anatolia, Syria, and Egypt known at present are much more extensive than biblical literature, we may

[107] Gray, *1 and 2 Kings,* 33.

[108] Cf. the prophetical literature in *ANET,* 441–52, and the references to non-Israelite prophecy in H. B. Huffmon, "The Origins of Prophecy," in *Magnalia Dei: The Mighty Acts of God,* ed. F. M. Cross, W. E. Lemke, and P. D. Miller, Jr. (Garden City: Doubleday, 1976) 172–86.

hazard the conjecture that such stories will not appear in the future either, for these were apparently never written. Thus, though it is probable that in Mesopotamia, too, stories were told about wonders performed by this *āšipu* or that *baru*, they were never recorded in written form or preserved as cherished traditions.[109]

In other words, there are *no parallel* prophetic "legends" known at this time. Rofé justifies classifying the texts as "legends" because of tales that grew up in later periods.[110] If the literary forms from Israel are the only known evidence for prophetic legends, and if the literary details for the proposed legends do not differ from historical accounts, as has been argued, then one must conclude that the miraculous elements of the texts are the chief difference between "legends" and "history." It is therefore relevant to address the plausibility of miracles.

Theological reflection leaves open the possibility of miracles within a historical framework. Four reasons lead to this conclusion. First, if God created the heavens and the earth, then it is likely that God controls and safeguards the natural order. As Keil concludes, if Yahweh is "Creator and Lord of all creatures, even the voracious ravens are made subservient to His plans of salvation."[111] The God who created and sustains nature can certainly factor in and control any changes in nature caused by a miracle. Second, if God is all powerful, then the Lord certainly can do anything that does not contradict his own character. Third, if Yahweh truly cared for Israel and Elijah, then a selective famine and a selective feeding that led to both's spiritual and physical well-being might indeed fit God's character. Fourth, Scripture indicates that miracles occur in crisis times in lives and history. The insertion of Baalism into Israelite culture was such a time. Such arguments may not *prove* that the miracles occurred, but they make the miraculous plausible within a theological context. This context is especially important if the miraculous is the major argument for calling the stories "legends."

There are also philosophical reasons for the possibility of miracles. R. Swinburne, R. Purtill, and N. Geisler[112] claim that miracles are plausible

---

[109] Rofé, *The Prophetical Stories,* 9.

[110] Ibid.

[111] C. F. Keil, "I and II Kings," COT, trans. J. Martin (1876; reprint, Grand Rapids: Eerdmans, 1980) 3:237.

[112] R. Swinburne, *The Concept of Miracle* (London: Macmillan, 1970); Swinburne offers a sophisticated philosophical defense of miracles; R. L. Purtill, "Miracles: What If They Happen?" in *Thinking about Religion: A Philosophical Introduction to Religion* (Englewood Cliffs, N.J.: Prentice-Hall, 1978); N. L. Geisler, *Miracles and Modern Thought* (Grand Rapids: Zondervan, 1982). Other evangelical examinations of the concepts include F. J. Beckwith, *David Hume's Argument against Miracles: A Critical Analysis* (Lanham, Md.: University Press of America, 1989); and C. Brown, *Miracles and the Critical Mind* (Grand Rapids: Eerdmans, 1984). I am indebted to R. D. Geivett for sharing these bibliographical sources and his thoughts on the rationality of miracles.

unless one adopts naturalistic, nonsupernaturalistic presuppositions. If the possibility of the existence of God is allowed, however, then the very nature of the concept of "God" as powerful, sustaining, and creative leaves open the possibility of miracles as well. In other words, a naturalistic dogmatism that refuses to consider theism as an option is as close minded as any fideistic theism. If God's existence can be argued for in a rational philosophic manner, as many philosophers conclude, then one must remain open to the miraculous and the supernatural. C. S. Lewis makes similar points in his more popular *Miracles*.

In conclusion, each person must decide whether or not to accept the veracity of the accounts of miraculous events in 1, 2 Kings. What is unacceptable is to decide the matter based on faulty arguments. Except for the miraculous elements, the stories themselves do not portray these events in any significantly different way than other types of information are conveyed. It is more likely, then, that the author of 1, 2 Kings believed these miracles occurred in real, space-and-time history. Theological evidence for the occurrence of the miraculous can be forwarded. Philosophical analysis yields a rational defense of miracles. Therefore, no reader need fear being obscurantist or nonintellectual due to a belief in the miraculous stories in 1, 2 Kings. One might not accept that they actually happened but must do so for reasons based on something other than historical literary or theological data.

Introduction to Literary Issues

Since 1969 a growing number of scholars have stressed the importance of analyzing the literary aspects of biblical books. Some of these authors have separated literary and historical concerns, while others have attempted to mesh the two. Much of the discussion has focused on narrative, which impacts the interpretation of 1, 2 Kings. Many literary elements of the books deserve extensive treatment, but only selected segments can be introduced here. These aspects will be highlighted further in the commentary itself. This portion of the introduction discusses five essential elements of narrative literature: genre, structure, plot, characterization, and point of view. These details explain both the contents and authorial perspective of 1, 2 Kings.

1. The Genre of 1, 2 Kings

A first step in interpreting any piece of literature is to determine what genre, or type of writing, it may be. Ancient, medieval, renaissance, neoclassical, and modern writers have all seen the need to know what a text *is* in order to hear what it *says*.[113] In other words, genre studies help illuminate the text's purpose and method of presentation. As C. S. Lewis claims:

> The first qualification for judging any piece of workmanship from a corkscrew to a cathedral is to know *what* it is—what it was intended to do and how it is meant to be used . . . as long as you think the corkscrew was meant for opening tins or the cathedral for entertaining tourists you can say nothing to the purpose of them.[114]

Since 1, 2 Kings contain history, theology, and story, it is reasonable to explore how the author combines these items to arrive at a genre for the books.

(1) Narrative Literature

First and Second Kings display all the characteristics found in quality narrative literature. They present engaging, compelling characters. They develop an interesting story from start to finish. They use standard storytelling techniques, such as foreshadowing, backtracking, and telescoping. Irony and sarcasm appear. Dialogue and editorial comments are interspersed. Time progresses from one era to the next. Without question, then, the books read like much modern writing.

Indeed, R. Alter concludes that this type of Old Testament narrative should be called "fiction."[115] Why? Because it reads more like a modern novel or short story than like ancient Near Eastern history.[116] It also displays too much authorial artistry to be classified as pure, "objective" history. Alter does not mean that the historical accounts are not true but rather that they are best explicated by analyzing Scripture through methods that have "illuminated, for example, the poetry of Dante, the plays of Shakespeare, the novels of Tolstoy."[117]

M. Sternberg warns against creating divisive categories when discussing biblical narratives. For instance, he thinks Alter unnecessarily pits history against fiction by calling historical narratives "fiction."[118] After all, no detailed history simply lists facts and no fictional work is totally false.[119] Both require creativity and truthfulness. Thus, it is best to seek other ways to

---

[113] For a succinct survey of issues in genre studies, see P. R. House, *Zephaniah—A Prophetic Drama,* JSOTSup 97/BALS 27 (Sheffield: Sheffield Academic Press, 1988) 23–29.

[114] C. S. Lewis, *A Preface to Paradise Lost* (London: Oxford University Press, 1959) 1.

[115] R. Alter, *The Art of Biblical Narrative* (New York: Basic, 1981) 23–24.

[116] Most Assyrian and Babylonian historical texts focus on lists of kings and their conquests. Some events are explained as acts of the gods. Still, the plot and character development evident in Hebrew narrative is clearly lacking. Cf. *ANET,* 265–317.

[117] Alter, *The Art of Biblical Narrative,* 13.

[118] M. Sternberg, *The Poetics of Biblical Narrative: Ideological Literature and the Drama of Reading* (Bloomington: Indiana University Press, 1985) 24.

[119] Cf. Sternberg, *The Poetics of Biblical Narrative,* 25–30.

describe what biblical narrative is and does than to call it fiction.

Both Alter and Sternberg contribute valuable insights into the genre discussion. Alter correctly claims that biblical narrative is lively, interesting literature. Sternberg agrees with Alter's assessment of the literature itself, yet properly cautions against creating categories for biblical narratives that erect mental barriers in readers' minds. History can be as creative as fiction in the hands of a skilled author who knows how to tell the truth with enthusiasm.

(2) *Historical Narrative*

The author of 1, 2 Kings wrote a compelling story of Israel. This individual wrote the story to tell readers what actually happened to Israel. Thus, many commentators have called 1, 2 Kings "historical narrative." S. DeVries observes that only Israel, among all its ancient neighbors, "defined themselves in historical rather than mythological language."[120] Only Israel claimed to have made a covenant with their God, and that the consequences of keeping or breaking that covenant were made plain in history. So only Israel believed their God determined the events of history.

What did the Israelites mean by "history"? They certainly at least meant that books like 1, 2 Kings depicted real people doing what they actually did in the centuries the books cover. DeVries writes that 1, 2 Kings are historical because they use "authenticated sources," "trace an organic line of development from beginning to end," and "show the interactions of cause and effect in a realistic way."[121] Sternberg adds that Israelite history believes that "the remembrance of the past devolves on the present and determines the future," that history is headed in a meaningful direction, and that the Bible claims its view of events is *the truth* about what really happened.[122] Clearly, then, the fact that 1, 2 Kings unfold in a story-like manner in no way detracts from its claim to be "real history." The creative storyteller told the truth about Israel's story.

(3) *Theological Narrative*

One issue that has troubled some scholars is how 1, 2 Kings can be considered historical when the books take clear theological positions.[123] The author attributes many events to the sovereignty of God, often without noting how secular matters affected what occurred. Kings are judged more by their relationship to God and opposition to idolatry than by their economic or military

[120] DeVries, *1 Kings,* xxxii.

[121] Ibid., xxxiii.

[122] Sternberg, *The Poetics of Biblical Narratives,* 107.

[123] For example, J. Skinner finds it necessary to separate source material from the author's own comments (*I and II Kings*, [8–9]). What he implies is that the source material is more valuable because it is more objective and unbiased.

capabilities. Events seem to be selected more for how they fit the author's theological explanation of Israel's disintegration than for their impact on the overall structure of ancient history. Is such writing historical?

Three issues help answer this question. First, no history is totally "objective." Every historian, no matter how careful and well-trained, has personal beliefs that affect his or her writing of history.[124] Second, a historian's personal perspective must be judged in part by whether the view of cause and effect fits the actual events. The author of 1, 2 Kings notes how all the threats made in Deuteronomy 27–28 come true, and shows that what the prophets predicted did happen. Thus, the author's ideology does match what took place. Third, an author's theology should reflect accurately how people really act. Certainly Israel's deeds do bring about the nation's downfall. Political corruption and shortsightedness, coupled with moral depravity, is a deadly sociological *or* theological combination. There is no telling reason, then, to minimize the historical value of 1, 2 Kings because of its theological nature.

(4) Prophetic Narrative

There was one movement in Israel that united narrative, a concern for history, and the belief that failure to live up to theological agreements caused the nation's destruction. The prophetic movement incorporated these various components in order to make sense of history. Prophets preached the Word and wrote the Word. Prophets predicted the future and explained the past. Prophets anointed kings and denounced kings. The very existence of the Old Testament proves that long after the prophets had died, people came to agree with their interpretations of Israel's actions and accepted their writings as the Word of God.

In many ways, it is probably most accurate to call 1, 2 Kings "prophetic narrative." After all, the prophets' lives and predictions help structure the books (see section two below). Prophetic theological themes such as covenant, sin, punishment, and renewal, permeate 1, 2 Kings (see "Introduction to Theological Issues").[125] Understanding God's work in history is as important to the prophets as it is to the author of 1, 2 Kings. Perhaps, then, the historical and theological issues discussed above can actually be better encompassed by the term "prophetic" than by a modern term like "fiction" or a hybrid term like "sacred narrative."

Prophetic narrative has at least five distinguishing characteristics. First, it assesses the past based on God's covenant with Israel. Second, it predicts the future by noting how God has blessed or punished Israel in the past and by

---

[124] A careful reading of several biographies of the same person proves this point.

[125] See Beckwith, *The Old Testament Canon of the New Testament Church,* 110–234 for a thorough discussion of the structure, order, and naming of the various parts of the Hebrew canon.

noting what promises God has made to individuals (e.g., David in 2 Sam 7:7–17) or to the nation as a whole. Third, it creates its plot by emphasizing events that fulfill a prophetic view of the past and future. Fourth, it assesses characters based on how they accelerate or retard the blessings or judgments God sends to Israel. Fifth, like the prophets did when they preached in Israel, prophetic narrative instructs its audience to turn to the Lord so they can receive blessing instead of punishment. These characteristics are evident throughout Joshua–Kings and also in Isaiah, Jeremiah, Ezekiel, and the minor prophets.

Though 1, 2 Kings are written as prophetic narrative, it is not necessary to argue that a prophet wrote the books.[126] The prophetic movement almost certainly had great influence after 587 B.C. when the people saw that the prophets' dire predictions about defeat and exile had come true. Still, though prophecy itself continued to flourish (cf. Haggai, Zechariah, Malachi), its principles were accepted by many nonprophets (e.g., Ezra) who hoped for Israel's renewal. The author of 1, 2 Kings clearly appreciated the prophetic heritage, yet incorporated its ideals and historical heritage with the monarchy's history rather than simply preaching a prophetic message. In this way the result was prophetic narrative rather than another book of prophecy.

2. The Structure of 1, 2 Kings

Virtually every aspect of a literary work is uncovered by its structure or framework. Effective structural schemes unite a work's themes, images, ideas, characters, plots, point of view, and time sequence. Good frameworks are thereby one with the other elements of the art form. They hold artistic pieces together. As E. V. Roberts summarizes, "Structure is a matter of the relationship among parts that are usually described in terms of cause and effect, position in time, association, symmetry, and balance and proportion."[127]

Obviously, authors can choose more than one means of structuring their work. The only absolute criterion is that the structure be logical and sequential. Roberts observes, "In a good work of literature, the parts are not introduced accidentally. One part demands another, sometimes by logical requirement."[128] Ideas, time, or characters may provide this logic. Whatever method of organization is chosen, however, must help the text's progression from beginning to conclusion.

B. Long has stated that 1, 2 Kings are logical and sequential, but they do

[126] Cf. n. 36.

[127] E. V. Roberts, *Writing Themes about Literature,* 3d ed. (Englewood Cliffs, N.J.: Prentice-Hall, 1973) 119.

[128] Ibid., 120.

not necessarily conform to modern conceptions of order. Indeed, according to Long, insisting on modern notions of structural order has led some scholars to reach incorrect conclusions about the book's authorship.[129] Long thinks 1, 2 Kings utilize a form of *paratactic* style, a compositional method used later by the ancient Greek historian Herodotus.[130] G. B. Caird states that Hebrew poetry and narrative often use parataxis, which means they "set two ideas side by side and allow the one to qualify the other without bothering to spell out in detail the relation between them."[131]

What this conclusion means for 1, 2 Kings is that two rival kingdoms, two or more theological themes, and two destructions of capital cities existing side-by-side may reflect conscious structuring devices rather than multiple authors at work. These diverse, yet related, elements could coexist to make a cumulative impression on readers. Further, Long clarifies Caird's definition of parataxis by listing linguistic, temporal, and thematic elements the author uses to link the books' parallel threads.[132] Finally, M. Noth observed that the author used key speeches and summaries to tie together the story's many segments.[133] It is appropriate, then, given the nature of the literature in 1, 2 Kings, to highlight characters, events, speeches, and themes when presenting a structural outline of the books.

Scholars have offered various types of structures for 1, 2 Kings, some that acknowledge their diversity, and some that do not do so. Many have simply divided the books into their three broad historical eras: the united kingdom (1 Kgs 1–11), the divided kingdom (1 Kgs 12–2 Kgs 17), and Judah alone (2 Kgs 18–25).[134] R. D. Nelson separates the books into five parts based on significant themes that summarize important time periods.[135] S. J. DeVries and T. R. Hobbs combine important characters and events in their divisions of 1, 2 Kings.[136] G. Savran suggests that a chiastic structure best unfolds the

---

[129] Long, *1 Kings,* 16–18.

[130] Ibid., 19–20. For other ways that Old Testament narrative differs from modern narrative consult B. Long, "Framing Repetitions in Biblical Historiography," *JBL* 106/3 (1987) 385–99.

[131] G. B. Caird, *The Language and Imagery of the Bible* (Philadelphia: Westminster, 1980) 118.

[132] Long, *1 Kings,* 24–28.

[133] Noth, *The Deuteronomistic History,* 76.

[134] Cf. Gray, *I and II Kings,* 5–8; Jones, *1 and 2 Kings,* 1:82–85 (though Jones does separate 1 Kgs 1–2 from 1 Kgs 3–11); Patterson and Austel, "1 and 2 Kings," 21–24; and Long, *1 Kings and 2 Kings,* FOTL 10 (Grand Rapids: Eerdmans, 1991) 3–4.

[135] R. D. Nelson, *First and Second Kings,* IBC (Louisville: John Knox, 1987) vii–viii. Nelson divides the books as follows: A Kingdom of Shalom (1 Kgs 1–10), Shalom Is Broken (1 Kgs 11–16), Israel under the Prophetic Word (1 Kgs 17:1–2 Kgs 8:15), Israel's Last Chance and the End (2 Kgs 8:17–17:41), Judah: Paradox of Promise and Punishment (2 Kgs 18–25).

[136] DeVries, *1 Kings,* vii–viii; Hobbs, *2 Kings,* vii–viii.

books' major characters, conflicts, and historical developments.[137] The variety of opinions on this issue demonstrates the diverse nature of the books' contents. The similarities of these opinions demonstrates that there are unifying details in 1, 2 Kings.

This commentary follows a structure of 1, 2 Kings that incorporates the insights of Long, Nelson, and Savran. Hopefully, this structure reflects the books' historical, thematic, and literary richness. It notes both the importance of major, event-producing characters like Solomon, Elijah, and Elisha and of significant events such as the destruction of Samaria and Jerusalem. In so doing, it also focuses on the rise of prophecy and the prophets' war with idolatry and demonstrates how prophetic narrative unfolds.

OUTLINE OF THE BOOKS

I. The Rise of Solomon (1:1–2:46)
   1. David's Declining Health (1:1–4)
   2. Adonijah's Attempt to Become King (1:5–10)
   3. Solomon Becomes King (1:11–52)
   4. David Advises Solomon (2:1–9)
   5. David's Death (2:10–12)
   6. Solomon Consolidates His Power (2:13–46)

II. Solomon's Reign (3:1–11:43)
   1. God's First Appearance to Solomon (3:1–15)
   2. Solomon Demonstrates His Wisdom (3:16–4:34)
   3. Solomon Builds the Temple and Palace (5:1–7:51)
   4. Solomon Dedicates the Temple (8:1–66)
   5. God's Second Appearance to Solomon (9:1–9)
   6. Solomon's Pursuits (9:10–28)
   7. Solomon's Wisdom and Wealth (10:1–29)
   8. Solomon's Decline (11:1–43)

III. The Divided Kingdom and the Rise of Idolatry (12:1–16:34)
   1. The Rise and Fall of Jeroboam's Family (12:1–15:32)

---

[137] G. Savran, "1 and 2 Kings," in *The Literary Guide to the Bible,* ed. R. Alter and F. Kermode (Cambridge: Harvard University Press, 1987) 148. Savran offers the following chiastic arrangement:

A Solomon/United Monarchy – 1 Kgs 1:1–11:25
  B Jeroboam/Rehoboam; division of kingdom – 1 Kgs 11:26–14:31
    C Kings of Judah/Israel – 1 Kgs 15:1–16:22
      D Omride dynasty; rise and fall of Baal cult in Israel and Judah – 1 Kgs 16:23–2 Kgs 12
    C' Kings of Judah/Israel – 2 Kgs 13–16
  B' Fall of Northern Kingdom – 2 Kgs 17
A' Kingdom of Judah – 2 Kgs 18–25.

2. The Rise of Omri and Ahab (15:32–16:34)

IV. Elijah's Opposition to Idolatry and Oppression (1 Kgs 17:1–2 Kgs 1:18)
1. Elijah Battles Baalism (17:1–18:46)
2. Elijah Denounces Ahab (20:1–22:40)
3. Elijah's Final Days (1 Kgs 22:41–2 Kgs 1:18)

V. Elisha's Work as Prophet, Miracle Worker, and Kingmaker (2:1–13:25)
1. Elisha Succeeds Elijah (2:1–3:27)
2. Elisha Performs Miracles (4:1–6:23)
3. Elisha Predicts a Siege's End (6:24–7:20)
4. Elisha's Political Influence (8:1–9:13)
5. Jehu's Purge (9:14–10:35)
6. Joash's Reform (11:1–12:21)
7. Elisha's Final Days (13:1–25)

VI. Israel Disintegrates (14:1–17:41)
1. Judah Battles Israel (14:1–22)
2. Temporary Respite (14:23–15:7)
3. Israel's Political Upheaval (15:8–31)
4. Judah's Political Weakness (15:32–16:20)
5. Assyria Destroys Israel (17:1–41)

VII. Judah Disintegrates (18:1–25:30)
1. Hezekiah's Righteous Reign (18:1–20:21)
2. Manasseh and Amon's Wicked Reigns (21:1–26)
3. Josiah's Righteous Reign (22:1–23:30)
4. Judah's Political and Moral Decline (23:31–24:20)
5. Babylon Destroys Judah (25:1–26)
6. Jehoiachin Survives in Exile (25:27–30)

3. The Plot of 1, 2 Kings

"Plot" means more than simply what happens in a story. It goes beyond the happenings in a story to the reasons for these happenings. Plot relates the causes and effects in a story. Thus, the story line in 1, 2 Kings may be that Israel went into exile, but the plot is Israel went into exile because of its unfaithfulness to God.[138] To make cause and effect unfold, plots normally have at least two basic aspects: conflict and resolution. A plot's conflict is the tension in a story that makes it an interesting account, while a plot's resolution is the way the conflict is settled. How the author develops these two compo-

[138] This example is modified from an illustration in E. M. Forster, *Aspects of the Novel* (New York: Harcourt Brace Jovanovich, 1955) 86.

nents usually decides the shape and effectiveness of the plot.

Two basic types of action enhance plot. First, rising action brings the conflict to the breaking point. Rising action often foreshadows future events in ways calculated to create interest in the end of the story. Second, there is falling action, which forms pauses in the plot and concludes a story after the conflict and resolution have occurred. Falling action allows readers to reflect on what has happened. It also often provides an explanation of the resolution, or suggests possible scenarios for the future.

Most plots can either be described as tragic or comic. Tragedy presents a story in which a main character or characters achieve success, only to crash from the heights they have reached. Comedy, on the other hand, ends on a positive note. Major characters experience severe difficulties, yet overcome these problems by the end of the story. N. Frye therefore describes tragedy as an inverted U-shaped plot,[139] and comedy as a U-shaped plot. Comic plots slide into the bottom of the U-shape before moving up, while tragic plots reach the top of the inverted-U before crashing down. How the author integrates characterization, conflict, resolution, rising action, and falling action helps determine whether a plot is tragic or comic. Though it is problematic whether biblical writers wrote tragedies and comedies as Greek authors did,[140] it is correct to conclude that Old Testament plots are comic and tragic. Also, modern readers understand these concepts, which also makes them helpful for explaining 1, 2 Kings.

(1) Plot in Prophetic Narrative

Plots in prophetic narratives resemble the plots found in prophecies like Isaiah, Jeremiah, Ezekiel, and the Minor Prophets. In these books the conflict is between a righteous God, who has graciously redeemed Israel, and the rebellious nation, who breaks the Lord's law and takes their favored status for granted. Israel's rebellion can take many forms but at its heart consists of idolatry. Quite often Baal worship is the "idolatry of choice" for the people.[141] To combat the people's sin, God warns Israel by sending prophets who call them to repentance (Isa 6; Jer 1; Ezra 1–2). Usually the people refuse to listen,

---

[139] N. Frye, *The Great Code: The Bible and Literature* (New York: Harcourt Brace Jovanovich, 1982) 128–129. Also note Frye's discussion of the nature of tragedy and comedy in *Anatomy of Criticism* (New York: Atheneum, 1967) 163–186, 206–223.

[140] For a thorough discussion of the appropriateness of calling biblical narratives "tragic" or "comic," see the essays in *Semeia* 32 (1985).

[141] Writing about Zephaniah (ca. 625 B.C.), J. M. P. Smith asserts: "Baalism died hard in Israel. Yahweh never had the sole and undivided allegiance of Israel in the preexilic age. Notwithstanding the bitter opposition to Baalism on the part of Elijah, Hosea and all the succeeding prophets, it still called for the prophetic wrath of Zephaniah" (*A Critical and Exegetical Commentary on Micah, Zephaniah, Nahum, Habakkuk, Obadiah and Joel,* ICC [New York: Scribners, 1911] 187).

though there are notable exceptions to this rule (e.g., Isa 37:14–38; Hag 1:12–15; Zech 1:16).

The resolution in prophecies usually begins unpleasantly. When Israel or the nations refuse to repent, God threatens, then sends, a "day of the Lord," or judgment day (cf. Isa 2:6ff.; Jer 4:23–31; Zeph 1:8–18). This "day" will wipe out the wicked, purge the land, and leave only a righteous remnant. But punishment is only part of the resolution. After judgment God will restore Israel, then bring the nations to the Lord (cf. Zeph 3:8–20). God then begins again with people who will presumably obey their Lord (cf. Jer 31:31–34).

Clearly, prophecies incorporate both tragic and comic principles. Ultimately, however, the goal is restoration and renewal, so the comic outlook prevails. Still some horrible situations occur when judgment helps effect the resolution. Happy endings only emerge after a terrible price has been paid. Jeremiah envisions a new covenant but only long after Jerusalem's destruction. Ezekiel sees a new Jerusalem yet only because the city has been devastated. Therefore, the fact that hope remains does not negate the tragic consequences of Israel's actions.

(2) Plot in 1, 2 Kings

First and Second Kings fit into the overall plot of Joshua-Kings, yet they also present their own self-contained set of events. Joshua depicts Israel's struggle to conquer the land God promised to Abraham (Gen 12:1–9). Moses' generation refused to trust the Lord and invade Canaan (Num 13–14), but Joshua's armies succeed where their parents failed (cf. Josh 1–12). After this generation dies, however, the nation virtually becomes enslaved in their own homeland. Why? Because of idolatry (Judg 2:10–23). Because in Judges each person does whatever he or she sees fit (17:6, 21:25) rather than obeying God's Word. Israel seems to prefer defeat to victory.

What can change this situation? God grants Israel's request for a king in 1 Samuel 8–12. At first this king (Saul) succeeds, but soon he breaks God's commands just as the people do (1 Sam 15),[142] so the Lord makes David king (1 Sam 16:13–14). Once David's kingdom is established, God promises that David's dynasty will never end (2 Sam 7:1–17). His family will rule forever, which implies that the monarchy will help the nation be faithful, which in turn means God will let them keep their land.

Despite this expectation the promise to David acts as a paradox in 1, 2 Kings. David's line does endure, even if it is in exile by the story's end (cf. 2 Kgs 25:27–30). Thus, some long-term hope remains.[143] But the people

---

[142] D. Gunn takes a more sympathetic approach to Saul's life than commentators tend to do in *The Fate of King Saul,* JSOTSup 14 (Sheffield: Sheffield Academic Press, 1980).

[143] Cf. von Rad, *Studies in Deuteronomy,* 90–91.

maintain their rebellious ways, so God removes them from the land. The kings are usually as unfaithful as the populace, even while they remain the key to the brighter future. This tension allows the monarchy to be a key element in the plot's conflict and resolution.

First and Second Kings themselves present Israel's final slide into exile. After David's death Solomon rules the nation well for many years, then participates in idolatry himself (1 Kgs 11). Seasoned readers of Joshua-Samuel know that such activity will be punished. Soon both halves of the nation are idolatrous. God sends prophets, some famous and some nameless, to lead the people to repentance.[144] This group, coupled with the activities of the few righteous kings that emerge, provides pauses in the inevitable movement toward national devastation. Rising action occurs when Egypt, Assyria, and Babylon threaten Israel and Judah. Falling action is evident after Samaria and Jerusalem are destroyed.

Resolution occurs in the books' final chapter (2 Kgs 25). The conflict between rebellious Israel and the holy God is solved by Babylon's victory over Judah. Both people and monarch are punished. Still, Jehoiachin, David's "son," lives on in exile. Concern for the future is eased somewhat. All things considered, 1, 2 Kings portray God's people in the lowest level of the U-shape Frye describes.[145] These books mark the lowest ebb in Israel's national history.

4. Characterization in 1, 2 Kings

Characterization is vital to narrative. Literary scholars since Aristotle have noted that, alongside plot, characters are one of the main factors in believable, interesting stories. This fact is as true in historical narrative as in fiction, for how the author portrays a character and fits that character into the overall historical scheme in part determines the history's effectiveness. It is necessary to examine characterization, then, to have a proper understanding of 1, 2 Kings.

In fiction authors create their characters, since fictional worlds do not really exist. Even in fiction, though, characters may be drawn from real persons. In historical narrative authors must select what individuals to highlight. Thus, writers of fiction and history share the burden of bringing characters out of the shadows and including them in the composition. Once the selection of personages has been made, the account has one or more characters.

[144] Cf. Wolff, "The Kerygma of the Deuteronomic Historical Work," 97–99.
[145] Frye, *The Great Code*, 171.

"Characterization" is the way authors depict the characters they choose for their stories. E. V. Roberts states that characterization is the way an author draws "a personality who takes on actions, thoughts, expressions, and attitudes unique and appropriate to that personality and consistent with it."[146] E. Olson adds that characterization is the author's ability to describe characters who are appropriate, consistent, and useful to the plot.[147] Good characterization makes characters seem real. Good characterization develops dynamic, changing characters rather than flat, lifeless, or stereotypical ones.[148]

There are at least four ways to assess characters. First, it is important to judge characters by what they say and do, especially if speech and act contradict each other. Second, it is necessary to examine what other characters say about a character or how others react to the person. Third, it is advisable to note what the book's narrator/author says about a character. Fourth, it is also advisable to read what other biblical writers say about a character. Only when all these aspects are collected can true character be assessed. For instance, what Ahab says about himself, what Jezebel says about him, and what the narrator thinks of him are all different. Learning to interpret these various elements gives readers greater perspective on what 1, 2 Kings actually teach.

(1) Characterization Techniques in 1, 2 Kings

Characters are judged frequently in 1, 2 Kings. Indeed virtually every king is either praised or condemned by the author. Editorial comments on the people of the nation (treated as one of the characters) also appear. With so much commentary it is somewhat difficult to grasp how the author determines which character to stress at what time. Readers must remember, though, that prophetic narrative has certain points it wants to make. The author presents characters in ways that will highlight those particular ideas.

G. Savran outlines several ways characterization is achieved in 1, 2 Kings. Kings can be compared to other kings by characters in the story (1 Kgs 12:1–19). Characters can be portrayed negatively by their opposition to obviously positive personae, such as in the Ahab and Elijah accounts. Or a character may be presented as doing the right thing for the wrong reason (e.g., Jehu).[149] Of course, the more obvious means of determining character outlined above are also evident. Savran's observations demonstrate that the manner of characterization in 1, 2 Kings is much richer and more subtle than a quick reading of the material might indicate.

---

[146] Roberts, *Writing Themes about Literature,* 45.

[147] E. Olson, *Tragedy and the Theory of Drama* (Detroit: Wayne State University Press, 1966) 82.

[148] Note the thorough yet succinct analysis of characterization in C. H. Holman, *A Handbook to Literature,* 3d ed. (New York: Odyssey, 1972).

[149] Savran, "1 and 2 Kings," 149–55.

(2) *Types of Characters in 1, 2 Kings*

Both characters and character groups contribute to the plot of 1, 2 Kings. Four character groups can be identified—kings, prophets, Israelites, foreigners—which impact the whole story and affect portions of the whole. For example, there are many prophets in the books, but Elijah and Elisha are the most significant members of this group. The Lord is a dominant character in the story who does not, of course (in the author's view), fit into any larger grouping. Within each of these four categories are single characters who either contribute to the demise of Israel and Judah or stall the nations' decline.

Various kings are selected for special emphasis. Some of those chosen are obviously important in Israelite history, yet some are "surprise choices." Solomon and Jeroboam I are giant figures because of their pivotal role in the best years the people enjoy and for their contribution to the long downward slide of Israel and Judah. Hezekiah and Josiah are highlighted for their positive influence in Judah. Manasseh receives serious treatment because of his fifty-two-year reign but even more because of his gross wickedness. Yet Omri, the builder of Samaria and a man of high international fame,[150] is dismissed in eight verses (1 Kgs 16:21–28). Why? Probably because he plays no particularly significant role in Israel's decline. Again, characterization is based largely on its role in plot development, not on how it will or will not satisfy modern historians.

Two kinds of prophets appear in 1, 2 Kings. Good prophets, such as Elijah, Elisha, Micaiah, and Huldah, preach only God's word and only at God's command. These characters attempt to save their hearers from spiritual and financial disaster. Unfortunately, false prophets, like those who oppose Micaiah (1 Kgs 22), probably were more numerous and popular than righteous prophets. Their preaching in effect urges the kings to continue with their destructive leadership styles. They make sure God's word is not heard and that the covenant remains broken.

Similarly, faithful and wicked Israelites and foreigners participate in the story. Obadiah, the Shunammite woman, and others aid the prophets. Naaman the Syrian believes God's prophet and is thereby healed of leprosy. On the other hand, the vast majority of Israelites follow their kings, practice idolatry, and go to their doom. Foreign leaders, like the Assyrian official in 1 Kings 18, Ben-Hadad of Syria, and Nebuchadnezzar, the Babylonian conqueror, all detest God's people. They often blaspheme and gladly oppress other nations.

God is also portrayed as a king. The Lord rules the whole earth and therefore blesses and punishes according to the nations' obedience. Even Egypt,

---

[150] Assyrian records tend to refer to Israel's kings as sons of Omri and even calls Samaria "Omri-land." Cf. *ANET,* 280–81, 284–85.

Babylon, and Assyria are tools in God's hands. No nation, however great, acts autonomously. Rather, nations are subservient to the Great King. Unlike most of the monarchs portrayed in 1, 2 Kings, though, God is fair, merciful, faithful, and patient. Most of these characteristics are declared by the prophets and divulged by the author/narrator. God's words to the people through the prophets make the Lord ever-present in history, and the author's explanations of God's work in history make the Lord ever-present in the story.[151]

5. Point of View in 1, 2 Kings

According to Holman, "point of view" is a term that describes "the way in which the reader is presented with the materials of the story, or, viewed from another angle, the vantage point from which the author presents the actions of the story."[152] In other words, an analysis of a text's point of view uncovers who tells a story, how the story is told, and how accurately the story has been told. It should also determine the author's belief system, which is particularly important for interpreting Scripture. Point of view is a particularly vital topic for 1, 2 Kings because of the fact that the books' author selects the events, characters, and themes that he deems most important. Thus, the more interpreters understand about this author's perspective the better they can grasp and proclaim the books' message.

In 1, 2 Kings, as in most Old Testament narratives, the narrator appears to be omniscient. That is, the narrator knows everything about everyone in the story. A. Berlin says: "He can be anywhere and everywhere, even inside the minds of the characters. The reader's perception is formed by what the narrator reveals of his omniscience and the way it is revealed."[153] In fact, the narrator of 1, 2 Kings claims to know why *God* does certain things (cf. 1 Kgs 17). Without question this narrator has privileged information.[154] Fortunately, this information is shared, which means "the reader comes to see what the narrator sees."[155] Readers are thereby offered a vantage point even greater than that enjoyed by the story's characters.

---

[151] For an extended treatment of the OT's characterization of God, see D. Patrick, *The Rendering of God in the Old Testament* (Philadelphia: Fortress, 1981).

[152] Holman, *A Handbook to Literature,* 408.

[153] A. Berlin, *Poetics and Interpretation of Biblical Narrative,* BALS 9 (Sheffield: Almond Press, 1983) 52. Elsewhere narrators also can be limited, unreliable, or impersonal. Cf. W. C. Booth, *The Rhetoric of Fiction* (Chicago: University of Chicago Press, 1961), for explanations of these categories.

[154] Sternberg (*The Poetics of Biblical Narrative,* 12) theorizes that the omniscient author's comprehensive knowledge is consciously calculated by the author to emphasize the text's claim to be inspired by an all-knowing God.

[155] Berlin, *Poetics and Interpretation of Biblical Narrative,* 52.

This privileged position calls readers to decision. Biblical narrators are unashamedly ideological.[156] They intend to change lives by getting readers to accept their views of God's Word. As W. Booth observes, "From the author's viewpoint, a successful reading of his book must eliminate all distance between the essential norms of his implied author and the norms of his postulated reader."[157] Therefore, the original "implied audience"[158] the book addresses learned why and how Israel disintegrated. They then had to decide whether to imitate or to avoid that way of life. Likewise, today's readers will either accept the author's view of history and order their lives accordingly or they will ignore the text at their own peril.

Introduction to Canonical Issues

Clearly, historical and literary analysis are indispensable tools for understanding 1, 2 Kings. Left by themselves, however, they do not necessarily yield interpretations that make the books relevant and applicable to contemporary audiences. Historical criticism practiced in isolation tells readers what lies behind the written text. T. Keegan says focusing solely on the background of a text is like attempting "to see what is on the other side of the window without looking at the window itself, without recognizing that the canonical text is not merely something to be looked through, but that it is meant to be looked at."[159] Similarly, considering only a text's literary aspects leaves interpreters grasping for its theological and applicational importance. Readers could easily enjoy the Bible, a very positive reaction, yet fail to acknowledge its authority over their lives. Pastors, teachers, and scholars therefore need an exegetical step that links historical and literary reflections with doctrine and everyday life.

These and other concerns led to a new discipline in biblical studies during the 1970s and 1980s. Several scholars, led by B. Childs and J. Sanders, began to analyze how Old Testament books function within the Bible as a whole.[160]

---

[156] This is the main point of Sternberg's *Poetics of Biblical Narrative.* He correctly asserts that ancient authors did not consider disinterested objectivity a virtue. Rather, they considered presenting a distinct point of view a positive and necessary part of their writing task.

[157] Booth, *The Rhetoric of Fiction,* 157.

[158] The term "implied audience" is used by literary critics to describe the possible viewpoints and situation of whomever the author intended to address.

[159] T. J. Keegan, *Interpreting the Bible: A Popular Introduction to Biblical Hermeneutics* (New York: Paulist Press) 135.

[160] Key works in canonical criticism include Childs, *Introduction to the Old Testament as Scripture; The New Testament as Canon* (Philadelphia: Fortress, 1985); *Old Testament Theology in a Canonical Context* (Philadelphia: Fortress, 1986); Sanders, *Torah and Canon; Canon and Community: A Guide to Canonical Criticism* (Philadelphia: Fortress, 1984); and *From Sacred Story to Sacred Text* (Philadelphia: Fortress, 1987).

Though they disagreed over certain key points,[161] these "canonical critics" shared several basic convictions. First, they noted the tendency of historical criticism to divide the Old Testament into countless isolated pieces and desired to locate more unity among the books.[162] Second, they recognized that great pains were taken to select the canon, or list of books that constitute the Bible. Once chosen, the books were considered Scripture, which means they possess the authority to tell people how to live.[163] Third, they stressed that biblical books were often impacted by earlier scriptural writings and that each new work was in turn interpreted by its successors. For instance, 1, 2 Kings are influenced by Deuteronomy and complete a story begun in Joshua, Judges, and 1, 2 Samuel. Also, other books, such as 1, 2 Chronicles, Jeremiah, and Malachi, reflect 1, 2 Kings' point of view on important characters and events.[164] Fourth, they claimed that a book's placement and function in the canon has theological implications. Ideas such as covenant breaking and the wrath of God are prominent in 1, 2 Kings, for example, because the books are composed as and placed at the end of Israel's history.[165]

Fifth, and very vital for this commentary, the canonical critics emphasized that the Old Testament Scriptures were always meant to be preached and taught by communities of faith.[166] As a literary work the Old Testament tells Israel's story. As Scripture it becomes Israel's guidebook. As guidebook it states the theology that directs everyday godly living. These characteristics should encourage the church to affirm the value of the Old Testament in every generation.

---

[161] The chief disagreement between Childs and Sanders lies in which canonical text to analyze. Childs insists the final, literary form of the MT must be the source of exegesis (*Introduction,* 73), but Sanders argues that each stage of the canonical process within and outside of Scripture should be assessed (*From Sacred Story to Sacred Text,* 166–72). This commentary agrees with Childs on this point, chiefly because the final form of the OT is best preserved in the MT and because most reconstructions of the intertextual canonical process are uncertain at best.

[162] Childs, *Introduction,* 39–41; Sanders, *Torah and Canon,* ix.

[163] Sanders contends that the Bible's basic authority lies in its ability "to engage the two questions: who am I, or we, and what are we to do?" Thus, he says, "Canon functions, for the most part, to provide indications of the identity as well as the life style of the ongoing community that reads it" (*From Sacred Story to Sacred Text,* 17).

[164] For discussions of how Scripture refers to and interprets itself see P. R. Ackroyd, "Original Text and Canonical Text," *USQ* 32 (1977) 166–73; G. T. Sheppard, "Canonization: Hearing the Voice of the Same God through Historically Dissimilar Traditions," *Int* 37 (1982) 21–33; and J. Sailhamer, "The Canonical Approach to the Old Testament: Its Effect on Understanding Prophecy," *JETS* 30/3 (1987) 307–15.

[165] Writing about 1, 2 Kings, Childs says, "A canonical approach would see the intention of the biblical writer to describe the execution of the curses of Deuteronomy, which had been rehearsed by successive generations of prophets, against a disobedient covenant people" (*Introduction,* 300–301).

[166] Cf. Sanders, *From Sacred Story to Sacred Text,* 9–39.

Like most approaches to biblical interpretation, canonical criticism has critics as well as supporters. Some evangelicals accept the approach's basic tenets without accepting Childs and Sanders' view of biblical inspiration.[167] Several nonevangelicals critique canonical criticism at various strategic points.[168] This section uses positive features of the method to show how an emphasis on 1, 2 Kings' canonical shape and function helps interpret them. To achieve this purpose the books' placement, purpose, and usage in Scripture are discussed.

1. Canonical Placement of 1, 2 Kings

One of the major differences between the order of the books in the Hebrew and English canons is found in the historical books. The Hebrew text places here only four books (known as the Former Prophets): Joshua, Judges, Samuel, and Kings. English Bibles follow the Septuagint by adding Ruth and dividing Samuel and Kings into four books. The English Bible also includes 1, 2 Chronicles, Ezra, Nehemiah, and Esther in this section, which allows it to present Israel's history from the conquest of Canaan (ca. 1400 B.C.) to the Persian period (ca. 465 B.C.). The Hebrew Bible, on the other hand, places 1, 2 Chronicles, Ezra, Nehemiah, and Esther in the final section of the canon. Job, Psalms, and the other poetic and wisdom books follow Esther in the English Bible, while the prophets come after Kings in Hebrew texts.

Why mention these varying orders when the books themselves are inspired Scripture? Chiefly because the differing lists reveal two ways 1, 2 Kings have been read and interpreted. The English Bible presents the books primarily as historical accounts. Their placement next to 1, 2 Chronicles demonstrates the collectors' interest in detailing all the events of Israel's history. In contrast, the Hebrew Bible places Joshua-Kings with the prophets, which highlights their common viewpoints. This decision implies that 1, 2 Kings are being treated as proclamation *and* history. It also underlines 1, 2 Kings' belief that Israel's prophets should have been heeded. Both traditions tell Israel's story, but the Hebrew canon gives the story more bite by following it with a parade of the very people who warned that destruction was coming.

---

[167] J. Sailhamer's works take this approach, as do my own studies (*Zephaniah—A Prophetic Drama,* JSOTSup 97, BALS 18 [Sheffield: Sheffield Academic Press, 1988], and *The Unity of the Twelve,* JSOTSup, BALS 27 [Sheffield: Sheffield Academic Press, 1990]). J. Oswalt offers several cautions about the method in "Canonical Criticism: A Review from a Conservative Viewpoint," *JETS* 30/3 (1987) 317–25.

[168] J. Barr presents a lengthy critique of Childs' opinions in *Holy Scripture: Canon, Authority, Criticism* (Philadelphia: Westminster, 1983). Also note S. Fowl, "The Canonical Approach of Brevard Childs," *ExpTim* 96 (1985) 173–76.

2. Canonical Function of 1, 2 Kings

First and Second Kings play a pivotal role, then, in the Hebrew canon. On the one hand, they provide the tragic end of Israel's national story, a story that begins in Genesis. On the other hand, they introduce readers to the extensive prophetic influence in Israel, provide a prophetic interpretation of the nation's history, and thereby pave the way for the messages found in Isaiah, Jeremiah, Ezekiel, and the twelve Minor Prophets. In other words, 1, 2 Kings bring together the major concerns of Israel's religious heritage. Covenant obligations, divine promise, the monarchy's responsibility to God and the people, and the prophets' attempts to reconcile Israel to the Lord merge here.

Several vital Old Testament ideas and institutions reach their end in 1, 2 Kings.[169] The land God promises to Abraham (Gen 12:7; 15:1–16) is lost and can only be regained at an unspecified time in the future. Israel breaks the Mosaic Covenant, which forces them to accept the punishments set forth in Deuteronomy 27–28. David's family will have no kingdom to rule—a direct result of their own failure to provide Israel with righteous leadership. Thus, God's pledge of an eternal kingdom for David would have to be reinterpreted from a physical to a spiritual reality. Temple worship ends. Priests have no one to instruct and no place to offer sacrifices. With one exception, no positive element of Israel's heritage is left intact at the conclusion of 1, 2 Kings.

That one exception is the prophetic movement. Unencumbered by a need for king or cult, the prophets could preach wherever Israelites were scattered. Their message could also be collected and read even in exile, and their interpretation of Israel's demise could be widely disseminated. Given these facts, 1, 2 Kings prepared readers to grasp both the message and the importance of the prophetic books. For example, readers know of Isaiah's prominence from 2 Kgs 19:20 to 20:11. They are also prepared for his emphasis on Israel's failure to obey God, for Jeremiah's attempts to spur the people to repentance, and for Ezekiel's ministry in exile. As H. W. Wolff has observed, the insistence on repentance in 1, 2 Kings also prepares readers for the possibility of a bright future, an idea prevalent in Isaiah 40–66; Jeremiah 31–34; and Ezekiel 40–48.[170]

3. The Usage of 1, 2 Kings in Scripture

Generally speaking, 1, 2 Kings comment on previous biblical characters and events more than other books comment on similar elements. The pivotal nature of the books partially explains this tendency. Still, interpreters need to note how and where significant portions of 1, 2 Kings are reused to understand

---

[169] Cf. Childs, *Introduction,* 300–301.

[170] Cf. Wolff, "The Kerygma of the Deuteronomic Historical Work."

how other Scriptures interpret the repeated material. This practice will in turn offer suggestions about ways to explain 1, 2 Kings to contemporary audiences. There are at least four ways the books are utilized in the rest of the Bible.

First, they are used as information in 1, 2 Chronicles. Indeed the Chronicler uses the books as more than information, for they also operate as a brooding dialogue partner to the more upbeat history 1, 2 Chronicles present. The Chronicler includes most of the characters and events mentioned in 1, 2 Samuel and 1, 2 Kings yet shapes them in a much different way from the author of those books. Saul makes only a cameo appearance in 1, 2 Chronicles (cf. 1 Chr 9:35–10:14). David's importance is heightened. For example, he is given credit for collecting the materials to build the temple (1 Chr 28:1–29:20). Solomon's idolatry goes unmentioned, and even wicked Manasseh is portrayed in a partly positive manner. Jerusalem's fall receives only brief treatment (2 Chr 36:15–21), though the Chronicler does blame the people for the disaster (36:14).

Both 1, 2 Kings and 1, 2 Chronicles are needed for readers to have a balanced picture of Israel's history.[171] Though very different, both viewpoints are accurate. Certainly Israel's negative actions fueled its downfall, but the nation still had a proud and productive heritage. Placed at the end of the Hebrew canon, 1, 2 Chronicles encourage readers to maintain hope and to trust God to do great things for them again. Written earlier, and from a prophetic theological stance, 1, 2 Kings admonish the nation. Hope is based more on change than on the removal of doubt and discouragement. The Chronicler demonstrates how to soften the message of 1, 2 Kings when that perspective becomes appropriate.

Second, 1, 2 Kings provide vital background details for subsequent texts. The life settings and theological positions of the prophets are much more understandable after reading 1, 2 Kings. Likewise, texts like Lamentations and Psalm 137, which mourn the exile and its hardships, make more sense when 1, 2 Kings are kept in mind. The end of David's dynasty makes messianic texts even more poignant and urgent. In turn, such passages indicate the significance of what happened in 1, 2 Kings.

Third, 1, 2 Kings present prophets and the prophetic movement, two elements that affect the rest of Scripture. True and false prophets battle in 1, 2 Kings, a scenario that continues and one that particularly impacts Jeremiah. God's unique relationship with the prophets emerges. Perhaps Elijah has the most unusual tie to the Lord. He does not die, thereby becoming the ideal apocalyptic prophet in Mal 4:5–6 and Matt 17:1–8 and the model for John the Baptist. Prophecy lives on in the New Testament (e.g., Acts 21:1–15). Paul

[171] Cf. P. R. House, *Old Testament Survey* (Nashville: Broadman, 1992) 267–70, for a discussion of the Chronicler's view of Israel's history.

rates it as the highest of church-edifying spiritual gifts (1 Cor 14:1–25). None of these later ideas can be properly assessed until their roots in 1, 2 Kings have been examined.

Fourth, major theological ideas found in all of Scripture are prominent in 1, 2 Kings as demonstrated in the next section ("Introduction to Theological Issues"). Most of 1, 2 Kings' chief ideas support and enhance other texts where these emphases appear.

Introduction to Theological Issues

First and Second Kings are a storehouse of theological ideas. As the previous three sections have shown, theology impacts the books' historical, literary, and canonical aspects. After all, the author of 1, 2 Kings lived after Jerusalem's fall and therefore wrote a history for people dealing with national disgrace and exile. The stark reality of the people's situation called for a history with a viewpoint that explained why events had unfolded in such a negative way. Israel's national predicament also caused the people to wonder if any hope remained. In this setting history could not be told in some detached manner. Events had to be infused with meaning.

Further, the unusual nature of the books' literary details invites theological reflection. Indeed, a story that claims historical accuracy yet includes prophets who speak with God, miracles, and a narrator who claims to know God's thoughts and intentions demands theological analysis. These books boldly state that history and theology are inseparable. History gives theology a context, while theology gives history meaning. Literature portrays these truths creatively. No character, theme, or plot development in 1, 2 Kings makes sense outside of a theological perspective.

Finally, the canonical placement of 1, 2 Kings has theological implications. No careful reader of the Hebrew canon could possibly read Genesis-2 Kings without noting how the promises concerning land and nationhood seem to have been thwarted. Similarly, thoughtful readers could not help but wonder how the Former Prophets introduce or supplement the Latter Prophets (Isaiah-Malachi). Clearly, some vital issues seem to end, while others appear to begin, in 1, 2 Kings. How (not if) theology plays a part in the canonical function of 1, 2 Kings within the Old Testament is the question.

Though historical, literary, and canonical data reveal theological ideas, it is still necessary to summarize conclusions drawn from the data. The books' richness makes this process rewarding. Scholars have handled this task in a variety of ways, with some offering a list of themes and others integrating different concepts into one overriding category. This commentary presents major ideas that reflect 1, 2 Kings' status as prophetic narrative. Hopefully, this approach will be consistent with the books' literary character and will illuminate their theological unity and diversity at the same time. Each idea is presented with its opposite to show that the prophetic viewpoint was at odds with Israel's behavior.

1. Monotheism versus Idolatry

If Old Testament theology could be summarized in one sentence, it probably would read, "There is no god but the Lord." This theme begins with the Bible's opening declaration that "in the beginning God created the heavens and the earth" (Gen 1:1).[172] It is reemphasized in the Ten Commandments, when Israel is told to worship only the Lord (Exod 20:3) and is warned not to bow down to any idol (Exod 20:4–5). The idea appears again in Deut 6:4, where Israel's worship, home life, indeed its entire values system are based on God's oneness. In Judges idolatry is blamed for Israel's periodic descents into defeat and oppression. First and Second Samuel avoid any implication that what occurs on earth is not caused by the Lord. Virtually all the prophets condemn idol worship, with some even lampooning the practice (cf. Isa 44:6–23; 46:1–2; Jer 10:1–5).[173]

The author of 1, 2 Kings drives home the anti-idolatry, promonotheism theme repeatedly. Idolatry is blamed for the nation's division after Solomon's death (1 Kgs 11:9–13). Without exception the kings are judged by whether or not they promoted, curtailed, or eradicated idolatry in the land. A refusal to turn from idolatry ultimately leads to the destruction of both Israel and Judah (2 Kgs 17:7–41). Clearly, the people's theological failure results in their military failure.

Who was responsible for this descent into idolatry? Solomon deserves some blame for giving royal approval to polytheism (1 Kgs 11:1–13). Also the average Israelite often preferred Canaanite religion, particularly Baalism and its sexually charged rites, over the worship of Yahweh. Above everyone else, though, 1, 2 Kings blames Jeroboam I and Ahab for institutionalizing idolatry and paganism in the land.

Once he establishes the new, northern nation, Jeroboam starts a new religion, one that serves his own interests rather than those of God or his subjects. This alternative religion reverses Moses' teachings. Instead of rejecting idols, Jeroboam has two golden calves made, then teaches the nation that *these* gods delivered Israel from Egypt (1 Kgs 12:28–30; cf. Exod 32). Knowing that it is not politically expedient to allow his people to travel to Jerusalem to worship, he builds two local shrines where the new gods can be honored (1 Kgs 12:29–31). Other aspects of his novel religion are noted in the next section. It is obvious that his founding and spreading of this religion

---

[172] G. Hasel, "The Polemic Nature of the Genesis Cosmology," *EvQ* 46 (1974) 81–102.

[173] Note the various aspects of idol worship discussed in T. Jacobsen, "The Graven Image," in *Ancient Israelite Religion,* ed. P. Miller, P. Hanson, S. D. McBride (Philadelphia: Fortress, 1987) 15–32.

amounted to a devious institutionalizing of idolatry.

Ahab and Jezebel promoted and supported Baalism in Israel (1 Kgs 18:1–19:18). Jezebel employed 450 prophets of Baal (1 Kgs 18:22) and threatened the lives of God's prophets (1 Kgs 18:1–6; 19:1–2), while Ahab built a temple for Baal (1 Kgs 16:32–33). Their influence spread to Judah when their descendants intermarried with the royal family there (2 Kgs 8:18,25–27). It took Jehu's savage purge to stifle their work on behalf of Baalism (2 Kgs 9–10).

2. Central Worship versus the High Places

A by-product of idolatry was the people's tendency to offer sacrifices at "high places" (cf. 1 Kgs 3:3; 11:31–33; 13:33–34; 2 Kgs 10:28–29; etc). G. H. Davies notes that high places

> were situated on high hills and associated with green trees and leafy oaks. They could be open-air or roofed sanctuaries and were also frequently equipped with houses and halls or buildings of various kinds (I Kings 12:31; 13:32; II Kings 17:32; 23:9), including raised platforms as at Beth-shan and other places. Equipped with altars of sacrifice, incense, stone pillars, trees and/or poles, and water, they were the objects of Yahweh's wrath (Lev. 26:30; Ps. 78–58).[174]

Such locations were the places where Jeroboam's religion, Baalism, and other non-Mosaic cults were practiced. Thus, they symbolized the destructive presence of polytheism in Israel to the author of 1, 2 Kings.

Besides their obvious polytheistic implications, the high places were a direct rejection of Jerusalem as God's chosen worship center (Deut 12:5–26; 14:23–25; 15:20; 16:2; 17:8,10; 18:6; 26:2; 31:11).[175] When Solomon dedicates the temple, he asks God to "put his name there" (1 Kgs 8:16,44,48). In response the Lord agrees to place his name there "forever" (1 Kgs 9:3), then commands Solomon to show integrity and loyalty to God (1 Kgs 9:4). After Solomon permits idolatry, God divides the kingdom yet spares Judah for David's sake and for Jerusalem's sake (1 Kgs 11:13). Second Kings 21:7 reaffirms God's choice of Jerusalem, and 2 Kgs 23:27 declares that the city's destruction amounts to a temporary rejection of the chosen capital and its temple.

Therefore, every sacrifice offered at a high place is an act of rebellion against God's standards revealed through Moses. Such offerings also endanger Yahweh's continual blessing of David's family and heighten the chance that the Lord will punish the people. The author of 1, 2 Kings views the high places as symbols of national religious decadence. Only those kings who attempt to eliminate them receive unqualified praise (cf. 2 Kgs 18:1–4; 22:1–2; 23:1–25).

---

[174] G. H. Davies, "High Place, Sanctuary," *IDB* (Nashville: Abingdon, 1962) 2:602.

[175] For an examination of these and other texts that link ideas in Deuteronomy and 1, 2 Kings see M. Weinfeld, *Deuteronomy and the Deuteronomic School* (Oxford: Clarendon Press, 1972) 320–63.

3. Covenant Loyalty versus Spiritual Rebellion

Underlying the constant complaints about idol worship and the high places is the conviction that Israel and Judah have broken their covenant commitments to God. As has been stated, the author of 1, 2 Kings was committed to the teachings of the Pentateuch, particularly those found in Deuteronomy. Thus, the books include statements by David (1 Kgs 2:3), Solomon (1 Kgs 8:53,56), and the narrator (2 Kgs 14:6; 18:4,6,12; 21:8; 23:25) that stress the importance of Israel keeping the Mosaic covenant. In fact, except for 2 Kgs 14:6 and 18:4, each of these passages stresses the relationship between Israel's faithfulness to Moses' law and their ability to remain in the promised land. This belief coincides with the threats and promises made in Leviticus 26 and Deuteronomy 27–28. Other texts, most notably 2 Kgs 17:7–41, which summarizes *why* Israel fell to Assyria, emphasize the relationship between the people's disobedience and their subsequent loss of the land.

What was the nature and content of the covenant Israel broke? Over the past several decades scholars have debated the fine points of these issues.[176] Theories abound on the meaning of covenant terminology,[177] the relationship between covenant thinking and worship,[178] the use of covenant concepts in the prophets,[179] the obligations incumbent upon Israel within the covenant context,[180] and the origin of the covenant ideal in Israel.[181] These topics impact the

[176] See the excellent survey of opinions in R. A. Oden, Jr., "The Place of Covenant in the Religion of Israel," in *Ancient Israelite Religion,* ed. P. Miller, P. Hanson, S. D. McBride (Philadelphia: Fortress, 1987) 429–47.

[177] D. J. McCarthy correctly states that covenant means "relation and obligation, commitment and action" ("Berit and Covenant in the Deuteronomistic History," in *Studies in the Religion of Ancient Israel,* VTSup 23 (Leiden: Brill, 1972) 85. For an analysis of how the word's meaning developed over time, see M. Weinfeld, "berith," *TDOT* 2.254–79.

[178] Cf. E. G. Kraeling, "The Real Religion of Ancient Israel," *JBL* 47 (1928), and W. Eichrodt, *Theology of the Old Testament,* trans. J. A. Baker (Philadelphia: Westminster, 1961) 1:98–177.

[179] Cf. Weinfeld, "berith," 275–78; R. E. Clements, *Prophecy and Covenant,* SBT 43 (Napierville, Ill.: Allenson, 1965), and W. Eichrodt, "Prophet and Covenant: Observations on the Exegesis of Isaiah," in J. I. Durham and J. R. Porter, eds., *Proclamation and Presence: Old Testament Essays in Honour of Gwynne Henton Davies* (Richmond: John Knox, 1970) 167–88.

[180] For instance, scholars have argued over whether the covenant created mutual obligations between Yahweh and Israel (e.g., McCarthy, "Berit and Covenant in the Deuteronomistic History") or simply a pledge with no obligation attached (e.g., A. Jepsen, "Berith. Ein Beitrag zur Theologie der Exilszeit," in A. Kuschke, ed., *Verbannung und Heimkehr. Beiträge zur Geschichte und Theologie Israels im 6. und 5. Jahrhundert v. Chr., W. Rudolph zum 70. Geburstag* (Tübingen: Mohr-Siebeck, 1961) 161–79.

[181] The main issue here was whether or not Israel patterned its covenants after ancient treaty forms. The affirmative response was offered by G. E. Mendenhall, "Covenant Forms in Israelite Tradition," *BA* 17 (1954) 50–76; Kline, *The Treaty of the Great King;* and others. A mostly negative conclusion was reached by D. J. McCarthy, *Treaty and Covenant: A Study in Form in the Ancient Oriental Documents and in the Old Testament,* AB 21A, 2d ed. (Rome: Biblical Institute Press, 1978), and E. W. Nicholson, *God and His People: Covenant and Theology in the Old Testament* (Oxford: Clarendon, 1986).

covenant comments in 1, 2 Kings, but examining them at length here will not greatly enhance the fairly straightforward idea of covenant in 1, 2 Kings.

W. Eichrodt summarizes the basic meaning of the covenant idea in a way that accurately describes its usage in 1, 2 Kings. He notes five characteristics of "covenant" in the Old Testament. First, "the establishment of a covenant through the work of Moses especially emphasizes one basic element in the whole Israelite experience of God, namely *the factual nature of the divine revelation*."[182] That is, God communicated with Moses in history and stated objective standards for Israel to keep. Second, the covenant consists of both promise and demand.[183] God wants to bless Israel beyond their wildest imagination (Lev 26:1–13; Deut 28:1–14) yet will only do so when Israel obeys the covenant commands (Lev 26:3; Deut 28:1). Punishment will only be used as a corrective measure—a last resort—but will indeed come. If habitual disobedience occurs, the people will forfeit the land God has given as the most obvious sign of Israel's favored status (Lev 26:14–39; Deut 28:15–68). Only heartfelt repentance can restore them to the land (Lev 26:40–45).

Third, the covenant helps form Israel into a community. Either God's will "unites the tribes to one another and makes them a unified people with a strong sense of solidarity"[184] or the tribes will become a federation loosely linked by self-interest. Fourth, the covenant creates in Israel an "interior attitude to history,"[185] one that stresses God's activity in everyday life. Fifth, this historical, ethically oriented covenant rejects popular Canaanite notions that God is somehow inextricably bound to or dependent upon Israel.[186] God exists as a whole, infinite personality whether or not Israel obeys the covenant. God chose Israel for their sake, in mercy, not as an act of self-completion.

Each of these five concepts is significant for interpreting 1, 2 Kings. First, disobeying the covenant ignores God's merciful self-revelation and rejects the Lord's clear will for Israel. Second, Israel's consistent rebellion thwarts the blessings of God and warrants punishment. Israel loses the land because the people refuse to obey or repent (cf. 2 Kgs 17:7–41; 18:12; 21:7–15; 23:26–27; 24:18–20). Third, casting away the covenant led to the nation's division, which eventually helped speed the defeat of both parts. The division also made possible Jeroboam's plans for a worship system separate from Jerusalem. Fourth, Israel's covenant breaking signaled their unwillingness to allow a sovereign God to direct their everyday affairs. Fifth, the people's preference for idolatry and Baal worship linked them with nature religion. This type of worship was really an attempt to manipulate the gods into doing what the people wanted; the gods were

---

[182] Eichrodt, *Theology of the Old Testament,* 37.

[183] Ibid., 38. Eichrodt correctly assesses the nature of covenant obligation here. The OT concept of "covenant" clearly expects allegiance to God from Israel (cf. Lev 26; Deut 27–28).

[184] Ibid., 39.

[185] Ibid., 41.

[186] Ibid., 42–43.

honored so that crops would grow, animals would give birth, and babies would be born. Yahweh, who created the heavens and earth, who exists independently of human beings, cannot be "bought" through these or any other means.

4. True Prophecy versus "Lying Spirits"

The struggle between prophets who obeyed the Lord by speaking the truth about Israel's conduct and historical situation and those prophets paid by corrupt kings to speak soothing words to an unrepentant people recurs repeatedly in 1, 2 Kings. Some of the division between the prophets rests on religious grounds. Elijah, God's prophet, opposes the prophets of Baal, who are supported by Ahab and Jezebel. In this episode the prophets clearly serve two different deities: Yahweh and Baal. Other lines of dispute are more complicated. For instance, in 1 Kings 13 two prophets dominate the action. The first receives and delivers God's word against Jeroboam (1 Kgs 13:1–10) yet is killed by a lion when he does not follow God's explicit directions about how to return home (1 Kgs 13:20–25). He makes this fatal mistake because he listens to lies told by the second prophet (1 Kgs 13:11–19). This second prophet is unscrupulous, but he also receives accurate messages from God (1 Kgs 13:20–22). Here character separates the two prophets.

A third example may explain the most common differences between real and false prophets. In 1 Kings 22 the most extended account of the battle between true and false prophets appears. Ahab wants to go to war against Syria. He recruits Judah's king, Jehoshaphat, as an ally. Jehoshaphat asks that they first seek a positive word from God (1 Kgs 22:5). Ahab responds by producing four hundred court prophets who counsel the kings to proceed (1 Kgs 22:6). Unconvinced, Jehoshaphat forces Ahab to summon Micaiah, an imprisoned prophet who has no use for Ahab (1 Kgs 22:7–8).

Warned to say what Ahab wants to hear, Micaiah declares the chief principle of true prophecy. He states that he will only speak what God tells him (1 Kgs 22:13–14). Once in the kings' presence, Micaiah declares that the battle will be lost and Ahab will be killed (22:17). More important for current readers, Micaiah explains that God has allowed a "lying spirit" to infiltrate Ahab's prophets' mouths *so that* Ahab would go to his death (1 Kgs 22:19–23). Though the other (false) prophets continue to disagree (22:24–28), Micaiah's forecast comes true when a disguised Ahab is killed "by chance" in battle (22:29–40).

What can be learned from these three examples? First, prophets worked in many countries and for many gods. Prophecy was a widespread phenomenon in the ancient world.[187] Second, in Israel competition arose between advocates

[187] Cf. J. Lindblom, *Prophecy in Ancient Israel* (Philadelphia: Fortress, 1980) 29–32, for an analysis of visionary and ecstatic prophecy in the ancient world, and R. R. Wilson, *Prophecy and Society in Ancient Israel* (Philadelphia: Fortress, 1980) 89–134, for a study of the sociological significance of prophecy in ancient times.

of covenantal religion and proponents of Baalism. Third, the most formidable opponents of true prophecy were the kings' hired prophets who mixed Jeroboam's religion with Yahweh worship. These individuals were quite dangerous because they confused an already rebellious people. Fourth, not every prophet had sterling character. They were human beings with the failings of human beings. Fifth, a true prophet's predictions came to pass.

From these conclusions it is possible to draw a portrait of the true prophet. True prophets preached only what God told them to proclaim. Their messages focused on covenant issues, particularly how the practice of idolatry would result in punishment and, ultimately, expulsion from the land. Thus, Elijah challenged the people, "If the LORD is God, follow him; but if Baal is God, follow him" (1 Kgs 18:21); and the unnamed prophet in 1 Kgs 13:1–5 denounced Jeroboam's religion. Their declarations also emphasized future events.

In fact, their predictions and their subsequent fulfillments help structure the story. Ahijah predicts Jeroboam's rise to power in 1 Kgs 11:29–39, sees the oracle come true in 1 Kgs 12:15, then later predicts the destruction of Jeroboam's line, which occurs in 1 Kgs 15:29–30. More importantly, he states that Jeroboam's religion will cause Israel to be removed from the land (1 Kgs 14:14–16). Elijah's promise of no rain occupies 1 Kings 17–18. His prediction of Ahab's death and the ruin of his dynasty encompasses from 1 Kgs 21:20–24 until its completion in 2 Kgs 10:10. God promises Jehu four generations of dynastic rule in 2 Kgs 10:30, and the promise is kept by 2 Kgs 15:12. After this fulfillment Israel is conquered by Assyria, thereby completing the prediction made by Ahijah two hundred years earlier. Oracles by Isaiah (2 Kgs 19:20–20:21), by unnamed prophets (21:10–15), and by Huldah (22:15–20) complete the book. God makes sure that the words the true prophets declare come true because they are in fact his word.

In Deut 18:14–22 Moses teaches Israel that God's prophets mediate God to the people (18:14–16). They only say what they are commanded (18:17–20) to say. Their predictions are fulfilled (18:21–22). Certainly Ahijah, Elijah, Micaiah, and others meet these requirements. They indeed receive and dispense messages from God, while false prophets speak sermons "not imposed upon them in a special supernatural manner . . . but were visions which came from the human heart alone."[188] Though often unappreciated or outright persecuted, these individuals convey God's merciful calls to repent when only repentance can save Israel.

5. God's Covenant with David versus Dynastic Disintegration

God's covenant with David set forth in 2 Sam 7:1–17 helps unite the entire

[188] E. J. Young, *My Servants the Prophets* (Grand Rapids: Eerdmans, 1974) 149.

Old Testament. In this text a grateful David desires to build a temple for the Lord. Despite God's pleasure with David's request, however, he declines the offer. Instead, God declares his intention to build a "house," a royal dynasty, *for David* (2 Sam 7:11). This house will begin with a son who will continue David's work and who will also build a temple for the Lord (2 Sam 7:12–13). Solomon fits this description. He must obey God's law or face the consequences but will not forfeit David's ancestors' opportunity to rule Israel, a fate that befell Saul's family (2 Sam 7:14–15).

Beyond these fairly immediate promises lies a greater, long-term pledge. God tells David his kingdom will endure *forever* (2 Sam 7:13,16).[189] This promise complements the Lord's assurances to Abraham in Gen 12:1–9. W. C. Kaiser notes that the decision to make David's name great, plant Israel in the land, give David a covenant-bearing son, and be a special God to David parallels language and themes found in the Abraham narratives.[190] Abraham's seed and David's dynasty both have similar enduring qualities. In fact, the promise to Abraham that he would bless the whole earth is realized through this new pledge to his descendant David. As C. A. Briggs says, "The seed of David assumes the place and significance of the seed of the woman and the seed of Abraham."[191]

Several prophetic books and psalms interpret this covenant to mean that the Messiah will come through the Davidic lineage. Isaiah, Jeremiah, Ezekiel, Micah, Zechariah, and Malachi all highlight the concept.[192] Psalms 89 and 110 indicate the long-term implications of God's promise to David. Of course, the New Testament concludes that Jesus, a descendant of David, fulfills the Old Testament predictions about the Messiah.[193] Therefore, the Bible as a whole teaches that David's kingdom will endure forever because one of his descendants is the eternal Son of God.[194]

First and Second Kings use the Davidic Covenant to emphasize God's

---

[189] C. F. Keil comments that "however unmistakable the allusions to Solomon are, the substance of the promise is not fully exhausted in him. The threefold repetition of the expression 'for ever,' the establishment of the kingdom and throne of David for ever, points incontrovertibly beyond the time of Solomon, and to the eternal continuance of the seed of David" ("The Book of Samuel," COT, trans. J. Martin [1875; reprint, Grand Rapids: Zondervan, 1978] 2:346).

[190] W. C. Kaiser, Jr., *Toward an Old Testament Theology* (Grand Rapids: Zondervan, 1978) 153.

[191] C. A. Briggs, *Messianic Prophecy* (1889; reprint, Peabody, Mass.: Hendrickson, 1988) 128.

[192] Cf. Isa 7:14; 9:1–7; 11:1–9; Jer 23:5–7; 33:14–22; Ezek 34:11–31; Mic 5:2; Zech 9:9–13; Mal 4:1–6.

[193] Note that both Matthew and Luke trace Jesus' ancestry through David's lineage (Matt 1:1–17; Luke 3:23–37).

[194] H. W. Hertzberg, *I and II Samuel,* OTL, trans. J. S. Bowden (Philadelphia: Westminster, 1976) 287.

mercy and to expose Israel's and especially its monarchy's unfaithfulness to the Lord. Because of their privileged status as David's heirs, each king had the responsibility to lead the people to serve God by embodying the ideals in the law.[195] Though Solomon and all his successors except Hezekiah and Josiah displease Yahweh in some way, God spares the nation "for David's sake" (1 Kgs 11:12–13; 15:3–5). Ultimately, however, reprehensible kings like Manasseh cause God to give the people and their king over to judgment (2 Kgs 21:10–15). Unfortunately, as does the nation itself, the monarchy exhausts the Lord's patience through constant rebellion.

Despite the kings' sinfulness, the promise of an eternal Davidic kingdom is never revoked. Land and temple are lost, the monarchy grinds to an ignominious halt, yet the promise remains. Just how it will continue is not explained, though hints do emerge. Chief among these hints is the release in Babylon of the exiled king Jehoiachin after thirty-seven years in captivity. God continues to bless David's descendants, which reflects the never-ending nature of the Davidic Covenant. Israel has hope for the future as long as a Davidide exists.

6. God's Sovereignty versus Human Pride

God's absolute rule of all creation undergirds every theological emphasis in 1, 2 Kings. Israel lived in a covenant relationship because a sovereign God chose to reveal absolute standards to this small nation. Jerusalem is where Israel should worship simply because God decided to "place his name there." God called the prophets and chose David. Solomon received wisdom as a direct gift from the Lord.

Further, God rules all nations, not just Israel, and directs all human affairs. Even great nations, such as Egypt, Assyria, and Babylon, do not determine their own destinies. God sends them to do his will. They punish Israel only because the Lord wants them to do so. Otherwise, God can defend Jerusalem no matter what the circumstances (cf. 2 Kgs 19:35–37). The worst mistake Israel's enemies can make is to assume that Yahweh is a regional deity (cf. 1 Kgs 20:23–30). On the other hand, choosing to serve the Lord is the best decision a Gentile can make (2 Kgs 5:1–15).

Unfortunately, 1, 2 Kings sadly chronicles case after case of kings and nations who reject God's rule. Solomon chooses to worship idols. Manasseh practices child sacrifice (2 Kgs 21:6). Assyria claims to do Yahweh's bidding even though they believe in many gods (2 Kgs 18:17–37). Given the covenant threats in Leviticus 26 and Deuteronomy 27–28, such attitudes and actions can

---

[195] D. J. McCarthy, "Compact and Kingship: Stimuli for Hebrew Covenant Thinking," in *Studies in the Period of David and Solomon and Other Essays,* ed. T. Ishida (Winona Lake, Ind.: Eisenbrauns, 1982) 185.

only lead to destruction. A sovereign, gracious God cannot allow individuals and nations to worship false deities, lest the human race destroy itself spiritually and physically.

Introduction to Applicational Issues

It is impossible for a commentator to tell readers how to apply biblical texts in sermons and Bible lessons with total accuracy. After all, every commentary reader addresses a different audience, and each audience has unique theological, physical, sociological, psychological, and educational needs. Therefore, teachers and preachers bear the responsibility of communicating scriptural truth in an effective manner. Still, some universal principles do exist for collecting applicational data that will make 1, 2 Kings relevant for contemporary listeners. This section seeks to present these principles by offering a methodology for comparing ancient and modern audiences and presenting biblical information in teaching and preaching situations.

J. Stott observes that a "true sermon bridges the gulf between the biblical and the modern worlds, and must be equally earthed in both."[196] C. Fant agrees, and concludes that preaching must "restore the unity of Word and world."[197] To bridge this gap between the ancient text and the modern world, speakers must find where the two share some common ground. As H. Hendricks says: "Before we can communicate we must establish commonness, commonality. And the greater the commonality, the greater the potential for communication."[198] This commonality ought to exist between text and speaker, speaker and audience, and text and audience. Perhaps there are other ways to unite these concerns, but one very logical way is to ask the text a series of questions based on what the passage and the audience may or may not share in common.

Because the passage's original intended message is the key to application, it is necessary to review first the historical data gleaned from a text in 1, 2 Kings. Speakers should remember the chosen passage's original setting, purpose, and situation. Were the people in the story obeying or disobeying God? Did the original audience need correction, instruction, or both? Which of these needs does the text address, and how does it do so? Does the story occur in time of war, peace, prosperity, or economic privation? Modern listeners face similar situations and have many of the same attitudes and problems.

Second, speakers should review literary details such as plot and characterization. In the plot, how were the people living? What causes and effects

---

[196] J. R. W. Stott, *Between Two Worlds: The Art of Preaching in the Twentieth Century* (Grand Rapids: Eerdmans, 1982) 10.

[197] C. E. Fant, *Preaching for Today,* rev. ed. (New York: Harper & Row, 1987) 221.

[198] H. G. Hendricks, *Teaching to Change Lives* (Portland: Multonomah, 1987) 98.

placed them in their stated situation? What external factors (enemies, political intrigue, etc.) impacted their lives? What were the results of decisions that were made? Noting causes and effects in the stories in 1, 2 Kings helps interpreters to understand how and why current events occur and to grasp the impact similar events have on today's congregation. Characters' strengths, weaknesses, and attitudes should be examined. Presenting biblical characters allows modern audiences to identify with these ancient persons who, like themselves, have families to raise, careers to build, governments to serve, and relationships with God to maintain.

Third, preachers and teachers ought to analyze how other texts in the Old and New Testaments interpret their passage. How do the Prophets and the Gospels portray Elijah, for instance? How do Jeremiah, Ezekiel, Daniel, and the psalmists approach Jerusalem's destruction? How do these writers use the events described in 1, 2 Kings to encourage, admonish, or inform their audiences? Canonical analysis has the dual advantage of placing 1, 2 Kings in its own biblical context *and* of demonstrating how inspired preachers and writers proclaimed the material.

Fourth, themes should be gathered from theological reflection. What does the text say about sin, salvation, judgment, or God's nature? What significant Bible doctrines are supported by the text? Answering these questions helps speakers realize how audiences relate to God and others now. It also informs and instructs hearers about salvation, commitment, and service.

Fifth, speakers should examine the passage's original tone. Is the text told in a biting or ironic manner? If so, it should be presented that way. Is the story optimistic? If it is, it should be used to encourage hearers. The stories in 1, 2 Kings ought to warn audiences how easily individuals and nations can slide into long-term sin and, ultimately, disaster. In other words, the original presentation of the text can help the modern preacher know how to present the text now.

These steps attempt to bridge the gap between the ancient story and the modern audience. Different speakers will use the data in varying ways. Some will shape sermons and lessons in a traditional three-point format. These individuals should examine the data gleaned from the text, find three aspects of God's nature, three facets of good leadership, three attitudes that harm or build a relationship with God, etc. All points will come from the text and will fit the speaker's normal mode of proclamation. Other speakers will choose to utilize storytelling or dramatic techniques. These persons can glean a wealth of material from 1, 2 Kings, since the story format of the books themselves matches this preferred mode of presentation.

Thus, speakers who know their audiences well, who will read and analyze a chosen text carefully and accurately, and match their speaking style to the biblical material can preach and teach effectively from 1, 2 Kings. This achievement will only come as a result of courage, creativity, and discipline but will be very rewarding. Stories are very powerful, so preaching from stories may also be powerful. If modern listeners "hear the narrative the way the original listeners heard it,"[199] then speakers can live with the hope "that God's story is still being lived in our own time and experience and ever new insights might still flow from our encounter with a living Word."[200]

[199] S. Greidanus, *The Modern Preacher and the Ancient Text* (Grand Rapids: Eerdmans, 1988) 223.

[200] B. C. Birch, *Let Justice Roll Down: The Old Testament, Ethics, and Christian Life* (Louisville: Westminster/John Knox, 1991) 65.

SECTION OUTLINE

I. THE RISE OF SOLOMON (1:1–2:46)

Survey of Historical Details Related to 1 Kings 1–2

1. David's Declining Health (1:1–4)
2. Adonijah's Attempt to Become King (1:5–10)
   - (1) Adonijah's Strategy and Character (1:5–6)
   - (2) Adonijah's Supporters (1:7–8)
   - (3) Adonijah's "Coronation" (1:9–10)
3. Solomon Becomes King (1:11–52)
   - (1) Nathan and Bathsheba's Strategy (1:11–14)
   - (2) Nathan and Bathsheba's Audience with David (1:15–27)
   - (3) David Chooses Solomon (1:28–37)
   - (4) Solomon's Coronation (1:38–40)
   - (5) Adonijah's Fear of Solomon (1:41–53)
4. David Advises Solomon (2:1–9)
   - (1) Keep the Law (2:1–4)
   - (2) Avenge Your Father (2:5–9)
5. David's Death (2:10–12)
6. Solomon Consolidates His Power (2:13–46)
   - (1) Adonijah's Foolish Request and Execution (2:13–25)
   - (2) Solomon Banishes Abiathar (2:26–27)
   - (3) Solomon Executes Joab (2:28–34)
   - (4) Benaiah and Zadok Given Power (2:35)
   - (5) Shimei's Disobedience and Execution (2:36–46)

Canonical and Theological Implications of 1:1–2:46

Applicational Implications of 1:1–2:46

I. THE RISE OF SOLOMON (1:1–2:46)

The first two chapters of 1 Kings act as an important bridge between the careers of two extremely significant Old Testament kings. David's story, begun in 1, 2 Samuel, ends here, while Solomon's begins. These chapters describe the transition of power from father to son. This transition is far from smooth, however, because Adonijah, Solomon's older brother, attempts to succeed his father (1:1–10). Solomon eventually prevails but only because his mother (Bathsheba) and the prophet Nathan maneuver David into naming Solomon king (1:11–53). Before dying, David gives Solomon some sage advice about how to secure the kingdom (2:1–12). The new ruler follows this counsel, which requires eliminating several serious political enemies (2:13–46).

These episodes are told with great artistry, subtlety, and care. Characters are well developed and intriguing. Themes that appear repeatedly in 1, 2 Kings are introduced (e.g., 2:2–4), and the plot sets the stage for vital events in the rest of the story. Important issues such as the king's conduct, the survival of David's lineage, the use of power, and the nation's long-term well-being also are introduced. Readers are therefore ushered into the story through a final appearance of a familiar character, then thrust into the events and issues that will dominate the rest of 1, 2 Kings.

Survey of Historical Details Related to 1 Kings 1–2

Several scholars have noted that 1 Kings 1–2 provides the answer to a question first asked in 2 Samuel 9–20, namely, "Who will succeed David?"[1] Two serious challenges to the throne occur during David's lifetime. First, his son Absalom attempts to unseat him but fails to do so (2 Sam 14:1–19:8). Second, "a troublemaker named Sheba son of Bicri, a Benjamite" leads a rebellion that apparently seeks to recapture for Benjamin the power lost when Saul died (2 Sam 20:1–26). Both Absalom and Sheba are defeated by Joab, David's able yet unscrupulous army leader. The intervening years between 2 Samuel 20 and 1 Kings 1 are less threatening for David, but old age has left him infirm.

David has built an impressive kingdom to leave to his successor. During his reign (ca. 1010–970), David subdued old enemies such as Moab, Edom, Ammon, Syria, and Philistia (2 Sam 8:1–14; 10:1–19). Thus he effectively expanded Israel's borders and fattened its treasuries (cf. 2 Sam 8:5–12). He also captured Jerusalem, then turned this small (pop. 2,500) city into the nation's political and religious focal point (2 Sam 5:6–10; 6:1–23).[2] God had promised that David's kingdom would continue forever (2 Sam 7:7–17), and David responded by gathering materials for Solomon to use for building the temple (1 Chr 22:1–19; 29:1–9). Clearly, David would leave the nation better than he had found it.

Despite these gains, however, David was unable to resolve every tension in the land. The Sheba revolt revealed that the northern tribes had never sworn undying allegiance to David's family (2 Sam 20:1–2). During the Absalom

---

[1] These scholars tend to argue that the author of 1, 2 Kings possessed a "succession narrative," consisting of most of 2 Samuel 9–20 and 1 Kings 1–2, which he edited into Joshua-Kings. The most influential study of this nature is L. Rost, *The Succession to the Throne of David,* trans. M. D. Rutter and D. M. Gunn, *Historic Texts and Interpreters in Biblical Scholarship,* 1 (Sheffield: Almond, 1982). Cf. also R. N. Whybray, *The Succession Narrative: A Study of II Samuel 9–20; I Kings 1 and 2*, SSBT II, 9 (Naperville: Allenson, 1968).

[2] F. E. Peters, *Jerusalem* (Princeton: Princeton University Press, 1985) 11.

uprising, even Judah, David's native tribe, was not altogether loyal to him (2 Sam 19:11–14).[3] Thus, as J. Flanagan notes, "The underlying tensions that would eventually separate the kingdoms of Judah and Israel after Solomon's reign posed a threat to the dual monarchy even during the time of David."[4] His ability to overcome regional jealousies and overt coup attempts are a tribute to David's leadership ability. Later kings were not as skillful.

1. David's Declining Health (1:1–4)

[1]When King David was old and well advanced in years, he could not keep warm even when they put covers over him. [2]So his servants said to him, "Let us look for a young virgin to attend the king and take care of him. She can lie beside him so that our lord the king may keep warm."

[3]Then they searched throughout Israel for a beautiful girl and found Abishag, a Shunammite, and brought her to the king. [4]The girl was very beautiful; she took care of the king and waited on him, but the king had no intimate relations with her.

1:1 The story opens with David's physical health all but gone. Once a great fighter, politician, and lover, his circulation is not sufficient to keep him warm, even with the aid of blankets. With death imminent, it is obvious that a new leader must replace David. Who will this person be? How will he be chosen? What kind of character will he possess?

1:2–4 Before these questions are addressed, royal servants attempt to revive the aging monarch. They seek a "young virgin"[5] to nurse the king and to "lie beside him," which may be better translated "lie in your bosom" (NASB).[6] Their search yields "Abishag, a Shunammite"[7] of exceptional beauty. Indeed she does care for the king and see to his needs, but he has "no intimate relations with her."[8] Presumably he can no longer do so, which reinforces the emphasis on the king's irretrievably failing health. If not even a lovely young woman can stir David's blood, then he obviously is not long for the world. It is

---

[3] J. Bright, *A History of Israel*, 3d ed. (Philadelphia: Westminster, 1981) 209.

[4] J. W. Flanagan, "Court History or Succession Document? A Study of 2 Samuel 9–20 and 1 Kings 1–2," *JBL* 91 (1972) 181.

[5] The construction (נַעֲרָה בְתוּלָה) in 1:2 stresses Abishag's youth and virtue. She is called a "very beautiful" young woman (וְהַנַּעֲרָה יָפָה עַד־מְאֹד) in 1:4 with no reference to her virginity. The fact that the king has no "intimate relations" (לֹא יְדָעָהּ) with Abishag, however, probably underscores her virginal status.

[6] In Hebrew the text switches to second-person address in the second half of the verse. The LXX has the statement refer to David in third person, which makes better sense.

[7] According to *HBD* (1275), Shunem "was located southeast of Mt. Carmel." Obviously the search took them outside the near environs of Jerusalem.

[8] The phrase would be more literally "he did not know her," a common OT euphemism for a sexual relationship (cf. Gen 4:1,17, etc).

important to note, however, that the text makes no mention of senility. His *mind is still sound.*

2. Adonijah's Attempt to Become King (1:5–10)

While David "is cited for his shivering impotence . . . his markedly handsome son stands just beyond sight and hearing."[9] As in nearly every nation, a candidate for the throne presents himself before the old officeholder has had time to die. In this part of the story the candidate is Adonijah, David's oldest surviving son. Absalom, the thirdborn, dies in his revolt, but not before killing Amnon, the firstborn. The secondborn, Kileab, disappears from the story after the mention of his birth in 2 Sam 3:3. Thus, though Israel has no established accession system, it seems reasonable for Adonijah to assume he will be king. But what kind of man cannot wait for his father to die before seeking power?

(1) Adonijah's Strategy and Character (1:5–6)

[5]Now Adonijah, whose mother was Haggith, put himself forward and said, "I will be king." So he got chariots and horses ready, with fifty men to run ahead of him. [6](His father had never interfered with him by asking, "Why do you behave as you do?" He was also very handsome and was born next after Absalom.)

1:5–6 These two verses portray Adonijah as an aggressive, self-possessed person. He "put himself forward" would be more literally he was "lifting himself up,"[10] by emphatically stating, "I will be king." By declaring such intentions he breaks with the Israelite tradition of God choosing the king, then confirming the choice through a prophet's ministry. Neither Saul nor David sought the throne, yet God told Samuel to select these men for the task (1 Sam 10:9–27; 16:1–13). Not only is his arrogance shown through his "running for office," but it is further revealed by his choice of "fifty men to run ahead of him." He acts like a king before being made king.

Three reasons for this arrogance are offered. David, whom 2 Samuel 13–19 reveals as a rather ineffective father, never contradicted Adonijah. Adonijah was very handsome and also was the oldest living son. Good looks and a favored status, coupled with parental indulgence, rarely build strong character. Neither do they instill wisdom, as will become evident later in the story.

(2) Adonijah's Supporters (1:7–8)

[7]Adonijah conferred with Joab son of Zeruiah and with Abiathar the priest, and they gave him their support. [8]But Zadok the priest, Benaiah son of Jehoiada,

---

[9] B. O. Long, "A Darkness between Brothers: Solomon and Adonijah," *JSOT* 19 (1981) 84.

[10] מִתְנַשֵּׂא is a *hithpael* (passive) participle. It is an editorial comment strategically placed to reveal the motive behind his statements.

Nathan the prophet, Shimei and Rei and David's special guard did not join Adonijah.

1:7–8 Whatever his faults, Adonijah is able to recruit two powerful supporters: Abiathar the priest and Joab the great general. These two men had been with David since the beginning of his career (1 Sam 22:20; 2 Sam 2:13ff.). Joab was particularly important to David, for he conquered Jerusalem (1 Chr 11:4–6), led Israel's military triumphs (2 Sam 8:1–14; 10:1–19), and helped David through the Absalom episode. Yet he also murdered two men in cold blood who stood in the way of his personal goals (2 Sam 3:22–39; 20:9–10). These murders could be construed as done in the nation's best interests,[11] but they ultimately serve Joab's purposes more than the country's. Finally, Joab also killed Absalom after David had commanded he be spared (2 Sam 18:1–18), then counseled David to cease mourning his son's death, lest he lose his loyal soldiers (2 Sam 19:1–8). Joab is decisive, powerful, and politically dangerous.

Other influential leaders are either not asked or do not choose to follow Adonijah. Zadok, David's other priest (2 Sam 8:17), Benaiah, the head of David's elite guards, the Kerethites and Pelethites (2 Sam 8:18), Nathan, David's straightforward court prophet, and David's "special guard," or "mighty men," were not part of Adonijah's inner circle. Thus, Adonijah had some important advocates, but he did not have the unanimous support of every influential leader.

(3) Adonijah's "Coronation" (1:9–10)

[9]Adonijah then sacrificed sheep, cattle and fattened calves at the Stone of Zoheleth near En Rogel. He invited all his brothers, the king's sons, and all the men of Judah who were royal officials, [10]but he did not invite Nathan the prophet or Benaiah or the special guard or his brother Solomon.

1:9 Lacking a clear consensus, Adonijah pushes forward with his plans to become king. He offers sacrifices and invites strategically important persons to a meal, all of which is intended to unite the group.[12] His brothers are included so they can relinquish their right to the throne. The "men of Judah who were royal officials" are invited so that the most prestigious leaders in David's court can give Adonijah's claim more validity.[13]

1:10 Those not invited to this premature coronation are prominent persons. Three names are highlighted. Nathan has religious authority, while Benaiah bears the sword. They pose religious and military threats to Adonijah's

[11] Whybray reads Joab's actions this way (*The Succession Narrative*, 41).

[12] Cf. J. Gray, *I and II Kings,* OTL (Philadelphia: Westminster, 1963) 81.

[13] G. H. Jones, *1 and 2 Kings,* NCB (Grand Rapids: Eerdmans, 1984) 1:92.

plans. Solomon is also mentioned for the first time. This brief phrase "or his brother Solomon" deftly announces Adonijah's younger brother as potential heir to David's kingdom. Gray notes that the exclusion of these individuals meant that Adonijah relied on "the strength of his party to liquidate the opposition" rather than on any notion of negotiating peace with them.[14] How will those snubbed respond?

3. Solomon Becomes King (1:11–52)

When 1:10 ends, Adonijah sits eating with his supporters, seemingly in possession of his father's empire. Unfortunately for him, a less-public power play will soon begin. Those he expects to eliminate will move into action. Led by the seasoned prophet/politician Nathan, this group will install Solomon as coregent with his declining father. Before they achieve this goal, however, the plot will become more complicated.[15] Old characters will eventually rouse themselves and determine what younger persons will carry the story forward.

(1) Nathan and Bathsheba's Strategy (1:11–14)

[11]Then Nathan asked Bathsheba, Solomon's mother, "Have you not heard that Adonijah, the son of Haggith, has become king without our lord David's knowing it? [12]Now then, let me advise you how you can save your own life and the life of your son Solomon. [13]Go in to King David and say to him, 'My lord the king, did you not swear to me your servant: "Surely Solomon your son shall be king after me, and he will sit on my throne"? Why then has Adonijah become king?' [14]While you are still there talking to the king, I will come in and confirm what you have said."

1:11–14 Ignored by Adonijah, Nathan senses his own peril and that of Bathsheba and Solomon. Perhaps Bathsheba does not realize the danger, or perhaps she does not have the power necessary to help herself. Whatever the need to inform her, Nathan unfolds a two-part plan. First, Bathsheba must remind David that he promised the throne to Solomon. This pledge appears nowhere in 2 Samuel. Readers are left to judge whether Nathan fabricates the story,[16] uses it to remind David of his guilt in the Uriah episode, or reveals a detail the author has withheld as an authorial surprise. Second, Nathan says that he will confirm what she tells David, just in case the king does not under-

---

[14] Gray, *I and II Kings,* 83.

[15] For an excellent structural analysis of how the plot in 1:1–53 unfolds, see B. O. Long, *1 Kings, with an Introduction to Historical Literature,* FOTL 9 (Grand Rapids: Eerdmans, 1984) 35.

[16] R. D. Nelson, *First and Second Kings,* IBC (Louisville: John Knox, 1987) 16.

stand or agree. Clearly, this plan shows that Nathan is as aggressive as Adonijah yet is more cunning than the younger man.[17]

(2) Nathan and Bathsheba's Audience with David (1:15–27)

15So Bathsheba went to see the aged king in his room, where Abishag the Shunammite was attending him. 16Bathsheba bowed low and knelt before the king.

"What is it you want?" the king asked.

17She said to him, "My lord, you yourself swore to me your servant by the LORD your God: 'Solomon your son shall be king after me, and he will sit on my throne.' 18But now Adonijah has become king, and you, my lord the king, do not know about it. 19He has sacrificed great numbers of cattle, fattened calves, and sheep, and has invited all the king's sons, Abiathar the priest and Joab the commander of the army, but he has not invited Solomon your servant. 20My lord the king, the eyes of all Israel are on you, to learn from you who will sit on the throne of my lord the king after him. 21Otherwise, as soon as my lord the king is laid to rest with his fathers, I and my son Solomon will be treated as criminals."

22While she was still speaking with the king, Nathan the prophet arrived. 23And they told the king, "Nathan the prophet is here." So he went before the king and bowed with his face to the ground.

24Nathan said, "Have you, my lord the king, declared that Adonijah shall be king after you, and that he will sit on your throne? 25Today he has gone down and sacrificed great numbers of cattle, fattened calves, and sheep. He has invited all the king's sons, the commanders of the army and Abiathar the priest. Right now they are eating and drinking with him and saying, 'Long live King Adonijah!' 26But me your servant, and Zadok the priest, and Benaiah son of Jehoiada, and your servant Solomon he did not invite. 27Is this something my lord the king has done without letting his servants know who should sit on the throne of my lord the king after him?"

1:15–16 Bathsheba proceeds to carry out the plan. Two details stand out when she sees David: Abishag's presence and the fact that the king was very old.[18] It is ironic that Bathsheba has to see David with a younger woman. Bathsheba shows David great courtesy, for she bows and kneels before him. Not too feeble to acknowledge her presence, David inquires why she has come.

1:17–21 Bathsheba goes directly to the heart of the matter. She omits any insinuation that David approves of Adonijah's activity, reminds David of his promise to make Solomon king, then describes Adonijah's attempt to seize the throne.[19] Four comments are intended to stir the king to action. First, she suggests that he has lost touch with events in his kingdom (1:18). Second, she dis-

---

[17] Note the stimulating character analysis of Nathan in G. Rice, *Nations Under God: A Commentary on the Book of 1 Kings,* ITC (Grand Rapids: Eerdmans, 1990) 16–18.

[18] The author contrasts her youth and beauty with the king's age and infirmity, which highlights the urgency of Bathsheba's task.

[19] J. Skinner, *I and II Kings,* Century Bible (Edinburgh: T. C. & E. C. Jack, 1904) 63.

closes the identity of Adonijah's supporters (1:19). Third, she claims that "all Israel" waits to see whom he will choose as his successor (1:20). Fourth, Bathsheba states that she and Solomon "will be treated as criminals"[20] when David dies (1:21). This last plea may refer to the fact that Solomon was not invited to Adonijah's feast.

1:22–27 Nathan arrives as planned, which allows the king no time to dispute Bathsheba's view of the facts. He too prostrates himself before David, then repeats her speech. The only change is that he chides the king by asking him if he has "declared that Adonijah shall be king" (1:24) and if David has done so in secret (1:27). These two persons who share David's *most personal* secret have presented their case in a crafty, psychologically challenging fashion. Will, or can, the king respond?

(3) David Chooses Solomon (1:28–37)

[28]Then King David said, "Call in Bathsheba." So she came into the king's presence and stood before him.

[29]The king then took an oath: "As surely as the LORD lives, who has delivered me out of every trouble, [30]I will surely carry out today what I swore to you by the LORD, the God of Israel: Solomon your son shall be king after me, and he will sit on my throne in my place."

[31]Then Bathsheba bowed low with her face to the ground and, kneeling before the king, said, "May my lord King David live forever!"

[32]King David said, "Call in Zadok the priest, Nathan the prophet and Benaiah son of Jehoiada." When they came before the king, [33]he said to them: "Take your lord's servants with you and set Solomon my son on my own mule and take him down to Gihon. [34]There have Zadok the priest and Nathan the prophet anoint him king over Israel. Blow the trumpet and shout, 'Long live King Solomon!' [35]Then you are to go up with him, and he is to come and sit on my throne and reign in my place. I have appointed him ruler over Israel and Judah."

[36]Benaiah son of Jehoiada answered the king, "Amen! May the LORD, the God of my lord the king, so declare it. [37]As the LORD was with my lord the king, so may he be with Solomon to make his throne even greater than the throne of my lord King David!"

1:28–31 This complicated drama now reaches its climax.[21] Despite his well-chronicled physical problems, David rises to the occasion. He summons the woman he once risked his kingdom for and swears by the Lord that he will make Solomon king. Indeed, he will do the deed "today," or before his age and infirmity make the act impossible. The text does not mention another meeting

[20]The word here is חַטָּאִים (lit., "sinners"). Gray suggests the implication is that some "captious interpretation of the law would have been found for putting Solomon and his mother out of the way" (*I and II Kings,* 89).

[21]Cf. Long, *I Kings,* 35.

between these two persons who altered Israel's history by a single sexual liaison.

1:32–37 David still possesses a keen mind, for he knows exactly how to carry out his promise. Without hesitation he summons the men who can counter Adonijah's supporters. Solomon is to be placed on the king's own mule to demonstrate his new status. Next, Zadok and Nathan will anoint Solomon king, which will give him divine approval in addition to his royal approval. Finally, he is to be placed on David's throne, most likely as the older man's coregent.[22] Benaiah, the warrior, offers enthusiastic military approval of the proceedings. Jones astutely notes, "David's shrewdness in assembling such a well-chosen party of supporters contrasts with the picture . . . given in the previous verses."[23]

(4) Solomon's Coronation (1:38–40)

[38]So Zadok the priest, Nathan the prophet, Benaiah son of Jehoiada, the Kerethites and the Pelethites went down and put Solomon on King David's mule and escorted him to Gihon. [39]Zadok the priest took the horn of oil from the sacred tent and anointed Solomon. Then they sounded the trumpet and all the people shouted, "Long live King Solomon!" [40]And all the people went up after him, playing flutes and rejoicing greatly, so that the ground shook with the sound.

1:38–40 David's plan quickly gains popular support. Immediately following Solomon's anointing, which takes place near the tent housing the ark of the covenant,[24] a horn is blown and the people rejoice over the coronation. Apparently Nathan and Bathsheba correctly assessed the people's desire for David to name a successor. Solomon must still deal with Adonijah, but he can now operate from a position of strength.

Israel had never gotten a king in this way. Before, Saul and David had been identified by Samuel as God's chosen. Both men then had to prove themselves worthy in the people's eyes, and neither Saul nor David began to rule all twelve tribes immediately. The placing of Solomon on the throne signals the beginning of the Davidic dynasty, a royal lineage that will eventually produce Jesus Christ. God has begun to keep the promises made to David in 2 Sam 7:7–17. David *does* have a son on the throne, and that son will be blessed as long as he obeys the Lord.

(5) Adonijah's Fear of Solomon (1:41–53)

[41]Adonijah and all the guests who were with him heard it as they were finishing their feast. On hearing the sound of the trumpet, Joab asked, "What's the

[22] Coregency was a common ancient practice during an older king's declining years. Cf. E. R. Thiele, "Coregencies and Overlapping Reigns among the Hebrew Kings," *JBL* 93 (1974) 174–200.

[23] Jones, *1 and 2 Kings,* 1:98.

[24] Skinner, *I and II Kings,* 67.

meaning of all the noise in the city?"

42 Even as he was speaking, Jonathan son of Abiathar the priest arrived. Adonijah said, "Come in. A worthy man like you must be bringing good news."

43 "Not at all!" Jonathan answered. "Our lord King David has made Solomon king. 44 The king has sent with him Zadok the priest, Nathan the prophet, Benaiah son of Jehoiada, the Kerethites and the Pelethites, and they have put him on the king's mule, 45 and Zadok the priest and Nathan the prophet have anointed him king at Gihon. From there they have gone up cheering, and the city resounds with it. That's the noise you hear. 46 Moreover, Solomon has taken his seat on the royal throne. 47 Also, the royal officials have come to congratulate our lord King David, saying, 'May your God make Solomon's name more famous than yours and his throne greater than yours!' And the king bowed in worship on his bed 48 and said, 'Praise be to the LORD, the God of Israel, who has allowed my eyes to see a successor on my throne today.'"

49 At this, all Adonijah's guests rose in alarm and dispersed. 50 But Adonijah, in fear of Solomon, went and took hold of the horns of the altar. 51 Then Solomon was told, "Adonijah is afraid of King Solomon and is clinging to the horns of the altar. He says, 'Let King Solomon swear to me today that he will not put his servant to death with the sword.'"

52 Solomon replied, "If he shows himself to be a worthy man, not a hair of his head will fall to the ground; but if evil is found in him, he will die." 53 Then King Solomon sent men, and they brought him down from the altar. And Adonijah came and bowed down to King Solomon, and Solomon said, "Go to your home."

1:41–48 While finishing their feast, Adonijah and his guests hear the uproar.[25] The trumpet blast makes the veteran politician uneasy. A messenger brings the bad news that everything has turned against them. All has changed in a few hours' time. Every person Adonijah snubbed has been honored by David (1:42–45). Solomon has been established, the people approve, the royal officials have praised David for his choice, and the old king praises God for what has occurred (1:46–48).

1:49–53 Every man now attempts to save himself. Suddenly, Adonijah sits alone, the kingdom snatched from his grasp. Afraid for his own life, the loser of the power struggle takes desperate measures. Perhaps invoking Exod 21:12–14, Adonijah flees to the altar and holds its horns. There he begs for his life. Solomon lets him live, yet only with the stipulation that he prove himself to be "a worthy man" (1:52; cf. v. 42).[26] He clearly has little room to maneuver. This almost-certain future king must now humiliate himself before the

[25] In the repetition of the verb שׁמע ("hear"), readers sense these hearers' bewilderment and approaching desperation.

[26] The phrase is בֶּן־חַיִל ("son of worthiness"). The term חַיִל is used of physical power, wealth, bravery, and ability but also strength of character or virtue as here (cf. Ruth 3:11; 4:11; Prov 12:4; 31:10,29). The phrase בֶּן־חַיִל is used sixteen times with these various senses. See H. Eising, "חַיִל *chayil*," *TDOT* 4.348–55.

brother he disdained to invite to his "coronation" feast. The brothers declare a truce, but, Long notes, "In this moment one feels the story has a resting point, but not its end."[27]

4. David Advises Solomon (2:1–9)

These verses have troubled many readers and commentators. After all, they present David giving spiritual advice to Solomon on the one hand, then offering him cold-blooded political counsel on the other. Some scholars argue that this episode was written by a pro-Solomonic author who switches blame for the bloodshed from Solomon to David.[28] Other authors claim that the final writer of the history was pro-David and thus reworked the story by adding deuteronomic themes that soften David's harsh commands.[29] Each viewpoint attempts to salvage the reputation of one of the kings, thereby fixing blame for the events in 2:13–46 on the other.

Despite these critical opinions, the text makes both kings responsible for what happens.[30] The way the story is told fits the author's selective theological and storytelling perspective. The same author who finalized Joshua to 2 Kings presents David as a righteous king, adulterer, poor father, sage advisor, and political animal. This author also depicts Solomon as loyal son, wise king, "sage *par excellence*,"[31] and idolator. Thus, it is not unusual for David to speak of spiritual and political issues at the same time, nor is Solomon's response unexpected. Both do what they deem appropriate. The author simply details what occurs without commentary, and expects readers to decide the validity of the kings' actions themselves.[32]

(1) Keep the Law (2:1–4)

1When the time drew near for David to die, he gave a charge to Solomon his son.
2"I am about to go the way of all the earth," he said. "So be strong, show yourself a man, 3and observe what the LORD your God requires: Walk in his ways, and keep his decrees and commands, his laws and requirements, as written in the Law of Moses, so that you may prosper in all you do and wherever you go, 4and

---

27 Long, "A Darkness between Brothers," 87.

28 E.g., Jones, *1 and 2 Kings,* 1:106.

29 E.g., Gray, *I and II Kings,* 95; M. Noth, *Könige* (1. Teilband) BKAT 9/1 (Neukirchen–Vluyn: Neukirchener, 1968) 30; and S. J. DeVries, *1 Kings,* WBC 12 (Waco: Word, 1985) 30. W. T. Koopmans argues for the unity of 2:1–10 by treating it as poetic narrative ("The Testament of David in 1 Kings 2:1–10," *VT* 41 [1991] 429–49).

30 Cf. Skinner's conclusions in *I and II Kings,* 69–70.

31 J. L. Crenshaw, *Old Testament Wisdom: An Introduction* (Atlanta: John Knox, 1981) 42–54.

32 For an analysis of the author's political neutrality, note K. K. Sacon, "A Study of the Literary Structure of 'The Succession Narrative'" in *Studies in the Period of David and Solomon and Other Essays,* ed. T. Ishida (Winona Lake, Ind.: Eisenbrauns, 1982) 53–54.

that the LORD may keep his promise to me: 'If your descendants watch how they live, and if they walk faithfully before me with all their heart and soul, you will never fail to have a man on the throne of Israel.'

2:1 David's "charge"[33] to Solomon consists of two parts. The first deals with Solomon's commitments to the Lord (2:1–4), while the second covers ways the younger man can secure his kingdom. The order should be understood as significant, since the second without the first would be useless. Farewell speeches appear elsewhere in the Old Testament, such as when Jacob addresses his sons in Gen 47:29–49:33, and in Josh 23:1–16, where Joshua speaks to Israel's leaders.[34] David's directives to Solomon are similar to those given Joshua by the Lord (cf. Josh 1:1–9). All texts of this type move the story to new characters and events yet do so by providing continuity between the new situation and the old.

2:2–4 According to David, Solomon will only "be strong" and a "man" if he keeps the Mosaic covenant.[35] He must take great pains to "observe" what God demands.[36] This observing of God's standards should grow into a lifestyle, a "walking" in the ways of the Lord. How does one achieve this lifestyle? By adhering to the various elements of "the Law of Moses." "Decrees and commands" are the *specific* instructions God forwards, such as the prohibitions against idolatry, murder, adultery, coveting, etc. found in Exod 20:1–17. On the other hand, "laws and requirements" refer to the case laws the Mosaic covenant includes and to the rules for offering sacrifices.

David states that two vital benefits will result from Solomon's obedience. First, the new king will "prosper" in everything he attempts. This blessing is, of course, of great interest to Solomon, who would naturally want a successful reign. Second, obedience will ensure God's ongoing pleasure with David's family. All the promises made in 2 Sam 7:1–17 will be fulfilled, including the eternal nature of David's kingdom. This blessing is of particular interest to David, since it immortalizes his faith in God. It is also important to every generation of the text's readers, all of whom depend on David's messianic descendant for salvation.

(2) Avenge Your Father (2:5–9)

5"Now you yourself know what Joab son of Zeruiah did to me—what he did to the two commanders of Israel's armies, Abner son of Ner and Amasa son of

---

[33] "Gave a charge" can be translated "commanded," since וַיְצַו is the form used here. David was emphatic in his instructions.

[34] Cf. Long, *1 Kings*, 44. Koopmans notes verbal parallels between these verses and Josh 23:3,6,14,16 ("The Testament of David," 432).

[35] Note the similarity between David's wording and the phrasing in Josh 1:1–9.

[36] David employs a cognate accusative that could be rendered "keep the keepings," a play on words that emphasizes the seriousness of the obligations of the king before the Lord.

Jether. He killed them, shedding their blood in peacetime as if in battle, and with that blood stained the belt around his waist and the sandals on his feet. [6]Deal with him according to your wisdom, but do not let his gray head go down to the grave in peace.

[7]"But show kindness to the sons of Barzillai of Gilead and let them be among those who eat at your table. They stood by me when I fled from your brother Absalom.

[8]"And remember, you have with you Shimei son of Gera, the Benjamite from Bahurim, who called down bitter curses on me the day I went to Mahanaim. When he came down to meet me at the Jordan, I swore to him by the LORD: 'I will not put you to death by the sword.' [9]But now, do not consider him innocent. You are a man of wisdom; you will know what to do to him. Bring his gray head down to the grave in blood."

2:5–6 David's political advice begins with the elimination of Joab, David's effective, yet generally amoral, military chief (cf. comments on 1:7–8). Why does he tell Solomon to do what seems to be such a vindictive act? Skinner thinks David wants to squelch any notion that he ordered or approved of Joab's killing of Abner and Amasa.[37] P. Matheney states that "this charge . . . is not an expression of personal vengeance; it is rather the satisfaction of a primitive idea of the danger to the dynasty of unavenged innocent blood (cf. 2 Sam 21:6–9)."[38]

Two more possibilities also exist. First, Joab is indeed a powerful, crafty, and dangerous opponent of Solomon's accession to the throne. Solomon cannot afford to let him disturb the peace. Second, with Nathan and Bathsheba satisfied, Joab remains the lone individual who knows of David's adultery with Bathsheba and ordering of Uriah's death. David may simply want to remove the one person who could harm his reputation and Solomon's claim to the throne. Despite the charge's frank brutality and despite the painfully obvious fact that David never had the courage to punish Joab himself, he gives his son sound political advice. Joab represents the greatest threat to Solomon's shaky hold on the throne.

2:7 A note of kindness appears between two vengeful passages. David tells Solomon to reward old friends, which is also wise political counsel. Barzillai provided food and bedding when David ran from Absalom (2 Sam 17:27–29), and his family deserves to reap the benefits of loyalty and kindness offered in a stressful, uncertain time.

---

[37] Skinner, *I and II Kings,* 71.

[38] M. P. Matheney, "1 Kings," BBC (Nashville: Broadman, 1970) 3:163. Koopmans takes בְּשָׁלֹם in v. 5 ("in peace") as originally בשלמה ("on a cloak"). This better fits the verb וַיָּשֶׂם("he placed"), which the NIV translates "shedding." The clause would then read, "He placed the blood of battle on a cloak," which fits well with the following clause (Koopmans, "The Testament of David," 447–49).

2:8–9 On the other hand, Shimei, the pro-Saul Benjamite who cursed David when he fled from Absalom (2 Sam 16:5–14), must be dealt with in a different manner. David admits that he swore not to kill Shimei, yet he encourages Solomon to find a shrewd way to "bring his gray head down to the grave in blood." Certainly David does have personal revenge on his mind, but killing Shimei also lets the populace know that pro-Saul, anti-David sentiments will not be tolerated. Thus, David has told his successor how to reduce the risk that old factions will mount challenges to his authority.

5. David's Death (2:10–12)

10 Then David rested with his fathers and was buried in the City of David. 11 He had reigned forty years over Israel—seven years in Hebron and thirty-three in Jerusalem. 12 So Solomon sat on the throne of his father David, and his rule was firmly established.

2:10–12 David's death marks the end of the most glamorous and momentous reign in Israel's history. This great character, second only to Moses in importance in the Old Testament, is buried in the capital city he himself built. Most importantly for 1, 2 Kings, he has placed Solomon on the throne, "and his rule was firmly established." The promises the Lord made to David in 2 Samuel 7 are beginning to come true.

Besides noting his political accomplishments, it is also necessary to survey David's ongoing influence in 1, 2 Kings as a whole. Most of the references to David in 1, 2 Kings are in 1 Kings 1–11, where he places Solomon in power (1 Kgs 1–2), serves as the narrator's (3:3) and Solomon's (5:5; 8:18; 8:24–26) model for leadership, and remains God's ideal monarch (9:4–5). Beyond these chapters, David is the standard by which other kings are measured (1 Kgs 14:8; 15:11; 2 Kgs 14:3; 16:2). According to the author, David was faithful in his walk with the Lord, "except in the case of Uriah the Hittite" (1 Kgs 15:5). Indeed, David defends Jerusalem long after his death, since God spares the city for centuries simply for the sake of the promises made to David (2 Kgs 20:6).

6. Solomon Consolidates His Power (2:13–46)

Solomon now moves to do what David advised. He will deal carefully yet decisively with the enemies his father mentioned and with others he recognizes as threats to the authority he has gained. How he treats each situation demonstrates developing leadership skills and a bent toward wisdom, traits his father recognizes in 2:9.

(1) Adonijah's Foolish Request and His Execution (2:13–25)

13 Now Adonijah, the son of Haggith, went to Bathsheba, Solomon's mother. Bathsheba asked him, "Do you come peacefully?"

He answered, "Yes, peacefully." 14Then he added, "I have something to say to you."

"You may say it," she replied.

15"As you know," he said, "the kingdom was mine. All Israel looked to me as their king. But things changed, and the kingdom has gone to my brother; for it has come to him from the LORD. 16Now I have one request to make of you. Do not refuse me."

"You may make it," she said.

17So he continued, "Please ask King Solomon—he will not refuse you—to give me Abishag the Shunammite as my wife."

18"Very well," Bathsheba replied, "I will speak to the king for you."

19When Bathsheba went to King Solomon to speak to him for Adonijah, the king stood up to meet her, bowed down to her and sat down on his throne. He had a throne brought for the king's mother, and she sat down at his right hand.

20"I have one small request to make of you," she said. "Do not refuse me."

The king replied, "Make it, my mother; I will not refuse you."

21So she said, "Let Abishag the Shunammite be given in marriage to your brother Adonijah."

22King Solomon answered his mother, "Why do you request Abishag the Shunammite for Adonijah? You might as well request the kingdom for him—after all, he is my older brother—yes, for him and for Abiathar the priest and Joab son of Zeruiah!"

23Then King Solomon swore by the LORD: "May God deal with me, be it ever so severely, if Adonijah does not pay with his life for this request! 24And now, as surely as the LORD lives—he who has established me securely on the throne of my father David and has founded a dynasty for me as he promised—Adonijah shall be put to death today!" 25So King Solomon gave orders to Benaiah son of Jehoiada, and he struck down Adonijah and he died.

2:13–18 In contrast to Solomon's wisdom, Adonijah now makes a ridiculous request. He approaches Bathsheba with what he says is a peaceful question. With at least a trace of bitterness, he reminds the queen mother, using a bit of exaggeration, that "all Israel" had expected him to succeed David. In a massive understatement, he observes, "But things changed." Things are about to change even more, since he asks Bathsheba to secure Solomon's permission for him to marry Abishag, David's last concubine. Without expressing any verdict on Adonijah's request, Bathsheba agrees to carry the petition to Solomon.

2:19–22 Unfortunately for Adonijah, Bathsheba does what she promised. Using almost the same words as Adonijah, Bathsheba mentions "one small request," then pleads, "Do not refuse me" (cf. 2:16–17,20). When Solomon hears the request, he explodes in anger and ultimately decides to execute Adonijah. Why? Because Abishag was David's last concubine, and whoever possessed the harem controlled the kingdom (cf. 2 Sam 16:21–22). J. W. Wesselius observes, "Solomon not surprisingly saw this as a sign that Adonijah had not relinquished the thought of becoming king himself."[39] Solomon also continues to be suspicious of Abiathar and Joab.

Bathsheba never appears in the book again, so it is appropriate to assess her character now. Many commentators misjudge her. For example, Whybray calls Bathsheba "a good-natured, rather stupid woman who was a natural prey both to more passionate and to cleverer men."[40] Keil believes the implications of Adonijah's request escaped her.[41] Montgomery concludes that Bathsheba simply had a "womanly interest in his [Adonijah's] love-affair."[42] In response, for a stupid woman Bathsheba wielded great powers. She lived in the palace and was a major player in her son's rise to power. As for not realizing the significance of Adonijah's plea, who would understand harem politics more than the queen of the harem? Finally, why would she take a "womanly interest" in the future of her son's chief rival? Bathsheba is, rather, the first of several vital female characters in 1, 2 Kings. She cooperates with Nathan, exposes Adonijah, and generally makes prudent moves in the halls of power. Thus, it is evident that she understands the nature of Adonijah's request and prudently warns her son of his rival's inept power play.

2:23–25 Without hesitation Solomon sends Benaiah, his military leader, to kill Adonijah. He also has plans for Joab and Abiathar, as the next several verses reveal. Unlike Bathsheba, who survives through careful political activity, Adonijah dies on account of his own foolishness. He not only desires David's last concubine, but he also asks Solomon's mother to secure Abishag for him. This last political move is no more effective than his earlier ones. Ironically, Solomon becomes king by wisely following the advice of others, while the more active Adonijah fails at every turn.[43]

(2) Solomon Banishes Abiathar (2:26–27)

[26]To Abiathar the priest the king said, "Go back to your fields in Anathoth. You deserve to die, but I will not put you to death now, because you carried the ark of the Sovereign LORD before my father David and shared all my father's hardships." [27]So Solomon removed Abiathar from the priesthood of the LORD, fulfilling the word the LORD had spoken at Shiloh about the house of Eli.

2:26–27 Solomon banishes Abiathar for political reasons. After all, the priest had backed Adonijah's bid for the throne (cf. 1 Kgs 1:7–8). In

[39] J. W. Wesselius, "Joab's Death and the Central Theme of the Succession Narrative (2 Samuel 9–1 Kings 2)," *VT* 40/3 (1990) 338.

[40] Whybray, *The Succession Narrative,* 40.

[41] C. F. Keil, "I and II Kings," COT, trans. J. Martin (1876; reprint, Grand Rapids: Eerdmans, 1980) 3:31.

[42] J. A. Montgomery and H. S. Gehman, *A Critical and Exegetical Commentary on the Book of Kings,* ICC (1951; reprint, Edinburgh: T & T Clark, 1986) 92.

[43] Cf. Long, "A Darkness between Brothers," 87.

Solomon's mind, Abiathar remains a pro-Adonijah threat to the newly established order (cf. 2:22) and is only allowed to live because of his past association with David. To the author of 1, 2 Kings, however, this decision marks a direct fulfillment of a prophecy made by Samuel against Eli's descendants (cf. 1 Sam 2:27–36). The importance of prophecy as the direct word of God will grow as the account progresses.

(3) Solomon Executes Joab (2:28–34)

28When the news reached Joab, who had conspired with Adonijah though not with Absalom, he fled to the tent of the LORD and took hold of the horns of the altar. 29King Solomon was told that Joab had fled to the tent of the LORD and was beside the altar. Then Solomon ordered Benaiah son of Jehoiada, "Go, strike him down!"

30So Benaiah entered the tent of the LORD and said to Joab, "The king says, 'Come out!'"

But he answered, "No, I will die here."

Benaiah reported to the king, "This is how Joab answered me."

31Then the king commanded Benaiah, "Do as he says. Strike him down and bury him, and so clear me and my father's house of the guilt of the innocent blood that Joab shed. 32The LORD will repay him for the blood he shed, because without the knowledge of my father David he attacked two men and killed them with the sword. Both of them—Abner son of Ner, commander of Israel's army, and Amasa son of Jether, commander of Judah's army—were better men and more upright than he. 33May the guilt of their blood rest on the head of Joab and his descendants forever. But on David and his descendants, his house and his throne, may there be the LORD's peace forever."

34So Benaiah son of Jehoiada went up and struck down Joab and killed him, and he was buried on his own land in the desert.

2:28–29 Joab understands the implications of Adonijah's death and Abiathar's removal. The aging, politically astute warrior knows he must be next. Expecting the worst, he takes refuge by grasping "the horns of the altar." Regarding the horns, P. King writes, "Their symbolism is uncertain, but the holiness of the altar bore a special relationship to the horns of the altar; the altar was consecrated by rubbing the blood of the victims on the horns."[44] Joab is not a particularly religious man, but he apparently hopes he will not be killed in so holy a place. Solomon has no such scruples, though, so Joab's ploy fails.

2:30–34 Benaiah gets permission to kill Joab at the altar. Solomon's motive for eliminating Joab is to remove bloodguilt from David's dynasty. This concept is taken seriously, as 2 Sam 21:1–14 demonstrates. Besides granting

[44] P. J. King, *Amos, Hosea, Micah—An Archaeological Commentary* (Philadelphia: Westminster, 1988) 90.

one of David's last wishes, Joab's removal means that the political, religious, and military leaders of the anti-Solomon faction are no longer on the scene.

(4) Benaiah and Zadok Given Power (2:35)

35The king put Benaiah son of Jehoiada over the army in Joab's position and replaced Abiathar with Zadok the priest.

2:35 Solomon wisely rewards his supporters. Zadok replaces Abiathar, and Benaiah replaces Joab. Solomon has begun to display the organizational and political skills that will eventually make him a legendary figure.

(5) Shimei's Disobedience and Execution (2:36–46)

36Then the king sent for Shimei and said to him, "Build yourself a house in
Jerusalem and live there, but do not go anywhere else. 37The day you leave and
cross the Kidron Valley, you can be sure you will die; your blood will be on your own head."

38Shimei answered the king, "What you say is good. Your servant will do as my lord the king has said." And Shimei stayed in Jerusalem for a long time.

39But three years later, two of Shimei's slaves ran off to Achish son of Maacah,
king of Gath, and Shimei was told, "Your slaves are in Gath." 40At this, he sad-
dled his donkey and went to Achish at Gath in search of his slaves. So Shimei went away and brought the slaves back from Gath.

41When Solomon was told that Shimei had gone from Jerusalem to Gath and
had returned, 42the king summoned Shimei and said to him, "Did I not make you
swear by the LORD and warn you, 'On the day you leave to go anywhere else, you can be sure you will die'? At that time you said to me, 'What you say is good. I
will obey.' 43Why then did you not keep your oath to the LORD and obey the command I gave you?"

44The king also said to Shimei, "You know in your heart all the wrong you did
to my father David. Now the LORD will repay you for your wrongdoing. 45But
King Solomon will be blessed, and David's throne will remain secure before the LORD forever."

46Then the king gave the order to Benaiah son of Jehoiada, and he went out and struck Shimei down and killed him.

The kingdom was now firmly established in Solomon's hands.

2:36–38 Only one person on David's list of enemies remains. Shimei, whom the author of 1, 2 Samuel portrays as an angry pro-Saul, anti-David, backbiting individual (cf. 2 Sam 16:5–12), has yet to be addressed. As "a man of wisdom" (1 Kgs 2:9), Solomon deals with Shimei shrewdly. He limits this foe to living in Jerusalem and gets him to agree never to leave the city via crossing the Kidron Valley. This order is quite restricting, since at this time Jerusalem was "a small acropolis city, whose circumference has been estimated at 4500 feet."[45] By this means Solomon can either observe Shimei at all times, or he can eliminate him altogether.

2:38–45 Despite agreeing to Solomon's terms, Shimei foolishly leaves home to pursue some slaves who have fled to Gath, which was located about twenty-five miles from Jerusalem. Gray notes that Shimei "did not actually cross the Kidron" to chase the servants, which means "he did not violate the letter but the spirit of Solomon's ban."[46] Perhaps Shimei thinks he is more clever than Solomon.

If so, he has made a serious miscalculation. The king obviously interpreted the travel ban to be on going "anywhere else" rather than on a literal crossing of the Kidron Valley. By breaking his oath to God and to Solomon, the old curser of David has cursed himself. Solomon now reminds Shimei of the original reason for his displeasure, which is Shimei's verbal attack on David. God will punish all David's enemies, will bless Solomon, and will secure David's dynasty forever. Each of these assertions echoes 2 Sam 7:1–17.

2:46 With Benaiah's execution of Shimei, the "kingdom was now firmly established in Solomon's hands." This statement reaffirms the similar comment found in 2:12. All religious foes, supporters of Adonijah, and proponents of Saul's dynasty have been crushed. This political reality fulfills theological promises made to David long ago.

Canonical and Theological Implications of 1 Kgs 1:1–2:46

The major canonical and theological issue this section raises is the fulfillment of the Davidic Covenant. Within the canon this theme unites 1, 2 Samuel and 1, 2 Kings. It explains why God waits so long before punishing Judah (2 Kgs 20:6). More importantly, this emphasis explains why the prophets looked to David's dynasty to provide a righteous leader who would usher in the kingdom of God (cf. Isa 9:1–7).

Theologically, the canonical focus on the Davidic lineage leads to the Old Testament's hope for the Messiah. Every prophet who writes of the Messiah believes he will be a son of David (cf. Isa 9:1–7; 11:1–9; Jer 23:1–8; Mic 5:2) and that he will rule with a perfect mixture of power, righteousness, and kindness. The New Testament teaches that only Jesus, the son of David (Matt 1:1–17), the son of God (Luke 3:23–37), can make David's rule "eternal." These larger implications are not stated in 1 Kings 1–2, of course, but they do grow out of this beginning.

Applicational Implications of 1 Kgs 1:1–2:46

Several interesting applicational issues emerge from this segment. First,

[45] Montgomery and Gehman, *Kings*, 96.

[46] Gray, *I and II Kings*, 109.

God keeps all promises made to human beings. David's morality may have faltered, but God's never did. Second, people who serve the Lord, such as the prophets, need to take an active role in government affairs. G. Rice notes:

> The chapter is a summons to the man or woman of God to be in the midst of the rowdy, untidy push and shove of human striving where God's purposes are at stake and to act with the boldness and astuteness of a Nathan. Bad leadership and evil can succeed only with the consent of the righteous.[47]

Christians must decide what role they will play in the ongoing reformation of society.

Third, this section raises questions about the complexities of just governing. Some scholars consider Solomon and David rather brutal and manipulative in these stories.[48] Others point to tensions within David's family as the cause of the story's brutality.[49] Still others note the dangers inherent in any "one-party state."[50] Whatever one's conclusions about the propriety of Solomon's actions, it is unclear how else he could secure the kingdom. Just as Nathan was forced to make some hard personal choices in forcing David to name Solomon king, so Solomon had to make difficult decisions. In both cases the men served a higher end by actions that were at least partially defensible.[51]

Fourth, the text demonstrates how divisions within a country can eventually lead to dissolution, as J. Flanagan observes.[52] Fifth, the story's many ambiguities stress the need for intelligent and creative readings and discussion of Old Testament narrative.[53] Only then can the original author's subtle and provocative telling of these crucial events receive the insightful interpretation they deserve.[54]

---

[47] Rice, *Nations under God,* 17.

[48] E.g., A. G. Auld calls Solomon a "cynical manipulator" (*I and II Kings,* DSB [Philadelphia: Westminster, 1986] 20).

[49] Cf. Long, "A Darkness between Brothers," 87.

[50] Nelson, *First and Second Kings,* 23.

[51] For a survey of methods of ethical decision making, see N. Geisler, *Contemporary Options in Evangelical Ethics* (Grand Rapids: Baker, 1981).

[52] Flanagan, "Court History or Succession Document? A Study of 2 Samuel 9–20 and 1 Kings 1–2," *JBL* 91 (1972) 181.

[53] Consult D. A. Knight, "Moral Values and Literary Traditions: The Case of the Succession Narrative (2 Samuel 9–20; 1 Kings 1–2)," *Semeia* 34 (1985) 7–23, for suggestions about how the author of 1 Kings 1–2 encourages ethical thought without explicitly stating norms.

[54] Cf. Sacon, "A Study of the Literary Structure of 'The Succession Narrative,'" 53.

SECTION OUTLINE

II. SOLOMON'S REIGN (3:1–11:43)
- 1. God's First Appearance to Solomon (3:1–15)
  - (1) God Accepts Solomon's Sacrifice (3:1–5)
  - (2) Solomon Asks for Wisdom (3:6–9)
  - (3) God's Promises to Solomon (3:10–15)
- 2. Solomon Demonstrates His Wisdom (3:16–4:34)
  - (1) Solomon Solves the Prostitutes' Dilemma (3:16–28)
  - (2) Solomon Organizes His Government (4:1–19)
  - (3) Solomon Levies Taxes (4:20–28)
  - (4) Solomon Exhibits Great Breadth of Knowledge (4:29–34)

Canonical and Theological Implications in 1 Kgs 3:1–4:34
Applicational Implications of 1 Kgs 3:1–4:34
- 3. Solomon Builds the Temple and Palace (5:1–7:51)
  - (1) Hiram of Tyre Provides Temple Materials (5:1–12)
  - (2) Solomon Conscripts Workers (5:13–18)
  - (3) Building the Temple (6:1–10)
  - (4) God's Promises concerning the Temple (6:11–13)
  - (5) Finishing the Temple (6:14–38)
  - (6) Palace Construction (7:1–12)
  - (7) Furnishing the Temple (7:13–51)
- 4. Solomon Dedicates the Temple (8:1–66)
  - (1) Bringing the Ark to the Temple (8:1–13)
  - (2) Solomon's Thanksgiving (8:14–21)
  - (3) Solomon's Dedication Prayer (8:22–53)
  - (4) Solomon's Blessing (8:54–61)
  - (5) Solomon's Sacrifices (8:62–66)
- 5. God's Second Appearance to Solomon (9:1–9)

Canonical and Theological Implications of 1 Kgs 5:1–9:9
Applicational Implications of 1 Kgs 5:1–9:9
- 6. Solomon's Pursuits (9:10–28)

Survey of Historical Issues Related to 1 Kgs 9:10–11:43
  - (1) Foreign Relations (9:10–14)
  - (2) Forced Labor (9:15–23)
  - (3) Further Building (9:24)
  - (4) Worship (9:25)
  - (5) Shipping (9:26–28)
- 7. Solomon's Wisdom and Wealth (10:1–29)

(1) The Queen of Sheba's Visit (10:1–13)
(2) Solomon's Wealth (10:14–29)
8. Solomon's Decline (11:1–43)
(1) Solomon's Idolatry (11:1–13)
(2) Rebellions against Solomon (11:14–25)
(3) Ahijah Prophesies Division (11:26–40)
(4) Solomon's Death (11:41–43)

II. SOLOMON'S REIGN (3:1–11:43)

Having detailed Solomon's rise to power, the author next describes the new king's life and work. Now Solomon becomes the story's dominant character rather than simply a candidate for the throne or a young man in the shadow of his more famous father. His career unfolds in three distinct phases. These phases are definitely thematic in nature, but they may also reflect the historical stages of his reign. Each segment has a corresponding visitation from God or a message from a prophet.

The first phase (3:1–4:34) begins when Solomon offers sacrifices to God, who responds by granting Solomon's wish for wisdom (3:1–15). Then Solomon demonstrates his God-given wisdom in a series of decisions (3:16–4:34). In the second phase of the story (5:1–9:9) Solomon builds the temple and palace, projects that take thirteen years (5:1–7:51). After the temple is dedicated (8:1–66), the Lord appears to the king and reaffirms the Davidic Covenant (9:1–5). The Lord warns Solomon, however, to be faithful or face the consequences (9:6–9). During the final phase of the story (9:10–11:43), Solomon carries on the normal activities of a monarch (9:10–28) and enjoys the great fame and wealth associated with his wisdom (10:1–29); yet he degrades himself through idolatry (11:1–13). Because of this sin, God allows several enemies to chip away at Solomon's empire (11:14–40). Still, Solomon remains rich and powerful until his death (11:41–43). In the final segment God instructs Ahijah to prophesy the impending division of Israel. Solomon obviously does not heed the warnings in 9:6–9.

Though it is impossible to say whether or not the author used other selected sources, the text states explicitly that information has been gleaned from "the book of the annals of Solomon" (1 Kgs 11:41). This source was either available to the author or included in a larger source that was utilized. Either way, scholars generally agree that there is no reason to doubt the source's basic accuracy. The author no doubt adapted the material to fit the overall scheme of 1, 2 Kings, but this adaptation involved changes of emphasis, not of facts.[1]

---

[1] See comments on the author's selection of events in the Introduction to Literary Issues segment of the commentary's introduction.

Survey of Historical Issues Related to 1 Kgs 3:1–4:34

Because the second major section of 1 Kings is lengthy and unfolds in three phases, it is best to examine the historical data in three stages. First Kings 3–4 describes the first years of Solomon's rule and the fame he gains during this time. Foreign and domestic political situations are mentioned as are religious, literary, and commercial issues. If 1 Kings 1–2 establishes Solomon as the successor of David, then 1 Kings 3–4 indicates how Solomon begins to fill the rather large void his father left.

Most of the events in 1 Kings 3–4 apparently occur during the first four years of Solomon's rule (ca. 970–966 B.C.). At least they are all told before temple construction begins "in the fourth year of Solomon's reign" (1 Kgs 6:1). Three historical details deserve mention: Solomon's relationship to Egypt, Solomon's organization of Israel into twelve districts, and the extent and cost of Solomon's kingdom. These details are interspersed between the chapters' most important ideas, which are the origin, emergence, and fruits of Solomon's wisdom.

As has been stated, David left a significant kingdom to his son. He had built the nation largely through conquest. Philistia, Moab, Ammon, Edom, and Syria had fallen to his armies. These nations continued to be under Israel's authority during the first decades of Solomon's era, which presented the new king with an administrative problem, not a military one. Since he controlled virtually all the land between Egypt and the Hittite kingdom, Solomon was a major player in international affairs.

Egypt's pharaoh, "most probably Siamun (ca. 978–959),"[2] recognized Solomon's significance and made an alliance with him by marrying one of his daughters to Israel's king (1 Kgs 3:1). Perhaps Egypt was weak and needed Solomon's support at this time, or maybe Egypt thought it easier to gain access to Israel's trade routes through negotiation than through war. Whatever the reasons, peaceful relations existed between Egypt and Israel for "some twenty years—until the twenty-first dynasty was superseded by Shishak (ca. 945 B.C.)."[3] Having Egypt as an ally enhanced Solomon's status even more. When this alliance ceased, however, Egypt helped support the man who eventually split Israel into two rival nations (cf. 1 Kgs 11:26–40).

Before Solomon, Israel's government was fairly informal. Saul and David's kingdoms were not disorganized, but they were forced to focus on waging war rather than managing a peaceful empire. Solomon, on the other hand, was

---

[2] J. A. Soggin, "The Davidic-Solomonic Kingdom," in *Israelite and Judaean History,* ed. J. H. Hayes and J. M. Miller (Philadelphia: Westminster, 1977) 375.

[3] A. Malamat, "A Political Look at the Kingdom of David and Solomon and Its Relations with Egypt," in *Studies in the Period of David and Solomon and Other Essays,* ed. T. Ishida (Winona Lake, Ind.: Eisenbrauns, 1982) 200.

determined to accomplish normal peacetime goals, such as trading and building. Thus, he divided Israel into twelve districts, each of which was ruled by a governor, who "had to provide supplies for one month in the year" (1 Kgs 4:7). In other words, the governors collected taxes in their districts that went to support a central government. Bright observes that "these districts in some cases coincided roughly with the old tribal areas, more often tribal boundaries were disregarded."[4] Resentment over this redistricting undoubtedly arose, then grew as the districts struggled to pay their apportionment. As Bright concludes about the new system:

> In any event, this was a radical and decisive step, and that not only because it imposed upon the people an unprecedented burden. It meant that the old tribal system, already increasingly of vestigial significance, had been, as far as its political functioning was concerned, virtually abolished. In place of twelve tribes caring in turn for the central shrine were twelve districts taxed for the support of Solomon's court![5]

Without question, Solomon's court needed vast sums to support its many interests. Besides the king, his harem, and his officials, there were chariot horses and regular army horses to feed (1 Kgs 4:26). Too, the nation's population grew (1 Kgs 4:20), which necessitated further administrative costs. Since funds could not be gained through warfare, taxes and trade had to provide all the government's income. Only an extraordinarily wise king could fund all these various interests, and even this type of ruler could not do so for an indefinite period of time.

1. God's First Appearance to Solomon (3:1–15)

After the rather brutal events in 1 Kings 1–2, readers may wonder whether the Lord approves of Solomon's rise to power. Other than Nathan's support, Solomon has yet to receive any direct divine affirmation. Chapters 3 and 4 help alleviate this legitimate concern. In 3:1–15 the king has the first of two direct encounters with God. Both visions stress God's covenant with David and God's desire to bless Solomon if he will follow David's example of serving only the Lord.

(1) God Accepts Solomon's Sacrifice (3:1–5)

[1]Solomon made an alliance with Pharaoh king of Egypt and married his daughter. He brought her to the City of David until he finished building his palace and the temple of the LORD, and the wall around Jerusalem. [2]The people, however, were still sacrificing at the high places, because a temple had not yet been built for the Name of the LORD. [3]Solomon showed his love for the LORD by walk-

[4] J. Bright, *A History of Israel,* 3d ed. (Philadelphia: Westminster, 1981) 221–222.
[5] Ibid., 222.

ing according to the statutes of his father David, except that he offered sacrifices and burned incense on the high places.

4The king went to Gibeon to offer sacrifices, for that was the most important high place, and Solomon offered a thousand burnt offerings on that altar. 5At Gibeon the LORD appeared to Solomon during the night in a dream, and God said, "Ask for whatever you want me to give you."

3:1 The author presents information here that could puzzle, concern, and yet instill pride in the book's first readers. Solomon's ability to make a marriage alliance with Egypt demonstrates the king and nation's newfound prominence, which might produce some nationalistic arrogance. At the same time, marrying a foreign princess might bring destructive foreign religious and political ideas to Israel.[6] The author uses the queen's arrival in Jerusalem as an opportunity to introduce Solomon's most important building projects: the palace, the temple, and defensive walls around the capital city.

3:2–3 With no central worship site, the people "were still sacrificing at the high places." These shrines were located at slight elevations throughout the land, were quite often fairly elaborate in design and construction, and were roundly denounced by the author of 1, 2 Kings after the temple was built.[7] For now this practice is excusable, but Solomon's long-term commitment to the high places is contrary to God's law and David's example.

3:4–5 Solomon demonstrates his love for the Lord by journeying approximately seven miles northeastward to Gibeon and offering burnt offerings there. This text does not say why Gibeon was the most important high place, but 2 Chr 1:5–6 explains that while David had brought the ark to Jerusalem, the Mosaic tabernacle and "the bronze altar that Bezalel . . . had made" were still in Gibeon. The very necessity of going more than one place to use the traditional implements of worship underscores the need for a central sanctuary. God seems pleased at Solomon's piety, for the Lord appears in a dream and tells the king to ask for whatever he wants.

This offer amounts to a reaffirmation of the Davidic Covenant. Solomon has obeyed God, as David commanded in 2:2–4. Now the Lord decides to bless David's son. This verse also indicates that God approves of Solomon's rise to power, the issue left unresolved after chap. 2.

(2) Solomon Asks for Wisdom (3:6–9)

6Solomon answered, "You have shown great kindness to your servant, my father David, because he was faithful to you and righteous and upright in heart.

---

[6] See A. Malamat, "The Kingdom of David and Solomon in Its Contact with Egypt and Aram Naharaim," *BA* 21 (1958) 96–102; id., "The First Peace Treaty between Israel and Egypt," *BAR* (1979) 58–61.

[7] For a fuller description of "high places," see K. D. Schunk, בָּמָה, "bamah" *TDOT* 2.139–45.

You have continued this great kindness to him and have given him a son to sit on his throne this very day.

[7]"Now, O LORD my God, you have made your servant king in place of my father David. But I am only a little child and do not know how to carry out my duties. [8]Your servant is here among the people you have chosen, a great people, too numerous to count or number. [9]So give your servant a discerning heart to govern your people and to distinguish between right and wrong. For who is able to govern this great people of yours?"

3:6 Solomon prefaces his request by acknowledging the continuation of his father's covenant with God. The fact that he rules Israel stems from Nathan's prophecy in 2 Sam 7:12 and because his father David remained "faithful . . . and righteous and upright in heart." David's covenant loyalty matched God's own kindness to him. Whatever opportunities Solomon may have are based firmly on God's sovereign purpose for those who keep their covenant vows.

3:7–9 In light of the greatness of the Lord's relationship with David, Solomon humbles himself before the Lord. He admits that God is the cause of his rise to power.[8] Further, he says he is but a small child[9] who does not know "how to carry out my duties." This last statement in Hebrew literally says, "I do not know how to go and come," an idiom referring to the skills of leadership (cf. Num 27:17; Deut 31:2–3; Josh 14:11; 1 Sam 18:13,16; 29:6; 2 Kgs 11:8).

In contrast to his own personal and experiential lack of stature, Solomon must lead a people whose greatness is first measured by the fact that they were chosen by God. Solomon now becomes the head of the nation once led by Abraham, Moses, Joshua, Samuel, and David. According to Deut 17:14–20, he must embody God's standards for the people. Israel's greatness is also measured by its growing population. Solomon senses that perhaps old ways of governing may not meet the current needs of his subjects.

Given this personal dilemma, Solomon requests "a discerning heart." This phrase literally means "a listening heart" or "an obedient heart."[10] In the Old Testament "hearing" and "obeying" come from the same word, a linguistic trait with practical implications. Only those who obey authority figures have really *heard* them. Solomon must obey the Lord by keeping God's commands in order for his heart to be prepared to lead others. This listening to God will also enable him to listen to others.

Solomon's desire for an obedient, listening heart is based on his wish to

---

[8] The verb here (הִמְלַכְתָּ) is in the *hiphil,* or causative, stem. Solomon recognizes God's sovereignty over all the events in 1 Kings 1–2.

[9] Solomon uses the term נַעַר קָטֹן, which can refer to a dependent child (cf. Exod 2:6; 1 Sam 1:22) or to a youth not yet fully responsible for his own financial support (Gen 19:4; Hos 11:1). Jeremiah uses similar phrasing in Jer 1:6. Solomon acknowledges his utter dependence on God here.

[10] The Greek OT translates לִשְׁמֹעַ, which makes שׁמע an infinitive like the next two verbal forms.

administer justice in Israel. Justice can only emerge when the king is able "to distinguish between right and wrong" (lit., "good and evil"). Justice can become a quite complicated goal, as 3:16–28 proves. Only knowledge of what God considers fair and unfair can guide the king to act justly with any consistency. Though Solomon has already exhibited political craftiness, he knows that long-term wisdom and success reside where David found it—in an ongoing relationship with the Lord.

(3) God's Promises to Solomon (3:10–15)

10The LORD was pleased that Solomon had asked for this. 11So God said to him, "Since you have asked for this and not for long life or wealth for yourself, nor have asked for the death of your enemies but for discernment in administering justice, 12I will do what you have asked. I will give you a wise and discerning heart, so that there will never have been anyone like you, nor will there ever be. 13Moreover, I will give you what you have not asked for—both riches and honor—so that in your lifetime you will have no equal among kings. 14And if you walk in my ways and obey my statutes and commands as David your father did, I will give you a long life." 15Then Solomon awoke—and he realized it had been a dream.

He returned to Jerusalem, stood before the ark of the LORD's covenant and sacrificed burnt offerings and fellowship offerings. Then he gave a feast for all his court.

3:10–13 God is pleased with Solomon's attitude. Though Solomon could have asked for selfish favors such as wealth, long life, or revenge, he desires the ability to help others. Thus, in the first of four revelations to Solomon, God not only agrees to grant the request but makes promises beyond what Solomon imagined. He will indeed have "a wise and discerning heart," one that will set him apart for all times. Solomon's wisdom will exceed those before and after him. Further, though he did not ask for wealth and fame, these blessings will be his as well. What all kings want, yet rarely achieve, Solomon will have because of God's answer to his prayer.

3:14–15 "All" Solomon must do to secure these blessings is to follow David's example of adherence to the Sinai covenant. If he keeps the "statutes and commands," Solomon will honor his father and thereby have "a long life." This reference to Exod 20:12 underscores the continuity of God's covenant with Israel, with David, and with Solomon, the new generation. It also emphasizes the conditional nature of Solomon's kingship, an idea that is repeated every time God addresses Solomon directly (cf. 6:11–13; 9:3–9; 11:11–13). Long notes that in these four addresses "the editor-author(s) forged a kind of unity of exhortation out of the material, which then can be turned on end to become a deadly serious, twice-repeated message of conditions violated, promise lost, glory tarnished (ch. 11)."[11] God's covenant with David is eternal, but

[11] B. O. Long, *1 Kings, with an Introduction to Historical Literature,* FOTL 9 (Grand Rapids: Eerdmans, 1984) 59.

Solomon can be replaced with another "son of David" if he disobeys the Lord.

When the king awakes from this life-changing dream, the king seals the agreement. A celebration marked by sacrifices and a feast prove his sincerity and determination to keep the covenant. God's approval of Solomon has finally been clarified.

2. Solomon Demonstrates His Wisdom (3:16–4:34)

(1) Solomon Solves the Prostitutes' Dilemma (3:16–28)

16Now two prostitutes came to the king and stood before him. 17One of them said, "My lord, this woman and I live in the same house. I had a baby while she was there with me. 18The third day after my child was born, this woman also had a baby. We were alone; there was no one in the house but the two of us.

19"During the night this woman's son died because she lay on him. 20So she got up in the middle of the night and took my son from my side while I your servant was asleep. She put him by her breast and put her dead son by my breast. 21The next morning, I got up to nurse my son—and he was dead! But when I looked at him closely in the morning light, I saw that it wasn't the son I had borne."

22The other woman said, "No! The living one is my son; the dead one is yours."

But the first one insisted, "No! The dead one is yours; the living one is mine." And so they argued before the king.

23The king said, "This one says, 'My son is alive and your son is dead,' while that one says, 'No! Your son is dead and mine is alive.'"

24Then the king said, "Bring me a sword." So they brought a sword for the king. 25He then gave an order: "Cut the living child in two and give half to one and half to the other."

26The woman whose son was alive was filled with compassion for her son and said to the king, "Please, my lord, give her the living baby! Don't kill him!"

But the other said, "Neither I nor you shall have him. Cut him in two!"

27Then the king gave his ruling: "Give the living baby to the first woman. Do not kill him; she is his mother."

28When all Israel heard the verdict the king had given, they held the king in awe, because they saw that he had wisdom from God to administer justice.

3:16–23 This story is one of the best known in the whole Bible. Having been promised wisdom, Solomon will now have this wisdom tested. Israel's kings were sometimes called upon to settle particularly hard cases (2 Sam 12:1–6; 14:1–11), and this situation is quite perplexing. Two prostitutes[12] have

---

[12] Montgomery and Gehman note "some ancient texts try to modify or ignore the ugly noun" by reading the term as "Innkeeper" (*A Critical and Exegetical Commentary on the Book of Kings,* ICC [Edinburgh: T & T Clark, 1986] 109). Such changes are incorrect, since, as G. H. Jones observes, "harlots were unashamedly visited in ancient Israel (cf. Gen. 38; Jos 2:1)" (*1 and 2 Kings,* NCB [Grand Rapids: Eerdmans, 1984] 1:131).

had babies. One woman quite carelessly smothers her child in the night, then switches babies while her colleague sleeps. Now both women claim the living child as their own. Without other witnesses or evidence, Solomon must devise some way to solve the case. Will God's promised sagacity materialize? Will Solomon wilt under this newly imposed pressure?

3:24–28 The king quickly produces his own evidence. He decides to try the case based on the women's maternal instincts and human compassion. Calling for a sword, he orders the child cut into halves, with each woman getting an equal share. The real mother, who has already cared enough for her child to plead her case before the king, acts out of "compassion for her son." She begs Solomon to give the baby to the other woman. In startling contrast the careless, dishonest woman is willing to take her "half." Her cruelty has been revealed, just as the other mother's kindness has emerged.

Solomon can now give a just verdict. The compassionate woman is given the child. He has the insight to see the difference between just and unjust persons even when he has no corroborating evidence. When this verdict becomes public knowledge, the nation was in awe of (lit., "feared") the king. This comment reinforces the statement in 2:46 that the "kingdom is now firmly established in Solomon's hands." Most importantly, this respect stems from the knowledge that wisdom like Solomon's can come only from God. Israel now understands, as does the reader, that "the wisdom of God is in his heart to do justice."[13] If so, the nation will flourish under his leadership. So far Solomon has been faithful to the God who has kept the promises made to the new king.

(2) Solomon Organizes His Government (4:1–19)

1So King Solomon ruled over all Israel. 2And these were his chief officials:

Azariah son of Zadok—the priest;
3Elihoreph and Ahijah, sons of Shisha—secretaries;
Jehoshaphat son of Ahilud—recorder;
4Benaiah son of Jehoiada—commander in chief;
Zadok and Abiathar—priests;
5Azariah son of Nathan—in charge of the district officers;
Zabud son of Nathan—a priest and personal adviser to the king;
6Ahishar—in charge of the palace;
Adoniram son of Abda—in charge of forced labor.

7Solomon also had twelve district governors over all Israel, who supplied provisions for the king and the royal household. Each one had to provide supplies for one month in the year. 8These are their names:

Ben-Hur—in the hill country of Ephraim;

---

[13] Author's translation.

[9]Ben-Deker—in Makaz, Shaalbim, Beth Shemesh and Elon Bethhanan;
[10]Ben-Hesed—in Arubboth (Socoh and all the land of Hepher were his);
[11]Ben-Abinadab—in Naphoth Dor (he was married to Taphath daughter of Solomon);
[12]Baana son of Ahilud—in Taanach and Megiddo, and in all of Beth Shan next to Zarethan below Jezreel, from Beth Shan to Abel Meholah across to Jokmeam;
[13]Ben-Geber—in Ramoth Gilead (the settlements of Jair son of Manasseh in Gilead were his, as well as the district of Argob in Bashan and its sixty large walled cities with bronze gate bars);
[14]Ahinadab son of Iddo—in Mahanaim;
[15]Ahimaaz—in Naphtali (he had married Basemath daughter of Solomon);
[16]Baana son of Hushai—in Asher and in Aloth;
[17]Jehoshaphat son of Paruah—in Issachar;
[18]Shimei son of Ela—in Benjamin;
[19]Geber son of Uri—in Gilead (the country of Sihon king of the Amorites and the country of Og king of Bashan). He was the only governor over the district.

Solomon now uses his wisdom to organize the kingdom. Settling local disputes like the one between the prostitutes is essential to a successful reign, but his leadership expertise must extend to broader issues. Thus, the author presents whom the king chose to direct the nation's internal affairs. The book's subsequent references to Solomon's many successes indicate the appropriateness of his appointments.

4:1–6 After again highlighting Solomon's rule "over all Israel" (4:1; cf. 2:46), the text lists nine offices and those who held them. Certainly Solomon employed other appointed officials, but these are mentioned because of their prominence in earlier stories (e.g., Benaiah, Zadok, Abiathar) or because of their involvement in future episodes (e.g., Ahishar, Adoniram).[14]

The first reference, "Azariah son of Zadok—the priest," seems to overlap with the fifth notation, "Zadok and Abiathar—priests." Given Zadok and Abiathar's probable age, it is likely that Azariah succeeded Zadok, his father, then served for the majority of Solomon's era. Thus, it is understandable why Azariah is included with the older men. That he is listed first may demonstrate his, and the priesthood's, importance during these years.[15]

---

[14]Cf. Long, *1 Kings,* 72.

[15]Gray, following Montgomery and Gehman, observes that "Elihoreph" may not be a proper name. Instead, it may mean "over the year," which implies that Azariah may have been the priest in charge of an annual New Year festival (*1 and 2 Kings,* OTL [Philadelphia: Westminster, 1963] 128). Montgomery and Gehman further suggest that this officer may also have kept the king's calendar of events and that "the dated data scattered throughout our book" may come from these recorded documents" (*The Book of Kings,* 116). This possible reading has certain attractive features but unfortunately requires changing "sons" and "secretaries" to the singular, an alteration that has no support in the Hebrew manuscript tradition.

Several commentators claim that the next two offices may reflect Egyptian influence, a natural occurrence if Solomon looked to his father-in-law for administrative advice.[16] Though a variety of opinions exists on the actual scope of the "secretaries'" duties, they at least managed the king's home and foreign correspondence.[17] The "recorder," or "the one causing to remember,"[18] may have been "the official protocol officer,"[19] or one who "transmitted and explained royal commands."[20] In other words, the "recorder" was a liaison between the king and the public.

As 1 Kings 1–2 has already stated, Benaiah and Zadok are rewarded for their support of Solomon by being named commander and priest, respectively. Abiathar remains on the list as priest, despite his favoring of Adonijah. This retention of two priests may be due to the delicate political situation at the beginning of Solomon's reign.

Two of Nathan's sons are given high office. Azariah supervises the district officers chronicled in 4:7–19, and Zabud acts as special counsel to the king. No doubt they are both capable men, but it is impossible not to notice how the honest yet clever prophet has been rewarded for his help in Solomon's rise to power. Solomon definitely follows David's advice to punish enemies and repay friends.

Ahishar and Adoniram complete the list. Ahishar becomes quite important as the court expands to fill the new palace Solomon builds (cf. 1 Kgs 7:1–12). Likewise, Adoniram oversees the "forced labor" Solomon will draft from Israel and from vassal nations to work on his many construction projects. Adoniram's job must have made him unpopular, a fact the circumstances of his death illustrates (1 Kgs 12:18).

4:7–19 Because of Israel's size, diversity, and volatile nature, Solomon could not govern it, much less fulfill his later ambitious goals, without an extensive administrative system. Therefore, he names "twelve district governors" responsible for raising the revenue necessary for sustaining the central government. Four details about these appointments deserve further mention. First, Gray states that "the division of the country, if not ignoring the old tribal boundaries, was not rigidly bound by them"[21] (cf. "Survey of Historical Issues Related to 1 Kgs 3:1–4:34" on p. 107). Perhaps Solomon hoped to neutralize old enemies by linking them with nonallies.

---

[16] Cf. S. DeVries, *1 Kings,* WBC 12 (Waco: Word, 1985) 69; Gray, *1 and 2 Kings,* 128; and Jones, *1 and 2 Kings,* 1:135–36.

[17] Cf. Noth's discussion of options in Könige, BKAT 9/1 (Neukirchen-Vluyn: Neukirchener, 1968) 63–64. He concludes that one secretary may have dealt with home affairs and the other with foreign matters.

[18] The word here (הַמַּזְכִּיר) is a *hiphil* participle.

[19] DeVries, *1 Kings,* 69.

[20] Gray, *1 and 2 Kings,* 129.

[21] Ibid., 131.

Second, Solomon makes two of his sons-in-law, Ben-Abinadab and Ahimaaz, governors. Presumably these men could also negate enemies through their family loyalties. Third, Solomon entrusts some men with more territory than others. Though the king does reward his friends, he only places capable ones in power and allows the best of these to gain extensive authority. Again, these tendencies reveal the wisdom in Solomon's leadership style. Fourth, through his God-given ability, Solomon manages to rule all the territory God promised to Abraham. The land Moses desired, Joshua conquered, and David subdued now lay in the hands of a man of unsurpassed wisdom.

Modern readers normally miss the significance of such lists and summaries. What should interpreters gain from this passage? R. Nelson asserts: "The reader is intended to marvel at the complexity of a kingdom requiring such a sophisticated system." The lists also "provide the reader with a sense of reality and verisimilitude. This utopia was no never-never land. It involved real people and real geography."[22] It also involved a real God who provided a wise leader for the covenant nation.

(3) Solomon Levies Taxes (4:20–28)

20The people of Judah and Israel were as numerous as the sand on the seashore; they ate, they drank and they were happy. 21And Solomon ruled over all the kingdoms from the River to the land of the Philistines, as far as the border of Egypt. These countries brought tribute and were Solomon's subjects all his life.

22Solomon's daily provisions were thirty cors of fine flour and sixty cors of meal, 23ten head of stall-fed cattle, twenty of pasture-fed cattle and a hundred sheep and goats, as well as deer, gazelles, roebucks and choice fowl. 24For he ruled over all the kingdoms west of the River, from Tiphsah to Gaza, and had peace on all sides. 25During Solomon's lifetime Judah and Israel, from Dan to Beersheba, lived in safety, each man under his own vine and fig tree.

26Solomon had four thousand stalls for chariot horses, and twelve thousand horses.

27The district officers, each in his month, supplied provisions for King Solomon and all who came to the king's table. They saw to it that nothing was lacking.
28They also brought to the proper place their quotas of barley and straw for the chariot horses and the other horses.

4:20–21 Only prosperity keeps people from resenting large government and new taxes. Israel's population grew steadily during Solomon's era. Food was plentiful, and the nation was in good spirits. Solomon gained both divine and popular favor. Part of this prosperity stemmed from tribute money brought to the king by countries his father had subdued. This needed income came from every corner of the promised land and provided the material bless-

[22] R. D. Nelson, *First and Second Kings,* IBC (Louisville: John Knox, 1987) 40.

ings promised Abraham in Gen 12:1–9.[23]

4:22–26 Such an impressive government required vast resources to continue operations. Estimates of the number of persons Solomon sustained vary from fourteen thousand to thirty-two thousand.[24] Keil contends that these figures are not unusual given what other contemporaries of Solomon spent on their governments and given the many officials Solomon must have employed.[25] Coupled with the military expenditures related to the horses mentioned in 4:26, the money earmarked for the central government appears to be great. Still, the money may have been well spent, since the land was at peace.

4:27–28 As 4:7–19 has already explained, the twelve district governors collected taxes. Over time this burden became too great for the people to bear, so they asked Solomon's successor for relief (1 Kgs 12:1–4). For now, though, Israel seems content that they have finally reached the goal they set almost a century before when they asked Samuel for a king: they are like other prominent nations (cf. 1 Sam 8:5).

It is interesting to realize that at this point in the story the author expresses neither approval nor disapproval of Solomon's activities. Certainly the writer presents Solomon as a man made wise by the Lord. Of course, the people seem happy now. Yet Moses' warnings, especially the one against collecting "great numbers of horses" (cf. Deut 17:14–20), and Samuel's cautions against royal excesses (1 Sam 8:10–18) linger in the minds of seasoned readers. What long-term good can come of such traditionally non-Israelite practices?

(4) Solomon Exhibits Great Breadth of Knowledge (4:29–34)

29God gave Solomon wisdom and very great insight, and a breadth of understanding as measureless as the sand on the seashore. 30Solomon's wisdom was greater than the wisdom of all the men of the East, and greater than all the wisdom of Egypt. 31He was wiser than any other man, including Ethan the Ezrahite—wiser than Heman, Calcol and Darda, the sons of Mahol. And his fame spread to all the surrounding nations. 32He spoke three thousand proverbs and his songs numbered a thousand and five. 33He described plant life, from the cedar of Lebanon to the hyssop that grows out of walls. He also taught about animals and birds, reptiles and fish. 34Men of all nations came to listen to Solomon's wis-

---

[23] The LXX omits 4:20–21,25–26, and part of v. 24, apparently because its translators thought these texts are late explanatory glosses. Gray basically approves of the change (*1 and 2 Kings,* 135), while Montgomery and Gehman disagree because some of the same LXX material appears after 2:46 (*The Book of Kings,* 127). The Hebrew text makes sense as it stands, for the author answers a basic question for the reader, "How did the people feel about all these changes?" For now these new policies are popular.

[24] Cf. Jones, *1 and 2 Kings,* 1:146; and J. Skinner, *I and II Kings,* CB (Edinburgh: T. C. & E. C. Jack, 1904) 95.

[25] C. F. Keil, "I and II Kings," COT, trans. J. Martin (1876; reprint, Grand Rapids: Eerdmans, 1980) 3:52.

dom, sent by all the kings of the world, who had heard of his wisdom.

4:29–34 These verses demonstrate how faithfully God kept his promise to make Solomon wise (cf. Matt 12:42; Luke 11:31). The king's "wisdom and very great insight" have already been proven by his awareness of how to solve the prostitute dilemma and his skill in organizing the government. Now the text states that his wisdom exceeded that of all the wise men of the East, which is quite a compliment given the impressive wisdom writings produced in Babylon, Egypt, and other neighboring lands.[26] To emphasize the point, the author lists otherwise unknown great men Solomon surpassed.

Further, Solomon "spoke three thousand proverbs," or comparisons drawn from life,[27] and wrote 1,005 songs. Many of these proverbs appear in the Book of Proverbs, and the Song of Songs may be one of his compositions.[28] This notation indicates that Solomon's skill in judgment and speech was matched by his artistic gifts. Finally, Solomon possessed knowledge of botany and biology.[29] This type of encyclopedic knowledge was highly valued in the ancient Near East, so it is no wonder his fame spread to other countries.[30] Without question, God has been faithful to the king. Will this faithfulness be returned in kind?

Canonical and Theological Implications in 1 Kgs 3:1–4:34

Students of the whole of Scripture should be cautiously optimistic after reading these chapters. After all, the passage seems strategically placed to inform readers that promises made by God to Abraham about land and blessing (Gen 12:1–9), to David about succession and peace (2 Sam 7:7–17), and to Solomon about leadership skill have come true. Israel enjoys all the benefits that Deuteronomy 27–28 details.

At the same time, a canonical uneasiness lingers. As has been stated, Moses and Samuel warn against wealthy monarchs. Jeremiah expresses similar con-

---

[26] For a selection of wisdom writings from other nations, see *ANET,* 405–40. For surveys of ancient wisdom literature, see R. B. Y. Scott, *The Way of Wisdom in the Old Testament* (New York: Macmillan, 1971); J. L. Crenshaw, *Old Testament Wisdom, An Introduction* (Atlanta: John Knox, 1981) 212–35; J. H. Walton, *Ancient Israelite Literature in Its Cultural Context* (Grand Rapids: Zondervan, 1989) 169–200. See also D. J. Wiseman, "Israel's Literary Neighbors in the Thirteenth Century B.C.," *JNWSL* 5 [1977] 77–91).

[27] This definition of "proverb" seeks to draw together the many types of imagery found in the proverbs themselves. For a detailed study of the word, see W. McKane, *Proverbs,* OTL (Philadelphia: Westminster, 1970) 22–33.

[28] As D. Garrett points out, while the title (1:1) of the Song of Songs "seems to indicate Solomonic authorship," other interpretations are possible (see Garrett, *Proverbs, Ecclesiastes, Song of Songs,* NAC (Nashville: Broadman, 1993) 348–52.

[29] As D. J. Wiseman notes, the cedar of Lebanon was the greatest of trees, and the hyssop was the smallest, especially when stunted by growing from a wall (*1 & 2 Kings,* TOTC [Downers Grove: InterVarsity, 1993] 97).

[30] Cf. Scott, *The Way of Wisdom,* 36.

cerns (Jer 22:13–17). Common sense and human history should cause readers to wonder if power and money will not eventually corrupt the king. Still, God has assured that Solomon has divine approval as long as he keeps the covenant. Only then can this difficult balance between power and piety be maintained.

Several theological ideas converge in these two chapters. First, the whole notion of covenant emerges again, this time in conjunction with the Lord's decision to bless Solomon as long as he is willing to walk in God's ways and obey God's commands (1 Kgs 3:14). As always, the covenant offered entails both obligation and opportunity, and also includes both individual and community ramifications. Second, these texts illustrate the principle of promise-fulfillment in Scripture. Throughout the Bible the Lord pledges to bring certain beneficial events to pass. Sometimes these benefits materialize quickly, while at other times they take some time to occur. For instance, the promise to Abraham that his descendants would possess Canaan took over a thousand years, while Solomon received wisdom in a relatively short time frame. W. C. Kaiser observes that God's promises gave meaning to both the present and future of the Bible characters.[31]

Third, God gives individuals the wisdom to perform the tasks to which they are called. This principle extends into the New Testament, where Paul teaches that God equips believers for ministry (Rom 12:1–8; 1 Cor 12:1–11), and where James asserts that wisdom produces purity and peacemaking (Jas 3:13–18). Solomon correctly assumes that only the Lord can equip him to lead Israel. Fourth, godly leadership requires humility, commitment to God, and administrative insight. Again, these qualities must come from the Lord. Any kind of personal pride or national arrogance is therefore out of place, even dangerous.

Applicational Implications of 1 Kgs 3:1–4:34

Solomon's covenant with God illustrates the primacy of each individual's relationship to the Lord. Certainly the Bible teaches that God makes covenants with groups like Israel and the church, but it specifically teaches that the Lord also desires communion with individuals. Those who seek God's presence and help can indeed receive the wisdom they need to do God's will and serve God's people.

The fact that several promises are fulfilled in 1 Kings 3–4 demonstrates the importance of hope in human life. Abraham, Moses, and David could die in peace because they trusted in the hope of God's promises (cf. Heb 11). They learned to live as if promise and possession were the same. Solomon, on the other hand, enjoyed daily hope as he lived out the wisdom God gave him. He could also know that the Lord's ongoing blessings would benefit his kingdom. Likewise, Scripture offers past, present, and future promises to believers that

[31] W. C. Kaiser, *Toward an Old Testament Theology* (Grand Rapids: Zondervan, 1978) 35.

fit their individual circumstances.

Obviously, leadership is a major issue in the former prophets. The beginning of Solomon's career stands as a basically positive model for leaders who desire to honor God as the source of their ability to lead and who want to help others through their gift of leadership. Prayer and worship appear here as essential components of political, economic, and administrative ability, not as barriers to success in these areas. Still, the canon's previous warnings about leadership's potential excesses warn against thinking that prayer is some magic charm that wards off failure. Faithfulness and righteousness alone please God, and only God decides whether these traits will necessarily bring material wealth or personal recognition.

3. Solomon Builds the Temple and Palace (5:1–7:51)

Political, historical, and theological currents flow together throughout 1, 2 Kings but nowhere more so than in the temple-building stories. Solomon learned the political value of centralizing Israel's religion from David, who brought the ark of the covenant to Jerusalem (2 Sam 6:12–23). Along with placing the royal court in Jerusalem, this move helped solidify David's position as controller of Israel's military, religious, and government systems. Solomon's decision to construct a permanent home for the ark and the worship that surrounded it completed what his father had begun.

The time was right to build a temple. Historical events were never favorable to such an undertaking before, nor would they have been so in the future. Not only was Israel able to subdue their traditional enemies and make peace with Egypt, but David and Solomon had made an alliance with Tyre, a nation that could provide plans and material for a temple. Solomon was wise enough to seize this opportunity for an unprecedented building program.

Though politically advisable and historically possible, it is incorrect to think the temple would have been built regardless of Solomon's theological beliefs. The Davidic promise came as a result of David's desire to build God "a house" (2 Sam 7:1–2). In promising to build David a house (family) instead, the Lord stated that David's son would build the temple David had envisioned. First Chronicles 22:1–19 and 28:1–21 say that David collected some of the material for the project and told Solomon what some of the temple's implements should be. It is not so surprising, then, for Solomon to fulfill his portion of the covenant by finishing what David started. Besides this family concern, Solomon wanted God to bless the people, as 1 Kings 8 will demonstrate. Finally, several times in Deuteronomy Moses predicts that someday God would choose one central place for Israel to worship.[32] This centralization of

[32] Cf. Deut 12:5,11, etc. For a survey of texts in Deuteronomy, the former prophets, and the prophets that stress the central sanctuary, see M. Weinfeld, *Deuteronomy and the Deuteronomic School* (New York: Oxford University Press, 1972) 324ff.

worship would hopefully combat the rise of rival religions and the pollution of Mosaic-covenant faith.

Certainly Solomon's other building projects during this era were significant. His own palace took thirteen years to build (1 Kgs 7:1). He also constructed a hall of justice (1 Kgs 7:7) and a palace for pharaoh's daughter (1 Kgs 7:8). In later years he undertook other significant projects (1 Kgs 9:10–28). The fact that the text mentions these secular pursuits in passing while describing the temple's construction in great detail illustrates the author's writing strategy. For the author, palaces and law courts are not unimportant; they just do not help readers understand God's rule in history to the same extent as the temple. Again, history has been written, but it is a history that places God's activity at its core.

Historical Events Related to 1 Kgs 5:1–9:9

Virtually all of the historical details noted in the comments on 1 Kings 3–4 apply to 5:1–9:9 too, but in addition the reader will observe the importance of Tyre in these accounts. Chapter 5 says that "Hiram king of Tyre" had enjoyed good relations with David and thus sent envoys to Solomon, obviously hoping to continue the alliance (5:1). Solomon sends back a reply that states his plans to build a temple, asks for cedar, requests some laborers, and suggests payment for these favors (5:3–6). Who was Hiram, and why would he help Solomon?

Hiram ruled Tyre, the capital of Phoenicia, for over thirty years, from David's old age until he and Solomon were veteran kings.[33] DeVries observes: "Tyre had a mainland base but occupied also an offshore island, which kept it invulnerable to siege warfare up to the time of Alexander the Great, 333 B.C."[34] From its Mediterranean port Tyre was able to establish an impressive shipping fleet. Israel had aided Tyre's sailing efforts by defeating the Philistines, the other regional power traditionally involved in sea trade.[35] Therefore, an Israel-Tyre alliance was a natural, mutually beneficial result of Israel's newly won prominence. Together the two countries could create a monopoly by exploiting Israel's control of the land-based trade and Tyre's expertise in shipping.

Besides these national common interests, Solomon and Hiram were both aggressive young kings. Both used the historical situation to their advantage. They both expanded their capitals and built central worship centers.[36] Both desired to make their nation wealthy without military conquest, and both suffered when Egypt reasserted its power late in their reigns.

---

[33] Bright, *A History of Israel,* 212.

[34] DeVries, *1 Kings,* 81.

[35] B. Peckham, "Israel and Phoenicia," *Magnalia Dei: The Mighty Acts of God,* ed. F. M. Cross, W. E. Lemke, and P. D. Miller (Garden City: Doubleday, 1976) 231.

[36] Ibid., 232.

One other historical fact deserves mention. Israel's temple building was similar to what many nations were attempting before and during this time period. As was already stated, Hiram himself built worship centers. He "set up a golden pillar in the sanctuary of Baal Shamem, and built new temples to Melqart and Astarte."[37] In *I Have Built You an Exalted House*, his extremely thorough survey of ancient temple buildings, V. Hurowitz charts how nations like Sumeria, Assyria, Babylon, and the Canaanites constructed temples and how they wrote about their projects.[38] Hurowitz concludes, "As far as the thematic structure of the biblical building stories is concerned, it is possible to state that they are all typical, routine ancient Near Eastern building stories."[39]

Besides attesting to the accuracy of the biblical accounts, this observation reminds readers of the literary nature of 1, 2 Kings. Israel is not portrayed as doing odd, astounding things. Rather, their activities, which appear like those of other nations, are significant because of how they display or fail to display Israel's faith in God. They also reflect God acting in history through a chosen people. Thus, the uniqueness of the events lies in the inherent meaning that emerges from a people responding faithfully to the one true God who alone deserves worship.

(1) Hiram of Tyre Provides Temple Materials (5:1–12)

1When Hiram king of Tyre heard that Solomon had been anointed king to succeed his father David, he sent his envoys to Solomon, because he had always been on friendly terms with David. 2Solomon sent back this message to Hiram:

> **3"You know that because of the wars waged against my father David from all sides, he could not build a temple for the Name of the LORD his God until the LORD put his enemies under his feet. 4But now the LORD my God has given me rest on every side, and there is no adversary or disaster. 5I intend, therefore, to build a temple for the Name of the LORD my God, as the LORD told my father David, when he said, 'Your son whom I will put on the throne in your place will build the temple for my Name.'**
>
> **6"So give orders that cedars of Lebanon be cut for me. My men will work with yours, and I will pay you for your men whatever wages you set. You know that we have no one so skilled in felling timber as the Sidonians."**

7When Hiram heard Solomon's message, he was greatly pleased and said, "Praise be to the LORD today, for he has given David a wise son to rule over this great nation."

---

[37] Ibid.

[38] V. Hurowitz, *I Have Built You an Exalted House: Temple Building in the Bible in Light of Mesopotamian and Northwest Semitic Writing*, JSOTS 115 (Sheffield: Sheffield Academic Press, 1992). Also note the examination of kingship and temple building in B. Halpern, *The Constitution of the Monarchy in Israel*, HSM 25 (Chico, Cal.: Scholars Press, 1981) 19-24.

[39] Hurowitz, *I Have Built You an Exalted House*, 126.

[8]So Hiram sent word to Solomon:

"I have received the message you sent me and will do all you want in providing the cedar and pine logs. [9]My men will haul them down from Lebanon to the sea, and I will float them in rafts by sea to the place you specify. There I will separate them and you can take them away. And you are to grant my wish by providing food for my royal household."

[10]In this way Hiram kept Solomon supplied with all the cedar and pine logs he wanted, [11]and Solomon gave Hiram twenty thousand cors of wheat as food for his household, in addition to twenty thousand baths of pressed olive oil. Solomon continued to do this for Hiram year after year. [12]The LORD gave Solomon wisdom, just as he had promised him. There were peaceful relations between Hiram and Solomon, and the two of them made a treaty.

5:1–7 Second Samuel 5:11 records the fact that Hiram "sent messengers to David, along with cedar logs and carpenters and stonemasons, and they built a palace for David." This episode explains the "friendly terms" between Hiram and David. Eager to maintain his mutually beneficial relationship with Israel, Hiram sends his representatives to welcome Solomon to the throne. Like Solomon, Hiram makes wise decisions at key times.

Solomon seizes the chance for Tyre to help him as they once helped his father and to maintain the relationship between the nations. Long correctly states that Solomon's response to Hiram continues the text's emphasis on God's making the king wise (cf. 1 Kgs 3:12–13). Here Solomon is "wise in statecraft, gaining international agreements, establishing peaceful conditions in the kingdom, laying the groundwork for building activities."[40] So far the Lord has given Solomon judicial (3:16–28), administrative (4:1–28), intellectual (4:29–34), and political (5:1–7) skill. Any one of these abilities is impressive in its own right. As a group they are awe-inspiring. God's faithfulness is evident.

The letter to Hiram itself is structured in a common ancient format[41] but is composed in covenantal terms. For instance, Solomon says that David could not build the temple until "the LORD put his enemies under his feet." Then he adds that "the LORD my God has given me peace [lit., "rest"] on every side," language that reminds readers of Joshua's conquest of the promised land (cf. Josh 11:23). Finally, Solomon bases his desire to build on God's promises to David in 2 Samuel 7, which removes any notion that he only loves God because of the success he has enjoyed. It is a theological reading of history that encourages Solomon to seek Hiram's help, not just a sense of political expediency. With good reason, Hiram is pleased with Solomon's answer, and his own response in 5:7 affirms that God has kept all promises made to David.

---

[40] Long, *1 Kings,* 80.

[41] Hurowitz, *I Have Built You an Exalted House,* 109-10.

5:8–12 Hiram's return message basically agrees to Solomon's requests in 5:6. Tyre will provide "cedar and pine logs" by floating "them in rafts by sea to the place you specify." Two alterations are made in Solomon's request. The men from Tyre and Israel will not work together, and Hiram wants food for the "royal household" instead of wages for his workers.[42] These terms are met, the nations remain at peace, the kings make a treaty, and temple construction is under way. Again, this whole episode demonstrates God's gracious giving of wisdom to Solomon.

(2) Solomon Conscripts Workers (5:13–18)

[13]King Solomon conscripted laborers from all Israel—thirty thousand men. [14]He sent them off to Lebanon in shifts of ten thousand a month, so that they spent one month in Lebanon and two months at home. Adoniram was in charge of the forced labor. [15]Solomon had seventy thousand carriers and eighty thousand stonecutters in the hills, [16]as well as thirty-three hundred foremen who supervised the project and directed the workmen. [17]At the king's command they removed from the quarry large blocks of quality stone to provide a foundation of dressed stone for the temple. [18]The craftsmen of Solomon and Hiram and the men of Gebal cut and prepared the timber and stone for the building of the temple.

5:13–18 In order to have enough workers to complete his project, Solomon finds it necessary to institute the unpopular practice of drafting laborers. This imposition on commoners was used by many ancient nations. Even David used forced, or corvée, labor. R. D. Patterson and H. J. Austel explain: "In the list of David's officials, Adoniram is said to be over the forced labor. This would indicate that David used the corvée system to a limited degree. . . . Solomon, however, used it extensively. The more splendid the royal court, the greater the demand on the people."[43] At least those conscripted are allowed eight months at home alongside their four months of forced labor.

Scholars disagree about the identity of the thirty thousand Israelite laborers mentioned in 5:13. Part of the problem stems from 1 Kgs 9:20–22, which describes Solomon's forced labor, then states, "But Solomon did not make slaves of any of the Israelites" (9:22). Gray, Skinner, Matheney, and others think these two references (5:13–18 and 9:20–22) contradict each other.[44] Keil, Patterson and Austel, and Jones disagree.[45] Linguistic analysis may help explain the perceived contradiction, since the text uses different terminology

---

[42] Cf. Jones' discussion of the arrangements in *1 and 2 Kings,* 1:156.

[43] R. D. Patterson and H. J. Austel, "1, 2 Kings," EBC (Grand Rapids: Zondervan, 1988) 4:59.

[44] Gray, *1 and 2 Kings*, 148; Skinner, *I and II Kings*, 102; M. P. Matheney, "1 Kings," BBC (Nashville: Broadman, 1970) 3:172.

[45] Keil, "I and II Kings," 62-63; Patterson and Austel, "1, 2 Kings," 59; Jones, *1 and 2 Kings*, 1:157–58.

to describe the laborers in 5:13–18 and 9:20–22. In the former text they are called simply "laborers" (*mas*) while in the latter they are called "servant [slave] laborers" (*mas ʿobēd*). Apparently, the Israelite workers were required only to toil four months of the year until the task was done. Forced labor does not necessarily entail slavery. On the other hand, foreign workers were permanently assigned to forced labor.

Another difficulty arises when one compares 5:15–16; 1 Kgs 9:23; 2 Chr 2:17–18; 8:10. The first passage mentions 150,000 laborers beyond the 30,000 listed in 5:13 and also states that 3,300 foremen "supervised the project and directed the workmen." On the other hand, 1 Kgs 9:23 says 550 officials led the work project. Further, 2 Chr 2:17–18 states that the 150,000 were non-Israelites and that 3,600 foremen were assigned "to keep the people working." Finally, 2 Chr 8:10 claims 250 officials supervised the forced labor. Interestingly enough, Kings and Chronicles each arrives at 150,000 foreign workers and 3850 foremen, but by counting them differently. The exact numbers make an outright contradiction unlikely. Why the variance? Keil probably answers this question when he writes:

> We must therefore follow J. H. Michaelis, and explain the differences as resulting from a different method of classification, namely, from the fact that in the Chronicles the Canaanitish overseers are distinguished from the Israelitish (viz. 3600 Canaanites and 250 Israelites), whereas in the books of Kings the *inferiores et superiores prefecti* are distinguished. Consequently Solomon had 3300 inferior overseers and 550 superior (or superintendents), of whom 250 were selected from the Israelites and 300 from the Canaanites.[46]

The forced laborers had two simple yet time-consuming and backbreaking tasks. They were to quarry and fashion the temple's huge foundation stones. They also "cut and prepared the timber and stone" necessary for the main portion of the temple. Given the nature of this work, it is no wonder many men were needed, and it is no wonder only conscripted men would attempt the task.

(3) Building the Temple (6:1–10)

1In the four hundred and eightieth year after the Israelites had come out of Egypt, in the fourth year of Solomon's reign over Israel, in the month of Ziv, the second month, he began to build the temple of the LORD.

2The temple that King Solomon built for the LORD was sixty cubits long, twenty wide and thirty high. 3The portico at the front of the main hall of the temple extended the width of the temple, that is twenty cubits, and projected ten cubits from the front of the temple. 4He made narrow clerestory windows in the temple. 5Against the walls of the main hall and inner sanctuary he built a structure around the building, in which there were side rooms. 6The lowest floor was

---

[46] Keil, "I and II Kings," 62.

five cubits wide, the middle floor six cubits and the third floor seven. He made offset ledges around the outside of the temple so that nothing would be inserted into the temple walls.

[7]In building the temple, only blocks dressed at the quarry were used, and no hammer, chisel or any other iron tool was heard at the temple site while it was being built.

[8]The entrance to the lowest floor was on the south side of the temple; a stairway led up to the middle level and from there to the third. [9]So he built the temple and completed it, roofing it with beams and cedar planks. [10]And he built the side rooms all along the temple. The height of each was five cubits, and they were attached to the temple by beams of cedar.

Scholars particularly interested in the author's use of source material are often perplexed by certain features of the building accounts in chaps. 6–7. First of all, the Greek translation omits certain verses and rearranges the chapters.[47] Second, the temple building stories are "interrupted" by details about the palace's construction. Third, the author includes some editorial comments on the events described. Each of these tendencies is common in 1, 2 Kings and is discussed in the introduction to this commentary. Therefore, it is sufficient at this point to say that in many places the Septuagint attempts to "smooth" texts yet sometimes, as in chaps. 6–7, really only confuses matters. Further, the fact that the author presents the material in a selective order and comments upon it is hardly surprising. Placing the sacred alongside the secular is one of the book's common narrative strategies. Finally, this selectivity in no way compromises the account's historical integrity. Indeed, the temple's size and design coincide with similar buildings of that era,[48] a fact that testifies to the story's accuracy.

6:1 Solomon starts building the temple 480 years after the exodus. This reference reminds readers that the permanent worship center is one more proof that God has given Israel the promised land.[49] The tabernacle was a portable shrine, but the temple reflects permanence. Israel once moved from place to place, but now they have settled down with the intention of never wandering again.

Because the actual date of the exodus continues to be debated, commentators differ on the meaning of the 480 years. This disagreement crosses normal traditional and nontraditional boundaries.[50] Those who believe in a ca. 1450

---

[47] DeVries summarizes the situation by noting that the LXX "omits MT vv 11–13, 18, 21a, 22a, 31b–33a, 38b, and rearranges the text so that English/MT material appears in the sequence: 1, 6–7, 9–15, 8, 16–34, 4–5" (*1 Kings,* 87).

[48] Hurowitz, *I Have Built You an Exalted House,* 251–56.

[49] Cf. Keil, "I and II Kings," 66–67.

[50] For arguments for a thirteenth-century exodus see R. K. Harrison, *Introduction to the Old Testament* (Grand Rapids: Eerdmans, 1969) 174–77; K. A. Kitchen, *Ancient Orient and Old Testament* (Chicago: InterVarsity, 1966) 57–75. A fifteenth-century date is argued by J. J. Bimson, *Redating the Exodus and Conquest,* 2d ed., JSOTSup 5 (Sheffield: Almond, 1981); G. L. Archer, *A Survey of Old Testament Introduction,* rev. ed. (Chicago: Moody, 1979) 223–34; E. H. Merrill, *Kingdom of Priests* (Grand Rapids: Baker, 1987) 58–75.

B.C. date for the exodus think the 480 years is a rounded, yet accurate number,[51] while those who date the exodus ca. 1290–1250 B.C. argue that the author has approximated the years from the number of generations between the exodus, the temple's construction, and the exile, or that the number has symbolic significance. It is not the purpose of this volume to settle exodus issues, so it suffices to state that the important reference for this study is that construction began in Solomon's fourth year (ca. 966 B.C.). No one seriously questions that notation's accuracy. Early in his reign Solomon built the temple, which represented God's placement of Israel in the land and which fulfilled David's wishes.

6:2–10 DeVries observes that "in vv 2–10 . . . the narrator tells about the temple, the porch, the windows, the platform, and the stories, with door and stairway."[52] These items' dimensions are also listed. A more detailed description of the interior appears in 6:14–38. Certain features deserve to be summarized. First, the temple was about ninety feet long, thirty feet wide, and forty-five feet high.[53] By modern standards it was a fairly small worship center. Second, it had a portico, or porch (6:3), which ran "the width of the temple" and projected out "from the front of the temple" (6:3). Third, it was a three-story complex (6:6).[54] Fourth, its various portions were carefully shaped at their quarries, then fitted, without hammering, on site (6:7). Fifth, its frame and beams were cedar (6:9). Sixth, the facility included a number of "side rooms" (6:10) that probably were set aside for the priests' use. In other words, the building was attractive, yet functional.

(4) God's Promises concerning the Temple (6:11–13)

[11]The word of the LORD came to Solomon: [12]"As for this temple you are building, if you follow my decrees, carry out my regulations and keep all my commands and obey them, I will fulfill through you the promise I gave to David your father. [13]And I will live among the Israelites and will not abandon my people Israel."

6:11–13 Throughout the Solomon stories the author presents an activity, then waits until later to state God's approval or disapproval of it. For example, 3:1–15 expresses approval of Solomon's rise to power in chaps. 1–2, and 5:12 explains that the decisions in 5:1–7 demonstrate God-given wisdom. This strategy continues here, where, through some unspecified manner, Solomon

---

[51] Patterson and Austel, "1, 2 Kings," 61.

[52] DeVries, *1 Kings*, 95.

[53] This approximation is based on the general assumption that a cubit was about eighteen inches long.

[54] See the diagram in D. J. Wiseman, *1 & 2 Kings*, TOTC (Downers Grove: InterVarsity, 1993) 108. A more thorough study of architectural details may be found in C. J. Davey, "Temples of the Levant and the Buildings of Solomon," *TynBul* 31 (1980) 107-46.

receives God's word about the temple.

Once more the Lord bases Solomon's (and Israel's) success on covenant faithfulness. As David told him in 2:1–4, Solomon must obey God's word. Only then can the temple have lasting significance, and only then can the nation as a whole enjoy God's favor. This reminder of the Mosaic and Davidic covenants, and of earlier texts such as 2:1–4 and 3:10–15, reemphasizes the nature of Israel's place in history. Great kings and great buildings can and will be replaced if disobedience becomes a way of life. On the other hand, eternal blessings will result from consistent obedience. Solomon must not forget these things in the midst of all his busy success.

(5) Furnishing the Temple (6:14–38)

[14]So Solomon built the temple and completed it. [15]He lined its interior walls
with cedar boards, paneling them from the floor of the temple to the ceiling, and
covered the floor of the temple with planks of pine. [16]He partitioned off twenty
cubits at the rear of the temple with cedar boards from floor to ceiling to form
within the temple an inner sanctuary, the Most Holy Place. [17]The main hall in
front of this room was forty cubits long. [18]The inside of the temple was cedar,
carved with gourds and open flowers. Everything was cedar; no stone was to be
seen.

[19]He prepared the inner sanctuary within the temple to set the ark of the cov-
enant of the LORD there. [20]The inner sanctuary was twenty cubits long, twenty
wide and twenty high. He overlaid the inside with pure gold, and he also overlaid
the altar of cedar. [21]Solomon covered the inside of the temple with pure gold, and
he extended gold chains across the front of the inner sanctuary, which was over-
laid with gold. [22]So he overlaid the whole interior with gold. He also overlaid with
gold the altar that belonged to the inner sanctuary.

[23]In the inner sanctuary he made a pair of cherubim of olive wood, each ten
cubits high. [24]One wing of the first cherub was five cubits long, and the other
wing five cubits—ten cubits from wing tip to wing tip. [25]The second cherub also
measured ten cubits, for the two cherubim were identical in size and shape. [26]The
height of each cherub was ten cubits. [27]He placed the cherubim inside the inner-
most room of the temple, with their wings spread out. The wing of one cherub
touched one wall, while the wing of the other touched the other wall, and their
wings touched each other in the middle of the room. [28]He overlaid the cherubim
with gold.

[29]On the walls all around the temple, in both the inner and outer rooms, he
carved cherubim, palm trees and open flowers. [30]He also covered the floors of
both the inner and outer rooms of the temple with gold.

[31]For the entrance of the inner sanctuary he made doors of olive wood with
five-sided jambs. [32]And on the two olive wood doors he carved cherubim, palm
trees and open flowers, and overlaid the cherubim and palm trees with beaten
gold. [33]In the same way he made four-sided jambs of olive wood for the entrance
to the main hall. [34]He also made two pine doors, each having two leaves that

turned in sockets. [35]He carved cherubim, palm trees and open flowers on them and overlaid them with gold hammered evenly over the carvings.

[36]And he built the inner courtyard of three courses of dressed stone and one course of trimmed cedar beams.

[37]The foundation of the temple of the LORD was laid in the fourth year, in the month of Ziv. [38]In the eleventh year in the month of Bul, the eighth month, the temple was finished in all its details according to its specifications. He had spent seven years building it.

6:14–28 Having given a general description of the edifice's exterior, the author now focuses on its interior. After a comment that all inside stones were covered with cedar panels (6:15), the holy of holies or "Most Holy Place" is described. This was the resting place of the ark of the covenant and the scene of the annual atonement for the nation's sin (cf. Lev 16). Thirty feet were set aside at the rear of the sanctuary for this special room, so it occupied one-third of the temple's space (6:16). Like the rest of the interior, the most holy place was overlaid with gold.

Two cherubim, each about fifteen feet high, grace the most holy place. From one extreme wing tip to the other the two carved pieces span the width of the room. Perhaps these figures are guardians of the ark, since cherubim guard Eden in Gen 3:24 and Ezek 28:13–14.[55] Other possibilities include that these creatures represent God's personal chariot (cf. 2 Sam 22:8ff. and Ps 18:8ff.) or even his throne.[56] All of these theories stress God's presence in the temple. God will choose to dwell wherever the ark rests.

6:29–36 The other sixty feet of the sanctuary are also overlaid with gold. Carvings of "cherubim, palm trees and open flowers" cover the walls and inner doors. Clearly, Solomon intends to decorate his temple as attractively as possible. He thereby competes well with other kings involved in similar projects.

6:37–38 About seven years and six months are needed to complete the temple.[57] Though not his largest or most ornate construction, this is the most important facility Solomon ever builds. It stands for nearly four centuries and is the only Solomonic structure the Israelites rebuild after the exile. As time passes, the nation learns to look to the temple as a sign of their relationship to God. For now, however, the people will have to make the transition from a more austere place of worship to this new, ornately decorated temple.

(6) Palace Construction (7:1–12)

[1]It took Solomon thirteen years, however, to complete the construction of his palace. [2]He built the Palace of the Forest of Lebanon a hundred cubits long, fifty

---

[55] Cf. Gray, *1 and 2 Kings,* 161–62.

[56] Montgomery and Gehman, *Kings,* 155–56.

[57] DeVries, *1 Kings,* 96.

wide and thirty high, with four rows of cedar columns supporting trimmed cedar beams. [3]It was roofed with cedar above the beams that rested on the columns—forty-five beams, fifteen to a row. [4]Its windows were placed high in sets of three, facing each other. [5]All the doorways had rectangular frames; they were in the front part in sets of three, facing each other.

[6]He made a colonnade fifty cubits long and thirty wide. In front of it was a portico, and in front of that were pillars and an overhanging roof.

[7]He built the throne hall, the Hall of Justice, where he was to judge, and he covered it with cedar from floor to ceiling. [8]And the palace in which he was to live, set farther back, was similar in design. Solomon also made a palace like this hall for Pharaoh's daughter, whom he had married.

[9]All these structures, from the outside to the great courtyard and from foundation to eaves, were made of blocks of high-grade stone cut to size and trimmed with a saw on their inner and outer faces. [10]The foundations were laid with large stones of good quality, some measuring ten cubits and some eight. [11]Above were high-grade stones, cut to size, and cedar beams. [12]The great courtyard was surrounded by a wall of three courses of dressed stone and one course of trimmed cedar beams, as was the inner courtyard of the temple of the LORD with its portico.

7:1–12 Inserted between the building and furnishing of the temple, this palace construction story shows that Solomon's secular interests never cease and that these interests cost more than his religious one. The palace takes nearly twice as long to finish. Presumably it is also larger and more costly. Some of these differences are natural, given the constant use of the royal residence and hall of justice. Still, the close proximity of 6:37–38 and 7:1 make the contrast quite obvious, even startling. The author again leaves doubt about the king in the reader's mind, much as was done in the slave labor and taxation passages.

Solomon's palace complex consisted of five parts: "the Palace of the Forest of Lebanon," a hall of pillars, "the Hall of Justice," a palace for himself, and a palace for Pharaoh's daughter.[58] Positioned adjacent to the temple,[59] these connected buildings provided living quarters for the royal family and their retainers as well as a place for the king to decide cases. Since she is given such preferential treatment, Pharaoh's daughter is either the primary queen or simply a wife whose father must not be disappointed.

Fine stone and wood are used in these structures. Indeed, Solomon has built himself an impressive home. Is this project self-indulgence or another example of God's blessing? The author does not comment, though readers must wonder if this extravagance is in keeping with Moses' declaration that kings "must not accumulate large amounts of silver and gold" (Deut 17:17). At least it is quite possible that DeVries is correct in writing: "He did everything imaginable to

[58] The linguistic construction אֶת־כָּל־בֵּיתוֹ implies a joined structure.

[59] Bright, *A History of Israel*, 217–18.

show that, as Yahweh was a great God, he was a great king. What is displayed here is far more Solomon's 'riches and honor' than his 'wisdom.' His was undoubtedly the piety of worldly success."[60]

(7) Furnishing the Temple (7:13–51)

13King Solomon sent to Tyre and brought Huram, 14whose mother was a widow from the tribe of Naphtali and whose father was a man of Tyre and a craftsman in bronze. Huram was highly skilled and experienced in all kinds of bronze work. He came to King Solomon and did all the work assigned to him.

15He cast two bronze pillars, each eighteen cubits high and twelve cubits around, by line. 16He also made two capitals of cast bronze to set on the tops of the pillars; each capital was five cubits high. 17A network of interwoven chains festooned the capitals on top of the pillars, seven for each capital. 18He made pomegranates in two rows encircling each network to decorate the capitals on top of the pillars. He did the same for each capital. 19The capitals on top of the pillars in the portico were in the shape of lilies, four cubits high. 20On the capitals of both pillars, above the bowl-shaped part next to the network, were the two hundred pomegranates in rows all around. 21He erected the pillars at the portico of the temple. The pillar to the south he named Jakin and the one to the north Boaz. 22The capitals on top were in the shape of lilies. And so the work on the pillars was completed.

23He made the Sea of cast metal, circular in shape, measuring ten cubits from rim to rim and five cubits high. It took a line of thirty cubits to measure around it. 24Below the rim, gourds encircled it—ten to a cubit. The gourds were cast in two rows in one piece with the Sea.

25The Sea stood on twelve bulls, three facing north, three facing west, three facing south and three facing east. The Sea rested on top of them, and their hindquarters were toward the center. 26It was a handbreadth in thickness, and its rim was like the rim of a cup, like a lily blossom. It held two thousand baths.

27He also made ten movable stands of bronze; each was four cubits long, four wide and three high. 28This is how the stands were made: They had side panels attached to uprights. 29On the panels between the uprights were lions, bulls and cherubim—and on the uprights as well. Above and below the lions and bulls were wreaths of hammered work. 30Each stand had four bronze wheels with bronze axles, and each had a basin resting on four supports, cast with wreaths on each side. 31On the inside of the stand there was an opening that had a circular frame one cubit deep. This opening was round, and with its basework it measured a cubit and a half. Around its opening there was engraving. The panels of the stands were square, not round. 32The four wheels were under the panels, and the axles of the wheels were attached to the stand. The diameter of each wheel was a cubit and a half. 33The wheels were made like chariot wheels; the axles, rims, spokes and hubs were all of cast metal.

---

60 DeVries, *1 Kings,* 103.

**[34]Each stand had four handles, one on each corner, projecting from the stand.
[35]At the top of the stand there was a circular band half a cubit deep. The supports
and panels were attached to the top of the stand. [36]He engraved cherubim, lions
and palm trees on the surfaces of the supports and on the panels, in every available space, with wreaths all around. [37]This is the way he made the ten stands.
They were all cast in the same molds and were identical in size and shape.**

**[38]He then made ten bronze basins, each holding forty baths and measuring
four cubits across, one basin to go on each of the ten stands. [39]He placed five of
the stands on the south side of the temple and five on the north. He placed the Sea
on the south side, at the southeast corner of the temple. [40]He also made the basins
and shovels and sprinkling bowls.**

So Huram finished all the work he had undertaken for King Solomon in the temple of the LORD:

[41]the two pillars;
the two bowl-shaped capitals on top of the pillars;
the two sets of network decorating the two bowl-shaped capitals on top of the pillars;
[42]the four hundred pomegranates for the two sets of network (two rows of pomegranates for each network, decorating the bowl-shaped capitals on top
of the pillars);
[43]the ten stands with their ten basins;
[44]the Sea and the twelve bulls under it;
[45]the pots, shovels and sprinkling bowls.

**All these objects that Huram made for King Solomon for the temple of the
LORD were of burnished bronze. [46]The king had them cast in clay molds in the
plain of the Jordan between Succoth and Zarethan. [47]Solomon left all these
things unweighed, because there were so many; the weight of the bronze was not
determined.**

[48]Solomon also made all the furnishings that were in the LORD's temple:

the golden altar;
the golden table on which was the bread of the Presence;
[49]the lampstands of pure gold (five on the right and five on the left, in front of the inner sanctuary);
the gold floral work and lamps and tongs;
[50]the pure gold basins, wick trimmers, sprinkling bowls, dishes and censers; and the gold sockets for the doors of the innermost room, the Most Holy Place, and also for the doors of the main hall of the temple.

[51]When all the work King Solomon had done for the temple of the LORD was finished, he brought in the things his father David had dedicated—the silver and gold and the furnishings—and he placed them in the treasuries of the LORD's temple.

7:13–14 In order to furnish the temple properly, Solomon once again looks to Tyre for assistance. He secures Hiram,[61] a workman of mixed Israelite and Tyrian descent. Hiram is "filled with wisdom, and understanding, and knowledge to do all sorts of work in bronze."[62] This threefold ability is reminiscent of Bezalel and Oholiab, the men who made the furnishings for the tabernacle (cf. Exod 31:1–11; 35:30ff.). The author wants readers to know that a man of similar skill is on the job now. Careful artistry can be expected.

7:15–22 Hiram fashions four basic items and their accessories in 7:15–47. Each of these items is cast in bronze. The first is "two bronze pillars," which he fits with "bowl-shaped capitals," "interwoven chains," that fix the capitals on the pillars, and "pomegranates . . . to decorate the capitals on top of the pillars." These pillars are placed "at the portico of the temple." One is placed to the south and is named Jakin, while one is erected to the south and is called Boaz. The name Jakin, which does not appear prominently elsewhere in Scripture, means "he establishes." Of course, Boaz ("by him he is mighty") is David's grandfather, so this pillar most likely refers in some way to the Davidic dynasty.

It is not entirely clear what these pillars represent. Keil believes they symbolize the strength and stability of the kingdom of God in Israel.[63] Gray suggests they "may symbolize the presence and permanence of Yahweh and the king."[64] Jones combines these two ideas, for he argues that the pillars "symbolized the covenant between God and his people, and especially between him and the Davidic dynasty."[65] Certainly worshipers would see the impressive monuments and reflect on all these ideas. God's strength and Israel's stability are both highlighted in the Davidic Covenant. Any real future the nation has depends on both God's power and the line of David's faithfulness to the Lord and the people.

7:23–26 Next, Hiram fashions a large holding tank for water called "the Sea" (7:23). Round in shape and lipped at the top, this basin could hold about 11,500 gallons of water. Despite the Sea's being seven feet high, 2 Chr 4:6 states that it "was used by the priests for washing" themselves. It therefore had the symbolic function of being the place where the priests could cleanse themselves before and after performing their duties.

Twelve bulls undergirded the Sea. Gray thinks these bulls represent the infil-

[61] Though the NIV reads "Huram," here the name is spelled חִירָם, which is identical to the name for the king of Tyre. Second Chronicles 2:13 and 4:16 give the name "Huram" (חוּרָם) for this workman yet spell the king's name "Huram" as well in 2 Chr 2:11. Thus, both books are consistent in their rendering of the men's names.

[62] Author's translation.

[63] Keil, "I and II Kings," 103.

[64] Gray, *1 and 2 Kings,* 175.

[65] Jones, *1 and 2 Kings,* 1:183.

tration of Baal imagery into Israel's religion.[66] It is more likely, however, that the twelve bulls represent either the twelve tribes of Israel or Solomon's twelve administrative districts.[67] Certainly Solomon was not above using patterns from other cultures, or the temple would never have been built. Still, the number of bulls cautions against automatically accepting Gray's interpretation.

7:27–39 Hiram's third project was to make "ten movable stands" to hold basins for water needed in the various temple rituals. Bulls, cherubim, and lions appeared on carved side panels. Each of the stands had four wheels, so they could be used in different parts of the temple court. The top of the stand was decorated with cherubim, lions, and palm trees. Even these utterly functional objects were given elegance, style, and beauty. Holy objects in this temple were useful *and* attractive, a combination rare in the history of ritual and worship.

Ten bronze basins, each able to hold about 230 gallons of water, were then fashioned "to go on each of the ten stands." Five units were placed on the south side of the temple and five on the north. Along with the Sea, these vessels held sufficient water for priestly cleansing, the ritual washing of animals, and the removal of blood and refuse from the area.

7:40–47 Fourth, and finally, Hiram made the smaller basins, as well as "shovels and sprinkling bowls." Such implements were used where temple ceremonies required less water. The summary of Hiram's work presented in 1 Kgs 7:41–45 reminds readers of the size of his task and of the quality of his work. His craftsmanship took planning and skill and required him to know how to transport his molds and finished products from "the plain of the Jordan" to the capital city. Surely this man on loan from Tyre deserves to be remembered with Oholiab and Bezalel as one whose wisdom was revealed through the art work and practical items he creatively crafted.

7:48–51 Solomon completes the temple's furnishing by having its internal utensils made. Most of these items correspond to virtually identical furnishings in the tabernacle. Four implements and two types of decorations are mentioned. First, "the golden altar" is not described at length but "probably was an altar of incense like that described in Exod 30:1–4, and it probably stood in front of the Most Holy Place."[68] The Exodus passage indicates that this altar was "for burning incense" (Exod 30:1), a practice that most likely symbolized Israel's prayers rising to God day and night. Second, Solomon made "the golden table on which was the bread of the Presence." This bread represented the Lord's presence among, and provision for, the chosen people (cf. Exod 25:30).

Third, ten lampstands are fashioned. Five were placed on each side of the

[66] Gray, *1 and 2 Kings,* 178.
[67] Cf. Jones, *1 and 2 Kings,* 1:184.
[68] R. L. Hubbard, *First and Second Kings,* EBC (Chicago: Moody Press, 1991) 51.

"front of the inner sanctuary." A similar lampstand existed in the tabernacle (cf. Exod 25:31–40). R. Honeycutt concludes that that lampstand "served three purposes: (1) functional, for it gave light to an otherwise dark place; (2) aesthetic, lending 'glory and beauty' to the holy place, for which there is a proper and continuing need; and (3) symbolic, conveying the concept of life through both the tree of life and light."[69] Certainly this newer light source had similar significance. Gold floral patterns decorated the lampstand.

Fourth, "basins, wick trimmers, sprinkling bowls, dishes and censers" were made for the various rituals in the temple. Like all the other major furnishings and adornments, these small items were made of gold. Finally, the author notes the various "sockets for the doors" that were fashioned.

One last task remains. Solomon brings all the items David dedicated for the temple (cf. 2 Sam 8:11; 1 Chr 22:14) to the temple's treasury. This action was practical, since these riches were an endowment that helped with temple expenses. Solomon's act here also honors his father's long-term commitment to the Lord and the Lord's house. David's dream of building a temple is finally realized years after his death. Thus, his faith continues to be a witness to Israel and to the readers of 1, 2 Kings.

4. Solomon Dedicates the Temple (8:1–66)

Chapter 8 is one of the most theologically significant texts in 1, 2 Kings. Here readers encounter more than the pomp, ceremony, and ritual associated with major religious building dedications. The author certainly includes these details yet also selects the aspects of the ceremony that underscore Israel's theological heritage. Whether in describing the procession to the temple, Solomon's prayers and speeches, or the Lord's reaction to the scene, the writer interweaves into the story awe, theological history, warnings, and encouragements. This chapter also acts as a completion of the promises God made to Abraham, Moses, and David as well as a warning of how the nation will disintegrate.

Two narratives frame three orations in this chapter. How the ark of the covenant was brought from the tent of meeting is described first (8:1–13), and the sacrifices offered after the orations complete the dedication (8:62–66). In between these accounts Solomon first gratefully tells the audience of God's greatness (8:14–21). Next, the king offers a prayer that contains seven petitions for himself and the people (8:22–53). These petitions contain a summary of the major elements of the Lord's covenant with Israel. Finally, Solomon exhorts the people to receive God's blessings by keeping their covenant with the Lord (8:54–61). Clearly, this section is carefully crafted to express the theological importance of an event that is historically significant in its own right.

---

[69] R. L. Honeycutt, "Exodus," BBC (Nashville: Broadman, 1973) 1:67.

(1) Bringing the Ark to the Temple (8:1–13)

**[1]Then King Solomon summoned into his presence at Jerusalem the elders of
Israel, all the heads of the tribes and the chiefs of the Israelite families, to bring
up the ark of the LORD's covenant from Zion, the City of David. [2]All the men of
Israel came together to King Solomon at the time of the festival in the month of
Ethanim, the seventh month.**

**[3]When all the elders of Israel had arrived, the priests took up the ark, [4]and
they brought up the ark of the LORD and the Tent of Meeting and all the sacred
furnishings in it. The priests and Levites carried them up, [5]and King Solomon
and the entire assembly of Israel that had gathered about him were before the
ark, sacrificing so many sheep and cattle that they could not be recorded or
counted.**

**[6]The priests then brought the ark of the LORD's covenant to its place in the
inner sanctuary of the temple, the Most Holy Place, and put it beneath the wings
of the cherubim. [7]The cherubim spread their wings over the place of the ark and
overshadowed the ark and its carrying poles. [8]These poles were so long that their
ends could be seen from the Holy Place in front of the inner sanctuary, but not
from outside the Holy Place; and they are still there today. [9]There was nothing in
the ark except the two stone tablets that Moses had placed in it at Horeb, where
the LORD made a covenant with the Israelites after they came out of Egypt.**

**[10]When the priests withdrew from the Holy Place, the cloud filled the temple
of the LORD. [11]And the priests could not perform their service because of the
cloud, for the glory of the LORD filled his temple.**

**[12]Then Solomon said, "The LORD has said that he would dwell in a dark
cloud; [13]I have indeed built a magnificent temple for you, a place for you to dwell
forever."**

8:1 Every segment of Israelite leadership—the "elders," the "heads," and the "chiefs"—helps bring the ark to its new resting place. Israel's "elders" were older, respected leaders who advised the king on various national matters. The "heads of the tribes" were also mature older men. Hubbard says, "They were the titular 'chiefs of the Israelite families,' the ones responsible for learning the law and leading their families to obey it."[70] These individuals were to clans and villages what the elders were to the nation as a whole. All the common men join the procession too (v. 2), so Solomon clearly has broad-based support for moving the heart of Israel's national worship to the new site.

The ark had previously been housed in "Zion, the City of David," a fact already established by Solomon's offering sacrifices there in 3:15. This description of Jerusalem again emphasizes God's choice of Jerusalem and David as major theological ideas in 1, 2 Samuel and 1, 2 Kings (cf. 2 Sam 5:7).[71] It also reminds readers that the temple and palace were constructed out-

[70] Hubbard, *First and Second Kings*, 52.

[71] Noth, *Könige*, 177.

side the confines of David's Jerusalem. Solomon seizes this opportunity to enlarge the capital city's borders.

8:2 Solomon chooses to dedicate the temple during the Feast of Booths, which traditionally took place "in the month of Ethanim, the seventh month." Patterson and Austel observe that this harvest feast "celebrated the end of the wilderness wanderings and the fact that God had brought his people home into the Land of Promise, i.e., had given them rest (Deut 12:8–11)."[72] During this feast Moses renewed the covenant with the second generation of freed Israelites. He also commanded them to read the law at this observance every seven years (Deut 31:9–13). Solomon's choice of the Feast of Booths for the dedication, then, was strategic in that it was a traditional time of national gathering, a reminder of Israel's conquest of Canaan, and a time of religious renewal.

Commentators suggest three possibilities for the timing of this particular Feast of Booths. Certain factors figure in their calculations. First Kings 6:38 says the temple was finished in "the eighth month," while 1 Kgs 8:2 states that the dedication took place in "the seventh month." Thus, there is a gap in time between completion and dedication. Further, 1 Kgs 9:1 indicates that God approves of the temple only after the palace and temple are both finished, which could be understood as meaning many years passed before the temple's dedication occurred.

Given these considerations, Ewald thinks that Solomon dedicated the temple a month before the building was finished.[73] The main difficulty with this idea is that 1 Kgs 7:51 says the project was finished before the ark was brought to the temple. Keil first disagrees with Ewald based on 7:51. He then reads 1 Kgs 9:1–12 to mean that the dedication ceremony must have happened thirteen years after its completion, or when the palace was finished. Finally, Keil notes that the Septuagint prefaces 1 Kgs 8:1 with "and it happened that when Solomon finished building the house of the LORD and his own house after 20 years," a phrase that harmonizes 8:1; 9:1–2, and 9:10. Thus, he concludes that the dedication took place twenty years after the project was begun.[74] Most scholars accept the third possibility, which is that Solomon dedicated the temple eleven months after it was constructed. He simply waited until the symbolic Feast of Booths occurred and used the extra months to furnish the worship center and allow the priests to make necessary arrangements.[75]

This third possibility seems the most likely explanation. The first option does not square with the clear flow of the narrative. Keil's arguments are not without weight but fail on two points. First, God could have waited some years to warn Solomon against idolatry, as 1 Kgs 9:1–9 indicates. Tentative divine

---

[72] Patterson and Austel, "1 and 2 Kings," 79.

[73] Ewald, as cited in Keil, "I and II Kings," 118, and Patterson and Austel, "1 and 2 Kings," 79.

[74] Keil, "I and II Kings," 118.

[75] Gray, *1 and 2 Kings,* 193.

approval of the project comes in 1 Kgs 6:11–13, so the comments in 9:3–10 may have other functions in the narrative, as is discussed below. Second, the Septuagint reference is an interpretative attempt to collate all the dates and is therefore most likely not in the original Hebrew text.[76] An eleven-month wait for the dedication does not seem extreme given the practical and theological reasons for waiting.[77]

8:3–5 With all the supportive secular leaders in place, it now becomes the priests' privilege to carry the ark, and the Levites' privilege to carry the sacred utensils, to the temple. Würthwein, Noth, and Jones believe that these details were added to the original text by priestly editors who desired to protect their role in Israelite society.[78] These commentators think the priestly laws were mostly written in the fifth century B.C., rather than by Moses, and that the distinct separation of the priests' roles in worship from those of nonpriests was a later development in Israel's history.

Though of obvious scholarly substance, this approach to the account does not fit the overall emphases of the former prophets or the practices of other ancient nations. The priests were the ones who carried the ark into the promised land in Josh 3:3. Eli and Samuel, both priests, care for the ark in 1 Samuel 1–6. Uzzah, a nonpriest, was struck dead for touching the ark while it was being carried to Jerusalem (2 Sam 6:1–8). Certainly, then, the information in 1 Kgs 8:3 coincides with the rest of the former prophets. Too, nations besides Israel had distinct roles for priests and nonpriests. Such practices demonstrate a respect for the priest, the holy objects, and worship itself. They can degenerate into a power struggle but do not have to do so.

What emerges in 8:3–5 is a picture of a respectful, solemn people. Each person accepts a proper role. Solomon contributes money and expertise to the project. The elders and clan chiefs pledge religious and community support. Levites accept their responsibility for assisting the priests (cf. Num 4:15). The priests assume the awesome, even dangerous (cf. Lev 10:1–20), privilege of leading worship. Everyone involved offers sacrifices both in recognition of individual and national sin and in praise of the God who forgives, gives them a homeland, and provides a place for worship celebration.

8:6–9 Now the ark reaches its destination. It is placed in the "inner sanctuary," the chamber in the temple described in 1 Kgs 6:19–28. Indeed, with the ark there, the room becomes "the Most Holy Place," the place where God will meet the high priest once a year and forgive Israel's sins (cf. Lev 16). The ark

---

[76] Cf. C. F. Burney, *Notes on the Hebrew Text of the Books of Kings* (Oxford: Clarendon Press, 1903) 104; he concludes, "The form of the gloss was determined by 9:1, and the time notice μετὰ εἴκοσι ἔπη derived from the addition of שֶׁבַע שָׁנִים 6:38, and שְׁלֹשׁ עֶשְׂרֵה שָׁנָה 7:1."

[77] Cf. Patterson and Austel, "1 and 2 Kings," 79, and Gray, *1 and 2 Kings,* 192–94.

[78] E. Würthwein, *Das Erste Buch der Könige*, Kapitel 1–16, ATD 11, 1 (Göttingen: Vandenhoeck & Ruprecht, 1977) 85–86; Noth, *Könige*, 177; Jones, *1 and 2 Kings,* 1:193.

comes to rest under the wings of the cherubim that stretch from wall to wall (cf. 1 Kgs 6:27). These cherubim cover the ark, thus protecting it and approximating God's "throne room" in heaven.

It is not easy to grasp just how the ark's carrying poles were visible in the sanctuary. Montgomery and Gehman suggest that perhaps the poles could have been seen "projecting right and left by one standing near the narrow door of the sanctuary, but not from a greater distance."[79] Maybe "the doors of the Most Holy Place were kept open so that a worshipper looking in could see the ends of the poles."[80] Whatever the case, the author finds it necessary to stress that the poles are "still there today." As the introduction to this commentary discusses, this reference is the author's way of stressing the text's accuracy.[81]

Inside the ark there "was nothing except the two stone tablets that Moses had placed in it at Horeb." This emphatic comment probably is intended to clear up the possible misconceptions that Aaron's rod (Num 17:10) and a jar of manna (Exod 16:33) were there as well. These items were placed alongside the ark but never in it, and by Solomon's time they were no longer available for placement in the most holy place. The presence of Moses' tablets underscores Israel's ties to the Sinai (Horeb) covenant. God's presence, God's word, and God's covenant with Israel are inextricably linked.

8:10–11 Once the priests leave the ark in the most holy place, "the cloud" fills the temple, thus making their work impossible. This was the cloud of God's glory that led Israel in the wilderness (Exod 16:10), the cloud that filled the tabernacle when Moses dedicated that earlier worship center (Exod 40:34–35). N. Snaith notes that the cloud of glory indicates the reality of the Lord's presence. This presence protects (Exod 14:19–20) and guides (Exod 33:9) Israel in the Exodus stories.[82] Here the glory demonstrates divine approval of Solomon's temple. Just as God was with Moses, so now God is with this new generation of Israelites. Such continuity reaffirms the Lord's never-changing character, desire to have fellowship with human beings, and ongoing commitment to the chosen people.

8:12–13 Solomon responds in awe at God's decision to descend to the temple. Normally the Lord dwells "in a dark cloud" or where human beings cannot see him. Such is the mystery of God's ways (cf. Pss 18:11; 97:2). In this instance, however, the Lord chooses to descend to earth and relate to Israel directly. As Gray notes, he is the Creator and at the same time "the God of Israel who has condescended to fix his throne in the midst of his people

---

[79] Montgomery and Gehman, *Kings,* 189.

[80] J. Robinson, *The First Book of Kings,* CBC (Cambridge: Cambridge University Press, 1972) 95.

[81] See the commentary Introduction.

[82] N. H. Snaith, "The First and Second Books of Kings, Introduction and Exegesis," *IB* (Nashville: Abingdon, 1954) 3:71.

Israel." Consequently, "his nearness and readily-experienced power and grace never exhaust his revelation (cf. v. 27)."[83]

Solomon has been faithful in providing a place for worship, and the Lord has been faithful in honoring the king's commitment. God's pledge made in 6:11–13 has been kept.

(2) Solomon's Thanksgiving (8:14–21)

14While the whole assembly of Israel was standing there, the king turned around and blessed them. 15Then he said:

> **"Praise be to the LORD, the God of Israel, who with his own hand has fulfilled what he promised with his own mouth to my father David. For he said, 16'Since the day I brought my people Israel out of Egypt, I have not chosen a city in any tribe of Israel to have a temple built for my Name to be there, but I have chosen David to rule my people Israel.'**
>
> **17"My father David had it in his heart to build a temple for the Name of the LORD, the God of Israel. 18But the LORD said to my father David, 'Because it was in your heart to build a temple for my Name, you did well to have this in your heart. 19Nevertheless, you are not the one to build the temple, but your son, who is your own flesh and blood—he is the one who will build the temple for my Name.'**
>
> **20"The LORD has kept the promise he made: I have succeeded David my father and now I sit on the throne of Israel, just as the LORD promised, and I have built the temple for the Name of the LORD, the God of Israel. 21I have provided a place there for the ark, in which is the covenant of the LORD that he made with our fathers when he brought them out of Egypt."**

Now Solomon explains to his people what he, the author, and the readers already know. He states that the events they are witnessing are part of God's ongoing love for Israel. The completion of the temple marks the end of the striving for a homeland. It also stresses the Davidic covenant and the Lord's presence among the chosen people. These affirmations set the stage for more detailed theological statements later in the chapter.

8:14–21 All the groups and individuals described in 8:1–5 are addressed here. They hear the king give God credit for this significant day. His praise focuses on three significant concepts. First, he bases the Lord's covenant with David on the earlier deliverance of Israel from Egypt. That concrete historical evidence of God's commitment to saving the chosen people paved the way for future saving events. Included in these subsequent saving acts is God's eternal covenant with David.

Second, Solomon reflects on the delay between Israel's entry into Canaan and the building of the temple. Moses taught the people that eventually the

83 Gray, *1 and 2 Kings,* 212.

Lord would choose a central place of worship (Deut 12:1–28), but before Solomon's reign the nation was too preoccupied with external enemies and internal disorganization to have the luxury of building a temple. Further, Solomon indicates the delay also was tied to God's plan to use David's family to achieve this goal. Third, the king celebrates the Lord's choice of him and his father to rule Israel and his provision of a central sanctuary for the people. David's desire to build the temple was a God-honoring act of gratitude, and the Lord's approval of Solomon's accession to power and of his building plans are tied directly to David's appropriate attitude. Solomon's praise concludes with a reference to the ark of the covenant, which is yet another tie with the exodus heritage. Thus, he begins and ends with the historical basis of Israel's relationship with God.

(3) Solomon's Dedication Prayer (8:22–53)

22Then Solomon stood before the altar of the LORD in front of the whole assembly of Israel, spread out his hands toward heaven 23and said:

"O LORD, God of Israel, there is no God like you in heaven above or on earth below—you who keep your covenant of love with your servants who continue wholeheartedly in your way. 24You have kept your promise to your servant David my father; with your mouth you have promised and with your hand you have fulfilled it—as it is today.

25"Now LORD, God of Israel, keep for your servant David my father the promises you made to him when you said, 'You shall never fail to have a man to sit before me on the throne of Israel, if only your sons are careful in all they do to walk before me as you have done.' 26And now, O God of Israel, let your word that you promised your servant David my father come true.

27"But will God really dwell on earth? The heavens, even the highest heaven, cannot contain you. How much less this temple I have built! 28Yet give attention to your servant's prayer and his plea for mercy, O LORD my God. Hear the cry and the prayer that your servant is praying in your presence this day. 29May your eyes be open toward this temple night and day, this place of which you said, 'My Name shall be there,' so that you will hear the prayer your servant prays toward this place. 30Hear the supplication of your servant and of your people Israel when they pray toward this place. Hear from heaven, your dwelling place, and when you hear, forgive.

31"When a man wrongs his neighbor and is required to take an oath and he comes and swears the oath before your altar in this temple, 32then hear from heaven and act. Judge between your servants, condemning the guilty and bringing down on his own head what he has done. Declare the innocent not guilty, and so establish his innocence.

33"When your people Israel have been defeated by an enemy because they have sinned against you, and when they turn back to you and confess your name, praying and making supplication to you in this temple, 34then hear from heaven and forgive the sin of your people Israel and bring them back to

the land you gave to their fathers.
35“When the heavens are shut up and there is no rain because your people
have sinned against you, and when they pray toward this place and confess
your name and turn from their sin because you have afflicted them, 36then
hear from heaven and forgive the sin of your servants, your people Israel.
Teach them the right way to live, and send rain on the land you gave your people for an inheritance.
37“When famine or plague comes to the land, or blight or mildew, locusts
or grasshoppers, or when an enemy besieges them in any of their cities, whatever disaster or disease may come, 38and when a prayer or plea is made by
any of your people Israel—each one aware of the afflictions of his own heart,
and spreading out his hands toward this temple— 39then hear from heaven,
your dwelling place. Forgive and act; deal with each man according to all he
does, since you know his heart (for you alone know the hearts of all men), 40so
that they will fear you all the time they live in the land you gave our fathers.
41“As for the foreigner who does not belong to your people Israel but has
come from a distant land because of your name— 42for men will hear of your
great name and your mighty hand and your outstretched arm—when he
comes and prays toward this temple, 43then hear from heaven, your dwelling
place, and do whatever the foreigner asks of you, so that all the peoples of the
earth may know your name and fear you, as do your own people Israel, and
may know that this house I have built bears your Name.
44“When your people go to war against their enemies, wherever you send
them, and when they pray to the LORD toward the city you have chosen and
the temple I have built for your Name, 45then hear from heaven their prayer
and their plea, and uphold their cause.
46“When they sin against you—for there is no one who does not sin—and
you become angry with them and give them over to the enemy, who takes
them captive to his own land, far away or near; 47and if they have a change of
heart in the land where they are held captive, and repent and plead with you
in the land of their conquerors and say, ‘We have sinned, we have done
wrong, we have acted wickedly’; 48and if they turn back to you with all their
heart and soul in the land of their enemies who took them captive, and pray to
you toward the land you gave their fathers, toward the city you have chosen
and the temple I have built for your Name; 49then from heaven, your dwelling
place, hear their prayer and their plea, and uphold their cause. 50And forgive
your people, who have sinned against you; forgive all the offenses they have
committed against you, and cause their conquerors to show them mercy; 51for
they are your people and your inheritance, whom you brought out of Egypt,
out of that iron-smelting furnace.
52“May your eyes be open to your servant’s plea and to the plea of your
people Israel, and may you listen to them whenever they cry out to you. 53For
you singled them out from all the nations of the world to be your own inheritance, just as you declared through your servant Moses when you, O Sovereign LORD, brought our fathers out of Egypt.”

8:22–26 Having encouraged the people by stressing God's past saving acts, Solomon now begins the process of asking the Lord to save Israel in the future. The whole prayer is grounded firmly in texts like Leviticus 26 and Deuteronomy 27–28, where Moses tells Israel that God will richly bless them for obeying the covenant but will punish severely all rebellion.[84] This prayer takes on significance beyond its dedicatory context later in 1, 2 Kings, when it becomes a reminder of why the Lord allows the covenant nation to be defeated by Assyria and Babylon.

Solomon begins with a confession: God is unique in his unchanging faithfulness. God keeps the "covenant of love" with all who "continue wholeheartedly" in his ways. This affirmation mirrors Deut 7:7–9, which focuses on the Lord's loving, gracious choice of Israel. Indeed, Deut 7:9 reads, "Know therefore that the LORD your God is God; he is the faithful God, keeping his covenant of love to a thousand generations of those who love him and keep his commands." Not obligation, not legalism, nor a desire to control others for personal gain motivates God. Every miracle, saving act, or law flows from divine mercy and grace.

David's life illustrates this grace. God made him king, selecting him above all his brothers (1 Sam 16:1–13). Further, God made his son, Solomon, king in his place and allowed the temple to be built. Solomon now requests that the last part of the Davidic Covenant come to pass. He asks that their line never lose power. No doubt he could not fully conceive of an eternal kingdom, yet he knows that God can make even this promise come true.

8:27–30 A crucial theological issue emerges before Solomon begins his specific petitions. If God is unique "in heaven above or on earth below" (8:23), and if "even the highest heaven cannot contain" the Lord, then Solomon correctly exclaims, "How much less this temple I have built!" Though Moses was a man "whom the LORD knew face to face" (Deut 34:10), he was not allowed to see all God's glory (Exod 33:7–23). God's magnitude would simply overwhelm a human's capacity to grasp it. Tokens of the Lord's presence, such as clouds and pillars of fire (Exod 40:34–38; 1 Kgs 8:10–11), appear, of course, and people cannot stay near *them*. On what basis, then, can Solomon hope that God will dwell on earth, in this temple? How will the Lord "live among the Israelites and . . . not abandon" (1 Kgs 6:13) them?

Solomon's confidence in God's willingness to condescend to human level must ultimately emerge from four principles. First, he knows God has revealed himself in the past, particularly in the lives of Moses, Joshua, and David (cf. 1 Kgs 8:21–26). Thus, Solomon does not pray for a brand new occurrence. Second, the king understands that the covenant described in written Scripture, in the Pentateuch, teaches that God desires a relationship with Israel as a

[84] Keil, "I and II Kings," 125.

nation and with individual Israelites (cf. Deut 7:7–9; 1 Kgs 8:23). He can approach God in prayer because he is the Lord's "servant" and because Israel is the Lord's people (8:30). Such assurance comes from the covenant itself.

Third, Solomon can expect God to fulfill the promise made in Deut 12:4–11 to "put his Name" (Deut 12:5) in a central worship site. Fourth, he can hope for God's presence because of what he knows about God's character. Since God is loving (1 Kgs 8:23), faithful (8:24), consistent (8:25), and relational (8:30), it is reasonable to assume that he will continue to meet human beings where they live. God is lofty, holy, and mysterious, yet approachable and personal at the same time. The temple will serve as the physical symbol of these divine realities. Here the unapproachable Lord becomes approachable and ready to help those who worship, sacrifice, and pray.

8:31–32 This first specific petition focuses on the certainty of neighbor mistreating neighbor, in itself a violation of Lev 19:18—"Love your neighbor as yourself"—which Jesus calls the second great command (Mark 12:28–34). More specifically, the situation appears to be that one neighbor accuses another without any witnesses to confirm the accusation.[85] It therefore becomes the Lord's sole responsibility to judge between the guilty and the innocent. So Solomon recognizes that the Lord, the heavenly King, must decide cases that he, the earthly king, cannot possibly solve. This is quite an admission from the man who settled the prostitute case in 1 Kgs 3:16–28!

8:33–34 According to Lev 26:17 and Deut 28:25, one of the ways God will punish Israel is by allowing their enemies to defeat them. Israel's defeat by lowly Ai (Josh 7:1–11), constant losses in Judges, and humiliation at the hand of Philistia (1 Sam 4:1–11) illustrate this principle. Solomon knows both the teachings in the Pentateuch and the people's not-so-glorious past.

He understands that such national defeats are the result of rebellion against the covenant God. Solomon also knows that Moses teaches that military losses can either serve as warnings that remove pride and stubbornness (Lev 26:18–19) or as catastrophic defeats that lead to loss of land (1 Kgs 8:34; Lev 26:33; Deut 28:36–37). Deportation and exile were a fact in ancient military life. How Israel understands God's perspective on history will determine their response to their situation.

All Solomon can pray for is that the people will come to their senses after such catastrophes. He hopes they will "turn back," or repent,[86] and "confess" their allegiance to their Lord. Such repentance and acknowledgment of God's lordship must come through prayer. The logical central place for these prayers is the temple. Surely the God whose character is so eloquently described in

---

[85] Matheney, "1 Kings," 181.

[86] The word here is וְשָׁבוּ, which derives from שׁוּב, the simple yet distinctive Heb. word used to describe all types of "turnings," including turnings of individuals' hearts and actions.

8:14–30 will forgive the chosen people and restore them to the promised land.

8:35–36 Having concluded the last petition with a reference to the land God "gave to their fathers" (8:34), Solomon prays for the land itself. Reflecting on Moses' warning that national disobedience will force the Lord to "make the sky above you like iron and the ground beneath you like bronze" (Lev 26:19; cf. Deut 28:23), Solomon prays for drought relief. As with the defeats in 8:33–34, the droughts he mentions are not normal, uncaused events. Rather, they are direct natural punishment from the Creator of heaven and earth for the people's rebellion.

Once Israel turns from its sin, forgiveness will come in the form of rain. Solomon hopes that such obvious correlation between human prayer and divine response will "teach them the right way to live." Thus, punishment will have a positive, not negative, function. God corrects in order to effect needed changes, not to vent personal anger. Throughout his prayer Solomon balances a sense of realism about sin and his desire that sin and the punishment that necessarily follows it never be the final word in Israel. As G. McConville notes, Solomon's basis for such cautious optimism probably derives from texts like Deut 30:1–10, where Moses soberly warns the Israelites of that era about the harsh facts of punishment for sin.[87] Solomon does hope, then, and his hope is founded on God's Word; but that hope is not wishful thinking or giddy optimism spawned by the excitement of the moment. Rather, it is the real hope that comes from applying the realistic word of a realistic God. Anything else is not true hope.

8:37–40 Solomon continues the land motif in this fourth petition, yet he also includes the significant notion of individual forgiveness. Until now he has stressed humanly unresolvable cases (8:31–32) and national sin and correction (8:33–36). Here he again notes the many ills that can afflict the land, such as famine, plague, blight, mildew, insects, and enemies. Each of these could occur because of national sin, as has already been stated.

Unlike 8:33,35, which emphasizes corporate repentance, this passage recognizes the importance of the prayers of every individual worshiper. Solomon asks God that "any of your people Israel," that is, anyone "aware of the afflictions of his own heart," may turn back the devastations 8:38 describes. The prayers of individuals matter in the Old Testament. Abraham's prayers save Lot's life (Gen 18:22–33; 19:29). Moses successfully intercedes on Israel's behalf after the golden calf incident in Exodus 32–34. Elijah will stop a drought later in 1 Kings. In each of these cases the individual not only represents himself but humanity and all of Israel as well.[88] The king hopes that such persons will always be heard.

---

[87] G. McConville, "1 Kings VIII 46–53 and the Deuteronomic Hope," *VT* XLII, 1 (1992) 77–79.

[88] For a provocative study of the OT's concept of the individual as representative of all Israel, see B. Childs, *Old Testament Theology in a Canonical Context* (Philadelphia: Fortress, 1986) 99–103.

As in 8:36, Solomon aims at an ongoing positive result. God's response to an individual prayer for the corporate body proves that God, and God alone, knows "the hearts of all men." Once this truth is understood, Solomon prays, Israel "will fear you all the time they live in the land you gave our fathers." Fear, or respect, will lead to obedience, love, and service (Deut 10:12). This basic attitude of worship should in turn guard against future rebellion.

8:41–43 During this great moment of national significance it would be easy for Solomon to pray only for *his* people. Instead, he prays "for the foreigner who does not belong to your people Israel," for those who will be drawn to Jerusalem because of the Lord's fame. Perhaps he recalls that non-Israelites like Rahab and Ruth, both of whom accepted the Lord as their God (Josh 2:11; Ruth 1:16), are his grandmothers. Maybe Jethro (Exod 18:1–12) or even Hiram affect his thinking.

Regardless of his personal motivation, Solomon knows that all nations need to know the Lord and that Israel must mediate this knowledge. Indeed, God envisioned this role for Israel when promising Abraham that all nations would be blessed through him (Gen 12:2–3). Knowledge of God includes grasping God's character and standards. This knowledge will lead to proper worship based on a healthy fear of the Lord. Therefore any lack of this active knowledge is dangerous, for it separates people of all nations from God (cf. Hos 4:1–3; Amos 8:11–12). Rather than contributing to this disaster, Solomon prays that Israel and its temple will teach the nations God's will.

8:44–45 The sixth petition is for the success of Israel's armies. Why should God "uphold their cause"? Because they are God's people praying toward God's city and God's temple. Apparently Solomon restricts his prayer to when Israel's cause is God's cause, as it was during the conquest of Canaan.

8:46–51 For his last petition Solomon returns to an idea he mentions in 8:34. Again he recalls the ultimate punishment God may use against Israel—expulsion from the very land that the Lord has given the chosen people as a major proof of their favored status (cf. Lev 26:27–35; Deut 28:36–37,49–68). Again he asks that God forgive their sin and return them to the land if they recognize their errors and repent.

Besides its original significance as a warning to his own people, Solomon's prayer takes on particular importance for the author's audience. Remember that 1, 2 Kings was written for people who had lost the land in the very manner Solomon describes. For them, then, this seventh petition acts as a call to repentance and a program for prayer. It teaches the readers how to restore their relationship with God. At the same time, it provides hope that exile is not God's final word for Israel. The chosen people can return to the promised land when they return to the covenant Lord who gave them the land. In this way Solomon's prayer redeems the time for the book's original, hurting audience.[89]

8:52–53 Solomon's prayer concludes as it began, with hope for the present and future based on the Lord's past covenant loyalty to Israel. He asks that the Lord pay the utmost attention to his requests. Why? Solely because God "singled them out from all the nations of the world," then sealed the relationship through Moses' teachings and the exodus itself. Clearly, Solomon believes that Israel's past is a monument to God's grace, and any future benefits the people will receive must also come from their merciful Lord.

(4) Solomon's Blessing (8:54–61)

54When Solomon had finished all these prayers and supplications to the LORD, he rose from before the altar of the LORD, where he had been kneeling with his hands spread out toward heaven. 55He stood and blessed the whole assembly of Israel in a loud voice, saying:

> **56"Praise be to the LORD, who has given rest to his people Israel just as he promised. Not one word has failed of all the good promises he gave through his servant Moses. 57May the LORD our God be with us as he was with our fathers; may he never leave us nor forsake us. 58May he turn our hearts to him, to walk in all his ways and to keep the commands, decrees and regulations he gave our fathers. 59And may these words of mine, which I have prayed before the LORD, be near to the LORD our God day and night, that he may uphold the cause of his servant and the cause of his people Israel according to each day's need, 60so that all the peoples of the earth may know that the LORD is God and that there is no other. 61But your hearts must be fully committed to the LORD our God, to live by his decrees and obey his commands, as at this time."**

8:54–55 All petitions and praises ended, the king rises "from before the altar of the LORD, where he had been kneeling with his hands spread out toward heaven." Nelson observes: "The reader remembers that the prayer began with him standing (v. 22) and can only conclude that under the weight of his petitions Solomon had sunk to a kneeling position, an act of submission (19:18; II Kings 1:13; Isa. 45:23)."[90] This whole worship experience has been overwhelming for the priests (1 Kgs 8:10–11) and the king, yet not so overwhelming that Solomon forgets the people, for he rises to dismiss them with another blessing.

8:56 Solomon prefaces his blessing with a confession of God's faithful-

---

[89] As Long observes, the author "offered a paradigmatic moment from which the past and future, especially that longed for by the temple-shorn and landless exiles, derived its value and significance" (*1 Kings,* 104).

[90] Nelson, *First and Second Kings,* 55.

ness. This faithfulness is revealed by the fact that the Lord "has given rest to his people Israel just as he promised." In Solomon's mind "rest" refers to peaceful settlement in the land of promise. It means freedom from enemies (Deut 12:10) and God's presence in Israel's midst (Exod 33:14). It means total reliance on God's word, which never fails. Finally, it means that what the Lord promised through Moses has come true nearly five centuries after it was first pledged. Solomon can bless the people with the confidence that an absolutely steadfast God stands behind the king's statements.

8:57–60 The blessing has three parts. First, Solomon encourages the people to recognize the importance of God's presence in their lives. When God calls Moses to lead Israel, the Lord's major promise is "I will be with you" (Exod 3:12). Joshua (Josh 1:9), Gideon (Judg 6:16), and Jeremiah (Jer 1:8,19) receive the same promise. God's constant presence will enable Solomon's subjects to occupy the temple and the promised land in a way that will please the Lord. Thus, it will be evident that the Lord is with them as he was with their ancestors and that God will "never leave . . . nor forsake" them.

Second, Solomon hopes that God will "turn our hearts to him." Moses teaches in Deut 6:4–9; 11:18; 30:14; and 32:46 that Israel's relationship with God begins in the heart and moves outward to obedience. Only through an internal commitment can Israel "walk in all his ways and . . . keep the commands, decrees and regulations" that Moses taught in the Pentateuch. Legalistic servitude is foreign to Old Testament faith.

Third, the king desires God to uphold Israel's cause. Why? Not for national prominence or royal pride but so "all the peoples of the earth may know that the Lord is God and that there is no other." This concern for monotheism is at the heart of all Old Testament theology. Israel must confess that God is one (Deut 6:4); that idols are mere works of human hands (Exod 20:3–4; 32:1–4); and that the Lord alone has created the earth (Gen 1:1), delivered Israel (Exod 15:1–18), and established the Davidic monarchy. God's plan of blessing all nations through Abraham (Gen 12:2–3) will then be fulfilled as Israel teaches others about the only true God.

8:61 Just as Solomon began the blessing with a confession of the one who is faithful, he now closes his comments with a plea that Israel be faithful to the Lord. The language of full commitment is similar to that in covenant renewal ceremonies like the one in Joshua 24, where Joshua commands Israel to "fear the LORD and serve him with all faithfulness" (24:14). Each new generation must choose to follow the Lord. Abraham, Moses, Joshua, and David have shown Solomon and his subjects how to obey the Lord, but they must now follow their ancestors' example.

(5) Solomon's Sacrifices (8:62–66)

62Then the king and all Israel with him offered sacrifices before the LORD.

63Solomon offered a sacrifice of fellowship offerings to the LORD: twenty-two thousand cattle and a hundred and twenty thousand sheep and goats. So the king and all the Israelites dedicated the temple of the LORD.

64On that same day the king consecrated the middle part of the courtyard in front of the temple of the LORD, and there he offered burnt offerings, grain offerings and the fat of the fellowship offerings, because the bronze altar before the LORD was too small to hold the burnt offerings, the grain offerings and the fat of the fellowship offerings.

65So Solomon observed the festival at that time, and all Israel with him—a vast assembly, people from Lebo Hamath to the Wadi of Egypt. They celebrated it before the LORD our God for seven days and seven days more, fourteen days in all.
66On the following day he sent the people away. They blessed the king and then went home, joyful and glad in heart for all the good things the LORD had done for his servant David and his people Israel.

After the dedicatory prayer, Solomon leads the nation in an unforgettable festival of tabernacles. Sacrifices are offered at the new sanctuary. All the people participate in a joyful feast and then return happily to their homes. Few moments in biblical history surpass this scene in hope, gladness, and glory.

8:62–63 Solomon and the people slaughter "twenty-two thousand cattle and a hundred and twenty thousand sheep and goats." Though some Septuagint texts omit the numbers, both this passage and 2 Chr 8:5 record these amounts, so the count has solid support in the Hebrew textual tradition. These sacrifices are "fellowship offerings,"[91] or "peace offerings," which traditionally were "shared, with the blood, fat and entrails being devoted to God, and the community eating the flesh."[92] Directions for offering this type of sacrifice appear in Lev 3:1–17 and 7:11–38. The goal of the offering was to unite the people with their leaders and their God.

Scholars differ over the plausibility of such a large number of sacrificed animals. Montgomery and Gehman deem the figures "exaggerations" for effect,[93] Matheney believes they seem "excessively large,"[94] and DeVries thinks they are "utterly fantastic."[95] Noth, Jones, and Gray take a mediating approach by observing that a special seven-day feast involving all the tribes of Israel might indeed require such a large number of sacrifices.[96] Keil argues that the number of celebrants, the length of the festival, and the fact that the people helped kill and dispose of fellowship offerings make the number rea-

---

[91] The Hebrew word is הַשְּׁלָמִים, which corresponds nicely to the king's name (שְׁלֹמֹה) and to the word rendered "fully committed" (שָׁלֵם) in 8:61.

[92] Jones, *1 and 2 Kings,* 1:207.

[93] Montgomery and Gehman, *Kings,* 200.

[94] Matheney, "1 Kings," 184.

[95] DeVries, *1 Kings,* 127.

[96] Noth, *Könige,* 191; Jones, *1 and 2 Kings,* 1:207; Gray, *1 and 2 Kings,* 216.

sonable.[97] Hurowitz cites a Mesopotamian inscription about a banquet for sixty thousand people that makes the count appear within the realm of possibility.[98] It seems logical, then, to affirm the text's credibility.

8:64–66 Due to the large amount of sacrifices, the "middle part of the courtyard in front of the temple" is pressed into service as a site for the other types of sacrifices being offered. The whole celebration is so historically and symbolically important that the festival lasts fourteen days. When the people finally leave, they praise the Lord and bless the king for all that has happened. Indeed, this entire event has served to unify Israel as one people, under one king, serving the one true God.

5. God's Second Appearance to Solomon (9:1–9)

[1]When Solomon had finished building the temple of the LORD and the royal palace, and had achieved all he had desired to do, [2]the LORD appeared to him a second time, as he had appeared to him at Gibeon. [3]The LORD said to him:

"I have heard the prayer and plea you have made before me; I have consecrated this temple, which you have built, by putting my Name there forever. My eyes and my heart will always be there.

[4]"As for you, if you walk before me in integrity of heart and uprightness, as David your father did, and do all I command and observe my decrees and laws, [5]I will establish your royal throne over Israel forever, as I promised David your father when I said, 'You shall never fail to have a man on the throne of Israel.'

[6]"But if you or your sons turn away from me and do not observe the commands and decrees I have given you and go off to serve other gods and worship them, [7]then I will cut off Israel from the land I have given them and will reject this temple I have consecrated for my Name. Israel will then become a byword and an object of ridicule among all peoples. [8]And though this temple is now imposing, all who pass by will be appalled and will scoff and say, 'Why has the LORD done such a thing to this land and to this temple?' [9]People will answer, 'Because they have forsaken the LORD their God, who brought their fathers out of Egypt, and have embraced other gods, worshiping and serving them—that is why the LORD brought all this disaster on them.'"

This episode provides a conclusion for the book's account of the first twenty years of Solomon's reign (cf. 9:10). God's initial appearance to Solomon occurs after his rise to power yet before he actually begins his work as king. That theophany, or divine self-revelation, indicated God's pleasure with Solomon's request for wisdom. Similarly, this second appearance expresses the Lord's satisfaction with the king's prayers for the people and

[97] Keil, "I and II Kings," 135.

[98] Hurowitz, "I Have Built You an Exalted House," 276.

for the temple. First Kings 6:11–13 states that Solomon had received a "word of the LORD" concerning the temple, but this "word" differs from the second theophany in that this second appearance is more of a vision than a prophetic exhortation. Still, the word and the vision agree. God will honor the eternal side of the Davidic Covenant. The temporal portion of the covenant, the part about Solomon and his descendants, however, is dependent on human obedience.

9:1–3 Some unspecified amount of time after the dedication services, God "appeared to [Solomon] a second time, as he had appeared to him at Gibeon." The Lord both answers the king's prayer and reemphasizes the conditions for continued blessing. God assures Solomon that his prayers have been heard, for the Lord has "consecrated" the temple, or "caused it to be holy," by deciding to place his name there forever and by deciding to watch over and love the place always. This commitment to the central place of worship serves as a clear answer to Solomon's comments in 8:14–21 and his petitions in 8:22–53.

9:4–9 Exhortations and warnings permeate this text. God reminds Solomon that he must obey God by keeping the divine commands and decrees. Solomon's obedience, however, must be motivated by "integrity of heart," not by a mere external observance of God's word. Such heartfelt commitment to the Lord will result in Solomon's sons ruling Israel after him. This promise coincides with similar comments in 3:14–15 and 6:11–13.

On the other hand, an embracing of other gods will result in the most devastating consequences listed in Leviticus 26 and Deuteronomy 27–28. If idolatry occurs, God will "cut off Israel from the land," "reject this temple," and make Israel "a byword and an object of ridicule among all peoples" (cf. Lev 26:27–39; Deut 28:36–37). Patterson and Austel note the seriousness of the language of these threats. They state that "cut off" is used in texts "where a person is cut off or excluded from the fellowship of God's people (e.g., Lev 17:4,9; Num 19:20)." God's use of "reject" implies "divorce." Finally, becoming a byword in ancient times was a calamity, since all personal and national self-respect or international respect disappeared.[99] Even strangers in the land would know that these disasters came about because of Israel's unfaithfulness to their covenant with their Lord.

Without question the book's intended audience would have understood this warning as God's grace to Solomon. All the king had to do was remain obedient to the Lord, shun idols, and continue to enjoy God's favor. The first readers also knew that Solomon does not accept this grace. Eventually he will adopt habits that will lead to disaster, a fact the hurting readers knew all too well.

[99] Patterson and Austel, "1 and 2 Kings," 94.

Canonical and Theological Implications in 1 Kgs 5:1–9:9

This section's emphasis on the temple serves some vital canonical functions. First, it provides the historical fulfillment of Moses' prediction that God would someday choose a single place to be the focal point of Israel's worship (cf. Deut 12:5,11,14,18,21,26; 14:23–25; 15:20; 16:2,6–7,11). Moses believed that having a central sanctuary would guard against idolatry (cf. Deut 12:1–7). Related to the first idea is a second theme. The building of the temple completed the promise of land made to Abraham, taught by Moses, and secured by Joshua and David (cf. 1 Kgs 6:1 and 8:50–51). These two themes, then, help readers grasp how the temple's completion helps conclude *the law's* emphasis on covenant worship and the reception of the promised land.

Third, the temple's completion illustrates the twin themes of Israel's faithfulness and God's enduring presence among the people. These ideas are particularly significant in the *prophetic segment* of the canon. Solomon's decision to build the temple stemmed from his gratitude to God and his desire to honor his father's memory. This former motivation emerges again after the exile when Haggai and Zechariah urge the people to rebuild the destroyed temple as a token of their esteem for the Lord. Ezekiel and Malachi stress the temple as a place where God is present among faithful worshipers (cf. Ezek 40–48; Mal 3–4). Indeed, Ezekiel envisions the temple as the most important place in the new Jerusalem, the city of God, for the temple will be where God's glory resides (Ezek 43:1–12).

Fourth, the restoration of the fallen temple symbolizes Israel's postexilic restored fortunes in *the writings*. Ezra in particular stresses this point (Ezra 1–6). In fact, the Hebrew canon concludes with the Chronicler's challenge to rebuild the temple (2 Chr 36:23). Only through this rebuilding can Israel's humiliation in exile truly cease. Only then can the promises to Abraham and the teachings of Moses reenter the nation's history as key components of Israel's future.[100]

Fifth, the temple's presence stands as a reminder of the importance of worship throughout Israel's history and throughout the Old Testament. Certainly the psalms stress the temple as the most important place where worship occurs, as does 1, 2 Chronicles. Books such as Jeremiah, Zechariah, and Malachi highlight the value of pure, faithful temple worship. Anything less dishonors God, defiles Israel, and leads to judgment (cf. Jer 7:1–8:3; 26:1–24). God will honor Israel with his presence but only if the people take worship seriously.

These canonical details have theological significance. At least three major

[100] See J. D. Levenson, "From Temple to Synagogue: I Kings 8," *Traditions, Transformations, and Turning Points in Biblical Faith,* ed. B. Halpern and J. D. Levenson (Winona Lake, Ind.: Eisenbrauns, 1981) 165–66, for a discussion of how exiles viewed the temple's rebuilding as evidence of God's restored favor.

themes, each with subpoints, emerge in these chapters. The first of these ideas is the presence, nearness, or immanence of God. If God is not close to and accessible to those who desire to worship him, then temple building, prayers, and sacrifices are absurd practices. On the other hand, if God is real, created the earth, and cares about human beings, then honoring the Lord not only makes sense but it also strengthens one's relationship with him. One caution deserves mention. Such worship does not control or manipulate God in any way. As Nelson explains:

> God is "really present" in the temple in cloud, glory, and ark (vv. 3:13). Yet lest this be misunderstood as suggesting that God is automatically at Israel's beck and call, Solomon insists that even the whole universe cannot contain God. God is only "symbolically present" in the temple through the divine name.[101]

Israel must freely worship the Lord, who freely chooses to dwell among them.

God's presence is manifested in various ways in 1 Kgs 5:1–9:9. As has been mentioned, the Lord's presence is evident in the cloud described in 8:10–11. Solomon also believes God will choose to dwell, or be present, in the new temple (8:12–13). Further, God's presence is demonstrated by his covenants with David (8:14–21,25–26) and with Israel as mediated through Moses (8:56–61). Israel's deliverance from Egypt shows how powerful God's presence was in Moses' day (8:50–51). Finally, the Lord is present in direct, verbal communication in 6:11–13 and 9:3–9. God not only comes near to the human race but also speaks to people, thus making his will known to them.

Human worship is the second major theological concept in these chapters. Here, as in the whole of Scripture, worship consists of praise (8:14–21), confession (8:23–51), petition (8:46–53), and humility (8:54). This worship assumes the existence of a personal God who is near, who acts on behalf of faithful worshipers, and who makes binding covenants with those he loves. Solomon's petitions also depict a God who does judge those who sin yet who also forgives the penitent (8:34). Though powerful, this God is not unapproachable. The covenant God is a loving Lord.

Worship may occur anywhere, but the focus in this story is on the temple. Proper temple worship includes prayer, sacrifice, and the ministry of the Levites. The centralizing of worship in this one place is intended to bring order and uniformity to Israel's religion without suppressing love and devotion for God. By no means does the temple's existence imply that God can be contained in one place (8:27). Nor does it mean the people can take God for granted, as occurred over time (cf. Jer 7:1–15; 26:1–15).[102] Rather, worship must be consistent as each new generation arises, a truth illustrated by

[101] Nelson, *First and Second Kings*, 59.

[102] Cf. G. Rice, *Nations under God: A Commentary on the Book of 1 Kings*, ITC (Grand Rapids: Eerdmans, 1990) 72.

Solomon's constant references to his father, David (8:14–21,25–26).

Leadership is the third theme this text describes. Throughout the books the author of 1, 2 Kings transforms this seemingly secular concept into a theological issue. God is a model of faithful, consistent, just leadership. Similarly, David led the people to be faithful to the one living God. He thereby helped Israel to enjoy the blessings of God. At this point in his career, Solomon follows in his father's footsteps. He worships God and leads the people to do the same. God rewards this faithfulness primarily through his presence but also through blessing Solomon with wisdom and political gain.

Applicational Implications of 1 Kgs 5:1–9:9

The canonical and theological conclusions lead to some extremely important life applications. First, understanding that the covenant God is personal and present should affect believers' behavior. Solomon's prayer indicates that God observes all of life's activities. God knows when oppression (8:31–32), war (8:33–34), natural disaster (8:35–40), or exile (8:46–51) occur. Thus, the people must be careful to keep their covenant with the Lord. They can also know that they may call on their God in whatever type of distress they find themselves.[103]

Second, worship is vital for faithful living. In fact, it is so important that it must be taken very seriously,[104] for people will not enjoy worship until they do take it seriously. Joy will result when prayer, confession, praise, and petition are offered with an earnestness like Solomon's. This recognition of the importance of serious worship will guard against taking God for granted. It will remind worshipers that God blesses them with his presence. The Lord chooses to be present, though he has no obligation to do so. Finally, poor worship leads to improper ethical behavior, then to punishment (8:31–51). Worship is not an obligation. Rather, it is a blessing that unites the worshiper with God and guarantees correct relationships in the community.

Third, godly leaders possess certain character traits. They choose projects that reflect the Lord's past and present faithfulness. They lead others *in* worship, which in turn leads others *to* worship. They seek the Lord's will for themselves and their followers. In other words, their leadership style flows from their commitment to the God who leads them.

---

[103] Ibid., 73.

[104] For an explanation of the relationship between the gravity and joy of worship consult J. Piper, *Desiring God: Meditations of a Christian Hedonist* (Portland: Multnomah, 1986) 9, 61ff.; and *The Supremacy of God in Preaching* (Grand Rapids: Baker 1990) 47–66.

6. Solomon's Pursuits (9:10–28)

Twenty-four years of Solomon's reign, over half of it, have now been discussed. The king has enjoyed success in every area of his life. He has subdued his rivals, organized the nation, built himself a palace and the Lord a temple, made beneficial alliances with Tyre and Egypt, and given his people rest from war. Clearly, he has excelled in both foreign and domestic affairs. Solomon has had an impressive start to his reign. Can he sustain this level of excellence? Will he remain faithful to the Lord? Are these issues related? Only time will tell.This section begins a six-part analysis of the second portion of Solomon's era. The first segment offers an overview of all the king's activities, including his building, domestic policy, and trade agreements (9:10–28). Next, the famous queen of Sheba story demonstrates Solomon's wisdom (10:1–13) and is followed by a chronicle of his wealth (10:14–29). Chapter 11 presents Solomon's slide into idolatry (11:1–13), the opposition God allows to hinder Solomon (11:14–25), and the man who will eventually divide the nation (11:26–43). Clearly, the author of 1, 2 Kings does not think the second half of Solomon's reign is as successful as the first, a fact emphasized by the shorter account that appears.

Because of its placement between the successful completion of the temple and the nation's irreversible division, this passage acts as an important bridge between Israel's last happy days as a united country and the contention and weakness that follow. Clues to Solomon's faults have surfaced already. Now they become evident. Even a brilliant, gifted king must follow the Lord. Failure to do so constitutes a breach of the covenant standards outlined in 3:14; 6:11–13; and 9:3–9.

Survey of Historical Details Related to 1 Kgs 9:10–11:43

Certain foreign, domestic, economic, and religious factors changed during Solomon's last sixteen years. First, Israel's relationship with Egypt deteriorated over time. Though 9:16 states that the Pharaoh, possibly Siamun,[105] conquered Gezer and "gave it as a wedding gift to his daughter, Solomon's wife," by 11:14–25 a new Pharaoh, probably Shishak, supports Solomon's enemies. Unlike his immediate predecessors, Shishak was able to unite Egypt and then mount aggressive campaigns against neighboring countries.[106] Eventually Shishak invaded Jerusalem itself during the reign of Rehoboam, Solomon's son

---

[105] See the comments on 1 Kgs 3:1.

[106] Cf. Malamat, "A Political Look at the Kingdom of David and Solomon and Its Relations with Egypt," 203. For more information on Shishak's power and policies consult H. D. Lance, "Solomon, Siamun, and the Double Ax," *Magnalia Dei: The Mighty Acts of God,* ed. F. M. Cross, W. E. Lemke, and P. D. Miller (Garden City: Doubleday, 1976) 209–23, and D. B. Redford, *Egypt, Canaan, and Israel in Ancient Times* (New Jersey: Princeton University Press, 1992), 312–15.

(cf. 1 Kgs 14:25; 2 Chr 12:2). Similarly, Solomon's influence in Syria was weakened when Rezon seized control of Damascus (1 Kgs 11:23–25) and when Hadad became king of Edom (1 Kgs 11:14–22). Probably Rezon's power threatened Israel more than Hadad's.[107] Still, coupled with Egypt's new attitude, Edom and Syria's rebellions presented Solomon with foes on all sides.

Domestic tensions grew as well. J. A. Soggin argues that the northern tribes began to feel that they were shouldering more than their share of the tax and conscripted labor burden.[108] Perhaps they believed Judah received special treatment for being David's clan. Soggin's assertion fits with the north's complaints after Solomon's death (1 Kgs 12:1–4). Probably not even Judah appreciated the taxes that all Solomon's projects required (cf. 1 Kgs 4:1–28). Jeroboam, a young and vigorous opponent, arose as an alternative to Solomonic rule (1 Kgs 11:26–28). Because of Solomon's idolatry, God supported Jeroboam's rise to power, as did Shishak of Egypt, though for less religious reasons (1 Kgs 11:29–40).

Despite such complications, however, Solomon was able to maintain order, mostly because of his economic prowess. Israel enjoyed prosperity for most of these years because of Solomon's ability to utilize the trade potential that remained at his disposal. For instance, he sustained his shipping partnership with Hiram of Tyre. Solomon built the ships, but Hiram's men commanded and sailed them (1 Kgs 9:26–28).[109] This arrangement must have benefited Hiram, since he continued the relationship even after he felt Solomon's payment of Galilean towns was "Cabul," or "worthless" (1 Kgs 9:10–14). Solomon also strengthened his caravan trade by improving relations with the queen of Sheba, a nation that had come to "dominate the trade in spice and incense for which southwestern Arabia was famous."[110] Since Solomon controlled part of the land route and had shipping interests as well, it was in the queen's best interest to pay Israel's king a visit.[111] All these financial ventures bought Solomon peace at home, as the presence of luxury items often does (cf. 1 Kgs 10:14–29).

All of these details contribute to the author's accurate historical portrait of Solomon's final years in power. As in the whole book, however, the major issue is Solomon's faithfulness to the Lord. Unfortunately, he is quite lacking in this area. Unlike David, Solomon worships other gods, in particular those his many wives favor (1 Kgs 11:1–13). This decision breaches the Mosaic and

---

[107] Bright, *A History of Israel*, 214.

[108] J. A. Soggin, "Compulsory Labor under David and Solomon," in *Studies in the Period of David and Solomon and Other Essays*, ed. T. Ishida (Winona Lake, Ind.: Eisenbrauns, 1982) 264–67.

[109] Peckham, "Israel and Phoenicia," 232.

[110] Bright, *A History of Israel*, 215; G. W. Van Beek, "Frankincense and Myrrh," *BA* (1960) 69–95.

[111] Ibid.

Davidic Covenants and leaves Solomon open to the punishments implicit in each of God's conversations with him. Earlier a prophet (Nathan) helped Solomon become king. Now a prophet named Ahijah will predict the end of the Davidic dynasty's exclusive rule over Israel (1 Kgs 11:29–39). Solomon's dynasty could have weathered foreign, domestic, and economic challenges, but idolatry makes the Lord an enemy. How can the dynasty survive?

(1) Foreign Relations (9:10–14)

10 At the end of twenty years, during which Solomon built these two buildings—the temple of the LORD and the royal palace— 11 King Solomon gave twenty towns in Galilee to Hiram king of Tyre, because Hiram had supplied him with all the cedar and pine and gold he wanted. 12 But when Hiram went from Tyre to see the towns that Solomon had given him, he was not pleased with them. 13 "What kind of towns are these you have given me, my brother?" he asked. And he called them the Land of Cabul, a name they have to this day. 14 Now Hiram had sent to the king 120 talents of gold.

9:10–14 Solomon and Hiram's friendship lasts as long as both men live. Only Solomon's death and Shishak's expansionist policies interrupt their trade agreement.[112] These verses demonstrate the strength of the alliance's bonds, for Solomon is not presented in a favorable way here. Apparently he has offered Hiram cities instead of the food that was given in previous years (cf. 1 Kgs 5:10–12). These cities were "Cabul," meaning "worthless," constituting a poor payment to a "brother" (9:13). Hiram had sent gold to Solomon and received "Cabul" in return. This episode shows a conniving side of Solomon. Readers may wonder whether he is completely trustworthy. Still, Hiram continues to work with Solomon (cf. 9:26–28).

(2) Forced Labor (9:15–23)

15 Here is the account of the forced labor King Solomon conscripted to build the LORD's temple, his own palace, the supporting terraces, the wall of Jerusalem, and Hazor, Megiddo and Gezer. 16 (Pharaoh king of Egypt had attacked and captured Gezer. He had set it on fire. He killed its Canaanite inhabitants and then gave it as a wedding gift to his daughter, Solomon's wife. 17 And Solomon rebuilt Gezer.) He built up Lower Beth Horon, 18 Baalath, and Tadmor in the desert, within his land, 19 as well as all his store cities and the towns for his chariots and for his horses—whatever he desired to build in Jerusalem, in Lebanon and throughout all the territory he ruled.

20 All the people left from the Amorites, Hittites, Perizzites, Hivites and Jebusites (these peoples were not Israelites), 21 that is, their descendants remaining in the land, whom the Israelites could not exterminate—these Solomon conscripted

---

[112] Peckham, "Israel and Phoenicia," 233.

for his slave labor force, as it is to this day. [22]But Solomon did not make slaves of any of the Israelites; they were his fighting men, his government officials, his officers, his captains, and the commanders of his chariots and charioteers. [23]They were also the chief officials in charge of Solomon's projects—550 officials supervising the men who did the work.

9:15–23 Several thousand workers were needed for Solomon's many building projects. Besides the temple and the palace, Solomon commissioned work on "the supporting terraces," which Burney concludes was "a massive fortress or tower built into that part of the city wall where such a protection was specially needed."[113] He also had defensive walls strengthened in Jerusalem, Hazor, Megiddo, and Gezer. Indeed, Gezer needed serious reconstruction because it had been destroyed by Pharaoh, then presented to Solomon as a wedding gift. Further, he decided to construct "store cities and the towns for his chariots and for his horses." Obviously, there was some building project under construction throughout Solomon's reign. Conscripted labor was the cheapest means for the king to complete his building goals.

Who comprised this nonvoluntary labor force? As the comments on 1 Kgs 4:1–6 and 5:13–18 state, scholars disagree about the identity of this group. Those texts state that Adoniram was in charge of the corvée workforce, a notion 1 Kgs 12:18–19 supports, and that thirty thousand Israelites spent up to four months per year working on the king's projects. The confusion arises from 9:22, which says, "But Solomon did not make slaves of any of the Israelites." Rather, it was the remaining Canaanite peoples that were "his slave labor force" (9:20–21). Again, 9:21 and 9:22 use different words for the services rendered.[114] The distinction is a technical one. The Canaanites were *permanent* corvée workers, while the Israelites were *temporary* draftees. Regardless of the technical differences, the northern tribes came to resent the practice bitterly, as later texts reveal.

(3) Further Building (9:24)

[24]After Pharaoh's daughter had come up from the City of David to the palace Solomon had built for her, he constructed the supporting terraces.

9:24 This verse draws together statements made in 1 Kgs 3:1; 7:8; and 9:15. The first text indicates that Pharaoh's daughter lived in Jerusalem until the temple, palace, and defensive walls were completed. The second text simply states that Solomon built a separate palace for his Egyptian-born queen after his major works were done. In 2 Chr 8:11 Solomon says she could not live in David's palace "because the places the ark of the LORD has entered are

[113] Burney, *Notes on the Hebrew Text of the Books of Kings*, 136.
[114] See notes on this section.

holy." Such concern for purity becomes ironic later when the king worships his wives' gods. Finally, the third text notes that "the supporting terraces" were built to help fortify Jerusalem. Patterson and Austel theorize that besides the explanation noted in 2 Chr 8:11 probably "the construction activities would have been at or near the site of her temporary home. It also appears likely that existing structures may have been razed to allow the construction over a large area of this buttressing work."[115]

Besides these basic historical details, 1 Kgs 9:24 reminds readers that this foreign-born wife requires special considerations. For whatever reason, the nation must bear the expenses for a new, separate palace. Pharaoh's daughter worships different gods from the Israelites (2 Chr 8:11). So far she is the only non-Israelite royal wife mentioned. The problems she causes will multiply by chap. 11, where the author finally reveals the extent of the king's harem. Then the full implications of Solomon's marriage to women who share neither his national nor religious heritage become clearer.

(4) Worship (9:25)

[25]Three times a year Solomon sacrificed burnt offerings and fellowship offerings on the altar he had built for the LORD, burning incense before the LORD along with them, and so fulfilled the temple obligations.

9:25 At least for now Solomon honors the Lord by offering sacrifices at the new temple. Three occasions for sacrifices are mentioned. These times were most likely the Feasts of Unleavened Bread, Weeks, and Booths (cf. Exod 23:14–19). By offering the required sacrifices at these specified times, Solomon demonstrates his faithfulness to the covenant. All his subjects could then follow his lead.

The last sentence in 9:25, which the NIV renders "and so fulfilled the temple obligations," is somewhat difficult to translate. Literally the text reads "and he finished the house."[116] Burney thinks the phrase is a copyist's error.[117] Montgomery and Gehman suggest, however, that this phrase parallels Ps 76:11, where a similar construction refers to the paying of vows.[118] Keil adds that "and so fulfilled" may be a continuation of "burning incense."[119] Furthermore, the preceding description of Solomon's ritual activities favors the NIV translation. Solomon met all religious obligations set by the Mosaic law and implied by the building of a central sanctuary.

---

[115] Patterson and Austel, "1 and 2 Kings," 97.

[116] The clause is וְשִׁלַּם אֶת־הַבָּיִת.

[117] Burney says, "It seems not improbable that the letters ושלם are a mistaken repetition of ושלמים in the earlier part of the verse" (*Notes on the Hebrew Text of the Books of Kings,* 142).

[118] Montgomery and Gehman, *Kings,* 215.

[119] Keil, "I and II Kings," 147.

(5) Shipping (9:26–28)

[26]King Solomon also built ships at Ezion Geber, which is near Elath in Edom, on the shore of the Red Sea. [27]And Hiram sent his men—sailors who knew the sea—to serve in the fleet with Solomon's men. [28]They sailed to Ophir and brought back 420 talents of gold, which they delivered to King Solomon.

9:26–28 Solomon's partnership with Hiram emerges again. Israel built the ships, Tyre sailed them, and both nations took home gold. Perhaps only 1 Kgs 10:11–12 approximates this passage's ability to illustrate how both kings benefited from their alliance. Ezion Geber no longer exists as a port, due to changes in the coastal line.[120] Ophir was an ancient city virtually synonymous with the production of gold.[121] Solomon's success in shipping also led to prosperous land trade, as the next passage indicates.

7. Solomon's Wisdom and Wealth (10:1–29)

If any doubts about Solomon's greatness remain after chap. 9, surely 1 Kgs 10:1–29 removes them. So far the text has presented the monarch's exploits from an Israelite's point of view. In 10:1–13, however, an outsider's opinion is included. The queen of Sheba travels some 1,500 miles to examine his wisdom.[122] Perhaps she also wanted to explore future trading ventures as well (cf. 1 Kgs 10:11–12), but her primary purpose "was to verify Solomon's reputation for wisdom and devotion to Yahweh (v. 1)."[123] She is not disappointed. Solomon exceeds her expectations. The author follows up this story with more data intended to convince readers of Solomon's political, financial, and military splendor (1 Kgs 10:14–29).

(1) The Queen of Sheba's Visit (10:1–13)

[1]When the queen of Sheba heard about the fame of Solomon and his relation to the name of the LORD, she came to test him with hard questions. [2]Arriving at Jerusalem with a very great caravan—with camels carrying spices, large quantities of gold, and precious stones—she came to Solomon and talked with him about all that she had on her mind. [3]Solomon answered all her questions; nothing was too hard for the king to explain to her. [4]When the queen of Sheba saw all the wisdom of Solomon and the palace he had built, [5]the food on his table, the seating of his officials, the attending servants in their robes, his cupbearers, and the burnt offerings he made at the temple of the LORD, she was overwhelmed.

[6]She said to the king, "The report I heard in my own country about your

[120] Gray, *1 and 2 Kings,* 236–37.

[121] Jones, *1 and 2 Kings,* 1:220.

[122] Matheney, "1 Kings," 188.

[123] Hubbard, *First and Second Kings,* 63.

**achievements and your wisdom is true. 7But I did not believe these things until I
came and saw with my own eyes. Indeed, not even half was told me; in wisdom
and wealth you have far exceeded the report I heard. 8How happy your men must
be! How happy your officials, who continually stand before you and hear your
wisdom! 9Praise be to the LORD your God, who has delighted in you and placed
you on the throne of Israel. Because of the LORD's eternal love for Israel, he has
made you king, to maintain justice and righteousness."**

10And she gave the king 120 talents of gold, large quantities of spices, and precious stones. Never again were so many spices brought in as those the queen of Sheba gave to King Solomon.

**11(Hiram's ships brought gold from Ophir; and from there they brought great
cargoes of almugwood and precious stones. 12The king used the almugwood to
make supports for the temple of the LORD and for the royal palace, and to make
harps and lyres for the musicians. So much almugwood has never been imported
or seen since that day.)**

13King Solomon gave the queen of Sheba all she desired and asked for, besides what he had given her out of his royal bounty. Then she left and returned with her retinue to her own country.

10:1–5 Two reasons for the queen's journey are given. First, she "heard about the fame of Solomon" (cf. 2 Chr 9:1). His abilities have earned him the reputation of being the wisest man in the ancient world (1 Kgs 4:29–34). This very rich, very successful woman intends to see if he deserves such acclaim. Second, she comes because of Solomon's "relation to the name of the LORD."[124] In other words, she recognizes that only a great God could produce such a great king. C. F. Burney explains:

> The meaning is that the fame of Yahweh's name led to a diffusion of a report concerning the wise and prosperous king who enjoyed His favor and protection; and this is in full accordance with the prominence which the queen in this story assigns to Yahweh as the chooser and supporter of Solomon (v. 9).[125]

She decides "to test him with hard questions," or "riddles," such as those mentioned in Prov 1:6 or the one posed by Samson in Judg 14:12–14. Gray comments that "such tests of practical sagacity and poetic susceptibility were part of the diplomatic encounters of the day."[126] However, she may seek more than intellectual combat. She may also desire "truths hidden in some of the enigmatic sayings known to her."[127] Indeed, she seeks spiritual insight from one famous for possessing the Lord's wisdom.

The queen's arrival must have caused a commotion in Jerusalem. Her ques-

---

124 The Hebrew text reads וּמַלְכַּת־שְׁבָא שֹׁמַעַת אֶת־שֵׁמַע שְׁלֹמֹה לְשֵׁם יְהוָה. This construction makes God the focus for both Solomon's wisdom and his reputation.

125 Burney, *Notes on the Hebrew Text of the Books of Kings*, 142.

126 Gray, 1 and 2 Kings, 241.

127 Patterson and Austel, "1 and 2 Kings," 101.

tions, on the other hand, may have been difficult, but they were not "too hard for the king to explain to her." Thus, she *hears* his wisdom in an unmistakable way. Furthermore, the queen *observes* Solomon's wise decisions and organizational genius in his palace, his court, and the temple. Solomon's words are matched by his deeds. Given the king's brilliance, the queen realizes he has won the battle of wits. She is "overwhelmed," or "totally out of breath, or spirit."[128] There are no more questions.

10:6–10 Before she actually meets Solomon, the queen finds the reports of Solomon's wisdom and wealth too fantastic to be believed. After this encounter, however, she admits to him, "You have far exceeded the report I heard." His servants are privileged to be in earshot of his wise speeches. As a token of the queen's esteem, she gives Solomon a large amount of gold and an even greater amount of spices. In this way she pays tribute to one she considers her superior (cf. Gen 14:20).

Between the confession of Solomon's greatness and the offering of the gifts, the queen makes an important statement about the Lord. She claims that God deserves praise for choosing him to rule Israel. In fact, the presence of Solomon on the throne proves "the LORD's eternal love for Israel." This love has motivated God's choice of Israel (Deut 7:7–8), David (2 Sam 7:15–16), and now Solomon. How must Solomon reflect God's love? By maintaining justice and righteousness in the land, the very gift Solomon requested in 1 Kgs 3:1–9. These comments are similar to those Hiram makes in 1 Kgs 5:7. Both non-Jewish monarchs recognize God's primacy in Israel's history. Quite ironically, Solomon and future kings of Israel choose to ignore what even noncovenant rulers seem to know is true: God rules Israel, and God blesses obedient Israelite kings.

10:11–12 These verses remind readers of the Hiram-Solomon trading practices mentioned in 9:26–28. Probably the author wants to remove any doubts the preceding verse may have raised about Solomon's ability to bring gold and spices to Jerusalem. He and Hiram were able to accomplish this task effectively on their own. Therefore, the queen's gift grows in significance given the magnitude of Solomon's trading successes.

10:13 Now the story ends amiably. Solomon gives the queen tangible gifts to supplement the intellectual and spiritual gifts he has given her, and she returns to her country.

Various interpretations of this story arose over time in Jewish, Ethiopic, and Christian circles. One Jewish legend holds that Solomon fathered a son for the queen, which was her ultimate "desire." Ethiopic tradition parallels the Jewish tradition, for it claims "the royal Abyssinian line was founded by the offspring

[128] The phrase וְלֹא־הָיָה בָהּ עוֹד רוּחַ. It could also be translated "and there was no longer any spirit in her."

of Solomon and the queen of Sheba."[129] Neither of these traditions has any historical basis, nor can they be substantiated by the biblical text. Jesus uses the queen as an example of the effort one should be willing to make to hear God's truth (Matt 12:42). She traveled 1,500 miles to question Solomon, but Jesus' audience refuses to listen to the Son of God himself.

(2) Solomon's Wealth (10:14–29)

14The weight of the gold that Solomon received yearly was 666 talents, 15not including the revenues from merchants and traders and from all the Arabian kings and the governors of the land.

16King Solomon made two hundred large shields of hammered gold; six hundred bekas of gold went into each shield. 17He also made three hundred small shields of hammered gold, with three minas of gold in each shield. The king put them in the Palace of the Forest of Lebanon.

18Then the king made a great throne inlaid with ivory and overlaid with fine gold. 19The throne had six steps, and its back had a rounded top. On both sides of the seat were armrests, with a lion standing beside each of them. 20Twelve lions stood on the six steps, one at either end of each step. Nothing like it had ever been made for any other kingdom. 21All King Solomon's goblets were gold, and all the household articles in the Palace of the Forest of Lebanon were pure gold. Nothing was made of silver, because silver was considered of little value in Solomon's days. 22The king had a fleet of trading ships at sea along with the ships of Hiram. Once every three years it returned, carrying gold, silver and ivory, and apes and baboons.

23King Solomon was greater in riches and wisdom than all the other kings of the earth. 24The whole world sought audience with Solomon to hear the wisdom God had put in his heart. 25Year after year, everyone who came brought a gift—articles of silver and gold, robes, weapons and spices, and horses and mules.

26Solomon accumulated chariots and horses; he had fourteen hundred chariots and twelve thousand horses, which he kept in the chariot cities and also with him in Jerusalem. 27The king made silver as common in Jerusalem as stones, and cedar as plentiful as sycamore-fig trees in the foothills. 28Solomon's horses were imported from Egypt and from Kue—the royal merchants purchased them from Kue. 29They imported a chariot from Egypt for six hundred shekels of silver, and a horse for a hundred and fifty. They also exported them to all the kings of the Hittites and of the Arameans.

10:14–17 Solomon's annual tax revenues were enormous during his glory days. Many tons of gold ("666 talents") flowed into the treasury each year. As with most of the numbers reported in 1, 2 Kings, scholars dispute whether the amount of gold listed here is exaggerated or accurate. Those who question the total wonder if the "666 talents" is compiled by adding figures

[129] Patterson and Austel, "1 and 2 Kings," 102.

mentioned in 9:14,28; 10:10.[130] Those who accept the total think the numbers are not fantastic given the fact that they include all Solomon's major pursuits.[131] The lesser income mentioned in 10:15 simply made the revenue greater. Soggin explains that Solomon "functioned as a middleman," connecting and profiting greatly from the economic interests of Egypt, Syria, Arabia, and the Mediterranean world. He was thus a key figure in international trade.[132]

Given the variety and extent of these endeavors, it appears impossible to contradict the biblical witness. Besides, had the author intended to emphasize the king's wealth by exaggeration here, he could have done as the Chronicler does in 2 Chr 1:15 ("The king made silver and gold as common in Jerusalem as stones") as he does later in the passage at vv. 21,27.

Because of the influx of gold, Solomon was able to make shields of gold, which were probably used during ceremonial occasions (cf. 1 Kgs 14:26–28).[133] These shields were kept in the summer palace, "the Palace of the Forest of Lebanon." Perhaps the shields were also a good way of stockpiling gold without having to utilize the treasury itself.

10:18–22 Solomon used ivory gathered during Hiram's three-year voyages to build a magnificent throne. There does not seem to be any particular significance in Israelite religion to the number of steps or the presence of lions on the throne. Gray thinks the design reflects Phoenician influence, which is logical given this same influence on the temple's construction.[134] What remains unclear is whether such designs reflected non-Yahwistic beliefs.

Verses 21–22 reemphasize the abundance of gold mentioned in 10:14–17. Even Solomon's drinking vessels were made of gold. Much of the gold came from far away since Hiram's ships brought it to Israel. Such was the availability of gold that "silver was considered of little value in Solomon's day." This statement would make the poor, exiled original audience of 1, 2 Kings gasp. The contrast between their present experience and the way things once had been could hardly be more obvious or telling. Such also is the spiritual bankruptcy caused by sin.

10:23–25 These verses offer the final confirmation that God has indeed kept his promise to make Solomon wiser than all who came before or follow after him (1 Kgs 3:12). As in 1 Kgs 4:29–34, Solomon's wisdom is said to exceed "all the other kings of the earth." Just as the queen of Sheba seeks his wisdom in 10:1–13, so now other kings come to hear his instruction. Those who come bring gifts, which both shows their appreciation for Solomon and

[130] Cf. Montgomery and Gehman, *Kings,* 219, and Noth, *Könige,* 228.

[131] Cf. Keil, "I and II Kings," 161.

[132] Soggin, "The Davidic-Solomonic Kingdom," 374–75.

[133] Montgomery and Gehman, *Kings,* 220.

[134] Gray, *I and 2 Kings,* 247.

swells his treasury. Will he continue to serve God as the natural response to the Lord's faithfulness? Will he remain wise to the end?

10:26–29 Solomon's wealth, as depicted in these and earlier verses, is further proof of the Lord's covenant keeping (cf. 1 Kgs 3:13). The king has horses for an army that he barely has to use. Metaphorically speaking, he becomes so gold-laden that silver seems "as common in Jerusalem as stones." His horses and chariots are quite expensive, though some costs are recovered by resale to other nations.

A more positive financial picture could hardly be imagined. Still, readers must ask if Solomon will keep his end of the covenant. God has kept all promises (cf. 1 Kgs 3:12–13). Will Solomon follow David's example by keeping God's commands (cf. 1 Kgs 3:14–15)? As R. Hubbard observes, "The chapter offers one last picture of Solomon at his best—the king above all ancient kings. . . . Its point is that Solomon enjoyed God's special favor."[135] The point of the book's next episode is to explore what Solomon did with this favor during his last years in power.

8. Solomon's Decline (11:1–43)

One final assessment of Solomon now appears. Unlike the earlier ones, this account lays bare the faults and frailties of this brilliant man. These failings affect the king himself, of course, but they affect the nation more. So far the people have certainly worked hard and have enjoyed the material success their leader's wisdom brings them. They seem to have remained faithful to the Lord, at least in part because of the presence of the temple. Like their king, Israel is riding a crest of power and influence previously unknown. To be sure, hints of problems appear in the text, yet such potential difficulties appear to be annoyances, not threats.

Unfortunately, the plot takes a tragic turn. Solomon and Israel have risen to great heights only to fall into idolatry, division, decay, and, ultimately, exile. The four episodes in 1 Kings 11 begin this sorry decline. Each stage of Israel's deterioration is made all the more regrettable because of its avoidability. Covenant faithfulness would have allowed the covenant people blessing and safety, but their disobedience leaves a just God no alternative except to punish. Solomon's sin may have begun small. It may have developed in stages over time. However it started, however it was fueled, it began a national disintegration that was at times slowed but never completely halted.

(1) Solomon's Idolatry (11:1–13)

[1]King Solomon, however, loved many foreign women besides Pharaoh's daugh-

[135] Hubbard, *First and Second Kings,* 66.

ter—Moabites, Ammonites, Edomites, Sidonians and Hittites. [2]They were from nations about which the LORD had told the Israelites, "You must not intermarry with them, because they will surely turn your hearts after their gods." Nevertheless, Solomon held fast to them in love. [3]He had seven hundred wives of royal birth and three hundred concubines, and his wives led him astray. [4]As Solomon grew old, his wives turned his heart after other gods, and his heart was not fully devoted to the LORD his God, as the heart of David his father had been. [5]He followed Ashtoreth the goddess of the Sidonians, and Molech the detestable god of the Ammonites. [6]So Solomon did evil in the eyes of the LORD; he did not follow the LORD completely, as David his father had done.

[7]On a hill east of Jerusalem, Solomon built a high place for Chemosh the detestable god of Moab, and for Molech the detestable god of the Ammonites. [8]He did the same for all his foreign wives, who burned incense and offered sacrifices to their gods.

[9]The LORD became angry with Solomon because his heart had turned away from the LORD, the God of Israel, who had appeared to him twice. [10]Although he had forbidden Solomon to follow other gods, Solomon did not keep the LORD's command. [11]So the LORD said to Solomon, "Since this is your attitude and you have not kept my covenant and my decrees, which I commanded you, I will most certainly tear the kingdom away from you and give it to one of your subordinates. [12]Nevertheless, for the sake of David your father, I will not do it during your lifetime. I will tear it out of the hand of your son. [13]Yet I will not tear the whole kingdom from him, but will give him one tribe for the sake of David my servant and for the sake of Jerusalem, which I have chosen."

11:1–3 After the glowing report in 10:14–29, these verses are the literary equivalent of a blow to the face. Despite all his obvious strengths, the king has a very evident weakness for women, especially foreign women.[136] Besides Pharaoh's daughter, he loves Moabite, Ammonite, Edomite, Sidonian, and Hittite women. Altogether he accumulates "seven hundred wives of royal birth and three hundred concubines." Like the marriage to the Egyptian

---

[136]The LXX version of this passage is somewhat different than the MT. Gray comments: "The opening sentence in G, for instance, merely states that Solomon was fond of women. No censure is implied as in MT, which states that he loved many alien women (v. 1) of the races with whom Israel was forbidden to mix" (*1 and 2 Kings,* 252). Still, Gray concludes that the LXX "betrays obvious traces of smoothing out of a complex text which had many obvious elaborations and accretions, hence it is to be followed with extreme caution" (ibid.). Montgomery and Gehman take the changes more seriously and even offer a possible original text that lies behind the received text (*Kings,* 231–32). Burney also offers a proposed reconstruction of the text's transmission (*Notes on the Hebrew Text of the Book of Kings,* 153–55). Perhaps the LXX smooths over the rough edges of Solomon's reputation here, as it surely does later in the chapter. Without question, though, thoughtful readers would have made the connection between the wives and Deut 7:3–4 and Exod 34:15–16 with or without an editorial comment. It appears likely, then, that the MT is original, for it portrays Solomon honestly and presents the obvious ramifications of his actions.

princess, most of these unions probably were politically motivated.[137] Such linking of nations was intended to foster peaceful relations between normally combative countries. In a straightforward secular kingdom this practice would be good politics.

There are several problems, however, with what Solomon has done. First, he has disobeyed Moses' law for marriage, which constitutes a breach of the agreement Solomon makes with God in 1 Kgs 3:1–14; 6:11–13; and 9:1–9. Moses says in Deut 7:3–4 and Exod 34:15–16 that Israelites must not intermarry with noncovenant nations. Why? Because God says "they will turn your sons away from following me to serve other gods" (Deut 7:4). Judgment will then result. Second, Solomon has broken Moses' commands for kings (cf. Deut 17:14–20). Moses explicitly says, "He must not take many wives or his heart will be led astray" (Deut 17:17). Indeed, all of Moses' dire predictions come true in Solomon's case. His wives do lure him into idolatry. Solomon, however, is responsible for his own actions. He knows better but does not act on this knowledge.

Third, Solomon has evidently fallen into the emotional trap of wanting to be like pagan kings. Moses counsels kings to remain as close to the people as possible (Deut 17:14–20). Kings who become too wealthy desire possessions and women more than they desire to serve God and the people, Moses warns (Deut 17:14–20). Solomon has clearly forgotten this admonition. He has competed with other kings and queens in wisdom and splendor and has won (cf. 1 Kgs 4:29–34; 10:1–13,23–25). These victories are gifts from God (1 Kgs 3:10–15). Competing in wives is outside of God's will and promise to bless, though, so the process can have no positive result.

11:4–8 What occurs in this passage must have sickened the author of 1, 2 Kings and any original readers committed to the Lord. In Solomon's old age his wives influence his devotion to God, and he worships "other gods." How did this outrage occur? "His heart was not fully devoted to the LORD his God, as the heart of David his father had been." In other words, his heart was no longer wholly God's. The Lord had ceased to be the major factor in his life. Once this shift occurred, the next steps into idolatry became more natural and easier to accept.

Other than their link to his wives, Solomon's choice of gods makes no sense. In the ancient world polytheists tended to worship the gods of nations who had conquered their armies or at least the gods of countries more powerful than their own. Ironically, Solomon worships the gods of people he has conquered and already controls. What could he possibly gain from such activity? The whole episode makes no sense, just as idolatry itself makes no sense.

[137] Bright, *A History of Israel*, 211.

Who were these gods Solomon worshiped? The fertility goddess Ashtoreth had been a stumbling block to the Israelites since they arrived in Canaan (Judg 2:13). Perhaps it is fitting for Solomon to worship a sex goddess. Molech was an astral deity (Zeph 1:5) to whom human sacrifices were offered (Lev 20:2–5; 2 Kgs 23:10; Lev 18:21; Jer 32:35).[138] Chemosh, like Molech, probably was also an astral god. Besides these deities, Solomon probably worshiped other gods as well (1 Kgs 11:8). Thus, the miraculously blessed heir of David, leader of the covenant people, has broken the most fundamental command of all: "You shall have no other gods before me" (Exod 20:3).

11:9–13 Of all the sins recorded in Scripture, God takes idolatry the most seriously, for no other sin has the capability of wrecking the entire covenant by itself. When this sin is committed, God acts swiftly, justly, and redemptively, as Israel discovers in Exodus 32–34; Numbers 20; and the entire Book of Judges. It is natural, then, to read that God "became angry with Solomon." The Lord has revealed himself to Solomon, blessed him, and honored him. In return Solomon has turned his back on the Lord.

Therefore, God speaks to Solomon again. Unlike 1 Kgs 3:1–15; 6:11–13; and 9:1–19, however, the Lord now censures Solomon. God says, "Since this is your attitude . . . I will most certainly tear the kingdom away from you and give it to one of your subordinates." This declaration reminds readers of 1 Sam 13:13–14, where Saul's sin leads Samuel to tell Saul his kingdom will not endure, for "the LORD has sought out a man after his own heart and appointed him leader of his people, because you have not kept the LORD's command" (13:14). Whereas David ascended to power because of Saul's power, now David's son has sinned in a way that causes God to limit the kingdom of David's descendants.

Only one thing keeps Solomon on the throne at all, and that is the promise the Lord made to David in 2 Sam 7:1–17. For David's sake the Lord allows Solomon to remain in power. Further, for David's sake his descendants will continue to rule a fragment of the covenant nation. Despite these concessions to David's memory, however, the punishment is clear, irrevocable, and stunning. Solomon's sin will soon cause the nation to crash from the heights it has achieved. His idolatry will lead to idolatry among the people. Israel has begun the long road to exile, though they do not know yet that their actions entail such consequences.

(2) Rebellions against Solomon (11:14–25)

[14]Then the LORD raised up against Solomon an adversary, Hadad the Edomite, from the royal line of Edom. [15]Earlier when David was fighting with Edom,

[138] On Ashtoreth, Molech, and Chemosh see Gray, *1 and 2 Kings,* 257–258; Jones, *1 and 2 Kings,* 1:236.

Joab the commander of the army, who had gone up to bury the dead, had struck down all the men in Edom. [16]Joab and all the Israelites stayed there for six months, until they had destroyed all the men in Edom. [17]But Hadad, still only a boy, fled to Egypt with some Edomite officials who had served his father. [18]They set out from Midian and went to Paran. Then taking men from Paran with them, they went to Egypt, to Pharaoh king of Egypt, who gave Hadad a house and land and provided him with food.

[19]Pharaoh was so pleased with Hadad that he gave him a sister of his own wife, Queen Tahpenes, in marriage. [20]The sister of Tahpenes bore him a son named Genubath, whom Tahpenes brought up in the royal palace. There Genubath lived with Pharaoh's own children.

[21]While he was in Egypt, Hadad heard that David rested with his fathers and that Joab the commander of the army was also dead. Then Hadad said to Pharaoh, "Let me go, that I may return to my own country."

[22]"What have you lacked here that you want to go back to your own country?" Pharaoh asked.

"Nothing," Hadad replied, "but do let me go!"

[23]And God raised up against Solomon another adversary, Rezon son of Eliada, who had fled from his master, Hadadezer king of Zobah. [24]He gathered men around him and became the leader of a band of rebels when David destroyed the forces [of Zobah]; the rebels went to Damascus, where they settled and took control. [25]Rezon was Israel's adversary as long as Solomon lived, adding to the trouble caused by Hadad. So Rezon ruled in Aram and was hostile toward Israel.

11:14–22 Just because the Lord leaves Solomon on the throne does not mean Solomon encounters no consequences of his sin. God raises up an adversary,[139] an Edomite named Hadad, to oppose Solomon. Hadad was the only surviving member of Edom's royal family after David's crushing victory over that nation (cf. 2 Sam 8:13–14; 1 Chr 18:11–13). Having fled to Egypt, it is understandable for him to grow up hating Israel. Apparently the Pharaoh had no problem nurturing Hadad while maintaining favorable relations with Solomon at the same time.[140] Eventually Hadad returns home to harass Solomon, who could no longer expect total cooperation from this vassal state.

11:23–25 God also raises up a second adversary. This individual, Rezon, began his career, like David, as a leader of a band of rebels. Later he took control of Damascus, from which he caused Solomon much trouble. David had defeated Syria earlier (cf. 2 Sam 8:3–9), so Rezon's hatred of Israel was similar to Hadad's. Together they posed an ongoing threat to Israel's interests in Solomon's latter years. As Patterson and Austel note, Rezon "was Solomon's troublemaker in the north while Hadad caused problems in the south (v. 25)."[141]

---

[139] Literally a satan (שָׂטָן), or "adversary."
[140] Gray, *1 and 2 Kings,* 265.
[141] Patterson and Austel, "1, 2 Kings," 109.

(3) Ahijah Prophesies Division (11:26–40)

26 Also, Jeroboam son of Nebat rebelled against the king. He was one of Solomon's officials, an Ephraimite from Zeredah, and his mother was a widow named Zeruah.

27 Here is the account of how he rebelled against the king: Solomon had built the supporting terraces and had filled in the gap in the wall of the city of David his father. 28 Now Jeroboam was a man of standing, and when Solomon saw how well the young man did his work, he put him in charge of the whole labor force of the house of Joseph.

29 About that time Jeroboam was going out of Jerusalem, and Ahijah the prophet of Shiloh met him on the way, wearing a new cloak. The two of them were alone out in the country, 30 and Ahijah took hold of the new cloak he was wearing and tore it into twelve pieces. 31 Then he said to Jeroboam, "Take ten pieces for yourself, for this is what the LORD, the God of Israel, says: 'See, I am going to tear the kingdom out of Solomon's hand and give you ten tribes. 32 But for the sake of my servant David and the city of Jerusalem, which I have chosen out of all the tribes of Israel, he will have one tribe. 33 I will do this because they have forsaken me and worshiped Ashtoreth the goddess of the Sidonians, Chemosh the god of the Moabites, and Molech the god of the Ammonites, and have not walked in my ways, nor done what is right in my eyes, nor kept my statutes and laws as David, Solomon's father, did.

34 "'But I will not take the whole kingdom out of Solomon's hand; I have made him ruler all the days of his life for the sake of David my servant, whom I chose and who observed my commands and statutes. 35 I will take the kingdom from his son's hands and give you ten tribes. 36 I will give one tribe to his son so that David my servant may always have a lamp before me in Jerusalem, the city where I chose to put my Name. 37 However, as for you, I will take you, and you will rule over all that your heart desires; you will be king over Israel. 38 If you do whatever I command you and walk in my ways and do what is right in my eyes by keeping my statutes and commands, as David my servant did, I will be with you. I will build you a dynasty as enduring as the one I built for David and will give Israel to you. 39 I will humble David's descendants because of this, but not forever.'"

40 Solomon tried to kill Jeroboam, but Jeroboam fled to Egypt, to Shishak the king, and stayed there until Solomon's death.

11:26 A third adversary is introduced. This man, named Jeroboam, comes from Israel itself. In fact, this opponent emerges from Solomon's own court, for Jeroboam is "one of Solomon's officials." Two other items are mentioned. First, he is from the tribe of Ephraim, a northern clan. Thus, he can possibly muster a power base that will rival Solomon's southern-based coalition. He would be less of a threat if he were from Solomon's own region. Second, he is a widow's son. The Greek translation turns his mother into a harlot, a move clearly aimed at defaming Jeroboam at his mother's expense.[142] Evidence is insufficient to accept this alteration. The Greek

[142] For other LXX variations in the Jeroboam story see the discussion of chap. 12.

translators appear to lessen Solomon's and his family's roles in Israel's downfall. Jeroboam's identity, however, is not as significant as how he rises to prominence.

11:27–33 Verse 27 announces that what follows details how Jeroboam rebelled against Solomon, then eventually gained power. At some unstated period of time after "Solomon had built the supporting terraces" and repaired Jerusalem's walls (Cf. 1 Kgs 9:24), Jeroboam impresses the king. Jeroboam is "a man of standing," which perhaps means that he has received an inheritance from his deceased father.[143] He is still a "young man," so the king's decision to "put him in charge of the whole labor force of the house of Joseph" demonstrates just "how well" he does his work. His ties with "the house of Joseph," the northern tribes, will become significant when the rebellion actually occurs. Ironically, Solomon chooses, promotes, and gives a power base to the man who will end the Davidic dynasty's rule over Northern Israel.

Now God acts decisively to inform Jeroboam that he will one day have his own kingdom. Ahijah the prophet takes a new cloak and meets Jeroboam outside Jerusalem. At this apparently unplanned meeting, Ahijah tears the cloak into twelve pieces, gives Jeroboam ten pieces, and explains that Israel will be divided. David's descendants from the tribe of Judah will have one other tribe (Benjamin) to rule. Jeroboam will govern the remaining ten tribes. Israel will remain in the promised land but in a divided, weakened condition.

Ahijah explains two extremely important theological ideas that impact Israel's future. These ideas come as direct words from the Lord. First, he says that it is only because of God's faithfulness to David and choice of Jerusalem that Judah will continue as a kingdom. Second, the prophet asserts that the division will occur as a judgment of Solomon and the people's idolatry. Clearly, sin impacts a country's so-called secular existence. Despite Solomon's unfaithfulness, however, the Lord will remain faithful. Promises made to David in 2 Samuel 7 will be kept, as will the pledges made to Solomon in 1 Kings 3; 6; and 9. The reader senses at this point that ongoing national sin will lead to still greater punishment, such as exile and the other consequences described in Deuteronomy 27–28 and Leviticus 26.

11:34–40 Ahijah continues God's message to Jeroboam by commenting further on Jerusalem's importance in Judah's survival. Not only has God chosen David, the Lord has chosen Jerusalem. His purpose there was to glorify his name through unified and committed worship at the temple (cf. 1 Kgs 9:1–9) and through the witness of a people wholly committed to a personal, relational, just, covenant God.

As for Jeroboam, God promises him a kingdom and, startlingly, "a dynasty as enduring as the one I built for David." To receive these blessings,

---

[143] Gray, *1 and 2 Kings,* 273.

however, Jeroboam must act like David. He must obey God, keep the commandments, and walk in God's ways. Only then will he be blessed as David has been blessed. Implicit in these promises is the notion that any idolatry will bring this covenant to a halt. Jeroboam must emulate David, not Solomon. Ahijah concludes the message by stating that all these things happen to "humble David's descendants," not to eliminate the promise of an eternal kingdom. The messianic promise remains in effect, for the punishment will not last "forever."[144]

The episode ends with Jeroboam fleeing to Egypt to avoid Solomon's desire to kill him. He finds refuge in Shishak's court, a fact that alerts readers to changes in Egypt's leadership.[145] Shishak is not as friendly to Solomon as Siamun was in the past. Perhaps the new Pharaoh resents paying Solomon's tolls, or perhaps he attempts to build a new power base that will serve his own interests. Either way the Davidic lineage is in trouble. Jeroboam has a constituency in Israel, a significant foreign ally, and God's promise to place him in power. Without question, then, he will soon be the major force in Israelite politics.

Ahijah's prominence in this story begins the prophets' role as major players in the history of Israel. Of course, earlier prophets impact Israel's story, such as Samuel and Nathan, but the prophetic movement now becomes even more significant. In the rest of 1, 2 Kings the prophets act as God's spokespersons, as anointers of new kings, as miracle workers, and as Israel's overall covenant conscience. Scholars disagree about how, when, and why the prophetic movement emerged in Israel. Still, much work has been done that illuminates these unusual servants of God. More specifically, how the prophets received their messages,[146] what the prophets taught,[147] the forms their messages took,[148] the prophets' place in society,[149] the prophets' historical set-

---

[144] The Heb. reads לֹא כָל־הַיָּמִים. The LXX omits the words "and will give Israel to you. I will humble David's descendants because of this, but not forever" (1 Kgs 11:38b–39). Certainly this promise is in keeping with the book's message to this point and is repeated later, so its originality seems quite plausible. Still, the differences between the MT and the LXX in the Jeroboam stories are significant, so interpreters must be cautious at this point.

[145] Cf. "Survey of Historical Details Related to 1 Kgs 9:10–11:43" on p. 155.

[146] In this and the next five footnotes space allows only a few foundational works to be cited. Cf. G. Hölscher, *Die Profeten: Untersuchungen zur Religionsgeschichte Israels* (Leipzig: J. C. Hinrichs, 1914), and J. Lindblom, *Prophecy in Ancient Israel* (Philadelphia: Fortress, 1962), for examinations of the ecstatic nature of prophecy.

[147] Analyses of prophetic theology include G. von Rad, *Old Testament Theology,* vol. 2, trans. D. M. G. Stalker (New York: Harper & Row, 1965); B. Duhm, *Theologie der Propheten* (Bonn: Adolph Marcus, 1875); and R. Clements, *Prophecy and Covenant*, SBT 43 (London: SCM, 1965).

[148] Cf. C. Westermann, *Basic Forms of Prophetic Speech* (Philadelphia: Westminster, 1967), and J. Hayes, "The History of the Form-Critical Study of Prophecy," *Society of Biblical Literature Seminar Papers 1973: Vol One,* ed. G. MacRae (Cambridge: SBL, 1973) 60–99.

[149] R. R. Wilson, *Prophecy and Society in Ancient Israel* (Philadelphia: Fortress, 1980).

ting,[150] and the prophets' literary artistry[151] have all been treated thoroughly over the past several decades. These analyses testify to the depth and diversity inherent in the prophetic tradition. Without these individuals it is difficult to conceive of an Israelite religion.

(4) Solomon's Death (11:41–43)

[41]As for the other events of Solomon's reign—all he did and the wisdom he displayed—are they not written in the book of the annals of Solomon? [42]Solomon reigned in Jerusalem over all Israel forty years. [43]Then he rested with his fathers and was buried in the city of David his father. And Rehoboam his son succeeded him as king.

11:41–43 The author uses what will become a familiar formula to mark Solomon's passing. First, the author mentions the source for the information found in chaps. 1–11. No one knows the exact contents of "the book of the annals of Solomon," but this "book" probably contained both narrative and chronological materials. Second, the length of Solomon's reign (forty years) is duly noted. Solomon rules for the same number of years as his father (cf. 1 Kgs 2:11), which at least implies that the Lord has kept his promise to David to place his son on the throne and his promise of long life to Solomon (cf. 1 Kgs 3:14). Third, Solomon's death and the name of his successor are mentioned. Rehoboam will become king, but he does not know what the reader knows: Solomon's son will govern a greatly reduced kingdom. Israel's glory days are over.

With Solomon's death one of the book's major characters leaves the story. Only Elijah, Elisha, and, perhaps, Hezekiah and Josiah approach Solomon's prominence in the overall scheme of 1, 2 Kings. What kind of man was Solomon? How does the author characterize him? Certainly Solomon has some positive traits. Chief among these good qualities is his wisdom. He has the ability to gather knowledge on a wide range of topics, organize the information gathered, write his conclusions, live by his conclusions, and finally teach

---

[150] For a recent historical-critical analysis of how the prophets worked within their historical environment consult B. Peckham, *History and Prophecy: The Development of Late Judean Literary Traditions* (Garden City: Doubleday, 1993). Virtually every commentary on the prophetic books that has been written in the last century has been enriched by information gathered through archaeological discoveries.

[151] Both canonical and literary studies have appeared. For the former, see R. Clements, "Patterns in the Prophetic Canon," in *Canon and Authority*, ed. G. W. Coats and B. O. Long (Philadelphia: Fortress, 1977) 42–55, and B. Childs, *Biblical Theology of the Old and New Testaments: Theological Reflection on the Christian Bible* (Minneapolis: Fortress, 1992) 167–180. For treatments of the latter read J. D. W. Watts, *Isaiah 1–33*, WBC (Waco: Word, 1985) and *Isaiah 34–66*, WBC (Waco: Word, 1987), and P. R. House, *The Unity of the Twelve*, JSOT 97/BALS 27 (Sheffield: Almond Press, 1990).

others what he has learned (cf. 1 Kgs 4:29–34; 10:1–13). Most importantly, at his best Solomon is able to do all these things in *spiritual* matters. Early in his career Solomon applies his knowledge of Scriptures and his experiences with God in a way that helps him obey God. He keeps the Lord's commands, judges justly, and builds the temple. Thus, wisdom means the ability to obey God's truth, and Solomon is quite able to be wise.

Three other positive characteristics demonstrate Solomon's wisdom in so-called secular realms. First, he is an organizational genius. He is able to order, tax, and govern a fairly extensive political and financial empire. Solomon's cognitive abilities make this success possible. Second, he implements an effective foreign policy, which demonstrates his adaptability and willingness to compromise and improvise. Third, Solomon is humble enough to ask for God's help and thoughtful enough to pray for Israel, both in his time and in the future, and for other nations as well. Despite his failings in later years these good traits should not be forgotten.

Sadly, no character sketch of Solomon is complete without an analysis of his flaws. He is capable of expressing his ambition to be a great king through the acquiring of vast wealth and numerous wives. Eventually these twin desires for prestige and sensuality lead to his nation's downfall. Solomon is not beyond using oppressive measures to get what he wants, as the institution of forced labor indicates, nor is he beyond cheating a friend, as his giving of worthless towns to Hiram proves. Worst of all, Solomon condones and even practices idolatry. Thus, he is capable of irrational thinking, ingratitude, and covenant infidelity. At his worst, then, this wise leader of Israel acts no better than the most foolish of his subjects. He thereby serves as a warning to those who take their God-given gifts for granted or, worse, come to believe they have achieved greatness on their own.

Canonical and Theological Implications of 1 Kgs 9:10–11:43

This passage acts as a bridge in the Old Testament canon in several ways. First, it provides a conclusion for the promises of land, rest, and unhindered worship that were first made in Gen 12:1–9. Israel possesses Canaan, has subdued its enemies, has built its temple, and enjoys every material success. In other words, the blessings mentioned in Deuteronomy 27–28 and Leviticus 26 are theirs. Second, unfortunately the text also leads to the downfall of Israel and the loss of the promised land. Idolatry by king and populace will lead to disintegration of the nation, then to defeat, and finally to exile.

Third, because of Israel's sin the prophetic movement now increases in importance. God will send Ahijah, Elijah, Elisha, and Isaiah to warn the people to repent in 1, 2 Kings. In the rest of the prophets segment of the canon, Jeremiah, Ezekiel, and the Twelve join these earlier prophets in their difficult, unappreciated, lonely work as God's messengers to a disobedient populace. Indeed the prophetic viewpoint becomes the guiding narrative force in 1, 2 Kings as the story moves toward its tragic conclusion.

Fourth, the Writings also reflect the seriousness of Israel's decline and fall. Laments in the Books of Psalms and Lamentations chronicle the results of the covenant people's unwillingness to live as God's people. Proverbs, Ecclesiastes, and Song of Solomon depict Solomon at his best yet also at his worst, which reinforces the rather complex portrait of the man 1, 2 Kings presents. Not until the time of Ezra and Nehemiah will Jerusalem begin to recuperate from the ultimate consequences of Solomon's actions.

Theologically, the passage reemphasizes God's faithfulness. This time the author depicts the Lord as the God who keeps promises even when the person who is the object of the promise fails to be righteous. For David's sake, and for the sake of Solomon, the Lord refuses to obliterate the nation. Despite this mercy, however, Israel must still face the consequences of idolatry. God does judge. Related to the merciful/just nature of the Lord is the emergence of the prophets. God communicates with sinners through the Scriptures, through answered prayer, through historical events, and through messengers such as Ahijah. The Lord is faithful to his own merciful character as he warns Israel to avoid punishment and true to his sovereignty when he chooses Jeroboam to punish Solomon.

Further, the text stresses how a leader's sin can impact others. Although it is doubtful that Solomon can be held responsible for introducing idolatry into Israel (cf. the Book of Judges), his religious open-door policy serves to legitimize the practice in a way that no commoner's similar actions could. Just as one holy person, such as Abraham or Moses, can bless a whole people, so one significant idolater can create spiritual cancer in a people. Had Solomon continued to seek God's favor rather than wealth and power, he could have helped Israel continue to enjoy prosperity. Instead, he illustrates the principle that sin always affects others.

Finally, it is important to observe that God requires fidelity to the covenant in a pluralistic, multicultural society. Solomon's wives embody the various religious worldviews that existed at that time. God allows no rivals, since no other gods are real. Neither new ideas, new philosophies, new situations, nor new national status change this truth. God alone has created the earth. God alone rules history. God alone blesses and punishes men, women, and nations.

Applicational Implications of 1 Kgs 9:10–11:43

Individuals and churches often come to pivotal moments in their lives. Actions and decisions at these strategic times need to be sound, or their consequences may be unpleasant. This section of 1, 2 Kings illuminates what readers or hearers of its words may expect when faced with life's turning points. Therefore, the first point of emphasis is that persons and congregations must learn to discern when a pivotal moment has arisen. For some the moment occurs after a time of great success, while for others it comes after a failure, and for still others after one of life's normal passages, such as marriage, graduation, or retirement. Proper assessment should help faithful persons stay on course.

Second, when people disappoint us, it is important to remember that God remains trustworthy regardless of how unstable people may be. God made eternal promises to David and made sure those promises were kept. God's people can be confident, then, that the Lord never judges incorrectly, never breaks faith, and never holds a grudge. God's word is certain and thus a foundation for hope.

Third, God's use of prophets indicates that the Lord always finds ways to reveal warnings, encouragement, and counsel. Chief among these means, of course, is Scripture, as the author's repeated allusions to the Pentateuch indicate. Yet God also uses persons to confront or to counsel other persons. The prophets are good examples of the difficulty, yet importance, of sharing God's truth with other persons.

Fourth, the ramifications of Solomon's actions should give us further food for thought when we are tempted to sin. Individual sin affects the whole community, especially when that sin is committed by the leader of a group, whether of a nation, a church, or a family. Each person must therefore examine the wider consequences of his or her actions. This principle is particularly true in spiritual matters, since one's relationship to God is more important than any other issue in life.

Fifth, Solomon's idolatry in his time emphasizes the need for faithfulness in today's postmodern, pluralistic society. Multiculturalism, competing worldviews, and fear of appearing narrow minded are not new. Biblical characters from Abraham and Moses, to Daniel and Esther, to Paul and John faced the same problems. Unlike these persons, Solomon chose to please his wives, give in to competing religions, and worship other gods. Monotheism in its Christian expression insists that anyone may trust Christ but also that there is no other way of salvation (Exod 20:3–11; Deut 6:4–9; Acts 4:12). People of faith may suffer for this conviction, yet the effort must be made for the world to come to God.

SECTION OUTLINE

III. THE DIVIDED KINGDOM AND THE RISE OF IDOLATRY (12:1–16:34)
  Survey of Historical Details Related to 1 Kgs 12:1–16:34
  1. The Rise and Fall of Jeroboam's Family (12:1–15:32)
     (1) Rehoboam Divides the Nation (12:1–24)
     (2) Jeroboam Institutionalizes Idolatry (12:25–33)
     (3) An Unnamed Prophet Denounces Jeroboam (13:1–34)
     (4) Ahijah Prophesies against Jeroboam (14:1–18)
     (5) Jeroboam's Death (14:19–20)
     (6) Rehoboam's Reign (14:21–31)
     (7) Abijah's Reign (15:1–8)
     (8) Asa's Reign (15:9–24)
     (9) Nadab's Reign (15:25–31)
  2. The Rise of Omri and Ahab (15:32–16:34)
     (1) Baasha's Early Career (15:32–34)
     (2) Jehu Prophesies against Baasha (16:1–4)
     (3) Baasha's Death (16:5–7)
     (4) Elah's Reign (16:8–14)
     (5) Zimri's Coup and Death (16:15–20)
     (6) Omri's Reign and the Founding of Samaria (16:21–28)
     (7) Ahab's Ascension and Wickedness (16:29–34)
  Canonical and Theological Implications of 1 Kgs 12:1–16:34
  Applicational Implications of 1 Kgs 12:1–16:34

III. THE DIVIDED KINGDOM AND THE RISE OF IDOLATRY (12:1–16:34)

Solomon's death leaves a gigantic hole in Israel's leadership structure. David's son, the man who gave Israel political cohesion, wealth, prestige, and religious unity, is dead. Who could possibly fill his place? The text has already introduced what will occur. God will continue to honor the covenant with David, so Solomon's son will have a two-tribe kingdom (1 Kgs 11:32–36). Because of Solomon's idolatry, however, Jeroboam will rule the other ten tribes (1 Kgs 11:26–31). The Lord has sent these infallible promises through Ahijah the prophet, so the predictions must come true. What remains to be seen is *how* they will come to pass.

Sadly, Solomon's son Rehoboam's lack of political skill opens the door for the split (12:1–24). Just as sadly, Jeroboam does not appreciate what God has done for him, for he will establish an alternative religion in his new kingdom

(12:25–33). Though the Lord sends prophets to warn Jeroboam to change his ways, he refuses to do so (13:1–10). Thus, God condemns Jeroboam's actions (14:1–18) and ends his dynasty after a few short generations (15:29–30). Jeroboam's deeds are particularly unacceptable to God because he was told that he came to power because of Solomon's disobedience (1 Kgs 11:26–31). Indeed, Jeroboam's sins are so far-reaching and repulsive that the author uses him as the example of how to define a morally deficient king (cf. 1 Kgs 16:7,9,26).

After Jeroboam passes from the scene, several rather nondescript kings come to power in Israel, and David's dynasty continues to rule Judah. Of Judah's kings only Asa impresses the author in a positive way (15:9–24). None of the northern kings are righteous, yet one is significant. Omri builds a new capital, makes an alliance with Tyre, and places his son, Ahab, on the throne (16:21–28). He thereby provides a stable dynasty for Israel. Ahab will become one of the major characters in the rest of 1 Kings.

Overall, these chapters present a picture of decline among God's people. Certainly the nation's division spells political decline. More importantly, Jeroboam's decision to form a new religion tears the people from God, which means their political situation will get even worse. Prophets rebuke the kings but are ignored. A confrontation between the Lord's messengers and the monarchs surely looms in the future.

Survey of Historical Details Related to 1 Kgs 12:1–16:34

Four issues need special consideration. First, the division of the nation into two parts has a tremendous impact on Israel's history. The separate entities never regain the prestige David and Solomon had established. They are also less able to repel foreign invaders. Of course, 1 Kgs 11:1–40 discusses the religious roots of the breakup. This text also notes that Jeroboam, a northerner, was already a likely candidate to take Solomon's place. His position as supervisor over a forced labor project (11:27–28) underscores why northern Israelites were tired of Solomon's policies. They were drafted to work in the south, their tax burden was heavier than Judah's, and their love for the Davidic dynasty was always tenuous at best.[1] As H. Tadmor observes, the very fact that Rehoboam felt compelled to go to Shechem to speak to the northern tribes "is evidence of deep unrest and ferment among the people."[2] Only spiritual commitments could keep the nation united, and those commitments had already been weakened by Solomon.

Second, because of the dissolution of Solomon's kingdom other nations

---

[1] H. Donner, "The Separate States of Israel and Judah," *Israelite and Judean History*, ed. J. H. Hayes and J. M. Miller (Philadelphia: Westminster, 1977) 384.

[2] H. Tadmor, "Traditional Institutions and the Monarchy: Social and Political Tensions in the Time of David and Solomon," in *Studies in the Period of David and Solomon and Other Essays*, ed. T. Ishida (Winona Lake, Ind.: Eisenbrauns, 1982) 253.

moved against Judah and Israel. That Shishak of Egypt favored Jeroboam meant that Solomon's trade pact with Egypt was no longer valid. In fact, in Rehoboam's fifth year Shishak attacked Judah with such force that only the payment of high tribute induced him to withdraw (cf. 1 Kgs 14:25–28).[3] This invasion also greatly diminished the Israel-Tyre trade cartel.[4] Egypt's era of abject weakness was over. To make matters worse, smaller nations rebelled against their former masters. Syria became impossible for Israel to control and soon became a threat in the north. Judah could hold neither Ammon nor Philistia, and only Moab continued to pay tribute money.[5] Each part of the divided kingdom had to face the future with less income from trade, with more external threats from small and large countries, and with turmoil between each other. A difficult future lay ahead.

Third, Jeroboam's new religion made covenant keeping even more difficult than it had been. Jeroboam was clever enough to realize that if his subjects traveled to Jerusalem for religious observances their loyalty might revert to the house of David (cf. 1 Kgs 12:26–27). Therefore, he set up shrines in Dan on his extreme northern border and a more significant one at Bethel on his southern boundary (cf. 2 Kgs 17:24–28; Amos 7:10–13).[6] Jerusalem's uniqueness in God's sight was ignored. Jeroboam also set up golden calves to represent God's presence in the new sanctuaries.[7] These images quickly became used as idols (1 Kgs 12:28–30), thus shattering the first two of the Ten Commandments (Exod 20:3–6). New priests were appointed who were not Levites (1 Kgs 12:31), and a new festival was instituted (1 Kgs 12:33). Jeroboam's innovations were a compromise between Canaanite idolatry and traditional Yahwism. Such syncretism led to loyalty for neither tradition. Ultimately, this religion sapped Israel's spiritual fiber to the extent that they did not have enough character to endure as a nation.

Fourth, the prophetic movement began to have more importance in both kingdoms. Ahijah, the prophet who declared Jeroboam's rise to power in chap. 11, returns in 1 Kgs 14:1–18 to denounce Jeroboam and predict the end of the king's dynasty. Unnamed prophets reaffirm God's sovereignty over kings and governments in chap. 13. Given the tension that already exists between monarchs and prophets, greater conflicts in the future appear to be inevitable.

---

[3] J. Bright, *A History of Israel*, 3d ed. (Philadelphia: Westminster, 1981) 233–34.

[4] B. Peckham, "Israel and Phoenicia," *Magnalia Dei: The Mighty Acts of God*, ed. F. M. Cross, W. E. Lemke, and P. D. Miller, Jr. (Garden City: Doubleday, 1976) 233.

[5] M. Noth, *The History of Israel*, 2d ed., trans. P. R. Ackroyd (New York: Harper & Row, 1960) 227–28.

[6] Donner, "The Separate States of Israel and Judah," 387.

[7] For several scholarly opinions on Jeroboam's motivation for erecting the calves and pillars and these cult items' actual symbolism, see the discussion of 1 Kgs 12:28–30.

1. The Rise and Fall of Jeroboam's Family (12:1–15:32)

No intrigue like what brought Solomon to the throne occurs after Solomon's death. Rehoboam seems to have no rivals, so he automatically assumes power in Jerusalem. His right to govern the northern tribes is far from automatic, however, so he goes to Shechem to consolidate his control over the whole nation. Decisions he makes at this point make Ahijah's prophecies come true. Jeroboam will reign over ten tribes. How long he and his sons stay in power will depend on their faithfulness to God's word (cf. 1 Kgs 11:37–38).

(1) Rehoboam Divides the Nation (12:1–24)

**1Rehoboam went to Shechem, for all the Israelites had gone there to make him
king. 2When Jeroboam son of Nebat heard this (he was still in Egypt, where he
had fled from King Solomon), he returned from Egypt. 3So they sent for Jeroboam, and he and the whole assembly of Israel went to Rehoboam and said to
him: 4"Your father put a heavy yoke on us, but now lighten the harsh labor and
the heavy yoke he put on us, and we will serve you."**

**5Rehoboam answered, "Go away for three days and then come back to me."
So the people went away.**

**6Then King Rehoboam consulted the elders who had served his father Solo-
mon during his lifetime. "How would you advise me to answer these people?" he
asked.**

**7They replied, "If today you will be a servant to these people and serve them
and give them a favorable answer, they will always be your servants."**

**8But Rehoboam rejected the advice the elders gave him and consulted the
young men who had grown up with him and were serving him. 9He asked them,
"What is your advice? How should we answer these people who say to me,
'Lighten the yoke your father put on us'?"**

**10The young men who had grown up with him replied, "Tell these people who
have said to you, 'Your father put a heavy yoke on us, but make our yoke
lighter'—tell them, 'My little finger is thicker than my father's waist. 11My father
laid on you a heavy yoke; I will make it even heavier. My father scourged you with
whips; I will scourge you with scorpions.'"**

**12Three days later Jeroboam and all the people returned to Rehoboam, as the
king had said, "Come back to me in three days." 13The king answered the people
harshly. Rejecting the advice given him by the elders, 14he followed the advice of
the young men and said, "My father made your yoke heavy; I will make it even
heavier. My father scourged you with whips; I will scourge you with scorpions."
15So the king did not listen to the people, for this turn of events was from the
LORD, to fulfill the word the LORD had spoken to Jeroboam son of Nebat through
Ahijah the Shilonite.**

**16When all Israel saw that the king refused to listen to them, they answered
the king:**

"What share do we have in David,
what part in Jesse's son?

To your tents, O Israel!
Look after your own house, O David!"
So the Israelites went home. [17]But as for the Israelites who were living in the towns of Judah, Rehoboam still ruled over them.

[18]King Rehoboam sent out Adoniram, who was in charge of forced labor, but all Israel stoned him to death. King Rehoboam, however, managed to get into his chariot and escape to Jerusalem. [19]So Israel has been in rebellion against the house of David to this day.

[20]When all the Israelites heard that Jeroboam had returned, they sent and called him to the assembly and made him king over all Israel. Only the tribe of Judah remained loyal to the house of David.

[21]When Rehoboam arrived in Jerusalem, he mustered the whole house of Judah and the tribe of Benjamin—a hundred and eighty thousand fighting men—to make war against the house of Israel and to regain the kingdom for Rehoboam son of Solomon.

[22]But this word of God came to Shemaiah the man of God: [23]"Say to Rehoboam son of Solomon king of Judah, to the whole house of Judah and Benjamin, and to the rest of the people, [24]'This is what the LORD says: Do not go up to fight against your brothers, the Israelites. Go home, every one of you, for this is my doing.'" So they obeyed the word of the LORD and went home again, as the LORD had ordered.

12:1 Perhaps Rehoboam does not sense the depth of northern dissatisfaction with Solomon's policies. Maybe he assumes that since David and Solomon did not gain consensus support immediately that he would have to win over those who doubted him. Whatever his mind-set, he does not handle the situation well. The people await him in Shechem, and there is no reason to believe that they are determined to reject Rehoboam.

12:2–5 Jeroboam returns from Egypt when he hears of the assembly on what is friendly ground to him.[8] Obviously he does not fear Rehoboam as he had Solomon. Once home, Jeroboam is chosen to approach Rehoboam with the people's requests. Conscripted labor is the major complaint. Northerners have been forced to build southern projects, a fact Jeroboam, the former taskmaster (1 Kgs 11:28), knows quite well. When asked to lighten their load, Rehoboam asks for three days to formulate a decision. Sectionalism, with all its force and fury, has backed Rehoboam into a corner.[9]

12:6–11 In order to make his decision, Rehoboam consults two sets of advisors. The elders tell him to give a "favorable" (lit., "good") response. If he will serve the people, then they will serve him. These seasoned political veterans seem to know exactly what the young king is facing. They realize it is time to accede to the crowd's wishes.

---

[8] On textual problems in the Jeroboam account see Introduction, "The Text of 1, 2 Kings."

[9] For a discussion of the pressures caused by sectionalism, consult B. Halpern, "Sectionalism and the Schism," *JBL* 93 (1974) 519–32.

But Rehoboam rejects the elders' advice and consults with the counselors his own age. Like Rehoboam, they are young, ambitious, proud, and insecure. They tell him to intimidate the crowd by declaring that he is tougher than Solomon. Their theory is that servant leadership will not work. Only a bully can handle a diverse kingdom. As Nelson observes, "Rehoboam chooses slogans over wisdom, machismo over servanthood."[10]

12:12–15 When the three days are over, Rehoboam delivers the harsh message. The author explains why "the king did not listen to the people." This lack of judgment and its results, this "turn of events,"[11] "was from the LORD" so that God's word through Ahijah could come true. Nothing occurs here because of "chance." There is no "chance." God is sovereign. Still, Rehoboam's decision is his own. The text maintains the tension between God's sovereignty and human responsibility that pervades all of Scripture.[12]

12:16–20 Without hesitation the people reject Rehoboam's authority over them. They deny any responsibility to David's dynasty and leave Rehoboam to rule Judah. One incredibly poor decision tears down in a few days what David and Solomon labored eighty years to build. DeVries notes, "Possibly this passage's most important lesson is how much easier it is to break up what belongs together than it is to restore what is broken."[13]

Rehoboam makes one final, futile attempt to maintain control over the north. He sends Adoniram, the longtime head of forced labor (cf. 1 Kgs 4:6), to the people. Regardless of whether he sent Adoniram to effect a compromise, threaten the people, or conduct business as usual, the result was the same. Rehoboam again miscalculates the northerners' depth of anger, for Adoniram is stoned to death.[14] The "king" flees for his life. Jeroboam becomes the popular choice for king in the north, and God's word is fulfilled.

12:21–24 At home Rehoboam gathers a massive force, intent on invading the north. At this point, however, another prophetic voice surfaces. Shemaiah, simply designated as "the man of God," a title that takes on growing significance in the story (see below), warns the king to stay home. Why? Because God says, "This is my doing." Rehoboam obeys God in this matter. Israel has

---

[10] R. D. Nelson, *First and Second Kings,* IBC (Louisville: John Knox, 1987) 79.

[11] The word for "turn of events" (סבה) only appears in this verse in the OT, so a contextual study is difficult. A variation of the word (נְסִבָּה) occurs in the parallel account in 2 Chr 10:15, which may indicate the Chronicler's use of 1 Kings in writing his own account.

[12] For a classical Reformed study of this issue see C. A. Hodge, *Systematic Theology: Abridged Edition,* ed. E. N. Gross (1872; reprint, Grand Rapids: Eerdmans, 1992) 313–19. For a contemporary evangelical, Baptist discussion of the matter consult M. J. Erickson, *Christian Theology* (Grand Rapids: Baker, 1992) 345–63.

[13] S. J. DeVries, *1 Kings,* WBC (Waco: Word, 1985) 159.

[14] Cf. R. Case II, "Rehoboam: A Study in Failed Leadership," *Presbyterion: Covenant Seminary Review* 14/1 (1988) 62, for an analysis of Rehoboam's lack of leadership skills in this critical situation.

been irreparably split into northern (ten tribes) and southern (two tribes) segments. The year is ca. 930 B.C.[15]

(2) Jeroboam Institutionalizes Idolatry (12:25–33)

[25]Then Jeroboam fortified Shechem in the hill country of Ephraim and lived there. From there he went out and built up Peniel.

[26]Jeroboam thought to himself, "The kingdom will now likely revert to the house of David. [27]If these people go up to offer sacrifices at the temple of the LORD in Jerusalem, they will again give their allegiance to their lord, Rehoboam king of Judah. They will kill me and return to King Rehoboam."

[28]After seeking advice, the king made two golden calves. He said to the people, "It is too much for you to go up to Jerusalem. Here are your gods, O Israel, who brought you up out of Egypt." [29]One he set up in Bethel, and the other in Dan. [30]And this thing became a sin; the people went even as far as Dan to worship the one there.

[31]Jeroboam built shrines on high places and appointed priests from all sorts of people, even though they were not Levites. [32]He instituted a festival on the fifteenth day of the eighth month, like the festival held in Judah, and offered sacrifices on the altar. This he did in Bethel, sacrificing to the calves he had made. And at Bethel he also installed priests at the high places he had made. [33]On the fifteenth day of the eighth month, a month of his own choosing, he offered sacrifices on the altar he had built at Bethel. So he instituted the festival for the Israelites and went up to the altar to make offerings.

12:25 Jeroboam's first concern is to solidify his position in Shechem, so he fortifies that city, then does likewise in Peniel. Shechem was not only an important ancestral location (Gen 12:6), but it also guarded the Northern Kingdom's west-east pass and commanded the road "through the hills of Manasseh to Bethshan."[16] Even when the capital was moved, first to Tirzah and finally to Samaria, the locations were not far from this strategic point.[17] Keil says that Peniel "was on the caravan road, which led through Gilead to Damascus," so Jeroboam probably fortifies the city "to defend his sovereignty over Gilead against hostile attacks from the northeast and east."[18] Such activity indicates that Jeroboam understands the precarious nature of his new kingdom and moves to protect it through reasonable and appropriate measures.

12:26–27 Having secured his military and economic interests, Jeroboam now moves to protect his religious concerns. The all-knowing narrator

[15] For an additional treatment of the nation's division, note the "Introduction to Historical Issues" section of this commentary's Introduction.

[16] J. Gray, *1 and 2 Kings,* OTL (Philadelphia: Westminster, 1963) 289.

[17] Ibid.

[18] C. F. Keil, "I and II Kings," COT, trans. J. Martin (1876; reprint, Grand Rapids: Eerdmans, 1980) 3:198.

divulges what the king thinks to himself: if northerners sacrifice in Jerusalem, then their allegiance might return to Rehoboam. This fear amounts to a lack of faith, since surely the God who brought him to power can protect him from harm. God had promised him a dynasty as enduring as David's if he would keep God's commandments (1 Kgs 11:38). But Jeroboam does not find the Lord's pledge sufficient for his life needs.

12:28–30 Bad advice again mars a king's life (cf. 1 Kgs 12:10–11). "After seeking advice," Jeroboam introduces a new form of religion that in effect institutionalizes idolatry. On the pretense of being concerned for the people's travel capacities, he erects "two golden calves" that supposedly represent the "gods" who redeemed Israel from Egypt. They may worship one of these images in either Bethel, the ancient place where Jacob had his stairway to heaven dream (Gen 28:10–22), or in Dan, the northernmost city in the country.

Scholars debate Jeroboam's motivation for building these shrines. H. Donner thinks the calves were set up "certainly not as cult objects but—remotely comparable to the ark of Yahweh—as animal-shaped pedestals for Yahweh, who was thought to be standing on them invisibly."[19] Similarly, Noth agrees that the calves probably were pedestals for an unseen God:

> They were part of the worship of the God of Israel who had done great things for Israel and "brought Israel up out of the land of Egypt" (I Kings xii, 28, cf. Exod. xxxii, 4); and they were probably not intended to be thought of as divine images, especially as theriomorphic images were unknown in the Near East—as opposed to Egypt.[20]

Noth even uses the books' ongoing disgust with Jeroboam's practices as evidence that the author presents a stereotypical, not historical, portrait of Israel's history.[21]

Though Bright and DeVries also question the exactitude of the text's assessment of the calves, they locate a significant problem with the new symbols. Bright correctly observes that the "bull symbol . . . was too closely associated with the fertility cult to be safe."[22] The use of Canaanite cult symbols led to "a confusion of Yahweh and Ba'al, and to the importation of pagan features into the cult of the former."[23] In other words, idolatrous practices were mixed into Yahweh worship. DeVries concurs:

> Such a symbol had to create problems for those who were just progressing in the biblical understanding of God. All around Israel, and in the numerous Canaanite enclaves within its territory, were half-Yahwists to whom the calf or

[19] Donner, "The Separate States of Israel and Judah," 387.
[20] Noth, *History of Israel,* 232.
[21] Ibid., 233–34.
[22] Bright, *History of Israel,* 238.
[23] Ibid.

> bull was the symbol of male fecundity. Officially or unofficially, Baalism was in the land; it was destined in the days of Ahab to gain the mastery. Thus the golden calf could have done nothing but confuse and mislead.[24]

Israel's monotheistic faith was not an easy sell at any time, so Jeroboam's actions made it harder for Yahwism to survive in any recognizably distinct form.

Surely the author's account of the scene makes sense. Jeroboam knew the prohibitions against idolatry in Israel because Ahijah told him Solomon's idolatry led to God's placing him in power (cf. 1 Kgs 11:33). He also knew of the temple's importance as a central sanctuary. If readers living thousands of years later could see the similarities between Baalism and his new cult, Jeroboam likely could as well. It seems probable, then, that the compromises were deliberate. Finally, he had indeed lived in Egypt (1 Kgs 11:40), where depictions of gods were common.[25] Perhaps Jeroboam did not intend the harm he caused, but he should have foreseen that the only "positive" by-product of the new cult was supposedly to help him stay in power by manipulating the people.

12:31–33 Besides constructing national shrines at Bethel and Dan, Jeroboam institutes local worship sites at "high places"[26] throughout the land. This action further dilutes worship. He also appoints non-Levite priests in direct opposition to Mosaic standards (cf. Exod 28–29) and sets a new time for the Feast of Tabernacles, switching from the seventh month, fifteenth day to the eighth month, fifteenth day. Keil suggests that Jeroboam may have rationalized this change on the basis that crops ripened later in the north but that the real reason was to separate the two religious groups by regions.[27]

The institutionalization of a non-Mosaic religion is now complete. A syncretistic mix of Yahwism and Baalism is in place. Northerners will have to make a special effort just to worship the Lord. Just as there are now two nations, two capitals, two governments, and two kings, there are also two religions. The major differences are as follows:

JUDAH	ISRAEL
No images of God	Veneration of calves
Levitical priesthood	Multitribe priesthood
Central sanctuary	Local and regional sanctuaries
Separatist cult	Syncretistic cult

(3) An Unnamed Prophet Denounces Jeroboam (13:1–34)

[1]By the word of the LORD a man of God came from Judah to Bethel, as Jero-

[24] DeVries, *1 Kings,* 162.
[25] Cf. Noth, *History of Israel,* 232.
[26] See the discussion of "high places" in the commentary on 1 Kgs 3:2–3.
[27] Keil, "I and II Kings," 200–201.

**boam was standing by the altar to make an offering. 2He cried out against the
altar by the word of the LORD: "O altar, altar! This is what the LORD says: 'A son
named Josiah will be born to the house of David. On you he will sacrifice the
priests of the high places who now make offerings here, and human bones will be
burned on you.'" 3That same day the man of God gave a sign: "This is the sign
the LORD has declared: The altar will be split apart and the ashes on it will be
poured out."**

**4When King Jeroboam heard what the man of God cried out against the altar
at Bethel, he stretched out his hand from the altar and said, "Seize him!" But the
hand he stretched out toward the man shriveled up, so that he could not pull it
back. 5Also, the altar was split apart and its ashes poured out according to the
sign given by the man of God by the word of the LORD.**

**6Then the king said to the man of God, "Intercede with the LORD your God
and pray for me that my hand may be restored." So the man of God interceded
with the LORD, and the king's hand was restored and became as it was before.**

**7The king said to the man of God, "Come home with me and have something
to eat, and I will give you a gift."**

**8But the man of God answered the king, "Even if you were to give me half
your possessions, I would not go with you, nor would I eat bread or drink water
here. 9For I was commanded by the word of the LORD: 'You must not eat bread
or drink water or return by the way you came.'" 10So he took another road and
did not return by the way he had come to Bethel.**

**11Now there was a certain old prophet living in Bethel, whose sons came and
told him all that the man of God had done there that day. They also told their
father what he had said to the king. 12Their father asked them, "Which way did
he go?" And his sons showed him which road the man of God from Judah had
taken. 13So he said to his sons, "Saddle the donkey for me." And when they had
saddled the donkey for him, he mounted it 14and rode after the man of God. He
found him sitting under an oak tree and asked, "Are you the man of God who
came from Judah?"**

"I am," he replied.

15So the prophet said to him, "Come home with me and eat."

**16The man of God said, "I cannot turn back and go with you, nor can I eat
bread or drink water with you in this place. 17I have been told by the word of the
LORD: 'You must not eat bread or drink water there or return by the way you
came.'"**

**18The old prophet answered, "I too am a prophet, as you are. And an angel
said to me by the word of the LORD: 'Bring him back with you to your house so
that he may eat bread and drink water.'" (But he was lying to him.) 19So the man
of God returned with him and ate and drank in his house.**

**20While they were sitting at the table, the word of the LORD came to the old
prophet who had brought him back. 21He cried out to the man of God who had
come from Judah, "This is what the LORD says: 'You have defied the word of the
LORD and have not kept the command the LORD your God gave you. 22You came
back and ate bread and drank water in the place where he told you not to eat or
drink. Therefore your body will not be buried in the tomb of your fathers.'"**

[23]When the man of God had finished eating and drinking, the prophet who had brought him back saddled his donkey for him. [24]As he went on his way, a lion met him on the road and killed him, and his body was thrown down on the road, with both the donkey and the lion standing beside it. [25]Some people who passed by saw the body thrown down there, with the lion standing beside the body, and they went and reported it in the city where the old prophet lived.

[26]When the prophet who had brought him back from his journey heard of it, he said, "It is the man of God who defied the word of the LORD. The LORD has given him over to the lion, which has mauled him and killed him, as the word of the LORD had warned him."

[27]The prophet said to his sons, "Saddle the donkey for me," and they did so. [28]Then he went out and found the body thrown down on the road, with the donkey and the lion standing beside it. The lion had neither eaten the body nor mauled the donkey. [29]So the prophet picked up the body of the man of God, laid it on the donkey, and brought it back to his own city to mourn for him and bury him. [30]Then he laid the body in his own tomb, and they mourned over him and said, "Oh, my brother!"

[31]After burying him, he said to his sons, "When I die, bury me in the grave where the man of God is buried; lay my bones beside his bones. [32]For the message he declared by the word of the LORD against the altar in Bethel and against all the shrines on the high places in the towns of Samaria will certainly come true."

[33]Even after this, Jeroboam did not change his evil ways, but once more appointed priests for the high places from all sorts of people. Anyone who wanted to become a priest he consecrated for the high places. [34]This was the sin of the house of Jeroboam that led to its downfall and to its destruction from the face of the earth.

Chapter 13 has received a good deal of critical attention because of the unusual nature of the story it tells. Commentators have discussed the nature of the account as it appeared in the original source, the story's main theme, and the role of the chapter in the overall strategy of 1, 2 Kings.[28] This commentary focuses on the latter two concerns. If indeed an author living ca. 550 B.C. wove this text into the overall fabric of the history,[29] then it is important to determine how this account complements and expands what has occurred already and what will happen later in the story.[30] Basically, 1 Kings 13 continues the book's emphases on proper worship, the prophetic word, and the slow demise

[28] Note the bibliography of works on the chapter in D. W. Van Winkle, "1 Kings XIII: True and False Prophecy," *VT* 29/1 (1989) 43, and the survey of ideas the text has generated in U. Simon, "I Kings 13: A Prophetic Sign-Denial and Persistence," *HUCA* 47 (1976) 81–86, and W. E. Lemke, "The Way of Obedience: I Kings 13 and the Structure of the Deuteronomistic History," *Magnalia Dei: The Mighty Acts of God,* ed. F. M. Cross, W. E. Lemke, and P. D. Miller, Jr. (Garden City: Doubleday, 1976) 303–4.

[29] Cf. discussion of 1, 2 Kings authorship in the introductory segment of this commentary.

[30] For a good analysis of how the text fits its literary context, see J. T. Walsh, "The Contexts of I Kings XIII," *VT* 29/3 (1989) 355–70.

of the covenant people. It also begins to analyze the difference between true and false prophecy.[31]

13:1–3 The story begins by introducing the two characters who dominate the action in the first scene. A nameless "man of God"[32] comes from Judah to confront Jeroboam, who is standing by the altar that 1 Kgs 12:33 says he has created for his new cult. In fact, the prophet catches Jeroboam in the act of sacrifice. When he received his last prophetic message, Jeroboam was pleased, for it placed him on the throne (1 Kgs 11:26–40). What will he think now?

The prophet presents a message with three implications. First, he cries out "against the altar," presumably because it has no legitimacy in God's eyes. Second, he predicts a descendant of David named Josiah will someday defile the altar. This declaration suggests the eventual demise of Jeroboam's dynasty and the Northern Kingdom's loss of sovereignty. Third, he offers a sign to authenticate his message: the altar "will be split apart, and the ashes on it will be poured out." All of these implications are told without introduction and with stunning swiftness. God has denounced Jeroboam's brand of religion and announced Jeroboam's failure to receive the promises God had made him in 11:38. In doing so he predicts by name the rise of a king who is born almost three centuries after this account occurs. This feat is paralleled in the Old Testament only by Isaiah's eighth-century B.C. prediction of the career of the sixth-century B.C. Persian ruler Cyrus (Isa 44:28; 45:1,13).

13:4–10 Jeroboam attempts to stop the prophet and thus also to obliterate the word of God. But Jeroboam finds that he cannot withstand God's prophet. As Keil notes, "Thus Jeroboam experienced in the limbs of his own body the severity of the threatened judgment of God."[33]

Now Jeroboam changes tactics. He first begs the man of God to intercede for his withered hand, which the prophet does, and the hand is restored.[34] This second miracle reaffirms the prophet's authenticity and demonstrates God's grace. Next, the king attempts to win the prophet's favor by offering him food and a gift. His offer is refused because God has told him not to eat in Bethel or return the way he came. Prophets must not be for sale, nor should they tread the path everyone else walks. U. Simon demonstrates that "not to return by the

---

[31] Note the importance of true and false prophecy in T. B. Dozeman, "The Way of the Man of God from Judah: True and False Prophecy in the Pre-Deuteronomic Legend of 1 Kings 13," *CBQ* 44 (1982) 379–93; Van Winkle, "1 Kings XIII: True and False Prophecy;" and Simon, "I Kings 13: A Prophetic Sign-Denial and Persistence," 92–98.

[32] The simple phrase אִישׁ אֱלֹהִים grows in importance as 1, 2 Kings continues.

[33] Keil, "I and II Kings," 204.

[34] The phrase literally states that "it was returned to him." The governing verb form comes from שׁוּב. Lemke observes that some variation of "return" occurs sixteen times in the story and that the variations can mean "to return an object to its former state," to return by the same direction, to repeat an action, or to change behavior ("The Way of Obedience: I Kings 13 and the Structure of the Deuteronomistic History," 310).

way you came" is a fairly common Old Testament way of saying "be different" or "avoid past mistakes."[35]

So far the prophet has been obedient. He has heard God's word, opposed the king, and rebuffed Jeroboam's not-so-subtle bribe. Therefore he embodies the ideal of a prophet who stands for truth against those who pervert it.[36]

13:11–19 At this point a third important character enters the story. A "certain old prophet" hears of the exploits of the man of God from his sons and rides off to find him. When he meets the man of God, he invites him to a meal. Again the man of God refuses to eat; again he repeats God's instructions. Strangely, the old prophet *lies* to the man of God, claiming further conflicting revelation. Satisfied with the old man's explanation, the man of God goes with him, thus disobeying God's commands.

13:20–25 A new word from the Lord comes to the man of God, this time through the old prophet. Because of his disobedience the man will die. This word comes true when the man of God leaves and a lion kills him. Sadly, like Jeroboam (cf. 1 Kgs 12:28) the man of God has listened to bad counsel rather than heeding a direct word of God. Jeroboam was certain, despite the Lord's promise to the contrary, that he would lose his authority unless he formed a new cult. The man of God believed that an angelic message contradicted God's earlier word. Both men make incorrect choices based on bad advice and personal uncertainty.

13:26–32 When the old prophet hears of the death, he retrieves the body, brings it back, and buries the man of God "in his own tomb." Given what happened at the sanctuary and what happened to the man "who defied the word of the LORD" (13:26), the old prophet knows his acquaintance's words will come true. He therefore instructs his sons to bury him with the man of God. It is as if the old prophet has been on a quest to find a real word from God or as if he set out to be the personal tester of the man of God. Whatever his motives, and it is impossible to know them for sure,[37] the old man is a mixture of curiosity, dishonesty, accuracy, and conviction.

13:33–34 Not even a string of miracles deters Jeroboam from his path to idolatry.[38] He still sanctions high places, non-Levitical priests, and non-Mosaic-inspired sacrifices. The narrator explains Jeroboam's downfall according to Ahijah's warning in 11:38 and the judgment following in chap. 14 (esp. vv. 11–12). Jeroboam's religious heterodoxy leads to his dynasty's destruction.

Several important themes emerge from this text. First, God opposes idolatry,

---

[35] Simon, "I Kings 13," 90–91.

[36] On the opposition motif in the story, see Walsh, "The Contexts of 1 Kings XIII," 357–59.

[37] Cf. W. Gross, "Lying Prophet and Disobedient Man of God in 1 Kings 13: Role Analysis as an Instrument of Theological Interpretation of an OT Narrative Text," *Semeia* 15 (1979) 122.

[38] See the discussion of 1 Kgs 17:1–6 for an analysis of the historicity and plausibility of miracles in 1, 2 Kings.

semi-idolatry, or any form of non-Mosaic religion. Religious pluralism for pluralism's sake does not impress God. Second, the Lord shares his word with the prophets, who are then responsible for preaching it and keeping it. Third, it is important to discern whether a so-called word from the Lord is true or false prophecy. T. Dozeman thinks a prophecy may be tested by whether it is fulfilled (cf. Deut 18:22; 1 Kgs 13:5, 23–24), confirmed by other words or by signs (cf. 1 Kgs 13:20–22), or lived out with integrity by the prophet.[39] D. W. Van Winkle agrees but adds the criterion of "obedience to the command of Yahweh." By this he means that God changes circumstances when people repent, a principle the Lord announces from the outset of every promise (cf. 1 Kgs 8; 11:39), but that God is never "portrayed as instructing his prophets to encourage disobedience to his commandments."[40] The true prophet preaches fidelity to God's word based on God's merciful character. False prophets claim new, contradictory revelation and may even claim angelic guidance for doing so.

Fourth, God's word will come true no matter what the circumstances. Jeroboam, the old prophet, and the man of God all learn this lesson in rather hard ways. In about three hundred years Josiah will be born and fulfill the prophet's prediction. As Simon concludes, God's word will come true "in its due time, having transcended the weakness of its bearer and converted its violators into confirmants."[41] Fifth, God's word must be obeyed, whether or not it is attended by miracles. Jeroboam failed to believe when he saw wonders. On the other hand, the man of God failed to believe when he trusted the unusual over his personal convictions. It is the Lord's instructions themselves that matter most. All else may be important yet remains peripheral to the main issue—God's word. Sixth, Israel continues to march toward disaster. Jeroboam leads them astray, but they follow. By the time the promised Josiah arises, it will be too late for the north to follow his leadership.

(4) Ahijah Prophesies against Jeroboam (14:1–18)

1 At that time Abijah son of Jeroboam became ill, 2 and Jeroboam said to his wife, "Go, disguise yourself, so you won't be recognized as the wife of Jeroboam. Then go to Shiloh. Ahijah the prophet is there—the one who told me I would be king over this people. 3 Take ten loaves of bread with you, some cakes and a jar of honey, and go to him. He will tell you what will happen to the boy." 4 So Jeroboam's wife did what he said and went to Ahijah's house in Shiloh.

Now Ahijah could not see; his sight was gone because of his age. 5 But the LORD had told Ahijah, "Jeroboam's wife is coming to ask you about her son, for he is ill, and you are to give her such and such an answer. When she arrives, she will pretend to be someone else."

---

[39] Dozeman, "The Way of the Man of God from Judah," 392–93.

[40] Van Winkle, "1 Kings XIII," 40.

[41] Simon, "I Kings 13," 116.

**6So when Ahijah heard the sound of her footsteps at the door, he said, "Come in, wife of Jeroboam. Why this pretense? I have been sent to you with bad news.
7Go, tell Jeroboam that this is what the LORD, the God of Israel, says: 'I raised you up from among the people and made you a leader over my people Israel. 8I
tore the kingdom away from the house of David and gave it to you, but you have not been like my servant David, who kept my commands and followed me with all his heart, doing only what was right in my eyes. 9You have done more evil than all who lived before you. You have made for yourself other gods, idols made of metal; you have provoked me to anger and thrust me behind your back.**

10"'Because of this, I am going to bring disaster on the house of Jeroboam. I will cut off from Jeroboam every last male in Israel—slave or free. I will burn up the house of Jeroboam as one burns dung, until it is all gone. 11Dogs will eat those belonging to Jeroboam who die in the city, and the birds of the air will feed on those who die in the country. The LORD has spoken!'

**12"As for you, go back home. When you set foot in your city, the boy will die.
13All Israel will mourn for him and bury him. He is the only one belonging to Jeroboam who will be buried, because he is the only one in the house of Jeroboam in whom the LORD, the God of Israel, has found anything good.**

14"The LORD will raise up for himself a king over Israel who will cut off the family of Jeroboam. This is the day! What? Yes, even now. 15And the LORD will strike Israel, so that it will be like a reed swaying in the water. He will uproot Israel from this good land that he gave to their forefathers and scatter them beyond the River, because they provoked the LORD to anger by making Asherah poles. 16And he will give Israel up because of the sins Jeroboam has committed and has caused Israel to commit."

17Then Jeroboam's wife got up and left and went to Tirzah. As soon as she stepped over the threshold of the house, the boy died. 18They buried him, and all Israel mourned for him, as the LORD had said through his servant the prophet Ahijah.

14:1–3 For the third time prophecy impacts Jeroboam's life. On this occasion he is desperate for a word about his son's illness, so he disguises his wife, arms her with some presents, and sends her to Ahijah. It is ironic that he seeks help from the very prophet who predicted his rise to power yet who also warned him to keep the Lord's commands. It is also ironic that he tries to disguise his wife's identity from a man whom he expects to divulge whether his son will live or die and furthermore that a king should send such a paltry gift, apparently because he fears to reveal who needs the information.

14:4–18 Ahijah's physical sight has failed due to old age. Perhaps this fact helps explain why Jeroboam thought he could be fooled. Since Ahijah is a prophet, though, he can see things no one else can see. Jeroboam obviously thinks so or he would not seek from him a prediction about the future. How does the prophet discern such secrets? Because the Lord tells him what will occur, right down to the details of her visit. Truly the prophets are privileged persons who receive direct information from the Lord.

When Jeroboam's wife arrives, she finds Ahijah ready to identify her and give her five bits of bad news. First, he condemns Jeroboam for making idols, which makes God consider him "more evil than all who lived before" him. Second, "every last male" in Jeroboam's line will die. Jeroboam's sin disqualifies him from the enduring dynasty Ahijah said would result from covenant obedience (cf. 1 Kgs 11:38). Third, Ahijah states that her sick boy will die, be mourned in Jerusalem, and will be buried. Because of the second statement, this boy's early death makes him fortunate, since he will not have to suffer horrible death and the humiliation of not being buried.[42] Fourth, with Jeroboam's family gone, Israel will obviously receive a new royal dynasty. Fifth, Ahijah makes the long-term promise that Israel will go into exile because of their adherence to Jeroboam's religion and for their acceptance of fertility cults. This last prediction will take two hundred years to occur, but it is as certain as the short-range promises.

As soon as the woman returns home, the third prediction comes true, which serves as a pledge that the others will also be fulfilled. Readers now have some short and long-term promises to guide them in the text. The man of God predicted Josiah's reign, which does not occur until 640–609 B.C., or until 2 Kings 22–23. Ahijah's prediction of Israel's fall is not fulfilled until 2 Kings 17, which describes events in 722 B.C. Of course, the deaths of Jeroboam's sons will take place much sooner, by 1 Kgs 15:29 (ca. 908 B.C.). Obviously exilic readers already knew about the devastation of Israel and about Josiah's reign. What the author wanted them to know was that sin caused the fall, that not even Josiah could save Jerusalem, and that the prophets spoke God's word, which was the truth, from the start of Israel's history.

(5) Jeroboam's Death (14:19–20)

19The other events of Jeroboam's reign, his wars and how he ruled, are written in the book of the annals of the kings of Israel. 20He reigned for twenty-two years and then rested with his fathers. And Nadab his son succeeded him as king.

14:19–20 Here the author reveals that one of his sources for the data on Jeroboam's life was "the annals of the kings of Israel," a document that includes details of major events, wars, and decisions in Jeroboam's reign. He ruled for twenty-two years (ca. 930–909) and was succeeded by Nadab, his son.[43]

Jeroboam is a tremendously important character in 1, 2 Kings. Indeed, one

[42] Nelson notes that the lack of a proper burial was considered a horrible fate in the ancient world (*First and Second Kings,* 92).

[43] The book's regular formula for the passing of kings appears in 1 Kgs 2:10–12 and 11:41–43, of course, but becomes especially prominent in the story from this point. Alterations in the formula may reveal something about the story or the author's attitude toward an individual character.

could argue that he is more significant for the story than Solomon, Hezekiah, or Josiah. After all, it was Jeroboam who was God's instrument for punishing Solomon's sins, which also ended Davidic rule over all Israel. Jeroboam's religion had such a negative impact on Israel and Judah that it was a major factor in both countries' demise. Finally, this clever yet unfaithful man's life helped demonstrate the prophets' significance. These individuals now emerge as the only reliable bearers of God's word, as those who know the future, and therefore as those who should be consulted before important decisions are made.

(6) Rehoboam's Reign (14:21–31)

21Rehoboam son of Solomon was king in Judah. He was forty-one years old when he became king, and he reigned seventeen years in Jerusalem, the city the LORD had chosen out of all the tribes of Israel in which to put his Name. His mother's name was Naamah; she was an Ammonite.

22Judah did evil in the eyes of the LORD. By the sins they committed they stirred up his jealous anger more than their fathers had done. 23They also set up for themselves high places, sacred stones and Asherah poles on every high hill and under every spreading tree. 24There were even male shrine prostitutes in the land; the people engaged in all the detestable practices of the nations the LORD had driven out before the Israelites.

25In the fifth year of King Rehoboam, Shishak king of Egypt attacked Jerusalem. 26He carried off the treasures of the temple of the LORD and the treasures of the royal palace. He took everything, including all the gold shields Solomon had made. 27So King Rehoboam made bronze shields to replace them and assigned these to the commanders of the guard on duty at the entrance to the royal palace. 28Whenever the king went to the LORD's temple, the guards bore the shields, and afterward they returned them to the guardroom.

29As for the other events of Rehoboam's reign, and all he did, are they not written in the book of the annals of the kings of Judah? 30There was continual warfare between Rehoboam and Jeroboam. 31And Rehoboam rested with his fathers and was buried with them in the City of David. His mother's name was Naamah; she was an Ammonite. And Abijah his son succeeded him as king.

14:21 Having offered a detailed description of the new situation in Israel, the author now discusses three kings of Judah. Of course, Rehoboam is treated first, and three items are highlighted. First, he governs for seventeen years (ca. 930–913). Second, as opposed to Jeroboam his reign occurs in Jerusalem, "the city the LORD had chosen." Third, his mother was an Ammonite, a fact that further underscores Solomon's love for foreign women (note the repetition in v. 31).

14:22–24 Judah's conduct during Rehoboam's era clearly disgusts and angers the narrator. Judah's sins stir up "God's jealous anger,"[44] a phrase that

[44] The phrase in Heb. is וַיְקַנְאוּ אֹתוֹ.

troubles many readers of Scripture who consider jealousy a solely negative trait. Jealous protection of what is rightly one's own, however, is justified. For example, most marriage partners do not want their spouses violated sexually. They are justifiably protective of an exclusive sexual relationship. Most parents are jealous concerning the right to raise their child, so they are justifiably protective of their parental responsibilities. In these examples jealousy is a good and normal trait.

God's jealousy is equally positive in this verse. Judah is part of the Lord's chosen people. The Lord chose Abraham, delivered Israel from Egypt, gave Moses the covenant, provided Israel a new home in Canaan, and established David and Solomon as their leaders. Israelites are God's people, and Yahweh is Israel's God. For him to be jealous of this exclusive relationship is no character flaw. Instead it magnifies God's righteousness, concern, and covenant loyalty. Anything less than this kind of justifiable protectiveness would indicate a careless attitude toward destructive behavior like idolatry and sensuality.

Judah's religious sins exceed even those of Israel at this point. Jeroboam's cult mixed several Yahwistic and Canaanite practices, but Judah goes one step further here and simply adopts Canaanite religion. The probability that some legitimate Mosaic, covenantal worship still occurred hardly softens the shock of any of God's people acting in such a manner. Besides "high places," the people worshiped "sacred stones and Asherah poles." Skinner says that the stones were pillars that were considered symbolic of a god's presence and that the Asherah poles were wooden poles that were identified as representations of a goddess.[45] Asherah was often seen as the female consort, wife or otherwise, of male gods. Obviously, this "coupling" of gods had strong sexual overtones. Thus, the presence of "prostitutes" at sacred Canaanite shrines was not unusual. Such prostitutes were present so worshipers could fulfill their obligations to fertility gods. Snaith explains:

> There were prostitutes of either sex within the temple in the service of the deity. This custom was common and recognized everywhere in Phoenician cults and in the cults (e.g., that of Aphrodite) which were influenced by them. The custom was a feature of Canaanite religion and was common in Mesopotamia from early times.[46]

By practicing such sins, Judah becomes no better than the nations they have replaced in the land.

Three types of worship now exist in the land, and the author refers to these types throughout the rest of the story. The first type is monotheistic Yahwism as revealed in the Mosaic Covenant. The second is Jeroboam's syncretistic,

---

[45] J. Skinner, *I and II Kings*, CB (Edinburgh: T. C. & E. C. Jack, 1904) 204–5.

[46] N. H. Snaith, "The First and Second Books of Kings, Exegesis," *IB* (Nashville: Abingdon, 1954) 3:130–31.

anti-Jerusalem cult, and the third is Canaanite idolatry, usually practiced in the form of a fertility cult. Kings will be judged subsequently based on what form of religion they practice *and* by what sorts of religions they allow to continue during their reigns.

14:25–28 Egypt's invasion of Judah signals the end of Jerusalem's autonomy. Rehoboam and all his successors must deal with political and military vulnerability. Bright states that friendly relations between Israel and Egypt ended when, "Late in Solomon's lifetime (ca. 935) the weak Twenty-first Dynasty, with which Solomon had been allied, was overthrown by a Libyan noble named Shishak (Shoshenq) who founded the Twenty-second (Bubastite) Dynasty."[47] Shishak hoped to reestablish Egyptian power in Asia, so it was in his interest to support Jeroboam as a way of undermining Solomon.[48]

Though this text only mentions Shishak's movements against Jerusalem, the invasion probably was a widespread operation. In fact, Gray notes that Shishak's Karnak inscription claims the Egyptians fought in about "150 places both in Israel and Judah from north of the Plain of Esdraelon to the extreme south of the settled land in the Negeb."[49] Cities great and small were affected by this operation. Rehoboam is forced to relinquish the temple treasures just to get rid of Shishak. Paying invaders to leave will become standard practice in Judah. Idolatry has political consequences.

14:29–31 Rehoboam's death comes after a lifetime of struggle. His humiliation at the hands of Shishak, coupled with "continual warfare" with Jeroboam, means that he had no rest until he "rested with his fathers." Sadly, Rehoboam pales in comparison to these fathers. Unlike David, he could not defeat his enemies. Unlike Solomon, he was unable to collect wisdom, wealth, or prestige. Unlike both men, he was unable to keep the nation together. The decline of the monarchy coincides with the decline of the nation as a whole and the decline of the nation's spiritual commitment.

(7) Abijah's Reign (15:1–8)

**1In the eighteenth year of the reign of Jeroboam son of Nebat, Abijah became
king of Judah, 2and he reigned in Jerusalem three years. His mother's name was
Maacah daughter of Abishalom.**

**3He committed all the sins his father had done before him; his heart was not
fully devoted to the LORD his God, as the heart of David his forefather had been.
4Nevertheless, for David's sake the LORD his God gave him a lamp in Jerusalem by
raising up a son to succeed him and by making Jerusalem strong. 5For David had
done what was right in the eyes of the LORD and had not failed to keep any of the**

[47] Bright, *History of Israel,* 233.
[48] Ibid.
[49] Gray, *1 and 2 Kings,* 314.

LORD's commands all the days of his life—except in the case of Uriah the Hittite.
6 There was war between Rehoboam and Jeroboam throughout [Abijah's] life-
time. 7 As for the other events of Abijah's reign, and all he did, are they not writ-
ten in the book of the annals of the kings of Judah? There was war between
Abijah and Jeroboam. 8 And Abijah rested with his fathers and was buried in the
City of David. And Asa his son succeeded him as king.

15:1–8 Abijah succeeds his father and governs in Jerusalem only three years (ca. 913–910). He too opposes Jeroboam throughout his reign. In fact, 2 Chr 13:1–20 states that Abijah defeated Jeroboam in Ephraim (ca. 912 B.C.), then took "Bethel, Jeshanah and Ephron, with their surrounding villages" (13:19). Thus, he was able to gain some relief from the northern threat. Still, he commits all the sins his father practiced (cf. 1 Kgs 14:25–28). Why, then, does God allow him to rule at all? Why does God abide Judah's existence? Again, the answer lies in the Lord's grace and his covenant with David. The Lord will continue David's dynasty and protect Jerusalem because of David's faithfulness. Certainly David sinned in the Bathsheba/Uriah incident, yet he never turned to idols as Solomon, Rehoboam, and now Abijah have done. God keeps his promises even when David's descendants do not.

(8) Asa's Reign (15:9–24)

9 In the twentieth year of Jeroboam king of Israel, Asa became king of Judah,
10 and he reigned in Jerusalem forty-one years. His grandmother's name was
Maacah daughter of Abishalom.
11 Asa did what was right in the eyes of the LORD, as his father David had
done. 12 He expelled the male shrine prostitutes from the land and got rid of all
the idols his fathers had made. 13 He even deposed his grandmother Maacah from
her position as queen mother, because she had made a repulsive Asherah pole.
Asa cut the pole down and burned it in the Kidron Valley. 14 Although he did not
remove the high places, Asa's heart was fully committed to the LORD all his life.
15 He brought into the temple of the LORD the silver and gold and the articles that
he and his father had dedicated.
16 There was war between Asa and Baasha king of Israel throughout their
reigns. 17 Baasha king of Israel went up against Judah and fortified Ramah to pre-
vent anyone from leaving or entering the territory of Asa king of Judah.
18 Asa then took all the silver and gold that was left in the treasuries of the
LORD's temple and of his own palace. He entrusted it to his officials and sent
them to Ben-Hadad son of Tabrimmon, the son of Hezion, the king of Aram, who
was ruling in Damascus. 19 "Let there be a treaty between me and you," he said,
"as there was between my father and your father. See, I am sending you a gift of
silver and gold. Now break your treaty with Baasha king of Israel so he will with-
draw from me."
20 Ben-Hadad agreed with King Asa and sent the commanders of his forces
against the towns of Israel. He conquered Ijon, Dan, Abel Beth Maacah and all
Kinnereth in addition to Naphtali. 21 When Baasha heard this, he stopped build-

ing Ramah and withdrew to Tirzah. [22]Then King Asa issued an order to all Judah—no one was exempt—and they carried away from Ramah the stones and timber Baasha had been using there. With them King Asa built up Geba in Benjamin, and also Mizpah.

[23]As for all the other events of Asa's reign, all his achievements, all he did and the cities he built, are they not written in the book of the annals of the kings of Judah? In his old age, however, his feet became diseased. [24]Then Asa rested with his fathers and was buried with them in the city of his father David. And Jehoshaphat his son succeeded him as king.

15:9–15 Asa's forty-one-year reign (ca. 910–869) probably includes a three-year coregency with his son Jehoshaphat,[50] perhaps made necessary by Asa's illness mentioned in 1 Kgs 15:23.[51] The author presents Asa in a positive light, even commenting that he serves the Lord as David had done. This reference means that Asa has no use for idols. Only the fact that he does not remove the high places mars the narrator's assessment of Asa's career.

Besides serving God himself, Asa attempts to end the pagan practices Rehoboam and Abijah allowed, even encouraged. He rids the land of the sacred prostitutes that his father and grandfather had ignored (cf. 14:25–28; 15:3) and removes "the idols his father had made." Asherah poles are forbidden to the extent that Asa deposes his grandmother "from her position as queen mother" because she worshiped one of these idols. He also supports the temple, for he collects gold and silver for its maintenance. Only two other kings (Hezekiah and Josiah) receive higher commendations than Asa.

15:16–22 Asa's religious fervor does not exempt him from military threats. Though no date is specified, the Chronicler writes that Asa repels a Cushite invasion during his reign (2 Chr 14:9–15). He and Baasha, Jeroboam's eventual successor (cf. 1 Kgs 15:33–16:7), fight "throughout their reigns." Baasha poses such a threat that Asa pays Syria's Ben-Hadad to break his alliance with Baasha and come rescue him. Perhaps Ben-Hadad agrees in order to weaken his neighbor's military capability. Although 2 Chr 16:7–10 recounts a prophetic rebuke that Asa received for relying on treaties for security, Kings does not mention it. Asa uses this respite to fortify Ramah, only four miles north of Jerusalem on the main route to the coastal plain. Clearly, Asa senses that his capital is too vulnerable in an ongoing hostile environment. The Syrians will be heard from again, next time as a foe of Israel.

15:23–24 Asa's death marks the end of Judah's first great reforming king.[52] He built cities, fought battles, and enjoyed other achievements, but his

[50] E. R. Thiele, *The Mysterious Numbers of the Hebrew Kings,* 3d ed. (Grand Rapids: Zondervan, 1983) 83–87.

[51] DeVries, *1 Kings,* 190.

[52] For an analysis of Judah's reforming monarchs, see R. H. Lowery, *The Reforming Kings: Cults and Society in First Temple Judah,* JSOTSup 120 (Sheffield: Sheffield Academic Press, 1991).

spiritual attainments matter most to the author of 1, 2 Kings. Unfortunately, faulty worship and idolatry never die easily in Israel. His son, Jehoshaphat, who follows him on the throne, will have to address many of the same problems during his own time in power (cf. 1 Kgs 22:46).

(9) Nadab's Reign (15:25–31)

25Nadab son of Jeroboam became king of Israel in the second year of Asa king of Judah, and he reigned over Israel two years. 26He did evil in the eyes of the LORD, walking in the ways of his father and in his sin, which he had caused Israel to commit.

27Baasha son of Ahijah of the house of Issachar plotted against him, and he struck him down at Gibbethon, a Philistine town, while Nadab and all Israel were besieging it. 28Baasha killed Nadab in the third year of Asa king of Judah and succeeded him as king.

29As soon as he began to reign, he killed Jeroboam's whole family. He did not leave Jeroboam anyone that breathed, but destroyed them all, according to the word of the LORD given through his servant Ahijah the Shilonite— 30because of the sins Jeroboam had committed and had caused Israel to commit, and because he provoked the LORD, the God of Israel, to anger.

31As for the other events of Nadab's reign, and all he did, are they not written in the book of the annals of the kings of Israel?

Now the story shifts to the Northern Kingdom, where it will stay until the last verses of 1 Kings. Two issues dominate the next several verses. First, rapid turnover of leadership becomes commonplace in Israel. As Bright observes, "Nothing is more characteristic of the northern state than its extreme internal instability."[53] Few failures could be more damaging to a new nation. Second, the power of the prophetic word emerges again. Predictions old and new come true. Prophets old and new call on kings to account for their actions, which indicates that God has not abdicated his role as Lord of history.

15:25–31 Nadab continues the sins begun by his father, Jeroboam. He attempts no reform like the one initiated by his counterpart in Judah, and he only reigns for two years (ca. 909–908). While besieging a Philistine town, Nadab is struck down by Baasha, who has not been introduced previously in the text. To remove all Jeroboamite claims to the throne, Baasha kills Jeroboam's entire family. Baasha's action fulfills Ahijah's prediction (cf. 1 Kgs 14:10–11) that Jeroboam's sin would cost his descendants their lives. Persons who lead a nation to embrace empty religious and ethical systems often create an environment of violence, greed, and oppression. Their children and grandchildren reap the harvest of their actions. God did not force this murder to occur. Rather, the prediction simply declared to Jeroboam the results of the decisions he had made.

---

[53] Bright, *History of Israel,* 238.

2. The Rise of Omri and Ahab (15:32–16:34)

Out of the chaos portrayed in this section will come Omri, a man who will stabilize the Northern Kingdom, establish a new capital, and begin a new dynasty. His family will rule through 2 Kings 10. They will therefore occupy more of the story than any other northern dynasty. Omrides will also serve as active opponents of the prophets and as patrons of idolatry, especially of Baal worship. Before Omri's ascent, however, Israel must face turbulent political times.

(1) Baasha's Early Career (15:32–34)

33In the third year of Asa king of Judah, Baasha son of Ahijah became king of all Israel in Tirzah, and he reigned twenty-four years. 34He did evil in the eyes of the LORD, walking in the ways of Jeroboam and in his sin, which he had caused Israel to commit.

15:32–34 Baasha assassinates Nadab in Asa's third year, then rules for twenty-four years (ca. 908–885). He is the first of several individuals in the north who come to power, at least briefly, by killing a king (cf. 1 Kgs 16:15–16; 2 Kgs 10:1–17; 15:10–13,14–16,25–26,30–31). In all but the long account of Jehu's revolt in 2 Kings 10 a standard form is followed for describing the uprising, so the author probably had a source that reported such activities the same way.[54] Once in control Baasha simply follows in Jeroboam's footsteps. He is able to enjoy royal powers yet does little with his opportunity except continue the sectional rivalry with Judah by fighting Asa "throughout their reigns."

(2) Jehu Prophesies against Baasha (16:1–4)

1Then the word of the LORD came to Jehu son of Hanani against Baasha: 2"I lifted you up from the dust and made you leader of my people Israel, but you walked in the ways of Jeroboam and caused my people Israel to sin and to provoke me to anger by their sins. 3So I am about to consume Baasha and his house, and I will make your house like that of Jeroboam son of Nebat. 4Dogs will eat those belonging to Baasha who die in the city, and the birds of the air will feed on those who die in the country."

16:1–4 Because Baasha squanders his chance to remove Jeroboam's religious legacy as well as his physical lineage, God sends a prophet to condemn him. This time Jehu brings God's word to the king. Essentially, he claims that

[54] Cf. G. H. Jones, *1 and 2 Kings,* NCB (Grand Rapids: Eerdmans, 1984) 1:47. Jones lists five statements that occur in conspiracy texts: (1) conspiracy noted, (2) conspirator and his father named, (3) assassination recounted, (4) king's death noted, and (5) conspirator named as new monarch.

the Lord has given Baasha the chance to bring Israel back to covenant faith, but instead he has acted like those he replaced. Thus, he is no better than Jeroboam and will share Jeroboam's fate.

(3) Baasha's Death (16:5–7)

**5As for the other events of Baasha's reign, what he did and his achievements,
are they not written in the book of the annals of the kings of Israel? 6Baasha rested
with his fathers and was buried in Tirzah. And Elah his son succeeded him as king.
7Moreover, the word of the LORD came through the prophet Jehu son of
Hanani to Baasha and his house, because of all the evil he had done in the eyes of the LORD, provoking him to anger by the things he did, and becoming like the house of Jeroboam—and also because he destroyed it.**

16:5–7 Besides providing information on Baasha's death, these verses reemphasize the author's theological approach to history. Three issues deserve mention. First, God's word dictates history, a fact Jehu's prophetic rebuke and prediction divulges. Second, Jeroboam and Baasha are judged unfavorably because they use their God-given political authority to preserve their own position rather than to glorify God among the people. Third, the text stresses cause and effect, not fatalistic determinism. God gives both Jeroboam and Baasha the opportunity to follow the covenant. Baasha eliminates Jeroboam's family, as God said would happen, yet becomes like Jeroboam, which makes him a murderer, not a reformer. Both men fulfill God's word by coming to power, but both men fail to do God's will in their reigns. They match the Lord's goodness with evil. Again, the Lord's sovereignty and human responsibility are both vital for understanding history.

(4) Elah's Reign (16:8–14)

8In the twenty-sixth year of Asa king of Judah, Elah son of Baasha became king of Israel, and he reigned in Tirzah two years.

**9Zimri, one of his officials, who had command of half his chariots, plotted against him. Elah was in Tirzah at the time, getting drunk in the home of Arza, the man in charge of the palace at Tirzah. 10Zimri came in, struck him down and
killed him in the twenty-seventh year of Asa king of Judah. Then he succeeded him as king.**

**11As soon as he began to reign and was seated on the throne, he killed off Baasha's whole family. He did not spare a single male, whether relative or friend.
12So Zimri destroyed the whole family of Baasha, in accordance with the word of
the LORD spoken against Baasha through the prophet Jehu— 13because of all the
sins Baasha and his son Elah had committed and had caused Israel to commit, so that they provoked the LORD, the God of Israel, to anger by their worthless idols.
14As for the other events of Elah's reign, and all he did, are they not written in the book of the annals of the kings of Israel?**

16:8–10 Yet another man ascends the northern throne during Asa's era. Baasha's son, Elah, becomes king and governs for two years (ca. 885–884). He dies a rather ignoble death. While he is getting drunk in the home of a high official, he is murdered by Zimri, "one of his officials, who had command of half his chariots." At least Nadab was assassinated during a military campaign rather than during a drinking spree!

16:11–14 Zimri follows Baasha's example. He fulfills a prophetic prediction by killing every one of his predecessor's heirs. He leaves no living rival to the throne. Baasha and Elah could have avoided this disaster by serving the Lord instead of idols but chose another path. Apparently the northern kings do not believe it is possible to govern the people if they insist on righteous behavior and proper worship. Obedience, not knowledge, is their problem.

(5) Zimri's Coup and Death (16:15–20)

15In the twenty-seventh year of Asa king of Judah, Zimri reigned in Tirzah seven days. The army was encamped near Gibbethon, a Philistine town. 16When the Israelites in the camp heard that Zimri had plotted against the king and murdered him, they proclaimed Omri, the commander of the army, king over Israel that very day there in the camp. 17Then Omri and all the Israelites with him withdrew from Gibbethon and laid siege to Tirzah. 18When Zimri saw that the city was taken, he went into the citadel of the royal palace and set the palace on fire around him. So he died, 19because of the sins he had committed, doing evil in the eyes of the LORD and walking in the ways of Jeroboam and in the sin he had committed and had caused Israel to commit.

20As for the other events of Zimri's reign, and the rebellion he carried out, are they not written in the book of the annals of the kings of Israel?

16:15–20 Zimri is only able to stay in power for seven days, which means his only claim to fame is that he ruled the shortest period of time in Israelite history. When the army, which is encamped "near Gibbethon, a Philistine town," hears of the assassination, they proclaim their leader, Omri, king. The army then shuts up Zimri in Tirzah, where he commits suicide by setting the palace on fire. According to the author, he was no better than earlier kings, for he followed Jeroboam's religion. This comment reflects Zimri's overall life and activity, not just his brief reign.

More important than the details about Zimri is the emergence of Omri in the story. He is a leader and a fighter. Several challenges await him. First, there are the ongoing conflicts with Judah and Philistia. Second, Tirzah, the capital city, has been besieged from without and burned from within. Third, Israel has suffered for some time from political instability due to rapid turnover of leadership. Finally, the next passage indicates that Omri has a rival to the throne. How will he solve these social and political problems? Will he have any interest in solving Israel's religious woes?

(6) Omri's Reign and the Founding of Samaria (16:21–28)

[21]Then the people of Israel were split into two factions; half supported Tibni son of Ginath for king, and the other half supported Omri. [22]But Omri's followers proved stronger than those of Tibni son of Ginath. So Tibni died and Omri became king.

[23]In the thirty-first year of Asa king of Judah, Omri became king of Israel, and he reigned twelve years, six of them in Tirzah. [24]He bought the hill of Samaria from Shemer for two talents of silver and built a city on the hill, calling it Samaria, after Shemer, the name of the former owner of the hill.

[25]But Omri did evil in the eyes of the LORD and sinned more than all those before him. [26]He walked in all the ways of Jeroboam son of Nebat and in his sin, which he had caused Israel to commit, so that they provoked the LORD, the God of Israel, to anger by their worthless idols.

[27]As for the other events of Omri's reign, what he did and the things he achieved, are they not written in the book of the annals of the kings of Israel? [28]Omri rested with his fathers and was buried in Samaria. And Ahab his son succeeded him as king.

16:21–22 Omri must overcome "Tibni son of Ginath" to become king. All the political intrigue has led to factionalism within Israel. Omri's ability to gain control of the situation is a tribute to his military and administrative skill.

16:23–26 At first glance the chronology for Omri's reign seems wrong. The text says he ruled twelve years, beginning with Asa's thirty-first year. Of course, Asa served forty-one years (1 Kgs 15:10), which seems to create a gap of two years. What has occurred, however, is that the author reflects the "coreign" of Tibni and Omri (ca. 885–880) *and* the length of time Omri ruled on his own (ca. 880–874). Thiele states that in this case the author utilizes a dual dating procedure "that is used for all three of the overlapping reigns in Israel and for two in Judah."[55] Thus, Omri comes to power in Asa's twenty-seventh year after Zimri's murder of Elah (1 Kgs 16:15), fights Tibni until the thirty-first year of Asa (1 Kgs 16:23), and dies in Asa's thirty-eighth year, a total of twelve years by the northern means of reckoning reigns.

Probably Omri's most impressive achievement is his construction of a new capital city, Samaria. This city was placed on "a strategic and centrally located site overlooking the chief commercial routes of the Esdraelon Plain."[56] It was therefore easily defended and quite accessible to merchants and traders. Samaria remained Israel's capital until Assyria plundered the city in 722 B.C.

Besides his military and civic achievements, Omri was able to stabilize the turbulent political climate in the north by beginning a dynasty that lasted until about 842 B.C. By secular standards he and his descendants were fairly effec-

[55] Thiele, *The Mysterious Numbers of the Hebrew Kings,* 62.

[56] R. D. Patterson and H. J. Austel, "1, 2 Kings," EBC (Grand Rapids: Zondervan, 1988) 4:135.

tive monarchs; for they kept foreign armies at bay, gave the people a religion they liked, and made foreign alliances through marriage. He and his sons stopped fighting Judah. Indeed his accomplishments were so considerable that Moabite and Assyrian records attest his greatness. Assyrian documents refer to Israel as "the land of Omri" as late as 733–732 B.C.[57]

What is the author's assessment of Omri? The author is unimpressed. According to the text, Omri walked in all the ways of Jeroboam "and sinned more than all those before him," perhaps because he, like Baasha, had an opportunity to lead the people in new directions. His failure to do so makes him even more culpable than the average nondescript monarch.

(7) Ahab's Ascension and Wickedness (16:29–34)

[29]In the thirty-eighth year of Asa king of Judah, Ahab son of Omri became king of Israel, and he reigned in Samaria over Israel twenty-two years. [30]Ahab son of Omri did more evil in the eyes of the LORD than any of those before him. [31]He not only considered it trivial to commit the sins of Jeroboam son of Nebat, but he also married Jezebel daughter of Ethbaal king of the Sidonians, and began to serve Baal and worship him. [32]He set up an altar for Baal in the temple of Baal that he built in Samaria. [33]Ahab also made an Asherah pole and did more to provoke the LORD, the God of Israel, to anger than did all the kings of Israel before him.

[34]In Ahab's time, Hiel of Bethel rebuilt Jericho. He laid its foundations at the cost of his firstborn son Abiram, and he set up its gates at the cost of his youngest son Segub, in accordance with the word of the LORD spoken by Joshua son of Nun.

16:29–33 Ahab succeeds his father with the kingdom in the best shape since Jeroboam's times. He rules for twenty-two years (ca. 874–853), but few if any of these years please the author, who condemns Ahab as the worst northern king yet. Ahab not only allows Jeroboam's cult to continue, but he also marries Jezebel of Tyre, a Baal worshiper. Jezebel becomes the great patroness of Baal in Israel. Her husband erects a temple for Baal, an image of Baal in the temple, and Asherah poles.[58] Full-blown fertility rites have come to Israel.

---

[57] J. A. Montgomery and H. S. Gehman, *A Critical and Exegetical Commentary on the Book of Kings,* ICC (1951; Edinburgh: T & T Clark, 1986) 284–85.

[58] Note the description of these cult objects in P. K. McCarter, Jr., "Aspects of the Religion of the Israelite Monarchy: Biblical and Epigraphical Data," *Ancient Israelite Religion,* ed. P. D. Miller, Jr., P. Hanson, and S. D. McBride (Philadelphia: Fortress, 1987) 146. Indeed the notion that Yahweh has a female consort, or Asherah, probably became part of syncretistic worship in Judah. Cf. M. S. Smith, *The Early History of God: Yahweh and the Other Deities in Ancient Israel* (San Francisco: Harper Collins, 1990) 80–114; and R. S. Hess, "Yahweh and His Asherah? Epigraphic Evidence for Religious Pluralism in Old Testament Times," in *One God, One Lord in a World of Religious Pluralism,* ed., A. D. Clarke and B. W. Winter (Cambridge: Tyndale, 1991) 5–33. For the other side of the issue see A. Le Maire, "Who or What Was Jahweh's Asherah?" *BAR* 10 (1984) 42–51.

Idolatry as an institution has become even more entrenched than in the past.

16:34 On the surface this verse seems to have little reason for occupying its present position. It reads like a curious aside about Jericho, yet it reveals two important points. First, in the polytheistic climate in Ahab's Israel, a man feels free to offer his children as sacrifices to build a city. DeVries believes: "The foundation sacrifice, revealed by modern archaeology, is probably what was involved. The children named were probably infants, dead or alive, placed in jars and inserted into the masonry, propitiating the gods and warding off evil."[59] Second, this wicked event reminds readers of God's word through Joshua that rebuilding Jericho would bring death to the builder's family (Josh 6:26). God's word is still active in history according to the author. Despite all the sin in Israel, the Lord is still in charge. The events that follow in 1 Kings 17–22 highlight this truth.

Canonical and Theological Implications of 1 Kgs 12:1–16:34

At least three major canonical turning points begin in 1 Kings 12–16. The first of these points is the division of the kingdom into two parts. This fracture marks the beginning of the eventual loss of the land promised to Abraham (Gen 12:1–9), sought by Moses (Exod–Deut), conquered by Joshua (Josh 1–12), secured by David (2 Sam 5–24), and given peace by Solomon (1 Kgs 1–10). Isaiah (10:20–23), Jeremiah (3:18; 31:9), Ezekiel (37:15–17), and Amos (9:11–15) looked forward to the time when a reunited Israel would once again serve the Lord after exile. Just as the division pointed to a time of disintegration and deserved punishment, so the nation's restoration will signal God's renewed promise of a holy land for a holy people. Certainly Ezra, Nehemiah, and the psalmists (e.g., 107; 126) read Israel's return to the land in this way.

Second, the vital matter of true prophecy versus false prophecy begins in earnest here. False prophets like Balaam[60] (cf. Num 22–24) have always existed, of course, but with competing kingdoms and competing religions the issue of who speaks God's word takes on even greater significance. First Kings 13 presents a problem that the prophetic writings address repeatedly. Here the true prophet possesses God's word, opposes any form of idolatry, and refuses to be bribed by the king. On the other hand, the false prophet protects Jeroboam by lying to the true prophet. Above all, true prophecy carries the full impact of the power of God's word. The true prophet prospers when he preaches and obeys the word yet dies when he listens to an oracle that contradicts it. Here, Childs says: "Timing and hermeneutics have nothing to do with the true and the false. The distinction is unrelated to the ethical sensitivity of

---

[59] DeVries, *1 Kings,* 205.

[60] R. Allen, "The Theology of the Balaam Oracles," in *Tradition & Testament: Essays in Honor of Charles Lee Feinberg*, ed J. S. and P. D. Feinberg (Chicago: Moody, 1981) 81–119.

an alert prophet, but measured completely by the effect of the word of God."[61] The Lord's word comes true regardless of who opposes it.

Perhaps no Old Testament book struggles with true and false prophecy more than the Book of Jeremiah. People of Jeremiah's day tried to force him to stop prophesying in the Lord's name because they hated his message (cf. Jer 11:21–23; 20:1–6). False prophets opposed him (Jer 28:1–17), and kings listened to false prophets instead of to him (Jer 37:18–20). He tells Hananiah, a lying prophet, that true prophets preach unpopular messages of war and turmoil. Messages of peace and safety are the exception (Jer 28:7–9). Words truly from God come to pass, a fact the Babylon invasion proved. The true prophet in 1 Kings 13 forgot these principles, even as the lying prophet was reminded of their validity.

New Testament texts also pursue this topic. Prophets appear in Acts 11:27–30; 13:1; 21:10–11, and elsewhere. Each time the prophet is portrayed as a person who is doctrinally sound and totally accurate in his or her predictions. Paul mentions prophecies in 1 Cor 14:29 and commands the congregation to make certain about their accuracy. There do not appear to be different standards for prophets in either testament. In both the Old and New Testaments prophets must have a word from God and state sound doctrine; 100 percent accuracy is required for any predictions made. Anything that does not meet these standards is not prophecy (cf. Deut 13:1–11; 18:14–22).

Third, 1 Kings 12–16 focuses on legitimate versus nonlegitimate worship. Syncretism and idolatry are discussed throughout the rest of the canon as threats to covenant loyalty. Isaiah lampoons idols as the works of men's hands (Isa 44:6–20), burdens to be carried (46:1–7), and snares to the people of God (46:8–13). Jeremiah and Hosea consider Israelite idolatry spiritual adultery (cf. Jer 2:1–11; Hos 2:1–13). Amos thinks idolatry merits punishment (Amos 2:4–5). Ezekiel denounces idolatry in any form (cf. Ezek 8:1–18). Psalm 78, the great psalm of Israel's history, blames constant covenant breaking and idolatry as the chief reasons for the people's exile (Ps 78:56–64). Clearly, Jeroboam's cult began the process of an ever-growing breach between the nation and their God, who had created them in the first place.

Given these canonical implications, perhaps it is best to summarize their theological counterparts by noting the author's portrayal of God, the prophets, and the kings. Much of what has already been said about the Lord applies in these chapters as well. God is fully sovereign in history, a fact that his sending of prophets to make predictions conveys (cf. 1 Kgs 12:21–24; 13:1–32; 14:1–18). This work through the prophets also underscores God's willingness to communicate with people. It further proves the Lord's mercy, for the prophets'

[61] B. S. Childs, *Old Testament Theology in a Canonical Context* (Philadelphia: Fortress, 1986) 142.

warnings seek to prevent, not hasten, judgment. Since the Lord cautions the kings through the prophets, whatever punishment ensues demonstrates God's righteousness. Truth, integrity, power, and mercy are all aspects of the Lord's character in these chapters.

The prophets' chief role is as God's messengers to the kings and the people. These messengers are Judah's only hope of avoiding Jeroboam's apostasy and thus of surviving disaster. Unfortunately, 1 Kings 13 shows that Judah will act like Israel, indeed will act like the good prophet who heeds the false prophet's lies. Barth observes:

> All Jerusalem and all Judah will do as this man of Judah has done. They will weigh the commission entrusted to them . . . against the commission of another. They will listen to supposed angelic voices from far and near. And their decision, too, will be false. They will become tolerant and then disobedient. They will eventually fall into every kind of apostasy.[62]

The Lord's messengers may fail to convince their hearers of the truth of God's word, but that word's power will inexorably surface as sin grows and the Lord punishes. What has been promised will be fulfilled.[63]

Because of the importance of God's word through the prophets in this section, obedience to divine direction and testing prophetic utterances are foundational applicational principles here. Divine direction is given to benefit its hearers. Rehoboam realizes this truth when he listens to Shemaiah's warnings not to invade Israel. God's word restrains from foolish mistakes.[64] On the other hand, Jeroboam's unwillingness to obey God's command made through Ahijah and the unnamed prophet leads to death for his family and the nation he founded. True prophets may be known by adherence to the covenant and by accuracy (Deut 18:14–22; 1 Kgs 13). They can be expected to carry difficult, even threatening, messages. They do not bring words of comfort, ease, and accommodation. There can be no fellowship between the true prophet, who agrees with and executes Yahweh's plans, and the false prophet, who creates his own oracles and uses them to distort the truth and harm God's people (cf. 1 Kgs 13).[65]

Except for Asa, the kings are not positive figures in these stories. Jeroboam in particular serves as an example of how pervasive sin can be. His religion affects others adversely. His sin becomes their sin, and his cult leads to an easy

---

[62] K. Barth, *Church Dogmatics II, 2: The Doctrine of God* (Edinburgh: T & T Clark, 1957) 401.

[63] Cf. H. N. Wallace, "The Oracles against the Israelite Dynasties in 1 and 2 Kings," *Bib* 67 1 (1986) 21–40.

[64] Cf. G. Rice, *Nations Under God: A Commentary on the Book of 1 Kings,* ITC (Grand Rapids: Eerdmans, 1990) 103.

[65] Barth, *Church Dogmatics II,* 2, 401.

acceptance of Baalism. Even in Judah, where David's descendants rule, only Asa adheres to David's legacy of single-minded devotion to Yahweh. Rather than obey God, respond positively to the prophets, and reject falsehood, they opt for Jeroboam's religion, or worse. Disregarding Moses' command to be different from the Canaanite kings, they adopt pagan practices for political reasons.[66] None of these decisions fulfills Moses' ideal of a king who honors and safeguards God's word (cf. Deut 17:14–20). The kings too often use theology as a political tool. Only Asa acts on behalf of Yahweh. He is not perfect, but he is faithful.

Related to these principles is the necessity of individual and national unwillingness to compromise the essentials of covenantal faith. What were the essentials in the author's mind? Simply put, the writer believed Yahweh alone is God; idols are therefore as dangerous as they are ridiculous; one temple must be maintained as the focal point of this single-minded worship; one priestly clan should serve as the teachers and intercessors at this one central worship center (cf. 1 Kgs 12:25–33). Implied in each of these convictions is the notion that Israel must follow the single covenant revealed to Moses. Jeroboam's religion deviated from the essentials slightly in some ways yet greatly in others.[67] Any deviation, however, not only could but did lead to ever-growing corruption.

Applicational Implications of 1 Kgs 12:1–16:34

Today's community of faith must decide what ideas, practices, and attitudes erode, then obliterate, biblical faith.[68] Certainly some worldviews, lifestyles, theologies, and associations are antithetical to distinctive Christianity. Basically, such attachments deny the uniqueness of God's covenant with the church, encourage adherence to or worship of other things or gods, or obliterate the authority of God in daily life. Certainly individuals must decide for themselves what constitutes essential faith, but some broad guidelines exist in 1 Kings 12–16. Whatever leads one away from clear biblical teaching about the Lord constitutes an opportunity for losing distinctive faith.

One way of not turning from covenantal faith is to have gratitude for what God has done. Jeroboam and Baasha illustrate this truth. Both men are ele-

---

[66] Note the discussion of how Jeroboam's idolatry breaks Moses' commands in C. M. Carmichael, *Law and Narrative in the Bible: The Evidence of the Deuteronomic Laws and the Decalogue* (Ithaca: Cornell University Press, 1985) 55–58.

[67] See T. Jacobsen, "The Graven Image," in *Ancient Israelite Religion,* ed. P. D. Miller, Jr., P. Hanson, and S. D. McBride (Philadelphia: Fortress, 1987) 15–29, for a variety of opinions on what ancient worshipers considered "real" or "symbolic."

[68] Cf. D. F. Wells, *No Place for Truth, or Whatever Happened to Evangelical Theology* (Grand Rapids: Eerdmans, 1993), for an incisive study of how Christianity can think and act more like the secular world than like the biblical writers.

vated to the throne through the Lord's direct intervention, yet neither man serves the Lord, which Ahijah and Jehu consider rank ingratitude (1 Kgs 14:8–9; 16:1–2). These kings fail to remember that responsibility and privilege go together, and this "amnesia" begins when they do not thank the Lord for their position by serving him exclusively.

Persons who disobey God, reject the covenant, adopt a syncretistic attitude toward their faith, and are ungrateful contribute to long-term problems in their lives, their family's lives, and their nation's life. Each of the northern kings helps guarantee their country's demise by what they do. Jeroboam and Baasha create an atmosphere of rebellion and violence that harms their descendants. Omri's plan for national expansion and security includes an alliance with Tyre, which includes Baalism, which ultimately causes Israel more problems than it solves. Sin leads to both short-term and long-term tragedy. Asa's life demonstrates, though, that the reverse is also true. Those who choose to follow God, even falteringly, ennoble Israel in the long run. They are not shielded from battles, fears, and hard decisions (cf. 1 Kgs 15:16–22), yet they do more good than harm.

R. Nelson observes that modern readers have a hard time accepting the notion "that the real fabric of history is not the interplay of economics or the march of national destiny, but the issue of faithfulness to God."[69] Certainly most rational people understand that actions have consequences. Still, many hope that somehow individual and national sin will not lead to tragedy. Nelson correctly states that 1, 2 Kings does not have a mechanistic theory of retribution. Rather, the author seeks to warn apostates and give hope to the faithful.[70] The books' original readers needed to know that they suffered for a reason but that their situation was not permanent if they obeyed the Lord in their own era. Today's reader needs to hear the same message.

---

[69] Nelson, *First and Second Kings,* 104.
[70] Ibid.

SECTION OUTLINE

IV. ELIJAH'S OPPOSITION TO IDOLATRY AND OPPRESSION (1 Kgs 17:1–2 Kgs 1:18)
- Historical Details Related to 1 Kgs 17:1 to 2 Kgs 1:18
- 1. Elijah Battles Baalism (17:1–18:46)
  - (1) Elijah Predicts Drought (17:1)
  - (2) God Provides for Elijah (17:2–6)
  - (3) Elijah's Miraculous Powers (17:7–24)
  - (4) Elijah Seeks Ahab (18:1–15)
  - (5) Elijah's Victory on Mount Carmel (18:16–40)
  - (6) Drought Ends (18:41–46)
  - (7) Elijah Flees Jezebel (19:1–8)
  - (8) God Reassures Elijah (19:9–18)
  - (9) Elisha's Call (19:19–21)
- 2. Elijah Denounces Ahab (20:1–22:40)
  - (1) Ahab Defeats Syria (20:1–34)
  - (2) An Unnamed Prophet Denounces Ahab (20:35–43)
  - (3) Ahab and Jezebel Murder Naboth (21:1–16)
  - (4) Elijah Denounces Ahab (21:17–29)
  - (5) Micaiah Denounces Ahab (22:1–28)
  - (6) Ahab's Death (22:29–40)
- 3. Elijah's Final Days (1 Kgs 22:41–2 Kgs 1:18)
  - (1) Jehoshaphat's and Ahaziah's Reigns (22:41–53)
  - (2) Elijah Denounces Ahaziah (1:1–18)
- Canonical and Theological Implications of 1 Kgs 17:1 to 2 Kgs 1:18
- Applicational Implications of 1 Kgs 17:1 to 2 Kgs 1:18

IV. ELIJAH'S OPPOSITION TO IDOLATRY AND OPPRESSION (1 Kgs 17:1–2 Kgs 1:18)

A new character enters the story at this point to challenge the spread of Baalism. This individual is not just *a* prophet but as time passed came to be considered *the* great prophet, the man who stands as the pattern for other prophets (cf. Mal 4:5–6). This man named Elijah appears on the scene without being announced (1 Kgs 17:1). He prays for a drought that will demonstrate Yahweh's power over Baal (17:1), receives divine sustenance (17:2–6), and performs miracles (17:7–24). The drought ends only after he wins a telling victory over the prophets of Baal, a victory that should, yet does not, eradicate Baalism in Israel (18:16–40). Despite his prowess, however, Elijah is a very human figure. He can be afraid, and he can become discouraged (19:1–18). Elijah is no superman.

Two extraordinary characters oppose Elijah in these accounts: King Ahab and his wife Jezebel. Ahab views Elijah as his enemy and as a "troubler of Israel" (18:17). Jezebel retaliates against Elijah's killing of Baal's prophets by threatening Elijah's life (19:1–2). Together Ahab and Jezebel conspire to kill Naboth, an honest man who refuses to sell some land to the king (21:1–26). Elijah immediately condemns Ahab for this murder and announces that Ahab's house will suffer the same fate as Jeroboam's and Baasha's (21:22). An unnamed prophet also denounces Ahab (20:35–43), as does Micaiah (22:1–28). Ahab does win some military victories (20:1–30) yet manages to allow Syria's king to live and fight another day (20:31–34). The only redeeming characteristic of this opponent of God's messenger is his willingness to repent, at least temporarily, during one portion of his life (21:27–29).

By the time Elijah is miraculously transported to heaven (2 Kgs 2:11–12), Ahab has already been killed (1 Kgs 22:29–40). Jezebel will survive another eight years or so only to be put to death by the avenging reformer Jehu (2 Kgs 9:30–37). The contrast between the deaths of Elijah and his enemies could hardly be any more stark. Elijah, the faithful servant of God, ascends to heaven. Ahab and Jezebel, the sworn enemies of Yahwism and the prophets, die at the hands of their foes. God's word continues unchecked, while the wicked receive the consequences of their actions. Baalism will not prevail ultimately.

Historical Details Related to 1 Kgs 17:1 to 2 Kgs 1:18

Since the struggle between Yahwish and Baalism permeates these chapters, it is necessary to have at least a basic understanding of Baalism to appreciate the texts. Baalism existed as a religion for several centuries in various ancient Near Eastern countries. Its prominence in Canaan and Phoenicia is especially important for understanding 1, 2 Kings, since it is from those cultures that the major influence on Israel and Judah came. M. Smith concludes that "the Phoenician baal of Ahab and Jezebel was a storm-god. The extrabiblical evidence indicates that the baal of Carmel and Baal Shamem were also storm gods."[1] Thus, Baal worshipers believed that their god made rain, which is a quite important detail in an agricultural community. Elijah apparently prays for a drought to prove that Yahweh, not Baal, is in charge of crop-enriching rains.

Given the lack of rain in specific seasons of the year in that region, Baal

[1] M. Smith, *The Early History of God: Yahweh and the Other Deities in Ancient Israel* (San Francisco: Harper Collins, 1990) 44.

cultists had to explain why Baal could not guarantee rain at all times. They said that Baal submitted to Mot, the god of death, each year, which caused drought and barrenness to the land. Eventually Anat defeated Mot and freed Baal, which restored fertility. A. Hauser believes: "The Canaanites' equating of fertility with the presence of a live and vibrant Baal, who as the storm god sent the life-preserving rains onto the land, and their equating of drought and famine with the periodic death of Baal, set the stage for the stories in 1 Kings 17–19."[2] Elijah must find a way to expose Baal as a nonentity and at the same time reestablish Yahweh as sovereign in the people's minds.

Baalism and Israel's government became linked as never before when the Tyrian princess Jezebel married Ahab. She and her retainers were allowed to continue to worship as they had in their homeland, and Ahab built a temple to Baal for her, which "was no more than Solomon had done for his foreign wives (ch. 11:1–8)."[3] But Jezebel was not satisfied with the prerogative of private worship. Rather, she insisted on attempting to promote Baal as a replacement for Yahweh and took steps to silence opposition to her goals (1 Kgs 18:1–15; 19:1–10). Her successes moved Israel beyond tolerance of high places and syncretism to outright worship of another god.

It is also important to note that the marriage of Ahab and Jezebel was part of a plan to improve Israel's foreign policy. Like Solomon, Omri and Ahab hoped to gain more favorable trading conditions as a result of marrying a foreign princess. In particular, both nations intended to "offset the growing influence of Damascus" through this alliance.[4] Concerning the benefits of the agreement, Bright comments:

> The alliance was mutually advantageous. Tyre was at the height of her colonial expansion (Carthage was founded later in the century); being partly dependent on imports of foodstuffs, she offered to Israel both an outlet for agricultural products and numerous commercial opportunities. Tyre, for her part, desired both a counterbalance to the power of Damascus and the reactivation of trade with Israel, and, via Israel, with the lands of the south.[5]

Both Tyre and Israel had reason to neutralize Syria if they could. Under the capable leadership of Ben-Hadad, the Syrian kingdom of Damascus had become the dominant power in Syria-Palestine. Asa had felt compelled to hire Ben-Hadad to defeat Baasha (1 Kgs 15:20–22). Now because both Judah and Israel realized Syria's power, they stopped fighting one another and joined forces against Ben-Hadad (1 Kgs 22:1–5).[6] Therefore, Israel made a new ally

---

[2] A. J. Hauser and R. Gregory, *From Carmel to Horeb: Elijah in Crisis,* JSOTSup 85/BALS 19 (Sheffield: Sheffield Academic Press, 1990) 11.

[3] J. Bright, *A History of Israel,* 3d ed. (Philadelphia: Westminster, 1981) 245.

[4] M. P. Matheney, "1 Kings," BBC (Nashville: Broadman, 1970) 3:206–7.

[5] Bright, *History of Israel,* 241–42.

[6] Cf. M. Noth's discussion of the situation in *The History of Israel,* 2d ed., trans. P. R. Ackroyd (New York: Harper & Row, 1960) 240–41.

in Tyre and ceased old disputes with their southern "brothers."

Not only were foreign relationships improving but domestic peace was restored as well. Ahab's succession of his father helped stabilize the government, as did the existence of one permanent capital (Samaria). In fact, Omri's ability to build such a city indicates that the nation's economic health was vibrant.[7] Perhaps only the religious scene remained in flux, and from Ahab's perspective most of that turmoil could have ended if Elijah and the Yahwist prophets had stopped their protests against Baalism and syncretistic cults.

Judah hardly enters the picture at all in these chapters. Only Jehoshaphat, Asa's son, really figures in the story and then only as an ally of Ahab who seeks a word from the Lord. Jehoshaphat continued his father's reforms (cf. 1 Kgs 22:46) and brought a measure of peace by stopping the conflict with Israel. Still, the religious threat posed by high places remained in place (1 Kgs 22:43), and Judah's lack of size precluded any permanent sense of military peace and economic freedom.

Finally, prophetism grew as a religious, social, and political factor in Israel. Groups of prophets emerge in the text. Up to four hundred prophets of Baal, four hundred prophets of Asherah, and four hundred so-called prophets of Yahweh were sustained by Ahab and Jezebel (1 Kgs 18:19; 22:6). These court prophets tended to say whatever the king wanted to hear (cf. 22:6,24). Separatist monotheists were threatened and impoverished (18:1–15), persecuted and pursued (19:1–10), and imprisoned (22:7–8). Somehow, however, they persevered. The prophetic movement continued to grow in size yet now consisted of rival factions competing for a hearing. Syncretistic Yahwists and Baalistic prophets coexisted, and the separatist prophets fought the other two factions, although with limited physical and economic means.

1. Elijah Battles Baalism (17:1–18:46)

Without question Elijah is one of the most distinctive and diversely talented individuals in the Bible. He is prophet, preacher, political reformer, and miracle worker all at the same time. At the heart of this multifaceted person, though, rests one overriding conviction. Elijah hates Baalism as much as Jezebel loves the cult, and he desires to magnify Yahweh over Baal and defeat the interloping religion once and for all.[8] He makes it his mission to teach that Yahweh lives, that Baal does not exist, and that ethical standards flow from a commitment to the living God.

---

[7] Bright, *History of Israel,* 243–44.

[8] Note the excellent treatment of Elijah's monotheism in L. Bronner, *The Stories of Elijah and Elisha as Polemics against Baal Worship,* Pretoria Oriental Series 6 (Leiden: Brill, 1968).

(1) Elijah Predicts Drought (17:1)

[1]Now Elijah the Tishbite, from Tishbe in Gilead, said to Ahab, "As the LORD, the God of Israel, lives, whom I serve, there will be neither dew nor rain in the next few years except at my word."

17:1 The prophet barges into the story unannounced. He is an unknown quantity from a town scholars can no longer locate with certainty.[9] His name declares his theological mission, for it means "Yahweh is my God."[10] Quite dramatically, he claims there will be no rain until he says so. He bases this declaration on the fact that his God lives and on the notion that he serves this living God, which means his prayers will be heard.

Why choose a drought? Why emphasize that Yahweh lives? Elijah determines to attack Baalism at its theological center. Baal worshipers believed that their storm god made rain, unless, of course, it was the dry season and he needed to be brought back from the dead. To refute this belief Elijah states that Yahweh is the one who determines when rain falls, that Yahweh lives at all times, and that Yahweh is not afraid to challenge Baal on what his worshipers consider his home ground.

(2) God Provides for Elijah (17:2–6)

[2]Then the word of the LORD came to Elijah: [3]"Leave here, turn eastward and hide in the Kerith Ravine, east of the Jordan. [4]You will drink from the brook, and I have ordered the ravens to feed you there."

[5]So he did what the LORD had told him. He went to the Kerith Ravine, east of the Jordan, and stayed there. [6]The ravens brought him bread and meat in the morning and bread and meat in the evening, and he drank from the brook.

17:2–6 Regardless of harsh physical circumstances, the Lord provides for the prophet. The drought has begun, but Elijah has resources because his God controls all natural resources. God directs him to a brook that has water and where ravens will feed him. Also God has protected Elijah by taking him out of Ahab's reach (cf. 18:10).[11] Nothing he needs has been withheld, a point that must be recalled for future reference.

(3) Elijah's Miraculous Powers (17:7–24)

[7]Some time later the brook dried up because there had been no rain in the land. [8]Then the word of the LORD came to him: [9]"Go at once to Zarephath of Sidon and stay there. I have commanded a widow in that place to supply you with

---

[9] Cf. S. Cohen, "Tishbe," *IDB* (Nashville: Abingdon, 1962) 4:653–54.

[10] Roughly divided "Eli" means "my God," and "jah" means "Yahweh" (אֵלִי יָהוּ).

[11] J. A. Montgomery and H. S. Gehman, *A Critical and Exegetical Commentary on the Book of Kings,* ICC (1951; reprint, Edinburgh: T & T Clark, 1986) 294.

food." [10]So he went to Zarephath. When he came to the town gate, a widow was there gathering sticks. He called to her and asked, "Would you bring me a little water in a jar so I may have a drink?" [11]As she was going to get it, he called, "And bring me, please, a piece of bread."

[12]"As surely as the LORD your God lives," she replied, "I don't have any bread—only a handful of flour in a jar and a little oil in a jug. I am gathering a few sticks to take home and make a meal for myself and my son, that we may eat it—and die."

[13]Elijah said to her, "Don't be afraid. Go home and do as you have said. But first make a small cake of bread for me from what you have and bring it to me, and then make something for yourself and your son. [14]For this is what the LORD, the God of Israel, says: 'The jar of flour will not be used up and the jug of oil will not run dry until the day the LORD gives rain on the land.'"

[15]She went away and did as Elijah had told her. So there was food every day for Elijah and for the woman and her family. [16]For the jar of flour was not used up and the jug of oil did not run dry, in keeping with the word of the LORD spoken by Elijah.

[17]Some time later the son of the woman who owned the house became ill. He grew worse and worse, and finally stopped breathing. [18]She said to Elijah, "What do you have against me, man of God? Did you come to remind me of my sin and kill my son?"

[19]"Give me your son," Elijah replied. He took him from her arms, carried him to the upper room where he was staying, and laid him on his bed. [20]Then he cried out to the LORD, "O LORD my God, have you brought tragedy also upon this widow I am staying with, by causing her son to die?" [21]Then he stretched himself out on the boy three times and cried to the LORD, "O LORD my God, let this boy's life return to him!"

[22]The LORD heard Elijah's cry, and the boy's life returned to him, and he lived. [23]Elijah picked up the child and carried him down from the room into the house. He gave him to his mother and said, "Look, your son is alive!"

[24]Then the woman said to Elijah, "Now I know that you are a man of God and that the word of the LORD from your mouth is the truth."

17:7–9 So far God's miraculous powers have benefited the prophet. In the next few episodes, though, the Lord works miracles *through* Elijah, which establishes his status as a "man of God" (cf. 1 Kgs 13:1–5, etc; 17:18,24). R. Cohn observes that the next three stories "form a clear literary sequence in which the author charts the rise of Elijah's prophetic powers. In each episode he confronts an increasingly more difficult problem which must be solved."[12]

To begin this sequence, the Lord instructs the prophet to leave the brook that once sustained him and that has now "dried up." He must go to "Zarephath of Sidon," where a widow will give him food. Zarephath is located in Phoenicia,

[12] R. L. Cohn, "The Literary Logic of 1 Kings 17–19," *JBL* 101/3 (1982) 335.

the very heart of Baalism. Here Yahweh will defeat Baal in his own territory.[13] Here God's people will fare better than Baal's. F. C. Fensham asserts that in fact the main purpose of this narrative is "to demonstrate on Phoenician soil, where Baal is worshiped, that Yahweh has power over things in which Baal has failed." Since Baal worshipers explained the drought as a sign that Baal was dead, he could not help the widow and her son. "In the absence of Baal who lies impotent in the Netherworld, Yahweh steps in to assist the widow and the orphan, and this is even done in the heartland of Baal, Phoenicia."[14] It is also done in Jezebel's native land. Because Yahweh exists and Baal does not, Elijah possesses power Jezebel and her prophets do not.

17:10–16 When Elijah encounters the widow, he discovers that the drought has reduced her resources to a bit of flour, a dab of oil, and a few sticks of wood. She expects to starve to death along with her son. Elijah promises that her flour and oil will not run out until the drought ends. This promise comes true, so the widow and her son are saved by this miraculous provision. God's people have what they need and what Baal cannot provide.

17:17–24 Another problem threatens the woman, however, when her son becomes so sick he stops breathing. The woman fears her sin has brought about her son's death and wonders if Elijah has been sent to punish her. Perhaps if he had not come, her son would have lived (forgetting, of course, that he would have starved).[15] Elijah also questions whether the Lord has repaid evil for good. Has the boy been spared hunger only to die from disease? Has God lost the ability to sustain life in the homeland of Baalism?

Elijah's faith in the midst of uncertainty allows God to use him to demonstrate God's life-giving power, his constant watchfulness, and his compassion even on those outside the elect nation (Luke 8:40–56). Elijah stretches himself on the child, thereby seemingly transferring life from himself to the sick one. Regardless of the method used, the important fact is that God raises the boy from the dead. The child revives because Yahweh hears Elijah's plea, not because of the prophet's prowess. Yahweh is God, not Baal, not Elijah.

Still, the miracle helps the woman know that Elijah is a man who represents and is sent by the Lord. She understands that the same God who provided the oil has provided life for her son. Baal may be dead, but Yahweh is not, nor is her son. Hauser comments: "Thus, as the challenges by death grow in intensity, God himself becomes more actively involved in the life-sustaining process, no longer commanding others, but himself taking the initiative against death and overcoming death's challenges."[16] Death cannot thwart Yahweh's purposes.

---

[13] Steck, *Uberlieferung und Zeitsgeschichte in den Elia-Erzählungen*, 128–30.

[14] F. C. Fensham, "A Few Observations on the Polarisation between Yahweh and Baal in I Kings 17–19," *ZAW* 92 (1980) 234.

[15] R. H. Dilday, *1, 2 Kings*, CC 9 (Waco: Word, 1987) 205.

[16] Hauser, *From Carmel to Horeb*, 22.

(4) Elijah Seeks Ahab (18:1–15)

[1]After a long time, in the third year, the word of the LORD came to Elijah: "Go and present yourself to Ahab, and I will send rain on the land." [2]So Elijah went to present himself to Ahab.

Now the famine was severe in Samaria, [3]and Ahab had summoned Obadiah, who was in charge of his palace. (Obadiah was a devout believer in the LORD. [4]While Jezebel was killing off the LORD's prophets, Obadiah had taken a hundred prophets and hidden them in two caves, fifty in each, and had supplied them with food and water.) [5]Ahab had said to Obadiah, "Go through the land to all the springs and valleys. Maybe we can find some grass to keep the horses and mules alive so we will not have to kill any of our animals." [6]So they divided the land they were to cover, Ahab going in one direction and Obadiah in another.

[7]As Obadiah was walking along, Elijah met him. Obadiah recognized him, bowed down to the ground, and said, "Is it really you, my lord Elijah?"

[8]"Yes," he replied. "Go tell your master, 'Elijah is here.'"

[9]"What have I done wrong," asked Obadiah, "that you are handing your servant over to Ahab to be put to death? [10]As surely as the LORD your God lives, there is not a nation or kingdom where my master has not sent someone to look for you. And whenever a nation or kingdom claimed you were not there, he made them swear they could not find you. [11]But now you tell me to go to my master and say, 'Elijah is here.' [12]I don't know where the Spirit of the LORD may carry you when I leave you. If I go and tell Ahab and he doesn't find you, he will kill me. Yet I your servant have worshiped the LORD since my youth. [13]Haven't you heard, my lord, what I did while Jezebel was killing the prophets of the LORD? I hid a hundred of the LORD's prophets in two caves, fifty in each, and supplied them with food and water. [14]And now you tell me to go to my master and say, 'Elijah is here.' He will kill me!"

[15]Elijah said, "As the LORD Almighty lives, whom I serve, I will surely present myself to Ahab today."

18:1–6 Nearly three years pass, then God decrees to end the drought. In order for the rains to come, however, Elijah must go present himself to Ahab for some unspecified purpose. Before this meeting takes place, the author introduces a character named Obadiah, a faithful man who, though one of Ahab's officials, has protected some of the Lord's prophets from Jezebel.

Obadiah is in a tough position. He desires to serve the Lord, yet must serve Ahab as well.[17] Ahab sends him to find pasture during the worsening drought, yet Obadiah may know that the king is the reason the drought has come. He is a man who has tried to live his life in two worlds, and he may not be able to do so much longer.

18:7–15 Obadiah's situation worsens when he comes upon Elijah, who commands him to summon his master. He sees the prophet's order as sure

---

[17] Ibid., 25.

death. Ahab has made a thorough search for Elijah but has not found him. Yahweh's protection has been quite effective. Obadiah fears Yahweh will hide him again, which will leave the king's servant with the king's wrath. He has already put his life in jeopardy by feeding the threatened prophets. Why must he place himself in further danger? Elijah is as confident as Obadiah is frightened.[18] He swears that he will not run, nor will he hide, for he stands ready to end the drought. Elijah has decided whom *he* will serve.

(5) Elijah's Victory on Mount Carmel (18:16–40)

16So Obadiah went to meet Ahab and told him, and Ahab went to meet Elijah.
17When he saw Elijah, he said to him, "Is that you, you troubler of Israel?"
18"I have not made trouble for Israel," Elijah replied. "But you and your father's family have. You have abandoned the LORD's commands and have followed the Baals.
19Now summon the people from all over Israel to meet me on Mount Carmel. And bring the four hundred and fifty prophets of Baal and the four hundred prophets of Asherah, who eat at Jezebel's table."
20So Ahab sent word throughout all Israel and assembled the prophets on Mount Carmel.
21Elijah went before the people and said, "How long will you waver between two opinions? If the LORD is God, follow him; but if Baal is God, follow him."

But the people said nothing.

22Then Elijah said to them, "I am the only one of the LORD's prophets left, but Baal has four hundred and fifty prophets.
23Get two bulls for us. Let them choose one for themselves, and let them cut it into pieces and put it on the wood but not set fire to it. I will prepare the other bull and put it on the wood but not set fire to it.
24Then you call on the name of your god, and I will call on the name of the LORD. The god who answers by fire—he is God."

Then all the people said, "What you say is good."

25Elijah said to the prophets of Baal, "Choose one of the bulls and prepare it first, since there are so many of you. Call on the name of your god, but do not light the fire."
26So they took the bull given them and prepared it.

Then they called on the name of Baal from morning till noon. "O Baal, answer us!" they shouted. But there was no response; no one answered. And they danced around the altar they had made.

27At noon Elijah began to taunt them. "Shout louder!" he said. "Surely he is a god! Perhaps he is deep in thought, or busy, or traveling. Maybe he is sleeping and must be awakened."
28So they shouted louder and slashed themselves with swords and spears, as was their custom, until their blood flowed.
29Midday passed, and they continued their frantic prophesying until the time for the evening sacrifice. But there was no response, no one answered, no one paid attention.

30Then Elijah said to all the people, "Come here to me." They came to him,

[18] Cf. R. Gregory, *From Carmel to Horeb,* 108, for an excellent description of both men's attitudes.

and he repaired the altar of the LORD, which was in ruins. 31Elijah took twelve
stones, one for each of the tribes descended from Jacob, to whom the word of the
LORD had come, saying, "Your name shall be Israel." 32With the stones he built
an altar in the name of the LORD, and he dug a trench around it large enough to
hold two seahs of seed. 33He arranged the wood, cut the bull into pieces and laid it
on the wood. Then he said to them, "Fill four large jars with water and pour it on
the offering and on the wood."

34"Do it again," he said, and they did it again.

"Do it a third time," he ordered, and they did it the third time. 35The water
ran down around the altar and even filled the trench.

36At the time of sacrifice, the prophet Elijah stepped forward and prayed: "O
LORD, God of Abraham, Isaac and Israel, let it be known today that you are God
in Israel and that I am your servant and have done all these things at your com-
mand. 37Answer me, O LORD, answer me, so these people will know that you, O
LORD, are God, and that you are turning their hearts back again."

38Then the fire of the LORD fell and burned up the sacrifice, the wood, the
stones and the soil, and also licked up the water in the trench.

39When all the people saw this, they fell prostrate and cried, "The LORD—he
is God! The LORD—he is God!"

40Then Elijah commanded them, "Seize the prophets of Baal. Don't let anyone
get away!" They seized them, and Elijah had them brought down to the Kishon
Valley and slaughtered there.

18:16–19 When the two men meet, Ahab calls Elijah the "troubler [*'ōkēr*][19] of Israel," blaming the drought on him, but he does not attempt immediately to have him killed. Elijah returns the accusation, stating fearlessly that Ahab's family's commitment to Baal has forced Yahweh to withhold rain, thus proving the Lord's power over the storm god. Now Elijah suggests a contest to determine who benefits Israel and who troubles the land. The site will be Mount Carmel, a place that may have long held significance for both worshipers of Yahweh and adherents of Baalism.[20] What better place to decide who is God, what prophets tell the truth, and what leaders benefit or harm the people?

18:20–21 Ahab apparently is satisfied with the odds and expects this to be an excellent way to rid himself of this troublesome prophet and separatistic Yahwism at the same time. So Ahab obliges Elijah by sending for the people and the prophets.[21] They wait to see who will win and who can help them the most. Will it be Baal or Yahweh? The prophet challenges the people to stop

---

[19] The word עָכַר describes the harmful effects one's bad behavior has on others. Cf. Gen 34:30; Josh 6:18; 7:25; see C. Schultz, "עָכַר (*'ākar*)" *TWOT* 666.

[20] Cf. H. H. Rowley, "Elijah on Mt. Carmel," *BJRL* 43/1 (1960) 199–200.

[21] The Hebrew text allows for no significant time lapse between Elijah's command in 18:19 (וְעַתָּה שְׁלַח) and Ahab's obedience (וַיִּשְׁלַח אַחְאָב) in 18:20.

limping (*pāsaḥ*, translated "waver")[22] between two opinions—to decide who is God and then act on that decision. Obadiah is a good man trapped between two competing worldviews. Ahab is a king who may be wondering if his "ancestral" God is more powerful than his wife's deity. The people are noncommittal at best. They "limp" along without conviction, wanting to follow halfheartedly one god and then the other.

18:22–25 Only Elijah and, ironically, the prophets of Baal have any conviction. Both Elijah and his counterparts believe their god to be the solution to Israel's problems. Elijah is supremely confident that there is no god but Yahweh. His experiences in Phoenicia have confirmed to him this truth. Despite what some scholars argue, Elijah does not accept the existence of many gods, thinking only that Yahweh is the strongest. Rather, as L. Bronner argues:

> It is true that the faith of many of his contemporaries was of this rudimentary order; the clash between God and Baal was to them a real struggle between rival deities. But Elijah's lofty conception of God virtually excludes all other objects of worship and makes all the gods idols. Elijah apparently proved by his actions that he believed the God of Israel not to be limited by the territory of Israel, and he demonstrated that God can perform miracles in Phoenicia as well, thus showing his belief in a universal deity.[23]

Elijah wants to eliminate Baal from consideration whenever Israel decides theological matters.

To achieve this goal Elijah suggests a contest. He says that a sacrifice should be offered and that the real God must come take it by fire. The people like this contest, and the text does not indicate the Baalists object at all. Again, at least the prophets of Baal do not lack conviction. As storm god Baal was thought to be responsible for lightning as well as rain, so this should be an easy contest.

18:26–29 Baal's prophets attempt to rouse him from the dead. They shout, but no one responds. Next, they "dance" or "limp" (*pāsaḥ*) around the altar, again trying to get the god's attention. This ritual dance also gets no response.[24] At noon Elijah begins to taunt them, suggesting Baal is preoccupied in some

---

[22] The verb פסח occurs only three times, the first time as a *niphal* in 2 Sam 4:4, where it describes Mephibosheth, who "became crippled." A synonym, נְכֵה, "lame," is used there, confirming the meanings "limp/be lame or crippled." The second occurrence is in 1 Kgs 18:21 (a *qal*), and the third is in v. 26 (*piel*), describing the way the Baal priests "danced," apparently a pun ridiculing their behavior. In v. 21 it describes a mind as wobbly and uncertain as the legs of someone lame. The word סְעִפִּים, "opinions," occurs only here, but related words have suggested the translation "crutches" (KB, 663; DeVries, *1 Kings,* 228).

[23] Bronner, *The Stories of Elijah and Elisha,* 25. Bronner rejects the arguments of Wellhausen and Gunkel that Elijah was a henotheist, worshiping only one god but acknowledging the existence of others.

[24] Cf. Rowley's discussion of ritual dances in Baalism and other ancient Near Eastern countries in "Elijah on Mt. Carmel," 199–200.

manner. G. E. Saint-Laurent demonstrates that ancient Baal worshipers indeed did imply in their writings that not only could Baal die, but he also could go on a journey, fall asleep, or even resort to bloody self-mutilation.[25]

Desperate now, their authority at stake, the Baalists cut themselves and practice frenzied prophesying, not unlike self-hypnosis.[26] Though they try for hours, the text says as explicitly as it can that their god is unable to answer because he is not real.

18:30–40 Very dramatically, Elijah rebuilds the altar now damaged by the frantic Baalistic rites. He then soaks it with water to remove any doubt about the miracle that will soon occur. When he prays for the fire to fall, he asks the Lord to remind the people that he is the covenant God of Israel. Without Yahweh there would be no Israel. Elijah also prays that he will be vindicated as the prophet of the covenant God. Finally, he asks that the people know Yahweh is God and that they have the opportunity to repent at once. This prayer incorporates concern, then, for God's reputation, the validity of the prophet's work, and for the people's well-being.

Fire falls without delay. It consumes the altar and the sacrifice. In the immediacy of the moment, with fear in their hearts, the people confess "the LORD is God!" They see no validity in any of Baal's claims at this point and have become, temporarily at least, strict Yahwistic monotheists. Thus, Elijah has taken the first step in showing the people who is God.

To affirm their belief the people slay the prophets of Baal. Perhaps this execution occurs in accordance with Deut 13:1–11, where Moses counsels Israel to purge by stoning prophets who lead the nation away from the covenant God into idolatry. Those who lead others astray in this manner are held *more* accountable than mere followers of heresy, though the followers are forced to choose the correct way as well.

(6) Drought Ends (18:41–46)

41And Elijah said to Ahab, "Go, eat and drink, for there is the sound of a heavy rain." 42So Ahab went off to eat and drink, but Elijah climbed to the top of Carmel, bent down to the ground and put his face between his knees.

43"Go and look toward the sea," he told his servant. And he went up and looked.

"There is nothing there," he said.

Seven times Elijah said, "Go back."

[25] Note the listing of various Baal myths in G. E. Saint-Laurent, "Light from Ras Shamra on Elijah's Ordeal upon Mount Carmel," in *Scripture in Context,* ed. C. D. Evans, W. W. Hallo, J. B. White (Pittsburgh: Pickwick, 1980) 133–35.

[26] Such behavior is recounted in the Canaanite myth "Baal and Mot" on the part of the high god El, who mourns the death of Baal. See J. C. L. Gibson, *Canaanite Myths and Legends,* 2d ed. (Edinburgh: T & T Clark, 1978) 73.

[44]The seventh time the servant reported, "A cloud as small as a man's hand is rising from the sea."

So Elijah said, "Go and tell Ahab, 'Hitch up your chariot and go down before the rain stops you.'"

[45]Meanwhile, the sky grew black with clouds, the wind rose, a heavy rain came on and Ahab rode off to Jezreel. [46]The power of the LORD came upon Elijah and, tucking his cloak into his belt, he ran ahead of Ahab all the way to Jezreel.

18:41–46 With his enemies dispatched, Elijah demonstrates one last time that Yahweh is Lord. It is time for rain. He counsels Ahab to hurry home so he will not be caught in the rain. When the rains come, the Lord's victory is complete. God sustains and protects his prophets, while Baal lets his die. Yahweh feeds the orphans and widows and raises the dead, while Baal lets the needy suffer and requires Anat to raise him from death. Yahweh can send fire or rain from heaven, but Baal cannot respond to his most valiant worshipers. A god like Baal is no God at all. A God like Yahweh must be God of all. Rain is not just rain here but evidence of the Lord's absolute sovereignty over nature and human affairs.

(7) Elijah Flees Jezebel (19:1–8)

[1]Now Ahab told Jezebel everything Elijah had done and how he had killed all the prophets with the sword. [2]So Jezebel sent a messenger to Elijah to say, "May the gods deal with me, be it ever so severely, if by this time tomorrow I do not make your life like that of one of them."

[3]Elijah was afraid and ran for his life. When he came to Beersheba in Judah, he left his servant there, [4]while he himself went a day's journey into the desert. He came to a broom tree, sat down under it and prayed that he might die. "I have had enough, LORD," he said. "Take my life; I am no better than my ancestors." [5]Then he lay down under the tree and fell asleep.

All at once an angel touched him and said, "Get up and eat." [6]He looked around, and there by his head was a cake of bread baked over hot coals, and a jar of water. He ate and drank and then lay down again.

[7]The angel of the LORD came back a second time and touched him and said, "Get up and eat, for the journey is too much for you." [8]So he got up and ate and drank. Strengthened by that food, he traveled forty days and forty nights until he reached Horeb, the mountain of God.

19:1–2 So far, Elijah has encountered serious yet less-than-overpowering opposition. At this point in the story, though, he meets the one person as committed to Baal as he is to Yahweh. What Jezebel hears from Ahab causes her to threaten Elijah's life. She swears by the "gods" that Elijah will die. Jezebel has killed Yahweh's prophets before (cf. 1 Kgs 18:4,13), so Elijah has no reason to doubt her threats indicate her true intentions.[27] This woman has the fierceness

[27] Matheney, "1 Kings," 213.

Ahab lacks, the civil authority the prophets of Baal lacked, and a freshness for battle that Elijah no longer possesses. She is as worthy an opponent as God's servants ever face in Scripture. Who, or what, can defeat her?

19:3–8 For whatever reason—fatigue, lack of faith, or a sense of resignation at the prospect of never having peace—Elijah flees. He fears death the way Obadiah did (18:9-14).[28] DeVries thinks "Elijah interprets Jezebel's personal attack on him as the end of his ministry."[29] Indeed, the fact that he dismisses his servant in Beersheba, the southernmost point in Judah, then goes a day's journey farther may indicate he has given up his ministry altogether.[30] Elijah's flight in 19:1–3 changes the face of the story. A. Hauser explains:

> In three short verses the writer has totally changed the flow of the story. Victory seems to be transformed into defeat, the brave prophet into a cowering refugee, and the victory over death and Baal into an opportunity for death to reassert itself through Jezebel's oath to take Elijah's life.[31]

How will the Lord prove to be God now? This question remains *the* fundamental issue in the story.

After "a day's journey into the desert," an exhausted Elijah says he wants to die, which, ironically, is the opposite desire to what he expressed by fleeing into the desert in the first place. Now God begins to renew his faith by miraculously feeding him. In other words, the Lord ministers to him as in the past. Twice an angel feeds him, thereby giving him strength to travel to "Horeb, the mountain of God." Elijah knows God exists in Israel, Phoenicia, and the desert. He knows God revealed himself at Horeb, the mountain of Moses' calling and the giving of the covenant (cf. Exod 3–4; 20–24). Here at another mountain Elijah will decide for himself if the Lord is God.

(8) God Reassures Elijah (19:9–18)

9There he went into a cave and spent the night.
And the word of the LORD came to him: "What are you doing here, Elijah?"
10He replied, "I have been very zealous for the LORD God Almighty. The Israelites have rejected your covenant, broken down your altars, and put your prophets to death with the sword. I am the only one left, and now they are trying to kill me too."
11The LORD said, "Go out and stand on the mountain in the presence of the LORD, for the LORD is about to pass by."

---

[28] Hauser, *From Carmel to Horeb,* 61. On Elijah's flight see also R. B. Allen, "Elijah the Broken Prophet," *JETS* 22 (1979) 195–201. He argues that Elijah was broken, not frightened by Jezebel.

[29] DeVries, *1 Kings,* 235.

[30] Ibid.

[31] Hauser, *From Carmel to Horeb,* 63.

Then a great and powerful wind tore the mountains apart and shattered the rocks before the LORD, but the LORD was not in the wind. After the wind there was an earthquake, but the LORD was not in the earthquake. [12]After the earthquake came a fire, but the LORD was not in the fire. And after the fire came a gentle whisper. [13]When Elijah heard it, he pulled his cloak over his face and went out and stood at the mouth of the cave.

Then a voice said to him, "What are you doing here, Elijah?"

[14]He replied, "I have been very zealous for the LORD God Almighty. The Israelites have rejected your covenant, broken down your altars, and put your prophets to death with the sword. I am the only one left, and now they are trying to kill me too."

[15]The LORD said to him, "Go back the way you came, and go to the Desert of Damascus. When you get there, anoint Hazael king over Aram. [16]Also, anoint Jehu son of Nimshi king over Israel, and anoint Elisha son of Shaphat from Abel Meholah to succeed you as prophet. [17]Jehu will put to death any who escape the sword of Hazael, and Elisha will put to death any who escape the sword of Jehu. [18]Yet I reserve seven thousand in Israel—all whose knees have not bowed down to Baal and all whose mouths have not kissed him."

19:9–10 Besides feeding the prophet, the Lord reassures Elijah with the book's most certain comfort—God's word, which never fails. The first "word of the LORD" asks him why he is at Horeb. He replies that Israel is apostate, they kill the prophets, and he alone stands for covenant faith. Again, he sees no real reason to continue. Apparently he had hoped that the Mount Carmel episode would produce a final victory over Baalism.

19:11–13a A second word of the Lord invites the prophet to "stand on the mountain in the presence of the LORD," for God will pass by there. This theophany, or appearance of the Lord, reminds readers of Exod 33:18–22, where Moses desires to see God's glory and is rewarded by being allowed to view "the back" of the Lord's splendor. God places Moses in the rock and covers him with a divine "hand" to protect him. Here, Elijah waits for God's word through tearing wind, ground shaking earthquake, and roaring flame. The Lord does not speak, however, through these natural phenomena. Certainly Elijah has experienced God's sovereignty over nature, and has benefited from miraculous fire, but what he needs now is a definitive word from the Lord.

He receives this word in "a gentle whisper."[32] Perhaps the Lord attempts to teach Elijah not to expect always the miraculous and wondrous deliverance from problems.[33] Maybe God wants "to signify to the prophet that He did not work in His earthly kingdom with the destroying zeal of wrath, or with the pitiless severity of judgment."[34] Or the Lord may simply try to explain to Elijah

[32]For a discussion of this fairly odd Heb. phrase, consult J. Lust, "A Gentle Breeze or a Roaring Thunderous Sound?" *VT* 25/1 (1975) 110–15.

[33]Cf. Gray, *1 and 2 Kings,* 365; and Dilday, *1, 2 Kings,* 220.

[34]Keil, "I and II Kings," 258.

that he works in small ways at this time. God speaks in a quiet voice here to a prophet drained of strength. The next passage will reveal still further the Lord's willingness to labor with relatively limited human resources. Regardless of the meaning of the natural wonders, however, it is God's word alone that will heal the prophet in this moment of crisis.

19:13b–18 The voice asks Elijah why he has come to the mountain. R. Gregory says that this repetition of the question asked in 19:9 forces Elijah to consider carefully his current position and his future destiny. "The first time this statement of defense is presented to the audience, the emphasis falls on Elijah's feelings (informative) but the precise reiteration exhibits Elijah's inflexibility and egocentrism (elucidating)."[35] God has fed him as before, and God has spoken to him as in the past. Why has he fled?

Elijah answers as in 19:10: Israel has rejected the covenant, Israel has become idolatrous, he is the only prophet left, and Jezebel plans to kill him. Implied in this response is Elijah's doubts that the Lord can save him or turn the nation back to the covenant. Who has God become in the prophet's life? Only a restatement and reassessment of his theology can extricate him from this pit of fear and depression.

The Lord's word to him reaffirms God's uniqueness, his sovereignty over all nations, and the importance of the prophetic word. God tells him, "Go back the way you came," a command that calls Elijah back into active service of the Lord.[36] He must anoint Hazael king of Syria, which declares Yahweh's lordship over that non-Israelite country. Similarly, he must anoint Jehu king of Israel, thus reestablishing the Lord's rule over the Northern Kingdom. Finally, Elijah must anoint Elisha to take his place. This command, coupled with the Lord's comment that he has selected, or caused to remain,[37] seven thousand persons who do not worship Baal, reminds Elijah that God's word cannot be silenced. It remains the force that produces the remnant, protects the remnant, and empowers the remnant. As a part of this remnant, Elijah can expect God's protection and empowerment.

(9) Elisha's Call (19:19–21)

19So Elijah went from there and found Elisha son of Shaphat. He was plowing with twelve yoke of oxen, and he himself was driving the twelfth pair. Elijah went up to him and threw his cloak around him. 20Elisha then left his oxen and ran after Elijah. "Let me kiss my father and mother good-by," he said, "and then I will come with you."

---

[35] Gregory, *From Carmel to Horeb,* 134.

[36] R. B. Coote, "Yahweh Recalls Elijah," in *Traditions in Transformation: Turning Points in Biblical Faith,* ed. B. Halpern and J. D. Levenson (Winona Lake, Ind.: Eisenbrauns, 1981) 119.

[37] The Heb. word is וְהִשְׁאַרְתִּי, a *hiphil* stem meaning "I caused to remain."

"Go back," Elijah replied. "What have I done to you?"

[21]So Elisha left him and went back. He took his yoke of oxen and slaughtered them. He burned the plowing equipment to cook the meat and gave it to the people, and they ate. Then he set out to follow Elijah and became his attendant.

19:19–21 Elijah accepts the Lord's reassurances and anoints Elisha. Like the widow (17:24), the people on Mount Carmel (18:39–40), and Ahab (18:41–19:1), Elijah has experienced the power and healing of God.[38] So he sets out to obey God, fully aware that God is his strength and his word will not fail.[39] Elijah throws his cloak, or mantle, upon Elisha, a symbolic way of transferring the prophetic power from one man to the next. Elisha says farewell to his family, then slaughters his oxen and burns his plow, which demonstrates the clear break between his old and new lives. Jesus reflects on this type of separation when he states, "No one who puts his hand to the plow and looks back is fit for service in the kingdom of God" (Luke 9:62). Elisha seems to know he must take a single-minded approach to the difficult task he will assume. For now he recedes into the background of the story but will step forward again in 2 Kgs 2:1.

2. Elijah Denounces Ahab (20:1–22:40)

Before Elijah, Ben-Hadad, or Ahab "retire," however, Ahab and Ben-Hadad will fight one another on three occasions (20:1–34; 22:1–40). Elijah will oppose Ahab after the king has an innocent man killed (21:17–29), and other prophets will correct him as well (20:35–43; 22:1–28). It will be Elijah who predicts Ahab's demise (21:17–29). In all these stories the issues remain the same as in 1 Kings 17–19: Who is God? Who rules the earth? Who speaks for God? What does it mean to be king over the Lord's people?

The Septuagint reverses chaps. 20–21. Shenkel claims, "The Greek arrangement is superior, however, because it keeps all the stories about Elijah and Ahab together."[40] Burney concurs, stating that the Septuagint is "no doubt correct in placing this narrative immediately after *ch.* 19."[41] He also suggests that the Hebrew text may be in its current order "due to the desire to bring the prophecy of Ahab's death (21:19) nearer to the account of its occurrence (22:35ff.) and perhaps in a minor degree to the description of the king's mood as סַר וְזָעֵף in 20:43 as in 21:4."[42]

[38] Cohn, "The Literary Logic of 1 Kings 17–19," 343.

[39] DeVries, *1 Kings,* 237.

[40] J. D. Shenkel, *Chronology and Recensional Development in the Greek Text of Kings* (Cambridge: Harvard University Press, 1968) 88.

[41] C. F. Burney, *Notes on the Hebrew Text of the Book of Kings* (Oxford: Clarendon Press, 1903) 210.

[42] Ibid.

D. W. Gooding questions whether the Septuagint's only goal was to keep the Elijah-Ahab stories intact. He notes that the Greek text not only has a different order but also "a decidedly different picture of Ahab from that painted by the MT."[43] In the Septuagint, Ahab's repentance in 1 Kgs 21:27–29 is part of sorrow he feels in 18:45b and after Naboth dies (LXX, 20:27–29).[44] Thus, the Greek text portrays Ahab as a man grieved over wickedness *before* Elijah speaks. It is certainly hard to see how this picture of the king fits the one in 1 Kgs 18:1–15 or 22:1–28. Consequently, Gooding correctly decides that if the Septuagint order came from a Hebrew tradition it was from one inferior to the Masoretic Text. More probable, however, "the changed order and the undue emphasis on Ahab's repentance originated with the LXX 'translation-interpretation.'"[45]

Besides Gooding's observations, it is important to note the coherence of the Hebrew text. As has been stated, the major issues from 1 Kings 17–19 carry over into chap. 20. Further, the king's attitude does link 20:43 and 21:4. Finally, the Hebrew order presents a cumulative reason for Ahab's change of heart. Given all these considerations, it seems reasonable to interpret the next two chapters in their Hebrew canonical order.

(1) Ahab Defeats Syria (20:1–34)

1Now Ben-Hadad king of Aram mustered his entire army. Accompanied by thirty-two kings with their horses and chariots, he went up and besieged Samaria and attacked it. 2He sent messengers into the city to Ahab king of Israel, saying, "This is what Ben-Hadad says: 3'Your silver and gold are mine, and the best of your wives and children are mine.'"

4The king of Israel answered, "Just as you say, my lord the king. I and all I have are yours."

5The messengers came again and said, "This is what Ben-Hadad says: 'I sent to demand your silver and gold, your wives and your children. 6But about this time tomorrow I am going to send my officials to search your palace and the houses of your officials. They will seize everything you value and carry it away.'"

7The king of Israel summoned all the elders of the land and said to them, "See how this man is looking for trouble! When he sent for my wives and my children, my silver and my gold, I did not refuse him."

8The elders and the people all answered, "Don't listen to him or agree to his demands."

9So he replied to Ben-Hadad's messengers, "Tell my lord the king, 'Your servant will do all you demanded the first time, but this demand I cannot meet.'" They left and took the answer back to Ben-Hadad.

---

43 D. W. Gooding, "Ahab according to the Septuagint," *ZAW* 76 (1964) 271–72.

44 Ibid., 273.

45 Ibid., 277.

[10]Then Ben-Hadad sent another message to Ahab: "May the gods deal with
me, be it ever so severely, if enough dust remains in Samaria to give each of my
men a handful."
[11]The king of Israel answered, "Tell him: 'One who puts on his armor should
not boast like one who takes it off.'"
[12]Ben-Hadad heard this message while he and the kings were drinking in their
tents, and he ordered his men: "Prepare to attack." So they prepared to attack
the city.
[13]Meanwhile a prophet came to Ahab king of Israel and announced, "This is
what the LORD says: 'Do you see this vast army? I will give it into your hand
today, and then you will know that I am the LORD.'"
[14]"But who will do this?" asked Ahab.
The prophet replied, "This is what the LORD says: 'The young officers of the
provincial commanders will do it.'"
"And who will start the battle?" he asked.
The prophet answered, "You will."
[15]So Ahab summoned the young officers of the provincial commanders, 232
men. Then he assembled the rest of the Israelites, 7,000 in all. [16]They set out at
noon while Ben-Hadad and the 32 kings allied with him were in their tents getting
drunk. [17]The young officers of the provincial commanders went out first.
Now Ben-Hadad had dispatched scouts, who reported, "Men are advancing
from Samaria."
[18]He said, "If they have come out for peace, take them alive; if they have come
out for war, take them alive."
[19]The young officers of the provincial commanders marched out of the city
with the army behind them [20]and each one struck down his opponent. At that, the
Arameans fled, with the Israelites in pursuit. But Ben-Hadad king of Aram
escaped on horseback with some of his horsemen. [21]The king of Israel advanced
and overpowered the horses and chariots and inflicted heavy losses on the Arameans.
[22]Afterward, the prophet came to the king of Israel and said, "Strengthen
your position and see what must be done, because next spring the king of Aram
will attack you again."
[23]Meanwhile, the officials of the king of Aram advised him, "Their gods are
gods of the hills. That is why they were too strong for us. But if we fight them on
the plains, surely we will be stronger than they. [24]Do this: Remove all the kings
from their commands and replace them with other officers. [25]You must also raise
an army like the one you lost—horse for horse and chariot for chariot—so we can
fight Israel on the plains. Then surely we will be stronger than they." He agreed
with them and acted accordingly.
[26]The next spring Ben-Hadad mustered the Arameans and went up to Aphek
to fight against Israel. [27]When the Israelites were also mustered and given provisions, they marched out to meet them. The Israelites camped opposite them like
two small flocks of goats, while the Arameans covered the countryside.
[28]The man of God came up and told the king of Israel, "This is what the LORD
says: 'Because the Arameans think the LORD is a god of the hills and not a god of

the valleys, I will deliver this vast army into your hands, and you will know that I am the LORD.'"

29For seven days they camped opposite each other, and on the seventh day the battle was joined. The Israelites inflicted a hundred thousand casualties on the Aramean foot soldiers in one day. 30The rest of them escaped to the city of Aphek, where the wall collapsed on twenty-seven thousand of them. And Ben-Hadad fled to the city and hid in an inner room.

31His officials said to him, "Look, we have heard that the kings of the house of Israel are merciful. Let us go to the king of Israel with sackcloth around our waists and ropes around our heads. Perhaps he will spare your life."

32Wearing sackcloth around their waists and ropes around their heads, they went to the king of Israel and said, "Your servant Ben-Hadad says: 'Please let me live.'"

The king answered, "Is he still alive? He is my brother."

33The men took this as a good sign and were quick to pick up his word. "Yes, your brother Ben-Hadad!" they said.

"Go and get him," the king said. When Ben-Hadad came out, Ahab had him come up into his chariot.

34"I will return the cities my father took from your father," Ben-Hadad offered. "You may set up your own market areas in Damascus, as my father did in Samaria."

[Ahab said,] "On the basis of a treaty I will set you free." So he made a treaty with him, and let him go.

20:1–12 Israel's old foe Syria rouses itself again (cf. 1 Kgs 15:16–22). Fully armed and accompanied by a coalition of thirty-two kings, Ben-Hadad[46] attempts to capture Samaria. Ahab agrees to give money, women, and children in return for a retreat. Ben-Hadad goes beyond this concession and asks for the right to loot the palace and the homes of Ahab's officials. Because of this humiliating demand the Israelites decide to fight rather than surrender. A war Israel seems destined to lose appears to be inevitable.

20:13–22 An unnamed prophet changes this seemingly disastrous situation. He tells Ahab God will give the Syrians "into your hand today." Why? So that the king will know Yahweh is God. The Lord continues to give Ahab opportunities to serve the covenant God. Desperate, Ahab wonders how the victory can be achieved. The prophet says the "young officers" will win the battle but that Ahab must lead them out.

Meanwhile, Ben-Hadad and his allies sit getting drunk, much as Elah had

[46] Gray (*1 and 2 Kings,* 374) and DeVries (*1 Kings,* 248) doubt that the same Ben-Hadad mentioned in 1 Kings 15 can be meant in this passage. They prefer to argue that "Ben-Hadad" is a throne name taken by a later monarch. Keil ("I and II Kings," 261) thinks this Ben-Hadad is the son of the king mentioned in 1 Kings 15, but Bright (*History of Israel,* 235, 240) indicates that the same person appears in both accounts. The evidence is quite difficult to assess, and any of these conclusions is possible; but this commentary adopts Bright's viewpoint.

done before Zimri assassinated him (cf. 1 Kgs 16:9–10). In fact, the text mentions this drinking twice to emphasize their condition (1 Kgs 20:12,16). The author also notes where they do this drinking. The word translated "tents" may also refer to the ancient city of Succoth. Yadin argues that interpreting the word as Succoth helps explain Ben-Hadad's location, the time lapse between the sending and receiving of messages, and the strategy Ahab employs.[47] Either way the story presents Ben-Hadad as drunk, surly, and in no condition to make sound decisions. He is also about to send chariots into hilly country where they are least effective.

Israel wins the battle, though Ben-Hadad manages to escape. The story presents a contrast between the king who has a word from God to direct his affairs and the king who depends on wine for his courage (Eph 5:18). One king submits to the Lord's messenger, while the other proudly believes he will conquer no matter what happens. Despite this victory the Syrians will not quit. Another prophetic word tells Ahab the enemy will regroup and strike again in the spring.

20:23–30 Syria misunderstands the nature of their first defeat and attributes the loss to the notion that Israel's "gods are gods of the hills." Thus, they decide to engage Israel on the plains and mass a great army for that purpose.

God sends Ahab another message. Syria must learn the Lord exists everywhere and controls all terrain, so Israel will defeat the larger army again. As in 1 Kings 17–19, the Lord is portrayed here as sovereign over all matters in all nations.[48] Israel's victory is so complete that Ben-Hadad is forced to flee and hide from Ahab. By now Ahab should know who his God is, who God's messengers are, and who his enemies are. Unfortunately, he remains oblivious to the implications of what he has seen and experienced.

20:31–34 Ben-Hadad pleads for his life and has his request granted. Inexplicably, Ahab makes a treaty with this long-term foe who has twice sought to devastate Ahab and his people. All Ahab gains is the "restoration of captured cities and the right to extraterritorial bazaars in Damascus."[49] Perhaps the cities taken in 1 Kgs 15:18–22 will revert to Israel, but that is a high price to pay for guaranteeing a dedicated foe will survive. Apparently Ahab hopes to buy peace and friendship. He may have his eye on the Assyrians, hoping that a treaty with Syria will strengthen him against this threatening eastern power. He will in fact go to battle with Syria against Shalmaneser III at Qarqar in 853 B.C.[50] Whatever advantages he may imagine his mercy will gain, he soon learns the price he will pay.

---

[47] Y. Yadin, "Some Aspects of the Strategy of Ahab and David (I Kings 20; II Sam. 11)," *Bib* 36/3 (1955) 332–51.

[48] Robinson, *The First Book of Kings,* 224–25.

[49] Montgomery and Gehman, *Kings,* 325; E. H. Merrill, *Kingdom of Priests* (Grand Rapids: Baker, 1987) 348.

[50] Patterson and Austel, "1, 2 Kings," 4:157.

(2) An Unnamed Prophet Denounces Ahab (20:35–43)

35By the word of the LORD one of the sons of the prophets said to his companion, "Strike me with your weapon," but the man refused.

36So the prophet said, "Because you have not obeyed the LORD, as soon as you leave me a lion will kill you." And after the man went away, a lion found him and killed him.

37The prophet found another man and said, "Strike me, please." So the man struck him and wounded him. 38Then the prophet went and stood by the road waiting for the king. He disguised himself with his headband down over his eyes. 39As the king passed by, the prophet called out to him, "Your servant went into the thick of the battle, and someone came to me with a captive and said, 'Guard this man. If he is missing, it will be your life for his life, or you must pay a talent of silver.' 40While your servant was busy here and there, the man disappeared."

"That is your sentence," the king of Israel said. "You have pronounced it yourself."

41Then the prophet quickly removed the headband from his eyes, and the king of Israel recognized him as one of the prophets. 42He said to the king, "This is what the LORD says: 'You have set free a man I had determined should die. Therefore it is your life for his life, your people for his people.'" 43Sullen and angry, the king of Israel went to his palace in Samaria.

20:35–43 The prophetic voice is strangely quiet in vv. 31–34. It returns here, however, and informs Ahab what the future holds. Two scenes prepare an unnamed prophet to address Ahab. In the first the prophet orders a fellow prophet to strike him. When the man refuses, the first prophet predicts a lion will kill him, not unlike what happens to the good prophet in 1 Kings 13. God's word must be obeyed. Another prophet obliges the first prophet by striking and wounding him. Two details are settled in these scenes. First, this prophet does have a word from God. Second, his wound makes him look like the survivor of a battle. He now disguises himself and goes to meet the king.

When Ahab passes by, the prophet acts like a common soldier who has allowed a prisoner to escape. Ahab cannot know, of course, that "the petitioner is a prophet bent on some secret mission, the appeal a ruse, the problem fictitious, the motives ulterior."[51] Like David in the famous Nathan scene (2 Sam 12:1–10), Ahab pronounces his own sentence (note the irony of v. 40). The prophet explains that Ahab let Ben-Hadad go when God had given him the Syrian through extraordinary circumstances, so Ahab will lose his life, a prediction that becomes a fact in 1 Kgs 22:29–40. Upon hearing his sentence the king stalks away "sullen and angry." This propensity for pouting (cf. 21:4) will not serve Ahab well in the last two major episodes of his life.

---

[51] Long, *1 Kings,* 221.

(3) Ahab and Jezebel Murder Naboth (21:1–16)

[1]Some time later there was an incident involving a vineyard belonging to Naboth the Jezreelite. The vineyard was in Jezreel, close to the palace of Ahab king of Samaria. [2]Ahab said to Naboth, "Let me have your vineyard to use for a vegetable garden, since it is close to my palace. In exchange I will give you a better vineyard or, if you prefer, I will pay you whatever it is worth."

[3]But Naboth replied, "The LORD forbid that I should give you the inheritance of my fathers."

[4]So Ahab went home, sullen and angry because Naboth the Jezreelite had said, "I will not give you the inheritance of my fathers." He lay on his bed sulking and refused to eat.

[5]His wife Jezebel came in and asked him, "Why are you so sullen? Why won't you eat?"

[6]He answered her, "Because I said to Naboth the Jezreelite, 'Sell me your vineyard; or if you prefer, I will give you another vineyard in its place.' But he said, 'I will not give you my vineyard.'"

[7]Jezebel his wife said, "Is this how you act as king over Israel? Get up and eat! Cheer up. I'll get you the vineyard of Naboth the Jezreelite."

[8]So she wrote letters in Ahab's name, placed his seal on them, and sent them to the elders and nobles who lived in Naboth's city with him. [9]In those letters she wrote:

> **"Proclaim a day of fasting and seat Naboth in a prominent place among the people. [10]But seat two scoundrels opposite him and have them testify that he has cursed both God and the king. Then take him out and stone him to death."**

[11]So the elders and nobles who lived in Naboth's city did as Jezebel directed in the letters she had written to them. [12]They proclaimed a fast and seated Naboth in a prominent place among the people. [13]Then two scoundrels came and sat opposite him and brought charges against Naboth before the people, saying, "Naboth has cursed both God and the king." So they took him outside the city and stoned him to death. [14]Then they sent word to Jezebel: "Naboth has been stoned and is dead."

[15]As soon as Jezebel heard that Naboth had been stoned to death, she said to Ahab, "Get up and take possession of the vineyard of Naboth the Jezreelite that he refused to sell you. He is no longer alive, but dead." [16]When Ahab heard that Naboth was dead, he got up and went down to take possession of Naboth's vineyard.

21:1–3 Of all Ahab's failings the text has never accused him of oppression or brutality against his people. But here the king proves himself to have even less character than was demonstrated previously, and his wife is the catalyst for this decline. Ahab desires to buy Naboth's vineyard, a property located close to the palace in Jezreel. Unlike Ahab, Naboth remains true to his ancestors' heritage and refuses to sell the land. For him it is a matter of honor to keep what has been passed on to him. Ahab, on the other hand, has few convictions about the religious or administrative heritage of men like David. He operates here based on momentary wishes.

21:4–7 Ahab responds to Naboth's refusal in a spoiled, immature fashion. He knows Israelite kings are supposed to be merciful to foreigners (cf. 1 Kgs 20:31) and to their own subjects (Deut 17:14–20). They are supposed to be different from the normal ancient despot, and this knowledge, coupled with his desire for Naboth's land, drives Ahab to despair.

Jezebel has no such scruples. She finds his sulking as despicable as the reader does and decides to settle the matter. DeVries comments that she "has been trained in the absolutistic traditions of the Phoenician city-states. To her Ahab seems a weakling."[52] Jezebel tells her husband to act like a king, to be a man! She then promises to show him how a real monarch gets what he or she wants. Readers surely sense that she cannot keep her promise through legitimate means.

21:8–16 In effect, Jezebel now assumes Ahab's role, his authority, even his name. She concocts a plot against Naboth's life by ordering "a day of fasting," then commanding the city's elders to seat two men who are willing to lie about Naboth next to him. At the right moment these two men do indeed say he has cursed God (blasphemy) and the king (treason). Thus, the people take the innocent man and stone him to death. All these things occur while Jezebel coopts the king's seal. Ahab does nothing to check his wife's scheming or even to express disapproval of her deed.

Once she hears Naboth is dead, Jezebel commands Ahab himself to "take possession" of the murdered man's land. He dutifully follows her orders, having seen how to be the kind of king Jezebel respects. Ahab and his queen have added murder, stealing, and oppression to their already-serious religious sins.

(4) Elijah Denounces Ahab (21:17–29)

17Then the word of the LORD came to Elijah the Tishbite: 18"Go down to meet Ahab king of Israel, who rules in Samaria. He is now in Naboth's vineyard, where he has gone to take possession of it. 19Say to him, 'This is what the LORD says: Have you not murdered a man and seized his property?' Then say to him, 'This is what the LORD says: In the place where dogs licked up Naboth's blood, dogs will lick up your blood—yes, yours!'"

20Ahab said to Elijah, "So you have found me, my enemy!"

"I have found you," he answered, "because you have sold yourself to do evil in the eyes of the LORD. 21'I am going to bring disaster on you. I will consume your descendants and cut off from Ahab every last male in Israel—slave or free. 22I will make your house like that of Jeroboam son of Nebat and that of Baasha son of

[52] DeVries, *1 Kings,* 257.

Ahijah, because you have provoked me to anger and have caused Israel to sin.'
[23]"And also concerning Jezebel the LORD says: 'Dogs will devour Jezebel by the wall of Jezreel.'
[24]"Dogs will eat those belonging to Ahab who die in the city, and the birds of the air will feed on those who die in the country."
[25](There was never a man like Ahab, who sold himself to do evil in the eyes of the LORD, urged on by Jezebel his wife.
[26]He behaved in the vilest manner by going after idols, like the Amorites the LORD drove out before Israel.)
[27]When Ahab heard these words, he tore his clothes, put on sackcloth and fasted. He lay in sackcloth and went around meekly.
[28]Then the word of the LORD came to Elijah the Tishbite:
[29]"Have you noticed how Ahab has humbled himself before me? Because he has humbled himself, I will not bring this disaster in his day, but I will bring it on his house in the days of his son."

21:17–19 The Lord reveals to Elijah the prophet what the royal couple have done (cf. Amos 3:7). God instructs the prophet to expose Ahab's sins of murder and stealing and to announce to the king that dogs will lick up his blood where dogs had drunk Naboth's blood. God knows everything, so Ahab has nowhere to hide, no excuse to make.

21:20–26 Ahab greets Elijah much like he does in 1 Kgs 18:17, where he called the prophet the "troubler of Israel." Now he calls him his "enemy," a defensive posture that emerges again in 1 Kgs 22:8 and one that demonstrates his self-centeredness. Elijah responds much as he did in the earlier encounter, claiming that he has only pursued Ahab because of the king's evil deed.

Elijah delivers God's word. Because of his ongoing wickedness Ahab will die and his dynasty will cease. His wife will die for her sins. In fact, dogs will eat her, which "was a fate worse than Ahab's, for it implied denial of a decent burial."[53] This second announcement intensifies the earlier prediction of death made by the unnamed prophet in 20:41–43. At this point in the narrative the author repeats the denunciation of Ahab first stated in 1 Kgs 16:30–33. Ahab's actions have validated that first negative assessment.

21:27–29 Quite unexpectedly, Ahab humbles himself, which is his most positive act in the book. Again he does not posture like a king, but this time penitence overwhelms petulance, and he does the right thing. God forgives him and postpones the judgment on his family, which demonstrates the Lord's overwhelming grace and mercy.[54] It has always been the Lord's desire to turn Ahab's heart. Unfortunately, Ahab does not fully learn how to listen to God and God's messenger.

---

[53] R. L. Hubbard, Jr., *First and Second Kings,* EvBC (Chicago: Moody, 1991) 113.

[54] Patterson and Austel, "1, 2 Kings," EBC (Grand Rapids: Zondervan, 1988) 4:160.

(5) Micaiah Denounces Ahab (22:1–28)

[1]For three years there was no war between Aram and Israel. [2]But in the third year Jehoshaphat king of Judah went down to see the king of Israel. [3]The king of Israel had said to his officials, "Don't you know that Ramoth Gilead belongs to us and yet we are doing nothing to retake it from the king of Aram?"

[4]So he asked Jehoshaphat, "Will you go with me to fight against Ramoth Gilead?"

Jehoshaphat replied to the king of Israel, "I am as you are, my people as your people, my horses as your horses." [5]But Jehoshaphat also said to the king of Israel, "First seek the counsel of the LORD."

[6]So the king of Israel brought together the prophets—about four hundred men—and asked them, "Shall I go to war against Ramoth Gilead, or shall I refrain?"

"Go," they answered, "for the LORD will give it into the king's hand."

[7]But Jehoshaphat asked, "Is there not a prophet of the LORD here whom we can inquire of?"

[8]The king of Israel answered Jehoshaphat, "There is still one man through whom we can inquire of the LORD, but I hate him because he never prophesies anything good about me, but always bad. He is Micaiah son of Imlah."

"The king should not say that," Jehoshaphat replied.

[9]So the king of Israel called one of his officials and said, "Bring Micaiah son of Imlah at once."

[10]Dressed in their royal robes, the king of Israel and Jehoshaphat king of Judah were sitting on their thrones at the threshing floor by the entrance of the gate of Samaria, with all the prophets prophesying before them. [11]Now Zedekiah son of Kenaanah had made iron horns and he declared, "This is what the LORD says: 'With these you will gore the Arameans until they are destroyed.'"

[12]All the other prophets were prophesying the same thing. "Attack Ramoth Gilead and be victorious," they said, "for the LORD will give it into the king's hand."

[13]The messenger who had gone to summon Micaiah said to him, "Look, as one man the other prophets are predicting success for the king. Let your word agree with theirs, and speak favorably."

[14]But Micaiah said, "As surely as the LORD lives, I can tell him only what the LORD tells me."

[15]When he arrived, the king asked him, "Micaiah, shall we go to war against Ramoth Gilead, or shall I refrain?"

"Attack and be victorious," he answered, "for the LORD will give it into the king's hand."

[16]The king said to him, "How many times must I make you swear to tell me nothing but the truth in the name of the LORD?"

[17]Then Micaiah answered, "I saw all Israel scattered on the hills like sheep without a shepherd, and the LORD said, 'These people have no master. Let each one go home in peace.'"

[18]The king of Israel said to Jehoshaphat, "Didn't I tell you that he never

prophesies anything good about me, but only bad?"

[19]Micaiah continued, "Therefore hear the word of the LORD: I saw the LORD sitting on his throne with all the host of heaven standing around him on his right and on his left. [20]And the LORD said, 'Who will entice Ahab into attacking Ramoth Gilead and going to his death there?'

"One suggested this, and another that. [21]Finally, a spirit came forward, stood before the LORD and said, 'I will entice him.'

[22]" 'By what means?' the LORD asked.

" 'I will go out and be a lying spirit in the mouths of all his prophets,' he said.

" 'You will succeed in enticing him,' said the LORD. 'Go and do it.'

[23]"So now the LORD has put a lying spirit in the mouths of all these prophets of yours. The LORD has decreed disaster for you."

[24]Then Zedekiah son of Kenaanah went up and slapped Micaiah in the face. "Which way did the spirit from the LORD go when he went from me to speak to you?" he asked.

[25]Micaiah replied, "You will find out on the day you go to hide in an inner room."

[26]The king of Israel then ordered, "Take Micaiah and send him back to Amon the ruler of the city and to Joash the king's son [27]and say, 'This is what the king says: Put this fellow in prison and give him nothing but bread and water until I return safely.' "

[28]Micaiah declared, "If you ever return safely, the LORD has not spoken through me." Then he added, "Mark my words, all you people!"

22:1–9 Another voice soon joins the chorus of prophets condemning Ahab. He speaks three years after the episodes recounted in 21:35–43. Ahab solicits help from Jehoshaphat, Asa's successor in Judah, to recapture Ramoth Gilead from the Syrians.[55] Ahab has waited three years for the Syrian king to make good his promise to restore Ramoth Gilead (about thirty miles southeast of the Sea of Galilee), apparently one of the cities referred to in the treaty of Aphek (20:34). The three years may have been used preparing for the battle of Qarqar (853 B.C.) in which, according to the "Kurkh stele," the Assyrian king Shalamaneser III was opposed by a Syrian coalition including "Ahab the Israelite." Although Shalmaneser claims an overwhelming triumph, his failure to proceed farther south suggests that the coalition's opposition succeeded at least in discouraging his advance.[56] It may be immediately following the battle that Ahab appeals to Jehoshaphat for help against Syria. Jehoshaphat and Ahab are allied by marriage (2 Chr 18:1), which may explain why Jehoshaphat agreed to the plan. But Jehoshaphat wants a word from God before proceed-

[55] G. H. Jones, however, argues that this episode occurs ca. 799 B. C. and that Ahab was not the king involved in the battle (*1 and 2 Kings,* NCB [Grand Rapids: Eerdmans, 1984] 1:336–39).

[56] J. Finegan, *Light from the Ancient East,* 2d ed. (Princeton: Princeton University Press, 1959) 204–5; Merrill, *Kingdom of Priests*, 349.

ing, an attitude in line with the author's portrayal of him in 22:41–50 (but cf. 2 Chr 19:2).

Ahab has all sorts of prophets at his disposal. Earlier he could muster 450 prophets of Baal and four hundred prophets of Asherah (1 Kgs 18:19), and now he produces "about four hundred men" who claim to speak for Yahweh. All these prophets say the Lord will give the kings victory. As in 1 Kings 13 and 1 Kings 18 the word "prophet" is a generic definition. The issue is whether or not these men have a word from the Lord.

Jehoshaphat seems unimpressed, or at least unconvinced, by the prophets' unanimity and requests another opinion. Ahab has only one man left, and the king whines that this one never says anything good about him. His self-consumed temperament emerges again. Still, this new prophetic voice is summoned, and the kings wait for Micaiah to be brought. A possible tension waits to surface. Will this voice agree with the four hundred, or will it offer a different word of the Lord?

22:10–12 While the kings wait for Micaiah, the other prophets stress their conviction that the Syrians will be defeated. Zedekiah acts out a prophetic drama for the monarchs.[57] He takes iron horns that represent how the Israelite armies will gore the Syrians to death. All the others agree with Zedekiah, which may indicate that he is their leader or that he simply steps forward to speak for the whole group. These verses offer an impressive scene. Ahab and Jehoshaphat sit on their thrones near the gate where major decisions are made, dressed in their robes, watching "Yahweh's prophets" preach the word. It is hard to imagine anything upsetting this magnificent setting.

22:13–28 Quite unknown to the reader, Ahab has sent for just the man to disturb everyone, maybe even the reader. As he is brought before the monarchs, Micaiah is encouraged to agree with the other men. His reply marks him as potentially a man of God, for he claims he can speak only as the Lord directs him (cf. Deut 13:1–11; 18:14–22). So far Micaiah says nothing against anyone. He simply awaits the chance to speak.

First, Micaiah troubles the kings. When asked his opinion of the potential invasion, he initially repeats exactly what the other prophets have said. Either he speaks too quietly or too sarcastically or Ahab becomes suspicious of this one who had always opposed him. He is admonished to speak only the truth, a rebuke totally absent after the other men's speeches. This time he shares a vision of Israel scattered like sheep with "no master." He either claims Israel has no leadership with Ahab in power or predicts that Ahab will die. Neither possibility could please Ahab very much.

Second, in continuing his comments, Micaiah may disturb readers. He

---

[57] For a discussion of scenes of prophetic drama, consult D. Stacey, *Prophetic Drama in the Old Testament* (London: Epworth, 1990).

recounts a vision about God wishing to eliminate Ahab, whose death has already been predicted in 1 Kgs 20:41–43; 21:17–29. To entice Ahab into the battle that will be his last, the Lord allows a lying spirit to speak through Ahab's prophets. Does Micaiah simply share a parable? Does he believe God tells lies? Are these prophets good men the Lord uses to eliminate Ahab? In short, what does this story say about God? What does it say about the biblical writer?

Micaiah's account has sparked a great deal of scholarly discussion, much as 1 Kings 13 has done. In an excellent survey of the history of the passage's interpretation, W. Roth notes three basic ways the text has been treated. First, scholars like Wellhausen (1876–1877) and Noth (1943) used the story as a means of separating possible sources and determining oral traditions.[58] Second, Kittel (1900), Gressmann (1921), and Montgomery (1951) argued that this text was a fairly primitive stage in the history of Israel's religious evolution.[59] In this view the story was evidence of a primitive notion that a sovereign God must do questionable things to keep order in an imperfect world. Eventually the Israelites came to hold higher views of Yahweh. Third, according to Würthwein (1967) and Rofé (1976), the account helps scholars determine how classical prophecy debated such theological issues as true versus false prophecy and the character of a worthy prophet.[60]

Besides these opinions, R. Goldenberg (1982) has stated how rabbinical texts attempted to explain the problem of two prophets possessing God's word, yet only one of them being worthy of obedience.[61] Goldenberg claims the text says: "It is not enough to identify the prophet sent by the Lord. You must also know *why* the Lord has sent that prophet and the result the prophecy in question was designed to produce."[62] D. Robertson (1982) concludes that the narrator of 1 Kings 22 "distances himself from all the characters, Yahweh included."[63] That is, the author simply tells the story yet never passes judgment on the truthfulness of any of the information given.

Disentangling every critical issue here is not possible, but certain points should be kept in mind when interpreting this story. First, Micaiah clearly

---

[58] Cf. W. Roth, "The Story of the Prophet Micaiah (1 Kings 22) in Historical-Critical Interpretation 1876–1976," in *The Biblical Mosaic Changing Perspectives,* ed. R. M. Polzin and E. Rothman (Philadelphia: Fortress, 1982) 106–10, 117–21, 131.

[59] Ibid., 110–17, 121–23.

[60] Ibid., 123–31.

[61] R. Goldenberg, "The Problem of False Prophecy: Talmudic Interpretations of Jeremiah 28 and 1 Kings 22," in *The Biblical Mosaic Changing Perspectives,* ed. R. M. Polzin and E. Rothman (Philadelphia: Fortress, 1982). For another insightful analysis of the difficulty of separating true prophecy from false prophecy, read S. J. DeVries, *Prophet against Prophet: The Role of the Micaiah Narrative (1 Kings 22) in the Development of Early Prophetic Tradition* (Grand Rapids: Eerdmans, 1978).

[62] Goldenberg, "The Problem of False Prophecy," 94.

[63] D. Robertson, "Micaiah ben Imlah: A Literary View," in *The Biblical Mosaic,* 146.

shapes his account of the lying spirit as a denunciation of the four hundred prophets. These are not faithful and sincere prophets of the Lord but court prophets on the king's payroll who live to please him. They are in striking contrast to the prophets of the Lord mentioned in 1 Kgs 18:1–15 who must be hidden to survive. Israel has "no master," and Ahab has only lying prophets. Micaiah's words are certainly taken as an insult by Zedekiah and Ahab. Second, it is difficult to call the Lord a liar in the story[64] when he announces *before* Ahab goes to battle that a lying spirit has been placed in the prophets' mouths. God warns the king through Micaiah not to listen to these prophets, but "he let himself be deceived to fight against Ramoth, he was killed in action in spite of the precautions he took, and lost the city to the Arameans."[65] Ahab should have known from past experience that the solitary prophet may well speak for God. Third, as in earlier difficult passages in the former prophets (e.g., 1 Sam 16:13–14; 2 Sam 24:1–17) this text focuses on God's sovereignty. Nothing escapes the Lord's notice, and no one operates outside of the Lord's jurisdiction.

Therefore, this account portrays God giving Ahab a chance to respond to a true prophet, which is consistent with other similar, earlier opportunities (e.g., 1 Kgs 18:16–19:2; 21:17–29). The story reveals a group of unanimous prophets who are clearly not part of the separatist Yahweh movement already unveiled in the book (1 Kgs 18:1–15; 19:15–18). *They* have not hidden from Jezebel. It also presents Ahab as the same moody, inconsistent person that readers have come to know. This account has some troubling aspects but can become less troubling when read as part of the whole story instead of as an isolated tradition separate from its canonical context.

Having troubled the kings and readers, Micaiah's story finally enrages the prophets. Zedekiah strikes Micaiah and sarcastically asks how God's Spirit got from him to Micaiah.[66] The solitary prophet responds that Zedekiah will know who has God's Spirit when he hides in fear. Terror will be Zedekiah's instructor.

Ahab has had enough of Micaiah, so he sends him to prison with nothing but bread and water and promises to return from battle. Micaiah once again places himself under Moses' standards for a prophet (cf. Deut 18:21–22). If his words do not come true, then he is not the Lord's prophet. One last time, then, he warns Ahab in the strongest terms available to a prophet that he has spoken the truth. He stakes his calling and reputation on the veracity of his comments. With such warnings made and with Ahab's past experiences in place, Ahab is no victim of divine duplicity or prophetic malice.[67] Rather, he now acts as one responsible for his own decision.

---

[64] As Robertson implies is possible (ibid., 146).

[65] H. Gressmann, *Die älteste Geschichtsschreibung und Prophetie Israels,* 280; quoted in Roth, "The Story of the Prophet Micaiah," 116.

[66] The interrogative phrase אֵי־זֶה also is found in 1 Sam 9:18; 1 Kgs 13:12; Isa 66:1.

[67] Contra Robertson, "Micaiah ben Imlah: Literary View," 146; and Long, *1 Kings,* 236.

(6) Ahab's Death (22:29–40)

29 So the king of Israel and Jehoshaphat king of Judah went up to Ramoth Gilead. 30 The king of Israel said to Jehoshaphat, "I will enter the battle in disguise, but you wear your royal robes." So the king of Israel disguised himself and went into battle.

31 Now the king of Aram had ordered his thirty-two chariot commanders, "Do not fight with anyone, small or great, except the king of Israel." 32 When the chariot commanders saw Jehoshaphat, they thought, "Surely this is the king of Israel." So they turned to attack him, but when Jehoshaphat cried out, 33 the chariot commanders saw that he was not the king of Israel and stopped pursuing him.

34 But someone drew his bow at random and hit the king of Israel between the sections of his armor. The king told his chariot driver, "Wheel around and get me out of the fighting. I've been wounded." 35 All day long the battle raged, and the king was propped up in his chariot facing the Arameans. The blood from his wound ran onto the floor of the chariot, and that evening he died. 36 As the sun was setting, a cry spread through the army: "Every man to his town; everyone to his land!"

37 So the king died and was brought to Samaria, and they buried him there. 38 They washed the chariot at a pool in Samaria (where the prostitutes bathed), and the dogs licked up his blood, as the word of the LORD had declared.

39 As for the other events of Ahab's reign, including all he did, the palace he built and inlaid with ivory, and the cities he fortified, are they not written in the book of the annals of the kings of Israel? 40 Ahab rested with his fathers. And Ahaziah his son succeeded him as king.

22:29–38 One last time Ahab prepares to engage his old enemy Syria in battle. He disguises himself before going to battle, however, either because he knows how much Ben-Hadad hates him, or because of knowledge gained from spies,[68] or due to a desire to circumvent Micaiah's prediction.[69] Jehoshaphat, on the other hand, dressed as a king normally would in battle.

Ahab's fears are not unfounded. Syria's king orders his soldiers to focus on killing Ahab. At first they chase Jehoshaphat, the only properly attired king, a detail that creates some tension in the story.[70] The Syrians realize their mistake, however, and stop chasing the wrong monarch (cf. 2 Chr 18:31). They seemingly have no one to pursue.

Just when it seems that Ahab will escape, an archer shoots an arrow "at random"[71] that hits and mortally wounds Israel's king. Ahab slowly bleeds to death as the battle continues. When the army goes home, they park his chariot,

---

[68] F. W. Farrar, *The First Book of Kings,* EB (New York: A. C. Armstrong & Sons, 1905) 494.

[69] J. Skinner, *I and II Kings,* CB (Edinburgh: T. C. & E. C. Jack, 1904) 267.

[70] DeVries, *1 Kings,* 269.

[71] The Heb. word לְתֻמּוֹ means "at random" (NIV), "in his innocence" (Skinner, *1, 2 Kings,* 268), or "in his wholeness" (Gray, *1 and 2 Kings,* 405). All these possibilities stress that the archer had no specific intention to kill Ahab.

and the dogs lick up his blood. Of course, this event has not been a "random" death in battle but a divine judgment. Elijah predicted what would happen (1 Kgs 21:19), the king ignored Micaiah's warning, and Ahab paid the price for both his complicity in the killing of Naboth and his rejection of the Lord's merciful word. He could not hide from the results of his own decision.

22:39–40 The author lists certain of Ahab's achievements before moving on with the history. Ahab built an ivory-laden palace (cf. Amos 6:4)[72] and fortified some cities. These comments support the earlier accounts of Ahab's palace in Jezreel and his victories over Syria. His son Ahaziah succeeds him as king, thus continuing the Omride dynasty, but he does so with Elijah's prediction of the dynasty's destruction (1 Kgs 21:17–29) weighing on the reader's mind.

Without question Ahab is characterized as a complex, inconsistent man. He is capable of positive action, such as listening to prophets, repenting of sin, and defeating Israel's foes. He builds a strong military force and constructs a beautiful palace. At the same time, however, he is equally capable of bowing to Jezebel's master plan for expansion of Baalism, of benefiting from her killing Naboth, and of ignoring the Lord's prophets. He fights battles yet sulks when things do not please him. Ultimately, he is judged as a man who heard from God yet did not act on the revelation he received. This character thereby allows more wickedness than he intended, perhaps, yet an amount of wickedness Israel could not afford. He wavers at a time when decisive persons around him like Elijah and Jezebel know full well how high the religious and political stakes are at this point in Israel's history.

1. Elijah's Final Days (1 Kgs 22:41–2 Kgs 1:18)

Though Elijah has already picked his successor, he still carries out his own prophetic ministry. His last acts demonstrate the same concerns he has expressed through the years. Elijah declares God's sovereignty and denounces monarchs who disobey the Lord (2 Kgs 1:1–18). Above all else, he is a "man of God" (2 Kgs 11:9–18), a prophet who embodies the power and greatness of the Lord.

(1) Jehoshaphat's and Ahaziah's Reigns (22:41–53)

[41]Jehoshaphat son of Asa became king of Judah in the fourth year of Ahab king of Israel. [42]Jehoshaphat was thirty-five years old when he became king, and

---

[72] About 200 pieces of carved ivory dating from about the time of Ahab were found in the royal acropolis at Samaria. They are mostly plaques which were probably inlays in palace furniture. See A. Mazar, *Archaeology of the Land of the Bible 10,000–586* B.C. (New York: Doubleday, 1990) 503–5; N. Avigad, "Samaria," *EAEHL*, 4:1044–46.

he reigned in Jerusalem twenty-five years. His mother's name was Azubah daughter of Shilhi. [43]In everything he walked in the ways of his father Asa and did not stray from them; he did what was right in the eyes of the LORD. The high places, however, were not removed, and the people continued to offer sacrifices and burn incense there. [44]Jehoshaphat was also at peace with the king of Israel.

[45]As for the other events of Jehoshaphat's reign, the things he achieved and his military exploits, are they not written in the book of the annals of the kings of Judah? [46]He rid the land of the rest of the male shrine prostitutes who remained there even after the reign of his father Asa. [47]There was then no king in Edom; a deputy ruled.

[48]Now Jehoshaphat built a fleet of trading ships to go to Ophir for gold, but they never set sail—they were wrecked at Ezion Geber. [49]At that time Ahaziah son of Ahab said to Jehoshaphat, "Let my men sail with your men," but Jehoshaphat refused.

[50]Then Jehoshaphat rested with his fathers and was buried with them in the city of David his father. And Jehoram his son succeeded him.

[51]Ahaziah son of Ahab became king of Israel in Samaria in the seventeenth year of Jehoshaphat king of Judah, and he reigned over Israel two years. [52]He did evil in the eyes of the LORD, because he walked in the ways of his father and mother and in the ways of Jeroboam son of Nebat, who caused Israel to sin. [53]He served and worshiped Baal and provoked the LORD, the God of Israel, to anger, just as his father had done.

22:41–50 Finally the author takes up Judah's history again. Jehoshaphat is mentioned first in 1 Kgs 15:24, where the text notes that he succeeds his father, Asa. He is also prominent in 1 Kgs 22:1–38, of course, and appears again in 2 Kings 3, a story that affirms his basic moral superiority to the northern kings (2 Kgs 3:12–14). The author introduces Jehoshaphat and his era here, even including his death and successor, then tells events that occur during his reign. He remains the Judahite king of record until 2 Kgs 8:16.

The text says that Jehoshaphat's reign lasts twenty-five years. Thiele concludes that this total includes a three-year coregency with Asa (872–869 B.C.) and a five-year coregency with Jehoram (853–848 B.C.).[73] These calculations coordinate the statements about these men's reigns made in 1 Kgs 15:24; 22:51–52; 2 Kgs 1:17; 3:1; 8:16–24. They also link their reigns with the northern kings of the same era and perhaps explain who ruled Israel during the disease Asa suffered that 2 Chr 16:11–12 describes.

Jehoshaphat receives the same sort of favorable evaluation that his father does. Like his father, he follows the Lord, his only defect being his allowing the high places to remain in place. He also purges "the land of the rest of the male shrine prostitutes who remained there even after the reign of his father Asa." Non-Yahwistic religion died hard throughout Israel's history. Jehosha-

[73] E. R. Thiele, *The Mysterious Numbers of the Hebrew Kings,* 3d ed. (Grand Rapids: Zondervan, 1983) 96–101.

phat also reestablishes Judah's authority over Edom. Apparently he sets his own "deputy" over Edom, who is the "king" who so readily marches with Judah and Israel in 2 Kings 3.[74] His shipping ventures are not as successful as Solomon's, but at least he tries to recapture some of the glory of his ancestor's era. According to 2 Chr 20:35–37, the reason Jehoshaphat is not successful is that he enters the venture jointly with King Ahaziah of Israel. Jehoram follows Jehoshaphat in Jerusalem, thus continuing the Davidic line.

In Samaria, Ahaziah succeeds his father Ahab but only governs for two years (ca. 853–852 B.C.). The author has nothing good to say about him. Ahaziah continues to allow both Jeroboam's religion and Baalism to flourish. He dies in 2 Kgs 1:16–18 while seeking a prophetic word from "Baal-Zebub, the god of Ekron." Clearly, he is no better than his mother and father, the people who remain the major influences in Israel.

(2) Elijah Denounces Ahaziah (1:1–18)

1After Ahab's death, Moab rebelled against Israel. 2Now Ahaziah had fallen through the lattice of his upper room in Samaria and injured himself. So he sent messengers, saying to them, "Go and consult Baal-Zebub, the god of Ekron, to see if I will recover from this injury."

3But the angel of the LORD said to Elijah the Tishbite, "Go up and meet the messengers of the king of Samaria and ask them, 'Is it because there is no God in Israel that you are going off to consult Baal-Zebub, the god of Ekron?'
4Therefore this is what the LORD says: 'You will not leave the bed you are lying on. You will certainly die!'" So Elijah went.

5When the messengers returned to the king, he asked them, "Why have you come back?"

6"A man came to meet us," they replied. "And he said to us, 'Go back to the king who sent you and tell him, "This is what the LORD says: Is it because there is no God in Israel that you are sending men to consult Baal-Zebub, the god of Ekron? Therefore you will not leave the bed you are lying on. You will certainly die!"'"

7The king asked them, "What kind of man was it who came to meet you and told you this?"

8They replied, "He was a man with a garment of hair and with a leather belt around his waist."

The king said, "That was Elijah the Tishbite."

9Then he sent to Elijah a captain with his company of fifty men. The captain went up to Elijah, who was sitting on the top of a hill, and said to him, "Man of God, the king says, 'Come down!'"

10Elijah answered the captain, "If I am a man of God, may fire come down from heaven and consume you and your fifty men!" Then fire fell from heaven and consumed the captain and his men.

[74] Cf. Jones, *1 and 2 Kings,* 2:374, 394.

[11]At this the king sent to Elijah another captain with his fifty men. The captain said to him, "Man of God, this is what the king says, 'Come down at once!'"

[12]"If I am a man of God," Elijah replied, "may fire come down from heaven and consume you and your fifty men!" Then the fire of God fell from heaven and consumed him and his fifty men.

[13]So the king sent a third captain with his fifty men. This third captain went up and fell on his knees before Elijah. "Man of God," he begged, "please have respect for my life and the lives of these fifty men, your servants! [14]See, fire has fallen from heaven and consumed the first two captains and all their men. But now have respect for my life!"

[15]The angel of the LORD said to Elijah, "Go down with him; do not be afraid of him." So Elijah got up and went down with him to the king.

[16]He told the king, "This is what the LORD says: Is it because there is no God in Israel for you to consult that you have sent messengers to consult Baal-Zebub, the god of Ekron? Because you have done this, you will never leave the bed you are lying on. You will certainly die!" [17]So he died, according to the word of the LORD that Elijah had spoken.

Because Ahaziah had no son, Joram succeeded him as king in the second year of Jehoram son of Jehoshaphat king of Judah. [18]As for all the other events of Ahaziah's reign, and what he did, are they not written in the book of the annals of the kings of Israel?

1:1–8 The author continues the account of Ahaziah begun in the previous three verses. Two difficulties befall Ahaziah. First, Moab rebels against Israel, an issue that will resurface in 2 Kgs 3:1. Second, Ahaziah injures himself in a domestic accident. Because of the injuries he incurs, he sends messengers to Baal-Zebub of Ekron to ask if he will recover. This Philistine god's name literally means "lord of the flies," but scholars have been unable to discover anything at all about Baal-Zebub. Most believe it to be an intentional corruption of the title "Baal Zebul," that is, "Baal the prince" (cf. Matt 10:25). Apparently the king believes this "Baal" is in charge of healing.[75]

It is the Lord, however, who is in charge of all things, including healing and death. This point was made repeatedly in 1 Kings 17–22. Thus, God instructs Elijah to confront one last king, this time with the message that the Lord reigns and that the monarch will die. Elijah meets the messengers headed for Ekron and shares God's word of judgment. When Ahaziah's messengers report to him, the king knows his parents' old enemy has condemned him, just as he had done to his father. How will this new monarch respond?

1:9–12 Rather than repenting, Ahaziah sends a squad of fifty and its captain to detain Elijah. The king seems to think he can control and intimidate this prophet, but he is mistaken. Jezebel made Elijah run once, but he refuses to run

[75] Cf. M. Cogan and H. Tadmor, *II Kings,* AB 11 (Garden City: Doubleday, 1988) 25. Also see Patterson and Austel, "1, 2 Kings," 4:172.

now. Instead, he calls fire down from heaven that consumes the first two groups sent to take him. This ability to get fire once again marks Elijah as "a man of God," a true possessor and proclaimer of God's word.

1:13–15 A third captain takes a very practical approach to bringing Elijah to Ahaziah. Rather than order him to come, as the previous two captains had done, he begs for his life and the lives of his men and confesses that he knows Elijah has the power to kill them all. This man understands that the prophet serves an authority other than the king and that he cannot manipulate the Lord's messenger. Because of the captain's humility and because God's angel instructs him to go, Elijah goes to see the king.

1:16–18 Once in the king's presence, Elijah delivers his life's message one last time. He declares that the Lord and his prophets have the only divine word. Seeking direction from other so-called gods is foolish. Again, it is this message that matters most to the man of God, and any judgment he pronounces is secondary to this truth. Still, he delivers what C. Westermann calls a "prophetic judgment-speech to individuals," a speech that includes a commissioning of the messenger (2 Kgs 1:3–4), an accusation (1:16), and an announcement of judgment (1:16).[76] Because of his idolatry, Ahaziah will die, just as his father before him died because of willful theological rebellion. Joram succeeds him, and no other specific achievements are mentioned.[77] Elijah has demonstrated Yahweh's sovereignty over Baal (1 Kgs 17–19). The unnamed prophets showed that the Lord rules hill and valley (1 Kgs 20). Elijah and Micaiah claimed that the Lord punishes sin and directs battles (1 Kgs 21–22). But the prophets' messages fall on deaf ears, and truth must be taught all over again in each new situation.

At this stage it is appropriate to note how the plot of this historical narrative has unfolded. So far, four major characters have piloted the action: David, Solomon, Jeroboam, and Elijah. They have been "supported" by strong minor characters like Nathan, Bathsheba, Hiram, Rehoboam, Ahijah, Ahab, Jezebel, and Micaiah. David passed on both covenant and kingdom to Solomon, who managed to maintain distinctive faith, particularly through temple building, almost to the end of his life. Sadly, Solomon's idolatry opens the door to further idolatry, a door Jeroboam opens for the whole nation. Elijah attempts to close this door and eliminate idolatry's most formidable form, Baalism. The fact that he is unable to do so should make readers apprehensive about the future.

Will Israel follow the way of Jeroboam or the way of Elijah? Will the people be blessed or punished? With no repentance in sight, the answer appears obvious. The prophets and reforming kings can stall the slide into idolatry but

[76] C. Westermann, *Basic Forms of Prophetic Speech*, trans. H. C. White (Philadelphia: Westminster, 1967) 129–36.

[77] The LXX omits 1:17b–18 and places 2 Kgs 3:1–3 here. Apparently the Greek translators wanted to bring more accession data together rather than spreading this information from 1 Kgs 22:51 to 2 Kgs 3:3.

cannot stop it. Therefore, the plot continues its inexorable movement downward to further idolatry, further disintegration, and, ultimately, the loss of the land. Readers are left to ponder the seeds of this destruction, the turning points in the tragedy.

Canonical and Theological Implications of 1 Kgs 17:1 to 2 Kgs 1:18

Many of the canonical and theological issues raised in 1 Kings 12–16 are expanded and elaborated upon in this section of the book. Idolatry, prophecy, kingship, and cult have been mentioned before yet surface again in new and challenging ways. First, idolatry's detrimental effect on Israel remains a canonical issue in 1 Kings 17 to 2 Kings 1. Starting at least in Exod 20:3, if not from the very first verse of Scripture, the Lord declares there are no other gods and Israel must worship him. Deuteronomy 6:4–9 calls for a wholehearted commitment to the Lord, and Josh 24:15 challenges Israel to choose what God/god they will serve. B. Childs says that 1 Kings 18 focuses on this choice between monotheism and polytheism. Indeed, "the essence of Israel's idolatry is reflected in Elijah's contest on Mount Carmel (1 Kings 18). The issue is not that Israel wanted to reject Yahweh and choose Baal, but rather to serve them both. Elijah called for an either/or decision."[78] Though the people decide for the Lord on Mount Carmel, this decision is temporary, a fact magnified in the canon by the frustrations with idolatry expressed by Isaiah, Jeremiah, Ezekiel, Hosea, Amos, the psalmists, Ezra, and others.[79]

Second, this segment of the book raises prophecy to a new level of importance. True and false prophecy remains a serious issue, and most of the same difficulties raised in texts like Num 12:1–8; 22–24; Deut 13:1–11; 18:13–33; and 1 Kings 13 linger. True prophets speak God's exact word, adhere to the covenant, and have the confidence to say, with Micaiah, "If my words do not come true, then I am not a prophet" (cf. 1 Kgs 22:28). False prophets may possess a hint of God's will but eventually always lead their hearers astray.

Beyond true and false prophecy, though, God's prophets in 1 Kings 17–22 become Israel's theological and moral conscience. Elijah displays a straightforward, unvarnished faith. He claims that the Lord is God, while Baal remains a myth, and that the Lord can be trusted.[80] Elijah and the anonymous prophets press these claims upon Ahab, yet with only limited success (cf. 1 Kgs 21:27–29). Some later prophets exceed their success, such as when Isaiah turns Hezekiah to the Lord (2 Kgs 18–20; Isa 37–39) or when Haggai convinces Israel and its leaders to build a new temple (Hag 1). Others, though,

[78] B. S. Childs, *Old Testament Theology in a Canonical Context* (Philadelphia: Fortress, 1986) 65.

[79] Cf. Isa 1:2–4; 44:6–20; 46:1–13; Jer 2–3; 44; Ezek 8–9; 16; Hos 1–4; Amos 2:4–5; 4:1–13; Pss 78; 97; Ezra 9:10–12.

[80] Cf. H. Heater, Jr., "A Theology of Samuel and Kings," *A Biblical Theology of the Old Testament,* ed. R. B. Zuck (Chicago: Moody Press, 1991) 133–34.

including Isaiah (cf. Isa 7:1–17), and most particularly Jeremiah (Jer 22; 34, 36), have no success at turning either king or nation to the Lord. But they are a voice nonetheless. These idealists break into sinful reality with their message of what ought to be in place of what is.

Third, proper kingship continues to confront readers. Over time Israel's kings embody more of Jezebel's ideals for kings (e.g., 1 Kgs 21:5–16) than those Moses sets forth (cf. Deut 17:14–20). Ahab becomes the first of many monarchs who hear God's word, maybe even believe it yet refuse to act on the truth they have been given. Ahaz (Isa 7:1–17), Zedekiah (Jer 34:37–38), and Jehoiakim (Jer 36) may fit this mold. Certainly the monarchs Elisha encounters respond to God's word like Ahab. Godly leaders are hard to find in 1, 2 Kings, though Jehoshaphat is a pleasant surprise in the stories of faulty leadership in 1 Kings 17 to 2 Kings 1.

Fourth, the prophets' message of commitment to the Lord and his word leads back to the matter of worship. As has been stated, Elijah's monotheism demands a choice. God has acted in history in a way that elicits a confession of faith.[81] Such confession must lead to loyal, exclusivistic worship. In fact, one could argue that Israel should have the kind of commitment to Yahweh that Jezebel has for Baal. This type of dedication leads to the faith that survives even persecution and exile, a truth argued forcefully in Jeremiah 40–45; Ezekiel 37–48; Psalms 138–139; Lamentations; Esther; and Daniel 1–6. Those who make a choice and take a stand are the only truly secure people according to the Hebrew canon. Fear does not paralyze them, and circumstances do not ultimately overwhelm them.

Each of these four canonical issues can be translated into theological statements. First, the anti-idolatry emphasis in 1 Kings 17 to 2 Kings 1 stresses the idea that God is unique. That is, there is no God like Yahweh because there is no God but Yahweh. W. Eichrodt claims that in 1 Kgs 18:21 "Elijah's words embody the certainty, that apart from the God of Israel there are in reality no gods worthy of the name; in other words we are manifestly at the stage of practical monotheism."[82] What Baal can only do in mythology Yahweh can do in history. Israel failed to learn and embrace this truth, but the biblical writers continued to make the point nonetheless. The Lord rules Israel, Judah, Phoenicia, Syria, and Philistia in these texts. Before the end of 2 Kings the author will argue that he also rules Assyria, Babylon, and Egypt, or, in other words, the whole earth.

Second, the prophets' ministries demonstrate that God warns and judges the earth's peoples. The Lord reveals himself as he speaks to and through the

---

[81] G. E. Wright, *God Who Acts: Biblical Theology as Recital,* SBT 8 (London: SCM, 1952) 84–85.

[82] W. Eichrodt, *Theology of the Old Testament: Volume One,* 6th ed., trans. J. A. Baker (Philadelphia: Westminster, 1961) 225.

prophets, whether this speaking comes through fire or a quiet voice.[83] Each of these self-revelations intends to express divine personality in a way that will encourage Israel to keep its covenant with the Lord. When these merciful warnings are ignored, however, the Lord becomes Israel's judge, a role God does not wish to play. The prophets' statements to the kings are particularly important in this regard, for the king's responsibility is to guarantee the place of the covenant in the nation's everyday life (Deut 17:14–20). When he fails to do so and fails to administer the law properly, the Lord becomes the judge who protects the oppressed. As R. Mason observes:

> No evildoers are too strong to oppose him. No one can deceive him nor blur his judgement by bribery. He will champion the cause of the poor and needy. His justice is perfect, his judgments all-wise. For the widow, the orphan, the poor and the immigrant, the God who is judge is in a real sense the God who is their deliverer.[84]

Certainly Ahab meets Yahweh the judge after the Naboth incident, as do the prophets of Baal on Mount Carmel, as do the Syrians when they limit Yahweh's sovereignty to one type of terrain.

Third, the story's contrast between Ahab's ruling style and God's righteousness declares that the Lord is king over the whole earth. Ahab remains king only as long as the cosmic king allows. Syria's king is chosen by the Lord (1 Kgs 19:15). Yahweh defends the weak (1 Kgs 19:1–18), cares for the widow and orphan (1 Kgs 17:7–24), and avenges the oppressed (1 Kgs 21:17–29; 22:29–38). He declares covenants and laws and expects these standards to be obeyed.

Fourth, Elijah's demand for the people's decision about who God is reminds readers that God alone deserves worship. Not even sincere, committed worship of another god is permitted, for the prophets of Baal and their patron Jezebel were certainly willing to die for their beliefs. Worshiping a nonexistent deity benefits no one. Of course, few Israelites believed this choice was necessary. After all, it was only religion, not something really important! G. von Rad astutely observes, "Elijah had to make a Herculean effort before he succeeded in forcing them to make a decision for which no one saw any need."[85] What the people failed to realize was that they were being presented with two opposite worldviews, two different ways of understanding nature, two separate notions of history, and two irreconcilable opinions about salvation and worship. J. Bright explains the crucial nature of the situation:

---

[83] Childs, *Old Testament Theology in a Canonical Context,* 41.

[84] R. Mason, *Old Testament Pictures of God,* Regent's Study Guides 2 (Macon, Ga.: Smyth & Helwys, 1993) 130.

[85] G. von Rad, *Old Testament Theology: Volume II,* trans. D. M. G. Stalker (New York: Harper & Row, 1965) 17.

> Clearly the question, Yahweh or Baal? was not a trivial one. We moderns tend to view it as a sort of denominational struggle, and to find the prophet [sic] hostility to Baal rather fanatical and narrow. But we are wrong. For these are not two rival religions, one of which was somewhat superior to the other; they were religions of wholly different sorts; they could have nothing to do with each other.[86]

Why? Because Yahwism was based on Israel's covenant relationship with Yahweh and the nation's obedience to God's word. Baalism, on the other hand, was based on belief in a god who had to be resurrected for the growing season each year, who appreciated sexual rituals that appealed to people's most sensual appetites, and who could be manipulated by worshipers. Bright concludes:

> As long as men take on the character of the gods they serve, so long does it greatly matter who those gods may be. Had Israel embraced Baal it would have been the end of her; she would no longer have lived as the peculiar people of God. Not one scrap of her heritage would have survived.[87]

Elijah saw this danger and committed his life to removing it.

Applicational Implications in 1 Kgs 17:1 to 2 Kgs 1:18

This section of 1, 2 Kings is one of the richest portions of Scripture for finding preaching and teaching material. The characters, events, and theological emphases found here lead in a variety of applicational directions. Perhaps it is best, then, to stay with the four canonical and theological issues already raised to keep the discussion focused. Still, a host of other options are available.

Since God is unique and since idols are condemned throughout Scripture, contemporary believers need to make a fearless inventory of idols in their lives. Whatever is worshiped ahead of, instead of, or alongside God needs to be removed. O. Guinness argues:

> In the biblical view, anything created—anything at all that is less than God, and most especially the gifts of God—can become idolatrous if it is relied upon inordinately until it becomes a full-blown substitute for God and, thus, an idol. The first duty of believers is to say yes to God; the second is to say no to idols. . . . We are under the searching demand of the truth at the heart of the gospel: There is one God, there is no god but God, and there is no rest for any people who rely on any god but God.[88]

This last comment should impact modern hearers. Idols create weariness, stress, and insecurity. Only those who serve the Lord can truly find rest (cf. 1 Kgs 18:21; Matt 11:28–29).

Because God warns in hopes of staving off judgment, true repentance

---

[86] J. Bright, *The Kingdom of God: The Biblical Concept and Its Meaning for the Church* (Nashville: Abingdon, 1953) 52.

[87] Ibid., 53.

[88] O. Guinness and J. Seel, eds., *No God but God: Breaking with the Idols of Our Age* (Chicago: Moody, 1992) 16.

becomes another way of finding rest and security. Even Ahab learned that any level of repentance is met by God's grace and forgiveness (1 Kgs 21:27–29). In fact, Elijah's continual confronting of Ahab proved God's grace. Foolishly, Ahab thought Elijah and Micaiah were his enemies when, quite the contrary, they were his only links to a future worth living. Today's readers of Scripture have the same option that was offered Ahab: they may hear and repent, or they may sulk and resent the messenger. An Ahab-like attitude eventually ruins the nation, for it sends Israel into exile.

God's sovereignty and kingship call people of all times to obedience and trust. Elijah himself learns this lesson in 1 Kings 17–19. God can feed the prophet (17:1–6), feed the widows and orphans, even raise the dead (17:1–24). God can provide safety for the persecuted (18:1–15), answer prayer in a miraculous fashion (18:16–40), and, again, keep the prophet safe (19:1–9). God dictates the future (19:11–18). If such things are true, then trust and obedience are logical responses to this God. Difficulties and persecutions will never disappear (cf. 1 Kgs 19:1–2), but God is faithful in these times just as he is in "easier" times. Like the ancient audience, today's audience can say "the LORD is God" (1 Kgs 18:39) with total confidence and with assurance that God cares for the faithful.[89]

Finally, if God alone deserves worship, the church must take worship and evangelism seriously. Not all Israel adopted separatist Yahwism by any means. Some no doubt continued to mix various forms of Yahwistic and Baalistic rites. Still, the prophets called for reform, and theirs was the most merciful voice. Taking a stand was the kindest thing they could do. Similarly, commitment and devotion to the Lord in worship benefits *the church* most. Telling everyone about Christ benefits *the world* most. Sincere worship of other gods is still idolatry and remains a detriment to people's souls. Believers must not be abrasive or offensive, but a multicultural society offers a great opportunity for witness, not for the church to adopt or accept new idols. Yahweh is still the only God, a truth that should lead not to pride or triumphalism but to an Elijah-like commitment to truth that heals its hearers.

[89] See the reference to Elijah in Jas 5:13–18 and K. Warrington, "The Significance of Elijah in James 5:13–18," *EvQ* 66 (1994) 217–27. He points especially to the necessity of personal righteousness and of attentiveness to the will of God in prayer.

SECTION OUTLINE

V. ELISHA'S WORK AS PROPHET, MIRACLE WORKER, AND KINGMAKER (2:1–13:25)

Historical Details Related to 2 Kgs 2:1–13:25

1. Elisha Succeeds Elijah (2:1–3:27)
   (1) Elijah Ascends to Heaven (2:1–12)
   (2) Elisha's First Miracles (2:13–25)
   (3) Elisha Predicts an Israelite Victory (3:1–27)
2. Elisha Performs Miracles (4:1–6:23)
   (1) Elisha Multiplies Oil (4:1–7)
   (2) Elisha Raises the Dead (4:8–37)
   (3) Elisha "Cures" Some Stew (4:38–41)
   (4) Elisha Feeds One Hundred People (4:42–44)
   (5) Elisha Heals Naaman (5:1–27)
   (6) Elisha Makes an Axhead Float (6:1–7)
   (7) Elisha Traps Syria's Army (6:8–23)
3. Elisha Predicts a Siege's End (6:24–7:20)
   (1) The Siege and Its Effects (6:24–33)
   (2) Elisha Predicts the Siege's End (7:1–2)
   (3) The Siege Is Lifted (7:3–20)
4. Elisha's Political Influence (8:1–9:13)
   (1) Elisha Helps Restore Land (8:1–6)
   (2) Elisha Predicts Syria's New King (8:7–15)
   (3) Jehoram's and Ahaziah's Reigns (8:16–29)
   (4) Elisha Anoints Jehu King (9:1–13)
5. Jehu's Purge (9:14–10:36)
   (1) Jehu Kills Joram and Ahaziah (9:14–29)
   (2) Jehu Kills Jezebel (9:30–37)
   (3) Jehu Kills Ahab's Family (10:1–17)
   (4) Jehu Kills Priests of Baal (10:18–27)
   (5) Israel's Decline (10:28–36)
6. Joash's Reform (11:1–12:21)
   (1) Athaliah's Rebellion (11:1–3)
   (2) Joash Becomes King (11:4–21)
   (3) Joash Repairs the Temple (12:1–16)
   (4) Joash Placates Syria (12:17–18)
   (5) Joash Dies (12:19–21)
7. Elisha's Final Days (13:1–25)
   (1) Jehoahaz's Reign (13:1–9)

(2) Elisha Predicts Syria's Demise (13:10–19)
(3) Elisha Dies (13:20–21)
(4) Syria's Defeat (13:22–25)

V. ELISHA'S WORK AS PROPHET, MIRACLE WORKER, AND KINGMAKER (2:1–13:25)

Over the past few chapters the writer of 1, 2 Kings has slowly set the stage for a new chapter in the history. Ahab has died, leaving behind a legacy of military strength, moral weakness, tolerance for Baalism and Jeroboam's cult, and a vicious queen who has yet to pass from the scene. Elijah remains in the picture, but he has already chosen Elisha to take his place as the Lord's spokesman (cf. 1 Kgs 19:16,19–21). Evidently he will soon give way to his successor, who has committed himself unreservedly to his calling but has not yet proven himself as a "man of God" or "prophet in Israel." Joram has followed Ahab's son Ahaziah on the throne, and readers await the fulfillment of Elijah's prediction that Ahab's whole household will be wiped out as a result of their "father's" sins (cf. 1 Kgs 21:21–22). Judah seems weak and silent. Syria despises their southern neighbors, which indicates more war will soon occur. Thus, the reader has now come to a pivotal point in the accounts. Old characters will be replaced; new dilemmas will arise.

In the midst of all this change, however, certain themes continue. First, God continues to work through the prophets. Again the Lord uses several prophets while blessing one person in an extraordinary manner. Many prophets are mentioned, but it is Elisha who follows Elijah as *the* man of God. He performs miracles (2 Kgs 2:13–25; 4:1–6:23), protects Israel (2 Kgs 6:24–7:20), and appoints kings in Israel *and Syria* (2 Kgs 8:1–9:13). One he anoints king, Jehu, leads a savage purge of northern and southern leadership (2 Kgs 9:14–10:36), which in turn makes reform possible in Judah (2 Kgs 11:1–12:21). Even Elisha's death is attended by unusual circumstances (2 Kgs 13:10–25). As before with Nathan, Ahijah, the unnamed prophet of 1 Kings 13, Shemaiah, and Elijah, it is Elisha who dominates the story and who dictates the flow of history by heralding God's decrees about the future.

Second, the prophets continue to stress that the Lord rules the earth. God sustains Israelite and Judahite armies in the desert of Edom (2 Kgs 3:8ff.); he heals a Syrian commander, Naaman, who declares that "there is no God in all the world except in Israel" (2 Kgs 5:15); and he determines who will be king in Syria (2 Kgs 8:7–15). Elijah's main concern continues to gain momentum. At every turn of the plot the reader finds the theology of monotheism demanding to be heard.

Third, prophets still confront kings when they disobey God. Elisha has no use for Joram and only receives him because Jehoshaphat is his ally (2 Kgs 3:14). He also weeps for the acts of violence Hazael of Syria will inflict on Israel (2 Kgs 8:7–15). Fourth, related to the third theme is the ongoing failure of Israel and Judah to turn from sin and return to a commitment to covenant keeping, regardless of numerous miraculous interventions by the Lord on their behalf (cf. 2 Kgs 3:15–27; 6:24–7:20). Signs and wonders do not produce faith in the hearts of this rebellious generation. Since no repentance occurs, defeat and exile remain the divided nations' logical fate, a fact Ahijah proclaimed as early in the story as 1 Kgs 14:15. Readers continue to follow a tragedy that need not happen.

Through this blending of the old and the new the story moves from about 850 B.C. to about 796 B.C. Roughly half of the years covered in the entire history will be covered by the end of this section. The writer continues to emphasize, then, what led to the disasters of 722 B.C. and 587 B.C. that the original audience knew so well. Causes receive more attention than results. Even as the story renews itself through new characters, settings, and events, readers are challenged to renew their lives by removing the aspects of their characters that may lead to disaster in their own eras.

Historical Details Related to 2 Kgs 2:1–13:25

Old and new historical details also mesh in these chapters. The division of Israel into two states continued to limit what either segment of Israelites could achieve during the last half of the ninth century B.C. Internal and external problems forced Judah and Israel into their lowest point of power and influence since the division itself. Vassals rebelled, old foes rose again, new foes emerged, land was lost, kings were assassinated, and armies were beaten time and time again. In the midst of this depressing scene the prophets, led by Elisha, attempted to demonstrate God's love and power to the people. Nothing they did worked, however, so the religious aspects of this era were little better than their political counterparts. Clearly, new leaders and some new nations populate the accounts, but the same old foreign and domestic difficulties plagued the covenant people.

Israel's external woes began with Moab's rebellion against its vassal status. During Ahab's reign Mesha, Moab's king, paid tribute in the form of lambs and wool to the Israelite monarch (2 Kgs 3:4). When Ahab died, however, Mesha withheld tribute, thus causing Joram, aided by Jehoshaphat, to invade Moab (2 Kgs 3:5–23). Despite suffering an initial defeat, Mesha was able to drive his enemies back to their home bases (2 Kgs 3:24–27), and apparently he never paid tribute again. Not only did he not return to vassal status, but according to the Moabite Stone, an inscribed monument from this period discovered in 1868, Mesha was able to capture Israelite lands as well.[1] Noth comments

[1] J. Bright, *A History of Israel,* 3d ed. (Philadelphia: Westminster, 1981) 248. Cf. *ANET,* 320ff.

that "Moab was able to seize the fertile tableland north of the Arnon, which had been in dispute between Israel and Moab for many years."[2] In fact, this land had been in Israelite hands since the time of David and Solomon. Now it belonged to a former Israelite vassal.

Syria caused Israel many more difficulties than Moab. This fact could be expected, given the constant warfare between Israel and Syria mentioned in 1 Kgs 15:16–22; 20:1–34; 22:1–38. Syria besieged Samaria during the latter years of Ben-Hadad's reign (2 Kgs 6:24–30). God delivered Israel at that time, but a new king arose whom Elisha recognized as fiercer than Ben-Hadad (2 Kgs 8:7–15). This man was Hazael, who ruled Syria about 842–806 B.C.[3] Hazael was busy with the Assyrian forces of Shalmaneser III (ca. 841–837 B.C.).[4] Once free of the Assyrian invaders, however, Hazael turned his attention to dominating his own immediate region. He defeated Jehu and seized Israelite territory (2 Kgs 10:32–33). He also invaded Philistia, then forced Judah to pay tribute or endure a siege of Jerusalem (2 Kgs 12:17–18). Jehoahaz, Jehu's son, had his army reduced to very small numbers by the Syrians. All the Israelite victories recounted in this section of the book were temporary respites from Hazael's power, not permanent reversals of his authority over the area. Only when Hazael died and Ben-Hadad II replaced him did Israel gain some relief from this opponent (2 Kgs 13:4–5,24–25).[5]

Assyria did not concern itself very much with Israel during this time, yet they did force Jehu to pay tribute when exacting similar payments from Tyre and Sidon.[6] This oppression occurred from about 841 to 837 B.C., or about the same time Assyria was battling Syria. Of course, Assyria became a more serious threat to Israel a century later and finally destroyed Samaria in 722 B.C.

Internal problems also plagued Israel. As has been stated, the prophets continued to oppose the monarchy's religious policies, though they did support the king in wartime (cf. 2 Kgs 3:4–27; 6:8–7:20; 13:14–19). Unlike during the earlier Jezebel-instigated persecutions, the prophets were allowed to flourish individually and in groups outside the palace. Prophetic guilds led by Elisha ate together (2 Kgs 4:38–41), worked together (6:1–7), and may have dressed alike or cut their hair the same (2 Kgs 2:23).[7] This organized group gave the king no comfort. They were different from the syncretistic court prophets

---

[2] M. Noth, *The History of Israel,* 2d ed., trans. P. R. Ackroyd (New York: Harper & Row, 1960) 244.

[3] Bright, *A History of Israel,* 250.

[4] Noth, *The History of Israel,* 248.

[5] Cf. H. Donner, "The Separate States of Israel and Judah," in *Israelite and Judean History,* ed. J. H. Hayes and J. M. Miller (Philadelphia: Westminster, 1977) 413.

[6] Cf. Bright, *A History of Israel,* 254, and *ANET,* 280.

[7] Note the discussion of prophetic guilds in J. D. Newsome, Jr., *The Hebrew Prophets* (Atlanta: John Knox, 1984) 5–9.

maintained by the king, though both types shared some of the same group dynamics.[8]

Even more serious than the prophetic opposition to the Omride regime was the emergence of military and popular discontent with the northern kings. In 841 B.C. Jehu, a military officer, was anointed king by a prophet sent by Elisha (2 Kgs 9:1–10), an event anticipated by readers since God's command to Elijah in 1 Kgs 19:16. Jehu received immediate support from the military (2 Kgs 9:11–13) and quickly gained the approval of Jehonadab, the leader of the Rechabites, a conservative clan committed to an agrarian lifestyle (cf. Jer 35:1–19). Noth states that the Rechabites "personified the 'nomadic ideal' in their way of life . . . thereby protesting against life in Palestine with its foreign religious influences. They thought Israel's task was to maintain its original, authentic way of life."[9] Such a group would hardly favor an entrenched monarchy, so it was not out of character for Jehonadab to join Jehu's uprising, nor is it unlikely that other groups opposed the Omrides as well.

Jehu wasted no time in disposing of the kings of Judah and Israel, Ahab's remaining family, including Jezebel, and the priests of Baal (2 Kgs 9:14–10:27). But this massacre was too extreme, according to Hos 1:4–5. Besides its brutality, the killings created a power vacuum that allowed the usurper Athaliah to seize the throne in Judah (2 Kgs 11:1–3). One must wonder whether Jehu was a reformer or a butcher. Regardless of his character, Jehu brought the military and civil discontent in Israel to a climax and furthered both Israel's history of instability and the reliability of the prophetic word.

Similar external problems plagued Judah but perhaps with less severity. Contrary to the divine will Jehoshaphat (2 Chr 18) pursued a policy of cooperation with Israel, fighting alongside both Ahab (1 Kgs 22:1–36) and Joram (2 Kgs 3:1–27). But he was a reformer about whom the author has few negative things to write (cf. 1 Kgs 22:43–44; 2 Kgs 3:14). His successor, Jehoram, however, extended his ties with Israel even further than his father by marrying Ahab's daughter and adopting Israel's religious policies (2 Kgs 8:18). Further, Edom rebelled against Judah's rule and managed to win independence (2 Kgs 8:20–22). Syria did not bother Judah in the same way it did its neighbor Israel. Still, Hazael did extract money from Joash, Athaliah's successor (2 Kgs 12:17–18). Joash's policy of appeasement would be copied by later southern leaders, especially a century later where Assyria was concerned.

Internally Jehu's purge disrupted the political stability brought Judah by Davidic succession. Athaliah, the mother of Ahaziah, the king Jehu killed, seized power, then killed all but one relative of Ahaziah (2 Kgs 11:1–3). This boy was Joash, who later became king through a priestly revolt (2 Kgs 11:4–

[8] Cf. R. R. Wilson, *Prophecy and Society in Ancient Israel* (Philadelphia: Fortress, 1980) 212.
[9] Noth, *The History of Israel,* 247.

21). Athaliah's reign was a low point in Judah's history, for she was a Baal worshiper, a northerner, and a murderer. She brought Jezebel-like qualities to David's throne.[10] Joash brought religious reform (2 Kgs 12:1–16), but no permanent gains were made in that area (cf. 2 Kgs 12:2). Judah was deteriorating from within, albeit at a slower rate than Israel.

1. Elisha Succeeds Elijah (2:1–3:27)

With so many unresolved spiritual problems still current in Israel, it is imperative that the prophetic movement remain vibrant. Thus, it is necessary for Elisha to assume Elijah's leadership role and for the other prophets to continue the type of work done by the unnamed prophet of 1 Kgs 20:35–43 and by Micaiah (1 Kgs 22:1–28). Without such ongoing opposition to idolatry and oppression, the nation has *no* chance of survival. For Elisha effectively to replace Elijah, though, he must show himself worthy of the "office." The next two chapters demonstrate that he is indeed a worthy successor to Elijah and that God will not leave Israel without a prophetic voice to guide them.

(1) Elijah Ascends to Heaven (2:1–12)

1When the LORD was about to take Elijah up to heaven in a whirlwind, Elijah
and Elisha were on their way from Gilgal. 2Elijah said to Elisha, "Stay here; the
LORD has sent me to Bethel."

But Elisha said, "As surely as the LORD lives and as you live, I will not leave you." So they went down to Bethel.

3The company of the prophets at Bethel came out to Elisha and asked, "Do you know that the LORD is going to take your master from you today?"

"Yes, I know," Elisha replied, "but do not speak of it."

4Then Elijah said to him, "Stay here, Elisha; the LORD has sent me to Jericho."

And he replied, "As surely as the LORD lives and as you live, I will not leave you." So they went to Jericho.

5The company of the prophets at Jericho went up to Elisha and asked him, "Do you know that the LORD is going to take your master from you today?"

"Yes, I know," he replied, "but do not speak of it."

6Then Elijah said to him, "Stay here; the LORD has sent me to the Jordan."

And he replied, "As surely as the LORD lives and as you live, I will not leave you." So the two of them walked on.

7Fifty men of the company of the prophets went and stood at a distance, facing
the place where Elijah and Elisha had stopped at the Jordan. 8Elijah took his
cloak, rolled it up and struck the water with it. The water divided to the right and to the left, and the two of them crossed over on dry ground.

9When they had crossed, Elijah said to Elisha, "Tell me, what can I do for you

[10] Bright, *A History of Israel,* 252–53.

before I am taken from you?"

"Let me inherit a double portion of your spirit," Elisha replied.

10"You have asked a difficult thing," Elijah said, "yet if you see me when I am taken from you, it will be yours—otherwise not."

11As they were walking along and talking together, suddenly a chariot of fire and horses of fire appeared and separated the two of them, and Elijah went up to
heaven in a whirlwind.
12Elisha saw this and cried out, "My father! My father! The chariots and horsemen of Israel!" And Elisha saw him no more. Then he took hold of his own clothes and tore them apart.

2:1 Readers have known since 1 Kgs 19:16 that Elisha will take Elijah's place, but how that transition would occur has remained a mystery. Now the author sets the scene by announcing that what follows recounts the events leading up to Elijah's being taken "to heaven in a whirlwind."[11] This miraculous event begins with the men journeying "from Gilgal." Scholars suggest two possible locations for the Gilgal mentioned here. "While the *Gilgal* between Jericho and Jordan (Jos. 4:19–20; modern Khirbet al-Mafjar) is the likely site in view of verse 19, others seek it at Jiljulieh, eleven kilometers north of Bethel, since from it they *went down* to Bethel ('House of God')."[12]

2:2–10 The trip from Gilgal to Bethel to Jericho to the Jordan retraces the first movements Israel made in the promised land (cf. Josh 1–8),[13] and the parting of the Jordan may also remind readers of the crossing of the Red Sea.[14] Such a scenario calls attention to the similarities of Elisha's succession of Elijah and Joshua's succession of Moses (Num 27:18–23; 1 Kgs 19:15–21).[15] Therefore, the text stresses the continuity of God's message and God's messengers in Israel's history and places Elijah on a par with Moses. The reverse tracing of Joshua's itinerary also serves as a reminder that every foot of the promised land belongs to God and is under the authority of God's word.

Elijah's more immediate purpose in moving from Gilgal to Bethel seems to be to see the "company of prophets" that reside in Bethel.[16] Next, Elijah makes a similar journey to Jericho. Though Elijah tells Elisha he may stay in Bethel (cp. 2:2 and 2:4), the younger prophet refuses, apparently because he wants to be near Elijah when his time on earth ends. Elisha's refusal to speak of the matter apparently shows his sorrow at the prospect of losing Elijah.

Fifty prophets serve as witnesses as Elijah and Elisha stop at the Jordan.

---

[11] Literally, the phrase בַּסְעָרָה הַשָּׁמָיִם says "in the storm of the heavens," which does not designate whether or not a "whirlwind" is meant. Cf. BDB, 704.

[12] D. J. Wiseman, *1 and 2 Kings: An Introduction and Commentary,* TOTC (Downers Grove: InterVarsity, 1993) 195.

[13] A. G. Auld, *I and II Kings,* DSB (Philadelphia: Westminster, 1986) 154.

[14] For a discussion of the historicity and plausibility of miracles in 1, 2 Kings see the discussion in 1 Kgs 17:1–6.

[15] T. R. Hobbs, *2 Kings,* WBC 13 (Waco: Word, 1985) 19.

[16] Cf. Hobbs, ibid., 25–27, for a detailed discussion of this phrase.

Elijah strikes the Jordan, the river parts, and the two men walk over on dry land. The fact that this group of prophets has seen this miracle becomes important later, for Elisha's repetition of the act will confirm in their minds that Elisha is truly Elijah's successor (cf. 2 Kgs 2:13–15).

Elijah senses that Elisha has followed him for a reason and therefore asks what Elisha wants. Elisha's request for a "double portion" of the spirit that possesses Elijah indicates his understanding that Elijah has a special relationship with God. Deuteronomy 21:17 says that the firstborn son must receive a "double portion" of his father's estate. If this privilege is what Elisha has in mind, then Jones may be correct in saying that "Elisha is asking that he be granted special privileges as his master's successor, possibly as the leader of a community of prophets."[17] Perhaps, then, Elisha desires both Elijah's spiritual strength and temporal responsibilities, or he may simply ask for the spiritual power to do the job he has known he would someday assume (cf. 1 Kgs 19:19–21).

2:11–12 Without warning "a chariot of fire and horses of fire" appear, which whisk Elijah to the heavens in a storm. As a way of showing his grief at his mentor's departure, Elisha calls Elijah his "father" and dubs him "the chariots and horses of Israel," which probably means Elijah's prophetic powers and spiritual depth are the nation's true strength.[18] Israel's king will use the same formula when Elisha dies (cf. 2 Kgs 13:14). Elisha also demonstrates his anguish by tearing his garment.

Elijah's "death" has proven as spectacular as his life. Just as fire from heaven once proved Yahweh is more powerful than Baal, so now a similar heavenly fire proves that Elijah is the prophet par excellence. And just as another fire from heaven protected him from wicked King Ahaziah (1:9–12), so now it removes Elijah permanently from any further dangers or discouragements. Cogan and Tadmor note that this nondeath "invested him with the quality of eternal life, surpassing even Moses, the father of all prophets, who died and was buried (albeit by God himself: Deut 34:5–6)."[19] Because he never dies, Elijah later becomes the symbol for great future prophets, including the forerunner of the Messiah (Mal 4:5–6). Several Jewish legends also rise up concerning him, and the New Testament patterns its portrayal of John the Baptist (Matt 3:1–12; John 1:19–23) and one of the two witnesses of Rev 11:1–14 after Elijah's ministry.[20]

Besides marking him as an extraordinary prophet, Elijah's death reminds

---

[17] G. H. Jones, *1 and 2 Kings,* NCB (Grand Rapids: Eerdmans, 1984) 2:385.

[18] For a detailed study of the phrase, see M. A. Beek, "The Meaning of the Expression 'The Chariots and the Horsemen of Israel,'" *OTS* 17 (1972) 1–10. Cf. also J. R. Lundblom, "Elijah's Chariot Ride," *JJS* 24/1 (1973) 47–48.

[19] M. Cogan and H. Tadmor, *II Kings,* AB (Garden City: Doubleday, 1988) 33–34.

[20] It is also important to note that Elijah appears with Moses on the mount of transfiguration (Matt 17:3), where he apparently represents all the OT prophets.

readers of Scripture of other unusual events. For example, his going skyward in a whirlwind reads much like Job 38:1, where God answers Job out of a similar storm. Unlike this mostly positive self-revelation to Job, God's presence in a storm means judgment in Jer 23:19; Zech 9:14; and Ps 83:15.[21] Earlier God had spoken to Elijah after a storm of sorts was over (1 Kgs 19:11–13). Also, this scene may be one last time where Yahweh proves stronger than Baal, for once again the Lord conquers death (cf. 1 Kgs 17:7–24), and once again he rules the storms instead of the supposed storm god Baal. Thus, rich irony, not unlike that so evident in the Mount Carmel episode, prevails to the end of the Elijah accounts.

(2) Elisha's First Miracles (2:13–25)

**13He picked up the cloak that had fallen from Elijah and went back and stood
on the bank of the Jordan. 14Then he took the cloak that had fallen from him and
struck the water with it. "Where now is the LORD, the God of Elijah?" he asked.
When he struck the water, it divided to the right and to the left, and he crossed
over.**

**15The company of the prophets from Jericho, who were watching, said, "The
spirit of Elijah is resting on Elisha." And they went to meet him and bowed to the
ground before him. 16"Look," they said, "we your servants have fifty able men.
Let them go and look for your master. Perhaps the Spirit of the LORD has picked
him up and set him down on some mountain or in some valley."**

"No," Elisha replied, "do not send them."

**17But they persisted until he was too ashamed to refuse. So he said, "Send
them." And they sent fifty men, who searched for three days but did not find him.
18When they returned to Elisha, who was staying in Jericho, he said to them,
"Didn't I tell you not to go?"**

**19The men of the city said to Elisha, "Look, our lord, this town is well situated,
as you can see, but the water is bad and the land is unproductive."**

**20"Bring me a new bowl," he said, "and put salt in it." So they brought it to
him.**

**21Then he went out to the spring and threw the salt into it, saying, "This is
what the LORD says: 'I have healed this water. Never again will it cause death or
make the land unproductive.'" 22And the water has remained wholesome to this
day, according to the word Elisha had spoken.**

**23From there Elisha went up to Bethel. As he was walking along the road,
some youths came out of the town and jeered at him. "Go on up, you baldhead!"
they said. "Go on up, you baldhead!" 24He turned around, looked at them and
called down a curse on them in the name of the LORD. Then two bears came out
of the woods and mauled forty-two of the youths. 25And he went on to Mount
Carmel and from there returned to Samaria.**

---

[21] Cf. Cogan and Tadmor's discussion of the relationship of these texts in *II Kings,* 31.

2:13–18 Only Elijah's cloak remains. Elisha takes it back to the Jordan and asks where Elijah's God is—the God who caused drought, brought fire from the sky, raised the dead, and took Elijah to heaven. When Elisha strikes the water with the cloak, he discovers that while Elijah is gone the Lord is not, for the water parts again. The prophets who witness the whole scene understand that Elijah's spirit, the spirit of zeal and power, now rests on Elisha. Still, they seek for Elijah for three days, then return to the new master prophet. Apparently there was still some doubt about whether Elisha could really replace Elijah, though it seems that he has at least laid claim to the status once reserved for Elijah among the company of the prophets.

2:19–22 A second miracle reveals Elisha's prominence to the men of Jericho. The city's water supply is bad, which renders the land as "unproductive" as a couple without children or robbed of children. Elisha purifies the water while performing a ritual involving salt. Gray notes that this use of salt most likely symbolized a break with the past, such as was declared when offerings were made holy by the rubbing of salt (Lev 2:13; Num 18:19; Ezek 43:24).[22] The fact that Elisha declares the water healed because of God's word indicates that no magic has occurred. Rather, the prophet has demonstrated the importance of the event through the use of a symbolic act and has then relayed a message concerning God's will on the matter. Two groups have now seen evidence of Elisha's special status.

2:23–25 A third, less respectful group learns of Elisha's power. Some young boys[23] from Bethel come out of the town to mock and jeer at the prophet. These boys parallel the soldiers in 1 Kgs 1:9–12 who order Elijah to come with them, for both groups seem to lack respect for the prophets' authority and position. The specific insult cast at Elijah is, "Go on up, you baldhead," a phrase that may refer to some physical marking Elisha took on as a prophet rather than to a literal baldness.[24] If this was the case, the insult was directed specifically at Elisha as a prophet and therefore at the Lord whom he represented. The jeering "Go on up!" may be a reference to Elijah's translation, with the sense of "Go away like Elijah," perhaps spoken in "contemptuous disbelief."[25]

Elisha pronounces a swift curse[26] on the group, and bears maul forty-two of

---

[22] J. Gray, *1 and 2 Kings,* OTL (Philadelphia: Westminster, 1963) 427.

[23] The phrase וּנְעָרִים קְטַנִּים can refer to youths from twelve to thirty years old (cf. 1 Sam 16:11–12; 2 Sam 14:21; 18:5), i.e., old enough to show respect for God's prophet. For a discussion of this story's influence on religious writing, read E. J. Ziolkowski, "The Bad Boys of Bethel: Origin and Development of a Sacrilegious Type," in *History of Religions,* 30:331–58.

[24] Cf. Gray, *1 and 2 Kings,* 480; contra Cogan and Tadmor, *II Kings,* 38–9; Wiseman, *1 and 2 Kings,* 198.

[25] W. C. Kaiser, Jr., *Hard Sayings of the Old Testament* (Downers Grove: InterVarsity, 1988) 124.

[26] The word קלל ("curse") means "punishment" or "consequence" in the OT, not "foul language" or "magical incantation" as it often does in current common English usage.

the boys. This punishment comes as a punishment of the Lord, in whose name the curse was offered (cf. Lev 26:21–22). The youths were typical of a nation that "mocked God's messengers, despised his words and scoffed at his prophets" (2 Chr 36:16). Some commentators think this story was originally meant "to frighten the young into respect for their reverend elders,"[27] while others believe the account is legendary and represents the worst notions of certain prophetic circles.[28] Cogan and Tadmor are more in touch with the story itself, for they argue that the account demonstrates Elisha's "effective use of the name of YHWH" and his role as new "father" of the prophets.[29] It is also true that the scornful have discovered Elisha is no more to be trifled with than Elijah was. Three groups of characters are now aware of Elisha's prominence. Others have yet to learn this fact, however, so further miracles may be required.

(3) Elisha Predicts an Israelite Victory (3:1–27)

[1]Joram son of Ahab became king of Israel in Samaria in the eighteenth year of Jehoshaphat king of Judah, and he reigned twelve years. [2]He did evil in the eyes of the LORD, but not as his father and mother had done. He got rid of the sacred stone of Baal that his father had made. [3]Nevertheless he clung to the sins of Jeroboam son of Nebat, which he had caused Israel to commit; he did not turn away from them.

[4]Now Mesha king of Moab raised sheep, and he had to supply the king of Israel with a hundred thousand lambs and with the wool of a hundred thousand rams. [5]But after Ahab died, the king of Moab rebelled against the king of Israel. [6]So at that time King Joram set out from Samaria and mobilized all Israel. [7]He also sent this message to Jehoshaphat king of Judah: "The king of Moab has rebelled against me. Will you go with me to fight against Moab?"

"I will go with you," he replied. "I am as you are, my people as your people, my horses as your horses."

[8]"By what route shall we attack?" he asked.

"Through the Desert of Edom," he answered.

[9]So the king of Israel set out with the king of Judah and the king of Edom. After a roundabout march of seven days, the army had no more water for themselves or for the animals with them.

[10]"What!" exclaimed the king of Israel. "Has the LORD called us three kings together only to hand us over to Moab?"

[11]But Jehoshaphat asked, "Is there no prophet of the LORD here, that we may inquire of the LORD through him?"

An officer of the king of Israel answered, "Elisha son of Shaphat is here. He used to pour water on the hands of Elijah."

[27] J. A. Montgomery and H. S. Gehman, *A Critical and Exegetical Commentary on the Book of Kings,* ICC (1951; Edinburgh: T & T Clark, 1951) 355.

[28] Gray, *1 and 2 Kings,* 428–29.

[29] Cogan and Tadmor, *II Kings,* 39.

[12]Jehoshaphat said, "The word of the LORD is with him." So the king of Israel
and Jehoshaphat and the king of Edom went down to him.
[13]Elisha said to the king of Israel, "What do we have to do with each other? Go
to the prophets of your father and the prophets of your mother."
"No," the king of Israel answered, "because it was the LORD who called us
three kings together to hand us over to Moab."
[14]Elisha said, "As surely as the LORD Almighty lives, whom I serve, if I did not
have respect for the presence of Jehoshaphat king of Judah, I would not look at
you or even notice you. [15]But now bring me a harpist."
While the harpist was playing, the hand of the LORD came upon Elisha [16]and
he said, "This is what the LORD says: Make this valley full of ditches. [17]For this is
what the LORD says: You will see neither wind nor rain, yet this valley will be
filled with water, and you, your cattle and your other animals will drink. [18]This is
an easy thing in the eyes of the LORD; he will also hand Moab over to you. [19]You
will overthrow every fortified city and every major town. You will cut down every
good tree, stop up all the springs, and ruin every good field with stones."
[20]The next morning, about the time for offering the sacrifice, there it was—
water flowing from the direction of Edom! And the land was filled with water.
[21]Now all the Moabites had heard that the kings had come to fight against
them; so every man, young and old, who could bear arms was called up and sta-
tioned on the border. [22]When they got up early in the morning, the sun was shin-
ing on the water. To the Moabites across the way, the water looked red—like
blood. [23]"That's blood!" they said. "Those kings must have fought and slaugh-
tered each other. Now to the plunder, Moab!"
[24]But when the Moabites came to the camp of Israel, the Israelites rose up and
fought them until they fled. And the Israelites invaded the land and slaughtered
the Moabites. [25]They destroyed the towns, and each man threw a stone on every
good field until it was covered. They stopped up all the springs and cut down every
good tree. Only Kir Hareseth was left with its stones in place, but men armed with
slings surrounded it and attacked it as well.
[26]When the king of Moab saw that the battle had gone against him, he took
with him seven hundred swordsmen to break through to the king of Edom, but
they failed. [27]Then he took his firstborn son, who was to succeed him as king, and
offered him as a sacrifice on the city wall. The fury against Israel was great; they
withdrew and returned to their own land.

3:1–3 Despite his successes among the prophets and the people, Elisha has yet to prove himself to the king as Elijah did in his time. This chapter fills this gap.[30] Joram is the king Elisha must "impress." While this monarch is slightly less evil than his father, Ahab, and his mother, Jezebel, he is hardly the reformer Israel needs. He does remove "the sacred stone of Baal that his father had made," an object clearly detested by the author, yet not mentioned elsewhere. On the negative side Joram continues to allow Jeroboam's religion to

[30]Read the commentary on 2 Kgs 1:17–18 for a discussion of textual variants related to this chapter.

exist. In other words, he is not a good king, but neither is he as bad as some other rulers the history describes.

3:4–19 Upon Ahab's death Mesha, king of Moab, seeks to stop being a vassal to Israel. Since such rebellions jeopardized ancient nations' treasuries, Joram decides to invade Moab in order to maintain his power there. As Ahab did in 1 Kings 22, Joram invites Jehoshaphat to attack with him. Joram marches south to join with Judah's army and will eventually march even further south to collect his vassal Edom's forces, then will eventually attack Moab from the south toward Kir Haresheth.[31] Again Jehoshaphat asks for a word from the Lord (1 Kgs 22:5) but only when the kings run out of water in the Edomite desert. To be more specific, he asks if there is "no prophet of the LORD" who can deliver God's word. Clearly, the kings are not yet aware of Elisha's ministry.

An unnamed officer reveals Elisha's name and his previous association with Elijah. This later detail satisfies Jehoshaphat that Elisha is the man they need to see. When the kings arrive, the prophet greets Joram rather roughly. Perhaps reflecting on 2 Kgs 1:1–2 as well as Joram's parents' love for syncretistic and Baalistic prophets, Elisha sarcastically urges the Israelite king to go to his parents' prophets, a practice that proved fatal to both Ahab and Jezebel.

Speaking like a good polytheist, Joram replies that Yahweh seems bent on destroying the kings, so they have come to the Lord's messenger. Elisha cannot hide his disgust for Joram's insinuation of God's evil intentions and overall faulty view of the Lord. He informs Joram that he would not even receive him if Jehoshaphat were not with him. Because Judah's ruler *is* present, though, Elisha agrees to seek God's will.

Elisha receives his word from the Lord while listening to a harpist play music. Lindblom and Wilson[32] contend that such practices were common in the ancient world. A prophet would receive ecstatic utterances after hearing music and would then speak out of a sort of trance. Old Testament prophets received their messages in a variety of ways, including through visions (e.g., Ezek 37:40–48), through hearing music (1 Sam 10:5), and through personal reflection (e.g., Jer 11:18–23). They presented messages quite simply at times yet in a much more complicated manner at others. Here Elisha simply makes use of one of the many ways prophets heard from God. There is no way to categorize and repeat these experiences now. The word Elisha receives is quite favorable to the coalition before him. He declares that their water problems will soon be solved not by rain in their area but by "flash floods caused by rain-

---

[31] For the route of this march consult the map in Cogan and Tadmor, *II Kings,* 41. For more details on Moab's resurgence see R. E. Murphy, "Israel and Moab in the Ninth Century B.C.," *CBQ* 15 (1953) 409–17; and J. Liver, "The Wars of Mesha, King of Moab," *PEQ* 99 (1967) 14–31.

[32] J. Lindblom, *Prophecy in Ancient Israel* (Philadelphia: Fortress, 1962) 58, 88; Wilson, *Prophecy and Society,* 33–35, 103–6, 129–30.

fall on the higher ground."[33] Their war against Moab will be successful to the point that they will devastate the land. This victory will be due to God's grace and Jehoshaphat's presence, of course, since Joram hardly pleases the Lord.

3:20–25 When morning comes, everything unfolds as Elisha predicted. Water does flow into the dry land. The Moabites mistake the sun's glow on the water for blood, deduce that the coalition has fought with one another, and attack. They are soundly defeated. Elisha proves to be an accurate prophet of the Lord. Kings now know who he is and to what extent Yahweh will use him.

3:26–27 Despite its initial success the victory proves to be temporary. To win the battle Mesha sacrifices his firstborn son, a practice that was common in other places at this time.[34] Jones states that this offering "was intended to pacify Chemosh, the Moabite deity, because the disasters that befell Moab were attributed to his anger, 'for Chemosh was angry with his land' (*Mesha Inscription* 1.5)."[35] After the sacrifice is made, "great fury" forces Israel to withdraw. Grays thinks the "fury" is that of Chemosh, which means the text preserves remnants of polytheistic theology.[36] Given the nature of the author's theology, however, it is much more likely either that the action inspired Moab's army to fight more fiercely[37] or that it caused Israel such indignation and sickness of heart that they lifted the siege.[38] Though the exact meaning is unclear, the result is the same: Israel withdraws without further disaster yet also without control of a former vassal.

2. Elisha Performs Miracles (4:1–6:23)

Elisha has now proven himself to the company of Yahwistic prophets, the men of Jericho, the disrespectful boys of Bethel, and the kings of Judah, Israel, and Edom. His ministry has benefited the covenant people materially and also has demonstrated that God's word remains authoritative and that God's prophets continue to mediate his word to anyone willing to hear. More miracles follow in 2 Kgs 4:1–6:23, each one furthering Elisha's influence and extending the knowledge that the Lord rules every nation and each area of life.

---

[33] Hobbs, *2 Kings,* 37.

[34] Montgomery and Gehman, *Kings,* 363.

[35] Jones, *1 and 2 Kings,* 2:400. See also Hobbs, *2 Kings,* 39–41, for a discussion of the Mesha Inscription's relationship to 2 Kings 3.

[36] Gray, *1 and 2 Kings,* 438. Jones agrees (*1 and 2 Kings,* 2:400).

[37] R. L. Honeycutt, "2 Kings," BBC (Nashville: Broadman, 1970) 3:235.

[38] Cf. Wiseman, *1 and 2 Kings,* 202; C. F. Keil, "I and II Kings," COT, trans. J. Martin (1876; reprint, Grand Rapids: Eerdmans, 1980) 3:307; Patterson and Austel, "1 and 2 Kings," 4:181–82.

(1) Elisha Multiplies Oil (4:1–7)

[1]The wife of a man from the company of the prophets cried out to Elisha, "Your servant my husband is dead, and you know that he revered the LORD. But now his creditor is coming to take my two boys as his slaves."

[2]Elisha replied to her, "How can I help you? Tell me, what do you have in your house?"

"Your servant has nothing there at all," she said, "except a little oil."

[3]Elisha said, "Go around and ask all your neighbors for empty jars. Don't ask for just a few. [4]Then go inside and shut the door behind you and your sons. Pour oil into all the jars, and as each is filled, put it to one side."

[5]She left him and afterward shut the door behind her and her sons. They brought the jars to her and she kept pouring. [6]When all the jars were full, she said to her son, "Bring me another one."

But he replied, "There is not a jar left." Then the oil stopped flowing.

[7]She went and told the man of God, and he said, "Go, sell the oil and pay your debts. You and your sons can live on what is left."

4:1–7 This story and the one that follows may be compared and contrasted with the account of the widow and Elijah in 1 Kgs 17:7–24. In both texts a woman is in need, and in both accounts oil helps solve a financial crisis. In the Elijah story, however, the widow receives oil and flour and has only one son, whereas the woman here gets only oil and has more than a single offspring. Finally, the same woman who is helped has her son die in 1 Kings 17, but a second woman suffers the loss in 2 Kgs 4:8–37. The stories share likenesses, therefore, but not enough of them to argue that the same story has been told twice.

A man from the company of the prophets has died, leaving his widow destitute and on the verge of having to sell her sons into slavery to pay her debts. That one of the prophets was married shows that these individuals led fairly normal lives. What remains unclear is "how they shared their time and commitments between the prophetic community and their own family and home."[39] The woman seeks help from Elisha because of his status as leader of the prophets.

At issue here is whether or not God will help the needy through Elisha as he did through Elijah (cf. 1 Kgs 17:7–24). The answer comes when Elisha learns the woman has a little oil. He instructs her to gather as many vessels as possible, then increases her oil until all jars are full. She sells the oil, which negates her need to sell her sons. Because of Elisha's actions, the text explicitly calls him "the man of God" (v. 7), a designation this needy woman surely must have affirmed. Without question the Lord ministers to the hurting through the prophet. What else will the Lord achieve through this man?

---

[39] Jones, *1 and 2 Kings,* 2:403.

(2) Elisha Raises the Dead (4:8–37)

[8]One day Elisha went to Shunem. And a well-to-do woman was there, who urged him to stay for a meal. So whenever he came by, he stopped there to eat. [9]She said to her husband, "I know that this man who often comes our way is a holy man of God. [10]Let's make a small room on the roof and put in it a bed and a table, a chair and a lamp for him. Then he can stay there whenever he comes to us."

[11]One day when Elisha came, he went up to his room and lay down there. [12]He said to his servant Gehazi, "Call the Shunammite." So he called her, and she stood before him. [13]Elisha said to him, "Tell her, 'You have gone to all this trouble for us. Now what can be done for you? Can we speak on your behalf to the king or the commander of the army?'"

She replied, "I have a home among my own people."

[14]"What can be done for her?" Elisha asked.

Gehazi said, "Well, she has no son and her husband is old."

[15]Then Elisha said, "Call her." So he called her, and she stood in the doorway. [16]"About this time next year," Elisha said, "you will hold a son in your arms."

"No, my lord," she objected. "Don't mislead your servant, O man of God!"

[17]But the woman became pregnant, and the next year about that same time she gave birth to a son, just as Elisha had told her.

[18]The child grew, and one day he went out to his father, who was with the reapers. [19]"My head! My head!" he said to his father.

His father told a servant, "Carry him to his mother." [20]After the servant had lifted him up and carried him to his mother, the boy sat on her lap until noon, and then he died. [21]She went up and laid him on the bed of the man of God, then shut the door and went out.

[22]She called her husband and said, "Please send me one of the servants and a donkey so I can go to the man of God quickly and return."

[23]"Why go to him today?" he asked. "It's not the New Moon or the Sabbath."

"It's all right," she said.

[24]She saddled the donkey and said to her servant, "Lead on; don't slow down for me unless I tell you." [25]So she set out and came to the man of God at Mount Carmel.

When he saw her in the distance, the man of God said to his servant Gehazi, "Look! There's the Shunammite! [26]Run to meet her and ask her, 'Are you all right? Is your husband all right? Is your child all right?'"

"Everything is all right," she said.

[27]When she reached the man of God at the mountain, she took hold of his feet. Gehazi came over to push her away, but the man of God said, "Leave her alone! She is in bitter distress, but the LORD has hidden it from me and has not told me why."

[28]"Did I ask you for a son, my lord?" she said. "Didn't I tell you, 'Don't raise my hopes'?"

[29]Elisha said to Gehazi, "Tuck your cloak into your belt, take my staff in your hand and run. If you meet anyone, do not greet him, and if anyone greets you, do not answer. Lay my staff on the boy's face."

30 But the child's mother said, "As surely as the LORD lives and as you live, I will not leave you." So he got up and followed her.

31 Gehazi went on ahead and laid the staff on the boy's face, but there was no sound or response. So Gehazi went back to meet Elisha and told him, "The boy has not awakened."

32 When Elisha reached the house, there was the boy lying dead on his couch.
33 He went in, shut the door on the two of them and prayed to the LORD. 34 Then he
got on the bed and lay upon the boy, mouth to mouth, eyes to eyes, hands to hands.
As he stretched himself out upon him, the boy's body grew warm. 35 Elisha turned
away and walked back and forth in the room and then got on the bed and stretched out upon him once more. The boy sneezed seven times and opened his eyes.

36 Elisha summoned Gehazi and said, "Call the Shunammite." And he did.
When she came, he said, "Take your son." 37 She came in, fell at his feet and
bowed to the ground. Then she took her son and went out.

4:8–17 Despite all he has done, Elisha has not yet matched Elijah's greatest feat, for he has not been used to raise the dead. Even this difference is removed when a second woman and her family enter Elisha's life. This woman confesses that Elisha is "a holy man of God" and convinces her husband that they ought to provide a room where the prophet can rest during his travels. Elisha determines to reward this hospitality. The woman has no need of political favors, but she and her husband are childless, so Elisha promises her a son. The promise is fulfilled despite her husband's advancing age.

This scenario is familiar to seasoned readers of Scripture. A childless couple endure the shame and pain of not having a son. Through a work of God they are able to conceive. Abraham and Sarah, Elkanah and Hannah, and Manoah and his wife face this situation in the Old Testament, and Zechariah and Elizabeth encounter it in the New Testament. As in nearly all these cases, although the boy in this story is cherished, his life will be endangered.

4:18–37 A crisis emerges when the boy feels pain in his head, then dies in his mother's lap. All at once the woman's joy is reversed. How will she respond to this crisis?

The woman formulates a plan to get her son back. First, she lays the boy in the prophet's room at her home. Second, seemingly without telling her husband the child is dead, she determines to go to the prophet. When her husband asks why she wants the prophet, she offers an evasive answer. Third, she travels to Mount Carmel, where the prophet lives. She refuses to reveal to Gehazi, Elisha's servant, what she wants. Clearly, she rests all her hopes on the man of God. Fourth, she clings to Elisha despite Gehazi's attempt to pull her away, a rather stunning break of decorum in the ancient world. Fifth, she reminds Elisha she did not ask for a son, which helps Elisha finally understand what has happened. Each of these actions demonstrates the woman's determined faith. She refuses to accept her child's death or at least refuses to do so until the prophet himself says nothing can be done. Her faith stands out in a history filled with descriptions of persons who reject belief and obedience.

Elisha heals the boy much like Elijah healed the child in 1 Kgs 17:7–24. Gehazi goes ahead and finds the boy dead. Elisha lies on the boy, the child recovers, and Elisha restores him to his mother. Elisha's work here proves the same points Elijah's healing demonstrated: the Lord controls death, and the Lord cares for the needy and hurting. This scene also shows that prophets not only are preachers of sin and repentance; they also are agents of God's healing mercy and kind compassion.

(3) Elisha "Cures" Some Stew (4:38–41)

38Elisha returned to Gilgal and there was a famine in that region. While the company of the prophets was meeting with him, he said to his servant, "Put on the large pot and cook some stew for these men."

39One of them went out into the fields to gather herbs and found a wild vine. He gathered some of its gourds and filled the fold of his cloak. When he returned, he cut them up into the pot of stew, though no one knew what they were. 40The stew was poured out for the men, but as they began to eat it, they cried out, "O man of God, there is death in the pot!" And they could not eat it.

41Elisha said, "Get some flour." He put it into the pot and said, "Serve it to the people to eat." And there was nothing harmful in the pot.

4:38–41 This story and the next illustrate that the Lord provides for his followers even during, or perhaps especially during, crisis times. In this way it parallels 1 Kgs 17:1–24 and 18:1–15, texts that stress God's provision for Elijah and other prophets during famine and persecution. Thus this "healing" of stew fits the overall context of the Elijah/Elisha accounts, provides hope and assurance for readers, and stresses the Lord's faithfulness.

(4) Elisha Feeds One Hundred People (4:42–44)

42A man came from Baal Shalishah, bringing the man of God twenty loaves of barley bread baked from the first ripe grain, along with some heads of new grain. "Give it to the people to eat," Elisha said.

43"How can I set this before a hundred men?" his servant asked.

But Elisha answered, "Give it to the people to eat. For this is what the LORD says: 'They will eat and have some left over.'" 44Then he set it before them, and they ate and had some left over, according to the word of the LORD.

4:42–44 As in the previous story, God uses Elisha to provide for faithful persons who have come to the end of their resources (note Elisha's instructions in v. 42 are almost identical to those in v. 41). Here the prophet causes twenty loaves of bread to be enough to feed one hundred people. An unnamed man brings the food to sustain the prophets. The man's bread is "baked from the first ripe grain," for such offerings were supposed to be given to Israel's priests (Num 18:13; Deut 18:4–5).[40] As R. L. Hubbard observes, "In this case, however, the man brought it to Elisha, bypassing in protest the apostate northern religious leaders at the sanctuary nearby at Bethel."[41] Not all Israelites adopted the religion of Jeroboam and Ahab. Faithful individuals supported the separatist Yahwist prophets (cf. 1 Kgs 18:1–15). The Lord did indeed reserve "seven thousand" who refused to worship Baal (cf. 1 Kgs 19:18).

This miracle is paralleled in the New Testament by Jesus' feeding of the multitudes. Such literary features as the questioning of whether there is enough bread to feed so many, the feeding of a large group, and the fact that there is "some left over" appear in Matt 14:13–21; Mark 6:30–42; 8:1–21; Luke 9:13–17; and John 6:12–13. Jesus hoped the miracle would demonstrate his power and mercy, which would in turn lead to faith in him. Unfortunately, people merely tended to look for more miracles (Mark 8:12), and even the disciples saw the feedings as temporary relief from hunger instead of evidence of Jesus' limitless provision (Mark 8:14–21). Elisha faced a similar problem, for his miracles helped preserve the faithful but never effected permanent change in the nation. Like Moses, Jesus and Elisha worked miracles that were signs of God's kingdom breaking into history, and both were ignored by all but a remnant of Israel. Still, the remnant did emerge, so their work was not totally in vain.

(5) Elisha Heals Naaman (5:1–27)

1 Now Naaman was commander of the army of the king of Aram. He was a great man in the sight of his master and highly regarded, because through him the LORD had given victory to Aram. He was a valiant soldier, but he had leprosy.

2 Now bands from Aram had gone out and had taken captive a young girl from Israel, and she served Naaman's wife. 3 She said to her mistress, "If only my master would see the prophet who is in Samaria! He would cure him of his leprosy."

4 Naaman went to his master and told him what the girl from Israel had said. 5 "By all means, go," the king of Aram replied. "I will send a letter to the king of Israel." So Naaman left, taking with him ten talents of silver, six thousand shekels of gold and ten sets of clothing. 6 The letter that he took to the king of Israel read: "With this letter I am sending my servant Naaman to you so that you may cure him of his leprosy."

7 As soon as the king of Israel read the letter, he tore his robes and said, "Am I God? Can I kill and bring back to life? Why does this fellow send someone to me to be cured of his leprosy? See how he is trying to pick a quarrel with me!"

8 When Elisha the man of God heard that the king of Israel had torn his robes, he sent him this message: "Why have you torn your robes? Have the man come to

---

[40] Keil, "I and II Kings," 316.

[41] R. L. Hubbard, Jr., *First and Second Kings,* EvBC (Chicago: Moody, 1991) 152.

**me and he will know that there is a prophet in Israel." 9So Naaman went with his
horses and chariots and stopped at the door of Elisha's house. 10Elisha sent a messenger to say to him, "Go, wash yourself seven times in the Jordan, and your flesh
will be restored and you will be cleansed."**

**11But Naaman went away angry and said, "I thought that he would surely
come out to me and stand and call on the name of the LORD his God, wave his
hand over the spot and cure me of my leprosy. 12Are not Abana and Pharpar, the
rivers of Damascus, better than any of the waters of Israel? Couldn't I wash in
them and be cleansed?" So he turned and went off in a rage.**

**13Naaman's servants went to him and said, "My father, if the prophet had told
you to do some great thing, would you not have done it? How much more, then,
when he tells you, 'Wash and be cleansed'!" 14So he went down and dipped himself in the Jordan seven times, as the man of God had told him, and his flesh was
restored and became clean like that of a young boy.**

**15Then Naaman and all his attendants went back to the man of God. He stood
before him and said, "Now I know that there is no God in all the world except in
Israel. Please accept now a gift from your servant."**

**16The prophet answered, "As surely as the LORD lives, whom I serve, I will not
accept a thing." And even though Naaman urged him, he refused.**

**17"If you will not," said Naaman, "please let me, your servant, be given as
much earth as a pair of mules can carry, for your servant will never again make
burnt offerings and sacrifices to any other god but the LORD. 18But may the LORD
forgive your servant for this one thing: When my master enters the temple of Rimmon to bow down and he is leaning on my arm and I bow there also—when I bow
down in the temple of Rimmon, may the LORD forgive your servant for this."**

19"Go in peace," Elisha said.

**After Naaman had traveled some distance, 20Gehazi, the servant of Elisha the
man of God, said to himself, "My master was too easy on Naaman, this Aramean,
by not accepting from him what he brought. As surely as the LORD lives, I will run
after him and get something from him."**

**21So Gehazi hurried after Naaman. When Naaman saw him running toward
him, he got down from the chariot to meet him. "Is everything all right?" he
asked.**

**22"Everything is all right," Gehazi answered. "My master sent me to say, 'Two
young men from the company of the prophets have just come to me from the hill
country of Ephraim. Please give them a talent of silver and two sets of clothing.'"**

**23"By all means, take two talents," said Naaman. He urged Gehazi to accept
them, and then tied up the two talents of silver in two bags, with two sets of clothing. He gave them to two of his servants, and they carried them ahead of Gehazi.
24When Gehazi came to the hill, he took the things from the servants and put
them away in the house. He sent the men away and they left. 25Then he went in
and stood before his master Elisha.**

"Where have you been, Gehazi?" Elisha asked.

"Your servant didn't go anywhere," Gehazi answered.

**26But Elisha said to him, "Was not my spirit with you when the man got down
from his chariot to meet you? Is this the time to take money, or to accept clothes,**

olive groves, vineyards, flocks, herds, or menservants and maidservants? [27]Naaman's leprosy will cling to you and to your descendants forever." Then Gehazi went from Elisha's presence and he was leprous, as white as snow.

Naaman's healing and conversion is one of the best known and most popular stories in 1, 2 Kings. This account may be compared to those in 1 Kings 1–2; 13; and 22 in that it offers a detailed plot that operates on several levels.[42] As many as ten characters or character groups interact with one another to create the undercurrents and subplots that make the plot so compelling.[43] Essential theological themes such as conversion, monotheism, the power of God's word, and the danger of covetousness emerge from the carefully woven story. Few texts in the Old Testament are as fertile ground for teaching, preaching, and personal challenge.

5:1 Naaman, the story's main character, is introduced as a great man who struggles to overcome a physical affliction. He is successful in his military career, for he commands Syria's army, a unit that allows Damascus to dominate the region.[44] His king duly praises him for his work. He exhibits courage. Only one issue mars his life: he is a leper. This leprosy may not have been an extremely advanced type, since he could continue his work;[45] but it was serious enough to him, as the text indicates later.

The author states that the Lord gave Naaman his victories. At first this claim may seem startling because Naaman is not an Israelite. However, 1, 2 Kings emphasize repeatedly God's sovereignty over all nations and all people. The Lord has already laid claim to ownership of Syria's political future (1 Kgs 19:15). Surely he can work on behalf of a Syrian, if only to discipline Israel for idolatry (cf. 2 Kgs 13:3). The Lord also has sent the prophets earlier to non-Israelites (1 Kgs 17:7–24), so it is not surprising for him to deal with Naaman here.

5:2–3 A rather obscure source becomes the key to Naaman's healing. Raiding parties into Israel have provided a servant girl for Naaman's wife. This girl tells her mistress that Naaman could be cured if he would see "the prophet who is in Samaria." Long notes the contrasts between the great man and the maid who helps him:

> She is an Israelite, he is an Aramean; she is a "little maiden" (*naʿărâ qĕtannâ*), he a "great man" (*ʾîš gādôl*); she is a captive servant, he a commander; he has

[42] Cf. B. O. Long, *2 Kings,* FOTL 10 (Grand Rapids: Eerdmans, 1991) 66–77, for a superb analysis of the chapter's plots and subplots.

[43] Note Hobbs, *2 Kings,* 58–62, for an excellent treatment of the author's presentation of the story's characters.

[44] Cf. the historical summary at the beginning of this section for more details about Syria's military prowess during Naaman's era.

[45] Auld, *I and II Kings,* 167.

> fame in the king's estimation, . . . she has none, for she simply "waited upon". . . Naaman's wife (cf. Deut 1:38; 1 Sam 19:7).[46]

Still, she shares the knowledge that her master needs most. Power and glory cannot save Naaman, but this information can.

Perhaps the book's first readers would have noted that the girl in the text is an exile too. Despite her captivity, she is not bitter or unhelpful. Rather, she shares what she knows about the Lord and the prophet out of concern for Naaman and her mistress and desire to see God's glory magnified. In this way she acts like Daniel, Mordecai, Ezra, Nehemiah, and other exiles who care for the spiritual and physical well-being of their conquerors.

5:4–7 Anxious for any possible avenue of healing, Naaman tells his king what the girl has said. Elisha's fame has spread from the lowest rung of society clear to the palace. Syria's king acts the only way he knows—like a king. He writes a letter of introduction and demand,[47] loads Naaman down with gifts, and sends his commander off to be healed. He does not know that true prophets do not work for money, nor are they paid by the king, nor does the king have authority over them. Thus, sending Naaman to Israel's king does Naaman no good.

Israel's king certainly understands the futility of the letter, for he knows he is no healer. He too thinks like a king and suspects that Syria is looking for an excuse to renew old hostilities. He has no idea that deep personal pain and a child's pure motives have caused this trip.

5:8–14 Elisha views Naaman's presence as an opportunity to prove there is a real prophet in Israel, which is the same as saying there is a real God in Israel. Like the servant girl in 5:2–3, he decides to use this difficult situation to help Naaman. His attitude also helps the king of Israel, since Elisha intends to show Naaman that while the monarch does not heal, someone in Israel can cure him.

When the Syrian arrives with his impressive entourage, the prophet does not come to meet him. Instead, he sends a messenger to instruct him to wash seven times in the Jordan if he wants to be healed. Why this aloof approach to the Syrian's problem? Jones suggests Elisha "may have been demonstrating that he was not a wonderworker who expected payment, or else indicating he wished no political involvement with Syria, or again be *[sic]* deliberately testing Naaman's faith."[48] Certainly it is a great test of humble faith and one that Naaman understandably misinterprets as an insult.[49] National pride and per-

---

[46] Long, *2 Kings,* 70.

[47] For an analysis of royal letter writing during this period read J. A. Fitzmyer, "Some Notes on Aramaic Epistolography," *JBL* 93 (1974) 201–25.

[48] Jones, *1 and 2 Kings,* 2:416.

[49] Gray, *1 and 2 Kings,* 454.

sonal expectations of a spectacular, magical display lead the commander to stomp away in rage.

Once again it is Naaman's servants who come to his rescue. They attack their master's pride with common sense.[50] He would do something difficult, they reason, so why not try this rather small possible cure? What can it hurt? Naaman follows their advice and is healed. His quest for healing has been fulfilled.

5:15–19a This text contains one of the great Gentile conversion accounts in the Old Testament. Like Rahab (Josh 2:9–13), Ruth (Ruth 1:16–18), and the sailors and Ninevites in Jonah (Jonah 1:16; 3:6–10), Naaman believes in the Lord. From Gen 12:2–3 onward in the Old Testament, God desires to bless all nations through Israel. This ideal becomes a reality here due to the witness of the Israelite servant girl and the work of the Israelite prophet.

Naaman's conversion includes a confession of faith. He states that no other god exists besides the Lord, a conclusion he draws from the fact that only the Lord can heal him. Hobbs correctly claims that Naaman's confession consists of "words which accord closely with Elisha's words in v 8. Following a major theme of these chapters, Naaman realizes that only in Israel, and through Israel's God, is healing to be found. Following this confession, Naaman's actions support his new-found faith."[51] Sadly, Naaman's confession of faith condemns most Israelites of that era, since they have rejected the one true God and embraced gods that cannot heal. Jesus makes this point while rebuking the people of Nazareth in Luke 4:23–30.

Naaman's conversion also leads to some new commitments on his part. First, he tries to give Elisha a gift, which indicates his gratitude for the human instrument of his healing. The prophet's refusal contrasts sharply with the typical court prophet and also with the actions of Gehazi, Elisha's servant, later in the story.[52] Second, he asks to take dirt home with him, with which he will build an altar to the Lord in his homeland.[53] Montgomery says that transporting "holy" dirt from one place to another was a fairly common ancient custom.[54] This practice is not unlike the modern tendency to take home significant personal souvenirs from the Holy Land.

Third, Naaman requests Elisha's indulgence on one point. He requests that the Lord forgive him for participating in worship of Rimmon when such participation is necessary to carry out his career responsibilities. Rimmon was a Syrian version of Baal. Naaman seems to say that this "worship" will not be real worship, since he has already confessed Yahweh's sole existence and sovereignty. His dilemma is not unlike the one Obadiah faced (cf. 1 Kgs 18:1–15),

---

[50] Long, *2 Kings,* 72.

[51] Hobbs, *2 Kings,* 65.

[52] Wiseman, *1 and 2 Kings,* 208.

[53] Jones, *1 and 2 Kings,* 2:418.

[54] Montgomery and Gehman, *Kings,* 377.

who also felt torn between prophet and king and between Yahweh and Baal. Even in this request, however, Naaman places himself under Elisha's authority and admits Yahweh's importance.

Elisha gives Naaman his blessing. Has the prophet been too lenient? Has Elisha given in to religious accommodationism? Three observations may help provide an answer. First, Keil notes that Naaman simply asks whether or not God will forgive him. He does not ask permission to worship Rimmon.[55] Second, Naaman has stated his opinion of Rimmon and has declared his intention to serve and offer sacrifices to Yahweh. Third, he must create what amounts to a personal outpost of Yahwism in Syria. He can pray, but there is no opportunity for community worship, nor is it likely that he can come back to Israel to worship. Elisha understands these realities and lays no more guilt on Naaman than Elijah did on Obadiah. Again, his commitment to the Lord is already greater than all but a remnant of the faithful.

5:19b–27 Gehazi certainly thinks Elisha has been too lenient, but he focuses on financial, not spiritual, leniency. He determines to get some of the goods "this Syrian" brought as a gift for Elisha. In this way he shows himself as greedy as Elisha is unaffected by wealth. Further, his greed contrasts the generosity shown by Naaman, who is "the humble and charitable healed one, who still, it develops, wishes to reward his benefactor."[56] Gehazi, on the other hand, appears "opportunistic and duplicitous, grasping at those outpourings of gratitude which a principled Elisha has refused."[57] When he catches up to Naaman, Gehazi lies to get silver and clothing, then stashes the loot before he sees his master.

Elisha confronts Gehazi by asking where he has been. Once more Gehazi lies, but this time he has lied to a man who knows he has lied. After reminding Gehazi of his special spirit, he rebukes him for accepting money for a healing ministry. Then Elisha pronounces a strict judgment. Gehazi will inherit Naaman's leprosy, just as Naaman seems to have inherited Gehazi's faith. One man goes away healed because of his obedience, while the other man, indeed the one who should have known what matters most, walks away with leprosy. Yet another Israelite has made the tragic mistake of choosing a substitute for the Lord, while a Gentile convert has discovered that what his servant girl said about the Lord's prophet is true.

(6) Elisha Makes an Axhead Float (6:1–7)

[1]The company of the prophets said to Elisha, "Look, the place where we meet with you is too small for us. [2]Let us go to the Jordan, where each of us can get a

[55] Keil, "I and II Kings," 321.
[56] Long, *2 Kings,* 74.
[57] Ibid.

pole; and let us build a place there for us to live."

And he said, "Go."

[3]Then one of them said, "Won't you please come with your servants?"

"I will," Elisha replied. [4]And he went with them.

They went to the Jordan and began to cut down trees. [5]As one of them was cutting down a tree, the iron axhead fell into the water. "Oh, my lord," he cried out, "it was borrowed!"

[6]The man of God asked, "Where did it fall?" When he showed him the place, Elisha cut a stick and threw it there, and made the iron float. [7]"Lift it out," he said. Then the man reached out his hand and took it.

6:1–7 Elisha's next miracle parallels the multiplying of the oil (2 Kgs 4:1–7), the curing of the stew (2 Kgs 4:38–41), and the feeding of one hundred (2 Kgs 4:42–44). Each of these stories portrays Elisha saving the prophets or the prophets' families from physical want or financial disaster. His miraculous powers help him to be the perfect "master" in these crisis situations.

Due to lack of space the company of the prophets decide to build a larger home. Wilson states that this building project, coupled with earlier texts, indicates that the company of the prophets lived together, ate together, and worked together yet maintained a separate family life.[58] During the community effort to build, one of the prophets loses an axhead in the Jordan River. This prophet bemoans the accident since "iron was expensive in Bible times, and the student-prophet was very poor."[59] Elisha removes the almost certain debt by making the axhead float. The text clearly presents the event as a miracle rather than as Elisha's ability to insert a stick into the axhead or to move the iron to shallower water.[60]

(7) Elisha Traps Syria's Army (6:8–23)

[8]Now the king of Aram was at war with Israel. After conferring with his officers, he said, "I will set up my camp in such and such a place."

[9]The man of God sent word to the king of Israel: "Beware of passing that place, because the Arameans are going down there." [10]So the king of Israel checked on the place indicated by the man of God. Time and again Elisha warned the king, so that he was on his guard in such places.

[11]This enraged the king of Aram. He summoned his officers and demanded of them, "Will you not tell me which of us is on the side of the king of Israel?"

[12]"None of us, my lord the king," said one of his officers, "but Elisha, the prophet who is in Israel, tells the king of Israel the very words you speak in your bedroom."

---

[58] Wilson, *Prophecy and Society,* 140–41.

[59] Hubbard, *First and Second Kings,* 157.

[60] Cf. Jones, *1 and 2 Kings,* 2:418, and Honeycutt, "2 Kings," 242, for variations of this type of explanation of the event. For further discussion of miracles in Kings see the comments at 1 Kgs 17:7–24.

[13]"Go, find out where he is," the king ordered, "so I can send men and capture him." The report came back: "He is in Dothan." [14]Then he sent horses and chariots and a strong force there. They went by night and surrounded the city.

[15]When the servant of the man of God got up and went out early the next morning, an army with horses and chariots had surrounded the city. "Oh, my lord, what shall we do?" the servant asked.

[16]"Don't be afraid," the prophet answered. "Those who are with us are more than those who are with them."

[17]And Elisha prayed, "O LORD, open his eyes so he may see." Then the LORD opened the servant's eyes, and he looked and saw the hills full of horses and chariots of fire all around Elisha.

[18]As the enemy came down toward him, Elisha prayed to the LORD, "Strike these people with blindness." So he struck them with blindness, as Elisha had asked.

[19]Elisha told them, "This is not the road and this is not the city. Follow me, and I will lead you to the man you are looking for." And he led them to Samaria.

[20]After they entered the city, Elisha said, "LORD, open the eyes of these men so they can see." Then the LORD opened their eyes and they looked, and there they were, inside Samaria.

[21]When the king of Israel saw them, he asked Elisha, "Shall I kill them, my father? Shall I kill them?"

[22]"Do not kill them," he answered. "Would you kill men you have captured with your own sword or bow? Set food and water before them so that they may eat and drink and then go back to their master." [23]So he prepared a great feast for them, and after they had finished eating and drinking, he sent them away, and they returned to their master. So the bands from Aram stopped raiding Israel's territory.

6:8–10 Just as Elisha saves the prophets physically and financially in several accounts, he now saves Israel's king and people in the next few stories. For some unstated reason, Syria once again makes war with Israel, this time by sending a series of raiding parties across the border.[61] Unfortunately for the Syrians, Elisha discerns where their armies will strike and tells Israel's king, which spoils all of Syria's plans. Elisha is Israel's best line of defense.

6:11–14 Syria's king draws the logical conclusion that he has a traitor in his court. Someone in his army must be divulging his movements. His officers explain that Elisha is the culprit, however, so he dispatches soldiers to Dothan, where the prophet is living. This expedition marks yet another vain attempt by a monarch to silence prophecy. Elijah withstood such threats (cf. 1 Kgs 17:1–24; 18:1–15; 19:1–18; 2 Kgs 1:1–15), and now Elisha must do so. Will God continue to protect his messenger?

6:15–23 When Elisha and his servant awake, they discover the city surrounded by Syrians. Like any "normal" person, the servant is afraid, but the

---

[61] Cf. Hubbard, *First and Second Kings,* 158.

prophet commands him to stay calm. Why? Because, he claims, their army is more numerous and powerful than the Syrian forces. After Elisha prays that his servant may see these "soldiers," the man indeed views "the hills full of horses and chariots of fire." At this point the Lord is defending Elisha from death by the same instrument with which Elijah was protected from death and taken to heaven. Such awareness of God's power must have soothed the servant's shattered nerves.

Not content with protection for himself, Elisha provides safety for all Israel. God strikes the Syrian army with blindness at Elisha's request, thus allowing the prophet to lead them to Samaria, about twelve miles north of Dothan.[62] Though Israel's king could exterminate these troops, Elisha counsels leniency, so the Israelites feed the Syrians and send them home, obviously humbled. In effect, then, Elisha brings peace through divine intervention. Everyone concerned receives safety from their enemies because of the prophet's ministry. Again Elisha aids those in distress over "small" matters, such as a lost axhead, and those concerned with larger, societal issues such as war.

3. Elisha Predicts a Siege's End (6:24–7:20)

This story is one of the most detailed accounts in the Elisha sections of 1, 2 Kings. It breaks with the material that comes immediately before it since it relates no miracle. Elisha himself goes beyond his prediction of Israel's deliverance from a Syrian siege. Still, this account maintains contact with the preceding episodes on the Israel-Syria conflict. It also offers an accurate prediction of the future as Jehu, Elijah, and Micaiah do before him and continues to portray Israel's kings as men who have little patience with the prophets and their message. This text also furthers the author's emphasis on how God uses Elisha to protect Israel in daily life and in battle. It integrates characters and plot tension in a way that creates suspense, sympathy, and anger. Thus the story not only presents Elisha at his best, but it also reveals the book's author at the height of his powers.

(1) The Siege and Its Effects (6:24–33)

24Some time later, Ben-Hadad king of Aram mobilized his entire army and marched up and laid siege to Samaria. 25There was a great famine in the city; the siege lasted so long that a donkey's head sold for eighty shekels of silver, and a quarter of a cab of seed pods for five shekels.

26As the king of Israel was passing by on the wall, a woman cried to him, "Help me, my lord the king!"

27The king replied, "If the LORD does not help you, where can I get help for

[62] Keil, "I and II Kings," 325; and Wiseman, *1 and 2 Kings,* 210.

you? From the threshing floor? From the winepress?" [28]Then he asked her, "What's the matter?"

She answered, "This woman said to me, 'Give up your son so we may eat him today, and tomorrow we'll eat my son.' [29]So we cooked my son and ate him. The next day I said to her, 'Give up your son so we may eat him,' but she had hidden him."

[30]When the king heard the woman's words, he tore his robes. As he went along the wall, the people looked, and there, underneath, he had sackcloth on his body. [31]He said, "May God deal with me, be it ever so severely, if the head of Elisha son of Shaphat remains on his shoulders today!"

[32]Now Elisha was sitting in his house, and the elders were sitting with him. The king sent a messenger ahead, but before he arrived, Elisha said to the elders, "Don't you see how this murderer is sending someone to cut off my head? Look, when the messenger comes, shut the door and hold it shut against him. Is not the sound of his master's footsteps behind him?"

[33]While he was still talking to them, the messenger came down to him. And [the king] said, "This disaster is from the LORD. Why should I wait for the LORD any longer?"

6:24–25 After an unspecified amount of time has passed, Ben-Hadad mounts yet another attack on Israel. This time the Syrians besiege Samaria itself rather than simply raiding chosen towns as in 2 Kgs 6:8–10.[63] The siege is so effective that Samaria's inhabitants are reduced to paying high prices for nonsavory items like a donkey's head or a few beans. It seems unlikely that the city can hold out much longer.

6:26–33 Just how desperate Samaria's citizens have gotten becomes apparent when two mothers approach Israel's king with a problem. Their dilemma is quite like the one brought to Solomon in 1 Kgs 3:16–28, for it involves two mothers, two sons, one of which has died and one of which is still living, and the future of the living child. In a cruel twist of the Solomon story, though, the mothers have agreed to eat their children; but one woman has broken the pact. The dead boy's mother wants the king to make the other woman keep her word. Syria's siege has led to the worst sort of atrocities.

The king blames Elisha for the siege, perhaps reasoning that Syria still wants to eliminate the prophet. Ironically, the king seems to forget how Elisha protected Israel from the Syrians in those instances. He is now acting toward Elisha the way Ahab acted toward Elijah (cf. 1 Kgs 18:1–15). He considers his chief asset a liability, his best friend an enemy, and swears to have the prophet killed.

Meanwhile, Elisha sits in his home, speaking with the city's leaders.[64] Gray thinks the leaders' presence in Elisha's home indicates their opposition to the

---

[63] Cf. Gray, *1 and 2 Kings,* 470.

[64] Samaria's "elders" were the respected leaders of that society. Cf. Ezek 20:1, etc.

king,[65] but Hobbs probably is right to infer rather that these men held Elisha in high regard.[66] Elisha instructs the visitors to lock the door to bar the king's assassin, but the man arrives too quickly. Once in Elisha's presence, however, the messenger does nothing. The author concludes this portion of the episode by noting the king now believes that the Lord has caused their problems, so there is no need to allow the Lord's prophet to live. Why not simply kill Elisha or turn him over to the Syrians and hope the enemy will leave?

(2) Elisha Predicts the Siege's End (7:1–2)

[1]Elisha said, "Hear the word of the LORD. This is what the LORD says: About this time tomorrow, a seah of flour will sell for a shekel and two seahs of barley for a shekel at the gate of Samaria."

[2]The officer on whose arm the king was leaning said to the man of God, "Look, even if the LORD should open the floodgates of the heavens, could this happen?"

"You will see it with your own eyes," answered Elisha, "but you will not eat any of it!"

7:1–2 Elisha makes two predictions about the lifting of the siege. First, he promises that food will be cheap and plentiful by the next day. This prediction seems incredible in light of their situation and suffering. Second, when the king's messenger doubts Elisha's word (reassuring that even an immediate rainfall would not solve their problems that fast; cf. Gen 7:11; 8:2), the prophet predicts that the man will see the plentiful food yet will not eat any of it. Eyes of faith reassured Elisha's servant in 2 Kgs 6:16–17, while here doubt will close the messenger's eyes in death before he can be rescued from hunger.

(3) The Siege Is Lifted (7:3–20)

[3]Now there were four men with leprosy at the entrance of the city gate. They said to each other, "Why stay here until we die? [4]If we say, 'We'll go into the city'—the famine is there, and we will die. And if we stay here, we will die. So let's go over to the camp of the Arameans and surrender. If they spare us, we live; if they kill us, then we die."

[5]At dusk they got up and went to the camp of the Arameans. When they reached the edge of the camp, not a man was there, [6]for the LORD had caused the Arameans to hear the sound of chariots and horses and a great army, so that they said to one another, "Look, the king of Israel has hired the Hittite and Egyptian kings to attack us!" [7]So they got up and fled in the dusk and abandoned their tents and their horses and donkeys. They left the camp as it was and ran for their lives.

[8]The men who had leprosy reached the edge of the camp and entered one of the tents. They ate and drank, and carried away silver, gold and clothes, and went off

---

[65] Gray, *1 and 2 Kings,* 471–72.

[66] Hobbs, *2 Kings,* 80.

and hid them. They returned and entered another tent and took some things from it and hid them also.

9Then they said to each other, "We're not doing right. This is a day of good news and we are keeping it to ourselves. If we wait until daylight, punishment will overtake us. Let's go at once and report this to the royal palace."

10So they went and called out to the city gatekeepers and told them, "We went into the Aramean camp and not a man was there—not a sound of anyone—only tethered horses and donkeys, and the tents left just as they were." 11The gatekeepers shouted the news, and it was reported within the palace.

12The king got up in the night and said to his officers, "I will tell you what the Arameans have done to us. They know we are starving; so they have left the camp to hide in the countryside, thinking, 'They will surely come out, and then we will take them alive and get into the city.'"

13One of his officers answered, "Have some men take five of the horses that are left in the city. Their plight will be like that of all the Israelites left here—yes, they will only be like all these Israelites who are doomed. So let us send them to find out what happened."

14So they selected two chariots with their horses, and the king sent them after the Aramean army. He commanded the drivers, "Go and find out what has happened." 15They followed them as far as the Jordan, and they found the whole road strewn with the clothing and equipment the Arameans had thrown away in their headlong flight. So the messengers returned and reported to the king. 16Then the people went out and plundered the camp of the Arameans. So a seah of flour sold for a shekel, and two seahs of barley sold for a shekel, as the LORD had said.

17Now the king had put the officer on whose arm he leaned in charge of the gate, and the people trampled him in the gateway, and he died, just as the man of God had foretold when the king came down to his house. 18It happened as the man of God had said to the king: "About this time tomorrow, a seah of flour will sell for a shekel and two seahs of barley for a shekel at the gate of Samaria."

19The officer had said to the man of God, "Look, even if the LORD should open the floodgates of the heavens, could this happen?" The man of God had replied, "You will see it with your own eyes, but you will not eat any of it!" 20And that is exactly what happened to him, for the people trampled him in the gateway, and he died.

7:3–11 Four lepers with nothing to lose become the first to enjoy the fulfillment of Elisha's prophecy. As lepers they had to live outside the city (Lev 13:46), but they stayed near the gate to beg for food. Ironically, just as the once-leprous Naaman led Syria to many victories over Israel, so now these lepers will lead Israel's looting of Syria's army. These men reason that the Syrians will kill them if the siege is effective, so they decide to cast themselves on the enemy's mercy. They will be no worse off no matter what happens.

When the lepers reach the edge of the Syrian camp, they discover the enemy has gone. God caused them to hear yet another unseen army (cf. 2 Kgs 6:17), which led them to retreat without taking their possessions. Not believing their good fortune, the lepers eat their fill, plunder the camp like a great four-man leprous army, and generally enjoy themselves. Eventually they feel they must share the good news or invite punishment, however, so they go back and report. This whole scene provides a delightful counterpart to the grim episode in 2 Kgs 6:24–33.[67]

7:12–16 The king finds it hard to believe this quartet of lepers. He reasons that the Syrians are attempting to lure the Israelites out of the city so they can kill them, "a tactic similar to that employed by his ancestors at Ai (Josh 8:3–28)."[68] One of the officers suggests they send a few horses and men out as decoys to see if the Syrians have indeed left. Like the lepers, he comments that if the men stay in the city they will die anyway, so they may as well test the king's theory.[69] When they do, the lepers' word proves true. The city plunders the enemy camp, and food does become cheap, just as Elisha predicted it would.

7:17–20 Elisha's second promise also comes to pass. The officer who doubted the prophet's word in 7:2 is crushed to death by the hungry mob that pours out of the city gate. His death stands as a testimony of the truthfulness of God's word through the prophet. It also reminds the book's readers to believe God's word, hope in God's provision, and count on God's deliverance.

4. Elisha's Political Influence (8:1–9:13)

Elisha wields as much political influence as any biblical prophet. Not only does he prod Israel's kings to do what is right, but he is also the person the Lord uses to determine who those kings will be. Further, in this section of the book he even determines who will rule *Syria*. Finally, it is Elisha who instigates Jehu's reform by sending a messenger to anoint Jehu king. Of course, he has already had a major impact on Israel's relationship with the Syrians (cf. 2 Kgs 5–7). Each episode in this section furthers the Lord's rule. God rules the prophets, the people, the kings, and the political process here, which clearly indicates his power and sovereignty.

(1) Elisha Helps Restore Land (8:1–6)

[1]Now Elisha had said to the woman whose son he had restored to life, "Go away with your family and stay for a while wherever you can, because the LORD has decreed a famine in the land that will last seven years." [2]The woman proceeded to do as the man of God said. She and her family went away and stayed in the land of the Philistines seven years.

---

[67] See Long, *2 Kings,* 93–94, for an insightful discussion of the contrast between the two stories.

[68] Wiseman, *1 and 2 Kings,* 212.

[69] In v. 13 virtually all of the ancient translations omit as a dittography the words "left here—yes, they will only be like all the Israelites" (NIV), so that the sentence reads: "Their plight will be like that of all the Israelites who are doomed." Cf. C. F. Burney, *Notes on the Hebrew Text of the Book of Kings* (Oxford: Clarendon Press, 1903) 292.

[3]At the end of the seven years she came back from the land of the Philistines and went to the king to beg for her house and land. [4]The king was talking to Gehazi, the servant of the man of God, and had said, "Tell me about all the great things Elisha has done." [5]Just as Gehazi was telling the king how Elisha had restored the dead to life, the woman whose son Elisha had brought back to life came to beg the king for her house and land.

Gehazi said, "This is the woman, my lord the king, and this is her son whom Elisha restored to life." [6]The king asked the woman about it, and she told him.

Then he assigned an official to her case and said to him, "Give back everything that belonged to her, including all the income from her land from the day she left the country until now."

8:1–2 Once again the author focuses on God's care for the poor, the widow, and the orphan. The woman whom Elisha helped in 2 Kgs 4:8–37 reappears. Acting on the prophet's advice, she spends seven years in Philistia in order to avoid a famine. This time away spares her the pain of famine, but it leaves her with no claim to her land and perhaps without her husband, who may have died since he was mentioned in 2 Kgs 4:8–37 but not here. G. H. Jones explains that "property left temporarily was taken over by the crown and was held in trust until reclaimed by the legal owner" (cf. Exod 21:2; 23:10ff.; Deut 15:1ff.).[70]

This situation would have been even more complicated, however, if her husband had died. In many ways, then, her situation parallels that of Naomi and Ruth. She has fled a famine, lost her main male supporter, and seems to be at the mercy of the political system.[71]

8:3–6 In a happy "coincidence" the king sits chatting with Gehazi about what Elisha did for the woman's son at the very moment she arrives with her request.[72] When she verifies the incident, the king orders an official to settle her case and restores whatever income may have been gleaned from it during the difficult years of her absence. Elisha does not even have to appear in order to help her. His very reputation and Gehazi's witness are enough to restore her financial security, and this restoration validates his advice about leaving the country in the first place.

(2) Elisha Predicts Syria's New King (8:7–15)

[7]Elisha went to Damascus, and Ben-Hadad king of Aram was ill. When the king was told, "The man of God has come all the way up here," [8]he said to Hazael, "Take a gift with you and go to meet the man of God. Consult the LORD through him; ask him, 'Will I recover from this illness?'"

---

[70] Jones, *1 and 2 Kings,* 2:440.

[71] Cf. Auld, *I and II Kings,* 178.

[72] This scene is either a "throwback" to Gehazi's preleprosy days or his leprosy was, like Naaman's, a type that did not require him to remove himself from society.

[9]Hazael went to meet Elisha, taking with him as a gift forty camel-loads of all the finest wares of Damascus. He went in and stood before him, and said, "Your son Ben-Hadad king of Aram has sent me to ask, 'Will I recover from this illness?'"

[10]Elisha answered, "Go and say to him, 'You will certainly recover'; but the LORD has revealed to me that he will in fact die." [11]He stared at him with a fixed gaze until Hazael felt ashamed. Then the man of God began to weep.

[12]"Why is my lord weeping?" asked Hazael.

"Because I know the harm you will do to the Israelites," he answered. "You will set fire to their fortified places, kill their young men with the sword, dash their little children to the ground, and rip open their pregnant women."

[13]Hazael said, "How could your servant, a mere dog, accomplish such a feat?"

"The LORD has shown me that you will become king of Aram," answered Elisha.

[14]Then Hazael left Elisha and returned to his master. When Ben-Hadad asked, "What did Elisha say to you?" Hazael replied, "He told me that you would certainly recover." [15]But the next day he took a thick cloth, soaked it in water and spread it over the king's face, so that he died. Then Hazael succeeded him as king.

8:7–8 For some unstated reason Elisha goes to Damascus (cf. 1 Kgs 19:15) and while there has the opportunity to predict who will be Syria's next king and what sort of person he will be. The long-lived Ben-Hadad has fallen ill. He is now an old man, for he has ruled Syria for nearly forty years,[73] but he still wants to know if he will recover. Thus, he sends Hazael, one of his lieutenants, to ask Elisha about the future. Unlike Ahaziah in 2 Kgs 1:1–18, Syria's king seems aware that the Lord's prophet is superior to any other prophetic "competitors."

8:9–13 Hazael receives more information than he expects. Like Naaman, he comes bearing gifts for the man of God, only to discover that this prophet cannot be bought or bribed. At first the message seems strange. He directs Hazael to tell Ben-Hadad that he will recover when, in fact, he knows he will die. The confusing message becomes clearer, however, when Elisha discloses Hazael's true nature. He will kill and maim Israelites *when* he becomes king, and the text reveals he will kill *to* become king. Therefore, the truth is that Ben-Hadad *could* recover yet will not because Hazael will kill him and take his place.

8:14–15 Hazael acts just as Elisha expects. He places a wet cloth, perhaps one used for a mosquito net,[74] over the king's face and suffocates him. The murderer probably replaced the cloth, which made the death seem a natural

[73] This interpretation of events follows the scheme in Bright, *A History of Israel,* 253. Other scholars, including Jones (*1 and 2 Kings,* 2:442–43) and Wiseman (*1 & 2 Kings,* 213), argue that Hadadeser is the king featured in this text, whose throne name was Ben-Hadad.

[74] Gray, *1 and 2 Kings,* 479.

one.[75] Just how or why Hazael was able to seize power is not clear, but his ability to do so continues Elijah's life work (cf. 1 Kgs 19:15), vindicates Elisha's prediction, and reinforces the Lord's authority over all nations.

As Montgomery and Gehman note, Assyrian records confirm that Hazael did control Syria by 842 B.C. and that he is called "a son of a nobody."[76] In other words, he was known as a usurper.[77] Hazael rules from about 842 to 806 B.C. and, despite some setbacks at the hands of Assyria, manages to wield serious military influence in his region.[78] Israel is forced to yield to him throughout his reign.

(3) Jehoram's and Ahaziah's Reigns (8:16–29)

16In the fifth year of Joram son of Ahab king of Israel, when Jehoshaphat was king of Judah, Jehoram son of Jehoshaphat began his reign as king of Judah. 17He was thirty-two years old when he became king, and he reigned in Jerusalem eight years. 18He walked in the ways of the kings of Israel, as the house of Ahab had done, for he married a daughter of Ahab. He did evil in the eyes of the LORD. 19Nevertheless, for the sake of his servant David, the LORD was not willing to destroy Judah. He had promised to maintain a lamp for David and his descendants forever.

20In the time of Jehoram, Edom rebelled against Judah and set up its own king. 21So Jehoram went to Zair with all his chariots. The Edomites surrounded him and his chariot commanders, but he rose up and broke through by night; his army, however, fled back home. 22To this day Edom has been in rebellion against Judah. Libnah revolted at the same time.

23As for the other events of Jehoram's reign, and all he did, are they not written in the book of the annals of the kings of Judah? 24Jehoram rested with his fathers and was buried with them in the City of David. And Ahaziah his son succeeded him as king.

25In the twelfth year of Joram son of Ahab king of Israel, Ahaziah son of Jehoram king of Judah began to reign. 26Ahaziah was twenty-two years old when he became king, and he reigned in Jerusalem one year. His mother's name was Athaliah, a granddaughter of Omri king of Israel. 27He walked in the ways of the house of Ahab and did evil in the eyes of the LORD, as the house of Ahab had done, for he was related by marriage to Ahab's family.

28Ahaziah went with Joram son of Ahab to war against Hazael king of Aram at Ramoth Gilead. The Arameans wounded Joram; 29so King Joram returned to Jezreel to recover from the wounds the Arameans had inflicted on him at Ramoth in his battle with Hazael king of Aram.

Then Ahaziah son of Jehoram king of Judah went down to Jezreel to see Joram son of Ahab, because he had been wounded.

---

[75] Jones, *1 and 2 Kings,* 2:445.

[76] Montgomery and Gehman, *Kings,* 392.

[77] Cf. Gray, *1 and 2 Kings,* 479; Jones, *1 and 2 Kings,* 2:445.

[78] Bright, *A History of Israel,* 254–56.

8:16–24 After not using the formula for the rise and death of kings since 2 Kgs 1:17–18, the author now turns to the data about Joram, Jehoram, and Ahaziah. The reason for the return to the earlier format is so the stage can be set for political intrigue, religious cleansing, and social upheaval.[79] Syria's usurping ruler will soon be joined by Jehu, a usurper who, like Hazael, was revealed in God's instructions to Elijah in 1 Kgs 19:15–17. This Jehu will strike a great, temporary blow against Baalism, which is another reason the author focuses on those Jehu kills.

Jehoram's eight-year reign (ca. 848–841 B.C.)[80] is characterized by three comments. First, he sins as did Ahab's house, primarily because he marries Ahab's daughter, Athaliah (cf. 2 Kgs 8:26), a woman who becomes quite important later in the story. Second, the writer claims that Yahweh only permits Jehoram and Judah to survive "for the sake of his servant David." This conclusion echoes sentiments already expressed in the text (cf. 1 Kgs 11:34–39; 15:3–5; cf. 2 Chr 21:4,10). Third, Jehoram is unable to put down an Edomite revolt and just manages to escape with his life. Like Israel's loss of its Moabite vassal (2 Kgs 3:1–27), this humiliation at the hands of the Edomites demonstrates how weak Judah has become since the glory days of David and Solomon.

8:25–29 Ahaziah succeeds his father in about 841 B.C. Chronicles explains that he was the youngest son but that all his older brothers had been killed (2 Chr 22:1). Four items highlight his reign. First, his mother is Athaliah, the daughter of Ahab (2 Kgs 8:18) and granddaughter of Omri. This second reference to Athaliah prepares the reader for her prominence in 2 Kgs 11:16. Second, Ahaziah acts like the house of Ahab because he is "related by marriage to Ahab's family." According to 2 Chr 22:3 his mother "encouraged him in doing wrong." Third, because of the family ties (2 Chr 22:4–5) he fights Syria alongside Joram of Israel. Fourth, he visits Joram when the Israelite king returns to Samaria to recover from wounds received while fighting Syria. This final item places Joram and Ahaziah at the same place at the same time, a fact that will matter a great deal in the next chapter.

(4) Elisha Anoints Jehu King (9:1–13)

1 The prophet Elisha summoned a man from the company of the prophets and said to him, "Tuck your cloak into your belt, take this flask of oil with you and go to Ramoth Gilead. 2 When you get there, look for Jehu son of Jehoshaphat, the son of Nimshi. Go to him, get him away from his companions and take him into an

---

[79] Honeycutt, "2 Kings," 246.

[80] E. R. Thiele states that the eight years counted are separate from a five-year coregency with Jehoshaphat (*The Mysterious Numbers of the Hebrew Kings,* 3d ed. [Grand Rapids: Zondervan, 1983] 99–101). For more details on the length of Jehoram's reign see this commentary's discussion of 2 Kgs 1:17 and 3:1.

**inner room. [3]Then take the flask and pour the oil on his head and declare, 'This is
what the LORD says: I anoint you king over Israel.' Then open the door and run;
don't delay!"**

**[4]So the young man, the prophet, went to Ramoth Gilead. [5]When he arrived, he
found the army officers sitting together. "I have a message for you, commander,"
he said.**

"For which of us?" asked Jehu.

"For you, commander," he replied.

**[6]Jehu got up and went into the house. Then the prophet poured the oil on
Jehu's head and declared, "This is what the LORD, the God of Israel, says: 'I
anoint you king over the LORD's people Israel. [7]You are to destroy the house of
Ahab your master, and I will avenge the blood of my servants the prophets and the
blood of all the LORD's servants shed by Jezebel. [8]The whole house of Ahab will
perish. I will cut off from Ahab every last male in Israel—slave or free. [9]I will
make the house of Ahab like the house of Jeroboam son of Nebat and like the
house of Baasha son of Ahijah. [10]As for Jezebel, dogs will devour her on the plot of
ground at Jezreel, and no one will bury her.'" Then he opened the door and ran.**

**[11]When Jehu went out to his fellow officers, one of them asked him, "Is every-
thing all right? Why did this madman come to you?"**

"You know the man and the sort of things he says," Jehu replied.

[12]"That's not true!" they said. "Tell us."

**Jehu said, "Here is what he told me: 'This is what the LORD says: I anoint you
king over Israel.'"**

**[13]They hurried and took their cloaks and spread them under him on the bare
steps. Then they blew the trumpet and shouted, "Jehu is king!"**

9:1–3 When Elijah departed the earth, he left a few things undone that Elisha had to finish. In 1 Kgs 19:15–17 the Lord tells Elijah to anoint Elisha to take his place (which he does in 1 Kgs 19:19–21), to anoint Hazael king of Syria (which *Elisha* does in 2 Kgs 8:7–15), and to anoint Jehu king over Israel (which has not yet been done). Further, Elijah predicts Ahab and Jezebel will die in certain ways because of their part in the Naboth incident, and Ahab's lineage will be obliterated (1 Kgs 21:17–24). Ahab has indeed perished in the prescribed manner (cf. 22:37–38), but Jezebel is still alive, and Ahab's lineage remains. Thus, Jehu must still become king, Jezebel must die, and Ahab's descendants must perish.

This section places Jehu in power, while a later account will complete the Jezebel story. Jehu's rise to power begins with no warning beyond the Lord's command to Elijah in 1 Kgs 19:15–17. Elisha summons one of the prophets and sends him on the rather difficult mission of anointing Jehu king over Israel. This mission appears to be dangerous, for Elisha instructs the prophet/messenger to run as soon as he anoints Jehu. Just why Elisha does not go himself is left unstated, but perhaps his presence would be too conspicuous.

9:4–10 The young prophet obediently travels to Jehu's camp in Ramoth Gilead. He identifies Jehu in a group of officers, despite the fact they have never met.[81] Perhaps this detail indicates some prophetic power. Jehu takes the prophet to a private place, where the messenger anoints him. Instead of running as soon as he declares him king, as Elisha has instructed him, the anointer tells Jehu that his rise to power will occur so that Elijah's predictions about Ahab's lineage and about Jezebel can come true. Indeed, this language in 9:10 sounds very much like 1 Kgs 21:23.[82] When he finishes this brief speech, the prophet exits, leaving Jehu to work out the details of the reform he will lead.

9:11–13 What has been done in secret now moves quickly into the public arena.[83] Jehu's "fellow officers" anxiously inquire about the prophet's message. Such an odd visitation could easily have disrupted the camp and troubled the soldiers.[84] At first Jehu dodges their question by calling the messenger a madman. Pressed for an answer, Jehu tells all and receives immediate, enthusiastic support. At least a certain segment of the military wants him to overthrow Joram. He is declared king, but he has much to do for the proclamation to be more than wasted breath.

For now Elisha fades from the scene. He will emerge again later, but the bulk of his work the author chooses to describe is over. Elisha has protected the company of the prophets, the widow and her family, and even the nation itself. He has modeled the Lord's grace by healing Naaman and has convinced Naaman that there are no other gods. Elisha has demonstrated the Lord's sovereignty over political affairs in Judah, Israel, and Syria. He has concluded the ministry of his mentor, Elijah. Without question he has proved a more-than-worthy successor to his master.

5. Jehu's Purge (9:14–10:35)

Few events in the history of the divided kingdom are as momentous as Jehu's purge of the political and religious leaders of Israel and Judah. This coup punishes Ahab's family for its idolatry and also effectively strips both nations of viable leadership, thus creating an unprecedented power vacuum. Neither country rebounds from the assassinations very quickly. Jehu's killings exceed reform and become atrocities, however, a fact Hos 1:4–5 makes clear. Eventually, Jehu becomes very much like those he replaces, which makes him more of a political opportunist than a catalyst for change.

(1) Jehu Kills Joram and Ahaziah (9:14–29)

[14]So Jehu son of Jehoshaphat, the son of Nimshi, conspired against Joram.

[81] Cogan and Tadmor, *II Kings*, 106.

[82] For a study of the relationship between this prophetic comment and the prediction in 1 Kgs 21:17–24, see H. N. Wallace, "The Oracles against the Israelite Dynasties in 1 and 2 Kings," *Bib* 67/1 (1986) 32.

[83] Long, *2 Kings*, 119.

[84] Cogan and Tadmor, *II Kings,* 108.

(Now Joram and all Israel had been defending Ramoth Gilead against Hazael king of Aram, 15but King Joram had returned to Jezreel to recover from the wounds the Arameans had inflicted on him in the battle with Hazael king of Aram.) Jehu said, "If this is the way you feel, don't let anyone slip out of the city to go and tell the news in Jezreel." 16Then he got into his chariot and rode to Jezreel, because Joram was resting there and Ahaziah king of Judah had gone down to see him.

17When the lookout standing on the tower in Jezreel saw Jehu's troops approaching, he called out, "I see some troops coming."

"Get a horseman," Joram ordered. "Send him to meet them and ask, 'Do you come in peace?'"

18The horseman rode off to meet Jehu and said, "This is what the king says: 'Do you come in peace?'"

"What do you have to do with peace?" Jehu replied. "Fall in behind me."

The lookout reported, "The messenger has reached them, but he isn't coming back."

19So the king sent out a second horseman. When he came to them he said, "This is what the king says: 'Do you come in peace?'"

Jehu replied, "What do you have to do with peace? Fall in behind me."

20The lookout reported, "He has reached them, but he isn't coming back either. The driving is like that of Jehu son of Nimshi—he drives like a madman."

21"Hitch up my chariot," Joram ordered. And when it was hitched up, Joram king of Israel and Ahaziah king of Judah rode out, each in his own chariot, to meet Jehu. They met him at the plot of ground that had belonged to Naboth the Jezreelite. 22When Joram saw Jehu he asked, "Have you come in peace, Jehu?"

"How can there be peace," Jehu replied, "as long as all the idolatry and witchcraft of your mother Jezebel abound?"

23Joram turned about and fled, calling out to Ahaziah, "Treachery, Ahaziah!"

24Then Jehu drew his bow and shot Joram between the shoulders. The arrow pierced his heart and he slumped down in his chariot. 25Jehu said to Bidkar, his chariot officer, "Pick him up and throw him on the field that belonged to Naboth the Jezreelite. Remember how you and I were riding together in chariots behind Ahab his father when the LORD made this prophecy about him: 26'Yesterday I saw the blood of Naboth and the blood of his sons, declares the LORD, and I will surely make you pay for it on this plot of ground, declares the LORD.' Now then, pick him up and throw him on that plot, in accordance with the word of the LORD."

27When Ahaziah king of Judah saw what had happened, he fled up the road to Beth Haggan. Jehu chased him, shouting, "Kill him too!" They wounded him in his chariot on the way up to Gur near Ibleam, but he escaped to Megiddo and died there. 28His servants took him by chariot to Jerusalem and buried him with his fathers in his tomb in the City of David. 29(In the eleventh year of Joram son of Ahab, Ahaziah had become king of Judah.)

9:14–16 Now the actual conspiracy to overthrow Joram is about to begin, so the author sets the stage. The king had been in Ramoth Gilead, a border town, defending it against the Syrians. Since he was wounded, Joram went to

Jezreel to recover, thus leaving Jehu at Ramoth Gilead and opening the door for Elisha's plans. This repetition of 2 Kgs 8:28–29 heightens readers' anticipation over what will occur. Jehu swears the men in Ramoth Gilead to secrecy, then drives his chariot toward Jezreel without stating exactly what he intends to do.

9:17–20 A lookout sees Jehu coming with "troops," whose existence is new information that confirms the conspiracy's strength. The identity and mission of the troops have not been identified, so the king sends a messenger to find out if the men come in peace. Jehu tells him there will be no peace today, and the messenger joins the rebel band. Obviously, this development does not satisfy or calm Joram, so he sends a second messenger. This individual repeats the king's question, hears Jehu repeat his response, and joins Jehu as the messenger before him has done. Suspense builds. The lookout finally identifies Jehu, but Joram still does not know why he has come. Joram waits anxiously as Jehu drives furiously. "The reader knows of Jehu's resolve, naturally infers hostile intent, and thus reads these signals (the riders who do not return and the wild rush of a man like Jehu) far less ambiguously. Joram faces a gathering epiphany of judgment."[85]

9:21–26 Finally, Joram decides to go meet Jehu himself. They come together at one of the most infamous places described in 1, 2 Kings, Naboth's vineyard. Readers must know by now that the last of Elijah's predictions will soon come true (cf. 1 Kgs 21:20–24). When the king asks if Jehu comes in peace, his commander responds by criticizing the "adulteries and witchcrafts" Jezebel propagates. The reference to "adulteries" repeats "the standard biblical metaphor for abandoning YHWH to take up the ways of foreign gods (e.g., Exod 34:16; Lev 17:7; Deut 31:16; Judg 2:7)."[86] Baalism's sexual content makes this metaphor an apt one. Montgomery and Gehman note, "By witchcrafts are meant the false cults, whose potency was ascribed to evil arts. For similar collocation of such terms see 17:17, 21:6, Dt. 18:10."[87]

Joram knows now that a rebellion is underway. He cries out to Ahaziah, who is also in Jezreel (cf. 2 Kgs 8:29; 2 Chr 22:7), that Jehu intends "treachery." Jehu wastes no time eliminating the Israelite king. When Joram turns to flee, Jehu shoots an arrow through his heart. Jehu orders "Bidkar, his chariot officer," to throw him on Naboth's field and reminds Bidkar how they heard Elijah's prophecy ten years earlier. Jehu has removed the major obstacle to his rise to power.

9:27–29 Ahaziah sees what has happened to Joram and runs for his life, heading south to Beth Haggan.[88] Jehu and his men pursue him and wound him

---

[85] Long, *2 Kings,* 121.

[86] Cogan and Tadmor, *II Kings,* 110.

[87] Montgomery and Gehman, *Kings,* 401–2.

[88] G. H. Jones says, "This is En-gannim of Jos. 19:21; 21:29, and is to be identified with modern Jenin to the south of Jezreel" (*1 and 2 Kings,* 2:461).

near Ibleam, which is halfway between Jezreel and Samaria. Here the account differs somewhat from that of 2 Chr 22:9. The Chronicler does not mention the wounding of Ahaziah, his fleeing to Megiddo, or the location of his death. He does add that at some point Ahaziah hid in Samaria, was "captured," and was "brought to Jehu and put to death." As Patterson and Austel explain, however, there is nothing in either passage that directly contradicts the other. Jehu apparently was in Megiddo, where Ahaziah was brought before he died.[89] No reason is given why Jehu kills him. Hobbs suggests that his marriage to Ahab's daughter, Athaliah, is enough motivation in Jehu's mind to commit the deed.[90] Gray thinks Jehu views Ahaziah as Joram's avenger, which means he could be a future threat if he is not eliminated.[91] Ahaziah only rules during 841 B.C., then, which is Joram's twelfth year by the northern method of counting years (2 Kgs 8:25) and the eleventh year of Joram's rule by the southern means of counting regnal years.[92]

(2) Jehu Kills Jezebel (9:30–37)

[30]Then Jehu went to Jezreel. When Jezebel heard about it, she painted her eyes, arranged her hair and looked out of a window. [31]As Jehu entered the gate, she asked, "Have you come in peace, Zimri, you murderer of your master?"

[32]He looked up at the window and called out, "Who is on my side? Who?" Two or three eunuchs looked down at him. [33]"Throw her down!" Jehu said. So they threw her down, and some of her blood spattered the wall and the horses as they trampled her underfoot.

[34]Jehu went in and ate and drank. "Take care of that cursed woman," he said, "and bury her, for she was a king's daughter." [35]But when they went out to bury her, they found nothing except her skull, her feet and her hands. [36]They went back and told Jehu, who said, "This is the word of the LORD that he spoke through his servant Elijah the Tishbite: On the plot of ground at Jezreel dogs will devour Jezebel's flesh. [37]Jezebel's body will be like refuse on the ground in the plot at Jezreel, so that no one will be able to say, 'This is Jezebel.'"

9:30–37 Jezebel will be killed next, but she will not die quietly. She puts on makeup, fixes her hair, and waits for Jehu by her window. This is no attempt to seduce the rebel. Rather, she does these things to look like, and die like, a queen.[93] When Jehu arrives, she sarcastically asks if he has come in peace. She

[89] Cf. Patterson and Austel, "1, 2 Kings," 208–9.

[90] Hobbs, *2 Kings,* 117–18.

[91] Gray, *1 and 2 Kings,* 494.

[92] Thiele, *The Mysterious Numbers of the Hebrew Kings,* 101.

[93] L. M. Barré thinks Jehu resists Jezebel's seductive charms (*The Rhetoric of Political Persuasion: The Narrative Artistry and Political Intentions of 2 Kings 9–11* [Washington, D.C.: The Catholic Biblical Association of America, 1988] 79), but Keil ("I and II Kings," 345) and Montgomery and Gehman (*Kings,* 403) think she insults Jehu after having prepared to die. On the motif of the woman at the window see R. D. Patterson, "The Song of Deborah," *Tradition and Testament,* ed. J. S. and P. D. Feinberg (Chicago: Moody, 1981) 141.

then insults him by calling him Zimri, the ineffectual, short-lived usurper of Elah's throne (cf. 1 Kgs 16:8–20). Of course, Jehu *is* the killer of his master, so it may be the insinuation of a brief reign that provides the bite to her accusation/insult.

As when killing Joram and Ahaziah, Jehu wastes no time. He identifies two or three "eunuchs," or "court officials,"[94] willing to betray her and orders them to throw her down. They comply. She bounces against the wall, lands in the street, and dies when horses trample her. Satisfied that she is dead, Jehu goes to eat. Almost as an afterthought and contrary to the prophet's word (9:10), he orders some men to bury her, since she was a king's daughter; but they find "nothing except her skull, her feet and her hands." Dogs have eaten the rest of her. Jehu recognizes that Elijah's predictions about Ahab and Jezebel have finally all come true. Naboth's death has been avenged. The only remaining prediction of Elijah regards the fate of Ahab's descendants.

(3) Jehu Kills Ahab's Family (10:1–17)

[1]Now there were in Samaria seventy sons of the house of Ahab. So Jehu wrote letters and sent them to Samaria: to the officials of Jezreel, to the elders and to the guardians of Ahab's children. He said, [2]"As soon as this letter reaches you, since your master's sons are with you and you have chariots and horses, a fortified city and weapons, [3]choose the best and most worthy of your master's sons and set him on his father's throne. Then fight for your master's house."

[4]But they were terrified and said, "If two kings could not resist him, how can we?"

[5]So the palace administrator, the city governor, the elders and the guardians sent this message to Jehu: "We are your servants and we will do anything you say. We will not appoint anyone as king; you do whatever you think best."

[6]Then Jehu wrote them a second letter, saying, "If you are on my side and will obey me, take the heads of your master's sons and come to me in Jezreel by this time tomorrow."

Now the royal princes, seventy of them, were with the leading men of the city, who were rearing them. [7]When the letter arrived, these men took the princes and slaughtered all seventy of them. They put their heads in baskets and sent them to Jehu in Jezreel. [8]When the messenger arrived, he told Jehu, "They have brought the heads of the princes."

Then Jehu ordered, "Put them in two piles at the entrance of the city gate until morning."

[9]The next morning Jehu went out. He stood before all the people and said, "You are innocent. It was I who conspired against my master and killed him, but who killed all these? [10]Know then, that not a word the LORD has spoken against the house of Ahab will fail. The LORD has done what he promised through his servant Elijah." [11]So Jehu killed everyone in Jezreel who remained of the house of Ahab, as well as all his chief men, his close friends and his priests, leaving him no survivor.

---

[94] Wiseman, *1 and 2 Kings,* 223.

[12]Jehu then set out and went toward Samaria. At Beth Eked of the Shepherds,
[13]he met some relatives of Ahaziah king of Judah and asked, "Who are you?"

They said, "We are relatives of Ahaziah, and we have come down to greet the families of the king and of the queen mother."

[14]"Take them alive!" he ordered. So they took them alive and slaughtered them by the well of Beth Eked—forty-two men. He left no survivor.

[15]After he left there, he came upon Jehonadab son of Recab, who was on his way to meet him. Jehu greeted him and said, "Are you in accord with me, as I am with you?"

"I am," Jehonadab answered.

"If so," said Jehu, "give me your hand." So he did, and Jehu helped him up into
the chariot. [16]Jehu said, "Come with me and see my zeal for the LORD." Then he
had him ride along in his chariot.

[17]When Jehu came to Samaria, he killed all who were left there of Ahab's family; he destroyed them, according to the word of the LORD spoken to Elijah.

10:1–5 One final, trembling obstacle remains in Jehu's path to total control of Israel. Seventy descendants of Ahab still live in Samaria, and any one of them could claim more right than Jehu to succeed Joram. Therefore, Jehu writes them a letter in which he "boldly challenges the leaders to appoint a new king and meet him in battle to decide who is to rule Israel."[95] Because of his military prowess the royals are too afraid to do as he commands, but the leaders of Samaria send Jehu word that they will do whatever he wishes. It is likely that the civic leaders want to spare the city an attack and that the palace officials want to save themselves. At any rate, Ahab's descendants are betrayed to Jehu without their knowledge.

10:6–11 In response to the offer for help, Jehu sends a second letter. This time he asks others to kill for him, demanding that the remaining royal heads be brought to him by the next day. Those asked to do the killing are the very men entrusted with "rearing" the potential kings. These individuals accede to Jehu's wishes and send the seventy heads to him in Jezreel, where he awaits the results of the rebellion in Samaria.

Jehu has the heads stacked "at the entrance of the city gate," the place that served as "the city's forum and market."[96] Gray notes that ancient kings often piled rivals' heads "to intimidate the inhabitants and discourage rebellion."[97] Besides scaring the people, this display also informs the Jezreelites that Samaria is now under the usurper's power. The *coup* has indeed succeeded, and any counterattack is useless.

When the people gather, Jehu uses the piled heads as evidence of God's approval of his rise to power. He himself killed his "master," but others killed

---

[95] Barré, *The Rhetoric of Political Persuasion,* 82.
[96] Montgomery and Gehman, *Kings,* 409.
[97] Gray, *1 and 2 Kings,* 500.

Ahab's other descendants. Elijah's prediction has come true, he reasons, and implies that the killing has been according to the Lord's will. Jehu is not totally honest at this point, for he leaves the impression that the men were killed not by his command but by divine decree. His goal is to make the people believe that opposing Jehu is the same as opposing God.[98] Apparently he succeeds, since future killings of persons not in Ahab's family occur without popular outcry.

10:12–17 In the midst of finishing off Ahab's family, Jehu also kills some of Ahaziah's relatives and gains further popular support. On his way to Samaria to finalize his assumption of power, Jehu meets forty-two men who claim to be relatives of Ahaziah. They are on their way to pay their respects to Israel's royal family and have obviously not heard about the rebellion. Jehu mercilessly slaughters these men without any real justification for doing so, unless he reasons that since Israel's and Judah's royal houses are related these individuals might have some claim to the throne.[99] Even this possibility stretches the limits of credibility, and it is probably these murders that cause Hosea to condemn what occurs in Jezreel (Hos 1:4–5). The prophecies of Elijah and Elisha say nothing about killing *David's* descendants.

Jehu's encounter with Jehonadab underscores popular dissatisfaction with Omri's dynasty. Jeremiah contrasts the loyalty of Jehonadab's descendants with Israel's rejection of the Lord's commands (cf. Jer 35:1–19). Cogan and Tadmor observe that

> The group's ascetic lifestyle—they did not cultivate the land, nor plant vineyards, did not drink wine nor build houses—represented an extreme rejection of all aspects of the civilization of the land of Canaan. Thus the joining of Jehonadab with Jehu to root out the cult of Baal would seem to have been a natural linking of interests.[100]

Jehonadab's belief in traditional national values led him to trust Jehu's show of "zeal for the LORD." Jehu's later actions probably both pleased and displeased Jehonadab and everyone like him who desired a complete overthrow of everything the Omrides represented.

(4) Jehu Kills the Priests of Baal (10:18–27)

[18]Then Jehu brought all the people together and said to them, "Ahab served Baal a little; Jehu will serve him much. [19]Now summon all the prophets of Baal, all his ministers and all his priests. See that no one is missing, because I am going to hold a great sacrifice for Baal. Anyone who fails to come will no longer live." But Jehu was acting deceptively in order to destroy the ministers of Baal.

---

[98] Cf. Keil, "I and II Kings," 347–48.

[99] R. D. Patterson and H. J. Austel, "1, 2 Kings," EBC (Grand Rapids: Zondervan, 1988) 4:211.

[100] Cogan and Tadmor, *II Kings,* 114.

[20]Jehu said, "Call an assembly in honor of Baal." So they proclaimed it. [21]Then he sent word throughout Israel, and all the ministers of Baal came; not one stayed away. They crowded into the temple of Baal until it was full from one end to the other. [22]And Jehu said to the keeper of the wardrobe, "Bring robes for all the ministers of Baal." So he brought out robes for them.

[23]Then Jehu and Jehonadab son of Recab went into the temple of Baal. Jehu said to the ministers of Baal, "Look around and see that no servants of the LORD are here with you—only ministers of Baal." [24]So they went in to make sacrifices and burnt offerings. Now Jehu had posted eighty men outside with this warning: "If one of you lets any of the men I am placing in your hands escape, it will be your life for his life."

[25]As soon as Jehu had finished making the burnt offering, he ordered the guards and officers: "Go in and kill them; let no one escape." So they cut them down with the sword. The guards and officers threw the bodies out and then entered the inner shrine of the temple of Baal. [26]They brought the sacred stone out of the temple of Baal and burned it. [27]They demolished the sacred stone of Baal and tore down the temple of Baal, and people have used it for a latrine to this day.

10:18–19 An act of deception completes Jehu's rise to power. Under the pretense of being a greater follower of Baal than Ahab, Jehu summons all the prophets, ministers, and priests of Baal to a special worship service in Baal's honor. This gathering parallels Elijah's calling together of the Baalists in 1 Kings 18, so the departed prophet's influence emerges again.[101] Ironically, Jehu threatens to kill any Baalist who does not come, when in fact he intends to kill them if they *do* appear. The narrator highlights the deception by announcing it in advance to the reader.[102]

10:20–24 Jehu's plans are carried off with the same secrecy and precision that marked his earlier, successful efforts to eliminate Ahab's family. He gathers the cult's leaders, then dresses them in special robes, which emphasizes his dedication to the worship event. Meanwhile, Jehu has instructed eighty men to kill the worshipers when he gives the command. He and Jehonadab will be on hand to witness the killing. Jehonadab's presence indicates Jehu's continuing desire to show his ally how serious he is about religious reform.

10:25–28 At the appointed time Jehu gives the order, and the Baalists are killed. Further, the sacred stone of Baal, which "represented Baal's presence in the temple,"[103] is destroyed (perhaps by heating it, then pouring water on it so that it cracked), as is the temple itself. This worship center was originally built by Ahab and is mentioned in 1 Kgs 16:32. To complete his denunciation of Baalism, Jehu turns the temple site into a latrine. One could hardly imagine a

[101] Wiseman, *1 and 2 Kings,* 227.
[102] Honeycutt, "2 Kings," 252.
[103] Hubbard, *First and Second Kings,* 179.

more thorough expurgation of Baalism. For now, Baalism has no place in Israelite culture. What Elijah began Jehu has finished.

(5) Israel's Decline (10:28–36)

[28]So Jehu destroyed Baal worship in Israel. [29]However, he did not turn away from the sins of Jeroboam son of Nebat, which he had caused Israel to commit—the worship of the golden calves at Bethel and Dan.

[30]The LORD said to Jehu, "Because you have done well in accomplishing what is right in my eyes and have done to the house of Ahab all I had in mind to do, your descendants will sit on the throne of Israel to the fourth generation." [31]Yet Jehu was not careful to keep the law of the LORD, the God of Israel, with all his heart. He did not turn away from the sins of Jeroboam, which he had caused Israel to commit.

[32]In those days the LORD began to reduce the size of Israel. Hazael overpowered the Israelites throughout their territory [33]east of the Jordan in all the land of Gilead (the region of Gad, Reuben and Manasseh), from Aroer by the Arnon Gorge through Gilead to Bashan.

[34]As for the other events of Jehu's reign, all he did, and all his achievements, are they not written in the book of the annals of the kings of Israel?

[35]Jehu rested with his fathers and was buried in Samaria. And Jehoahaz his son succeeded him as king. [36]The time that Jehu reigned over Israel in Samaria was twenty-eight years.

10:28–31 Despite his attacks against Baalism, Jehu does not lead the nation into separatist Yahwism. He allows the worship instituted by Jeroboam to continue. In effect, then, he expels the foreign religion (Baalism) in favor of the long-standing Israelite state religion begun by Jeroboam. Apparently he believes reform beyond the elimination of Ahab's children, Ahab's wife, and Ahab's religion, that is, what secures his power, does not concern him. Indeed he acts as the instrument of punishment against the corrupt Omride dynasty, but he does not operate out of Elijah-like motives. Rather, he is, like Syria, Assyria, and Babylon, an instrument that punishes but exhibits few personal moral strengths. Israel is now back to where it was before Ahab and Jezebel assumed leadership, but it has certainly not come back to the Lord.

10:32–33 These two short verses speak volumes about Israel's continued decline as a regional power, apparently because of Jehu's continued support of Jeroboam's cult. Once again the human agent for Israel's punishment is Syria, now led by Hazael. As it so happens, Hazael's domination of Jehu amounts to one usurper defeating another.

Besides the long-standing animosity between Israel and Syria, Jehu gives Hazael new reasons to seize his opponent's territory. As is noted in the introduction to the historical background of this section, Assyria invaded Syria more than once during the last half of the ninth century B.C. In 853 B.C., Assyria's Shalmaneser III was turned back at the battle of Qarqar, a conflict that found Israel fighting alongside Syria to defeat the common enemy. Ben-Hadad's failure to return Ramoth-Gilead to Israel as part of their anti-Assyrian treaty led to the battle that cost Ahab his life (cf. 1 Kgs 20:34; 22:3).[104] An even more serious invasion took place early in Hazael's reign when in 841 B.C. Assyria's "armies raged southward, defeated the Aramean forces and laid siege to Damascus, the gardens and groves of which they ravaged."[105] In this same year Jehu paid homage to Shalmaneser III, brought him tribute money, and began a pro-Assyrian policy that was followed by his descendants. These events are recorded both in Shalmaneser's annals and on a black obelisk that depicts Jehu bowing before the Assyrian monarch.[106] Clearly, Hazael would hardly have appreciated Jehu's support of Syria's foe.

What may have made Hazael the angriest is the possibility that Jehu may not have been *forced* to ally himself with Shalmaneser III. Elat argues that the black obelisk "shows the bearing of tribute only from those kings or countries which submitted without resistance, and perhaps at their own initiative."[107] If so, Jehu may have been taking what he considered were preventative measures, or he may have been supporting the enemy of his enemy. Whatever his motives, the result was that when Assyria left the region Jehu was left to face an angry Hazael, and by Jehu's death in 814 B.C. he "had lost the whole of Transjordan south to the Moabite frontier on the Arnon (II Kings 10:32 f.; cf. Amos 1:3)."[108] Indeed, the Lord did reduce the size of the Northern Kingdom!

10:34–36 Jehu's reign (841–814 B.C.) can best be described as tumultuous. He came to power through intrigue, conspiracy, and murder. He faced pressure from Hazael and sought relief through the fierce Assyrians. His religious reforms were likewise murderous, yet they only punished the cult most associated with the dynasty he overthrew. At least his death ushered in a new king without bloodshed. Jehu's legacy is a bloody one, so bloody, in fact, that the narrator seems unable to take much pleasure even in the purge of Baalism he undertakes. His acceptance of Jeroboam's cult seems to make him one more killer whose zeal for God extends only as far as his personal interests allow. Still, his actions prove once again the power of the prophetic word. Not one of Elijah's predictions about Ahab and Jezebel fail to come true.

6. Joash's Reform (11:1–12:21)

Extraordinary events also unfold in Judah. A usurper much more unusual than Jehu emerges in the south, for Athaliah, Jezebel's daughter, seizes control

---

[104] M. Elat, "The Campaigns of Shalmaneser III against Aram and Israel," *IEJ* 25 (1975) 30.

[105] Bright, *A History of Israel,* 254–56.

[106] M. C. Astour, "841 B.C.: The First Assyrian Invasion of Israel," *JAOS* 91 (1971) 388. Cf. *ANET,* 120–22.

[107] Elat, "The Campaigns of Shalmaneser III," 32.

[108] Bright, *A History of Israel,* 254.

during the crisis caused by Jehu's assassination of Ahaziah, Judah's king. After enduring her rule for six years, a counterrevolution removes her from power. David's dynasty will rule again, and all will seemingly be well. Reform comes to both nations, then, but in both nations it is a reform that leaves the author unimpressed with its ability to permanently uproot challenges to Yahwism.

(1) Athaliah's Rebellion (11:1–3)

[1]When Athaliah the mother of Ahaziah saw that her son was dead, she proceeded to destroy the whole royal family. [2]But Jehosheba, the daughter of King Jehoram and sister of Ahaziah, took Joash son of Ahaziah and stole him away from among the royal princes, who were about to be murdered. She put him and his nurse in a bedroom to hide him from Athaliah; so he was not killed. [3]He remained hidden with his nurse at the temple of the LORD for six years while Athaliah ruled the land.

11:1–3 Meanwhile, an extraordinary thing occurs in Judah. A usurper replaces David's descendants on the throne in Jerusalem, which is the only time such an event happens. Even more unusual is the fact that it is a woman, Ahaziah's mother, who seizes control. Of course, queen mothers are prominent in 1, 2 Kings, since each one in Judah is named with two exceptions,[109] but no other woman formally rules the nation. This daughter of Ahab (2 Kgs 8:18,27) certainly imitates Jezebel's decisiveness, cruelty, and sheer pluck. She thinks she has all heirs to the throne killed and assumes power. For six years she rules, never discovering that one of her grandsons, Joash, has escaped the cold-blooded *coup*. Only a baby (cf. 2 Kgs 11:3,21), Joash is hidden by a nurse.[110] God's promise of an eternal kingdom for David is kept alive, but just barely.

(2) Joash Becomes King (11:4–21)

[4]In the seventh year Jehoiada sent for the commanders of units of a hundred, the Carites and the guards and had them brought to him at the temple of the LORD. He made a covenant with them and put them under oath at the temple of the LORD. Then he showed them the king's son. [5]He commanded them, saying, "This is what you are to do: You who are in the three companies that are going on duty on the Sabbath—a third of you guarding the royal palace, [6]a third at the Sur Gate, and a third at the gate behind the guard, who take turns guarding the temple— [7]and you who are in the other two companies that normally go off Sabbath

---

[109] R. H. Lowery, *The Reforming Kings: Cult and Society in First Temple Judah,* JSOTSup 120 (Sheffield: Sheffield Academic Press, 1991) 105. The two exceptions are Jehoram (2 Kgs 8:17) and Ahaz (2 Kgs 16:20).

[110] The words "she put" in v. 2 are inserted from the parallel in 2 Chr 22:11. They are missing in the Hebrew text. The Hebrew phrase denoting the place he was hidden (חֲדַר הַמִּטּוֹת) may refer to a storeroom for bedding rather than a bedroom, where he surely would have been found (Patterson and Austel, "1, 2 Kings," 217).

duty are all to guard the temple for the king. [8]Station yourselves around the king, each man with his weapon in his hand. Anyone who approaches your ranks must be put to death. Stay close to the king wherever he goes."

[9]The commanders of units of a hundred did just as Jehoiada the priest ordered. Each one took his men—those who were going on duty on the Sabbath and those who were going off duty—and came to Jehoiada the priest. [10]Then he gave the commanders the spears and shields that had belonged to King David and that were in the temple of the LORD. [11]The guards, each with his weapon in his hand, stationed themselves around the king—near the altar and the temple, from the south side to the north side of the temple.

[12]Jehoiada brought out the king's son and put the crown on him; he presented him with a copy of the covenant and proclaimed him king. They anointed him, and the people clapped their hands and shouted, "Long live the king!"

[13]When Athaliah heard the noise made by the guards and the people, she went to the people at the temple of the LORD. [14]She looked and there was the king, standing by the pillar, as the custom was. The officers and the trumpeters were beside the king, and all the people of the land were rejoicing and blowing trumpets. Then Athaliah tore her robes and called out, "Treason! Treason!"

[15]Jehoiada the priest ordered the commanders of units of a hundred, who were in charge of the troops: "Bring her out between the ranks and put to the sword anyone who follows her." For the priest had said, "She must not be put to death in the temple of the LORD." [16]So they seized her as she reached the place where the horses enter the palace grounds, and there she was put to death.

[17]Jehoiada then made a covenant between the LORD and the king and people that they would be the LORD's people. He also made a covenant between the king and the people. [18]All the people of the land went to the temple of Baal and tore it down. They smashed the altars and idols to pieces and killed Mattan the priest of Baal in front of the altars.

Then Jehoiada the priest posted guards at the temple of the LORD. [19]He took with him the commanders of hundreds, the Carites, the guards and all the people of the land, and together they brought the king down from the temple of the LORD and went into the palace, entering by way of the gate of the guards. The king then took his place on the royal throne, [20]and all the people of the land rejoiced. And the city was quiet, because Athaliah had been slain with the sword at the palace.

[21]Joash was seven years old when he began to reign.

11:4–8 Jehoiada, whom the text later identifies as a priest (11:9), becomes the catalyst for restoring the Davidic dynasty to its historic place. It is significant that a religious leader institutes this counterrevolution, for his prominence in the new king's life will later lead to religious renewal (cf. 2 Kgs 12:1–16). Jehoiada utilizes the temple guards to overthrow Athaliah.[111] He shows the soldiers the seven-year-old Joash and commands them to protect the boy with their lives. Apparently Athaliah has no real military or religious sup-

[111] The "Carites" probably were mercenaries who served as the royal bodyguard. See 2 Sam 20:23.

port. The coup is to take place during the changing of the guard in order to maximize the military presence.

11:9–12 Everything unfolds as Jehoiada plans. The priest gives the men on duty the ceremonial shields, which were modeled after those made by David.[112] This initial symbolism in place, Jehoiada adds to the ceremony by placing a crown on the boy-king, then by presenting Joash with "a copy of the covenant," which contains at least the rules for kings found in Deut 17:14–20.[113] Finally, Jehoiada pronounces Joash king, a declaration met by popular approval. Thus, Joash is swept to power in a movement that includes popular, religious, and military support. His coronation, like his coalition, combines a commitment to the Davidic dynasty, to the Mosaic Covenant, and to the people. In other words, this scene embodies the best of Judah's sacred and secular institutions.

11:13–16 In a quite ironic scene, Athaliah the usurper learns of her own usurpation and cries "treason." Obviously she has no mandate to remain in power. Jehoiada has her killed "where the horses enter the palace grounds." This reference to horses reminds readers of how Jezebel met her fate in 2 Kgs 9:30–37. David's remaining descendant is on the throne, the northern-style usurper is removed, and religious reform seems visible on the horizon.

11:17 Jehoiada concludes the *coup* by binding the people to the Lord, the king to the Lord, and the people to the king. Literally the text says that Jehoiada "cut *the* covenant" (emphasis added),[114] which indicates that a previous covenantal model was followed. The covenant that is made between God and the people is a reminder and renewal of the pledges made in Exod 24:8 (cf. Deut 4:1–20; 27:9–10; and Josh 24:1–27). This ceremony also mirrors the covenant renewal that occurred during Asa's reform (cf. 2 Chr 15:12). The Israelites are God's special people, and they must live as such. Keil says, "The renewal of the covenant with the Lord was necessary, because under the former kings the people had fallen away from the Lord and served Baal."[115] In other words, they have forgotten who they are because they have forgotten who their God is. Covenant renewal restores, then, the proper sense of reality and identity for the people.

The covenant between God and the king is a renewal of the promises made to David in 2 Sam 7:1–17. Athaliah's reign interrupted the eternal dynasty but could not stop it entirely. Besides the reminder of God's promises to David, this passage reminds the king of the monarch's responsibility to rule according to the Lord's standards instead of the selfish standards that guided other ancient rulers. Moses establishes these codes of conduct in Deut 17:14–20,

[112] Cf. Gray's discussion of the shields in *1 and 2 Kings,* 517.

[113] Keil, "I and II Kings," 362.

[114] The Hebrew text reads וַיִּכְרֹת יְהוֹיָדָע אֶת־הַבְּרִית.

[115] Keil, "I and II Kings," 363.

and David reminds Solomon of them in 1 Kgs 2:1–4. Israel's rulers must serve, not oppress, the people, keep God's word near them as their guide, and be determined to please the Lord instead of themselves or the people. No doubt Jehoiada hopes the boy-king will embrace and model these principles his entire life.

The renewal of the covenant between king and people is also made necessary by Athaliah's usurpation, which broke the tradition of Davidic rulers succeeding one another.[116] Earlier in Israel's history David himself had confirmed his kingship by making a covenant with the nation's elders (2 Sam 5:3). Later Josiah will make a similar agreement with God and the people when he leads the nation in religious reform (2 Kgs 23:3). For now the people can expect Joash's faithfulness to the Lord to result in justice for them. They can hope, with Jehoiada, that this fresh start with a fresh king will yield long-term benefits.

11:18–21 All the covenant making leads to action against Baalism. The people tear down the Baal altar and execute Mattan, the Baal priest. Skinner states that Mattan is a common Phoenician name, so this person may have been imported for the job from other lands.[117] On the other hand, the name appears in 2 Kgs 24:17 for an Israelite, which means a native of Judah may have chosen this career.[118] Either option is possible, since Jezebel's influence was certainly felt in Judah through Athaliah and since Judah has a long pre-Jezebel history of Baal worship of their own by this time (cf. 1 Kgs 14:22–24).

This religious reform parallels Jehu's in some ways yet diverges in certain crucial areas. Baal's temple is destroyed in both instances, but only the leader of Baalism is killed in Judah's reform. Baalism is removed as the state religion in each case, yet the people dominate the reform in Judah, whereas the new king orchestrates the changes in Israel. Prophetic predictions fuel Jehu's purge, while a priest drives the people forward in Judah. In the north separatist Yahwism seems to have no real voice after the *coup*, and Jeroboam's cult appears to resume its earlier role as state religion. In Judah the high places are not removed (cf. 2 Kgs 12:3), but separatist Yahwism has been returned to the temple by its champion, Jehoiada. From this analysis it seems likely that the reform in the south has more popular support, more institutional backing, and more chance of long-term survival. Neither reform, though, goes as far as the narrator thinks is necessary.

A final parade of Joash's supporters concludes the story. In a phrase reminiscent of the Book of Judges, the narrator says that the city is quiet after the usurper's death.[119] Judah has survived an invasion of northern royalty, a turn

[116] Gray, *1 and 2 Kings,* 523.

[117] J. Skinner, *I and II Kings,* CB (Edinburgh: T. C. & E. C. Jack, 1904) 341.

[118] Cogan and Tadmor, *II Kings,* 130.

[119] Note the constant refrain in Judges "and the land had peace" after the defeat of a foreign enemy.

to Baalism, and a temporary overthrow of David's dynasty. Quiet now descends because of the reemergence of Yahwism, the priesthood, and the Davidic Covenant. How long will the "quiet" last? What can a seven-year-old king accomplish, even with the aid of a veteran priest/politician such as Jehoiada?

(3) Joash Repairs the Temple (12:1–16)

1In the seventh year of Jehu, Joash became king, and he reigned in Jerusalem forty years. His mother's name was Zibiah; she was from Beersheba. 2Joash did what was right in the eyes of the LORD all the years Jehoiada the priest instructed him. 3The high places, however, were not removed; the people continued to offer sacrifices and burn incense there.

4Joash said to the priests, "Collect all the money that is brought as sacred offerings to the temple of the LORD—the money collected in the census, the money received from personal vows and the money brought voluntarily to the temple. 5Let every priest receive the money from one of the treasurers, and let it be used to repair whatever damage is found in the temple."

6But by the twenty-third year of King Joash the priests still had not repaired the temple. 7Therefore King Joash summoned Jehoiada the priest and the other priests and asked them, "Why aren't you repairing the damage done to the temple? Take no more money from your treasurers, but hand it over for repairing the temple." 8The priests agreed that they would not collect any more money from the people and that they would not repair the temple themselves.

9Jehoiada the priest took a chest and bored a hole in its lid. He placed it beside the altar, on the right side as one enters the temple of the LORD. The priests who guarded the entrance put into the chest all the money that was brought to the temple of the LORD. 10Whenever they saw that there was a large amount of money in the chest, the royal secretary and the high priest came, counted the money that had been brought into the temple of the LORD and put it into bags. 11When the amount had been determined, they gave the money to the men appointed to supervise the work on the temple. With it they paid those who worked on the temple of the LORD—the carpenters and builders, 12the masons and stonecutters. They purchased timber and dressed stone for the repair of the temple of the LORD, and met all the other expenses of restoring the temple.

13The money brought into the temple was not spent for making silver basins, wick trimmers, sprinkling bowls, trumpets or any other articles of gold or silver for the temple of the LORD; 14it was paid to the workmen, who used it to repair the temple. 15They did not require an accounting from those to whom they gave the money to pay the workers, because they acted with complete honesty. 16The money from the guilt offerings and sin offerings was not brought into the temple of the LORD; it belonged to the priests.

12:1–3 As a prelude to the description of Joash's major works, the author offers a mostly favorable assessment of the king's work. Joash becomes king when seven years old (2 Kgs 11:21), which is Jehu's seventh year, then rules forty years in Jerusalem (ca. 835–796 B.C.). His mother was not only *not* a northerner, but she was, in fact, from Beersheba, the southernmost part of Judah. His reign could have lasted longer, but 2 Kgs 12:20 states that his own servants kill him and place his son on the throne. Thus, he comes into power as a result of a *coup*, and he dies due to the same type of activity.

According to the author, Joash governs well during his tenure, mostly because of Jehoiada's instruction. Patterson and Austel correctly observe that in light of 2 Chr 24:17–22, which says that after Jehoiada's death Joash allows outright idolatry to flourish, 1 Kgs 12:2 "is ominous in tone . . . and a reminder of the need for personal faith."[120] Quite significantly, the author credits a priest, not a prophet, with helping the king obey the Lord. This fact indicates that the writer values spiritual renewal in its various forms, not just when change arises from the prophetic movement.

Despite Jehoida's positive influence, however, Joash does not completely reform the religious scene, for he fails to remove the local high places that dot the landscape. As has been noted, 2 Chr 24:17–22 states that Joash eventually countenances Asherah worship as well. Still, the text seems to stress what the reader must surely appreciate: regardless of his flaws, Joash is a big improvement over the southerners influenced by the house of Ahab.

12:4–16 Joash's commitment to religious change is best seen in his attempts to repair the temple. The description of these attempts is quite straightforward, almost bland in comparison to other stories in 1, 2 Kings, and unfolds in nine parts.[121] In the first three scenes the king orders certain money be used for repairs (vv. 4–5). Next he discovers that the repairs have not been made (v. 6) and holds the priests in charge responsible for the delay (vv. 7–8). By now the temple is well over a century old and surely needs attention. Besides, 2 Chr 24:7 informs us that Athaliah's sons were looting it for Baal worship. Jones observes that until this time the temple expenses were met by the royal treasury, but Joash has transferred this obligation to the private sector.[122] Joash is not satisfied with the priests' progress in raising money, however (v. 8; cf. 2 Chr 24:5–6), and decides to take it out of their hands.

Because the priests fail to do their assigned task, in the next three segments Joash has Jehoiada institute a collection box system for collecting money (v. 9),[123] which thus raises the needed funds (v. 10; cf. 2 Chr 24:9–11, which adds that the box's presence and purpose was broadcast throughout the land), which in turn allows money to be distributed to workmen (vv. 11–12).

---

[120] Patterson and Austel, "1, 2 Kings," 221.

[121] Hobbs, *2 Kings,* 149.

[122] Jones, *1 and 2 Kings,* 2:490.

[123] Patterson and Austel explain that the box itself could not actually be "beside the altar" but as 2 Chr 24:8 clarifies was "against the altar wall at the entrance that lay to the right side of the altar, or the southern entrance to the middle court" ("1, 2 Kings," 222).

Finally, the text states that no money was made available for the manufacture of temple utensils until the temple repairs were finished (vv. 13–14 and 2 Chr 24:14), that the workmen were completely trustworthy (v. 15), and that certain monies were not allocated for the repairs (v. 16).[124] Part of this money that is not used for repairs is earmarked for the priests. It is hard to imagine that separatist Yahwist priests received any such subsidy during previous reigns, so this innovation alone signals a new day in Jerusalem's religious life. R. Hubbard notes that these developments are historically significant in at least two ways.

> First, it represented a major change in the procedures for handling Temple funds, which lasted until the Exile. Second, it reflected a shift of power over Temple affairs from the priests to the king. The project reminds the readers that God honored fidelity toward His temple.[125]

(4) Joash Placates Syria (12:17–18)

[17]About this time Hazael king of Aram went up and attacked Gath and captured it. Then he turned to attack Jerusalem. [18]But Joash king of Judah took all the sacred objects dedicated by his fathers—Jehoshaphat, Jehoram and Ahaziah, the kings of Judah—and the gifts he himself had dedicated and all the gold found in the treasuries of the temple of the LORD and of the royal palace, and he sent them to Hazael king of Aram, who then withdrew from Jerusalem.

12:17–18 Once again Syria interrupts Judahite plans, this time through invasion and direct threat of conquest. During an otherwise unknown campaign,[126] Hazael overruns the Philistine city Gath. Gray suggests that the Syrian's purpose may have been to control the southern trade routes.[127] Whatever his reasons, Hazael turns against Jerusalem, the capital of such old Syrian foes as David and Jehoshaphat. Given Syria's power, the threat is real.

To avoid the invasion, Joash plunders the temple treasuries to buy Hazael's retreat. Asa employed a similar strategy in 1 Kgs 15:18 when Ben-Hadad threatened him, and Hezekiah will use it when the Assyrians move against him (cf. 2 Kgs 18:15). Ironically, what Joash collected in 2 Kgs 12:4–16 he now spends. Indeed, the temple will never be safe from such usage. Judah's overall policy of appeasement emerges and resurfaces repeatedly in the rest of the history.

(5) Joash Dies (12:19–21)

[19]As for the other events of the reign of Joash, and all he did, are they not written in the book of the annals of the kings of Judah? [20]His officials conspired

[124] Hobbs, *2 Kings,* 149.

[125] Hubbard, *First and Second Kings,* 185.

[126] Montgomery and Gehman, *Kings,* 430.

[127] Gray, *1 and 2 Kings,* 533.

against him and assassinated him at Beth Millo, on the road down to Silla. [21]The officials who murdered him were Jozabad son of Shimeath and Jehozabad son of Shomer. He died and was buried with his fathers in the City of David. And Amaziah his son succeeded him as king.

12:19–21 Joash's career does not end as grandly as it begins. After forty years in power (cf. 2 Kgs 12:1) two of his officials murder him. No reason for the assassination is given here, but 2 Chr 24:17–25 offers more details on the matter, perhaps in order to explain what "the annotations on the book of the kings" (2 Chr 24:27) omits. The Chronicler says that after Jehoiada's death Joash allows idol worship, has a man (Zechariah, son of Jehoiada) stoned for opposing his acceptance of idolatry, and, as a result of these moral failures, is severely wounded by the Syrians in battle. His officials finish him as he lies recovering. Joash becomes so unpopular at the end of his life that he is denied burial in the tomb of his ancestors. His son Amaziah takes his place.

The decline in Joash's character is tragic. He does not fulfill his potential. Hubbard observes, "Once a promising, God-fearing young ruler, Joash died a disappointment. By bribing Hazael with Temple treasures, he tarnished his one great achievement, the Temple restoration."[128] Perhaps his problem was that he never learned to make solid decisions on his own. Honeycutt writes, "In the final analysis the individual, under God's leadership, must make his own decisions, create his own integrity, and achieve his own destiny."[129] Besides these flaws, Joash becomes proud and disloyal, even to the extent that he kills his mentor's son for preaching his mentor's message. It is hard to imagine a sadder case of moral failure.

7. Elisha's Final Days (13:1–25)

Though he has not figured in the story since the anointing of Jehu (2 Kgs 9:1–3), Elisha is still alive. His death ends the Elijah-Elisha era, which occupies over one-third of the text of 1, 2 Kings. Even after his death Elisha still performs miracles. Nothing can stop the power of God's word and God's Spirit in his life.

Israel's political fortunes do improve a bit. Hazael continues to oppress and harass the Northern Kingdom; but when he dies, his successor, Ben-Hadad III (807–780? B.C.), is unable to maintain Syria's dominance.[130] Syria's problems are compounded when Assyria reasserts itself in the region.[131] These events benefit Israel, yet the nation remains too weak at this time to take advantage of

[128] Hubbard, *First and Second Kings,* 185.

[129] Honeycutt, "2 Kings," 258.

[130] Bright, *A History of Israel,* 252.

[131] Donner, "The Separate States of Israel and Judah," 413–14.

the respite. Prosperity will come later. For now, Israel's kings are too weak and spiritually corrupt to achieve even secular success.

(1) Jehoahaz's Reign (13:1–9)

[1]In the twenty-third year of Joash son of Ahaziah king of Judah, Jehoahaz son of Jehu became king of Israel in Samaria, and he reigned seventeen years. [2]He did evil in the eyes of the LORD by following the sins of Jeroboam son of Nebat, which he had caused Israel to commit, and he did not turn away from them. [3]So the LORD's anger burned against Israel, and for a long time he kept them under the power of Hazael king of Aram and Ben-Hadad his son.

[4]Then Jehoahaz sought the LORD's favor, and the LORD listened to him, for he saw how severely the king of Aram was oppressing Israel. [5]The LORD provided a deliverer for Israel, and they escaped from the power of Aram. So the Israelites lived in their own homes as they had before. [6]But they did not turn away from the sins of the house of Jeroboam, which he had caused Israel to commit; they continued in them. Also, the Asherah pole remained standing in Samaria.

[7]Nothing had been left of the army of Jehoahaz except fifty horsemen, ten chariots and ten thousand foot soldiers, for the king of Aram had destroyed the rest and made them like the dust at threshing time.

[8]As for the other events of the reign of Jehoahaz, all he did and his achievements, are they not written in the book of the annals of the kings of Israel? [9]Jehoahaz rested with his fathers and was buried in Samaria. And Jehoash his son succeeded him as king.

13:1–3 Jehu's son, Jehoahaz, succeeds his father and rules from about 814 to 798 B.C.[132] God has promised Jehu a four-generation dynasty (2 Kgs 10:30), so Jehoahaz's ascent begins to complete this pledge. Jehoahaz adopts Jeroboam's cult, which his father also practiced (cf. 2 Kgs 10:28–31). Like his father, Jehoahaz suffers for his sins. Once again it is Syria who acts as God's instrument of discipline. God uses the unjust to punish the unjust here yet clearly does so to effect change, which will in turn initiate blessing (cf. Deut 27–28).

13:4–9 Jehoahaz sees the foolishness of continual disobedience, so he takes an unusual step for a northern monarch: he seeks the Lord's favor. Much as the Lord responds to Israel's cries for help in Exod 2:23–25, now God listens to the king because of the oppression they are enduring at the hands of the Syrians. This phraseology also sounds like that used to describe Israel's repentance and deliverance in Judges.[133] God's mercy and love dictates everything he does.

Because of this kindness he sends an unspecified deliverer to save Israel

---

[132] Cf. Thiele, *The Mysterious Numbers of the Hebrew Kings,* 105–6, for an explanation of the dates for Jehoahaz's reign.

[133] Hubbard, *First and Second Kings,* 187.

from Syria. Several opinions have been offered about the deliverer's identity, including Joash, Adadnirari III of Assyria, who invades Syria ca. 805 B.C., and Elisha.[134] Gray thinks Elisha is the deliverer, since he is the type of hero the Judges-like language suggests should arise.[135] Hobbs agrees with this assertion, and adds that 13:4–5 sounds very much like Deut 26:5–9, a text that magnifies Moses' work as God's agent of deliverance. Elisha therefore becomes the "new Moses" in this latest release from oppression.[136] Besides these observations, the passage that follows presents Elisha as "the chariots and horses of Israel" and as the man who predicts limited victories over the Syrians. It appears likely, then, that Elisha, the only figure in Israel's history who consistently makes Syria *fear him,* is indeed Israel's redeemer one last time.

Despite their release, the people fail to credit God for their peace and security. In return for the Lord's goodness, the nation continues in Jeroboam's cult and returns to Asherah worship. The futility of such worship is highlighted by the fact that Syria brought Israel to its knees by decimating its armies while they rebelled against the Lord. As in the times of Amos, it seems that the more the Lord does to change Israel's habits the more the people choose a destructive path (cf. Amos 4:6–12). When Jehoahaz dies, he is replaced by his son Jehoash, who becomes the second descendant of Jehu to rule. God continues to be faithful to Jehu.

(2) Elisha Predicts Syria's Demise (13:10–19)

[10]In the thirty-seventh year of Joash king of Judah, Jehoash son of Jehoahaz became king of Israel in Samaria, and he reigned sixteen years. [11]He did evil in the eyes of the LORD and did not turn away from any of the sins of Jeroboam son of Nebat, which he had caused Israel to commit; he continued in them.

[12]As for the other events of the reign of Jehoash, all he did and his achievements, including his war against Amaziah king of Judah, are they not written in the book of the annals of the kings of Israel? [13]Jehoash rested with his fathers, and Jeroboam succeeded him on the throne. Jehoash was buried in Samaria with the kings of Israel.

[14]Now Elisha was suffering from the illness from which he died. Jehoash king of Israel went down to see him and wept over him. "My father! My father!" he cried. "The chariots and horsemen of Israel!"

[15]Elisha said, "Get a bow and some arrows," and he did so. [16]"Take the bow in your hands," he said to the king of Israel. When he had taken it, Elisha put his hands on the king's hands.

[17]"Open the east window," he said, and he opened it. "Shoot!" Elisha said, and he shot. "The LORD's arrow of victory, the arrow of victory over Aram!" Elisha

---

[134] Cogan and Tadmor, *II Kings,* 143.

[135] Gray, *1 and 2 Kings,* 538.

[136] Hobbs, *2 Kings,* 167–68.

declared. "You will completely destroy the Arameans at Aphek."

[18]Then he said, "Take the arrows," and the king took them. Elisha told him, "Strike the ground." He struck it three times and stopped. [19]The man of God was angry with him and said, "You should have struck the ground five or six times; then you would have defeated Aram and completely destroyed it. But now you will defeat it only three times."

13:10 Jehoash's reign lasts sixteen years (ca. 798–782 B.C.) and is listed as having begun in Joash's thirty-seventh year. Jones states that this "detail is at variance with 2 Kgs 13:1 and 14:1, which make Joash's accession to the throne of Israel in the thirty-ninth year of Jehoash of Judah." He then claims it is best to agree with the Greek versions that in fact read "thirty-ninth year."[137] Rather than posit a textual error, Gray theorizes that the two-year gap could indicate a coregency between Jehoahaz and Jehoash.[138] Thiele offers a third option, which is that at this time both kingdoms shifted their system of reckoning lengths of reigns to the accession-year system, a practice that mirrored Assyria's method.[139] All of these possibilities have merit, but Thiele's theory explains why the text may be silent about a coregency and also helps explain other calculations that appear.[140]

13:11–13 At first the historian tells nothing about Jehoash that sounds impressive. Like his predecessors, he practices Jeroboam's religion. This religious failure brands him an evil man in the author's eyes. A war with Amaziah, Joash's successor in Judah, is mentioned, but details of that war are not given until 2 Kgs 14:8–14. Jeroboam succeeds him, yet comments on *his* reign are postponed until 2 Kgs 14:23–29. Jehoash's most important acts and those of his son are only revealed after, and because of, one final deed Elisha does on behalf of the nation. Narratives about the future are put on hold until Elisha predicts that future.

13:14–19 Despite his preference for Jeroboam's cult, Jehoash visits Elisha when the old prophet lies dying. In anguish the king weeps and calls Elisha "the chariots and horsemen of Israel," a title Elisha himself uses for Elijah in 2 Kgs 2:12. On the secular level the king may refer to Elisha's earlier efforts on behalf of Israel's army (cf. 2 Kgs 3:1–27; 6:8–7:20). Indeed Elisha seems to give Israel most of their all-too-few victories over Syria. M. A. Beek claims: "The prophet is the man whose prayer is better than chariots and horsemen. Trust in the words of the prophet means that horses and chariots can be abandoned."[141] Certainly Elisha echoes such sentiments about Elijah, and it is true

[137] Jones, *1 and 2 Kings,* 2:501.

[138] Gray, *1 and 2 Kings,* 540.

[139] Thiele, *The Mysterious Numbers of the Hebrew Kings,* 111–12.

[140] Cf. n. 132.

[141] Beek, "The Meaning of the Expression 'The Chariots and the Horsemen of Israel' (II Kings 2:12)," *OTS* 17 (1972) 8.

that Jehoash *ought* to feel this way about Elisha, but the ruler's spiritual condition makes the secular option more likely. Sadly, Jehoash chooses the lesser of the meanings of the phrase he utters.

As he invariably does throughout his life, Elisha helps the impious monarch, this time by employing two symbolic acts. First, he asks the king to shoot an arrow out the window. When Jehoash complies, he declares Israel will defeat Syria at Aphek, where Israel triumphs in 1 Kgs 20:26–34. In effect, Elisha predicts that good times will return.

Second, Elisha commands Jehoash to strike the ground with the arrows. Keil argues that a better translation is that the prophet orders Jehoash to shoot arrows into the ground, which would parallel the shooting in 13:17.[142] Perhaps Keil is correct, but the symbolic act is odd either way. People do not strike the ground with arrows, nor do they intentionally shoot them into the dirt. The king obeys yet hits the earth only three times. Angrily the prophet declares that now only three victories will occur, whereas hitting the ground more times would have annihilated the enemy completely. Apparently Jehoash should have struck the ground until Elisha gave him instructions to stop.

Though he does not make full use of his opportunity, Jehoash will still achieve some freedom from Syria's grip, a national luxury not enjoyed since Ahab's era. Really, though, the victory belongs to Elisha. He truly is the horses and chariots of Israel. God's prophets remain his instruments of warning, encouragement, mercy, and admonishment to Israel.

(3) Elisha Dies (13:20–21)

20 Elisha died and was buried.

Now Moabite raiders used to enter the country every spring. 21 Once while some Israelites were burying a man, suddenly they saw a band of raiders; so they threw the man's body into Elisha's tomb. When the body touched Elisha's bones, the man came to life and stood up on his feet.

13:20–21 Not even death stops this prophet's ministry. His predictions about Syria's defeat live on, of course, but so do his miraculous powers. A group of men burying a corpse are interrupted by Moabite raiders, which forces them to throw the body in a tomb that just happens to be Elisha's. The deceased man revives. This final Elisha story provides a fitting summary of the prophet and his ministry. Long says, "As he was a man of power in life (chaps. 2–7), moving and persuasive even in stories told about him (2 Kgs 8:1–6), so now his awesome powers continue working in death, confirming the prophet and foreshadowing the victory to come."[143] Elijah has gone to heaven without dying; Elisha has kept giving Israel life after he has died.

---

[142] Keil, "I and II Kings," 377.

[143] Long, *2 Kings,* 166.

(4) Syria's Defeat (13:22–25)

[22]Hazael king of Aram oppressed Israel throughout the reign of Jehoahaz. [23]But the LORD was gracious to them and had compassion and showed concern for them because of his covenant with Abraham, Isaac and Jacob. To this day he has been unwilling to destroy them or banish them from his presence.

[24]Hazael king of Aram died, and Ben-Hadad his son succeeded him as king. [25]Then Jehoash son of Jehoahaz recaptured from Ben-Hadad son of Hazael the towns he had taken in battle from his father Jehoahaz. Three times Jehoash defeated him, and so he recovered the Israelite towns.

13:22–23 Under normal political circumstances, Hazael would probably have finished Israel. All the pieces were in place for Syria to do what Assyria accomplishes later. This catastrophe does not occur yet, however, because of the Lord's grace, compassion, concern, and covenant faithfulness to Abraham, Isaac, and Jacob. "To this day," or to this point in history, the Lord refuses to give Israel over despite all they have done. Patience radiates from God's personal character. Israel's later destruction must therefore be seen as a last, desperate, just result of a nation's choosing punishment over blessing, death over life.

13:24–25 When Hazael finally dies, he is succeeded by Ben-Hadad II, who suffers the three losses Elisha predicted. Jehoash also opposes Syria by appeasing Assyria early in his reign, much as Jehu had done in his time.[144] Thiele writes that an Assyrian stele discovered in 1967 lists Jehoash as one of the kings who pays tribute to Adad-nirari III (ca. 809–782 B.C.)[145] and fixes the year of this tribute at 796 B.C., or two years into his reign.[146] Though some scholars are less certain than Thiele about the 796 B.C. date,[147] the impact of Jehoash's action remains the same: he adopts a pro-Assyria policy in hopes of defeating his Syrian enemies.

These victories signal the start of a new day in Israel, one that will bring military and economic success yet will leave the nation more religiously corrupt than ever before. How long can the Lord's patience last? How long can the people be protected by the greatness of their ancestors' relationship to the covenant God? Judgment looms on the horizon if no changes are made. Elisha is dead. How long can Israel survive without the necessary "chariots and horsemen"?

Canonical and Theological Implications of 2 Kgs 2:1–13:25

By this point in 1, 2 Kings several canonical and theological issues and categories have emerged and reemerged. These concepts are deepened and

[144] See this commentary's discussion of Jehu's relationship to Assyria in the comments on 2 Kgs 10:32–33.

[145] Hobbs, *2 Kings,* 167.

[146] Thiele, *The Mysterious Numbers of the Hebrew Kings,* 112.

[147] E.g., Wiseman, *1 and 2 Kings,* 240–41.

broadened in 2 Kings 2–13. Indeed, they become somewhat difficult to handle unless some familiar terms are retained. Thus, the following canonical comments will be structured by how they relate to God, the prophets, the kings, Israel, and the nations. The statements about the theological conclusions that surface from the canonical analysis follow the same format.

If one is familiar with the whole canon, the portrayal of God in 2 Kings 2–13 is hardly startling, though the situations described there provide new avenues of understanding. In these chapters the Lord acts primarily as sovereign and as source. God is the sovereign judge yet at the same time the source of salvation and protection, of miracles, and of self-revelation.

God's sovereignty has been established since Genesis 1–2, where the text claims that the God depicted in Scripture created the world and did so alone because no other gods exist. The Lord's rulership extends to all nations (Gen 1–11) but figures most prominently, as far as the text is concerned, with *Israel's* national destiny (Gen 12–50). Israel's deliverance, reception of the Mosaic Covenant, and occupation of Canaan (Exod-Josh) highlight the Lord's control of what occurs in history. Even God's punishment of Israel (Judges-1 Sam 7) proves this point, since God clearly has the inherent power to correct as well as to reward. Further, the rise of kingship in Israel itself arose under the Lord's supervision; and its ideals were envisioned through divine interaction with Moses (Deut 17:14–20), Samuel (1 Sam 8–10), Saul (1 Sam 8–12), David (1 Sam 13–1 Kgs 2), Solomon (1 Kgs 2–10), and individuals like Asa, Jehoshaphat, and Jehoiada. Finally, what happens to Israel and to other nations is determined by God's will. Whether by giving one army victory over another (2 Kgs 3; 6:8–7:20), supporting the faithful (2 Kgs 4), saving the lost (2 Kgs 5), appointing kings (2 Kgs 8:7–10:35), or sparing Israel (2 Kgs 13:22–23), it is God who dominates and dictates the action. The rest of Scripture continues this emphasis in great detail, so perhaps it is enough to mention the canonical trend to this point in the Old Testament.

Salvation, protection, miracles, and revelation occur repeatedly in 2 Kings 2–13. Each has God as its source. Just as God was the one calling the patriarchs and the one delivering the Israelites through the exodus, so in these chapters it is God who calls and delivers Elijah, Elisha, the sons of the prophets, the widow, and Naaman. God alone saves (2 Kgs 5:15). The rest of the prophets, the psalmists (cf. Ps 103), Job (cf. Job 19:19–25), Daniel, Ezra, and Nehemiah echo this truth. The Gospels present Jesus' death and resurrection as the focal points of this salvation. Acts 4:12 therefore speaks for the whole canon when it says, "Salvation is found in no one else, for there is no other name under heaven given to men by which we must be saved." All these texts insist a right relationship with God is the key to salvation, then proceed to insist just as strongly that this relationship impacts all of life.

Protection, especially when it comes through miracles, indicates the Lord is the source of safety and security for the faithful. Without his help Israel's armies have no chance of victory over Moab (2 Kgs 3), Syria (2 Kgs 5:1; 6:8–7:20; 13:22–25), or any other nation. This fact is repeated constantly in the Pentateuch, is emphasized almost above all else in Joshua and Judges, reaches its saddest depths in Jeremiah, Ezekiel, and Zephaniah, and generates reflection in Psalm 89, Daniel, and Lamentations. Without the Lord's help, individuals are equally destitute. With this help, however, widows (2 Kgs 4:1–7), mourning mothers (2 Kgs 4:8–37), hungry prophets (2 Kgs 4:38–44), lepers (2 Kgs 5), and poor prophets (2 Kgs 6:1–7) have an advocate who can meet any need. Jesus' ministry highlights God's concern for such persons, as does that of Paul, John, and James.

Humans can only know about God when the Lord acts as the source of this knowledge. He must speak to the prophets for them to prophesy here (cf. 2 Kgs 3:15), just as inspiration was necessary for Moses, Joshua, and Samuel to say anything substantive about God. Nature can become revelatory as well, especially when miracles alter what appears to be "natural." Scripture testifies that people need not worry that the revelation will not be sufficient for their needs, since God acts in history on behalf of individuals and nations for the purpose of meeting real-life spiritual, physical, intellectual, and emotional needs. Not even death provides an unbreachable barrier between God's help and God's people (cf. 2 Kgs 2:1–12).

The prophets are, of course, inextricably linked to the Lord in 2 Kings 2–13. As in the rest of the canon, the prophets are his messengers here.[148] They carry God's message to kings (2 Kgs 3:14–19; 6:8–7:20; 8:7–15; 9:1–10; etc) just as Moses (Exod 5–12), Samuel (1 Sam 12–13), Nathan (2 Sam 12:1–15), and the previous prophets in 1, 2 Kings have done. Later prophets such as Isaiah, Jeremiah, and Amos in the Old Testament, and John the Baptist in the New Testament likewise view themselves as mere messengers who convey to lesser lords what the great Lord wills. The general public also hears the messages, but the focus in 1, 2 Kings is on what the prophets tell Israel's leaders.

It is impossible to overemphasize the importance of the fact that it is *God's word* these messengers proclaim. Zimmerli notes that "God's hand," or "God's Spirit," must be upon the prophets or they have nothing worthy to say.[149] Elisha must wait for God's word (2 Kgs 3:15). When he receives that word it must be shared, however personally repugnant its message may be (2 Kgs 8:7–15). Though their lives can be threatened because their sharing of the word angers secular rulers (cf. 2 Kgs 6:8–15; 6:31), God has the resources to protect not only his word but also his messengers (2 Kgs 6:16–18; 6:32–7:2). All these

[148] Cf. the discussion of the messenger motif in G. von Rad, *Old Testament Theology: Volume II,* trans. D. M. G. Stalker (New York: Harper & Row, 1965) 36–39.

[149] W. Zimmerli, *Old Testament Theology in Outline,* trans. D. E. Green (Edinburgh: T & T Clark, 1993) 101–2.

principles are active in the lives of the other biblical prophets, but never more so than in the ministry of Jeremiah, who opposes peoples, nations, and rulers, has his life threatened constantly, yet enjoys God's deliverance repeatedly. In fact, all these adventures are promised him from his call to ministry onward (cf. Jer 1:1–19). Amos also suffers threats for faithfully sharing God's word (Amos 7:10–17). John the Baptist is murdered by a ruler (Mark 6:14–29), so the prophets sometimes pay the supreme price for their obedience to the Lord.

Not one word the prophets speak in God's name fails. Israel does win the battles Elisha says they will win (2 Kgs 3:15–25; 6:24–7:20, 13:24–25). Hazael does become king after Elisha says he will (2 Kgs 8:7–15). Older "predictions" God makes come true as well when Elisha succeeds Elijah, Hazael succeeds Ben-Hadad, and Jehu succeeds Joram (cf. 1 Kgs 19:15–18). As long as they share what God tells them, it is impossible for the prophets to say an erroneous phrase.

As for the kings in these chapters, they are supposed to heed God's covenant with the patriarchs (2 Kgs 13:22–23), lead the people back to temple-based separatist Yahwism (2 Kgs 12:1–18), reject Baal worship (2 Kgs 10:18–27), and follow the example set by David. In other words, they are to serve the people, which will thus fulfill Moses' requirements for monarchs (Deut 17:14–20). At their best David and Solomon rule as stewards, not despots, an example followed later in Israel's history by Hezekiah (2 Kgs 18–20; Isa 36–39) and Josiah (2 Kgs 22:1–23:30). Jehoshaphat and Joash (while under the tutelage of Jehoiada) lack only the elimination of high places to reach these canonical ideals.

At their worst, though, the kings in this section provide a negative pattern that readers of the whole canon recognize as traits of wicked rulers. Joram desires to hear God's blessings on his plans even though he does not serve the Lord (cf. 2 Kgs 3:11–14). In this way he reminds readers of Saul (cf. 1 Sam 28:1–25) and points them to Zedekiah (cf. Jer 34:1–7; 37:1–3; 38:14–28; 2 Kgs 24:18–25:7). Jehu kills innocent men (2 Kgs 10:1–14). Joash retreats from the God who makes him king (2 Kgs 12:2; 2 Chr 24:17–22), much as Solomon (1 Kgs 11:1–8) and Saul do. Such monarchs never please the Lord, for they ultimately lead God's people to their doom.

Israel's people remain divided between the remnant who serves God and the rebellious majority who do not. Certainly the prophets are the most famous members of the remnant in 1, 2 Kings, while Moses, Aaron, Joshua, Caleb, Samuel, Nathan, and David occupy that position earlier in Scripture. Later prophets, joined by Ezra, Nehemiah, Esther, and Ruth, glorify the term "remnant" by their commitment to the Lord. Still, several "minor" figures also help form the remnant. The unnamed prophets, especially those who undertake dangerous missions like anointing Jehu (2 Kgs 9:1–10), the widow, the Shunammite and her husband, and the man who feeds the faithful prophets

(2 Kgs 4:42–44) also deserve recognition. They make later canonical characters like Isaiah's children, Jeremiah's friend Baruch, Naomi, and Zerubbabel seem less like oddities and more like what the majority should have been. Similarly, individuals such as Joram, Jezebel, Jehu, and Athaliah embody all that was wrong in Israel, all that sent the chosen people into exile.

Finally, the nations also fulfill dual canonical roles. They are instruments of punishment for the Lord's rebellious nation (2 Kgs 10:32–33; 13:3), just as the foreign nations in Judges discipline an idolatrous Israel (Judg 2:1–23). Syria, of course, acts in this capacity most often in 2 Kings 2–13. Eventually, Assyria will assume Syria's role, followed by Babylon, then Persia. All subsequent prophetic books reflect on this procession of punishers, as do virtually all the books in the writings.

On the other hand, the Naaman story furthers a canonical emphasis on God's grace to the nations. From Abraham's call (Gen 12:1–9) onward God expects Israel to bless other nations. Moses marries a Cushite (Num 12:1); Ruth is from Moab; Rahab is a Canaanite; Jonah preaches to Assyrians; Daniel prophesies and witnesses to Babylonians. Yahweh, the only God, stands ready to accept Naaman without hesitation. The question is whether the covenant people are ready to share the covenant Lord. Surely this issue must have penetrated the minds of some of the original readers of 1, 2 Kings, and the servant girl's response to Naaman's pain sets a high standard of loving even captors enough to explain God's power to them.

Given these canonical patterns, it is possible to state several theological truths about the Lord. First, the phrase "the Lord is sovereign" means that no aspect of creation stands apart from God's rule. God governs nations, kings, nature, and death. There is nothing that escapes the Lord's notice, no one who retains personal autonomy, and no one who controls his or her departure from earth. Second, the fact that God protects, saves, and heals keeps his sovereignty from being a terrifying reality. The Lord is good in each of these stories. God never sanctions evil. Third, God's self-revelation is further evidence of divine goodness. The Lord could judge Israel based on past revelation alone yet continues to express his will through the prophets, through miracles, and through current events. This revelation indicates God is patient enough to delay punishment, but not oblivious to human sin.

The prophets are God's agents of revelation, whether the revelation comes through spoken words or miracles. These individuals proclaim an active word, one whose main thrusts never change yet are applied afresh to each new situation. Their orations contain timeless truths about sin, punishment, and restoration and at these same times carry new applications to new life settings. Miracles performed convey healing for the faithful but condemnation for those who fail to respond to the God who provides the power for miracles. Miracles, then, either inspire or harden their witnesses, depending on the witnesses' openness to the Lord. Thus, sermons and miracles both teach monotheism, reform, and hope, though in obviously different ways.

These chapters illustrate the kings' theological purpose in Israel. The kings are not simply stewards of a secular government, though that is part of their societal function. Rather, they are to guarantee the primacy of temple worship (cf. 2 Kgs 12:1–18) and keep the covenant themselves (cf. Deut 17:14–20). They are stewards of a holy land, a holy people, and a holy covenant. As such, they stand as earthly symbols of God's heavenly rule. When they allow anything besides separatist Yahwism to flourish, they are not pure symbols (cf. 2 Kgs 12:1–13). When they fight the Lord's will, they destroy the nation they exist to serve. Each new king, especially if the person is a Davidic king, is a proof of God's faithfulness to the people (cf. 2 Sam 7:1–17), so the monarchs ought to reciprocate with faithfulness of their own.

Israel and the nations share certain obligations and privileges because of God's nature. First, God's sovereignty and grace should lead people to worship the merciful Lord of creation. Israel's rebels fail to learn this lesson, but the remnant in Israel and Gentiles like Naaman recognize the Lord's worth. Second, God's sovereignty over all people means that God's grace extends to every nation and race. Again, Naaman, like the widow of Zarephath before him (cf. 1 Kgs 17:7–24), realizes that the God who heals must be the God who saves. His servant girl assumes correctly that Naaman's nationality does not matter to the prophet or to her compassionate God.

Third, Naaman's healing causes him to confess that "there is no God in all the world except in Israel" (2 Kgs 5:15). The fact that he makes this claim in a pluralistic, polytheistic culture is significant, for he is in no way sheltered from competing worldviews, nor has he failed to observe more than one belief system at close range. He has simply learned to discern the difference between a powerless idol and a personal God who meets worshipers' needs. Clearly, then, Naaman confesses what Israel fails to confess: the sovereign, saving God is the only God and therefore deserves worship. These truths have already been stated explicitly in 1, 2 Kings, yet in this section of the story they take on growing significance through a Gentile witness to an obviously declining covenant nation (cf. Matt 2:1–2).

Applicational Implications of 2 Kgs 2:1–13:25

Preaching and teaching from these chapters should begin with the nature of God. Who is this Yahweh? He is the ruler, the gracious Lord, the healer, the provider, the protector, the generous one, the believer's sole support, the personal God, the reason for communities of faith to exist, the savior, the conqueror of death, the Lord of historical events, the only God who exists. These pictures of God make every other truth meaningful and provide the foundation for all other vital principles in the text. Few sections of Scripture display the many facets of God's character in more detail or with more diversity of human response to that character.

Once God's personality and character are explained, the next obvious topic is human response to this personal Lord. Two very difficult-to-practice words shape this response: faith and obedience. Elisha's eyes of faith see God's ever-present protection, which leads him to live without fear of harm (2 Kgs 6:8–23). Naaman has enough faith in the God who has healed him to pledge life-long allegiance to the Lord (2 Kgs 5:15–18). Jehoiada's personal convictions lead him to take action against Athaliah and to propel Joash into power (2 Kgs 11:4–21). Thus he temporarily saves Judah from idolatry and reinstates David's family to the throne. The unnamed benefactor of the prophets acts out his faith by feeding the faithful (2 Kgs 4:42–44). In other words, faith leads to obedience in the forms of confident teaching and living (2 Kgs 6:8–23), complete commitment to God (2 Kgs 5:15–18), activity to restore godliness in society (2 Kgs 11:4–21), and generous giving to those serving the Lord (2 Kgs 4:42–44). In these texts faith obeys.

One other type of obedience deserves mention by itself. If God alone saves, then evangelism is essential. Certainly evangelism can take many forms. For instance, the slave girl simply tells Naaman where he can get help, yet she begins his healing and conversion journey (2 Kgs 5:1–3). On the other hand, Elisha tells Naaman how to be healed, which forces the Syrian to trust God, which in turn leads to a personal discovery of Yahweh. Both the prophet and the girl share a word appropriate in that situation, though, and this obedience, not some particular method to be used in every situation, is the heart of evangelism. Specific methods are useful when this central obedience exists but only then.

Obedient evangelism occurred in the ancient world in a pluralistic context. Many religions and worldviews vied for supremacy. Elisha and the other faithful followers of the Lord dared to claim that no other gods are real and that Yahweh alone can save. God then honored their faithfulness with discipline, protection, answered prayer, a convert or two, and miracles. In these ways these stories read very much like the way God blesses the early church in Acts. Both biblical books describe a remnant working to make God known, and both books record God's faithfulness to these remnants. Today's believers need to emulate the commitment of the biblical community to proclaiming the uniqueness of Jesus. They also need to have a rational defense of their faith,[150] one that leads them to stress commitment to Christ above cultural popularity, to risk appearing narrow or closeminded, to instruct members in a rational and compassionate worldview and social agenda, and to dare to speak of right and

[150] For an excellent group of essays that present such defenses of the faith read *Proceedings of the Wheaton Theology Conference,* 1 (1992).

wrong in a world like the one in 1, 2 Kings that believes truth is relative to its cultural and religious context.[151]

The value of communities of faith emerges repeatedly in 2 Kings 2–13 and remains vital today. The "sons of the prophets" ate together, worked together, and witnessed together. They shared a common calling, a common goal, and a common suffering. Their victories were also shared. Clearly, the primary elements of a confessional community transcend time and space. Churches can recapture their power only when they are unified under God's plan for Christ's body (cf. John 17; 1 Cor 12).

Finally, it is impossible to miss these stories' emphasis on the perils of disobedience. Jehu's murders, Gehazi's covetousness, Joash's ingratitude, the officer's lack of faith, and Athaliah's cruelty are all judged by God. Those who choose to sin in the ways these characters sin must be prepared to receive the kinds of punishments they endure. It is much better to choose the way of the remnant, even if that choice leads to short-term discomfort or outright persecution. All other paths lead to failure, corruption, defeat, and exile.

---

[151] J. R. Edwards, "A Confessional Church in the Pluralistic World," ibid., 95.

SECTION OUTLINE

VI. ISRAEL DISINTEGRATES (14:1–17:41)
Historical Details Related to 2 Kings 14–17
1. Judah Battles Israel (14:1–22)
2. Temporary Respite (14:23–15:7)
   (1) Jeroboam II's Reign (14:23–29)
   (2) Azariah's Reign (15:1–7)
3. Israel's Political Upheaval (15:8–31)
   (1) Zechariah's Reign and Assassination (15:8–12)
   (2) Shallum's Reign and Assassination (15:13–16)
   (3) Menahem's Reign and the Assyrian Threat (15:17–22)
   (4) Pekahiah's Reign and Assassination (15:23–26)
   (5) Pekah's Reign, Assassination, and the Assyrian Threat (15:27–31)
4. Judah's Political Weakness (15:32–16:20)
   (1) Jotham's Reign (15:32–38)
   (2) Ahaz's Reign (16:1–20)
5. Assyria Destroys Israel (17:1–41)
   (1) Hoshea's Reign and the Assyrian Conquest (17:1–6)
   (2) Reasons for Israel's Fall (17:7–23)
   (3) Samaria Resettled (17:24–41)

VI. ISRAEL DISINTEGRATES (14:1–17:41)

At the end of 2 Kings 13 Israel and Judah appear to have brighter prospects for the future after having suffered a great deal in their recent past. Unfortunately, an era of prosperity is not accompanied by faithfulness to the Lord, a fact the author makes plain (2 Kgs 14:24; 15:4) and canonical prophets such as Amos and Hosea emphasize. Without spiritual renewal this prosperity is merely a lull before the greatest storm the people have seen to this point in their history. As Noth observes, "The great power of Assyria loomed sinisterly in the background."[1]

By 745 B.C. a new and vigorous Assyrian leader named Tiglath-Pileser III has his nation on the march again. A succession of weak northern kings joins Syria in a futile attempt to hold off the Assyrian invaders (2 Kgs 15:17–31),

[1] M. Noth, *The History of Israel,* 2d ed., trans. P. R. Ackroyd (New York: Harper & Row, 1960) 250.

while Judah survives by adopting a pro-Assyrian policy (2 Kgs 16:1–18). In 722 B.C. Tiglath-Pileser's successor, Shalmaneser V (727–722 B.C.), overruns Israel, destroys Samaria, and sends the populace into exile (2 Kgs 17:1–6). Judah hangs by a thread, a mere trembling vassal of Assyria.

How did Israel come to such an end? Of course, Assyria's strength coupled with Israel's political and social instability made it improbable that the small country could survive. But the text stresses another factor: Israel fell because of its sin and its rejection of God's warnings graciously extended through the prophets (2 Kgs 17:7–23). Any other obstacle could have been overcome, but covenant unfaithfulness could not go unpunished forever (cf. Deut 27–28; Lev 26). Readers are left with the impression that God rules history. They are also left to wonder if Judah's own demise can tarry much longer.

Historical Details Related to 2 Kings 14–17

More than ever before, the international scene began to dictate what occurred in Judah and Israel. The first major incident to impact these nations' destiny was Assyria's defeat of Syria in 802 B.C. Hazael had died in 806 B.C., leaving the throne to his son Ben-Hadad II. Assyria's Adad-nirari III attacked the new king's armies repeatedly after Hazael's death and finally crushed Damascus, thus disposing of his longtime foe.[2] Adad-nirari did not follow up his victory by invading Israel, possibly because Jehoash paid him tribute money.[3] He also had problems with nations closer to home (e.g., Urartu), and occupation of lands so far from his capital was not part of his conquest policy.[4] Several much weaker rulers followed Adad-nirari, so Assyria did not bother the region for another fifty years.[5]

Israel and Judah took advantage of Syria's loss of capable leadership and their military weakness. Jehoash defeated a weakened Syria three times, thus regaining cities lost earlier (2 Kgs 13:25), as Elijah predicted (13:18–19). Amaziah was also active. He "defeated ten thousand Edomites in the Valley of Salt and captured Sela in battle," then renamed the city Joktheel (2 Kgs 14:7). Next, for no reason that is stated in the text other than pride, Amaziah challenged Jehoash. Second Chronicles 25:7–24 supplies some more information on the situation. The Chronicler states that Amaziah had hired some Israelite mercenaries to fight Edom but had sent them home because of advice he received from "a man of God" (2 Chr 25:7–9). Furious, the mercenaries killed Judahites and plundered Judean cities (2 Chr 25:10,13). Once finished with the Edomites, Amaziah sought to avenge his people but was humiliated instead,

---

[2] J. H. Hayes, *Amos the Eighth-Century Prophet: His Times and His Preaching* (Nashville: Abingdon, 1988) 21.

[3] *ANET,* 281ff.

[4] J. Bright, *A History of Israel,* 3d ed. (Philadelphia: Westminster, 1981) 256.

[5] Hayes, *Amos,* 24–25.

suffering even the invasion of Jerusalem and the robbing of its treasuries (2 Chr 25:23–24; 2 Kgs 14:11–14). The Chronicler says that this defeat was God's way of punishing Amaziah's idolatry (2 Chr 25:20). Israel clearly remained the more dominant of the two countries. Eventually Amaziah's subjects murder him and place his son Azariah (also called Uzziah) on the throne (2 Kgs 14:17–22). Jeroboam II replaces Jehoash when he dies (2 Kgs 14:23–29).

When the regional power vacuum continued, Jeroboam II (ca. 793–753 B.C.) and Uzziah (ca. 792–740 B.C.) extended their nations' authority even further. Bright explains that "Jeroboam was one of the strong military figures of Israel's history. Though we know of none of his battles (two victories in Transjordan are alluded to in Amos 6:13), he was able to place his northern frontier where Solomon's had been, at the entrance of Hamath (II Kings 14:25; cf. 1 Kings 8:65)."[6] Syria was no longer a factor in Israelite affairs. Uzziah also succeeded in expanding his country's borders. According to 2 Chr 26:1–23, he defeated the Philistines and forced Ammon to pay tribute, partly because of how well he rebuilt Judah's army. Uzziah also rebuilt Elath (2 Kgs 14:22), which means he extended Judah's southern border as well. Besides these achievements, he was able to act as coregent with Jotham, his son. This last act became necessary when he became "the only 'leper king' attested in antiquity,"[7] a disease he was afflicted with because he attempted to usurp the priests' authority by offering a sacrifice in the temple (2 Chr 26:16–21).

After the death of Jeroboam II Israel inherited a series of short-term monarchs. Zechariah followed Jeroboam II in 753 B.C. and reigned six months (2 Kgs 15:8). He was assassinated by Shallum, who ruled one month before Menahem killed him. Menahem governed for ten years but had no success like that enjoyed by Jeroboam II. Israel was crumbling at just the wrong time, for Assyria was about to ascend to its greatest national heights.

Tigath-Pileser III assumed power in Assyria in 745 B.C., while Menahem controlled Israel and while Uzziah and Jotham were governing Judah. He came to the throne as a usurper, quickly subdued Babylon, attacked Syrian outposts, and established the new policy of making conquered cities into Assyrian-administrated territories.[8] He usually forced a conquered monarch to swear allegiance to him or be replaced. Citizens of defeated nations were often deported and refugees from other places brought to take their place. Such practices allowed Assyria to control their subjects, extract money from them, and generally keep them confused and terrorized.[9] Though these were his general

---

[6] Bright, *A History of Israel,* 256.

[7] M. Cogan and H. Tadmor, *II Kings,* AB 11 (Garden City: Doubleday, 1988) 167.

[8] See W. W. Hallo and W. K. Simpson, *The Ancient Near East: A History* (New York: Harcourt, Brace, Jovanovich, 1971) 132–38.

[9] Cf. B. Obed, "Observations on Methods of Assyrian Rule in Transjordania after the Palestinian Campaign of Tiglath-Pileser III," *JNES* 29 (1970) 177–86.

practices, Tiglath-Pileser was wise enough to assess every situation individually and adapt his strategies to meet his goals in each separate place.[10]

During 743 to 738 B.C., "Tiglath-Pileser conquered and annexed north Syria: Arpad, Unqi, Hadrach, Simmira and its environs reaching as far as the desert east of Damascus."[11] These victories helped him subdue Urartu, an old border enemy of Assyria.[12] From 738 to 729 B.C. Tiglath waged war against the Medes and the Babylonians. He eventually conquered Babylon in 729 B.C., lived there as king Pul for two years, then died in 727 B.C.[13] Thus, Shalmaneser V (727–722 B.C.) inherited a vast and powerful kingdom when Tiglath-Pileser died.

Though some of the victories already mentioned constituted Tiglath-Pileser's greatest triumphs, another campaign impacted 1, 2 Kings more. For a time Israel avoided Assyria's wrath by paying tribute. Menahem (752–742 B.C.) levied taxes to pay Tiglath-Pileser to turn away from Israel in 743 B.C. (2 Kgs 15:19–20).[14] By 734 B.C., however, Israel had joined Syria in a coalition against Assyria. Edom and Philistia also were partners in the group. Judah, now under the authority of Ahaz, who allowed Jotham to rule as coregent as long as the older man lived, decided not to join the coalition. The allies attacked Judah from three sides and eventually threatened Jerusalem itself (16:5–6).

Ahaz asked Tiglath-Pileser III to beat back the coalition, and the Assyrian obliged. In 734 and 733 B.C. Tiglath-Pileser invaded Israel. Bright notes, "All Israelite lands in Galilee and Transjordan were overrun, portions of the population were deported (II Kings 15:29), and numerous cities (e.g., Megiddo, Hazor) destroyed."[15] Damascus fell in 732 B.C., which spelled the end of the coalition. Pekah (740–732 B.C.), who led Israel's opposition to Assyria, was murdered by Hoshea (732–722 B.C.), who took the throne of the Northern Kingdom. Unlike his predecessor, Hoshea served Assyria for a time.[16] Tiglath-Pileser divided Israel into three provinces and allowed Hoshea to remain in "power."[17] Ahaz's dependence on Assyria forced Judah to be Assyria's vassal

---

[10] Cf. M. Cogan, "Judah under Assyrian Hegemony: A Reexamination of Imperialism and Religion," JBL 112/3 (1993) 407.

[11] H. Tadmor and M. Cogan, "Ahaz and Tiglath-Pileser in the Book of Kings: Historiographical Considerations," *Bib* 60 (1979) 491.

[12] A. L. Oppenheim, "Urartu," *IDB,* 4:641.

[13] Hallo and Simpson, *The Ancient Near East,* 137.

[14] Cf. E. R. Thiele, *The Mysterious Numbers of the Hebrew Kings,* 3d ed. (Grand Rapids: Zondervan, 1983) 149–52; contra L. D. Levine's 738 B.C. date in "Menahem and Tiglath-Pileser: A New Synchronism," *BASOR* 206 (1972) 40–42.

[15] Bright, *A History of Israel,* 274.

[16] Ibid.

[17] Noth, *The History of Israel,* 261. For details on Assyria's administration of Israel after 734 B.C. consult Obed, "Observations on Methods of Assyrian Rule," and S. M. Paul, "Sargon's Administrative Diction in II Kings 17:27," *JBL* 88 (1969) 73–74.

as well. Neither kingdom was autonomous now.

When Shalmaneser V succeeded Tiglath-Pileser III, Hoshea decided to withhold tribute. He hoped Egypt would protect him against Assyria (2 Kgs 17:4). This foolish decision brought the wrath of Shalmaneser down upon Israel. Assyria invaded Israel and held Hoshea prisoner by 724 B.C., then captured Samaria in 722 B.C. after a three-year siege (2 Kgs 17:5).[18] Thus, Israel ceased to exist as a nation, while Judah survived because of Ahaz's pro-Assyrian policy. Ahaz was little more than an Assyrian puppet.

The author of 1, 2 Kings stresses that Israel and Judah suffered from spiritual woes as well. Not one Israelite king made any attempt to stop the moral decay caused by idolatry and syncretistic worship. Amos and Hosea claimed that not even the prosperity experienced under Jeroboam II turned the people toward the Lord. Judah was little better. Amaziah was basically a good king (2 Kgs 14:3), as were Uzziah (2 Kgs 15:3) and Jotham (2 Kgs 15:34), but none of these men removed the high places that stood as monuments to the nation's heterodox theology.[19] Ahaz, on the other hand, was an outright idolater who imported Assyrian gods into the land (2 Kgs 16:10–16). His guilt was compounded by the fact that this decision was most likely voluntary, not forced.[20] Ahaz apparently either worshiped these gods because he wanted to impress Tiglath-Pileser III or because he believed Assyria's gods were more powerful than Yahweh. Neither motivation was acceptable to the author of 1, 2 Kings, and Ahaz is condemned in the text (2 Kgs 16:1–4).

Besides these religious and political factors, Israel fell and Judah declined because of social and economic decay. The prosperity enjoyed in the first half of the century was shared by only a few. Amos complains that the rich got wealthy at the expense of the poor (cf. Amos 4:1–7; 6:1–7). Justice was perverted, and slavery flourished (Amos 2:6–7). No society can survive the strain of oppression, slavery, greed, and injustice for long, and Israel was no exception to this rule. Judah lasted a bit longer, yet finally succumbed due to similar types of corruption (cf. Jer 2–6).

Throughout, the prophets tried to turn Israel back to the Lord. Though they are not mentioned in 2 Kgs 14–17, Amos, Hosea, and Isaiah preached repen-

---

[18] Cf. J. H. Hayes and J. K. Kuan, "The Final Years of Samaria (730–720 B.C.)," *Bib* 72 (1991) 153–81.

[19] Cf. C. F. Graesser, "Standing Stones in Ancient Palestine," *BA* 35 (1972) 62.

[20] This comment follows the conclusions of J. McKay, *Religion in Judah under the Assyrians*, SBT/2,26 (Naperville, Ill.: Allenson, 1973); M. Cogan, *Imperialism and Religion: Assyria, Judah and Israel in the Eighth and Seventh Centuries* B.C.E., SBLMS 19 (Missoula, Mont.: Scholars Press, 1974); and M. Cogan, "Judah under Assyrian Hegemony: A Reexamination of Imperialism and Religion." These works argue that Assyria did not impose worship of its gods on defeated nations. For the opposite viewpoint consult T. Oestreicher, *Das deuteronomische Grundgesetz* BFCT 27/4 (Gütersloh, 1923); and H. Spieckermann, *Juda unter Assur in der Sargonidenzeit*, FRLANT 129 (Göttingen: Vandenhoeck & Ruprecht, 1982).

tance during these years, but to no avail. Only the predictions of judgment were left, and, sadly, these promises were fulfilled (2 Kgs 17:23). Tragically, Israel's fall could have been prevented. Judah could have learned from Israel's mistakes yet failed to do so. All the weight of the covenant people's sin finally came crashing down upon them. Assyria was the instrument of this destruction, but Israel was responsible for what happened to them.

1. Judah Battles Israel (14:1–22)

**[1]In the second year of Jehoash son of Jehoahaz king of Israel, Amaziah son of
Joash king of Judah began to reign. [2]He was twenty-five years old when he
became king, and he reigned in Jerusalem twenty-nine years. His mother's name
was Jehoaddin; she was from Jerusalem. [3]He did what was right in the eyes of the
LORD, but not as his father David had done. In everything he followed the example of his father Joash. [4]The high places, however, were not removed; the people
continued to offer sacrifices and burn incense there.**

**[5]After the kingdom was firmly in his grasp, he executed the officials who had
murdered his father the king. [6]Yet he did not put the sons of the assassins to
death, in accordance with what is written in the Book of the Law of Moses where
the LORD commanded: "Fathers shall not be put to death for their children, nor
children put to death for their fathers; each is to die for his own sins."**

**[7]He was the one who defeated ten thousand Edomites in the Valley of Salt and
captured Sela in battle, calling it Joktheel, the name it has to this day.**

**[8]Then Amaziah sent messengers to Jehoash son of Jehoahaz, the son of Jehu,
king of Israel, with the challenge: "Come, meet me face to face."**

**[9]But Jehoash king of Israel replied to Amaziah king of Judah: "A thistle in
Lebanon sent a message to a cedar in Lebanon, 'Give your daughter to my son in
marriage.' Then a wild beast in Lebanon came along and trampled the thistle
underfoot. [10]You have indeed defeated Edom and now you are arrogant. Glory in
your victory, but stay at home! Why ask for trouble and cause your own downfall
and that of Judah also?"**

**[11]Amaziah, however, would not listen, so Jehoash king of Israel attacked. He
and Amaziah king of Judah faced each other at Beth Shemesh in Judah. [12]Judah
was routed by Israel, and every man fled to his home. [13]Jehoash king of Israel
captured Amaziah king of Judah, the son of Joash, the son of Ahaziah, at Beth
Shemesh. Then Jehoash went to Jerusalem and broke down the wall of Jerusalem
from the Ephraim Gate to the Corner Gate—a section about six hundred feet
long. [14]He took all the gold and silver and all the articles found in the temple of
the LORD and in the treasuries of the royal palace. He also took hostages and
returned to Samaria.**

**[15]As for the other events of the reign of Jehoash, what he did and his achieve-
ments, including his war against Amaziah king of Judah, are they not written in
the book of the annals of the kings of Israel? [16]Jehoash rested with his fathers and
was buried in Samaria with the kings of Israel. And Jeroboam his son succeeded
him as king.**

17Amaziah son of Joash king of Judah lived for fifteen years after the death of Jehoash son of Jehoahaz king of Israel. 18As for the other events of Amaziah's reign, are they not written in the book of the annals of the kings of Judah?

19They conspired against him in Jerusalem, and he fled to Lachish, but they sent men after him to Lachish and killed him there. 20He was brought back by horse and was buried in Jerusalem with his fathers, in the City of David.

21Then all the people of Judah took Azariah, who was sixteen years old, and made him king in place of his father Amaziah. 22He was the one who rebuilt Elath and restored it to Judah after Amaziah rested with his fathers.

Two kings who already have been introduced dictate the action in this section. Jehoash of Israel, the ruler who finally ends Syria's dominance over his people (cf. 2 Kgs 13:24–25), and Amaziah of Judah, who comes to power when his father Joash is murdered (cf. 2 Kgs 12:19–21), lead their respective nations. Both men enjoy a measure of military success as a result of Syria's weakened condition. Unfortunately they also use their newly gained freedom to fight one another. Jehoash does not want the conflict, but his taunts do not quiet matters either. Neither country gains anything substantive from these hostilities, and readers are left to wonder how constructively the two countries might have used their respite from oppression. No real spiritual gains are made, so Israel and Judah squander a real opportunity to place themselves back on solid spiritual and governmental ground.

14:1–6 Perhaps Amaziah had nothing to do with his father's assassination (cf. 2 Kgs 12:19–21) since he punishes the killers, though it would not be totally unheard of for a king to kill those who gave him power. His official reign lasts twenty-nine years, or from about 796 to 767 B.C. However, most of these years he will not rule alone. It appears that he comes to power because the people do not want his father and that he becomes unpopular and is forced to accept a coregent. Thus he is a transitional figure who never leaves his own imprint on the nation.

Despite Amaziah's lack of permanent political success, the author does consider him better religiously than most of Judah's monarchs. Though not as faithful as David (cp. 2 Chr 25:2), the ultimate standard for rulers (cf. 1 Kgs 14:8; 15:4–5), he nonetheless continues Joash's emphasis on the temple's preeminence in worship. Still, he does not insist on Jerusalem's sole claim as the location for all worship, since he allows the high places to continue to exist. So on the one hand, he obeys Moses' laws concerning making only the sinner suffer for the sinner's wrongdoing (cf. Deut 24:16), unlike Jehu, who killed every relative of Ahab and Ahaziah that he could find. But on the other hand, Amaziah does not keep Moses' commands regarding the high places (e.g., Deut 16:1–8; 16:21–22). All in all, then, he is better than most kings, but not as strong morally as some future kings.

14:7 Amaziah's greatest military achievement is his defeat of Edom. The extent of his triumph is unknown,[21] but the victory is recorded here and in a longer description in 2 Chr 25:5–13. It is not possible to state with certainty where Sela was located.[22] What is certain is that Judah expands its southern border, which it has not done for some time.

The Chronicler offers information that helps explain why Amaziah challenges Jehoash after the victory in Edom. Amaziah hires mercenaries from Israel to help him fight the Edomites, then sends them home before the battle because of a prophetic word he receives (2 Chr 25:7–9). Enraged, the soldiers plunder Judahite towns all the way home (25:13) probably because their dismissal would mean forfeiting the plunder of battle.[23] Whatever their reasoning, the mercenaries' actions, coupled with Amaziah's pride over the recent triumph in Edom, lead to a confrontation that Judah will regret.

14:8–10 Amaziah uses a common royal style of presentation to challenge Israel formally.[24] Jehoash cites a familiar fable in response.[25] The Israelite chides Amaziah for his pride by comparing him to "a lowly thistle making pretentious demands against a great Lebanese cedar, only to be trampled under foot by a passing animal. How empty the boasting of such a puny antagonist!"[26] Jehoash counsels his counterpart to be happy with small victories and to avoid tangling with a nation that can whip Syria. Certainly Israel does not want a war, but Jehoash's words hardly constitute a soft answer calculated to turn aside Amaziah's wrath.

14:11–14 Just as Jehoash predicts, the confrontation proves a disaster for Judah. The Chronicler explains that the defeat was God's judgment on Amaziah for adopting the Edomite gods after the Sela victory (2 Chr 25:14–16,20). Israel attacks at Beth-shemesh, which was located about fifteen miles southwest of Jerusalem.[27] Dillard theorizes that Jehoash chooses this point of engagement so he could exercise "control over commerce to and from Jerusalem from the north and west."[28] If so, Jehoash is so confident of military victory that he intends to take over Judah's financial stronghold as well.

Israel quickly marches the fifteen miles to Jerusalem. They route Judah's army, capture Amaziah, take Jerusalem, break down parts of the city's defensive walls, and plunder the temple and palace. Hostages are taken, which Montgom-

---

[21] Bright, *A History of Israel,* 256–57.

[22] Cf. J. Gray, *1 and 2 Kings,* OTL (Philadelphia: Westminster, 1963) 548; and J. M. Myers, *II Chronicles,* 2d ed., AB (Garden City: Doubleday, 1973) 13:143.

[23] R. B. Dillard, *2 Chronicles,* WBC (Waco: Word, 1987) 15:200.

[24] Cogan and Tadmor, *II Kings,* 156, citing R. R. Wilson, *Genealogy and History in the Biblical World* (New Haven: Yale University Press, 1977) 58–60.

[25] D. J. Wiseman, *1 and 2 Kings,* TOTC (Downers Grove: InterVarsity, 1993) 245.

[26] R. D. Patterson and H. J. Austel, "1, 2 Kings," EBC (Grand Rapids: Zondervan, 1988) 4:228.

[27] Myers, *II Chronicles,* 143.

[28] Dillard, *2 Chronicles,* 202.

ery and Gehman observe is a unique occurrence in Old Testament history.[29] Thiele suggests that Amaziah himself is held hostage for years, though the text itself does not say so explicitly.[30] Although this suggestion is unprovable, it is clear that Amaziah has been completely humiliated. It is not difficult to imagine that he has lost any mandate for leadership he ever possessed.

14:15–16 Jehoash passes from the scene and is replaced by his son Jeroboam. Other than mentioning in passing his victory over Amaziah one last time, the author offers no critique of his reign, since 2 Kgs 13:10–11 has already done so. Jehoash continued Jeroboam's cult (2 Kgs 13:11), which is another way of saying he contributed to Israel's slide toward destruction. Readers must wonder if the new Jeroboam will be any different from his namesake.

14:17–22 Amaziah outlives his rival by fifteen years, but does not rule with any sole authority. His son Azariah (Uzziah) acts as coregent from about 792 to 767 B.C., perhaps because of discontent over the older man's ineptitude. Eventually Amaziah is a victim of a conspiracy. It is unclear what causes the discontent, though as Vos observes, "The opposition was widespread."[31] His final days are as hectic and dangerous as his confrontations with Jehoash.

Azariah succeeds his father, perhaps with Jehoash's blood on his hands. He rules from ca. 792–740 B.C., an era that includes coregencies with his father (ca. 792–767 B.C.) and his son Jotham (ca. 750–740).[32] Apparently he has widespread support when he assumes control, for the author stresses that "all the people of Judah" make him king. Azariah continues the recent southern expansion by restoring the port city Elath, a project his father may have begun.[33] In time the new king achieves even greater things, in part because he learns it is counterproductive to wage war against Israel. The time of these two small nations battling each other has ended, for now.

2. Temporary Respite (14:23–15:7)

When Jeroboam II becomes sole regent of Israel in 782 B.C.,[34] Israel has only a few decades left before its destruction in 722 B.C. His reign offers a respite, however, before the onslaught, a financial golden era before the Assyr-

---

[29] J. A. Montgomery and H. S. Gehman, *A Critical and Exegetical Commentary on the Book of Kings,* ICC (1951; reprint, Edinburgh: T & T Clark, 1986) 442.

[30] Thiele, *The Mysterious Numbers of the Hebrew Kings,* 115.

[31] H. F. Vos, *1, 2 Kings,* BSC (Grand Rapids: Zondervan, 1989) 181.

[32] Cf. Thiele, *The Mysterious Numbers of the Hebrew Kings,* 115; and Gray, *1 and 2 Kings,* 555.

[33] Montgomery and Gehman, *Kings,* 442.

[34] Cf. Thiele, *The Mysterious Numbers of the Hebrew Kings,* 116. He probably is coregent with Jehoash from 793 to 782 B.C., though Jehoash seems to have provided the actual leadership in this period.

ians ravage the land. Judah also has a time of prosperity under Azariah. Still, neither country learns any more from plenty than they do from want. This temporary break is, unfortunately, just that—temporary.

(1) Jeroboam II's Reign (14:23–29)

[23]In the fifteenth year of Amaziah son of Joash king of Judah, Jeroboam son of Jehoash king of Israel became king in Samaria, and he reigned forty-one years. [24]He did evil in the eyes of the LORD and did not turn away from any of the sins of Jeroboam son of Nebat, which he had caused Israel to commit. [25]He was the one who restored the boundaries of Israel from Lebo Hamath to the Sea of the Arabah, in accordance with the word of the LORD, the God of Israel, spoken through his servant Jonah son of Amittai, the prophet from Gath Hepher.

[26]The LORD had seen how bitterly everyone in Israel, whether slave or free, was suffering; there was no one to help them. [27]And since the LORD had not said he would blot out the name of Israel from under heaven, he saved them by the hand of Jeroboam son of Jehoash.

[28]As for the other events of Jeroboam's reign, all he did, and his military achievements, including how he recovered for Israel both Damascus and Hamath, which had belonged to Yaudi, are they not written in the book of the annals of the kings of Israel? [29]Jeroboam rested with his fathers, the kings of Israel. And Zechariah his son succeeded him as king.

14:23–25 Jeroboam II's reign is a long and "evil" one. Like his predecessors, he maintains the state religion instituted by Jeroboam I almost two centuries earlier. Thus, no move back to the Lord occurs. But despite his spiritual condition, God blesses him. Jonah, the prophet of the Book of Jonah, predicts Israel's borders will extend "from Lebo Hamath to the Sea of the Arabah." The designation of Lebo Hamath as Israel's northern border makes the new boundary equal to that managed by Solomon (cf. 1 Kgs 8:65).[35] As in the Elisha stories in 2 Kgs 13:14–19, it is the prophet, not the king, who gets credit for the expansion. God's patience is at work in the people's affairs.

Hosea and Amos, both of whom minister during this time period (Hos 1:1; Amos 1:1), reflect the author's emphasis on the Lord's patience and kindness toward the covenant people. Hosea compares God's love for straying Israel to his own commitment to Gomer, his adulterous wife (cf. Hos 1–3). Amos notes that God has tried to turn Israel from sin (Amos 4:6–13) and has delayed judgment more than once (Amos 7:1–6). Still the people reject the Lord, which means they will face punishment, just as Moses promises in Leviticus 26 and Deuteronomy 27–28 (cf. Amos 7:7–9; 8:1–9:10).

What sins do the people commit during these years? Hosea says they are spiritual adulterers (Hos 1:2; 4:1), thieves (4:2), and ungrateful children (11:1–

[35] Gray, *1 and 2 Kings,* 556.

7). In short, there is "no acknowledgment of God in the land" (Hos 4:1). God desires mercy (Hos 6:6) and monotheism (Hos 13:4) but receives only meaningless sacrifice and idolatry. Likewise, Amos finds oppression of the poor (Amos 2:6), injustice (2:7), and immorality (2:8). The people love wealth more than kindness (4:1–3), ease more than righteous character (6:1–7). How can the nation avoid divine wrath? God waits for change, then sends his prophets; yet he must still punish in the end.

14:26–29 The Lord's kindness emerges again in this text. As in 2 Kgs 13:22–23, the writer stresses that the Lord uses a quite imperfect ruler to extend grace to Israel. In language reminiscent of Exod 2:23–25, the text reminds readers that it is God's goodness, not the nation's, that allows Israel to survive. When Jeroboam II dies, Israel has lost its final chance to change. Assyria will soon march under Tiglath-Pileser III, Syria will regain some power under their king, Rezin, and Israel itself will suffer severe leadership crises. The respite is over.

(2) Azariah's Reign (15:1–7)

1In the twenty-seventh year of Jeroboam king of Israel, Azariah son of Amaziah king of Judah began to reign. 2He was sixteen years old when he became king, and he reigned in Jerusalem fifty-two years. His mother's name was Jecoliah; she was from Jerusalem. 3He did what was right in the eyes of the LORD, just as his father Amaziah had done. 4The high places, however, were not removed; the people continued to offer sacrifices and burn incense there.

5The LORD afflicted the king with leprosy until the day he died, and he lived in a separate house. Jotham the king's son had charge of the palace and governed the people of the land.

6As for the other events of Azariah's reign, and all he did, are they not written in the book of the annals of the kings of Judah? 7Azariah rested with his fathers and was buried near them in the City of David. And Jotham his son succeeded him as king.

15:1–4 Azariah, whom the text also refers to as Uzziah (cf. 2 Kgs 15:13,30,32,34),[36] succeeds in Judah much as Jeroboam II does in Israel. His reign is characterized in two ways. First, the text says he begins ruling in Jeroboam II's twenty-seventh year, or about 767 B.C. This notation is figured from the start of Jeroboam II's coregency with Jehoash but from the beginning of Azariah's sole regency. Second, the writer says Azariah rules fifty-two years, which reflects Azariah's coregency with Amaziah. Thus, including coregency Azariah serves ca. 792–740. Though such explanations seem strange to modern readers, the author's audience most likely understood why the form was

[36] For a list of biblical and Assyrian kings with both a personal name and a throne name, see Montgomery and Gehman, *Kings,* 446.

used and what type of information it conveyed.

Like Amaziah and Joash before him, Uzziah does "right in the eyes of the LORD." He does not remove the high places, however, so he is not an ideal ruler. Second Chronicles 26:16–20 adds other information about Uzziah that presents him as a less-than-perfect servant of the Lord. This text recounts that Uzziah enters the temple, burns incense on the altar, and is confronted by priests for usurping their role in worship. While he berates the priests, he breaks out in leprosy, which the Chronicler describes as a divine disciplinary affliction (2 Chr 26:20). Because of his leprosy he is forced to live separately and never enter the temple. Jotham is pressed into a coregency to help run the country (2 Chr 26:21).

Why does Uzziah offer incense? The Chronicler states that he becomes proud of his military victories, none of which are mentioned in 2 Kgs 15:1–7. According to 2 Chr 26:6–15, Uzziah defeats the Philistines and the Ammonites. He also rebuilds the walls of Jerusalem that Jehoash destroyed (cf. 2 Kgs 14:11–14). Clearly, Uzziah also benefits from Assyria's problems, Syria's weakness, and the opportunities that result from Israel's ascendancy. He does not fight Jeroboam II, so he contributes to overall stability in the region. According to Amos 2:4–5, though, many of the same sins found in Israel at this time are also present in Judah as well.

15:5–7 Two issues are emphasized here. First, Azariah is afflicted with leprosy by the Lord. The reason for the affliction is not stated, which may be why the Chronicler gives the rationale. Second, Jotham must take over for his father and rule the palace and govern the people. No statement about Azariah's ongoing involvement in an advisory capacity is mentioned, but such a possibility cannot be dismissed.[37] The practice of coregency is never stated more clearly than here. When Azariah dies, it is logical that Jotham succeed his father.[38] This coregency probably lasted ca. 750–740 B.C.

Judah could not have realized it at this time, but the nation has enjoyed one of its last peaceful periods. Except for a few years in Josiah's reign (640–609 B.C.), the people will now always be at the mercy of some other nation, or at least under constant pressure from some external force. It will indeed take longer for Judah to fall, but fall it will. Again the respite is over.

3. Israel's Political Upheaval (15:8–31)

Events now move swiftly, and none of them are kind to Israel. At just the moment that Assyria becomes a belligerent, conquering nation, Israel suffers through a succession of weak kings who come to power usually through

[37] Cf. Thiele, *The Mysterious Numbers of the Hebrew Kings,* 93–94.

[38] Although buried in Jerusalem, his body was not permitted in the royal tombs. See 2 Chr 26:23 and Patterson and Austel, "1, 2 Kings," 4:234.

intrigue and assassination. Of course, the author does not view these events as simply bad luck and poor timing. God is at work, punishing the sins of a stubborn people. Two hundred years of rebellion will soon be judged.

(1) Zechariah's Reign and Assassination (15:8–12)

8In the thirty-eighth year of Azariah king of Judah, Zechariah son of Jeroboam became king of Israel in Samaria, and he reigned six months. 9He did evil in the eyes of the LORD, as his fathers had done. He did not turn away from the sins of Jeroboam son of Nebat, which he had caused Israel to commit.

10Shallum son of Jabesh conspired against Zechariah. He attacked him in front of the people, assassinated him and succeeded him as king. 11The other events of Zechariah's reign are written in the book of the annals of the kings of Israel. 12So the word of the LORD spoken to Jehu was fulfilled: "Your descendants will sit on the throne of Israel to the fourth generation."

15:8–12 Zechariah's reign (ca. 753–752)[39] begins the swift downward plunge of the Northern Kingdom. As Jones observes, he was the last king descended from Jehu.[40] This observation underscores God's faithfulness in keeping the promise made to Jehu in 2 Kgs 9:30. God remains trustworthy no matter what humans may do. Zechariah's continuation of Jeroboam I's cult therefore magnifies God's grace, for the Lord allows Zechariah to rule for reasons other than merit.

Zechariah's reign also is noteworthy in that it begins an era of intrigue. Shallum becomes the first person of this current era to come to power through conspiracy and assassination. Of course, Baasha (1 Kgs 15:27–28), Zimri (16:10), Omri (16:15–20), and Jehu (2 Kgs 9–10) took this route to power earlier. Now kings will rarely use any other avenue to the throne. Israel's political scene becomes increasingly chaotic.

(2) Shallum's Reign and Assassination (15:13–16)

13Shallum son of Jabesh became king in the thirty-ninth year of Uzziah king of Judah, and he reigned in Samaria one month. 14Then Menahem son of Gadi went from Tirzah up to Samaria. He attacked Shallum son of Jabesh in Samaria, assassinated him and succeeded him as king.

15The other events of Shallum's reign, and the conspiracy he led, are written in the book of the annals of the kings of Israel.

16At that time Menahem, starting out from Tirzah, attacked Tiphsah and everyone in the city and its vicinity, because they refused to open their gates. He sacked Tiphsah and ripped open all the pregnant women.

---

[39] The reference to Azariah's thirty-eighth year reveals the author uses a dual dating scheme here. Cf. Thiele, *The Mysterious Numbers of the Hebrew Kings,* 123–24.

[40] G. H. Jones, *1 and 2 Kings,* NCB (Grand Rapids: Eerdmans, 1984) 2:520.

15:13–16 Shallum lasts even less time than the man he murders. His one-month monarchy is second shortest in Israel's history, with only Zimri serving fewer days (cf. 1 Kgs 16:15–20). So short is this reign that the author even fails to assess his merits or lack of redeeming characteristics. Gray notes that Assyrian records call Shallum "the son of a nobody," a designation that marks him as a usurper without rightful claim to the throne.[41]

Menahem's murder of Shallum receives more attention in the text than his predecessor's reign. Patterson and Austel theorize that Menahem "may have been a military commander under Zechariah"[42] who used support from Tirzah, the influential old capital city (1 Kgs 6:8–10), to overthrow his master. He extends his rebellion to include atrocities against a city that does not accept his sovereignty. The Hebrew text says the city is Tiphsah, which probably was located "on the bend of the Euphrates."[43] Some Greek texts read "Tappuah," a city only fourteen miles from Tirzah.[44] If the first city is intended, then Menahem seeks to consolidate northern gains made by Jeroboam II.[45] If the second possibility is accurate, he is concerned with squelching regional opposition to his ascendancy. In either case his brutality "is unparalleled in intertribal warfare in Israel, and matched only by the Ammonite barbarities mentioned in Amos."[46] Obviously Menahem's butchery marks a new low in how Israel's leadership conducts its affairs.

(3) Menahem's Reign and the Assyrian Threat (15:17–22)

17In the thirty-ninth year of Azariah king of Judah, Menahem son of Gadi became king of Israel, and he reigned in Samaria ten years. 18He did evil in the eyes of the LORD. During his entire reign he did not turn away from the sins of Jeroboam son of Nebat, which he had caused Israel to commit.

19Then Pul king of Assyria invaded the land, and Menahem gave him a thousand talents of silver to gain his support and strengthen his own hold on the kingdom. 20Menahem exacted this money from Israel. Every wealthy man had to contribute fifty shekels of silver to be given to the king of Assyria. So the king of Assyria withdrew and stayed in the land no longer.

21As for the other events of Menahem's reign, and all he did, are they not written in the book of the annals of the kings of Israel? 22Menahem rested with his fathers. And Pekahiah his son succeeded him as king.

15:17–18 Menahem's decade in power (ca. 752–742 B.C.) does not stabilize Israel. In fact, Menahem's activities lay the foundation for short-term and

---

[41] Gray, *1 and 2 Kings,* 562.
[42] Patterson and Austel, "1, 2 Kings," 235.
[43] Cogan and Tadmor, *II Kings,* 171.
[44] Gray, *1 and 2 Kings,* 563.
[45] R. L. Hubbard, Jr., *First and Second Kings,* EvBC (Chicago: Moody, 1991) 197.
[46] Gray, *1 and 2 Kings,* 563.

long-range disaster. Religiously, he does nothing to return Israel to its covenant roots, for he continues the destructive, morally deadening practices of Jeroboam I. His era proves one of the nation's last extended opportunities for renewal.

15:19–22 Menahem's political activities also place the nation in peril, though he probably believes he acts in the country's best interest. Tiglath-Pileser III invades the region 743–742 B.C. and fights there for as long as six years.[47] The text calls the Assyrian ruler "Pul" here, which was the throne name he took as Babylon's sovereign after he conquered that nation in about 729 B.C.[48] Therefore this designation for Tiglath-Pileser III was not in place when the events in these verses occurred but was current when the book was written. Menahem immediately pays the antagonist a large sum of money to leave, which Tiglath-Pileser III does, armed with the knowledge that Israel has neither the power nor the will necessary to oppose him. Menahem merely whets Assyria's appetite for expansion and oppression. Further, Menahem's levying of taxes for this appeasement begins the ongoing policy of draining Israel's resources, sometimes to fight Assyria and at other times to buy their favor. From now on the Northern Kingdom will never be rid of Assyria.

It is difficult to assess Menahem positively. While he does bring some stability to Israel's troubled political scene, he begins a tradition of unstable, ever-shifting foreign policy where Assyria is concerned. His religious policies do not help Israel heal its breach with the Lord. Thus his reign is but a longer episode in the swift decline of the northern people.

(4) Pekahiah's Reign and Assassination (15:23–26)

23In the fiftieth year of Azariah king of Judah, Pekahiah son of Menahem became king of Israel in Samaria, and he reigned two years. 24Pekahiah did evil in the eyes of the LORD. He did not turn away from the sins of Jeroboam son of Nebat, which he had caused Israel to commit. 25One of his chief officers, Pekah son of Remaliah, conspired against him. Taking fifty men of Gilead with him, he assassinated Pekahiah, along with Argob and Arieh, in the citadel of the royal palace at Samaria. So Pekah killed Pekahiah and succeeded him as king.

26The other events of Pekahiah's reign, and all he did, are written in the book of the annals of the kings of Israel.

15:23–26 The description of Pekahiah's two-year "era" (ca. 742–740 B.C.) sounds very much like that of Zechariah's and Shallum's reigns. The author merely states the length of the reign, Pekahiah's support of the cult of Jeroboam I, and the events surrounding his assassination. In other words, the historian notes that nothing has changed for the better. Assyria continues to

---

47 H. B. MacLean, "Menahem," *IDB*, 3:347.

48 Hallo and Simpson, *The Ancient Near East*, 137.

lurk in the shadows, waiting for a chance to extract more blood money; Israel's kings fail to lead the people in a positive spiritual direction; and grasping, greedy, power-hungry men kill monarchs and take their place. Nothing occurs to slow Israel's demise.

(5) Pekah's Reign, Assassination, and the Assyrian Threat (15:27–31)

27 In the fifty-second year of Azariah king of Judah, Pekah son of Remaliah became king of Israel in Samaria, and he reigned twenty years. 28 He did evil in the eyes of the LORD. He did not turn away from the sins of Jeroboam son of Nebat, which he had caused Israel to commit.

29 In the time of Pekah king of Israel, Tiglath-Pileser king of Assyria came and took Ijon, Abel Beth Maacah, Janoah, Kedesh and Hazor. He took Gilead and Galilee, including all the land of Naphtali, and deported the people to Assyria.
30 Then Hoshea son of Elah conspired against Pekah son of Remaliah. He attacked and assassinated him, and then succeeded him as king in the twentieth year of Jotham son of Uzziah.

31 As for the other events of Pekah's reign, and all he did, are they not written in the book of the annals of the kings of Israel?

15:27–28 Two issues require comment. First, the statements in 15:28 are by now so commonplace that the reader would be shocked if they were not present. Second, the twenty years given to Pekah causes some chronological difficulties. In fact, as Gray notes, this statement is "the first of the notorious chronological difficulties in the history of Israel and Judah from now until Hezekiah's time."[49] Though there are answers to these problems, such solutions must be offered with great humility, since the book's author uses information not now available to interpreters. Simply stated, though the chaos of the era makes it extremely difficult to reconstruct the exact order of events from Pekah's reign to Samaria's fall,[50] most scholars agree that Israel is conquered between 723–721 B.C. Thus, twenty years for Pekah and nine years for Hosea (2 Kgs 17:1) makes the date for the fall a decade too late. Since the author of 1, 2 Kings could also add and subtract, current interpreters are left to wonder what piece of explanatory information has been excluded. A textual error seems unlikely because 2 Kgs 16:1 uses Pekah's seventeenth year as a benchmark for Ahaz's ascendancy.[51]

Perhaps the most likely explanation for the twenty years is that Pekah exer-

[49] Gray, *1 and 2 Kings,* 567.

[50] Hobbs summarizes the problems by writing: "Although there is a wealth of material from Assyrian sources for this period of great Assyrian expansion into the west, this material serves at times only to confuse the picture. Much of the comparative data is fragmentary, readings are in dispute, and at the point where it could prove most helpful—that of chronology—it becomes less so. Many of the Assyrian texts are undated, and the problems of Hebrew chronology are compounded by the equally problematic chronology of the Assyrian sources" (*2 Kings,* 192).

[51] Cogan and Tadmor, *II Kings,* 174.

cised kinglike authority in the land before he actually seized power. Thiele theorizes that Pekah "began his twenty years in 752 as a rival of Menahem," that Gilead was "the probable site of Pekah's rival rule," and that "he could have come to terms with Pekahiah by accepting a prominent military post under him."[52] Obed suggests that Pekah "ruled over northern Transjordania on behalf of the king of Israel, cut his ties with Samaria and, voluntary or perforce, surrendered to Rezin northern Transjordania, in return for being placed on the throne in Samaria."[53] In other words, from about 752 to 740 B.C., Pekah was in effect a coregent, then became king through a coup backed by Syria. Though we presently are unable to verify such possibilities, something like these scenarios probably happened. If so, circumstances not unlike those described in 1 Kgs 16:21–22 may have resulted.

15:29–31 During Pekah's reign Israel opposes Assyria, a policy that results in the conflict known as the Syro-Ephraimite war. This war pits Israel (led by Pekah) and Syria (led by Rezin) against Tiglath-Pileser III. To strengthen their coalition, Israel and Syria seek to force Judah into joining them (cf. 2 Kgs 15:32–38). Judah resists, however, and calls upon Assyria for help, which Tiglath-Pileser III gladly provides (cf. 2 Kgs 16:7–9). Assyria enters the land, ravages the northernmost segment of Israel, and leaves Pekah with no mandate for leadership. This debacle leads to Pekah's being assassinated by Hoshea.

Israel cannot afford many more political miscalculations. Alternating appeasement of, then rebellion against, Assyria simply does not work. Poor leadership, coupled with spiritual and social decline, is proving a deadly combination. As Bright says, "Only uncommon wisdom could possibly have saved Israel in this desperate predicament, if indeed anything could have. But instead of exhibiting wisdom, her leaders manifested a complete inability to assess the realities of the situation."[54] Tiglath-Pileser III seems to understand the situation, though, so Israel is in deep trouble.

4. Judah's Political Weakness (15:32–16:20)

Judah's ultimate downfall only occurs more slowly than Israel's because its kings adopt a consistently pro-Assyrian policy. Otherwise, it is safe to say that Judah is weaker than Israel, almost as corrupt, and certainly no wiser than the Northern Kingdom. Its leaders fail to grasp the importance of covenant faithfulness. Though destruction comes later, the seeds of that devastation are sown as much in this era as in the decades that follow.

---

[52] Thiele, *The Mysterious Numbers of the Hebrew Kings,* 129.

[53] B. Obed, "The Historical Background of the Syro-Ephraimite War Reconsidered," *CBQ* 34 (1972) 162–63.

[54] Bright, *A History of Israel,* 273.

(1) Jotham's Reign (15:32–38)

32In the second year of Pekah son of Remaliah king of Israel, Jotham son of Uzziah king of Judah began to reign. 33He was twenty-five years old when he became king, and he reigned in Jerusalem sixteen years. His mother's name was Jerusha daughter of Zadok. 34He did what was right in the eyes of the LORD, just as his father Uzziah had done. 35The high places, however, were not removed; the people continued to offer sacrifices and burn incense there. Jotham rebuilt the Upper Gate of the temple of the LORD.

36As for the other events of Jotham's reign, and what he did, are they not written in the book of the annals of the kings of Judah? 37(In those days the LORD began to send Rezin king of Aram and Pekah son of Remaliah against Judah.) 38Jotham rested with his fathers and was buried with them in the City of David, the city of his father. And Ahaz his son succeeded him as king.

15:32–35 Jotham's spiritual commitments are similar to those of Uzziah, Amaziah, and Joash. During his sixteen years, ten of which probably are spent as coregent with Uzziah (ca. 750–740), the leprous king (cf. 2 Kgs 15:5), he worships the Lord yet does not use his position of authority to remove the high places. Once more a king does not understand the nature of true worship. Nothing less can save Judah and guarantee the people a reasonably secure future.

Second Chronicles 27:3–5 offers some further details about Jotham's building programs. Not only does he undertake the temple project, but he also repairs walls, builds new towns "in the Judean hills" (2 Chr 27:4), and establishes new "forts and towers" (2 Chr 27:4) near Jerusalem. He also conquers the Ammonites, forcing them to pay him tribute. The picture is of a mighty king blessed by God (2 Chr 27:6), one who takes measures to protect his kingdom, one who at least masters smaller countries, yet one who also knows serious enemies threaten him.

15:36–38 Before his death, however, Jotham begins to face the threat posed by Rezin of Syria and Pekah of Israel. Like the other Judahite kings before him, Jotham probably favors Assyria. Thus, the anti-Assyrian coalition led by Rezin and Pekah can hardly be happy with Jotham. No doubt they attempt to influence a change in policy but do not achieve their goal before Jotham dies.

(2) Ahaz's Reign (16:1–20)

1In the seventeenth year of Pekah son of Remaliah, Ahaz son of Jotham king of Judah began to reign. 2Ahaz was twenty years old when he became king, and he reigned in Jerusalem sixteen years. Unlike David his father, he did not do what was right in the eyes of the LORD his God. 3He walked in the ways of the kings of Israel and even sacrificed his son in the fire, following the detestable ways of the nations the LORD had driven out before the Israelites. 4He offered sacrifices and burned incense at the high places, on the hilltops and under every spreading tree.

**[5]Then Rezin king of Aram and Pekah son of Remaliah king of Israel marched
up to fight against Jerusalem and besieged Ahaz, but they could not overpower
him. [6]At that time, Rezin king of Aram recovered Elath for Aram by driving out
the men of Judah. Edomites then moved into Elath and have lived there to this day.**

**[7]Ahaz sent messengers to say to Tiglath-Pileser king of Assyria, "I am your
servant and vassal. Come up and save me out of the hand of the king of Aram and
of the king of Israel, who are attacking me." [8]And Ahaz took the silver and gold
found in the temple of the LORD and in the treasuries of the royal palace and sent
it as a gift to the king of Assyria. [9]The king of Assyria complied by attacking
Damascus and capturing it. He deported its inhabitants to Kir and put Rezin to
death.**

**[10]Then King Ahaz went to Damascus to meet Tiglath-Pileser king of Assyria.
He saw an altar in Damascus and sent to Uriah the priest a sketch of the altar,
with detailed plans for its construction. [11]So Uriah the priest built an altar in
accordance with all the plans that King Ahaz had sent from Damascus and finished it before King Ahaz returned. [12]When the king came back from Damascus
and saw the altar, he approached it and presented offerings on it. [13]He offered up
his burnt offering and grain offering, poured out his drink offering, and sprinkled
the blood of his fellowship offerings on the altar. [14]The bronze altar that stood
before the LORD he brought from the front of the temple—from between the new
altar and the temple of the LORD—and put it on the north side of the new altar.**

**[15]King Ahaz then gave these orders to Uriah the priest: "On the large new
altar, offer the morning burnt offering and the evening grain offering, the king's
burnt offering and his grain offering, and the burnt offering of all the people of
the land, and their grain offering and their drink offering. Sprinkle on the altar
all the blood of the burnt offerings and sacrifices. But I will use the bronze altar
for seeking guidance." [16]And Uriah the priest did just as King Ahaz had ordered.**

**[17]King Ahaz took away the side panels and removed the basins from the mov-
able stands. He removed the Sea from the bronze bulls that supported it and set it
on a stone base. [18]He took away the Sabbath canopy that had been built at the
temple and removed the royal entryway outside the temple of the LORD, in defer-
ence to the king of Assyria.**

**[19]As for the other events of the reign of Ahaz, and what he did, are they not
written in the book of the annals of the kings of Judah? [20]Ahaz rested with his
fathers and was buried with them in the City of David. And Hezekiah his son succeeded him as king.**

16:1–4 Ahaz's era is different from those that precede and follow it. He comes to power as a twenty year old, then rules officially for sixteen years. The text notes that he becomes king in Pekah's seventeenth year, which is 735 B.C., and rules sixteen years, though dates for later kings indicate his era ends in 715 B.C. R. Hubbard explains:

> Here the author applied a principle called "dual dating"; he dated Ahaz's reign by two different chronological references. The synchronism to Pekah's rule

marked the start of his coregency with his father, whereas the sixteen-year figure counted his years of sole rule.[55]

Given the calculations, Ahaz acts as coregent with Jotham during about 735–732 B.C., then serves as sole sovereign from 732 to 715 B.C.

Unlike David—indeed unlike Jotham, Uzziah, Amaziah, and Joash—Ahaz has little interest in serving the Lord. He not only duplicates the sins of Israel's kings, but he also sacrifices his son "in the fire," perhaps as an offering to the god Molech.[56] Though this is the initial mention of such "worship," the practice becomes more prominent "as an act of apostasy in the times of stress at the end of the monarchy of Israel (17:17) and in Judah under Manasseh (21:6; 23:10)."[57] Why does Ahaz do such a thing? Jones notes that these sacrifices often coincided with emergencies and suggests that Ahaz performs a child sacrifice when faced with the threat from Pekah and Rezin.[58] Ahaz also offers sacrifices "at the high places, on the hilltops and under every spreading tree." In other words, desperate to solve his political problems, Judah's king becomes a dedicated polytheist in hopes that some god may deliver him from his trouble. The author of 1, 2 Kings has no use for such behavior, of course, since such activity leads inexorably to destruction caused by God's judgment.

16:5–6 As has been mentioned, Ahaz inherits Jotham's problems with Israel and Syria during a time when Tiglath-Pileser III poses the greatest external threat to the small nations in the region. Syria has always fought Assyria, and now Pekah changes Israel's policy from a pro-Assyrian stance to one of hostility against the invaders. Judah is left as the sole appeaser of Assyria and endures a siege instituted by Pekah and Rezin ca. 733–732 B.C. Their purpose is to seize control of Judah and install a new ruler (Isa 7:6). Although Judah suffers heavy casualties (2 Chr 28:5–15), their enemies' overall purpose is thwarted. Rezin does drive Judah out of Elath and captures the city. Judah is in desperate straits. To whom will Ahaz turn?

16:7–9 Sadly, Ahaz decides to summon Tiglath-Pileser III to help him. Isaiah the prophet is active at this time, and he counsels the king to trust the Lord, even to ask for a sign that God will deliver Jerusalem from the invaders (Isa 7:1–10). When Ahaz declines the offer, Isaiah makes the famous Immanuel promise, then tells the king that Syria and Israel will retreat (Isa 7:11–20). God should get the credit for the deliverance, though, not the human instruments of that reprieve. Ahaz never responds positively to Isaiah's pleas. He prefers to pay the Assyrians to save him.

Tiglath-Pileser III responds by defeating both Syria and Israel by 732 B.C.

---

[55] Hubbard, *First and Second Kings,* 201.

[56] Wiseman, *1 and 2 Kings,* 260–61.

[57] Gray, *1 and 2 Kings,* 572.

[58] Jones, *1 and 2 Kings,* 2:534.

According to Assyrian records, he makes Israel into an Assyrian province at this time.[59] He conquers Damascus, which marks the end of Syria's role as a major power.[60] Judah, Ammon, and Moab benefit temporarily from Assyria's victory since they have "an opportunity to reassert their control of disputed territories and to extend their influence into regions that had previously been under the rule of . . . Aram and Israel."[61] Such "freedom" comes with a high price, however, since all these nations are now directly under Assyria's authority.

16:10–14 One of the most evident results of Ahaz's overtures to Tiglath-Pileser III is a commitment to Assyria's gods. After the Assyrian leader defeats Damascus, deports its inhabitants, and kills Rezin (2 Kgs 16:9), Ahaz journeys to Damascus to meet his "savior." While there he observes "an altar," presumably an Assyrian one, a replica of which he has made in Jerusalem. It is to this altar that he makes his sacrifices. He displaces the Lord's altar in favor of this new cultic object. Indeed, he operates, Long states, "as a royal priest, head of the state religion, like David and Solomon before him (cf. 2 Sam 6:17–18; 1 Kgs 8:63), or . . . like Jeroboam (1 Kgs 12:32–33)."[62] Readers could hardly miss the similarities between Jeroboam, the father of institutionalized idolatry in Israel, and Ahaz, the Judahite king who makes polytheism acceptable nationwide.

Scholars debate whether or not Ahaz's embracing of Assyria's gods is voluntary. Oestreicher[63] and Olmstead[64] argue that Assyria imposed acceptance of their gods on the nations they defeated. Ahaz sees an Assyrian altar in Damascus and rushes to produce one like it in Jerusalem, as a good vassal should. J. McKay[65] and M. Cogan[66] dispute this conclusion. They correctly argue that the Assyrians allowed some vassals to worship their own gods and to run their own affairs as long as they did not revolt against their masters.[67] Judah's idolatry was not limited to Assyrian deities.[68] Rather, after Ahaz's time Judah was not loyal to any particular system of worship. It appears, then, that Ahaz decides to serve other gods on his own. He may think that this adaptation is in his best interests and those of his country, but Tiglath-Pileser III does not force compliance.

---

[59] Noth, *The History of Israel,* 261.

[60] Montgomery and Gehman, *Kings,* 459.

[61] B. Obed, "Observations on Methods of Assyrian Rule in Transjordania after the Palestinian Campaign of Tiglath-Pileser III," *JNES* (1970) 177.

[62] B. O. Long, *2 Kings,* FOTL 10 (Grand Rapids: Eerdmans, 1991) 177.

[63] Cf. Oestreicher, *Das deuteronomische Grundgesetz,* 38.

[64] Cf. Olmstead, *History of Assyria,* 198, 632–34.

[65] McKay, *Religion in Judah under the Assyrians,* 67–73.

[66] Cogan, *Imperialism and Religion,* 1–7.

[67] Ibid., 42–61.

[68] J. McKay, *Religion in Judah under the Assyrians*, SBT/2,26 (Naperville, Ill.: Allenson, 1973) 45–59.

16:15–20 Ahaz orders Uriah the priest to make all major public sacrifices on the new altar. The "morning burnt offering and the evening grain offering" were the two basic sacrifices made at the temple. The "king's burnt offering and his grain offering" were made on Sabbaths and new moons (cf. Ezek 46), and the "burnt offering of all the people of the land, and their grain offering and their drink offering" were given daily for all the people.[69] Ahaz reserves the old altar for himself for "seeking guidance," perhaps by consulting entrails.[70] Pagan idolatry has displaced standard Yahwistic practices. Ahaz dismantles other worship implements so he can continue to pay tribute to Assyria and to keep from angering "the king of Assyria."

When Ahaz dies about 715 B.C., he is succeeded by Hezekiah, his son. He leaves a legacy of appeasement and syncretism unmatched to this time. Assyria can count on him for money, loyalty, and zealous acceptance of their gods. Judah's king seems genuinely pleased to serve a powerful master who can deliver him from regional foes. No doubt he feels safe, but the historian duly notes the ways in which he has exceeded Jeroboam's wickedness. If Jeroboam's practices are worth condemning, what will happen to a nation who rejects the Lord even more clearly?

5. Assyria Destroys Israel (17:1–41)

By now readers of 1, 2 Kings surely sense that a tragic story is unfolding. The once-great kingdom of Israel has been divided, has broken its covenant commitments, has suffered poor leadership, has seen its freedom taken away, and must certainly be destroyed altogether before much more time passes. Israel has risen to great heights but now rushes downward toward an awful catastrophe.[71] One political error could bring Assyria down on the head of either Israel or Judah, or both for that matter. That these errors are indeed made is sad, even tragic, for the whole debacle is avoidable, a viewpoint the author expresses quite clearly in this text.

(1) Hoshea's Reign and the Assyrian Conquest (17:1–6)

[1]In the twelfth year of Ahaz king of Judah, Hoshea son of Elah became king of Israel in Samaria, and he reigned nine years. [2]He did evil in the eyes of the LORD, but not like the kings of Israel who preceded him.

[3]Shalmaneser king of Assyria came up to attack Hoshea, who had been Shalmaneser's vassal and had paid him tribute. [4]But the king of Assyria discovered

[69] Jones, *1 and 2 Kings,* 2:540.

[70] Gray, *1 and 2 Kings,* 578.

[71] For a discussion of comic and tragic plots in Scripture, see Introduction, "The Plot of 1, 2 Kings" on p. 61.

that Hoshea was a traitor, for he had sent envoys to So king of Egypt, and he no longer paid tribute to the king of Assyria, as he had done year by year. Therefore Shalmaneser seized him and put him in prison. [5]The king of Assyria invaded the entire land, marched against Samaria and laid siege to it for three years. [6]In the ninth year of Hoshea, the king of Assyria captured Samaria and deported the Israelites to Assyria. He settled them in Halah, in Gozan on the Habor River and in the towns of the Medes.

17:1–2 After assassinating Pekah, Hoshea rules Israel nine years (ca. 732–722 B.C.). Though not as wicked as some of his predecessors, he will reap the consequences of their sins, their political blunders, and his own mistakes. Assyria's leadership changes during his era. Tiglath-Pileser III dies in 727 B.C. and is replaced by his son Shalmaneser V, who rules 727–722 B.C. After Shalmaneser's death in 722/721 B.C., Sargon II (ca. 722/721–705) governs Assyria.[72] Each of his successors continues Tiglath-Pileser's policies, so Hoshea deals with the same system despite the changes.

17:3–6 The author's description of Israel's fall is quite brief, much briefer, in fact, than the explanation of the defeat that follows. Five details frame the story. First, during the first part of his reign Hoshea, unlike the unfortunate Pekah, his predecessor, pays Shalmaneser V tribute. Second, Hoshea eventually withholds tribute, hoping that a new alliance with Egypt will set him free from Assyria's grip. The withholding of tribute and the envoys to Egypt seem to be twin actions in a single, fatal rebellious act.[73]

A Sudanese king named Piankhy managed in about 730 B.C. to restore a degree of unity to an Egypt previously divided between two Libyan dynasties (the twenty-second and twenty-third) and several independent city-states. Although he established the twenty-fifth dynasty, a rival dynasty was founded by a chieftain named Tefnakht, who was finally defeated by Piankhy. The last king of the twenty-second dynasty was named Osorkon IV. These three rulers, Piankhy, Tefnakht, and Osorkon IV, have all been candidates for the otherwise unknown "So King of Egypt."[74] Of the three Piankhy probably was in the best position to aid Hoshea, but in fact Egypt was no match for Assyria. Especially in the first half of the seventh century B.C., Egypt suffered several Assyrian defeats. Pinning any hopes on Egypt was foolish, to say the least.

---

[72] Bright, *A History of Israel,* 272–74.

[73] Hobbs, *2 Kings,* 230.

[74] For a history of the discussion and an argument for identifying him as Tefnakht, see J. Day, "The Problem of 'So, King of Egypt' in 2 Kings 17:4," *VT* 42 (1992) 289–301. On Egyptian history during this period see Hallo and Simpson, *The Ancient Near East,* 287–92; Kitchen, *Third Intermediate Period,* 362–77. A. R. W. Green, "The Identity of King So of Egypt—An Alternative Interpretation," *JNES* 52 (1993) 99–108, argues persuasively that *Sôʾ* is the equivalent of *Siwaʾ*, a short form of *Simaʾ-tawy*, the Horus name of Piankhy (cf. the month name *sîwān* in Esth 8:9 for the Babylonian *Simanu*).

Third, Shalmaneser V invades the land and kidnaps Hoshea. It appears that Hoshea is captured before the city itself capitulates.[75] Israel is left with no real leader. Fourth, the Assyrians besiege Samaria for three years, no doubt after having subdued every other significant Israelite city. Both Samaria and the invaders could have lasted three years.[76] No doubt the persons under siege hoped help would come before their walls could be breached. Fifth, when the city falls, Shalmaneser's forces deport the Israelites, scattering them to various parts of Assyria. Later, Samaria is resettled but by refugees from other lands. Such practices keep Assyria's enemies from rebelling against them. Israel ceases to exist as a nation.

A long time has passed since the prophet Ahijah told the wife of Jeroboam I that idolatry would lead to Israel's exile (1 Kgs 14:14–16). Over these two hundred years Israel has seemed determined to make this prophecy come to pass. No reform occurs. No real repentance emerges. No leader calls a halt to pagan worship. No prophet is taken seriously. Thus the spare, unadorned description of Samaria's fall is dramatic only in the sense that it is Israel's final scene. God's grace alone has delayed the fall this long.

(2) Reasons for Israel's Fall (17:7–23)

7All this took place because the Israelites had sinned against the LORD their God, who had brought them up out of Egypt from under the power of Pharaoh king of Egypt. They worshiped other gods 8and followed the practices of the nations the LORD had driven out before them, as well as the practices that the kings of Israel had introduced. 9The Israelites secretly did things against the LORD their God that were not right. From watchtower to fortified city they built themselves high places in all their towns. 10They set up sacred stones and Asherah poles on every high hill and under every spreading tree. 11At every high place they burned incense, as the nations whom the LORD had driven out before them had done. They did wicked things that provoked the LORD to anger. 12They worshiped idols, though the LORD had said, "You shall not do this." 13The LORD warned Israel and Judah through all his prophets and seers: "Turn from your evil ways. Observe my commands and decrees, in accordance with the entire Law that I commanded your fathers to obey and that I delivered to you through my servants the prophets."

14But they would not listen and were as stiff-necked as their fathers, who did not trust in the LORD their God. 15They rejected his decrees and the covenant he had made with their fathers and the warnings he had given them. They followed worthless idols and themselves became worthless. They imitated the nations around them although the LORD had ordered them, "Do not do as they do," and they did the things the LORD had forbidden them to do.

16They forsook all the commands of the LORD their God and made for themselves two idols cast in the shape of calves, and an Asherah pole. They bowed

---

[75] Cf. Hayes and Kuan, "The Final Years of Samaria (730–720 B.C.)," *Bib* 72 (1991) 163.

[76] Wiseman, *1 and 2 Kings,* 266.

**down to all the starry hosts, and they worshiped Baal. 17They sacrificed their sons
and daughters in the fire. They practiced divination and sorcery and sold themselves to do evil in the eyes of the LORD, provoking him to anger.**
**18So the LORD was very angry with Israel and removed them from his pres-
ence. Only the tribe of Judah was left, 19and even Judah did not keep the commands of the LORD their God. They followed the practices Israel had introduced.
20Therefore the LORD rejected all the people of Israel; he afflicted them and gave
them into the hands of plunderers, until he thrust them from his presence.**
**21When he tore Israel away from the house of David, they made Jeroboam son
of Nebat their king. Jeroboam enticed Israel away from following the LORD and
caused them to commit a great sin. 22The Israelites persisted in all the sins of Jeroboam and did not turn away from them 23until the LORD removed them from
his presence, as he had warned through all his servants the prophets. So the people of Israel were taken from their homeland into exile in Assyria, and they are
still there.**

17:7–13 Now the author summarizes why Israel has fallen. None of these reasons should surprise readers, for they have been mentioned over and over again. Israel's most fundamental error all along has been covenant breaking, the most obvious manifestation of which is idolatry. The people forgot the exodus and all it stood for: God's power and grace, God's acts on their behalf, and their responsibility to reciprocate God's goodness with faith, undivided allegiance, and pure worship. Instead, they worshiped local deities, adopted corrupt ethical practices, and ignored the Lord's prophets who were sent to warn them. By the time God's patience was exhausted and judgment fell, the rebellion was two hundred years old, thus fully mature.

17:14–20 The writer's frustration is evident as the summary continues. Israel has imitated the worst tradition of their fathers and "rejected his decrees and the covenant" (v. 15). They practiced worship rites connected with pagan deities. More specifically, they bowed down before Baal and the Canaanite astral gods. Some of them offered human sacrifices. In short, "They followed worthless idols and themselves became worthless." Unwilling to serve Yahweh, the only God, the Lord who gives life substance and meaning, they gave their lives to nonentities unable to ennoble a people.

Only Judah remains at this point in the history, and they act little better than their northern brothers and sisters. Plunderers like Egypt, Syria, and Assyria should have caused Israel and Judah to come to their senses, but God's covenant people decide to remain senseless. How long can Judah last?

17:21–23 Of course, Jeroboam I receives the most blame for Israel's religious decline. He takes the people away from the Davidic dynasty, institutes a new religion, and generally sets in motion destructive behaviors that become permanent. As God promises in Leviticus 26 and Deuteronomy 27–28, these sins can only lead to exile. Ultimately, then, Jeroboam I leads Israel to division from each other, from the Lord, and from the land.

(3) Samaria Resettled (17:24–41)

[24]The king of Assyria brought people from Babylon, Cuthah, Avva, Hamath and Sepharvaim and settled them in the towns of Samaria to replace the Israelites. They took over Samaria and lived in its towns. [25]When they first lived there, they did not worship the LORD; so he sent lions among them and they killed some of the people. [26]It was reported to the king of Assyria: "The people you deported and resettled in the towns of Samaria do not know what the god of that country requires. He has sent lions among them, which are killing them off, because the people do not know what he requires."

[27]Then the king of Assyria gave this order: "Have one of the priests you took captive from Samaria go back to live there and teach the people what the god of the land requires." [28]So one of the priests who had been exiled from Samaria came to live in Bethel and taught them how to worship the LORD.

[29]Nevertheless, each national group made its own gods in the several towns where they settled, and set them up in the shrines the people of Samaria had made at the high places. [30]The men from Babylon made Succoth Benoth, the men from Cuthah made Nergal, and the men from Hamath made Ashima; [31]the Avvites made Nibhaz and Tartak, and the Sepharvites burned their children in the fire as sacrifices to Adrammelech and Anammelech, the gods of Sepharvaim. [32]They worshiped the LORD, but they also appointed all sorts of their own people to officiate for them as priests in the shrines at the high places. [33]They worshiped the LORD, but they also served their own gods in accordance with the customs of the nations from which they had been brought.

[34]To this day they persist in their former practices. They neither worship the LORD nor adhere to the decrees and ordinances, the laws and commands that the LORD gave the descendants of Jacob, whom he named Israel. [35]When the LORD made a covenant with the Israelites, he commanded them: "Do not worship any other gods or bow down to them, serve them or sacrifice to them. [36]But the LORD, who brought you up out of Egypt with mighty power and outstretched arm, is the one you must worship. To him you shall bow down and to him offer sacrifices. [37]You must always be careful to keep the decrees and ordinances, the laws and commands he wrote for you. Do not worship other gods. [38]Do not forget the covenant I have made with you, and do not worship other gods. [39]Rather, worship the LORD your God; it is he who will deliver you from the hand of all your enemies."

[40]They would not listen, however, but persisted in their former practices. [41]Even while these people were worshiping the LORD, they were serving their idols. To this day their children and grandchildren continue to do as their fathers did.

17:24–28 Following their general conquest policy, the Assyrians replace the deported Israelites with refugees from other lands.[77] These new people do not know the Lord or how to worship him, so they presumably serve their own national gods. Thus, God sends lions against them to alert them to his displea-

[77] H. Donner, "The Separate States of Israel and Judah," in *Israelite and Judean History,* ed., J. H. Hayes and J. M. Miller (Philadelphia: Westminster, 1977) 434.

sure. Sadly, the foreigners respond to warnings better than the Lord's own people.[78] They desire priests who can teach them to please the God of that land. In this way they are somewhat like Naaman, who listened to a slave girl's words about the Lord during a time when Israel refused to heed the miracle-working Elisha. Some exiled priests return to the land and help them worship God.[79]

17:29–41 Despite this promising beginning, the new inhabitants of Samaria and the surrounding area soon revert to their national cultic rites. Now they imitate the Israelites' worst religious activities by initiating a truly syncretistic religious system. Deities from many lands are worshiped, and human sacrifice is practiced, yet the Lord is "served" as well. Individuals chosen from the new people groups act as priests for Yahweh worship.

Readers are warned that such worship is not worship at all.[80] They must adhere to their Lord and to the covenant, for only the covenant God freed them from Egypt and offered them guidance. Only the Lord can deliver them from their current enemies. Polytheism, syncretism, or simple neglecting of the Lord will ruin the current group of Israelites' present and future just as surely as these actions destroyed their nation's past. They must choose to break with the traditions of their ancestors and serve the Lord. Nothing can be done about the past, but the present and the future can be salvaged. The readers have the chance to learn from history.

Canonical and Theological Implications of 2 Kings 14–17

Unlike much of the material found in earlier sections of 1, 2 Kings, the details in these chapters are supplemented directly by information found elsewhere in Scripture. The most important sources of this information are the biblical prophecies of Hosea, Amos, and Isaiah. These eighth-century prophets add broader historical, sociological, and theological perspective to what the author of 1, 2 Kings describes. They also support many of the canonical emphases found in 1, 2 Kings. It is appropriate, then, to use these books as a canonical compass, to supplement their vision when necessary, and then to state the theological themes that emerge from this analysis.

All three prophets agree with 1, 2 Kings' opinion of idolatry in Israel. Isaiah says that the Lord's people have become immersed in idolatry (Isa 2:6–8), little realizing how foolish it is to bow down to a nonbeing made by human hands (Isa 44:9–20). Hosea claims that Israel is a nation of spiritual adulterers, each person lusting after "lovers" such as Baal (Hos 2:1–13). Without question Amos agrees with these assessments. Judah has gone after idols (Amos 2:4–5), while Israel focuses on the cult instituted by Jeroboam I (Amos 7:10–17).

---

[78] Hobbs, *2 Kings,* 237.

[79] Cf. S. Paul, "Sargon's Administrative Diction in II Kings 17:27," *JBL* 88 (1969) 73–74.

[80] Hubbard, *First and Second Kings,* 207.

Each prophet clearly states that judgment must come to punish such sins (cf. Isa 2:6–4:6; Hos 5:8–15; Amos 7:1–9:10). Samaria's fall would not have surprised any of them.

The author of 1, 2 Kings states often that some of the people are outright idolaters but that others worship Yahweh *and* other gods. Isaiah indicates that the nation sees no problem with bringing sacrifices to the Lord yet practicing divination at the same time (e.g., Isa 1:10–20; 2:6–8). Amos reproves his audience for supposedly serving God by supporting worship at the shrines at Bethel and Gilgal (Amos 4:4–5). Hosea's acquaintances offer sacrifices, but not in the proper place or in the proper way or with the proper attitude (Hos 6:4–10). Israel has no knowledge of how to please the Lord (Hos 4:1).

As a result of their idolatry, which amounts, of course, to covenant breaking of the worst sort (cf. Exod 20:3–6), the people no longer hold high ethical standards for how to treat one another. Oppression, greed, and brutality become common. Hosea notes that lies, wickedness, intrigue, and immorality are regular occurrences among both the people and their leaders (Hos 7:3–7). Amos claims Israel's women "crush the needy," "oppress the poor," and exhort their husbands to hurt the poor for material gain (Amos 4:1). The men, on the other hand, love luxury, are lazy, and care nothing about their country's moral decline (Amos 6:1–7). People are sold to pay petty debts (Amos 2:6–8). Similarly, Isaiah declares that justice is denied to the poor, the widow, and the orphan (Isa 1:17; 10:1–4). The false prophets do not restrain the people at all (Isa 28:7–13). None of these abuses are mentioned in 1, 2 Kings, so an awareness of their existence in this era helps readers understand that things were even worse than the author indicates. The people are as corrupt as their leaders.

As time passes, Israel and Judah become callous to the prophetic message, just as 2 Kgs 17:13–23 says. Amos and Hosea do not succeed in turning the hearts of the people back to the Lord, and Isaiah's success with Hezekiah is noticeable because it is so rare in the history of prophet-king relationships (cf. Isa 36:1–37:38; 2 Kgs 18:17–19:37). The prophets know they are God's agents of mercy to Israel (cf. Isa 1:18–20; Hos 11:1–11; Amos 3:7), and they know that the people's rejection of their message amounts to a rejection of the Lord who sends them (Amos 7:14–15; Hos 14:9; Isa 1:19–20). Certainly the writer of 1, 2 Kings agrees (2 Kgs 17:13–24), and it is partly this agreement that makes the books prophetic narratives.[81]

Theologically speaking, the issues that the canon reveals lead to some tremendous losses. Two covenants help shape the entire Old Testament: the covenant with Abraham and the covenant with David. In Gen 12:1–20 the Lord promises Abraham an heir that will eventually produce a nation, a relationship that leads to the Sinai covenant, and a homeland in Canaan.[82] God promises

[81] Cf. "Introduction to Literary Issues" on p. 54.

[82] Cf. D. J. A. Clines, *The Theme of the Pentateuch,* JSOTSup 10 (Sheffield: JSOT, 1978).

David an eternal kingdom in 2 Sam 7:7–17. All four of these vital items—nation, covenant, land, and kingship—are endangered by Israel's actions. Thus, readers of 1, 2 Kings need to be aware that the demise of Israel has tremendous implications. Indeed, Old Testament faith *seems* to fall under the weight of Israel's sin, though in reality God is not caught unprepared for the future.

Abraham's children are in trouble by the end of 2 Kings 17. Jeremiah says Rachel weeps for her children because they are no more (Jer 31:15). Ten of the twelve tribes have been ravaged by exile, and the two remaining clans are in danger of joining them (2 Kgs 17:18–20). To whom, then, will God's promises be given? To a remnant made up of people like David, Elijah, Elisha, the author of 1, 2 Kings, and, hopefully, the books' original readers. Isaiah 6:11–13, Hos 11:8–11, and Amos 9:11–15 also make this point. Abraham still has heirs, even though they exist in unnecessarily small numbers.

The covenant promised to Abraham that is given at Mount Sinai has been broken. Israel has rejected every detail of the covenant they promised to keep (2 Kgs 17:15,34–41). This covenant is based on a relationship, a long relationship at that, between God and Abraham's children.[83] Both Israel's obedience and the Lord's blessings are evidence the relationship is based on mutual love.[84] The Lord's love for Israel never fades, but Israel forgets all the love the Lord has lavished upon them (17:7). Their forgetfulness leads to idolatry, their idolatry devolves into immorality, oppression, and human sacrifice, and their constant wickedness leads to their destruction. Once the basic foundation for the relationship is broken through idolatry, all other types of covenant unfaithfulness become possible. Despite the pervasiveness of the covenant breaking, however, punishment does not have to last forever. Second Kings 17:39 indicates that God remains willing to turn back Israel's enemies. Thus, just as the nation could become more faithful and grow in numbers, so they could also return to the covenant and receive the blessings pledged in Deut 28:1–14.

Perhaps the thorniest theological problem is what happens to the promise of land when the people vacate Canaan. When God promises Abraham a homeland in Gen 12:7, then informs him in Gen 15:12–51 that it will be over four hundred years before this pledge is fulfilled, the stage is set for a large portion of the Pentateuch and the Former Prophets. When the land left unclaimed in Numbers 13–14 is finally taken in Joshua, the full blessings of possessing land fall on the Israelites. Responsibilities are also given to Israel. They must possess, care for, and protect the land. If they rebel against the Lord through idol worship and other forms of rebellion they will lose the land. E. Martens summarizes these issues:

> Land, then, is more than acreage or territory. It is a theological symbol, through which a series of messages are conveyed. It is the tangible fulfillment of the

[83] See W. J. Dumbrell, *Covenant and Creation: A Theology of Old Testament Covenants* (Nashville: Nelson, 1984) 16–20, for a study of the relational aspects of OT covenants.

[84] N. H. Snaith, *The Distinctive Ideas of the Old Testament* (New York: Schocken, 1975) 99.

> promise. Land is a gift from Yahweh, and Israel, through preoccupation with it, has her attention continually called to Yahweh. Land requires a specific and appropriate lifestyle. Responsibilities concerning social behavior are enjoined upon the people for the time when they will occupy the land, and they are warned that disobedience defiles the land and may result in loss of their privilege of tenancy.[85]

What happens when tenancy is revoked? How can Israel be Israel outside Israel? Will the people ever return? Some of these questions will be discussed in the last segment of this commentary, but a few observations are appropriate here. First, as has been said, the exile comes as a result of long-term covenant breaking and moral collapse. Israel has committed national suicide; they have not been kidnapped or taken prisoner by surprise. Second, readers must remember that 2 Sam 7:7–17 promises an eternal kingdom. Just how that kingdom will continue remains to be seen in Israel's history following the account in Kings, but it must emerge for God's word to come true. And if any lesson is taught in 1, 2 Kings it is that God's word *always* comes true. Third, the possibility of a return to the land exists (cf. 2 Kgs 17:39). Fourth, God rules everywhere, not just in Israel. Thus, the books' original readers should have taken solace in the fact that they could not be scattered to a place where God would not be or where he would not be their covenant Lord. In short, the loss of the land is a horrible catastrophe, yet it does not remove Israel's fundamental identity or responsibility. They are the Lord's people, and they have the privilege of knowing and serving the only God who exists.

Applicational Implications of 2 Kings 14–17

These texts offer preachers and teachers the opportunity to help audiences understand the consequences of unwise behavior. They also allow yet another opportunity for hearers to change their lives so they can avoid the mistakes the Israelites made. A diverse group of applications emerges along these standard lines.

First, the accumulated canonical data reveals the roots and results of social disintegration. Hosea, Amos, and Isaiah indicate that oppression, immorality, violence, deceit, and injustice contribute to the decline and fall of Israel that 2 Kings 14–17 describes. No nation, no matter how powerful or wealthy, can endure for long if its people mistreat one another. Suspicion, animosity, and civil strife will inevitably result. The country's leaders will find themselves unable to govern. Eventually the nation will sink either into obscurity, anarchy, or defeat by an aggressive enemy. History is filled with examples of such cases. The reason for this phenomenon is that a just God rules nations and directs history.

[85] E. A. Martens, *God's Design: A Focus on Old Testament Theology* (Grand Rapids: Baker, 1981) 115.

Second, the text underscores the necessity of faithful, continuous instruction of the community in God's truth. Second Kings 17:7–41 informs readers how idolatry, rebellion, neglect of the revealed prophetic word, and an *unwillingness to learn* contribute to Israel's disaster. The author's choice and use of prophetic narrative is in part due to an interest in teaching and encouraging. Pastors and teachers must never doubt the necessity and vitality of what they are doing. They must also stress teaching's importance to their audiences. Instruction changes lives, for it helps persons to be true disciples of the Lord (Matt 28:16–20). Despite the nation's discouraging past, the writer stakes a great deal of time and effort on the belief that the new generation need not repeat their ancestors' mistakes.

Third, the section reemphasizes the problems inherent in a blanket acceptance of pluralism by the covenant community. Perhaps Ahaz's actions illustrate this principle most clearly. If indeed he adopts Assyria's gods voluntarily (2 Kgs 16:10), then he probably does so in part because he thinks these gods make kings powerful. According to Isa 7:10–12 Ahaz also offers at least lip service to Yahweh, which implies that he courts the favor of whatever deity he thinks can help his cause. His subjects most likely held similar views, and the canon as a whole states that neither king nor people considered henotheism[86] or polytheism serious problems. Separatist Yahwists seemed overly zealous to them, yet the more Israel accepted not just the *presence* of the other religions but their *validity* as well, the more Yahwist worship became a mixture of truth and error and the more the people turned outright to other gods.

What should believers do in a pluralistic culture? What is at stake? As for the latter question, the future of Christian families and the future of the church is at stake. Competing religious voices abound in a world that enjoys extensive travel and advanced communication technology. Each succeeding generation is likely to have more and more contact with other religions and must find ways to be kind to adherents of these belief systems without accepting their convictions as equally valid as the truth revealed in the Old and New Testaments. As for the former question, part of its answer lies in the sort of vigilant instruction already mentioned. Each generation needs instruction. With so many religious options available, Christians can no longer *assume* persons will hear Christian teaching. Thus, instruction must be attractive and kind, of course, yet focused, purposeful, and accurate at the same time. Like the prophets, faithful teachers may gain few converts, but God does not judge the teacher on numerical success. Faithfulness is the standard.

Fourth, the historical, canonical, and theological data show that there are many dangers in idol worship beyond those already mentioned. Historically speaking, idolators were susceptible to psychological manipulation by their

[86] This term refers to a nation's commitment to only one God, while acknowledging the existence and legitimacy of other gods for other nations.

enemies. For instance, the Assyrians often placed a defeated nation's god in the fallen city's gates as the conquered people were marched off to exile. The intention was to leave the beaten persons with the impression that their gods approved of the Assyrian invasion. Assyria also created a mythology of invasion that was used as propaganda against their victims. In this mythology it was stated that the country's gods had already gone to Assyria to pay homage to Assyria's gods.[87] Why should the people not do so as well? Those who believed such rhetoric felt forsaken, helpless, and vulnerable. The message is clear: those who trust in images made by hands or in figments of false teachers' imaginations are ripe for psychological manipulation. Those who believe in a spiritual deity who is self-existent, nonmaterial, omniscient, personal, omnipresent, and all-powerful will have their own set of fears, no doubt, but will not fall prey to this type of religious sleight of hand.

Further, the accumulated canonical data demonstrates that human cruelty is a direct result of not serving the covenant God. Ahaz did not offer a human sacrifice to Yahweh (2 Kgs 16:3–4); rather, this outrage was done on behalf of other "deities." Amos's audience forgot that serving a merciful God includes showing mercy to others. Cruelty done in God's name is never God's will or God's work. God's strength, commitment to truth, and insistence on high ethical and moral standards includes high standards for kindness and truth on earth.

Finally, idolatry creates moral corruption, physical exhaustion, and physical weariness in people. Israel collapses under the weight of its own sickness. Idolatry leads to corruption, corruption ushers in decay, and decay results in death. Idol worship is not a neutral option for any society. It has consequences.

Fifth, 2 Kings 14–17 explains how to forfeit blessings. Throughout the story the author has made it clear that it takes a great deal to cause a patient God to punish. God brought Israel into a covenant relationship with himself that promised it nationhood and a homeland (Gen 12:1–9; 1 Kgs 8:23–61). He delivered these items and stood ready to do more (cf. Deut 27–28). No nation could take these things from Israel, for they were founded upon God's perfect character. But they could be forfeited, and Israel did so—day by day, decision by decision, sin by sin, rebellion by rebellion. Each forfeiture led to ultimate loss.

Sixth, these chapters surely invite reflection on what constitutes success in God's eyes. Again, it is not material or international prestige, otherwise Omri, Jeroboam II, and Tiglath-Pileser III would be called great men in these books. Ahab's diplomacy does not qualify him for greatness. Only reversing the attitudes unfolded in 2 Kings 17 can do so. Covenant faithfulness, in all its forms as expressed in the Old and New Testaments, makes persons pleasing to God. Such persons finally emerge in 2 Kings 18–25 too late to save Israel, but not too late to give the readers some positive examples to follow.

[87] Cf. Cogan, *Imperialism and Religion,* 9–21.

SECTION OUTLINE

VII. JUDAH DISINTEGRATES (18:1–25:30)
Historical Details Related to 2 Kings 18–25
1. Hezekiah's Righteous Reign (18:1–20:21)
   (1) Hezekiah's Devotion to God (18:1–8)
   (2) Hezekiah Attempts to Pacify Assyria (18:9–16)
   (3) Assyria Demands Surrender (18:17–37)
   (4) Hezekiah Prays for Deliverance (19:1–19)
   (5) Isaiah Predicts Deliverance (19:20–34)
   (6) God Defeats Assyria (19:35–37)
   (7) Hezekiah's Miraculous Healing (20:1–11)
   (8) Hezekiah Entertains Some Babylonians (20:12–21)
2. Manasseh and Amon's Wicked Reigns (21:1–26)
   (1) Manasseh's Unprecedented Wickedness (21:1–18)
   (2) Amon's Reign and Assassination (21:19–26)
3. Josiah's Righteous Reign (22:1–23:30)
   (1) The Law Is Found and Read (22:1–13)
   (2) Huldah Interprets the Law (22:14–20)
   (3) Josiah Leads Reform (23:1–27)
   (4) Egypt's Pharaoh Kills Josiah (23:28–30)
4. Judah's Political and Moral Decline (23:31–24:20)
   (1) Egypt Determines Judah's King (23:31–37)
   (2) Babylon Subjugates Judah (24:1–17)
   (3) Zedekiah's Wickedness (24:18–20)
5. Babylon Destroys Judah (25:1–26)
   (1) Babylon Conquers Jerusalem (25:1–7)
   (2) Babylon Burns the Temple and Takes Prisoners (25:8–21)
   (3) Babylon Appoints a Provisional Government (25:22–24)
   (4) Babylon's Governor Killed (25:25–26)
6. Jehoiachin Survives in Exile (25:27–30)
Canonical and Theological Implications of 2 Kings 18–25
Applicational Implications of 2 Kings 18–25

VII. JUDAH DISINTEGRATES (18:1–25:30)

Alone, small, and vulnerable, Judah now lives out the last 135 years of its history. At first, the nation's fortunes seem to improve. Hezekiah, a good king who receives unqualified praise from the writer (2 Kgs 18:3–8), takes the place of the compliant, idolatrous Ahaz ca. 715 B.C.[1] He institutes sweeping religious reforms (2 Kgs 18:4–8). The new king also breaks with Ahaz's pro-Assyrian policy, perhaps because the Assyrians were facing some problems of their own. These difficulties are soon overcome, though, and Hezekiah is forced to pay Assyria tribute to stave off annihilation (2 Kgs 18:13–16).

Either Assyria remains unsatisfied or Hezekiah rebels again, for the Assyrians invade Judah, place Jerusalem under siege, and demand surrender (2 Kgs 18:17–37). Greatly troubled, Hezekiah seeks the prophet Isaiah's advice, and prays for the Lord's help (2 Kgs 19:1–5; 14:19). Isaiah assures the king that the Lord will not allow Jerusalem to fall (2 Kgs 19:6–7). The prophet's word comes true when God causes the enemy to withdraw (2 Kgs 19:8–13) and slays 185,000 Assyrian troops in one evening (2 Kgs 19:35–37). One faithful king obeying the Lord is more effective in leading and saving Judah than all the wicked, yet politically skillful kings who precede him.

Yet not even a faithful king is immune from problems, and not even the presence of a righteous ruler in the land can stave off ultimate judgment. Isaiah warns Hezekiah to prepare for death (2 Kgs 20:1). The king asks God to spare him, however, and the Lord grants his petition (2 Kgs 20:2–11). Still, he must die sometime. What will happen to Judah then? At the end of his reign Hezekiah entertains a delegation from Babylon (2 Kgs 20:12–13). Once again Isaiah enters the picture, this time to predict that in the future it will be Babylon who destroys Judah (2 Kgs 20:14–19). But Hezekiah is allowed to die in peace (2 Kgs 20:20–21).

By the time Hezekiah dies in 687 B.C., his son Manasseh has been his coregent for a decade. Manasseh rules ca. 697–642 B.C., longer than any other monarch in Judah's history. Unfortunately, he chooses his grandfather Ahaz's approach to God, country, and foreign policy instead of his father's. He undoes all Hezekiah had done. He allows the high places to return, worships other gods, and reinstitutes payment of tribute to Assyria (2 Kgs 21:1–9). Because of his actions, some unnamed prophets claim that Jerusalem will in fact be destroyed (2 Kgs 21:10–16). The matter is settled. It may be delayed, but it is settled. Amon, Manasseh's son, takes over in 642 B.C., but only governs for two years before he is assassinated (2 Kgs 21:19–26). Judah appears on the brink of collapse, and only God's grace and another righteous king forestalls the coming devastation.

Josiah succeeds his father Amon and rules ca. 640–609 B.C. Only eight years old when he assumes the throne, Josiah decides to serve the Lord in his eighteenth year, or when he is about twenty-six years of age. This decision is fuelled by the discovery of "the book of the law in the house of the LORD" during a temple restoration initiated by the king (2 Kgs 22:3–8). When he hears God's

[1] See below for discussion of the dating difficulties associated with Hezekiah's era.

word, Josiah rips his clothing in shame and mourning, then sends envoys to Huldah the prophetess to learn the implications of the text's words for the nation (2 Kgs 22:9–14). Huldah pronounces bad news that the book's author surely seconds: Judah is finished. Because of his sensitivity to the Lord's word, however, Josiah will be allowed to die in peace. Afterwards, judgment will most certainly fall (2 Kgs 22:15–20). Again, the matter is settled.

Despite what he hears about ultimate doom, or perhaps because of it, Josiah institutes a religious reform that surpasses even the one undertaken in Hezekiah's era. Josiah has the book of the law read to the people (2 Kgs 23:1–2). He removes any sort of high place, idol, or aid to nonseparatist Yahwistic faith (2 Kgs 23:3–14). Moving north, he destroys the remnants of Jeroboam's religion in fallen Israel, all in accordance with the prophet's word in 1 Kgs 13:2. In fact, Josiah visits this prophet's grave (2 Kgs 23:15–19). Finally, he has the idolatrous priests killed (2 Kgs 23:20), then goes back to Jerusalem, where he orders that the Passover be observed (2 Kgs 23:21–23) and removes all sorcerers and practitioners of divination (2 Kgs 23:24).

Not even Josiah, though, can save Judah now. Truly he is a great and worthy Davidic king, but the prophetic word of God must come true (2 Kgs 23:25–28). Huldah's promise to Josiah also materializes. He dies in a battle with Neco, Egypt's Pharaoh (2 Kgs 23:29–30). Judah's last great hope is gone. Egypt now controls Judah's political position and policies.

Names like Jehoahaz, who rules only three months, Jehoiakim (ca. 609–598 B.C.), who switches allegiance from Egypt to Babylon when it is necessary, Jehoiachin, who also reigns only three months in 598–597 B.C., and Zedekiah, a weak man unable to act on his convictions, pass before readers' eyes in 2 Kgs 23:31–25:7. None of them embraces David's monotheism, nor Josiah's commitment to the Mosaic covenant. Thus, Babylon destroys Judah, including Jerusalem, because Zedekiah dares to rebel against his overlords (2 Kgs 25:8–26). Judah thereby joins Israel in exile.

After centuries of possessing the promised land, God's people now live either outside the land as exiles, or as tenants on their own ground. Only one bright spot remains for the author to report. Jehoiachin, exiled in 597 B.C., is elevated to favored status ca. 560 B.C. David's lineage still exists, albeit in Babylonian exile. Hope does remain.[2] Whenever God chooses, the people can return. However he chooses, the Davidic promise and kingdom can emerge. God is not weak, powerless, or in exile. Therefore, all who turn to this sovereign Lord may also look forward to strength, victory, and a home going.

[2] Cf. G. von Rad, *Studies in Deuteronomy,* trans. D. M. G. Stalker, SBT 9 (London: SCM, 1963) 74–91.

Historical Details Related to 2 Kings 18–25

Though this section's story line is quite clear, many of its historical details are tangled in intrigue or obscurity. The chronology of Hezekiah's reign is particularly notorious in this regard. It is somewhat difficult to chronicle the changing fortunes of the era's superpowers precisely. Given these, and other, problems, it is probably best to summarize events as they occur within the reigns of Judah's kings.

Hezekiah's reign (ca. 715–687) occurred during a period in which Assyria remained *the* great power in the region. Despite their continued role as oppressing giant, however, Assyria experienced some unsteady times due to turnover in leadership. When Tiglath-Pileser III died in 727 B.C. he was lord of all he surveyed, leaving his son Shalmaneser V (ca. 727–722 B.C.) a considerable kingdom. It was Shalmaneser V who finally captured Samaria after a three-year siege, and who defeated Tyre after a five-year siege.[3] In many ways, then, Shalmaneser V was truly his father's son.

The two Assyrian kings with whom Hezekiah had to deal faced more pressure than their immediate predecessors. Once they overcame their problems, though, they led Assyria to still-greater power. Sargon II (ca. 722–705 B.C.) encountered opposition from Babylon and Urartu almost immediately after he took the throne.[4] The Babylonian rebellion was led by "the sagacious and scheming Marduk-apla-id-dinna (the biblical Merodach-baladan,"[5] a man Sargon II was not able to subdue until 710 B.C. But subdue him he did. As for Urartu, Sargon II defeated them a few years earlier, but only after seven or eight years of conflict. He was also forced to squelch local rebellions in various places, such as Syria. Clearly, by 710 B.C. no nation was in a position to challenge the Assyrians' international prominence.[6]

Because of its problems with Babylon and Urartu, Assyria had not campaigned in Judah's territory for some time when Hezekiah came to power in 715 B.C. It is therefore possible that Judah's king thought the moment had come for his country to test the limits of Assyrian power.[7] He may also have sensed that his subjects were weary of foreign dominance.[8] Quite possibly he also may have had personal convictions about the religious implications of his nation's continued obeisance to a polytheistic state. Most likely a combination of factors motivated Hezekiah, but the result is the same. Hezekiah obviously

---

[3] J. H. Hayes and S. A. Irvine, *Isaiah the Eighth-Century Prophet: His Times and His Preaching* (Nashville: Abingdon, 1987) 25. The siege of Tyre occurred ca. 725–720 B.C.

[4] J. N. Oswalt, *The Book of Isaiah, Chapters 1–39,* NICOT (Grand Rapids: Eerdmans, 1986) 8.

[5] Hayes and Irvine, *Isaiah,* 25.

[6] Cf. Oswalt, *The Book of Isaiah,* 8–9; Bright, *A History of Israel,* 278; Hayes and Irvine, *Isaiah the Eighth-Century Prophet,* 26.

[7] Bright, *A History of Israel,* 281.

[8] J. A. Thompson, *The Book of Jeremiah,* NICOT (Grand Rapids: Eerdmans, 1980) 12.

desired to restore both Judah's political *and* religious autonomy, yet it appears that he instituted religious changes first, then waited for the right time to make the political break.

Apparently Hezekiah thought the correct time for revolt arrived when Sargon II was killed in battle and Sennacherib (ca. 705–681 B.C.) took his place. As Noth comments, "In the first years of his reign, his successor, Sennacherib, was preoccupied in various parts of his great empire, in enforcing his rule in the face of various rebellions."[9] Babylon was the chief rebel, led once again by the resilient Merodoch-baladan. Western nations, including Tyre (Phoenicia) and Judah, also withheld tribute (cf. 2 Kgs 18:7). To seemingly make the situation even brighter for the rebels, Egypt assured them of aid. It is possible that Hezekiah invaded Philistia at this time to force them to join the coalition against Assyria (cf. 2 Kgs 18:8). Freedom seemed to be possible. No doubt hopes were high.[10]

Sennacherib proved able to meet the challenge. By 702 B.C. he had driven Babylon's leaders into the swamps and regained control over his enemy for a time.[11] He was ready, then, to stop the western revolt. First he crushed Tyre and placed an Assyrian on the throne. Next, he exacted tribute from Philistia, Ammon, Moab, and Edom, who were anxious to avoid a full-blown invasion. Then, he captured numerous Judahite cities. Finally, he besieged Jerusalem itself.[12] Whatever hopes for independence Judah had harbored now seemed dashed. Survival had become a high goal.

Scholars debate the next series of events.[13] The Scriptures apparently say that Hezekiah agreed to pay whatever tribute the Assyrians demanded, yet when he paid the enemy did not retreat (2 Kgs 18:13–17). Rather, he demanded Jerusalem to surrender, perhaps to remove Hezekiah and replace him with an Assyrian as had been done in Babylon and Tyre.[14] Assyria left temporarily to meet a challenge from Egypt (2 Kgs 19:8–13), then returned later. In the midst of this grave situation, God performed the miracle of killing 185,000 Assyrian troops, a loss that forced the invaders to retreat (2 Kgs 19:35–37). Assyrian records do not state that such an event occurred, but they do say that Assyria left the area with Hezekiah still in power, which is quite

---

[9] M. Noth, *The History of Israel,* 2d ed., trans. P. R. Ackroyd (New York: Harper & Row, 1960) 265.

[10] Hayes and Irvine, *Isaiah,* 28; Bright, *A History of Israel,* 285; Noth, *The History of Israel,* 267; Oswalt, *The Book of Isaiah,* 10

[11] A. T. Olmstead, *History of Assyria* (Chicago: University of Chicago Press, 1923) 283–89; Oswalt, *The Book of Isaiah,* 11; Noth, *The History of Israel,* 267–68.

[12] These events are discussed in Olmstead, *History of Assyria,* 283–89; Oswalt, *The Book of Isaiah,* 11; Noth, *The History of Israel,* 267–68; Bright, *The History of Israel,* 286.

[13] Cf. A. K. Jenkins, "Hezekiah's Fourteenth Year: A New Interpretation of 2 Kings 18:13—19:37," *VT* 26/3 (1976) 284–86; and Bright, *The History of Israel,* 298–309.

[14] Olmstead, *History of Assyria,* 288; Oswalt, *The Book of Isaiah,* 11.

unusual given his constant opposition to Assyria.

When Manasseh assumed control of Judah upon his father's death in 687 B.C., he had already acted as coregent for ten years. Perhaps because of Isaiah's declaration of how long he would live (cf. 2 Kgs 20:1–7), "Hezekiah at the earliest opportunity associated Manasseh with himself on the throne to give him every possible training in carrying on the affairs of state."[15] The world situation had not changed drastically. From ca. 694–689 B.C. Babylon managed to defeat Assyria in several battles, but by 689 B.C. Assyria reasserted its authority over its ancient foe.[16] Egypt was more vital than it had been for years, yet it was still no threat to Assyria, nor any help to smaller countries like Judah for that matter.[17] For Judah to stand against Assyria, then, they had to stand alone.

Manasseh decided not to chance resisting Assyria again. At least two considerations seem to have motivated his thinking. First, Assyria was indeed a mighty nation, and Esarhaddon (ca. 681–669 B.C.), Sennacharib's successor, was at least as capable as his predecessors. Esarhaddon made sure Babylon behaved, then defeated Egypt quite soundly in 671 B.C.[18] Given this kind of might, no doubt Judah's king did not relish a confrontation with Assyria. Second, Manasseh had none of his father's spiritual convictions. He reinstituted high places, altars for Baal, pagan shrines like Ahaz's, and child sacrifice (2 Kgs 21:1–9). With no commitment to separatist Yahwism, opposing Assyria would appear just foolhardy. Thus, Manasseh's long reign (ca. 697–642) was marked by idolatry, compromise, and a pro-Assyrian foreign policy.

The fact that Esarhaddon's successor, Ashurbanipal (ca. 669–627), was also an effective monarch kept Manasseh in line. Only one possible rebellious moment occurred, an event described in 2 Chronicles 33:11–13, which says Manasseh was taken prisoner and brought to Babylon. R. Dillard believes that Manasseh was "suspected of complicity" during yet another Babylonian revolt that occurred ca. 652–648.[19] If so, Manasseh discovered firsthand how serious Ashurbanipal was about maintaining order. Apparently Manasseh learned his lesson, since he was allowed to return to his position of leadership.

After Manasseh's death, Amon served from 642–640 before being assassinated and succeeded by Josiah, who was a mere eight years old at the time. Josiah's long (ca. 640–609) and illustrious reign represented the last great days

[15] E. R. Thiele, *The Mysterious Numbers of the Hebrew Kings,* 3d ed. (Grand Rapids: Zondervan, 1983) 177.

[16] Olmstead, *History of Assyria,* 291–96.

[17] Bright, *A History of Israel,* 285.

[18] Ibid., 310.

[19] R. B. Dillard, *2 Chronicles,* WBC (Waco: Word, 1987) 15:265. J. M. Myers suggests Manasseh's journey may have occurred as early as 672 B.C. (*II Chronicles,* 2d ed., AB [Garden City: Doubleday, 1973], 13:198–99).

of Judah's nationhood. There were two basic reasons for this resurgence. First, Assyria collapsed as a major power in a surprisingly short period of time. Of course, Assyria always had enemies to fight, and this era was no exception. Babylon continued its stubborn determination to break free of its enemy's grip. The Medes were also restless, and Assyria was forced to make an alliance with Egypt, of all people.[20] This continued opposition came at a time when Assyria was experiencing a severe leadership crisis. After Ashurbanipal's death in 627 B.C., a struggle for the throne ensued that only placed Ashur-etil-ilani in control after fierce fighting.[21] Meanwhile, Nabopolassar seized power in Babylon in 626 B.C. and never relinquished it to the Assyrians.[22] The Medes joined the Babylonians, and by 616 B.C. these allies pushed the Assyrian army back to its home base.[23] In 612 B.C. Nineveh, the capital of Assyria, fell, and by 609 B.C. Assyria was finished as a world power.[24]

The second reason for Judah's resurgence under Josiah was that he expressed a definite commitment to separatist Yahwism in about 622 B.C., his eighteenth year on the throne (2 Kgs 22:3–7). In that year a copy of the Law was found during a temple restoration project. Upon hearing of the consequences of disobeying God's word, Josiah instituted sweeping reforms that included the removal of idols and a return to careful worship of the Lord (2 Kgs 22:8–23:30). Thus, during a time when foreign influence was removed a national religious and political renewal took place. Judah was certainly strengthened by these events. Josiah even pushed the reforms into the old nation of Israel (2 Kgs 23:15–20), which may have led to dreams of a reunited people of God (cf. Jer 3:6–18). Though the reform did not survive Josiah's death, it was nonetheless a great achievement.

Ironically, Josiah's death in 609 B.C. was also due in part to shifting alliances among world powers. In that year Pharaoh Neco was marching north to help Assyria fight at Haran. Josiah may have thought an Egyptian-Assyrian victory would place Judah back in its old vassal role, so he engaged Neco at Megiddo and was killed (2 Kgs 23:29–30).[25] Though Babylon won the battle at Haran, which forced Neco to retreat, the victors were not yet ready to occupy the smaller western nations. Therefore, Egypt took control of Judah.

Judah's next king, Jehoahaz, lasted only three months before Egypt replaced him with the more compliant Jehoiakim, who delivered high tribute payments to the Pharaoh (2 Kgs 23:31–35). Jehoiakim "ruled" from about 609 to 598 B.C., serving whomever could keep him king. Until 605 B.C. that nation was

---

[20] Bright, *A History of Israel,* 315.

[21] Olmstead, *History of Assyria,* 627.

[22] Bright, *A History of Israel,* 315.

[23] Noth, *The History of Israel,* 271.

[24] Bright, *A History of Israel,* 315–16.

[25] Thompson, *The Book of Jeremiah,* 22.

Egypt. In that year Babylon, now led by Nebuchadnezzar II (ca. 605–562 B.C.), asserted itself against Egypt. By the next year Jehoiakim had switched allegiance to Babylon (2 Kgs 24:1).[26] Captives were taken from Judah at this time, including Daniel and his friends (Dan 1:1–7). At the end of his career Jehoiakim apparently did rebel against Babylon but died before he was forced to pay for his actions (cf. 2 Kgs 24:1–10). Instead, his successor for three months, Jehoiachin (ca. 598–597), suffered for agreeing with Jehoiakim's policies.

Neither Jehoiakim nor Jehoiachin continued Josiah's reforms (2 Kgs 24:1–9). Idols and high places returned to the land, a fact Jeremiah and Ezekiel mourn in their prophecies. With religious and political distinctiveness gone, only a quest for survival fuelled national unity. Judah seemed to have run out of desirable options, for they could either rebel and die, or live in humiliation. The writer of 1, 2 Kings agreed with the prophets who proclaimed and wrote that Judah had brought this situation on themselves because of their covenant breaking.

Zedekiah (ca. 597–587 B.C.) acted as Judah's final monarch. He came to power as Babylon's replacement for Jehoiachin (2 Kgs 24:10–20) after a second deportation saw the king, other officials, and "professionals" like Ezekiel go into exile (cf. 2 Kgs 24:15–16; Ezek 1:1–3). Jeremiah portrays Zedekiah as a man who sought God's word through the prophets, probably believed those words, yet who found himself unable to obey what he was told (cf. Jer 21:1–7; 34:1–7; 37:1–10; 38:14–23). He was unable to effect moral government in the land (Jer 34:12–22).

For some unexplained reason, Zedekiah rebelled against Nebuchadnezzar. Bright thinks this refusal to pay tribute may have been a solitary decision, for there is virtually no evidence that other countries joined Judah in this action.[27] Babylon laid siege and captured Jerusalem in 587 B.C. Zedekiah attempted to flee, but he was taken, forced to watch his sons executed, and had his eyes gouged out (2 Kgs 25:1–7). Nebuchadnezzar looted the temple, burnt it, and killed or deported many people (2 Kgs 25:8–21). Gedaliah was appointed governor of the new Babylonian province (2 Kgs 25:22–26). Judah's last suicidal act was no more inexplicable than its earlier ones. Moral depravity and political-social decay go together.

Only one historical detail remains. Both 2 Kgs 25:27–30 and Jer 52:31–34 record the fact that ca. 560 B.C. the aged Jehoiachin remained in exile, but was treated well. G. von Rad thinks the conclusion is a positive one, for it shows that David's descendants may yet return to their ancestor's throne. All is not lost.[28] Still, the nation *is* in exile, and will remain so until 538 B.C., when

[26] Noth, *The History of Israel,* 281.

[27] Bright, *A History of Israel,* 327–30.

[28] Von Rad, *Studies in Deuteronomy,* 90–91.

Cyrus decrees they may return home (cf. Ezra 1:1–3). Hope exists, but it is a somber hope, clouded by a history of missed opportunities, tragic losses, bungling miscalculations, covenant infidelity, social decline, foreign oppression, and, in the end, defeat and exile. That any hope remains at all is a tribute to the Lord's grace and the faithful remnant's belief in that grace.

1. Hezekiah's Righteous Reign (18:1–20:21)

So far in the story not one monarch has met the author's high standards for a king: commitment to the Lord, rejection of idolatry, and removal of high places and all other remnants of non-Yahwistic religion. Now one of the two men who meet these criteria enters the story. Hezekiah is Ahaz's son, yet he rejects his father's approach to religion and statesmanship. His reform movement alone proves this point. His rejection of a pro-Assyrian foreign policy, which has always been the political equivalent of a pact with the devil, his sensitivity to Isaiah's prophetic word, and his personal relationship with the Lord simply heighten the contrast. Ultimately he does not save the nation from its permanent destruction, of course, but he does everything humanly possible to effect a stay of execution.

One of the unique features of this section is that it also appears with slight variations in Isa 36:1–39:8. That more than one author offers the same material supports the credibility of the account. The use of Isaiah's words and work by the author of Kings indicates a strong solidarity with the prophetic movement, which in turn influences the writing of prophetic history. Finally, the quotation of Isaiah's messages invites the comparison of other concepts in 1, 2 Kings with the Book of Isaiah.

(1) Hezekiah's Devotion to God (18:1–8)

1In the third year of Hoshea son of Elah king of Israel, Hezekiah son of Ahaz king of Judah began to reign. 2He was twenty-five years old when he became king, and he reigned in Jerusalem twenty-nine years. His mother's name was Abijah daughter of Zechariah. 3He did what was right in the eyes of the LORD, just as his father David had done. 4He removed the high places, smashed the sacred stones and cut down the Asherah poles. He broke into pieces the bronze snake Moses had made, for up to that time the Israelites had been burning incense to it. (It was called Nehushtan.)

5Hezekiah trusted in the LORD, the God of Israel. There was no one like him among all the kings of Judah, either before him or after him. 6He held fast to the LORD and did not cease to follow him; he kept the commands the LORD had given Moses. 7And the LORD was with him; he was successful in whatever he undertook. He rebelled against the king of Assyria and did not serve him. 8From watchtower to fortified city, he defeated the Philistines, as far as Gaza and its territory.

18:1–3 Exactly when Hezekiah takes the throne and how the author calculates that date remain quite difficult to determine. Scholars date his rise to sole power at 715 B.C. because of the events described from the divided kingdom until this point in the story, and because the reference to an enemy invasion in Hezekiah's fourteenth year (2 Kgs 18:13) seems to match Assyrian records of an incursion in 701 B.C. What puzzles interpreters most, then, are the comments that link Hezekiah's era with Hoshea's, the twenty-nine years given him in 2 Kgs 18:2, and the length of his successor's reign (cf. 2 Kgs 21:2).

Thiele thinks the references to Hoshea are a miscalculation.[29] Montgomery and Gehman date Hezekiah's era as 725–696 B.C. and state that the "fourteenth year" in 2 Kgs 18:13 "may be a scribal miswriting of '24,' which would give the correct date; or the figure was induced by the statement of the promise to Hezekiah of an additional 15 years of life (20:6), *i.e.*, 29–15 = 14."[30] If so, there is no other textual tradition that reflects the copyist's error. Perhaps R. Hubbard's comments on the text are the fairest way to address the matter:

> At present, the best solution is to concede that the problem lies in the synchronisms with Hoshea. It is possible that their dates are correct but calculated by some principles not clear to us. Though substantial, our knowledge of ancient chronological methods is imperfect. For the moment, one must concede that no good solution exists.[31]

As has been stated previously, interpreters must be humble as they attempt to reconstruct the history. But at present it seems appropriate to date Hezekiah's reign 715–687 B.C. and to wait for correctives to materialize.

The most startling editorial comment in this section is the favorable comparison of Hezekiah to David. Future verses verify the claim. This short statement is intended to make readers realize the magnitude of Hezekiah's achievements.

18:4–8 Hezekiah acts exactly how the author has wished other kings would. He removes high places, altars, Ashteroth, and an item from Moses' time that has come to be used as an idol (cf. Num 21:9). These changes make it possible for worship to be centralized in Jerusalem again. Jones notes that according to some commentators these reforms never took place, then he correctly states that such opinions are unfounded.[32] The writer of 1, 2 Kings is so

---

[29] Thiele, *The Mysterious Numbers of the Hebrew Kings,* 174–75.

[30] J. A. Montgomery and H. S. Gehman, *A Critical and Exegetical Commentary on the Book of Kings,* ICC (1951; reprint, Edinburgh: T & T Clark, 1986) 483.

[31] R. L. Hubbard, Jr., *First and Second Kings,* EvBC (Chicago: Moody Press, 1991) 208–9. See, however, the solution offered by E. H. Merrill, *Kingdom of Priests* (Grand Rapids: Baker, 1987) 402–5, 410, the third year of Hoshea, when he was eleven years old. He was twenty-five when he began his sole rule.

[32] G. H. Jones, *1 and 2 Kings,* NCB (Grand Rapids: Eerdmans, 1984) 2:561.

committed to high standards, and so ready to criticize those who do not meet them, that it seems unlikely that the author fabricates positive events now. In fact, the Chronicler adds details not in this text. According to 2 Chronicles 29–31 Hezekiah also repairs the temple, offers extensive dedicatory sacrifices when the renovation is complete, and celebrates Passover. J. Rosenbaum even suggests that these items are omitted to make Josiah's later reform seem even more impressive.[33] This possibility appears unlikely in light of 18:3, since the author bestows no higher compliment than to say that a king is like David. Thus, it is best to avoid the extremes of claiming either the events never happened or that more happened than the writer admits. As it stands the account deserves to be treated as an accurate statement of Hezekiah's basic reforms.

What motivates Hezekiah's reform? Noth says that the reform is a by-product of a political revolt,[34] but Gray believes that it is difficult to separate political and religious concerns.[35] Wiseman concludes that the need for unity in the face of the Assyrian threat, a desire to reestablish the Davidic and Solomonic empire, and Hezekiah's personal conviction fuel his policy.[36] Cogan and Tadmor, however, assess the situation accurately. They note that religious reforms of this magnitude could hardly be calculated to bring unity and coherence. Rather, they would cause upheaval at a time in which Hezekiah could least afford it. Therefore, the text properly states that the king acts from personal conviction and confidence in the Lord.[37]

Certainly Hezekiah's confidence in the Lord and his commitment to Moses' law does impact his public life, just as Moses said it should (cf. Deut 17:18–20). Eventually he does rebel against Assyria, a nation that is evil by any normal definition of the word.[38] Not serving this master indicates Hezekiah's spiritual standing more than his sense of diplomatic expediency, since he has no reason to believe such activity will please Assyria. Likewise, his success in invading Philistia is portrayed as the Lord's blessing, probably since the Philis-

[33] J. Rosenbaum, "Hezekiah's Reform and the Deuteronomistic Tradition," *HTR* 72 (1979) 41–43.

[34] Noth, *The History of Israel,* 266.

[35] J. Gray, *1 and 2 Kings,* OTL (Philadelphia: Westminster, 1963) 608.

[36] D. J. Wiseman, *1 and 2 Kings,* TOTC (Downers Grove: InterVarsity, 1993) 272.

[37] M. Cogan and H. Tadmor, *II Kings,* AB (Garden City: Doubleday, 1988) 11:219–20.

[38] I say "normal definition" knowing that many persons may think Assyria exercised its ideological and military options without being "evil." Assyria conquered by murdering, stealing, maiming, and starving men, women, and children in the process. After surveying similar atrocities in the Soviet Union, Alexander Solzhenitsyn writes, "Among progressive people, it is considered rather awkward to use seriously such words as 'good' and 'evil.' Communism has managed to persuade all of us that these concepts are old-fashioned and laughable. But if we are to be deprived of the concepts of good and evil, what will be left? Nothing but the manipulation of one another. We will sink to the status of animals" (*Warning to the West* [New York: Farrer, Straus & Giroux, 1976] 58).

tines are reluctant to oppose Assyria at this time.[39] Hezekiah acts on his convictions, and God blesses him for his faithfulness.

(2) Hezekiah Attempts to Pacify the Assyrians (18:9–16)

[9]In King Hezekiah's fourth year, which was the seventh year of Hoshea son of Elah king of Israel, Shalmaneser king of Assyria marched against Samaria and laid siege to it. [10]At the end of three years the Assyrians took it. So Samaria was captured in Hezekiah's sixth year, which was the ninth year of Hoshea king of Israel. [11]The king of Assyria deported Israel to Assyria and settled them in Halah, in Gozan on the Habor River and in towns of the Medes. [12]This happened because they had not obeyed the LORD their God, but had violated his covenant—all that Moses the servant of the LORD commanded. They neither listened to the commands nor carried them out.

[13]In the fourteenth year of King Hezekiah's reign, Sennacherib king of Assyria attacked all the fortified cities of Judah and captured them. [14]So Hezekiah king of Judah sent this message to the king of Assyria at Lachish: "I have done wrong. Withdraw from me, and I will pay whatever you demand of me." The king of Assyria exacted from Hezekiah king of Judah three hundred talents of silver and thirty talents of gold. [15]So Hezekiah gave him all the silver that was found in the temple of the LORD and in the treasuries of the royal palace.

[16]At this time Hezekiah king of Judah stripped off the gold with which he had covered the doors and doorposts of the temple of the LORD, and gave it to the king of Assyria.

18:9–12 This text repeats information already covered in 2 Kgs 17:1–6, with the intention of demonstrating Hezekiah's awareness of the dangers inherent in opposing Assyria.[40] The passage also reminds readers that the fundamental reason Samaria fell was its spiritual rebellion, not merely its refusal to obey Assyria any longer. Therefore, Hezekiah may not disobey the Lord and survive. The issue that awaits an appropriate answer is whether or not Hezekiah can serve the Lord, disobey Assyria, and survive. Since he cannot serve the Lord and maintain ties with an oppressive, murderous country, Hezekiah will be forced to discover the answer to this question. Indeed, as the next passage proves, God will not allow him to avoid finding out if the Lord will protect Judah against the Assyrians.

18:13–16 In 701 B.C. Sennacherib tires of Hezekiah's rebellious attitude and invades the land. The Assyrian has been thwarting Babylon's revolt since 705 B.C., so only now has time to deal with Judah, who has been leading an anti-Assyrian coalition of smaller nations since about the same time.[41] Sen-

[39] Bright, *A History of Israel,* 285.

[40] His Egyptian ally shows up later (19:9), but by then he has already sued for peace. See Merrill, *Kingdom of Priests,* 416.

[41] Oswalt, *The Book of Isaiah,* 10.

nacherib takes "all the fortified cities of Judah," but only after defeating Tyre and inspiring leaders from Byblos, Arvad, Ashdod, Moab, Edom, and Ammon to bring tribute.[42] Hezekiah realizes that he is quite alone in his opposition to Assyria. His allies are either unwilling or unable to help him.[43]

Given his desperate situation, Hezekiah attempts to make peace before the enemy reaches Jerusalem. He sends a message to Sennacherib at Lachish, where the Assyrians scored a triumph immortalized in Sennacherib's war art,[44] asking for terms of surrender. In response, the Assyrian demands an enormous amount of money, which Hezekiah attempts to raise by emptying Judah's treasuries and stripping the temple of its gold ornaments. According to 2 Chr 32:1–5,30 he also repairs Jerusalem's walls and provides water for a siege. Taken together, the biblical accounts leave the impression that Hezekiah is by no means certain about what Sennacherib will decide to do.

(3) Assyria Demands Surrender (18:17–37)

**17The king of Assyria sent his supreme commander, his chief officer and his
field commander with a large army, from Lachish to King Hezekiah at Jerusalem.
They came up to Jerusalem and stopped at the aqueduct of the Upper Pool, on the
road to the Washerman's Field. 18They called for the king; and Eliakim son of
Hilkiah the palace administrator, Shebna the secretary, and Joah son of Asaph the
recorder went out to them.**

19The field commander said to them, "Tell Hezekiah:

**"'This is what the great king, the king of Assyria, says: On what are you basing
this confidence of yours? 20You say you have strategy and military strength—but
you speak only empty words. On whom are you depending, that you rebel against
me? 21Look now, you are depending on Egypt, that splintered reed of a staff,
which pierces a man's hand and wounds him if he leans on it! Such is Pharaoh
king of Egypt to all who depend on him. 22And if you say to me, "We are depending on the LORD our God"—isn't he the one whose high places and altars Hezekiah removed, saying to Judah and Jerusalem, "You must worship before this
altar in Jerusalem"?**

**23"'Come now, make a bargain with my master, the king of Assyria: I will give
you two thousand horses—if you can put riders on them! 24How can you repulse
one officer of the least of my master's officials, even though you are depending on
Egypt for chariots and horsemen? 25Furthermore, have I come to attack and
destroy this place without word from the LORD? The LORD himself told me to
march against this country and destroy it.'"**

---

[42] Bright, *A History of Israel,* 286.

[43] "Hezekiah's fourth year" apparently refers to the fourth year of his coregency with Ahaz. It is thus a flashback that precedes the events of vv. 13–37 not by ten years, as it appears on the surface, but by almost thirty.

[44] Montgomery and Gehman, *Kings*, 484.

[26]Then Eliakim son of Hilkiah, and Shebna and Joah said to the field commander, "Please speak to your servants in Aramaic, since we understand it. Don't speak to us in Hebrew in the hearing of the people on the wall."

[27]But the commander replied, "Was it only to your master and you that my master sent me to say these things, and not to the men sitting on the wall—who, like you, will have to eat their own filth and drink their own urine?"

[28]Then the commander stood and called out in Hebrew: "Hear the word of the great king, the king of Assyria! [29]This is what the king says: Do not let Hezekiah deceive you. He cannot deliver you from my hand. [30]Do not let Hezekiah persuade you to trust in the LORD when he says, 'The LORD will surely deliver us; this city will not be given into the hand of the king of Assyria.'

[31]"Do not listen to Hezekiah. This is what the king of Assyria says: Make peace with me and come out to me. Then every one of you will eat from his own vine and fig tree and drink water from his own cistern, [32]until I come and take you to a land like your own, a land of grain and new wine, a land of bread and vineyards, a land of olive trees and honey. Choose life and not death!

"Do not listen to Hezekiah, for he is misleading you when he says, 'The LORD will deliver us.' [33]Has the god of any nation ever delivered his land from the hand of the king of Assyria? [34]Where are the gods of Hamath and Arpad? Where are the gods of Sepharvaim, Hena and Ivvah? Have they rescued Samaria from my hand? [35]Who of all the gods of these countries has been able to save his land from me? How then can the LORD deliver Jerusalem from my hand?"

[36]But the people remained silent and said nothing in reply, because the king had commanded, "Do not answer him."

[37]Then Eliakim son of Hilkiah the palace administrator, Shebna the secretary and Joah son of Asaph the recorder went to Hezekiah, with their clothes torn, and told him what the field commander had said.

18:17–18 It is hardly surprising that Sennacherib goes ahead with his plans to invade Jerusalem. After all, Hezekiah has paid tribute,[45] but his past record hardly qualifies him as a reliable vassal. Thus, Assyria wants further assurances of allegiance, more money, Hezekiah deposed, or a combination of these options. Tyre's king has already been replaced, and Assyria's historical pattern was to place Assyrians on the thrones of rebellious states.[46] So Hezekiah's removal may be the chief aim.

Sennacherib's officials bring the army, or a portion of it, to Jerusalem. They stop up some of the city's water supply, a standard procedure in siege warfare. Hezekiah is summoned, but he sends a contingent of three officials to match those dispatched by Sennacherib. Judah's king acts as if he demands to be treated as an equal in the negotiations.

[45] See, however, A. R. Millard's suggestion that Hezekiah had only promised payment ("Sennacherib's Attack on Hezekiah," *TynBul* 36 [1985] 71).

[46] Cf. Bright, *A History of Israel,* 287.

18:19–25 Assyria's spokesman[47] focuses on military and religious reasons Judah should surrender. First, he says quite correctly that Egypt is unable to rescue Jerusalem. Indeed, the Egyptians can only hurt those who depend on them. Assyria's "great king" (a rather common and arrogant self-designation)[48] can destroy any ally Judah possesses. His ability to defeat Judah almost goes without saying.

Second, the speaker tells the officials not to trust in the Lord either. Why? Because Hezekiah has angered the Lord by removing the high places in his honor and limited worship to one small place. Therefore, he claims the Lord has told Assyria to march against Jerusalem, to punish the people for such devaluation of their God/god. This sort of propaganda about other countries' deities abandoning their adherents was a standard Assyrian ploy when they invaded and conquered another nation. Cogan notes that the Assyrians routinely told their enemies that their gods were angry with them, that the gods had abandoned them, and that these gods counseled them to surrender to the Assyrians.[49] It is not unusual, then, for the spokesman to try such tactics on Judahites. What the speaker has not grasped, however, is that he addresses monotheists committed to separatist Yahwism, not the typical polytheists he is used to manipulating.

18:26–35 The second speech the Assyrian makes is directed at the city's defenders more than at the three immovable officials. He does so despite the officials' request that he speak only to them, which is one more evidence that the Assyrian treats Hezekiah and his envoys with contempt. He takes his propaganda directly to the people. This strategy was also a common Assyrian invasion technique.[50] The Assyrians pretend to have the "working class" warrior's interests in their minds, but history has left no trace of concrete evidence of any such benevolence.

As the spokesman continues, his determination to undermine Hezekiah becomes quite evident. Four times he denounces Judah's king, each time with the express purpose of belittling either his military capabilities or theological common sense. In other words, he expands his earlier comments to include direct attacks on Hezekiah. In the first two instances he warns them not to let their ruler "deceive" or "persuade" them. Hezekiah has no army to combat

---

[47] The Hebrew term רַב־שָׁקֵה can be translated "field commander" (NIV). Cf. R. D. Patterson and H. J. Austel, "1, 2 Kings," EBC (Grand Rapids: Zondervan, 1988) 4:258. Jones says, "The Heb. term Rabshakeh means 'chief butler,' but possibly the Assyrian title denotes 'chief officer' or 'chieftain' " (*1 and 2 Kings,* 2:569).

[48] Cogan and Tadmor, *II Kings,* 231.

[49] M. Cogan, *Imperialism and Religion: Assyria, Judah and Israel in the Eighth and Seventh Centuries* B.C.E., SBLMS 19 (Missoula, Mont.: Scholars Press, 1974) 9–21. Also see comments under "Applicational Issues Related to 2 Kings 14–17."

[50] Cf. Wiseman, *1 and 2 Kings,* 277, n. 2.

Assyria, and Yahweh will not deliver them either.

The final two denunciations of Hezekiah are elaborations of these concepts. He compares Hezekiah's empty promises to the benevolence of Assyria's king. A better life in a new land is promised, which is an interesting description of deportation to a place where you do not know the people, the language, the land, or the local customs (cf. 2 Kgs 17:24–41). Finally, he compares Yahweh unfavorably not only to Assyria's gods, but to the gods of nations already conquered. His argument fits polytheistic theology, for it measures the worth and power of individual gods by the success and grandeur of those who worship them. By his standards, Yahweh must be weaker than the gods of countries formerly more robust than Judah, so it is ludicrous to believe such a deity can save the city's people from disaster. His argument therefore makes sense given his presuppositions, but is Yahweh such a God/god? Are his people polytheists, or are they monotheists? Will they choose so-called pragmatism over covenant commitment?

18:36–37 The people remain silent because Hezekiah has anticipated such tactics and commanded them to do so. Too, they may not trust the speaker. Of course, the Assyrian line would be hard to sell anyway, since their reputation has preceded the invasion and other Judahite cities lie in ruins. While Hezekiah's officials report back to him, the Assyrians wait, the defenders wait, and the reader waits.

Some scholars have questioned the historical accuracy of these speeches. Montgomery and Gehman suggest they are "authentic in colour, even if literally fiction,"[51] and Auld concludes "that the narrative is more interested in the religious significance of events it records than in relating them exactly as they happened."[52] Childs thinks that the text sounds enough like other incidents in Assyrian history, though, to claim that the Assyrian's speech has its "setting in the diplomatic disputation and reflects a level of ancient historical tradition. However, there is another level of the oracle which is much younger and indicates later theological reflection on the tradition."[53] C. Cohen pursues Childs' historical points further and concludes, "It is therefore likely that a substantial part of the extant first speech may well have been ultimately based on the actual words of the Assyrian official."[54] Besides the historical parallels noted by Childs and Cohen, the theological perspective and political intentions implied in the passage are in keeping with Assyrian practice, as has already been stated. Therefore, it seems likely that the passage either reports the Assyrian's actual words or offers a telescoped summary of those words.

---

[51] Montgomery and Gehman, *Kings,* 487.

[52] A. G. Auld, *I and II Kings,* DSB (Philadelphia: Westminster, 1986) 214.

[53] B. S. Childs, *Isaiah and the Assyrian Crisis,* SBT/2, 3 (London: SCM, 1967) 85.

[54] C. Cohen, "Neo-Assyrian Elements in the First Speech of the Biblical *Rab-šaqê,*" *Israel Oriental Studies* IX, ed. Goldenberg (Tel-Aviv: Tel-Aviv University Press, 1979) 47.

(4) Hezekiah Prays for Deliverance (19:1–19)

[1]When King Hezekiah heard this, he tore his clothes and put on sackcloth and went into the temple of the LORD. [2]He sent Eliakim the palace administrator, Shebna the secretary and the leading priests, all wearing sackcloth, to the prophet Isaiah son of Amoz. [3]They told him, "This is what Hezekiah says: This day is a day of distress and rebuke and disgrace, as when children come to the point of birth and there is no strength to deliver them. [4]It may be that the LORD your God will hear all the words of the field commander, whom his master, the king of Assyria, has sent to ridicule the living God, and that he will rebuke him for the words the LORD your God has heard. Therefore pray for the remnant that still survives."

[5]When King Hezekiah's officials came to Isaiah, [6]Isaiah said to them, "Tell your master, 'This is what the LORD says: Do not be afraid of what you have heard—those words with which the underlings of the king of Assyria have blasphemed me. [7]Listen! I am going to put such a spirit in him that when he hears a certain report, he will return to his own country, and there I will have him cut down with the sword.'"

[8]When the field commander heard that the king of Assyria had left Lachish, he withdrew and found the king fighting against Libnah.

[9]Now Sennacherib received a report that Tirhakah, the Cushite king [of Egypt], was marching out to fight against him. So he again sent messengers to Hezekiah with this word: [10]"Say to Hezekiah king of Judah: Do not let the god you depend on deceive you when he says, 'Jerusalem will not be handed over to the king of Assyria.' [11]Surely you have heard what the kings of Assyria have done to all the countries, destroying them completely. And will you be delivered? [12]Did the gods of the nations that were destroyed by my forefathers deliver them: the gods of Gozan, Haran, Rezeph and the people of Eden who were in Tel Assar? [13]Where is the king of Hamath, the king of Arpad, the king of the city of Sepharvaim, or of Hena or Ivvah?"

[14]Hezekiah received the letter from the messengers and read it. Then he went up to the temple of the LORD and spread it out before the LORD. [15]And Hezekiah prayed to the LORD: "O LORD, God of Israel, enthroned between the cherubim, you alone are God over all the kingdoms of the earth. You have made heaven and earth. [16]Give ear, O LORD, and hear; open your eyes, O LORD, and see; listen to the words Sennacherib has sent to insult the living God.

[17]"It is true, O LORD, that the Assyrian kings have laid waste these nations and their lands. [18]They have thrown their gods into the fire and destroyed them, for they were not gods but only wood and stone, fashioned by men's hands. [19]Now, O LORD our God, deliver us from his hand, so that all kingdoms on earth may know that you alone, O LORD, are God."

19:1–4 Though it is not exactly clear what Hezekiah expects to hear from his officials, the news he receives distresses him. No doubt he hoped that the payment would satisfy Sennacherib, and now the money is gone and the enemy demands surrender, threatening to invade. As an act of humility, mourning, and supplication, Hezekiah puts on sackcloth and goes to the temple. His actions do not seem out of character, given the fact that he has been a reforming king for many years, but this dependence on God is a striking contrast to Ahaz's embracing of Assyrian gods when *he* was in trouble.

Hezekiah knows he needs a word from the Lord, so he sends Eliakim, Shebna, and some priests to the prophet Isaiah. Again, the king's behavior is extraordinary in light of past kings. Before, the prophets sought the kings, only to be rebuked. Now, the king actually *wants* a prophetic word. He is not simply acting out of desperation (Ahaz took quite another route when he was desperate. Hezekiah acts out his personal convictions).

The king's request focuses on the theological matter of how the Assyrians have ridiculed "the living God." He apparently concedes the point that he cannot field an army that can drive Assyria back home. What he rejects is the notion that the Lord is unable to do so. Therefore, he asks Isaiah to "pray for the remnant that still survives," clinging to the belief that hope has not disappeared permanently. Still, only the Lord can save them now.

19:5–7 Isaiah's response to the envoys' visit is clear, concise, confident, and comforting. He, too, reflects on the military and religious issues at hand, with the primary emphasis on the spiritual matters, which he in turn believes will decide the military concerns. Hezekiah need not fear, for the Lord will make himself known to the Assyrian king who has blasphemed him. Isaiah offers very specific promises, ones that will prove he is either a true prophet or a liar. His words also take Hezekiah one step further in his quest to serve the Lord. He knows now that the Lord promises to help him, yet he must believe this new promise, just as he has believed in the past.

19:8–13 Sennacherib's representative hears that his master has gone from Lachish to Libnah, so he goes there to report on the Jerusalem situation. Readers should expect an invasion to ensue, but no such event occurs. Instead, Sennacherib receives a report that Tirhakah of Egypt is marching out to fight him. Thus, Isaiah's mention of a troubling report takes concrete shape. Assyria is too busy to invade at this time. Hezekiah has at least a reprieve.

Gray argues that this reference to Tirhakah must describe a later campaign, since he "was much too young to have played such a role in 701. He was from the Sudan and became coregent in 689 and sole king in 686, ruling over Egypt till 664. It is noteworthy that he is not called Pharaoh, which may suggest a date somewhat earlier than 689."[55] Montgomery and Gehman disagree, stating, "Years before his elevation to the throne he was in active military service."[56] Wiseman agrees with Montgomery and Gehman, as do Patterson and Austel.[57] Hobbs summarizes these scholars' opinion when he concludes that

[55] Gray, *1 and 2 Kings,* 623–24.

[56] Montgomery and Gehman, *Kings,* 492.

[57] Cf. Wiseman, *1 and 2 Kings,* 279–80; Patterson and Austel, "1, 2 Kings," 264.

Tirhakah led Shabtaka's forces in this battle, then later became Pharaoh in his own right.[58] There is no overwhelming reason, then, to doubt the legitimacy of the text's claims.

In lieu of an actual invasion, Sennacherib threatens Hezekiah again. Once more he emphasizes Yahweh's inability to deliver them from his hand. No other gods have saved their people, so he sees no reason to think Judah's God/god is any different. His theology affects his decision-making processes, just as Hezekiah's affect his.

19:14–19 When Hezekiah receives Sennacherib's message he again turns to the Lord. His prayer consists of three parts, which Hubbard notes follow "a format typical of the most common kind of psalm, an 'individual complaint' (see Pss 6;13;102) to meet a personal need."[59] First, Hezekiah recognizes the Lord's greatness. He notes that the Lord is "enthroned between the cherubim," a reference to the ark of the covenant, the ancient symbol of the covenant between Israel and their God. Hezekiah furthers the image beyond Israel, though, by stating that the Lord is "God over all the kingdoms of the earth" because he has "made heaven and earth." If the Lord is creator and ruler of all nations, then Hezekiah can hope for deliverance in this seemingly impossible situation.

Second, Hezekiah explains his problem to the Lord. Again he speaks first about Assyria's insults against Yahweh, and only then addresses his military dilemma. He admits that Assyria has conquered the nations already mentioned, but he separates his God from those nations' deities on the grounds that they are not real. So how could they help their worshipers? Yahweh, on the other hand is not "fashioned by men's hands" and can therefore aid those who pray to him.

Third, Hezekiah asks directly for God's assistance against the Assyrians. Even in this direct petition, though, the king bases his request on a concern for God's honor, for he wants God to be worshiped because of the proposed great deliverance. Clearly, Hezekiah wants freedom for himself and for his people, yet he never loses sight of Israel's responsibility to bring recognition and glory to their Lord. Having prayed, he must wait to see what God will do, though he may expect the prophetic word already given to come true.

(5) Isaiah Predicts Deliverance (19:20–34)

[20]Then Isaiah son of Amoz sent a message to Hezekiah: "This is what the LORD, the God of Israel, says: I have heard your prayer concerning Sennacherib

[58] T. R.Hobbs, *2 Kings,* WBC (Waco: Word, 1985) 13:276. K A. Kitchen has shown that Tirhakah was in fact twenty or twenty-one in 701 B.C. (*The Third Intermediate Period in Egypt (1100–650 B.C.)* [Warminster: Aris & Phillips, 1973] 157–61.

[59] Hubbard, *First and Second Kings,* 215.

king of Assyria. 21This is the word that the LORD has spoken against him:

**"'The Virgin Daughter of Zion
despises you and mocks you.
The Daughter of Jerusalem
tosses her head as you flee.
22Who is it you have insulted and blasphemed?
Against whom have you raised your voice
and lifted your eyes in pride?
Against the Holy One of Israel!
23By your messengers
you have heaped insults on the LORD.
And you have said,
"With my many chariots
I have ascended the heights of the mountains,
the utmost heights of Lebanon.
I have cut down its tallest cedars,
the choicest of its pines.
I have reached its remotest parts,
the finest of its forests.
24I have dug wells in foreign lands
and drunk the water there.
With the soles of my feet
I have dried up all the streams of Egypt."**

**25"'Have you not heard?
Long ago I ordained it.
In days of old I planned it;
now I have brought it to pass,
that you have turned fortified cities
into piles of stone.
26Their people, drained of power,
are dismayed and put to shame.
They are like plants in the field,
like tender green shoots,
like grass sprouting on the roof,
scorched before it grows up.**

**27"'But I know where you stay
and when you come and go
and how you rage against me.
28Because you rage against me
and your insolence has reached my ears,
I will put my hook in your nose
and my bit in your mouth,
and I will make you return
by the way you came.'**

[29]"This will be the sign for you, O Hezekiah:

"This year you will eat what grows by itself,
and the second year what springs from that.
But in the third year sow and reap,
plant vineyards and eat their fruit.
[30]Once more a remnant of the house of Judah
will take root below and bear fruit above.
[31]For out of Jerusalem will come a remnant,
and out of Mount Zion a band of survivors.

The zeal of the LORD Almighty will accomplish this.

[32]"Therefore this is what the LORD says concerning the king of Assyria:

"He will not enter this city
or shoot an arrow here.
He will not come before it with shield
or build a siege ramp against it.
[33]By the way that he came he will return;
he will not enter this city, declares the LORD.
[34]I will defend this city and save it,
for my sake and for the sake of David my servant."

19:20–28 God answers the prayer through the prophet's words. Like Hezekiah's prayer, the response Isaiah sends also comes in three parts, the first of which also has three segments, and is composed as a "taunt or mocking song."[60] The poetic meter called *qinah* is typical of Hebrew laments. It was often used in mourning texts (e.g., Lamentations). Commenting on the report of this speech in Isa 37:31–35, A. Motyer writes, "In 36:5 Hezekiah received a word of the LORD in response to his approach to the prophet for prayer. Here he receives a word without any seeking on his part. His adoption of the way of faith opens the door whereby he speaks to God (14–20) and God speaks to him (21–35)."[61] J. Oswalt adds, "Sennacherib has spoken to Hezekiah concerning the Lord; Hezekiah has spoken to the Lord concerning Sennacherib; now the Lord speaks to Hezekiah concerning Sennacherib. It is always this last account which matters."[62]

God's response begins with the promise of a reversal of fortunes. Assyria has been oppressing Judah, and certainly expects to continue doing so. Their king has mocked Judah's king and Judah's God. But everything will soon change. Jerusalem is personified as a virgin daughter who tosses her head in disdain at the proud, once-powerful Assyrians, who believe they have made

[60] Cogan and Tadmor, *II Kings,* 236.

[61] J. A. Motyer, *The Prophecy of Isaiah: An Introduction and Commentary* (Downers Grove: InterVarsity, 1993) 282.

[62] Oswalt, *The Book of Isaiah,* 659.

themselves great. Indeed they have been great, but their reputation will not be "enhanced" by the rape of this virgin. Why? Because in insulting the virgin they have insulted the virgin's protector, who happens to rule the universe.

Next, the Lord corrects Assyria's prideful attitude about their enormous success. It is God who has ordained, planned, and brought to pass every victory they have achieved. They have been blessed by him, yet they have tried to take the credit themselves. Their enemies have been totally helpless, "drained of power." Before long Assyria itself will suffer the same fate (cf. Isa 10:5–19).

In the final segment of this first part of the Lord's response, God promises to make Assyria go home by the same route they came, a phrase that indicates a swift and direct return. The reference to the "hook" and "bit" reminds the original readers of the Assyrian practice of using these instruments to lead people into exile as if they were animals (cf. Amos 4:1–3).[63] Assyria will receive the sort of treatment they have given others. Their pride and rebellion against the Lord, who sent Jonah to warn them years before, will lead them to the same fate their vassals have endured.

19:29–31 The Lord's answer shifts at this point from a dirge directed against the Assyrians to a sign for Hezekiah. Keil argues that in the Old Testament a sign may be either "the prediction of natural events, which serve as credentials to a prediction" (e.g., Exod 3:12; 1 Sam 2:34; Jer 44:29), or an outright miracle offered as proof of God's work in history, as in Isa 7:14 and 38:7.[64] Here the sign is a natural event that will occur when the Assyrians leave. It it will take two full years for the land to be replenished after the invasion, but in the third year all will be well again.[65] This sign may not seem extraordinary at first, yet is remarkable considering Hezekiah is uncertain of three months of survival, let alone three years of recovery followed by an unspecified number of secure years. The sign means Judah has been healed from what appeared to be a terminal illness.

Like the crops that will grow in the third year, a "remnant" of surviving, faithful Judahites will grow up out of Jerusalem, and out of this experience. In Isa 10:20–23, the prophet defines the remnant as Israelite and Judahite "survivors" who "will no longer rely on him who struck them down but will truly rely on the LORD, the Holy One of Israel." These survivors will both return to the Lord and, if they are already in exile, return to the land. Here the faithful are not yet in exile. Indeed they will never be exiles. Many of their spiritual children will be exiles, however, a fact later events make clear.

19:32–34 The final portion of God's response quite specifically promises that the Assyrians will not conquer Jerusalem. In fact, their armies will not sur-

[63] Cf. Hobbs, *2 Kings,* 281.

[64] C. F. Keil, "I and II Kings," COT, trans. J. Martin (1876; reprint, Grand Rapids: Eerdmans, 1980) 3:454.

[65] Wiseman, *1 and 2 Kings,* 283.

round the city, lay a siege ramp, or shoot an arrow against it. Hezekiah's prayers are answered. Yahweh proves greater than the gods of defeated lands, and therefore is worthy of honor, praise, and worship. Jerusalem is spared. The king's faithfulness is rewarded. In fact, this faithfulness was "all" that was required for the victory. The Lord does the rest for "David's sake," to whom he has made eternal promises (cf. 2 7:7–17). In a way, then, David still serves his city, even from the grave, so great is the measure of his relationship with the Lord.

(6) God Defeats Assyria (19:35–37)

35That night the angel of the LORD went out and put to death a hundred and eighty-five thousand men in the Assyrian camp. When the people got up the next morning—there were all the dead bodies! 36So Sennacherib king of Assyria broke camp and withdrew. He returned to Nineveh and stayed there.

37One day, while he was worshiping in the temple of his god Nisroch, his sons Adrammelech and Sharezer cut him down with the sword, and they escaped to the land of Ararat. And Esarhaddon his son succeeded him as king.

19:35–37 Two separate events are described in this text. First, the Lord kills 185,000 Assyrian soldiers in a single, terrifying night. No other ancient texts record this event, which is not surprising in view of their consistently positive viewpoint. Normally only victories were recorded. Assyrian texts do refer to Sennacherib's return to Nineveh, and Herodotus shows that there was in Egypt the memory of an Assyrian retreat following a divine intervention.[66] Gray allows that this account may come from "an actual historical fact," but that the details cannot be confirmed.[67] Montgomery and Gehman declare the story "popular legend based on historical fact."[68] O. Kaiser believes a miracle occurs here, yet decides "the number given is far beyond what was possible at that time."[69] Attempts to lessen the numbers are not convincing, however,[70] so interpreters are left to determine whether or not the numbers are possible, and whether or not the miraculous is possible.

Keil and Oswalt defend the plausibility of 185,000 dead soldiers. Oswalt notes that Assyria's army was quite likely larger than this number, and could therefore have sustained such a loss.[71] Keil says that the Assyrians were probably based in more than one location, so the deaths would not decimate the entire army, thus leaving open the possibility of the orderly retreat implied in

---

[66] Wiseman, *1 and 2 Kings,* 284.

[67] Gray, *1 and 2 Kings,* 630.

[68] Montgomery and Gehman, *Kings,* 498.

[69] O. Kaiser, *Isaiah 13–39,* trans. R. A. Wilson, OTL (Philadelphia: Westminster, 1974) 395.

[70] Cf. Cogan and Tadmor, *II Kings,* 239.

[71] Oswalt, *The Book of Isaiah,* 669–670.

2 Kgs 19:36.[72] Obviously, the evidence can be assessed in more than one way.

What matters most is that the Lord miraculously delivers Judah from the Assyrians. If a miracle occurs, then the numbers involved are inconsequential unless they exceed the size of the Assyrian army, which is Kaiser's point. Since it is possible that the numbers are plausible, the account can be believed as it stands.[73] No doubt the event was as hard to comprehend when it happened as it is to grasp now. Sennacherib withdraws, tribute money in hand, but with his adversary Hezekiah still in power in Jerusalem.

The second event the text mentions occurs ca. 681 B.C., long after the invasion.[74] As Hubbard explains, "Apparently, Sennacherib had bypassed his older sons to designate his youngest son, Esarhaddon, as heir-apparent. Though details remain unclear, extrabiblical records suggest that those bypassed killed him in an attempted coup."[75] Isaiah's predictions have all come true now. Sennacherib has heard a rumor, has gone home, and has now been killed (cf. 2 Kgs 19:7). In other words, Isaiah's predictions are not just short-term in nature, they also cover long-term events. Thus, God is in control of all occurrences. Nothing happens outside the Lord's realm of authority, not even if it has no direct impact on Israel because contrary to Sennacherib's words the Lord is not a local deity nor a mere idol.

(7) Hezekiah's Miraculous Healing (20:1–11)

1 In those days Hezekiah became ill and was at the point of death. The prophet Isaiah son of Amoz went to him and said, "This is what the LORD says: Put your house in order, because you are going to die; you will not recover."

2 Hezekiah turned his face to the wall and prayed to the LORD,
3 "Remember, O LORD, how I have walked before you faithfully and with wholehearted devotion and have done what is good in your eyes." And Hezekiah wept bitterly.

4 Before Isaiah had left the middle court, the word of the LORD came to him:
5 "Go back and tell Hezekiah, the leader of my people, 'This is what the LORD, the God of your father David, says: I have heard your prayer and seen your tears; I will heal you. On the third day from now you will go up to the temple of the LORD.
6 I will add fifteen years to your life. And I will deliver you and this city from the hand of the king of Assyria. I will defend this city for my sake and for the sake of my servant David.'"

7 Then Isaiah said, "Prepare a poultice of figs." They did so and applied it to the boil, and he recovered.

8 Hezekiah had asked Isaiah, "What will be the sign that the LORD will heal me and that I will go up to the temple of the LORD on the third day from now?"

9 Isaiah answered, "This is the LORD's sign to you that the LORD will do what

[72] Keil, "I and II Kings," 457–58.

[73] Note the discussion of miracles in the Introduction to this commentary.

[74] Hayes and Irvine, *Isaiah,* 28.

[75] Hubbard, *First and Second Kings,* 217–18; Merrill, *Kingdom of Priests,* 416–17.

he has promised: Shall the shadow go forward ten steps, or shall it go back ten steps?"

[10]"It is a simple matter for the shadow to go forward ten steps," said Hezekiah. "Rather, have it go back ten steps."

[11]Then the prophet Isaiah called upon the LORD, and the LORD made the shadow go back the ten steps it had gone down on the stairway of Ahaz.

20:1–3 Sennacherib's future has now been declared. He will die at the hands of his sons. But what will happen to Hezekiah? What does his future hold? How will the God who determines all kings' destinies decide to conclude a faithful monarch's life?

At first, it appears that Hezekiah will not live to enjoy his God-given triumph over Assyria. He falls ill "in those days,"[76] and Isaiah, the bearer of the Lord's infallible word, tells him to prepare to die. Hezekiah refuses to accept this verdict as final, however, so he does what he has done before when in jeopardy—he prays. Just as in the previous episodes, he asks the Lord to change what seems to be a logical sequence of events. This time, though, his petition also includes a change in what is, apparently, what God intends to do. Following the Israelite tradition of personal laments, he cites his own character, the Lord's mercy, and the past as the bases for why he might receive what he requests. All three bases happen to be true, so he does not speak arrogantly.

20:4–11 God answers the prayer immediately, even before Isaiah leaves the temple premises. The Lord promises to heal the king within three days, add fifteen years to his life, and continue to deliver Jerusalem from Assyria. With Hezekiah, the only anti-Assyrian Judahite king of any substance, out of the picture, Judah could not last long against their powerful foe. Certainly the Lord's ability to defend Jerusalem is not circumscribed by the existence of one man, but God continues to use Hezekiah as the major instrument of this defense. Isaiah instructs Hezekiah's retainers to place "a poultice of figs" on the king's wound,[77] and he recovers.

Despite his recovery, Hezekiah asks for a sign that he will in fact go back to the temple in three days. Rather than an indication of unbelief, his request should be viewed against the background of Ahaz's refusal of a sign in Isa 7:12. Isaiah gladly offers Hezekiah a choice of signs: "Shall the shadow go forward ten steps, or shall it go back ten steps?" Though he chooses the far more difficult latter sign, it does occur. His healing thereby takes on miraculous proportions. He lives on under God's blessing, while Sennacherib lives under God's judgment. The Assyrian may be more successful by secular standards but certainly not in the eyes of God.

---

[76] This is apparently a reference to the general period of Hezekiah. Hezekiah's illness must have occurred before Sennacherib's invasion, perhaps in 713/712 B.C. (Patterson and Austel, "1, 2 Kings," 4:272) or 702/701 B.C. (Merrill, *Kingdom of Priests,* 417–18).

[77] See Gray, *1 and 2 Kings,* 634, for information on the ancient world's medicinal uses for figs.

(8) Hezekiah Entertains Some Babylonians (20:12–21)

[12]At that time Merodach-Baladan son of Baladan king of Babylon sent Hezekiah letters and a gift, because he had heard of Hezekiah's illness. [13]Hezekiah received the messengers and showed them all that was in his storehouses—the silver, the gold, the spices and the fine oil—his armory and everything found among his treasures. There was nothing in his palace or in all his kingdom that Hezekiah did not show them.

[14]Then Isaiah the prophet went to King Hezekiah and asked, "What did those men say, and where did they come from?"

"From a distant land," Hezekiah replied. "They came from Babylon."

[15]The prophet asked, "What did they see in your palace?"

"They saw everything in my palace," Hezekiah said. "There is nothing among my treasures that I did not show them."

[16]Then Isaiah said to Hezekiah, "Hear the word of the LORD: [17]The time will surely come when everything in your palace, and all that your fathers have stored up until this day, will be carried off to Babylon. Nothing will be left, says the LORD. [18]And some of your descendants, your own flesh and blood, that will be born to you, will be taken away, and they will become eunuchs in the palace of the king of Babylon."

[19]"The word of the LORD you have spoken is good," Hezekiah replied. For he thought, "Will there not be peace and security in my lifetime?"

[20]As for the other events of Hezekiah's reign, all his achievements and how he made the pool and the tunnel by which he brought water into the city, are they not written in the book of the annals of the kings of Judah? [21]Hezekiah rested with his fathers. And Manasseh his son succeeded him as king.

20:12–13 Judah may look forward to fifteen more years with Hezekiah on the throne, but what does the long-term future hold? Yet another episode that features Hezekiah and Isaiah answers this question. After Hezekiah's illness he receives a visit from emissaries of Merodach-Baladan (i.e., Marduk-upaliddina), who is fighting against Assyria to maintain power in Babylon. He may already have been deposed by 701 B.C.,[78] so perhaps he is scheming from exile to regain his place of authority,[79] for the purpose of the visit seems to be to court Hezekiah's favor (although the occasion was "to ask him about the miraculous sign" according to 2 Chr 32:31; cf. Isa 39:1). Perhaps having a mutual enemy can make the two leaders friends. Hezekiah gladly shows his visitors everything of substance in his kingdom.

20:14–18 Once the Babylonians have left, Isaiah uses the visit to predict the future. After learning that Hezekiah has shown the men everything, the prophet declares that some day Babylon will carry away everything of value in

---

[78] Bright, *A History of Israel,* 284; C. T. Begg, "2 Kings 20:12–19 as an Element of the Deuteronomistic History," *CBQ* 48 (1986) 29.

[79] Hobbs, *2 Kings,* 289.

the palace. Furthermore, Hezekiah's descendants, themselves "sons" of David, "will be taken away, and they will become eunuchs in the palace of the king of Babylon." Over a century will pass before this oracle will come true, but come true it will in 587 B.C. The peace and safety secured in Hezekiah's time will not last. Babylon will finally defeat Assyria, take their enemy's place as *the* major world power, and will defeat Judah at the appropriate time. Second Chronicles 32:31 indicates that the Lord uses this episode to test Hezekiah's commitment. This testing seems appropriate because of the king's earlier problems with pride (2 Chr 32:25–26). What remains unclear in either account is whether it is Hezekiah's action that causes Isaiah's declaration or whether the prophet uses this event as an opportunity to rebuke the king *and* state what will happen in the future.

20:19 Hezekiah's response to Isaiah's message is a bit difficult to assess. Unlike in earlier episodes, he does not petition the Lord about this matter at all. He merely asks an enigmatic question. P. Ackroyd suggests three possible ways to interpret the verse: (1) Hezekiah makes a smug, self-serving comment; (2) Hezekiah takes the message as a prayer that the disaster be delayed as long as possible; (3) Hezekiah accepts the inevitability of judgment, yet is grateful that the events will be delayed until after his death.[80] Though it is impossible to say with absolute certainty, the third option appears more in keeping with the king's character. On the one hand he sees destruction ahead, just as he sees death beyond the fifteen-year extension of his life, while on the other hand he appreciates this reprieve as much (or almost as much) as he has previous ones.

This account also plays an important function in the plot of 1, 2 Kings.[81] Judah has finally been led by a king like David.[82] Judgment has been averted, and opportunities for ongoing commitment to the Lord put in place. At this pivotal moment, however, readers are cautioned not to raise their hopes. The reforms will not last. Babylon will eventually punish the wayward people. A sure prophetic word guarantees judgment. What remains unclear is how and when Judah's demise will occur, not *if* it will happen. Their leaders will fail once again, and the people will fail with them and because of them.

20:20–21 By any standard, sacred or secular, Hezekiah's achievements are considerable. Besides his religious reforms and his own personal commit-

[80] Cf. Begg's analysis of this lack of intercession in "2 Kings 20:12–19," 35–38; P. R. Ackroyd, "An Interpretation of the Babylonian Exile: A Study of 2 Kings 20, Isaiah 38–39," *SJT* 27 (1974) 335–38.

[81] The same can be said of this account's role in Isaiah. Cf. Ackroyd, "An Interpretation of the Babylonian Exile," 338–39.

[82] For an analysis of the author's comparison of David and Hezekiah, read I. W. Provan, *Hezekiah and the Books of Kings: A Contribution to the Debate about the Composition of the Deuteronomistic History,* BZAW 172 (Berlin: Walter de Gruyter, 1988) 117–31.

ment to the Lord, he is one of the few kings of that era to oppose Assyria and live to rule another day. Some of the credit for the ability to withstand Assyria must go to his wisdom to prepare for the siege by bringing water into the city (cf. 2 Chr 32:30). Some credit must go to the strength of his will and the will of his people. Ultimately, though, God's will deserves the credit for his success, for it is the Lord who defeats Assyria, extends Hezekiah's life, and calls Isaiah to counsel the king. Perhaps Hezekiah's only serious flaw is his inability to prepare Manasseh, his successor, to be like himself. On the other hand, how can anyone guarantee the quality of their children's life choices?

2. Manasseh and Amon's Wicked Reigns (21:1–26)

Judah's next two kings manage to reverse nearly all of Hezekiah's achievements. Manasseh rules fifty-five years, longer than any other Judahite king, and the author thinks that every moment of those years makes Judah's death increasingly inevitable. Though he rules only two years, Amon also does great harm, mostly by emulating Manasseh. Amon does produce a son who will lead Judah effectively, so his life is not a total loss. These kings prove particularly distasteful after Hezekiah's positive example of how godliness and tenacity under pressure produce good results.

(1) Manasseh's Unprecedented Wickedness (21:1–18)

[1]Manasseh was twelve years old when he became king, and he reigned in Jerusalem fifty-five years. His mother's name was Hephzibah. [2]He did evil in the eyes of the LORD, following the detestable practices of the nations the LORD had driven out before the Israelites. [3]He rebuilt the high places his father Hezekiah had destroyed; he also erected altars to Baal and made an Asherah pole, as Ahab king of Israel had done. He bowed down to all the starry hosts and worshiped them. [4]He built altars in the temple of the LORD, of which the LORD had said, "In Jerusalem I will put my Name." [5]In both courts of the temple of the LORD, he built altars to all the starry hosts. [6]He sacrificed his own son in the fire, practiced sorcery and divination, and consulted mediums and spiritists. He did much evil in the eyes of the LORD, provoking him to anger.

[7]He took the carved Asherah pole he had made and put it in the temple, of which the LORD had said to David and to his son Solomon, "In this temple and in Jerusalem, which I have chosen out of all the tribes of Israel, I will put my Name forever. [8]I will not again make the feet of the Israelites wander from the land I gave their forefathers, if only they will be careful to do everything I commanded them and will keep the whole Law that my servant Moses gave them." [9]But the people did not listen. Manasseh led them astray, so that they did more evil than the nations the LORD had destroyed before the Israelites.

[10]The LORD said through his servants the prophets: [11]"Manasseh king of Judah has committed these detestable sins. He has done more evil than the

Amorites who preceded him and has led Judah into sin with his idols.
[12]Therefore this is what the LORD, the God of Israel, says: I am going to bring
such disaster on Jerusalem and Judah that the ears of everyone who hears of it
will tingle. [13]I will stretch out over Jerusalem the measuring line used against
Samaria and the plumb line used against the house of Ahab. I will wipe out
Jerusalem as one wipes a dish, wiping it and turning it upside down. [14]I will
forsake the remnant of my inheritance and hand them over to their enemies.
They will be looted and plundered by all their foes, [15]because they have done
evil in my eyes and have provoked me to anger from the day their forefathers
came out of Egypt until this day."

[16]Moreover, Manasseh also shed so much innocent blood that he filled Jerusalem from end to end—besides the sin that he had caused Judah to commit, so that they did evil in the eyes of the LORD.

[17]As for the other events of Manasseh's reign, and all he did, including the sin
he committed, are they not written in the book of the annals of the kings of
Judah? [18]Manasseh rested with his fathers and was buried in his palace garden,
the garden of Uzza. And Amon his son succeeded him as king.

21:1–6 After a brief introduction to Manasseh's reign, the historian produces an avalanche of negative comments about the new king. Manasseh's era spans about 697 to 642 B.C., a period that probably includes a coregency with Hezekiah from about 697 to 687, or when Manasseh was twelve to twenty-two years of age. His time of sole authority stretches, then, from about 687 to 642 B.C.

During this time Assyria's Sennacherib dies in about 681 B.C. and is followed first by Esarhaddon (ca. 681–669 B.C.), then by Ashurbanipal (ca. 669–627 B.C.). None of these men allows Assyria to lose its position as the world's dominant power. Bright states that though Manasseh rebels against Assyria at least once (cf. 2 Chr 33:10–13), he is "a loyal vassal of Assyria throughout his long reign. Esarhaddon lists him among twenty-two kings required to forward building materials for his building projects, while Ashurbanipal names him as one of a number of vassals who assisted his campaign against Egypt."[83] Judah's anti-Assyrian days are over. Manasseh adopts what he no doubt believes is a prudent policy.

Besides these "secular" matters, the text mentions at least seven separate religious offenses Manasseh commits. First, he reverts to worshiping idols in the same manner as the nations Israel expelled from the land. By doing so the covenant people prove as unworthy of the promised land as their predecessors. Second, Manasseh allows high places to flourish again. Now his standards are no higher than those of Jeroboam I. Third, he sinks to Ahab's religious level, reintroducing the worship of Baal and his consort Asherah (cf. 1 Kgs 30–33; Deut 16:21). Polytheism reenters Judahite society with royal approval.

---

[83] Bright, *A History of Israel,* 311. Cf. *ANET,* 291, 294.

Fourth, Manasseh also bows down "to all the starry hosts." Astral deities were popular throughout the ancient world before, during, and after this time. J. McKay believes "there can be no question that the Sun, the Moon and perhaps Venus were worshiped in Judah" and that "it can hardly be doubted that in this age of vassaldom Assyrian influence must have contributed much to the upsurge of the astral cults in Palestine."[84] Fifth, Manasseh builds altars to these gods in the temple of the Lord, as Ahaz his grandfather does in 2 Kgs 16:10–16. If these are Assyrian deities, he probably hopes to please the gods he thinks can make him as powerful as his masters, or at least he hopes to please his masters. Sixth, he also imitates Ahaz's practice of child sacrifice (cf. 2 Kgs 16:3), and, seventh, he consults "mediums and spiritists," both in direct violation of Moses' law (cf. Lev 18:21; Deut 18:9–13).

Given this summary, it is clear that Manasseh follows all the wrong role models. He imitates the detestable Canaanites, Jeroboam I the builder of high places, Ahab the advocate of Baal worship, Ahaz the proponent of child sacrifice, and Saul the visitor of mediums. It is hard to imagine a more damning critique (cp. vv. 3,6 with 17:16–17).

21:7–9 Stated simply, Manasseh, the representative of the royal house, violates three fundamental tenets of Old Testament life. First, he certainly fails to follow David's example, thus breaking the Davidic Covenant (cf. 2 Sam 7:7–17). Second, he defiles with idolatry the central sanctuary chosen by the Lord (cf. Deut 12:1–32; 1 Kgs 9:1–9), a sin that will lead to destruction and exile (cf. 1 Kgs 9:6–9). Third, he rejects Moses' covenant, which means the promised land will be forfeited (cf. Deut 28:49–63). Thus, Manasseh not only acts opposite of Hezekiah, but he also scorns the examples of Moses, Joshua, David, and Solomon as well.

21:10–16 God can hardly be silent during such times, so the prophets speak about the situation.[85] Though the names of specific prophets are not given, the messages outlined here are certainly similar to those in the canonical prophetic books. They are therefore also in agreement with the author's perspective on history. The prophetic rebuke of Manasseh in v. 11 may be compared to the rebuke of Ahab in 1 Kgs 21:26, where two of the same roots

[84] J. McKay, *Religion in Judah under the Assyrians,* SBT/2, 26 (Naperville, Ill.: Allenson, 1973) 48.

[85] W. M. Schniedewind ("History and Interpretation: The Religion of Ahab and Manasseh in the Book of Kings," *CBQ* 55 [1993] 656) notes that the phrase "his/my servants the prophets" occurs four times in Kings, twice in the account of Samaria's fall (17:13,23), and twice in accounts of the last days of Judah (21:10; 24:2). That the phrase itself suggests a backward look at God's attempts to draw Israel back to him is shown by the other passages in which it occurs (Jer 7:25; 25:4; 44:4; Zech 1:6; Dan 9:10; the exception is Amos 3:7).

occur[86] in addition to the comparison to the "Amorites." The announcement of judgment begins with the notion that the king's actions have set in motion a judgment so severe "the ears of everyone who hears of it will tingle" (cf. Jer 15:1–4). A great "plumb line" of assessment, the same one used to measure and punish Samaria, will be stretched out against Judah (cf. Amos 7:7–9). Not even Judah will be left, for in Hezekiah's absence they have done the same sort of evil that has brought the Lord's anger since the day the nation left Egypt.

The prophetic messages of warning have been shaped by theological reflection upon the covenants, the flow of Israelite history, and the activity of God within that history. They also speak from their knowledge of the Lord's character, such as his mercy, kindness, righteousness, and insistence on accountability. Therefore their words about the future are not only the product of divine revelation but are based upon their knowledge of God. As always the prophetic word does not fail, though in this case this fact saddens readers.

21:17–18 Manasseh's life is summarized in a few more comments. Besides all his other sins, he sheds "much innocent blood" (cf. 9:7,26), a reference that may lead to the legend that among Manasseh's victims is Isaiah, whom tradition says was sawn in two.[87] If not Isaiah in particular, the phrase may apply generally to "Manasseh's persecution of the prophets, suggested by the fact that, in contrast to prophetic activity since the middle of the ninth century and from the time of Josiah, there is total silence in the long reign of Manasseh."[88] The unnamed prophets of the previous passage may have paid for their honesty with their lives.

The Chronicler's account of Manasseh's life varies from the one in 2 Kgs 21:1–18 in one significant respect. Though 2 Chr 33:1–9 agrees with the completely negative assessment found in 2 Kgs 21:1–9, the Chronicler also recounts a time of repentance late in Manasseh's life (2 Chr 33:10–17). Oppression by Assyria initiates prayer and contrition on Manasseh's part, which leads to release from his immediate problem and a removal of idols he has erected. These reforms are portrayed as limited and short-lived, however, so the *results* of his reign remain the same.[89] His support of idolatry leads to

---

[86] Compare "he behaved in the vilest manner" (וַיַּתְעֵב מְאֹד) and "idols" (הַגִּלֻּלִים) in 1 Kgs 21:26 with "these detestable sins" (הַתֹּעֵבוֹת הָאֵלֶּה) and "with his idols" (בְּגִלּוּלָיו) in 2 Kgs 21:11. Schniedewind also points out that of the six times גִלּוּלִים occurs in Kings, five times it concerns the sins of Ahab and Manasseh (cf. 2 Kgs 21:21; 23:24). See Schniedewind, "History and Interpretation: The Religion of Ahab and Manasseh in the Book of Kings," 654–55.

[87] See *Martyrdom and Ascension of Isaiah* 5:1–16 in *OTP,* 2:163–64. For comments, see J. Skinner, *1–2 Kings,* CB, rev. ed. (London: T. C. & E. C. Jack, 1904) 409; Montgomery and Gehman, *Kings,* 521.

[88] Gray, *1 and 2 Kings,* 645–46.

[89] Dillard, *2 Chronicles,* 269.

corruption that Josiah will have to combat later, a point the Chronicler makes clear in the survey of Josiah's life (cf. 2 Chr 34:1–35:27). In both histories, then, Manasseh's long period of rule is portrayed as an ultimately damaging era in Israel's history at a moment when such leadership could not be afforded.

(2) Amon's Reign and Assassination (21:19–26)

[19]Amon was twenty-two years old when he became king, and he reigned in Jerusalem two years. His mother's name was Meshullemeth daughter of Haruz; she was from Jotbah. [20]He did evil in the eyes of the LORD, as his father Manasseh had done. [21]He walked in all the ways of his father; he worshiped the idols his father had worshiped, and bowed down to them. [22]He forsook the LORD, the God of his fathers, and did not walk in the way of the LORD.

[23]Amon's officials conspired against him and assassinated the king in his palace. [24]Then the people of the land killed all who had plotted against King Amon, and they made Josiah his son king in his place.

[25]As for the other events of Amon's reign, and what he did, are they not written in the book of the annals of the kings of Judah? [26]He was buried in his grave in the garden of Uzza. And Josiah his son succeeded him as king.

21:19–26 Unlike Manasseh, Amon imitates *his* father during his brief (ca. 642–640) reign. He follows his father's religious practices and political policies, either or both of which might have led to his assassination. B. Obed suggests that he may have been murdered "by factions who were faithful to the traditions of Israel and in favour of Hezekiah's reform," or "by factions opposed to Assyrian rule."[90] Regardless of the reasons, Josiah, a Davidic descendant, is placed on the throne. The fact that Josiah is only eight years old when he takes "control" indicates that some faction puts him in place and probably actually runs the country for some time. Judah's political future seems uncertain at this point but will clarify itself when Josiah comes of age.

3. Josiah's Righteous Reign (22:1–23:30)

It is difficult, if not impossible, to express adequately the magnitude of Josiah's achievements or those of others whose work was enhanced by his presence. While still a young man, though a veteran of eighteen years as Judah's king, Josiah leads a tremendous reform based on a prophetic interpretation of God's Word. This renewal at least matches the one initiated by Hezekiah. Josiah also manages to help Judah steer an independent political course during a turbulent time in international politics. He does not achieve all these things alone, however, for these are also the days of Huldah—who interprets the covenant for Josiah—of Jeremiah—who like Josiah is a young reformer—

[90] B. Obed, "Judah and the Exile," in *Israelite and Judaen History,* ed., J. H. Hayes and J. M. Miller (Philadelphia: Westminster, 1977) 456.

and of Nahum, Habakkuk, and Zephaniah, each of whom contributes significantly to the climate of reform in the land. In other words the years of Josiah's rule (ca. 640–609) are a glittering bright spot in the nation's tragic slide to destruction. As such they encourage readers concerning what is possible when obedience overrules rebellion.

(1) The Law Is Found and Read (22:1–13)

1Josiah was eight years old when he became king, and he reigned in Jerusalem thirty-one years. His mother's name was Jedidah daughter of Adaiah; she was from Bozkath. 2He did what was right in the eyes of the LORD and walked in all the ways of his father David, not turning aside to the right or to the left.

3In the eighteenth year of his reign, King Josiah sent the secretary, Shaphan son of Azaliah, the son of Meshullam, to the temple of the LORD. He said: 4"Go up to Hilkiah the high priest and have him get ready the money that has been brought into the temple of the LORD, which the doorkeepers have collected from the people. 5Have them entrust it to the men appointed to supervise the work on the temple. And have these men pay the workers who repair the temple of the LORD— 6the carpenters, the builders and the masons. Also have them purchase timber and dressed stone to repair the temple. 7But they need not account for the money entrusted to them, because they are acting faithfully."

8Hilkiah the high priest said to Shaphan the secretary, "I have found the Book of the Law in the temple of the LORD." He gave it to Shaphan, who read it. 9Then Shaphan the secretary went to the king and reported to him: "Your officials have paid out the money that was in the temple of the LORD and have entrusted it to the workers and supervisors at the temple." 10Then Shaphan the secretary informed the king, "Hilkiah the priest has given me a book." And Shaphan read from it in the presence of the king.

11When the king heard the words of the Book of the Law, he tore his robes. 12He gave these orders to Hilkiah the priest, Ahikam son of Shaphan, Acbor son of Micaiah, Shaphan the secretary and Asaiah the king's attendant: 13"Go and inquire of the LORD for me and for the people and for all Judah about what is written in this book that has been found. Great is the LORD's anger that burns against us because our fathers have not obeyed the words of this book; they have not acted in accordance with all that is written there concerning us."

22:1–2 Josiah's reign begins inauspiciously, since he is merely a child at his accession. From the start the author summarizes Josiah's life favorably. Like Hezekiah (cf. 2 Kgs 18:3), this man acts like David. He resolutely follows in his ancestor's footsteps. Given the religious climate Manasseh and Amon have created, and given the fact that Hezekiah's similarity to David led to reform, readers may expect some sort of renewal to ensue. When it will occur and how it will begin remain to be seen.

World politics shifted during Josiah's tenure. Ashurbanipal's death in 627 B.C. left Assyria with a leadership struggle that cost them control of Babylon in

626 B.C. From that year forward the Babylonians and their allies the Medes pressed Assyria. Nineveh fell in 612 B.C., despite the help of Egypt, and by 609 B.C. Assyria was finished. Thus, Josiah rules during years in which Assyria fades but also those in which Babylon is not yet ready to rule as far west as Judah and in a time when Egypt does not yet attempt to rule the smaller nations north of the border. Judah thereby gets a rest from its constant role as political football.

22:3–7 Serious reform begins in Josiah's eighteenth year of rule, or ca. 622 B.C. His desire to serve the Lord surfaces even earlier according to the Chronicler, who states that Josiah begins to "seek the God of his father David" in the eighth year of his rule (ca. 632 B.C.) and starts removing some "high places, Asherah poles, carved idols and cast images" in about 628 B.C., his twelfth year as king (2 Chr 34:3). Therefore, it is not strange that in his eighteenth year the king senses an obligation to repair the temple, an impulse felt by Joash years earlier (cf. 2 Kgs 12:1–16). Though the text does not divulge his motives for the repair, perhaps Josiah intends to promote worship at the central sanctuary (cf. Deut 12:1–32). Whatever his reasons, this project provides the impetus for greater reforms later.

22:8–10 Slowly, scene-by-scene, the author brings the story to the point at which sweeping reform begins. In the midst of the repair process, Hilkiah the high priest reports to Shaphan the king's secretary the discovery of the Book of the Law. Shaphan reads the book. He then takes the book with him to see the king and, after reporting on the work and the expenses related to it, reads the book to the king. God's Word emerges from God's house and confronts the king. How will Josiah respond? Like Ahab or like Hezekiah?

Scholars have debated the contents of the book for decades. Much of the discussion is linked to differing viewpoints on the authorship of the Pentateuch, since source critics date the theoretical "D" source partly by this discovery of the Book of the Law in about 622 B.C. S. R. Driver represents early proponents of this theory. In his 1895 commentary on Deuteronomy he first separates the book from the rest of the literature in the Pentateuch through a comparison of style and law codes.[91] He then dates the "D" material no later than 622 B.C.

> For the narrative of 2 Kgs 22–23 makes it plain that the book so found must have embraced Deuteronomy;[92] for although the bare description of its contents, and of the effect produced by it upon those who heard it (22:11,13,19) might suit Lev 26 equally with Deut 28, yet the allusions to the *covenant* con-

---

[91] S. R. Driver, *A Critical and Exegetical Commentary on Deuteronomy,* ICC (New York: Scribners, 1985) xxxiv–xliv.

[92] At this point he adds the following important note: "Or, at least, c. 5–26. 28. . . . It cannot be shown to have included more than Dt." (ibid., xlv).

> tained in it (23:2,3,21), which refer evidently to Deut (28:69 [29:1]: cf. 29:8,20,24 . . .), and the fact that in the reformation based upon it, Josiah carries out, step by step, the fundamental principles of Deut, leave no doubt upon the matter.[93]

By "fundamental principles" he means "the abolition of all heathen rites and superstitions, and the centralization of Jehovah's worship at Jerusalem,"[94] plus an emphasis on covenant keeping and covenant renewal. Other scholars who accept a late date for Pentateuchal authorship vary about whether or not Deuteronomy or some form of it was discovered in the temple and the extent to which this material impacted Josiah's reform. For example, G. von Rad thinks the book had some influence but that "King Josiah was certainly not stimulated to take action by Deuteronomy alone," since the reforms are not *identical* to Deuteronomy's teachings and since the political situation may have dictated the king's decisions more than religious convictions.[95]

M. Weinfeld believes that Deuteronomy was written over a period of time from the era of the Judges to Josiah's day and that this book was found in the temple. This discovery did indeed spur the reform to new heights by providing a definitive, authoritative book to follow.[96] A. D. H. Mayes, on the other hand, thinks a reform occurred, yet "the book of Deuteronomy, in any form, cannot be seen as basic to the reform of Josiah. It may have been in existence or in the course of preparation then, but there is no evidence of this."[97] The mention of the discovery of the book was, then, a literary device that emphasized the uniqueness of Josiah's reform.[98] M. Noth argues that a book was discovered that "was identical with the original form of the deuteronomic law which is preserved in the Old Testament."[99] This book was compiled in the seventh century B.C., then expanded and used as the beginning of a history that included Joshua, Judges, Samuel, and Kings.[100]

Of course, some scholars correctly understand what occurred as the rediscovery of God's law, which gave added impetus to reform but that the book dates from Moses. Certainly the author of 1, 2 Kings seems to indicate that all God's law was mediated through Moses, given the references to Moses in the books (e.g., 1 Kgs 2:3; 9:56; 2 Kgs 14:6; 18:12). Further, many scholars con-

---

[93] Ibid.

[94] Ibid.

[95] G. von Rad, *Deuteronomy,* trans. D. Barton, OTL (Philadelphia: Westminster, 1966) 27.

[96] M. Weinfeld, *Deuteronomy 1–11: A New Translation with Introduction and Commentary,* AB (New York: Doubleday, 1991) 5:37–84. Note esp. his summary of the issues on pp. 81–84.

[97] A. D. H. Mayes, *Deuteronomy,* NCB (Grand Rapids: Eerdmans, 1981) 102.

[98] Ibid., 103.

[99] Noth, *The History of Israel,* 275.

[100] Cf. M. Noth, *The Deuteronomistic History,* trans. D. Orton, JSOTSup 15 (Sheffield: Sheffield Academic Press, 1981).

tend that the Book of Deuteronomy is written in a treaty format more common in Moses' time than Josiah's.[101] Thus, any influence the book has can be traced to ancient roots. As R. K. Harrison argues, parts of the Pentateuch other than Deuteronomy may also influence Josiah's reform.[102]

The primary point to be made, however, is that Scripture greatly influenced Josiah's actions. Moses' writings were not obeyed through the centuries, but the reform restores them to prominence, at least for a brief time. Josiah's personal commitment grows when he determines that God spoke to Moses and made a covenant with Israel. He either hears at least a large portion of Deuteronomy or some other similar portion of the Pentateuch. This hearing motivates him to act. When he acts, it is with the confidence that he is doing God's will, based on God's Word, in service to God's people.

22:11–13 Josiah tears his garment when he hears God's law. Perhaps they read Deuteronomy 27–28 to him, since his response stresses God's wrath over the nation's disobedience. Most significantly, he seeks a prophetic word to interpret the ramifications of this disobedience. He admits the nation's sin, fears its results, and hopes it is not too late to change. He seems to reason that God may yet be merciful to an undeserving people.

(2) Huldah Interprets the Law (22:14–20)

14Hilkiah the priest, Ahikam, Acbor, Shaphan and Asaiah went to speak to the prophetess Huldah, who was the wife of Shallum son of Tikvah, the son of Harhas, keeper of the wardrobe. She lived in Jerusalem, in the Second District.

15She said to them, "This is what the LORD, the God of Israel, says: Tell the man who sent you to me, 16'This is what the LORD says: I am going to bring disaster on this place and its people, according to everything written in the book the king of Judah has read. 17Because they have forsaken me and burned incense to other gods and provoked me to anger by all the idols their hands have made, my anger will burn against this place and will not be quenched.' 18Tell the king of Judah, who sent you to inquire of the LORD, 'This is what the LORD, the God of Israel, says concerning the words you heard: 19Because your heart was responsive and you humbled yourself before the LORD when you heard what I have spoken against this place and its people, that they would become accursed and laid waste, and because you tore your robes and wept in my presence, I have heard you, declares the LORD. 20Therefore I will gather you to your fathers, and you will be buried in peace. Your eyes will not see all the disaster I am going to bring on this place.'"

So they took her answer back to the king.

---

[101] Cf. M. G. Kline, *Treaty of the Great King* (Grand Rapids: Eerdmans, 1963); P. C. Craigie, *The Book of Deuteronomy,* NICOT (Grand Rapids: Eerdmans, 1976) 24–29; E. H. Merrill, *Deuteronomy,* NAC (Nashville: Broadman & Holman, 1994) 27–37.

[102] R. K. Harrison, *Introduction to the Old Testament* (Grand Rapids: Eerdmans, 1969) 732.

22:14–20 Just as Hezekiah's representatives once sought Isaiah's advice, so now Josiah's men approach Huldah, God's representative. Two questions about Huldah arise: Why a woman? and, Why Huldah in particular? Honeycutt observes that the word "prophetess" occurs six times in the Old Testament (cf. also Exod 15:20; Judg 4:4; 2 Kgs 22:14; 2 Chr 34:22; Neh 6:14) as a designation for Miriam, Deborah, Huldah, and Noadiah.[103] Of these prophetesses, all but Noadiah are portrayed positively. Thus, though less common than male prophets, a female prophet is not unique to this situation. Indeed, Joel 2:28 looks forward to a time when "sons and daughters will prophesy," which Peter says does occur on the Day of Pentecost (Acts 2:14–21). As for why Huldah and not, for instance, Jeremiah, "We have to remind ourselves that judgments upon personalities vary between that of contemporaries and that of posterity. Indeed Jeremiah felt himself to be a forgotten man in his day. Huldah left no book."[104] Both were used by the Lord, and both must be judged on that basis.

Huldah's two-pronged message agrees with the pronouncements of the canonical prophets. First, she interprets God's word for the people. In short, their idolatry will lead to the consequences outlined in Deut 28:15–68. Second, Huldah offers a more positive word to Josiah. Because of his humility and grief over the nation's sin, he will die in peace before judgment falls. Whenever Isaiah's prediction about Babylon's ultimate victory over Judah comes true (cf. 2 Kgs 20:12–19), Josiah will not have to endure it. Like Hezekiah, it will not happen in *his* time, but it will happen. Once again God's word has been faithfully and accurately proclaimed, this time as an interpretation of the *written Word.*

(3) Josiah Leads Reform (23:1–27)

[1]Then the king called together all the elders of Judah and Jerusalem. [2]He went up to the temple of the LORD with the men of Judah, the people of Jerusalem, the priests and the prophets—all the people from the least to the greatest. He read in their hearing all the words of the Book of the Covenant, which had been found in the temple of the LORD. [3]The king stood by the pillar and renewed the covenant in the presence of the LORD—to follow the LORD and keep his commands, regulations and decrees with all his heart and all his soul, thus confirming the words of the covenant written in this book. Then all the people pledged themselves to the covenant.

[4]The king ordered Hilkiah the high priest, the priests next in rank and the doorkeepers to remove from the temple of the LORD all the articles made for Baal and Asherah and all the starry hosts. He burned them outside Jerusalem in the fields of the Kidron Valley and took the ashes to Bethel. [5]He did away with the

---

[103] R. L. Honeycutt, "2 Kings," BBC (Nashville: Broadman, 1970) 3:286.

[104] Montgomery and Gehman, *Kings,* 525.

pagan priests appointed by the kings of Judah to burn incense on the high places of the towns of Judah and on those around Jerusalem—those who burned incense to Baal, to the sun and moon, to the constellations and to all the starry hosts. 6He took the Asherah pole from the temple of the LORD to the Kidron Valley outside Jerusalem and burned it there. He ground it to powder and scattered the dust over the graves of the common people. 7He also tore down the quarters of the male shrine prostitutes, which were in the temple of the LORD and where women did weaving for Asherah.

8Josiah brought all the priests from the towns of Judah and desecrated the high places, from Geba to Beersheba, where the priests had burned incense. He broke down the shrines at the gates—at the entrance to the Gate of Joshua, the city governor, which is on the left of the city gate. 9Although the priests of the high places did not serve at the altar of the LORD in Jerusalem, they ate unleavened bread with their fellow priests.

10He desecrated Topheth, which was in the Valley of Ben Hinnom, so no one could use it to sacrifice his son or daughter in the fire to Molech. 11He removed from the entrance to the temple of the LORD the horses that the kings of Judah had dedicated to the sun. They were in the court near the room of an official named Nathan-Melech. Josiah then burned the chariots dedicated to the sun.

12He pulled down the altars the kings of Judah had erected on the roof near the upper room of Ahaz, and the altars Manasseh had built in the two courts of the temple of the LORD. He removed them from there, smashed them to pieces and threw the rubble into the Kidron Valley. 13The king also desecrated the high places that were east of Jerusalem on the south of the Hill of Corruption—the ones Solomon king of Israel had built for Ashtoreth the vile goddess of the Sidonians, for Chemosh the vile god of Moab, and for Molech the detestable god of the people of Ammon. 14Josiah smashed the sacred stones and cut down the Asherah poles and covered the sites with human bones.

15Even the altar at Bethel, the high place made by Jeroboam son of Nebat, who had caused Israel to sin—even that altar and high place he demolished. He burned the high place and ground it to powder, and burned the Asherah pole also. 16Then Josiah looked around, and when he saw the tombs that were there on the hillside, he had the bones removed from them and burned on the altar to defile it, in accordance with the word of the LORD proclaimed by the man of God who foretold these things.

17The king asked, "What is that tombstone I see?"

The men of the city said, "It marks the tomb of the man of God who came from Judah and pronounced against the altar of Bethel the very things you have done to it."

18"Leave it alone," he said. "Don't let anyone disturb his bones." So they spared his bones and those of the prophet who had come from Samaria.

19Just as he had done at Bethel, Josiah removed and defiled all the shrines at the high places that the kings of Israel had built in the towns of Samaria that had provoked the LORD to anger. 20Josiah slaughtered all the priests of those high places on the altars and burned human bones on them. Then he went back to Jerusalem.

[21]The king gave this order to all the people: "Celebrate the Passover to the LORD your God, as it is written in this Book of the Covenant." [22]Not since the days of the judges who led Israel, nor throughout the days of the kings of Israel and the kings of Judah, had any such Passover been observed. [23]But in the eighteenth year of King Josiah, this Passover was celebrated to the LORD in Jerusalem.

[24]Furthermore, Josiah got rid of the mediums and spiritists, the household gods, the idols and all the other detestable things seen in Judah and Jerusalem. This he did to fulfill the requirements of the law written in the book that Hilkiah the priest had discovered in the temple of the LORD. [25]Neither before nor after Josiah was there a king like him who turned to the LORD as he did—with all his heart and with all his soul and with all his strength, in accordance with all the Law of Moses.

[26]Nevertheless, the LORD did not turn away from the heat of his fierce anger, which burned against Judah because of all that Manasseh had done to provoke him to anger. [27]So the LORD said, "I will remove Judah also from my presence as I removed Israel, and I will reject Jerusalem, the city I chose, and this temple, about which I said, 'There shall my Name be.'"

23:1–3 To his credit Josiah is not content with waiting for his own peaceful death. Rather, out of gratitude for God's mercy in his own life he determines to attempt "to lead the whole nation to true conversion to the Lord, and thereby avert as far as possible the threatened curse of rejection, since the Lord in His word had promised forgiveness and mercy to the penitent."[105] This attempt begins with a covenant renewal ceremony that stands in the tradition of great renewals such as the one Deuteronomy itself represents and the one Joshua initiates (Josh 24:1–27).

The scene of the covenant renewal closely resembles Solomon's dedication of the temple (cf. 1 Kgs 8:1ff.). As in Solomon's ceremony the king, elders, priests, and people join together in the service. One new group is represented, however, the prophets (missing, however, from the parallel text in 2 Chr 34:30). Perhaps Huldah's role in Josiah's increased Yahwistic commitments helps elevate all the true prophets to their rightful place in Judah's religious community. Once in place the king and the people listen to "all the words of the Book of the Covenant, which had been found in the temple of the LORD." Now the assembly knows the privileges and obligations inherent in the relationship with the Lord. First, Josiah promises to keep the covenant, then the people follow his example. Each person pledges to obey God's "commands, regulations and decrees," a diverse enough list of types of laws to suggest they have heard a law code of some scope and substance.

23:4–14 Because of their renewed dedication to the Lord, the king and people remove non-Yahwistic worship sites and implements, first from Judah,

[105] Keil, "I and II Kings," 482.

then from the old Israelite territory.[106] N. Lohfink notes that ten separate items/issues are dealt with here.[107] First, Josiah orders the priests to remove from the temple all cultic vessels used in worship of other gods. When they complete the task, the king burns them all. Second, "he causes to cease"[108] the "pagan priests" who staff the high places where the people worship idols. These individuals may have existed with royal approval since Solomonic times (cf. 1 Kgs 11:1–8). Third, he burns the Asherah pole Manasseh placed in the temple. Fourth, Josiah demolishes the living quarters of "male shrine prostitutes," literally, "the separate ones" (*haqqĕdēšîm*) where materials for Asherah are also made. Since the text mentions both males and females, perhaps all these individuals engage in sacred prostitution, a common element in Baalism.

Next, the narrative recounts Josiah's efforts outside the temple area. Thus, his fifth act is to desecrate high places "from Geba to Beersheba," Judah's northern and southern boundaries.[109] Sixth, he demolishes shrines in the city gates.[110] Seventh, he defiles Topheth, where child sacrifices had been made in honor of Molech.[111]

The three remaining actions occur near the temple and just outside the city. Josiah's eighth reform is to take ornamental horses "dedicated to the sun" from the temple entrance.[112] Ninth, altars on roofs, probably set aside for worship of astral deities (cf. 20:11; 21:3–5; Zeph 1:5), are removed. Tenth, Josiah desecrates, then smashes, the high places Solomon built for his wives. With this last act Josiah rolls back the clock, so to speak, to preidolatry Jerusalem, to the glory days of David when images were not welcome in the capital city of the Lord's people. Monotheism is once again at least the official theology, whether or not the people in fact embrace what is, to them, a novel concept.

23:15–20 With Judah cleansed, Josiah moves north to Bethel, which had served as one of the major worship centers in Jeroboam's maverick cult (cf. 1 Kgs 12:25–13:5). He treats this place like the nonseparatist Yahwistic cultic

---

[106] For a study of one site Josiah destroys, consult Y. Yadin, "Beer-sheba: The High Place Destroyed by King Josiah," *BASOR* 222 (1976) 5–17.

[107] N. Lohfink, "The Cult Reform of Josiah of Judah: 2 Kings 22–23 as a Source for the History of Israelite Religion," in *Ancient Israelite Religion,* ed. P. D. Miller, P. D. Hanson, and S. D. McBride (Philadelphia: Fortress, 1987) 465.

[108] This is the literal translation of the verb form (a *hiphil* of שׁבת).

[109] Wiseman, *1 and 2 Kings,* 302.

[110] Patterson and Austel explain that while priests who had served at the high places were "admitted to the fellowship," they were not allowed to "officiate in the temple services" ("1, 2 Kings," 4:286).

[111] Contra some scholars who believe the text refers to an initiation rite, not actual human sacrifice. Cf. Jones, *1 and 2 Kings,* 2:622, for a discussion of these opposing viewpoints.

[112] Wiseman cites "models of *horses*, some with solar disks on their forehead, found east of Ophel and at Hazor and other sites" (*1 & 2 Kings,* 302–3).

shrines in Judah, thereby reclaiming all the promised land for the worship of the Lord. Again the author emphasizes restoration. Both parts of the divided kingdom are reunited spiritually, if not politically. Both sections of the land return to fidelity to the Lord and to an emphasis on worship at a central sanctuary.

In the midst of the Bethel cleansing, Josiah removes bones from priestly graves (2 Chr 34:5) and burns them on the altar to defile it. This desecration fulfills the prophecy made by the unnamed prophet of 1 Kings 13 (cf. 1 Kgs 13:1–13) who lived during Jeroboam I's reign (ca. 930–909 B.C.). Three centuries have passed, but God's word comes true because it cannot fail. This episode is but the latest example of the author's emphasis on the truthfulness of the prophetic utterances.

Josiah's defiling of northern altars continues with a purging of "all the shrines at the high places that the kings of Israel had built in the towns of Samaria that had provoked the LORD to anger." Part of this purging is the slaying of the priests who facilitate worship in those places. Gray concludes that this account is a "late elaboration" added to the text, since the killings constitute "an enormity which would have reflected no credit to Josiah."[113] One could wonder why they needed to be killed or why they are killed and Judah's priests are not (cf. 2 Kgs 23:8–9). Keil suggests that the punishment's severity results not only because the northern priests are not Levites, "but chiefly from the fact that they were really idolatrous priests."[114] In other words, the Judahite priests may have corrupted worship of Yahweh yet not have led in veneration of other gods, while the northern priests may have been polytheists or syncretists. Thus, Josiah does not just use geographical boundaries to determine who will live and who will die.

Still, why inflict the death penalty? The answer may lie in Josiah's interpretation of the Book of the Law. Deuteronomy 13:6–11 and 18:20 counsel Israel to put to death prophets who teach people to follow other gods, an admonition Elijah follows in 1 Kgs 18:40. Perhaps Josiah applies this principle to the priests here because of the seriousness of the consequences of idolatry for the nation (cf. Deut 28:15–68). On the other hand, he may follow the more general command in Exod 22:20. Whatever his motivation, and the author does not pass *direct* judgment on them, the effect of the purge remains clear. All the territory of Israel has been reclaimed for the covenant God. The national part of the spiritual agreement has been kept.[115]

23:21–23 Not all of Josiah's efforts are prohibitive in nature, for he also orders the Passover kept.[116] Again the festival will be kept because of what the

---

[113] Gray, *1 and 2 Kings,* 673.

[114] Keil, "I and II Kings," 490.

[115] This last point is crucial for applying this text to today's world. Those parts of the OT that apply only to Israel's context cannot be repeated today.

[116] Patterson and Austel, "1, 2 Kings," 286.

"Book of the Covenant" teaches.[117] Both Exod 12:1–11 and Deut 16:1–8 command Israel to keep the Passover on an annual basis as a reminder of their deliverance from Egypt. Unfortunately, for years this festival has not been observed in the manner intended.

Some commentators believe that v. 22 contradicts 2 Chr 30:1–27, which recounts the Passover observed in Hezekiah's time.[118] An examination of the Hezekiah and Josiah stories in 2 Chronicles, however, may help clarify the matter. After depicting the Hezekiah Passover, the Chronicler then summarizes Josiah's Passover in terms similar to 2 Kgs 23:22:

> The Passover had not been observed like this in Israel since the days of the prophet Samuel; and none of the kings of Israel had ever celebrated such a Passover as did Josiah, with the priests, the Levites and all Judah and Israel who were there with the people of Jerusalem. (2 Chr 35:18)

The distinction the Chronicler makes, then, may lie in the fact that "the numbers of offerings and celebrants at Josiah's Passover exceeded that of Hezekiah."[119] Unlike in Hezekiah's era, people from all the tribes appear for Passover, and Josiah's festival follows Moses' prescriptions more closely than Hezekiah's.[120] Given the Chronicler's data it seems that 2 Kgs 23:22 speaks more of this Passover's thoroughness and attention to covenant standards than of the absolute uniqueness of any Passover event whatsoever.

Josiah's emphasis on the Passover is one more attempt on his part to take the covenant nation back to their roots. It is as if he believes the nation has a chance to survive if the people will return to basics like an emphasis on God's Word, on covenant keeping, and on ceremonies that pass the faith from one generation to another. Despite Huldah's prophetic message that predicts Judah's doom, the king works to save the nation. In this way he acts like Moses, who serves God and Israel even after he knows that neither he nor his people will reach Canaan. Both leaders work to redeem the time and the remnant and to offer the witness that God is worth serving under any and all circumstances.

23:24–25 One last reform remains. Josiah rids the land of "mediums and spiritists," individuals skilled in "the art of alleged communication with the dead. This was, to judge from the condemnatory passages, a common problem in Israel (cf. Lev 19:31; 20:27; Deut 18:11)."[121] He also expunges idols "used in the practice of divination."[122] These actions remove not merely idolators but

[117] In 2 Kgs 22:11 the book is called סֵפֶר הַתּוֹרָה and in 23:21 סֵפֶר הַבְּרִית.
[118] E.g., Jones, *1 and 2 Kings,* 2:627–28.
[119] Dillard, *2 Chronicles,* 291; cf. 2 Chr 30:10–11.
[120] Keil, "I and II Kings," 491.
[121] Honeycutt, "2 Kings," 289.
[122] Hobbs, *2 Kings,* 338.

those who, because of their divination practices, compete with true prophets. The way is now clear for God's Word to flow directly to the people.

Josiah's reason for undertaking these reforms serves as his legacy to all readers of the text. He changes Judah "to fulfill the requirements of the law written in the book," a book that is synonymous with "the Law of Moses." Thus, he provides an example of what Davidic kings should do as the leaders of the Lord's people. He demonstrates proper motivation, proper sensitivity to God's Word, and proper obedience to the Lord.

23:26–27 Sadly, Josiah acts as Judah's last righteous king, and his death must have come as a great shock to his followers. The Lord's decision to judge Judah does not change. Huldah's words will come true. Any questions about the justness of this eventuality are answered by the future. The people revert to the worst parts of their past rather than continue in Josiah's ways. National suicide has been averted for a time by the sheer determination of the king and prophets, but the people go back to their old habits as soon as Josiah dies.

(4) Egypt's Pharaoh Kills Josiah (23:28–30)

28As for the other events of Josiah's reign, and all he did, are they not written in the book of the annals of the kings of Judah?

29While Josiah was king, Pharaoh Neco king of Egypt went up to the Euphrates River to help the king of Assyria. King Josiah marched out to meet him in battle, but Neco faced him and killed him at Megiddo. 30Josiah's servants brought his body in a chariot from Megiddo to Jerusalem and buried him in his own tomb. And the people of the land took Jehoahaz son of Josiah and anointed him and made him king in place of his father.

23:28–30 World events and questionable judgment combine to produce the circumstances surrounding Josiah's death. Judah has enjoyed a break from foreign dominance from at least 627 B.C. until 609 B.C., when this story occurs.[123] Now Pharaoh Neco II determines to march through Israel on his way to help Assyria try to recapture Haran from Babylon. Josiah decides to engage Neco at Megiddo in northern Israel. Why does he want to fight the Egyptians? Bright suggests that Josiah may have been pro-Babylonian, as Hezekiah apparently was (cf. 2 Kgs 20:12–19), or that Judah's king thinks an Egypt-Assyria victory could place him under Egypt's control.[124] Another possibility is that Josiah wishes to stake absolute claim to what was once Israel and considers the Egyptian movement a threat to that desire.

Regardless of his motives, the result is the same. Necho's army defeats Judah, killing Josiah in the process. Since Josiah's forces could not possibly have approximated Egypt's, his judgment appears questionable here. Maybe

---

[123] Note "Historical Details Related to 2 Kings 18–25" at the beginning of this chapter.

[124] Bright, *A History of Israel,* 324–25.

he expects a miracle like Hezekiah's. Again the result does not change with a clear answer. Josiah dies before the coming defeat of Jerusalem, a privilege Huldah promised him.

4. Judah's Political and Moral Decline (23:31–24:20)

Once again the author uses the strategy of presenting short reports of kings' reigns to make the story move quickly (cf. 1 Kgs 14:21–16:34; 2 Kgs 13:1–17:6). This time, however, the strategy is employed in effect to hasten Judah's destruction. Twenty-two years (ca. 609–587 B.C.) pass in quick succession, all without Judah's chances of survival improving. Babylon supplants Egypt as Judah's chief tormenter and eventually finishes the covenant people. The author is silent about any hope. Readers are forced to wait for Huldah's prophecy to come true, which places a cloud of inevitable gloom over the text.

(1) Egypt Determines Judah's King (23:31–37)

[31]Jehoahaz was twenty-three years old when he became king, and he reigned in Jerusalem three months. His mother's name was Hamutal daughter of Jeremiah; she was from Libnah. [32]He did evil in the eyes of the LORD, just as his fathers had done. [33]Pharaoh Neco put him in chains at Riblah in the land of Hamath so that he might not reign in Jerusalem, and he imposed on Judah a levy of a hundred talents of silver and a talent of gold. [34]Pharaoh Neco made Eliakim son of Josiah king in place of his father Josiah and changed Eliakim's name to Jehoiakim. But he took Jehoahaz and carried him off to Egypt, and there he died. [35]Jehoiakim paid Pharaoh Neco the silver and gold he demanded. In order to do so, he taxed the land and exacted the silver and gold from the people of the land according to their assessments.

[36]Jehoiakim was twenty-five years old when he became king, and he reigned in Jerusalem eleven years. His mother's name was Zebidah daughter of Pedaiah; she was from Rumah. [37]And he did evil in the eyes of the LORD, just as his fathers had done.

23:31–35 At first everything seems normal in Judah following Josiah's tragic death. His son Jehoahaz[125] succeeds him, so the Davidic dynasty continues. But he does not act like his father, for he does the same sort of evil his ancestors did. This reference probably reflects both his known lifestyle and his public policy, since his three-month reign during 609 B.C. could hardly leave him time to do more than relax his father's reforms.

Pharaoh Neco makes a drastic change of his own. He now determines who will be king in Judah. Jehoahaz is exiled, perhaps because of his anti-Egyptian

[125] Cogan and Tadmor (*II Kings*, 303) note that Jehoahaz is probably his throne name. Shallum is his given name (cf. Jer 22:10–12; 1 Chr 3:15).

policy, and is replaced by Eliakim, who seems to have no problem at all complying with Egypt's wishes.[126] Neco even determines that Eliakim adopt the throne name Jehoiakim, so complete is his control over his vassal. Thus, it is hardly surprising that Jehoiakim pays tribute to Neco nor that this collaborator taxes his own people heavily to raise these funds.

23:36–37 Jehoiakim rules from about 609 B.C. to 598 B.C. Nothing about him impresses the author. Jeremiah offers an even more scathing appraisal. He denounces the king as one who oppresses, extorts, and sheds innocent blood to get the money to build himself a new palace during tough economic times in Judah (Jer 22:13–17). Further, Jehoiakim kills or threatens truthful prophets (cf. Jer 26:1–24) and shows no regard for the prophetic word. Indeed, he burns a scroll of such words (Jer 36:20–26). Clearly, Josiah's reform is dead. Therefore Jeremiah declares that Jehoiakim "will have the burial of a donkey—dragged away and thrown outside the gates of Jerusalem." A more fitting end could hardly be imagined for so self-serving a king. Who would possibly mourn his passing?

(2) Babylon Subjugates Judah (24:1–17)

[1]During Jehoiakim's reign, Nebuchadnezzar king of Babylon invaded the land, and Jehoiakim became his vassal for three years. But then he changed his mind and rebelled against Nebuchadnezzar. [2]The LORD sent Babylonian, Aramean, Moabite and Ammonite raiders against him. He sent them to destroy Judah, in accordance with the word of the LORD proclaimed by his servants the prophets. [3]Surely these things happened to Judah according to the LORD's command, in order to remove them from his presence because of the sins of Manasseh and all he had done, [4]including the shedding of innocent blood. For he had filled Jerusalem with innocent blood, and the LORD was not willing to forgive.

[5]As for the other events of Jehoiakim's reign, and all he did, are they not written in the book of the annals of the kings of Judah? [6]Jehoiakim rested with his fathers. And Jehoiachin his son succeeded him as king.

[7]The king of Egypt did not march out from his own country again, because the king of Babylon had taken all his territory, from the Wadi of Egypt to the Euphrates River.

[8]Jehoiachin was eighteen years old when he became king, and he reigned in Jerusalem three months. His mother's name was Nehushta daughter of Elnathan; she was from Jerusalem. [9]He did evil in the eyes of the LORD, just as his father had done.

[10]At that time the officers of Nebuchadnezzar king of Babylon advanced on Jerusalem and laid siege to it, [11]and Nebuchadnezzar himself came up to the city while his officers were besieging it. [12]Jehoiachin king of Judah, his mother, his attendants, his nobles and his officials all surrendered to him.

In the eighth year of the reign of the king of Babylon, he took Jehoiachin

[126]Cf. Hobbs, *2 Kings,* 341.

prisoner. [13]As the LORD had declared, Nebuchadnezzar removed all the treasures from the temple of the LORD and from the royal palace, and took away all the gold articles that Solomon king of Israel had made for the temple of the LORD. [14]He carried into exile all Jerusalem: all the officers and fighting men, and all the craftsmen and artisans—a total of ten thousand. Only the poorest people of the land were left.

[15]Nebuchadnezzar took Jehoiachin captive to Babylon. He also took from Jerusalem to Babylon the king's mother, his wives, his officials and the leading men of the land. [16]The king of Babylon also deported to Babylon the entire force of seven thousand fighting men, strong and fit for war, and a thousand craftsmen and artisans. [17]He made Mattaniah, Jehoiachin's uncle, king in his place and changed his name to Zedekiah.

24:1–4 Whatever his faults, Jehoiakim could never be accused of non-adaptability. After serving Egypt for a few years, Judah's king switches his allegiance to Babylon in 605 B.C. because of that nation's decisive, clinching victory over Egypt at Carchemish and, more particularly, their march into Philistia.[127] Babylon takes some Judahite captives at this time, including Daniel and his friends (cf. Dan 1:1–5). To preclude any further penalties, Jehoiakim pays tribute to his new master, Nebuchadnezzar (cf. 2 Kgs 24:1 and Dan 1:2).

Three years pass, then Jehoiakim rebels. Obed suggests Jehoiakim does so "because of the failure of the Babylonian invasion of Egypt and in hopes of receiving significant support from Egypt."[128] Egypt may have been able to repel an invasion at this point but was hardly in any position to help its small northern allies. Nebuchadnezzar attacks his vassal by sending some Babylonian troops to join forces with Judah's traditional foes, Syria, Moab, and Ammon. This invasion is but the first of such military actions Judah must endure. Still, Judah somehow manages to survive until Jehoiakim dies in 598 B.C.[129]

The author believes Nebuchadnezzar's forays into Judah come as a direct judgment for the nation's sins. Manasseh's transgressions continue to be cited as the reason for divine displeasure, probably because of their seriousness yet also because of the prophets' promise of punishment offered in Manasseh's reign (cf. 2 Kgs 21:10–15). Certainly the final destruction awaits fulfillment at this point in the story, but Judah is being softened for the great assault to come.

24:5–7 By the time Jehoiakim receives his donkey's burial (Jer 22:19), Egypt no longer threatens Babylon. Judah, still reeling from constant pressure, must stand alone. Egypt has turned out to be as weak an ally as Assyria suggested (cf. 2 Kgs 18:21). Judah has no ally in the Lord either, since Jehoiakim has reversed all of Josiah's religious gains.

---

[127] Bright, *A History of Israel,* 326–27.

[128] Obed, "Judah and the Exile," 470.

[129] See Noth's discussion of possible scenarios in *The History of Israel,* 282.

24:8–12 It seems that Jehoiakim's final "service" to his country is to expire just in time to let his successors and those he has oppressed face Babylon's wrath. His son Jehoiachin, an inexperienced eighteen year old, succeeds him. The new king rules for only three months in late 598 B.C. and early 597 B.C.,[130] then pays for his father's political mistakes and his own sins. Nebuchadnezzar himself comes to participate in the capture of Jerusalem.

24:13–17 Babylon's domination of Judah could hardly be more complete. Jehoiachin is exiled, though he will appear in the story later. Nebuchadnezzer collects his unpaid tribute by raiding the temple treasury, takes Jerusalem's skilled workers and soldiers captive, and places Zedekiah on the throne. Ezekiel is one of the people taken to Babylon (cf. Ezek 1:1–3). Jones correctly concludes that the loss of such elite citizens must have furthered the disintegration of Judah's society.[131] Babylon runs Judah's affairs. Most of its societal leaders are gone, as is its military. Stripped of everything but an existence that lacks integrity and dignity, Judah stumbles closer to its end. Only a few faithful persons, most notably Jeremiah, attempt to change the people's hearts and the nation's destiny.

(3) Zedekiah's Wickedness (24:18–20)

18Zedekiah was twenty-one years old when he became king, and he reigned in Jerusalem eleven years. His mother's name was Hamutal daughter of Jeremiah; she was from Libnah. 19He did evil in the eyes of the LORD, just as Jehoiakim had done. 20It was because of the LORD's anger that all this happened to Jerusalem and Judah, and in the end he thrust them from his presence.

Now Zedekiah rebelled against the king of Babylon.

24:18–20 Zedekiah's lack of character during his ten-year reign (ca. 597–587 B.C.) destroys any chance of even delaying the inevitable. The author depicts him as no better than Jehoiakim, which at least means that he does not reinstate Josiah's policies. Further, Jer 21:1–2 indicates that he wants God to save Jerusalem even though he does not worship the Lord, while Jer 34:1–22 presents him as a man who hears and understands the prophet's warnings yet does not heed them. And he is presented as a king who first helps, then oppresses the poor in order to please the power brokers of Judah. Clearly, he lacks the moral fiber to be more than what he is, a man who gauges each situation by how long its results can keep him in power.

Eventually Zedekiah's indecisiveness and self-interest prove a deadly combination, for they lead him to rebel against Babylon. There are two probable causes for this ill-fated rebellion. First, after more than one aborted attempt, Egypt persuades Judah, Tyre, and possibly Ammon to join a revolt against

---

[130] Bright, *A History of Israel,* 327–28.

[131] Jones, *1 and 2 Kings,* 2:638.

Babylon about 589–588 B.C.[132] Jeremiah 27:1–11 indicates that Zedekiah has to be convinced of the "wisdom" of rebelling and that this counsel flies in the face of the prophet's. Thus, when he does finally rebel out of his inability to make and adhere to sound decisions, it is only with divided enthusiasm and divided loyalties.

Second, Zedekiah's own people are divided over whether to trust Egypt or obey Babylon. But his self-interest eventually leads him to give in to adventurous army officers spoiling for a fight and false prophets who implant "in the people the confidence that the God of Israel would not desert his people nor allow the destruction of the temple (Jer 5:12; 14:13)."[133] Zedekiah tries to please those who want to revolt, yet he also senses trouble. When the end comes, he is incapable of surrendering or standing up to his people (cf. Jer 38:14–28). So he considers his own situation so long that his future is decided for him.

Of course, these reasons for Jerusalem's fall are not as significant to the author as the nation's unrepentant rebellion against the Lord. It is God who destroys Judah in his anger (v. 20; cf. 2 Chr 36:15–16). Babylon only acts as the Lord's agent of justice. Hobbs notes that Babylon's power does not preclude Judah's survival, for God has allowed Judah's armies to triumph against larger forces in the past. Unfortunately, "a new element is expressed. Yahweh himself is fighting against his people, as the prophets have repeatedly warned. . . . To resist is useless. Herein lies the futility. It is a fight against Yahweh himself."[134] According to Jer 38:14–38, God's final act of mercy is to instruct Jeremiah to inform Zedekiah that surrender will avoid a bloodbath. But the king simply hopes the bearer of God's word is mistaken about the future.

5. Babylon Destroys Judah (25:1–26)

Finally, Nebuchadnezzar has seen enough. He sends his armies to Jerusalem, where they triumph after a wrenching siege. Every vestige of Judahite autonomy disappears. The monarchy is discontinued, the religious center, the temple, destroyed, and all but the poorest persons exiled. To Nebuchadnezzar this victory is just another conquest. To readers of Scripture, though, the triumph is a tragedy.

The author tells this story as an embarrassed, though somewhat saddened or angry, courtroom witness. Facts follow on facts, and disaster succeeds disaster, yet in an almost impersonally hasty fashion. Everything David and Solomon built collapses in a final flurry of brutality.[135] On the other hand, the storyteller

[132] Montgomery and Gehman, *Kings,* 560.

[133] Obed, "Judah and the Exile," 472.

[134] Hobbs, *2 Kings,* 356.

[135] R. D. Nelson, *First and Second Kings,* IBC (Louisville: John Knox, 1987) 261.

may simply suppress grief. After all, both author and original audience live in exile because of these events.

(1) Babylon Conquers Jerusalem (25:1–7)

[1]So in the ninth year of Zedekiah's reign, on the tenth day of the tenth month, Nebuchadnezzar king of Babylon marched against Jerusalem with his whole army. He encamped outside the city and built siege works all around it. [2]The city was kept under siege until the eleventh year of King Zedekiah. [3]By the ninth day of the [fourth] month the famine in the city had become so severe that there was no food for the people to eat. [4]Then the city wall was broken through, and the whole army fled at night through the gate between the two walls near the king's garden, though the Babylonians were surrounding the city. They fled toward the Arabah, [5]but the Babylonian army pursued the king and overtook him in the plains of Jericho. All his soldiers were separated from him and scattered, [6]and he was captured. He was taken to the king of Babylon at Riblah, where sentence was pronounced on him. [7]They killed the sons of Zedekiah before his eyes. Then they put out his eyes, bound him with bronze shackles and took him to Babylon.

25:1–7 Babylon's siege against Jerusalem begins in late 589 B.C.[136] and ends midyear of 587 B.C. After over a year the city runs out of food. A few days later the Babylonians break through Jerusalem's defensive walls, which signals the beginning of the end of the battle.[137]

When they are most needed, Judah's king and military flee. Indecisive Zedekiah meets a quite decisive Nebuchadnezzar when his master's men catch him. He is sentenced. His sons are killed. His eyes are put out so that their death will be the last visual image he ever receives. No one "deserves" such cruelty, though it must be noted that oppressive and self-serving leaders often run into tyrants like themselves. Zedekiah's suffering therefore partly results from how he has conducted his own life. Sadly, the same can also be said for the general population.

(2) Babylon Burns the Temple and Takes Prisoners (25:8–21)

[8]On the seventh day of the fifth month, in the nineteenth year of Nebuchadnezzar king of Babylon, Nebuzaradan commander of the imperial guard, an official of the king of Babylon, came to Jerusalem. [9]He set fire to the temple of the LORD, the royal palace and all the houses of Jerusalem. Every important building he burned down. [10]The whole Babylonian army, under the commander of the imperial guard, broke down the walls around Jerusalem. [11]Nebuzaradan the commander of the guard carried into exile the people who remained in the city, along

[136]Or early 588 B.C., as Wiseman (*1 and 2 Kings,* 312) suggests. See D. N. Freedman, "The Babylonian Chronicle," *BA* 19/3 (1956) 50–60, for an analysis of the Babylonian records related to these events.

[137]Cf. Hubbard, *First and Second Kings,* 235.

with the rest of the populace and those who had gone over to the king of Babylon. [12]But the commander left behind some of the poorest people of the land to work the vineyards and fields.

[13]The Babylonians broke up the bronze pillars, the movable stands and the bronze Sea that were at the temple of the LORD and they carried the bronze to Babylon. [14]They also took away the pots, shovels, wick trimmers, dishes and all the bronze articles used in the temple service. [15]The commander of the imperial guard took away the censers and sprinkling bowls—all that were made of pure gold or silver.

[16]The bronze from the two pillars, the Sea and the movable stands, which Solomon had made for the temple of the LORD, was more than could be weighed. [17]Each pillar was twenty-seven feet high. The bronze capital on top of one pillar was four and a half feet high and was decorated with a network and pomegranates of bronze all around. The other pillar, with its network, was similar.

[18]The commander of the guard took as prisoners Seraiah the chief priest, Zephaniah the priest next in rank and the three doorkeepers. [19]Of those still in the city, he took the officer in charge of the fighting men and five royal advisers. He also took the secretary who was chief officer in charge of conscripting the people of the land and sixty of his men who were found in the city. [20]Nebuzaradan the commander took them all and brought them to the king of Babylon at Riblah. [21]There at Riblah, in the land of Hamath, the king had them executed.

So Judah went into captivity, away from her land.

25:8–12 With the city defeated, Nebuzaradan, Nebuchadnezzar's representative, supervises Jerusalem's destruction. He torches the temple, the palace, the people's homes, indeed, "every important building he burned down." Next, he deports every notable person. Nebuzaradan excuses Jeremiah as a special exception (Jer 40:1–6). Finally, the Babylonian leaves a few poor people to tend vineyards, perhaps so they can "supply wine for the Babylonian forces and court."[138] Nothing remains of the glories of David and Solomon's era.

25:13–17 Not only does Solomon's kingdom disappear, but the temple and its articles are dismantled as well. In fact, the description of all the vessels, pillars, and implements closely parallels 1 Kgs 7:15–51.[139] No doubt Nebuchadnezzar seizes these items as payment of tribute previously withheld, and no doubt he extracts the last ounce of valuable metal, since Judah will no longer pay any serious tribute.

For covenant-minded readers the loss of the temple means much more than the destruction of a significant public building. To them the temple symbolizes God's presence in the midst of the chosen people, ongoing worship of Yahweh, the possibility of receiving forgiveness by the offering of sacrifice, and the opportunity to gather as a unified nation at festival time. Of course, the temple

---

[138] Wiseman, *1 and 2 Kings,* 314.

[139] Jones, *1 and 2 Kings,* 2:644.

was rarely used properly, yet as long as it stood, the *hope* for the ideal existed. Now what will happen to God's people?

25:18–21 To keep the exiles obedient and docile, Nebuzaradan executes several community leaders. Gray says: "Probably these executions were exemplary, certain leading men of the nationalist resistance party being selected from various sections of the people. The priests in those days of vassalage were the champions of nationalism."[140] With their leaders dead or deported, the city all but gone, and the people marched away, Judah's exile begins. This exile will last until 538 B.C. It fulfills Moses' threats (Deut 28:15–68), the unnamed prophets' predictions (2 Kgs 21:10–15), and Huldah's prophecy (2 Kgs 22:15–20).

(3) Babylon Appoints a Provisional Government (25:22–24)

22Nebuchadnezzar king of Babylon appointed Gedaliah son of Ahikam, the son of Shaphan, to be over the people he had left behind in Judah. 23When all the army officers and their men heard that the king of Babylon had appointed Gedaliah as governor, they came to Gedaliah at Mizpah—Ishmael son of Nethaniah, Johanan son of Kareah, Seraiah son of Tanhumeth the Netophathite, Jaazaniah the son of the Maacathite, and their men. 24Gedaliah took an oath to reassure them and their men. "Do not be afraid of the Babylonian officials," he said. "Settle down in the land and serve the king of Babylon, and it will go well with you."

25:22–24 Nebuchadnezzar appoints Gedaliah to govern what remains of Jerusalem. Cogan and Tadmor note that "Gedaliah was of a prominent Jerusalem family. His grandfather was the scribe during the reign of Josiah (2 Kgs 22:3), and his father was a member of the mission sent to Huldah . . . and later intervened to save Jeremiah from threatening the prophet's life (Jer 26:24)."[141] He seems to be an honorable, trusting person despite his willingness to serve Babylon (cf. Jer 40:7–16). His counsel to the people seems sound enough. If they settle down and make no trouble, all will be well. After all, Jeremiah has already predicted a seventy-year exile, beginning with 605 B.C. (cf. Jer 29:10), so why fight now?

(4) Babylon's Governor Killed (25:25–26)

25In the seventh month, however, Ishmael son of Nethaniah, the son of Elishama, who was of royal blood, came with ten men and assassinated Gedaliah and also the men of Judah and the Babylonians who were with him at Mizpah. 26At this, all the people from the least to the greatest, together with the army officers, fled to Egypt for fear of the Babylonians.

25:25–26 Gedaliah does not rule long, for a group of men led by a certain

[140] Gray, *1 and 2 Kings,* 700.

[141] Cogan and Tadmor, *II Kings,* 325.

Ishmael kills him. The reason for this murder is not altogether clear. It may be that this man of royal blood wants to claim power for himself. Jeremiah 40:13–14 states that the king of Ammon encourages Ishmael to kill Gedaliah, so regional rivalry contributes to this action. Either of these possible motives is equally foolish, since it is impossible to displace or even to bother Babylon at this time.

Many of those still left in Jerusalem flee in fear to Egypt. Jeremiah says this flight is unnecessary, but in response the people force him to go with them (cf. Jer 42–43). Obviously, their tendency to ignore prophets and make poor political decisions does not end with the city's destruction. Now Jerusalem has no one to tend to its future. Babylon's grip on the city and region has only been strengthened by this episode.

6. Jehoiachin Survives in Exile (25:27–30)

27In the thirty-seventh year of the exile of Jehoiachin king of Judah, in the year Evil-Merodach became king of Babylon, he released Jehoiachin from prison on the twenty-seventh day of the twelfth month. 28He spoke kindly to him and gave him a seat of honor higher than those of the other kings who were with him in Babylon. 29So Jehoiachin put aside his prison clothes and for the rest of his life ate regularly at the king's table. 30Day by day the king gave Jehoiachin a regular allowance as long as he lived.

Readers may have expected the story to end with Israel and Judah scattered to Assyria, Babylon, and Egypt. After all, the nation seems thoroughly crushed. David's dynasty appears completely cut off from power. Temple worship seems stopped forever. The land has apparently changed hands. How could anything change these potentially permanent realities?

But certain concepts need to be remembered. For instance, 2 Sam 7:7–17 promises David an eternal kingdom. Solomon has prayed for Yahweh to return any future exiled people to the land if they repent (1 Kgs 8:46–53), a request that Deut 30:1–10 indicates will be granted. Thus it is fair to ask how God will keep the Davidic covenant and if the people will ever repent and return home. Though 2 Kgs 25:27–30 does not answer these questions clearly, the text may offer some hints about these matters.

25:27–30 Quite unexpectedly, the book ends with a story about Jehoiachin, the king who rules for three months during 598–597 B.C.[142] He has survived thirty-seven years of exile and has outlived Nebuchadnezzar, who died in about 562 B.C.[143] Babylon's new king, Evil-Merodach (ca. 562–560

[142] J. D. Levenson, "The Last Four Verses in Kings," *JBL* 103 (1984) 353–61.

[143] Noth, *The History of Israel,* 281.

B.C.),[144] treats Jehoiachin well, giving him a place of honor among the exiled kings in Babylon and providing for his daily needs. Jehoiachin fares as well as an aged, imprisoned king possibly could.

Interpreters have read this text in a variety of ways. M. Noth thinks the passage simply ends Israel's tragedy with a note of benevolent finality. Jehoiachin and the other exiles exist, of course, but with no real chance of returning home.[145] G. von Rad disagrees. He argues that the prominence of God's covenant with David in 1, 2 Samuel and 1, 2 Kings indicates that Jehoiachin's survival means God may again raise up a house of David. This possibility "is just hinted at, and with great reserve,"[146] but it must be taken seriously since "the Deuteronomist saw yet another word as active in the history, namely, the promise of salvation in the Nathan prophecy, and it, as well as the threat of judgment, was effectual as it ran through the course of the history."[147] Cogan and Tadmor conclude that these verses are positive in that the original readers may have taken some solace in the good fortune of their aged king but that the author knew that no return to the land was imminent. Later members of the remnant would have "to guide the community of Israel in their search for return."[148]

Given the author's writings, perhaps some tentative conclusions are possible. First, the historian believes that though Israel's history has taken an ominous turn, better days are possible because they always were possible. Again, what makes this history so tragic is that things could have been so different. The author never writes of fate; rather, he writes of the results of choices made within a relationship between a small nation and the one God of heaven and earth. Thus, it is certainly possible for a new day to dawn, just as Deut 30:1–10 indicates. Second, on the other hand, the writer has no illusions about the people's propensities. They may, under good leadership, repent and turn to the Lord. It is more likely, though, that they will squander any new opportunity they are given. Third, the author believes David is the key to Israel's well-being. For whatever reason, God has chosen to stake the future on a relationship with David. So full restoration must include the Davidic lineage. Fourth, the writer also understands the kings' failings.

Thus these verses represent the unvarnished, clearheaded, realistic thinking the author exhibits throughout the history. The people are frail, sinful, and often unwilling to follow the Lord. But at their best they *can* do so. Hope for a better future still remains, then, because neither the Lord nor Israel's remnant

---

[144] Hobbs, *2 Kings,* 367.

[145] Noth, *The Deuteronomistic History,* 97.

[146] Von Rad, *Studies in Deuteronomy,* 90.

[147] G. von Rad, *Old Testament Theology: Volume I,* trans. D. M. G. Stalker (New York: Harper & Row, 1962) 343.

[148] Cogan and Tadmor, *II Kings,* 330.

are dead. God's word and God's promises to David remain in effect even if physical signs of the Yahweh-Israel relationship, such as the temple, no longer exist.

What does the writer tell the reader? Trust the Lord and find hope in him. If God can give the land once, God can give it again. If the Lord can raise up one David, another can come to take his ancestor's place. If people could be faithful in Hezekiah's and Josiah's reigns, then they can be obedient again. Even in exile the author believes in such possibilities. What he does not know, though, is when or if the potential will become reality. The decision, like the options, remains open.

Canonical and Theological Implications of 2 Kings 18–25

Canonically speaking, this part of 2 Kings may have more links with Scripture than any of its preceding sections. These chapters continue to reflect on the Pentateuch's teachings and interact with the prophets as well. Further, the events depicted here impact occurrences and interpretations in many other biblical books, so the pivotal nature of 1, 2 Kings in the canon becomes apparent again. Finally, the many correspondences between 2 Kings 18–25 and the rest of Scripture provide several theological points. These points summarize the teachings in 1, 2 Kings. Therefore an analysis of the eras of Hezekiah, Manasseh, Josiah, Jehoiakim, and Zedekiah will yield insights more cumulative than novel but significant all the same.

Hezekiah's reign offers readers their first glance since Solomon's best days at what can happen when divine sovereignty, law, prophecy, kingship, and worship mesh together. Above all else, God's sovereignty permeates 2 Kings 18–20. The Lord allows Hezekiah, a good man, to face great adversity. Why? To demonstrate that what Moses taught is true. Israel's God is one, unique, solitary in his sovereignty over earth (cf. Deut 6:4–9), despite what fearful Israelites and arrogant Assyrians may think (cf. 2 Kgs 18:17–37). Who will inform the king of the Lord's sovereignty? The prophet Isaiah prophesies that Judah is safe as long as they trust the Lord. The Lord causes nations to rise and fall (2 Kgs 19:1–34). The Lord gives life and sends death (2 Kgs 19:35–20:19). The Lord determines Judah's future (2 Kgs 20:12–19). How should people respond to such a God? With personal devotion (cf. 2 Kgs 19:14–19) and a commitment to serve only the Lord (2 Kgs 18:1–4).

This era of obedience occurs because of adherence to Moses' teachings (cf. 2 Kgs 18:5–7). Hezekiah agrees that there is no god but Yahweh and that idols must therefore be eliminated (cf. Exod 20:3–6; 2 Kgs 18:1–4). Hezekiah also agrees that worship should be centered in one place to guard against sliding into idolatry (cf. Deut 12:1–32; 2 Kgs 19:1–4,14–19). Moses instructs kings to keep God's word near them and to stay close to the people (Deut 17:14–20), advice Hezekiah seems to keep. Because Hezekiah obeys the Mosaic instructions, he compares favorably with David. Indeed by keeping Moses' commands he fulfills the basic requirement for keeping the Davidic dynasty in power (cf. 2 Sam 7:7–17; 1 Kgs 9:1–9).

The early portions of Isaiah's prophecy set the stage for Hezekiah's role in Judah's history. Isaiah clearly despises how Israel, Judah, Ahaz, the priests, the false prophets, and the nations disobey the Lord, worship idols, and act arrogantly (cf. Isa 1–35). Judgment must fall because of these sins (cf. Isa 2:6–4:1). Assyria will punish Israel (Isa 8:1–4), but Assyria and all other wicked nations must also face judgment, since they too reject Yahweh, their Creator (Isa 10:5–19; 13:1–23:18). Judah can only survive by consulting God's word (Isa 8:19–22) and by anticipating the emergence of the ideal Davidic king (Isa 7:14; 9:1–7; 11:1–9).

With these principles in place, Isaiah 36–39 states what also appears in 2 Kgs 18:17–20:19. Hezekiah's faithfulness and Isaiah's sensitivity to the Lord combine to give Judah victory over Assyria. This historical account then serves as a bridge to the hopeful yet quite stern passages in Isaiah 40–66. Hope and comfort, peace and safety occur only when king, people, priests, and prophets act in faith. Sennacherib's defeat proves that separatist Yahwism works because it is true. What could be more comforting (cf. Isa 40:9–31)?

On the other hand, Manasseh's era reminds readers of every disaster in Scripture. His idolatry is as destructive to the community as the golden calf incident (cf. Exod 32–34), the period of the Judges, or Ahaz's embracing of Assyria's gods (2 Kgs 16:1–18). Moses promises punishment for such activities (Deut 28:15–68), as do the prophets (2 Kgs 21:10–16; Isa 44:6–23). In the Writings, Psalms 78 and 89 note how idolatry brings punishment, and 2 Chr 33:1–20 indicates that Manasseh reverses Hezekiah's reform. No careful reader of Scripture could fail to grasp the implications of Manasseh's actions.

Josiah embodies the canonical ideal for kingship even more than Hezekiah. Besides following his predecessor's reforming instincts and willingness to listen to the prophets, he also obeys the teachings found in the Book of the Law (cf. Deut 17:14–20; 2 Kgs 23:1–30). His overall commitment to Yahweh also creates an atmosphere in which many prophets flourish. In additions to Jeremiah, Nahum, Habakkuk, and Zephaniah also work during his reign. Certainly these prophets agree with Josiah's reform, yet they also emphasize the need for heartfelt change in the people (cf. Jer 3:6–18; Hab 1:2–4; Zeph 1:2–18). Otherwise the renewal is merely public policy, not true confession and national transformation. Their concerns become quite relevant when Judah reverts back to Manasseh's policy after Josiah's death.

Jehoiakim and Zedekiah do not exceed Manasseh's sins, but their failings come at a more crucial time and receive more comment from the prophets. Of course, neither fulfills Moses' ideals for kingship (2 Kgs 23:36–24:4; 24:18–20). In fact, they make Samuel's worst fears about repressive and greedy kings come true (cf. 1 Sam 12:1–25). They have persisted in evil, and both king and people have been swept away (1 Sam 12:25). Jeremiah condemns Jehoiakim for selfish, oppressive "leadership" (cf. Jer 22:18–23), for allowing false worship, for killing true prophets (Jer 26:1–24), and for rejecting God's word (Jer 36:1–32). Similarly, Jeremiah warns Zedekiah to rule justly (Jer 22:1–5), to expect to surrender to Babylon (Jer 34:1–3), and to trust the Lord to help him (Jer 38:14–28). Because of Jehoiakim's misguided policies, Ezekiel ministers in exile, Habakkuk anticipates a Babylonian invasion, and Zephaniah predicts a massive punishment of God's people.

Finally, Judah's fall and subsequent exile provide perhaps the most important of all canonical signposts. This event is the most devastating punishment Moses can use to threaten people who desperately seek a home of their own (Deut 27–28). It is what Israel barely avoids in Judges, what Samuel warns the people about in 1 Samuel 12, and what Solomon fears in 1 Kgs 8:22–61. Isaiah predicts the exile (Isa 39:1–8), as do Jeremiah (Jer 7:1–15), Ezekiel (Ezek 20:1–49), Amos (Amos 2:4–5; 6:1–7), Micah (Mic 3:12), Habakkuk (Hab 1:5–11), and Zephaniah (Zeph 1:4–13). Jeremiah and Ezekiel live during the exile, while Haggai, Zechariah, and Malachi live in its aftermath. Clearly, it is one of *the* defining events in the Old Testament story.

Jerusalem's fall and the resulting exile play a vital role in the Writings as well. In Psalms the destruction and exile are the culmination of Israel's long-term covenant (cf. Pss 89–90). The end of the exile and the return to their land provides Israel's major cause for rejoicing in Psalms 107–150. Lamentations mourns the nation's demise. Daniel and Esther live in exile, while Ezra and Nehemiah attempt to facilitate the rebuilding of Jerusalem and Yahweh worship in postexilic times. The Chronicler closes history with a plea for all who will to go rebuild the temple (2 Chr 36:13). Thus, the Writings develop many of the daily implications of this tragic historical occurrence.

Since the events depicted in 2 Kings 18–25 have such canonical importance, it is necessary to consider the theological concepts that are developed there. It also is appropriate to note how this final section of 1, 2 Kings provides a theological summary for the books. Once again the text's major characters serve as windows into the story's significance.

The Hezekiah episodes magnify God's uniqueness and sovereignty. Without question, Hezekiah adopts a separatist Yahwist viewpoint. He may do so partly for anti-Assyrian reasons, but it is clear that he also sincerely believes that if Yahweh is the one true God, then all images and high places must be destroyed.[149] His convictions are put to the test, however, when the Assyrian official appears, claiming that Yahweh is no greater than other gods and has

---

[149] Cf. R. E. Clements, *Old Testament Theology: A Fresh Approach* (Greenwood, S.C.: Attic, 1978) 166–67.

told Assyria to conquer Judah (2 Kgs 18:19–25). This speech amounts to an attack on the Lord's "universality, omnipotence, and covenant-keeping grace to his people [that] has to be answered."[150] Thus, Hezekiah's prayer and God's response must respond to these charges. Assyria's devastating losses are certainly welcome political news, but their religious implications are even greater: Assyria's gods do not exist, the other countries' gods could not save them because these deities are not real, and Yahweh did not tell the Assyrians to invade (2 Kgs 19:1–7,14–19,20–37). To make the truth plain about these *most significant of matters*, the Lord delivers Jerusalem.[151] God heals the king and leads Isaiah to predict the exile for the same reasons. Divine uniqueness, sovereignty, worthiness, judgment, and mercy all combine here to teach readers the identity and nature of the loving God.

Two other theological themes emerge from the Hezekiah accounts. First, the all-powerful, all-knowing God answers prayer. Though there are no methods or formulae that guarantee answered prayer, Hezekiah's attitude and God's nature provide some clues about the basis on which the Lord grants requests. Hezekiah certainly wants relief from Assyria, yet his main concern is God's reputation in the world. In other words, the king prays out of a relational sense of respect for God. God answers for the same reasons. God and Hezekiah have a long-standing relationship that is recognized and honored. Part of honoring the relationship means Hezekiah will be healed (2 Kgs 20:1–11), but another part is healing the Lord's reputation in Judah, Assyria, and wherever this story is read. Both parties protect the relationship.

Second, no matter how many members of the covenant community rebel against God, there will always be a remnant of faithful servants of the Lord. Hezekiah thinks he and his followers constitute this remnant (2 Kgs 19:4). Isaiah reports that the Lord agrees and promises to increase and protect this small group (2 Kgs 19:29–31). The good news is that a remnant will always exist. The bad news is that it will be just a remnant, not a majority, and that the clearest way to identify the remnant is through the fires of persecution and through suffering punishment for the sake of the sinful majority. P. Hanson describes the glory and travail the remnant produces and faces in the following comments on Isa 8:22–9:7:

> Once judgment had broken the deceptive sense of self-confidence of the land, and had ended the succession of kings whose personal pride and refusal to submit to Yahweh made them unsuitable as leaders of God's people, a remnant would survive that would look to Yahweh with hope and trust. And the faithful survivors would not be disappointed, for Yahweh would act as in the days of

[150] H. Heater, Jr., "A Theology of Samuel and Kings," in *A Biblical Theology of the Old Testament,* ed. R. B. Zuck (Chicago: Moody, 1991) 137.

[151] Cf. Nelson, *First and Second Kings,* 241.

> Israel's birth as a people. Darkness would be turned to light, and in response to Yahweh's deliverance the grateful people would respond with great rejoicing.[152]

Manasseh's life and work demonstrate sin's far-reaching consequences. On one level his individual sin represents choices made by most Judahites of this era. Though the king may have been influenced by pro-Egyptian, nonseparatist Yahwist elements in the land,[153] it is still his own choice to pursue polytheism. Similarly, many people simply followed his lead in religious matters, but it was their choice to be part of the majority instead of a member of the remnant. The presence of unnamed prophets who denounce the king (cf. 2 Kgs 21:10–16) proves this point. On another level, however, it must be noted once again that a leader's transgressions impact others. Indeed, this ruler's sins make Judah's overthrow a certainty (2 Kgs 21:10–16; 22:15–20; 24:3–4). Put together, private and institutionalized sin create an atmosphere in which no nation can survive.

Josiah's obedience to the rediscovered Book of the Law and the prophetic word underscores the importance of God's Word and the benefits of practicing separatist Yahwism. Though it is impossible to say with certainty that no post-Solomonic kings did so, Josiah is the only monarch the author depicts obeying both the written and oral word of God. The written Word convicts his soul, and the interpretation Huldah gives changes his life's direction. From this point forward he attempts to return separatist Yahwism to its proper place in Judah and Israel, which results in national purpose, delayed judgment, and an honorable death for Josiah. Just as Hezekiah learns earlier, the world is truly secure, though not always quiet, only for those who serve Yahweh by embracing Yahweh's revelation unreservedly.

Since Jehoiakim and Zedekiah basically make the same sort of mistakes as Manasseh, it is best to focus on the theological importance of the major results of their errors—the fall of Jerusalem and the exile. Of course, it is appropriate to observe that the destruction occurs because of the covenantal disloyalty that virtually every prophet warns against. Similarly, the loss of land fulfills Moses' dire predictions about long-term sin (Deut 28:15–68). God waits and warns before punishing yet does punish when all else fails to turn the disobedient nation's heart (cf. Jer 18:1–12).

Taken as a whole, the theological concepts outlined here offer a theology of history that demands to be taken seriously. This theology integrates facts and prophetic interpretation. That is, the author of 1, 2 Kings does not present events he does not believe actually happened. Certainly parables and proverbs

---

[152] P. D. Hanson, *The People Called: The Growth of Community in the Bible* (San Francisco: Harper & Row, 1987) 192.

[153] Cf. Keil, "I and II Kings," 469.

appear but are clearly such (cf. 1 Kgs 22:18–28; 2 Kgs 14:9–10). The writer could have chosen a more mythic format, such as those adopted by Baalistic[154] or Assyrian[155] writers, but he does not do so. There is no pantheon of gods, no hierarchy of gods, no other gods at all. There is no cyclical approach to human events, no god who acts only slightly better or worse than human beings, no failure of character or nerve on Yahweh's part. There are no mythic human heroes either, no character who has to fool the gods into doing something they do not care to do, no hero or heroine who seems greater than mere mortals.[156] In fact, even the best humans in 1, 2 Kings are frail, fallible, and prone to make costly errors. They fear death; they betray others; they sin in their old age; they fight battles they cannot win. Instead, real people, real nations, real events populate these accounts. Clearly, Israel's "understanding of reality" differs from mythic concepts.[157] Indeed, if prophetic predictions and divine miracles were excluded from the history, then the books would read like many histories with a religiously interpretative bent.

But the historian includes miracles and predictions, always as a means of showing the difference between gods whose adherents *say* they rule nature, govern the nations, and so forth and *the* God who actually does these things. The historian also asserts that the Lord rules the earth, has made a covenant with Israel and with David, mediates guidance through the prophets, and punishes when mercy is rejected. This God allows no rivals, since to do so amounts to allowing people to live and die for a lie. The historian claims that ignoring this view of history leads to self-destruction and national devastation (2 Kgs 17:7–41). If adopting this viewpoint amounts to crucial theological thought, then certainly the author intends for every reader to become a theologian. Only those who become theologians of this stripe find hope for the future, for if the Lord is but one of many gods or is not like the text says, then why believe Israel will rise from oblivion? Why believe in a real future history if only a mythic past history, however well told, artistic, beautiful, and well meaning, lies in the past? Exile was real.

---

[154] Note the discussion of 1 Kgs 18:16–46 in this commentary and n. 123 in this section of this commentary.

[155] Cf. Cogan, *Imperialism and Religion,* 9–21.

[156] For a thorough discussion of various types of myths, read N. Frye, *Anatomy of Criticism* (New York: Atheneum, 1967) 131–239.

[157] B. S. Childs argues in *Myth and Reality in the Old Testament* ([Naperville, Ill.: Allenson, 1960] 17–29) that myth in ancient times was not so much a view of history as an "understanding of reality." While Childs makes many cogent points that moderate many parts of the myth debate, it is questionable whether "myth" works as a viable term for the OT writers' view of reality, since even Childs' work nuances the term beyond its normal literary meaning. Again, where 1, 2 Kings is concerned (and Childs does not deal with 1, 2 Kings in particular) only a conviction that predictions and miracles do not occur places the books anywhere near the mythic or legendary categories.

Applicational Implications of 2 Kings 18–25

Those who preach and teach texts from these chapters have an excellent opportunity to convey how to integrate theology and everyday living. Characters make decisions based on what they believe. Nations also act according to how their leaders lead and their people follow. Therefore, just as character analyses help illuminate canonical and theological issues, they also provide bridges from the ancient writer to the modern audience.

Two significant subjects that arise in the Hezekiah stories deserve explication. First, the whole series of reforms and the encounters with Assyria demonstrate how faith in a sovereign God gets tested. Progressively, step-by-step, Hezekiah must exercise ever-greater faith. He believes Yahweh alone is God, then must prove his beliefs by removing idols and high places. This obedience brings difficulties, not ease and acclaim, however, for Assyria threatens him. Thus, he prays, having been forced to believe his Lord can defeat Assyria, since he himself does not have the power to do so. God delivers Jerusalem yet turns around and tells Hezekiah he must die. Again the king prays, and again God grants life. Without question the life of faith allows Hezekiah no easy road to health and wealth. But it does teach him that the Lord gives life, delivers the remnant, and answers prayer. It teaches him that the Lord is the only hope worth clinging to in situations great or small.

Second, Hezekiah's prayers offer some insight into the difficult subject of answered and unanswered prayer. While it is inappropriate to theorize about "how to get what you want from God," as if prayer is a process of manipulating the Lord into doing or giving something he does not want to do or give, it is appropriate to note attitudes that fit Scripture's teaching about God-human relationships. First, Hezekiah prays with great humility. This fact does not mean he does not remind Yahweh of his past service (cf. 2 Kgs 20:2); rather, it means that he admits the situation is beyond his control. Second, Hezekiah's main concern in prayer is God's reputation (cf. 2 Kgs 19:14–19). If the author's monotheistic convictions are true, then nothing matters more in individual, national, or international history than God being fortified. All people benefit when God receives recognition, honor, praise, and glory, so Yahweh must make sure he glorifies himself. As J. Piper writes:

> God is the one Being in all the universe for whom seeking his own praise is the ultimately loving act. For him, self-exaltation is the highest virtue. When he does all things "for the praise of his glory," he preserves for us and offers to us the only thing in all the world which can satisfy our longings. God is for us! And the foundation of this love is that God has been, is now, and always will be, for himself.[158]

[158] J. Piper, *Desiring God: Meditations of a Christian Hedonist* (Portland: Multnomah, 1986) 37.

Third, Hezekiah's prayers focus on what benefits the whole community of faith (cf. 2 Kgs 19:5–7). Perhaps even his prayers for extended life fit this category. After all, he certainly knows what past kings have done. His ongoing commitment to God does benefit continued covenant fidelity in Judah.

Besides being a model for how one person's sins can impact a whole nation, Manasseh's life demonstrates the insecurity of following idols. When he determines not to adopt separatist Yahwism, Manasseh begins a lifetime of unrequited search for spiritual meaning and national deliverance. He worships astral deities, consults mediums, bows down to Baal and Asherah, and sacrifices his son (2 Kgs 21:1–9). He and the nation survive, but he as an Assyrian retainer and the nation as an Assyrian vassal. His father, the king dedicated to Yahweh, enjoyed dignity, freedom, and the chance to die with honor. Manasseh does as he is told, all the while trying to please nonexistent gods as fickle as his foreign overlords. In other words he allows polytheism to manipulate him.

Josiah serves as an example of how to seek, receive, and act on God's word. Though fairly simple in nature, his obedience to Yahweh is extraordinary given his situation. At least four points deserve mention. First, Josiah typically obeys fully what truth he possesses. Before the discovery of the book, he orders temple repair. When he receives the contents of the book, he knows all is not well, so he seeks Huldah's advice. Told what the book means, he enacts greater reforms. Second, Josiah accepts accurate interpretations for God's word as binding. He recognizes the proclamation of the law as an opportunity to hear and respond to Yahweh's will. Third, he does whatever he feels necessary to carry out that will. Fourth, though he knows Judah will be destroyed eventually, he still works to improve the people's commitment to Yahweh. In this way he imitates Moses, who prepares the second generation of postexodus Israelites to possess the promised land even after he knows he will not share this blessing. His short-term obedience does not depend on its long-term temporal effects.

The reigns of Jehoiakim and Zedekiah and the destruction they bring point to the two-sided nature of judgment.[159] On the one hand, judgment punishes (2 Kgs 21:10–16; 22:15–20; 24:3–4,18–20). Sin cannot go unchecked if the sovereign God is also good, holy, and righteous. God's people must be accountable for covenant agreements they have made. On the other hand, beyond judgment lies hope of renewal (cf. Deut 30:1–10; 2 Kgs 25:27–30). Part of the hope stems from knowing that evil will not always go unchecked, while another bit of hope emerges from the assurance that the righteous remnant will be rewarded for its faithfulness.[160]

---

[159] Cf. W. Brueggemann, *Old Testament Theology: Essays on Structure, Theme, and Text,* ed. P. D. Miller (Minneapolis: Fortress, 1992) 184–85.

[160] R. Mason, *Old Testament Pictures of God,* RSG 2 (Macon, Ga.: Smith & Helwys, 1993) 136.

Put another way, judgment falls because of broken covenantal commitments (Deut 27–28; 1 Kgs 11:9–13; 14:1–20; 20:35–43; 21:17–24; 2 Kgs 1:16; 17:7–41). The faithful remnant is forced to suffer during judgment, though they can take a grim satisfaction in knowing that evil has not triumphed. Beyond punishment, though, lies the possibility of renewal (Deut 30:1–10; 1 Kgs 8:22–53). Why? Because a faithful God will start over with the faithful remnant. Surely these concepts will help current believers accept the challenge to be part of the remnant, receive comfort over the defeat of wickedness, and look to the Lord for a brighter future.[161]

One final application remains. Audiences must decide whether or not they will accept a biblical view of history. Several options are available. One can believe the author's view of history, yet not turn to God in obedient faith. Or one can embrace the prophetic worldview and obey the Lord, if only as imperfectly as the best of the remnant characters in these stories. Still another option is to treat the books as exemplary, mythic, poetic, or culturally conditioned rather than as sober reality. In this scenario one can gain much from the stories yet may not be able to know where ideal and experience interact. One other possibility is to accept the vast majority of the author's viewpoint even while differing over a few details.

Preachers and teachers cannot force hearers to accept any one of these (or other available) options, but they can help audiences know what a biblical worldview consists of and help them realize they are indeed choosing *some* perspective on history. Such persons will never have the chance to face these facts, though, if those who teach them fail to absorb 1, 2 Kings, fail to integrate faith, practice, and history, fail to think theologically themselves. If those who preach and teach are as faithful as the historian, then the church may avoid faithlessness, idolatry, judgment, and exile. A true remnant may thrive.

[161] Nelson, *First and Second Kings,* 269.

Selected Subject Index

Person Index

Selected Bibliography

Ackroyd, P. "The Succession Narrative (so called)." *Int* 35 (1981): 383–98.

Allen, R. B. "Elijah, the Broken Prophet." *JETS* 22 (1979): 193–202.

Alter, R. *The Art of Biblical Narrative.* New York: Basic, 1981.

Andersen, F. I. "The Socio-Juridical Background of the Naboth Incident." *JBL* 85 (1966): 46–57.

Astour, M. C. "841 B.C.: The First Assyrian Invasion of Israel." *JAOS* 91 (1971): 383–89.

Auld, A. G. *I and II Kings.* DSB. Philadelphia: Westminster, 1986.

Brettler, M. "The Structure of 1 Kings 1–11." *JSOT* 49 (1991): 87–97.

Bright, J. *A History of Israel.* 3d ed. Philadelphia: Westminster, 1981.

Brindle, W. A. "The Causes of the Division of Israel's Kingdom." *BSac* 141 (1984): 223–33.

Bronner, L. *The Stories of Elijah and Elisha as Polemics against Baal Worship.* Leiden: Brill, 1968.

Burney, C. F. *Notes on the Hebrew Text of the Book of Kings.* Oxford: Clarendon Press, 1903.

Cogan, M. *Imperialism and Religion: Assyria, Judah and Israel in the Eighth and Seventh Centuries B.C.E.* SBLMS 19. Missoula, Mont.: Scholars Press, 1974.

———. Judah under Assyrian Hegemony: A Reexamination of Imperialism and Religion. *JBL* 112/3 (1993).

Cogan, M. and H. Tadmor. *2 Kings.* AB. Garden City: Doubleday, 1988.

Cross, F. M. *Canaanite Myth and Hebrew Epic.* Cambridge: Harvard University Press, 1973.

Davey, C. J. "Temples of the Levant and the Buildings of Solomon." *TynBul* 31 (1980): 107–46.

Davis, D. R. "The Kingdom of God in Transition: Interpreting 2 Kings 2." *WTJ* 46 (1984): 384–95.

Day, J. "The Problem of 'So, king of Egypt' in 2 Kings 17:4." *VT* 42 (1992): 289–301.

Dennison, J. T., Jr. "Elijah the Tishbite: A Note on I Kings 17:1." *WTJ* 41 (1978): 124–26.

DeVries, S. J. *1 Kings.* WBC. Waco: Word, 1985.

Dilday, R. H. *1, 2 Kings.* The Communicator's Commentary. Waco: Word, 1987.

Donner, H. "The Separate States of Israel and Judah." In *Israelite and Judean History.* Edited by J. H. Hayes and J. M. Miller. Philadelphia: Westminster, 1977.

Dozeman, T. B. "The Way of the Man of God from Judah: True and False Prophecy in the Pre-Deuteronomic Legend of 1 Kings 13." *CBQ* 44 (1982): 379–93.

Farrar, F. W. *The First and Second Books of Kings.* Minneapolis: Klock & Klock, 1981.

Fensham, F. C. "The Treaty between the Israelites and the Tyrians." *VTS* 17 (1968): 71–87.

Flanagan, J. W. "Court History or Succession Document? A Study of 2 Samuel 9–20 and 1 Kings 1–2." *JBL* 91 (1972).

Frisch, A. "The Narrative of Solomon's Reign: A Rejoinder." *JSOT* 51 (1991): 22–24.

———. "Structure and Its Significance: The Narrative of Solomon's Reign (1 Kings 1–12:24)." *JSOT* 51 (1991): 3–14.

Gooding, D. W. "Jeroboam's Rise to Power: A Rejoinder." *JBL* 91 (1972): 529–33.

———. "The Septuagint's Rival Versions of Jeroboam's Rise to Power." *VT* 17 (1967): 173–89.

Gordon, R. P. "The Second Septuagint Account of Jeroboam: History or Midrash?" *VT* 25 (1975): 368–93.

Gray, J. *1 and 2 Kings. A Commentary*. OTL. 2nd ed. Philadelphia: Westminster, 1970.

Green, A. R. "Regnal Formulas in the Hebrew and Greek Texts of the Books of Kings." *JNES* 42 (1983): 167–80.

Hallo, W. W. "From Qarqar to Carchemish: Assyria and Israel in the Light of New Discoveries." In *BAR 2*. Edited by D. N. Freedman and E. F. Campbell, Jr. Garden City: Doubleday, 1964.

Halpern, B. *The Constitution of the Monarchy in Israel.* HSM 25. Chico, Cal.: Scholars Press, 1981.

———. "Sectionalism and the Schism." *JBL* 93 (1974): 519–32.

Halpern, B. and D. S. Vanderhooft. "The Editions of Kings in the 7th–6th Centuries B.C.E." *HUCA* 62 (1991): 179–244.

Haran, M. "The Rise and Decline of the Empire of Jeroboam ben Joash." *VT* 17 (1967): 266–97.

Hauser, A. J. and R. Gregory. *From Carmel to Horeb: Elijah in Crisis.* JSOTS 85. Sheffield: Almond, 1990.

Hayes, J. H. and S. A. Irvine. *Isaiah the Eighth-Century Prophet: His Times and His Preaching.* Nashville: Abingdon, 1987.

Hayes, J. H. and J. K. Kuan. "The Final Years of Samaria (730–720 BC)." *Bib* 72 (1991): 153–81.

Hobbs, T. R. *2 Kings*. WBC. Waco: Word, 1985.

Holder, J. "The Presuppositions, Accusations, and Threats of 1 Kings 14:1–18." *JBL* 107 (1988): 27–38.

Hubbard, R. L., Jr. *First and Second Kings.* EBC. Chicago: Moody, 1991.

Hurowitz, V. *I Have Built You an Exalted House: Temple Building in the Bible in Light of Mesopotamian and North-West Semitic Writings.* JSOTSup 115. Sheffield: Academic Press, 1992.

Jenkins, A. K. "Hezekiah's Fourteenth Year." *VT* 26 (1976): 284–98.

Jones, G. H. *1 and 2 Kings*. NCB. 2 vols. Grand Rapids: Eerdmans, 1984.

Kaiser, W. C., Jr. *A History of Israel from the Bronze Age through the Jewish Wars.* Nashville: Broadman & Holman, 1998.

Keil, C. F. "I and II Kings." COT. Translated by J. Martin. 1876; reprint, Grand Rapids: Eerdmans, 1980.

Kitchen, K. A. "Shishak's Military Campaign in Israel Confirmed." *BAR* 15 (1989): 32–33.

———. "Where Did Solomon's Gold Go?" *BAR* 15 (1989): 30–31.

Klein, R. W. "Jeroboam's Rise to Power." *JBL* 89 (1970): 217–18; "Once More: 'Jeroboam's Rise to Power.'" *JBL* 92 (1973): 582–84.

Knoppers, G. N. "'There Was None Like Him': Incomparability in the Books of Kings." *CBQ* 54 (1992): 411–31.

Koopmans, W. T. "The Testament of David in 1 Kings 2:1–10." *VT* 41 (1991): 429–49.

Laato, A. *Josiah and David Redivivus: The Historical Josiah and the Messianic Expectations of Exilic and Postexilic Times.* Coniectanea Biblica, OT Series. Stockholm: Almqvist & Wiksell, 1992.

Lemke, W. E. "The Way of Obedience: I Kings 13 and the Structure of the Deuteronomistic History." In *Magnalia Dei: The Mighty Acts of God.* Edited by F. M. Cross, W. E. Lemke, and P. D. Miller, Jr. Garden City: Doubleday, 1976.

Levenson, J. D. "From Temple to Synagogue: I Kings 8." In *Traditions, Transformations, and Turning Points in Biblical Faith.* Edited B. Halpern and J. D. Levenson. Winona Lake: Eisenbrauns, 1981.

———. "The Last Four Verses in Kings." *JBL* 103 (1984): 353–61.

Long, B. O. *I Kings, with an Introduction to Historical Literature.* FOTL. Grand Rapids: Eerdmans, 1984.

Lowery, R. H. *The Reforming Kings: Cults and Society in First Temple Judah.* JSOTSup 120. Sheffield: Sheffield Academic Press, 1991.

———. "A Darkness between Brothers: Solomon and Adonijah." *JSOT* 19 (1981).

McCarthy, D. J. "II Samuel 7 and the Structure of the Deuteronomic History." *JBL* 84 (1965): 131–38.

———. "Compact and Kingship: Stimuli for Hebrew Covenant Thinking." In *Studies in the Period of David and Solomon and Other Essays.* Edited by T. Ishida (Winona Lake: Eisenbrauns, 1982.

McConville, J. G. "1 Kings 8:46–53 and the Deuteronomic Hope." *VT* 42 (1992): 67–79.

———. "Narrative and Meaning in the Books of Kings." *Bib* 70 (1989): 31–49.

McFall, L. "Some Missing Coregencies in Thiele's Chronology." *AUSS* 30 (1992): 35–58.

McKay, J. *Religion in Judah under the Assyrians.* SBT/2,26. Naperville, Ill.: Allenson, 1973.

McNeely, R. I. *First and Second Kings.* EBC. Chicago: Moody, 1978.

Malamat, A. "The First Peace Treaty between Israel and Egypt." *BAR* (1979): 58–61.

———. "The Kingdom of David and Solomon in Its Contact with Egypt and Aram Naharaim." *BA* 21 (1958): 96–102.

———. "A Political Look at the Kingdom of David and Solomon and Its Relations with Egypt." In *Studies in the Period of David and Solomon and Other Essays.* Edited by T. Ishida. Winona Lake: Eisenbrauns, 1982.

Matheney, M. P. "1 Kings," BBC. Nashville: Broadman, 1970.

Millard, A. "Does the Bible Exaggerate King Solomon's Golden Wealth?" *BAR* 15 (1989): 20–29, 34.

Miller, J. M. "The Fall of the House of Ahab." *VT* 17 (1967): 319–24.

Montgomery, J. A. and H. S. Gehman, *A Critical and Exegetical Commentary on the Book of Kings.* ICC. 1951; reprint, Edinburgh: T & T Clark, 1986.

Moore, R. D. *God Saves: Lessons from the Elisha Stories.* JSOTSup 95. Sheffield: JSOT, 1990.

Mullen, E. T., Jr. "The Royal Dynastic Grant to Jehu and the Structure of the Book of Kings." *JBL* 107 (1988): 193–206.

Nelson, R. D. *The Double Redaction of the Deuteronomistic History.* JSOTSup 18. Sheffield: Sheffield Academic Press, 1981.

———. *First and Second Kings.* IBC. Louisville: John Knox, 1987.

Newsome, J. D., Jr. *A Synoptic Harmony of Samuel, Kings, & Chronicles.* Grand Rapids: Baker, 1986.

Noth, M. *The Deuteronomistic History.* Translated by D. Orton. JSOTSup 15. Sheffield: Academic Press, 1981.

———. *The History of Israel,* 2d ed. Translated P. R. Ackroyd. (New York: Harper & Row, 1960.

Obed, B. "The Historical Background of the Syro-Ephraimite War Reconsidered." *CBQ* 34 (1972).

———. "Observations on Methods of Assyrian Rule in Transjordania after the Palestinian Campaign of Tiglath-Pileser III." *JNES* 29 (1970): 177–86.

Parker, K. I. "The Limits to Solomon's Reign: A Response to Amos Frisch." *JSOT* 51 (1991): 15–21.

———. "Repetition as a Structuring Device in 1 Kings 1–11." *JSOT* 42 (1988): 19–27.

Patterson, R. D. and H. J. Austel. "1 and 2 Kings." EBC. Vol. 4 (Grand Rapids: Zondervan, 1988.

Peckham, B. "Israel and Phoenicia." In *Magnalia Dei: The Mighty Acts of God.* Edited by F. M. Cross, W. E. Lemke, and P. D. Miller, Jr. Garden City: Doubleday, 1976.

Porten, B. "The Structure and Theme of the Solomon Narrative (1 Kings 3–11)." *HUCA* 38 (1967): 93–128.

Rad, G. von. *Studies in Deuteronomy.* SBT 9. Translated by D. Stalker. 1948; reprint, London: SCM Press, 1963.

Rice, G. *Nations Under God: A Commentary on the Book of 1 Kings.* ITC. Grand Rapids: Eerdmans, 1990.

Robinson, B. P. "Elijah at Horeb, 1 Kings 19:1–18: A Coherent Narrative." *RB* 98 (1991): 513–36.

Robinson, J. *The First Book of Kings.* CBC. Cambridge: Cambridge University Press, 1972.

Rofé, A. *The Prophetical Stories: The Narratives about the Prophets in the Hebrew Bible, Their Literary Types and History.* Translated by D. Levy. Jerusalem: Magnes, 1988.

Rost, L. *The Succession to the Throne of David.* Translated by M. D. Rutter, D. M. Gunn. Sheffield: Almond, 1982.

Sacon, K. K. "A Study of the Literary Structure of 'The Succession Narrative' " in *Studies in the Period of David and Solomon and Other Essays,* ed. T. Ishida (Winona Lake, Ind.: Eisenbrauns, 1982.

Savran, G. "1 and 2 Kings." In *The Literary Guide to the Bible.* Edited by R. Alter and F. Kermode. Cambridge: Harvard University Press, 1987.

Schley, D. G., Jr. "1 Kings 10:26–29: A Reconsideration." *JBL* 106 (1987): 595–601.

Schniedewind, W. M. "History and Interpretation: The Religion of Ahab and Manasseh in the Book of Kings." *CBQ* 55 (1993): 649–61.

———. "The Problem with Kings: Recent Study of the Deuteronomistic History." *RelSRev* 22 (1996): 22–27.

Shenkel, J. D. *Chronology and Recensional Development in the Greek Text of Kings.* Cambridge: Harvard University Press, 1964.

Simon, U. "I Kings 13: A Prophetic Sign-Denial and Persistence." *HUCA* 47 (1976): 81–86.

Skinner, J. *1, 2 Kings*. CB. Revised editon. Edinburgh: T & T Clark, 1904.

Snaith, N. H. "The First and Second Books of Kings, Introduction and Exegesis," *IB*. Nashville: Abingdon, 1954.

Soggin, J. A. "Compulsory Labor under David and Solomon." In *Studies in the Period of David and Solomon and Other Essays*. Edited by T. Ishida. Winona Lake: Eisenbrauns, 1982.

———. "The Davidic-Solomonic Kingdom." In *Israelite and Judaean History*. Edited by J. H. Hayes and J. M. Miller. Philadelphia: Westminster, 1977.

Steinmann, A. E. "The Chronology of 2 Kings 15–18." *JETS* 30 (1987): 391–97.

Sternberg, M. *The Poetics of Biblical Narrative: Ideological Literature and the Drama of Reading*. Bloomington: Indiana University Press, 1985.

Tadmor, H. "Traditional Institutions and the Monarchy: Social and Political Tensions in the Time of David and Solomon." In *Studies in the Period of David and Solomon and Other Essays*. Edited by T. Ishida. Winona Lake: Eisenbrauns, 1982.

Tadmor, H. and M. Cogan. "Ahaz and Tiglath-Pileser in the Book of Kings: Historiographical Considerations." *Bib* 60 (1979).

Talmon, S. *King, Cult and Calendar in Ancient Israel: Collected Essays*. Jerusalem: Magnes, 1986.

Talstra, E. *Solomon's Prayer: Synchrony and Diachrony in the Composition of 1 Kings 8:14–61*. Kampen: Kok Pharos, 1993.

Thiele, E. R. "Coregencies and Overlapping Reigns among the Hebrew Kings." *JBL* 93 (1974): 174–200.

———. *The Mysterious Numbers of the Hebrew Kings*. 3d ed. Grand Rapids: Zondervan, 1983.

Van Winkle, D. W. "1 Kings XIII: True and False Prophecy." *VT* 29/1 (1989).

Wallace, H. N. "The Oracles against the Israelite Dynasties in 1 and 2 Kings." *Bib* 67 1 (1986): 21–40.

Wallace, R. S. *Elijah and Elisha: Expositions from the Book of Kings*. Grand Rapids: Eerdmans, 1957.

Walsh, J. T. "The Contexts of I Kings XIII." *VT* 29/3 (1989): 355–70.

———. "Methods and Meanings: Multiple Studies of 1 Kings 21." *JBL* 111 (1992): 193–211.

Weinfeld, M. *Deuteronomy and the Deuteronomic School*. Oxford: Clarendon Press, 1972.

Wilson, R. R. "The Former Prophets: Reading the Books of Kings." In J. L. Mayes et al. eds. *Old Testament Interpretation:Past, Present, and Future: Essays in Honor of Gene M. Tucker*. Nashville: Abingdon, 1995, 83–96.

Wiseman, D. J. *1 & 2 Kings*. Downers Grove: InterVarsity, 1993.

———. "Israel's Literary Neighbors in the Thirteenth Century B.C." *JNWSL* 5 (1977): 77–91.

Wolde, E. van. "Who Guides Whom? Embeddedness and Perspective in Biblical Hebrew and in 1 Kings 3:16–28." *JBL* 114 (1995): 623–42.

Wolff, H. W. "The Kerygma of the Deuteronomic Historical Work." Translated by F. C. Prussner. In *The Vitality of Old Testament Traditions*. Edited by W. Brueggemann and H. W. Wolff. Atlanta: John Knox, 1975.

Scripture Index